D0071885

RICHARD S. HESS (PhD, Hebrew
Union College) is professor of Old Testament
at Denver Seminary. He is the author or edi-
tor of a dozen titles, including *Israel's Messiah
in the Bible and the Dead Sea Scrolls* and commentaries on the Song of Songs and Joshua.

Israelite
Religions

Israelite Religions

An Archaeological and Biblical Survey

Richard S. Hess

Baker Academic
Grand Rapids, Michigan

JKM Library
1100 East 55th Street
Chicago, IL 60615

© 2007 by Richard S. Hess

Published by Baker Academic
a division of Baker Publishing Group
P.O. Box 6287, Grand Rapids, MI 49516-6287
www.bakeracademic.com

and Apollos
(an imprint of Inter-Varsity Press)
Norton Street
Nottingham NG7 3HR, England
email: ivp@ivpbooks.com
website: www.ivpbooks.com

Printed in the United States of America

All rights reserved. No part of this publication may be reproduced, stored in a retrieval
system, or transmitted in any form or by any means—for example, electronic, photocopy,
recording—without the prior written permission of the publisher. The only exception is
brief quotations in printed reviews.

Library of Congress Cataloging-in-Publication Data
Hess, Richard S.
   Israelite religions : an archaeological and biblical survey / Richard S. Hess.
      p.   cm.
   Includes bibliographical references and index.
   ISBN 10: 0-8010-2717-9 (cloth)
   ISBN 978-0-8010-2717-8 (cloth)
   1. Judaism—History—To 70 A.D. 2. Jews—History—To 70 A.D. 3. Bible. O.T.—
Theology. 4. Bible. O.T.—Criticism, interpretation, etc. 5. Bible. O.T.—Antiquities.
I. Title.
BM165.H47 2007
296.09'01—dc22   2007012611

British Library Cataloguing in Publication Data
A catalogue record for this book is available from the British Library.
UK ISBN 978-1-84474-190-8

Scripture quotations are from the HOLY BIBLE, NEW INTERNATIONAL VERSION®.
NIV®. Copyright © 1973, 1978, 1984 by International Bible Society. Used by permission
of Zondervan. All rights reserved.

JKM Library
1100 East 55th Street
Chicago, IL 60615

Contents

Figures

Preface

The background to this study began in research that I had undertaken in the late 1980s after the appearance of studies concerning newly discovered Israelite inscriptions. Further research revealed a significant growth in the results of archaeological sites excavated and the study of various ancient Near Eastern documents, and a massive increase in the publications in the field of ancient Israelite religion. The former especially focused on newly published documents from Mari, Ugarit, and Emar. The results of all this material appeared to position the study of ancient Israelite religion as one of the most interesting and exciting areas in the study of the Hebrew Bible and the world in which Israel lived.

While I have learned much from my reading and research in this field, I sensed the need for a basic introduction that could provide a survey of methods of research, current syntheses and their relation to both the biblical text and other archaeological and textual evidence, and a critical review of the interpretation of what the religious world of ancient Israel was about. The present volume seeks to provide what may be an interim assessment of this changing and developing field. The choice of materials surveyed and the interpretations and scholars reviewed represents a fraction of the whole discipline. Nevertheless, some selectivity was necessary if the field was to be adequately covered. If the work succeeds at all it will be to provide a stimulus to the reader for further research in one or more aspects of this vast and growing field. It may also assist in making some sense out of the many questions and issues that surround the relationship between archaeological, biblical, and extrabiblical textual evidence. In the end the work should raise more questions than it answers and it is hoped that these questions will open new areas of research and understanding.

9

It remains to express my gratitude to the many who have made this study possible. I am grateful to Denver Seminary for sabbatical leave during 2004 that enabled me to undertake important research for this work. I thank Dr. Keith Wells, the seminary's librarian, and all the staff who kindly helped me with my every request and assisted my study. I thank my colleague, Dr. M. Daniel Carroll R., who looked over various parts of the manuscript and made helpful comments. I am grateful to the Institute of Biblical Research for the invitation to present the plenary lecture on November 21, 2003, in Atlanta, "Iron Age Religion in Israel and Its Neighbors: Any Distinctives in the Extrabiblical Evidence?" The interaction and feedback after that lecture provided me with important insights and motivation to pursue the research. In particular, Dr. Theodore Lewis, in his response to the lecture and in his later and more detailed interaction with an early draft of the manuscript, provided invaluable criticisms and perspectives that enabled me to improve this work in ways I would not otherwise have considered. I also thank Dr. Ziony Zevit for his willingness to read through the work and provide me with helpful comments. Further, thanks are due to Dr. Philip Johnston for his careful reading of the manuscript and for his detailed critique. I am grateful as well to Baker Academic for their willingness to publish this work and for the patience of Jim Kinney, Brian Bolger, and others as I attempted to complete it. All statements in this book remain my own responsibility and that of no one else.

I dedicate this work to my daughter, Fiona Jean Hess, whose graduation from college and beginning of seminary studies I celebrated during the years of research on the present work.

1

Introduction

Preliminary Perspectives

The purpose of this work is to survey the major elements of the study of ancient Israelite religion and the methods that have been used to study them. Interest in Israelite religion has recently enjoyed a renaissance. Why have so many books and articles been written on the subject with no indication of a reduction in their number in coming years? Several factors have contributed to this development: renewed interest in the areas of the history of the study of Old Testament theology; the explosion in the archaeological excavation of what is often called "the Holy Land"; and the broader philosophical and cultural trends of our era, especially postmodernism.

I begin with the "pedigree" of the study of Israelite religion vis-à-vis the study of the Old Testament and especially Old Testament theology. Dissatisfaction with traditional approaches to Old Testament theology can be traced to the end of a major movement in this field—the Biblical Theology Movement—in the mid-twentieth century. This dissatisfaction, along with a gradual shift away from the pursuit of a single unifying theological principle, led to the identification of a plurality of theologies, whose contradictory approaches and interpretations are nevertheless

11

grouped together within the collection of literature known as the Hebrew Bible.[1] This shift in thought led scholars to posit a radical disjunction between a late, idealized final edition of the Old Testament and its underlying multiplicity of parties and contentious views of worship and religious beliefs. From such a milieu, Israelite religion strengthened itself as a discipline independent of Old Testament theology. Those who studied it sought a path between two dangerous extremes: the Scylla of a "flattened out" Old Testament with no acknowledgment of its multiple voices and the Charybdis of an agnosticism that could not know anything about the history of early Israel and its religion.[2]

Thus Israelite religion as a modern discipline turned away from a fundamentally literary task aimed at distilling the principle teachings of the Old Testament for faith, life, and—especially in Christian contexts—a connection with the New Testament and Jesus Christ. In place of this, it focused on the growing body of textual and archaeological evidence addressing the subject of ancient Israel's life. This result is the second factor contributing to general interest in the religion of Israel. The analysis of cult centers and burials in Palestine emerged with the astonishingly intensive archaeological exploration and excavation of the region that has occurred during the past century. The discovery of cult centers, whether mere assemblages of religious artifacts and altars or larger architectural structures, led scholars to ask how they relate to the inhabitants of the land, and especially to Israel. The same was true of the burial sites, where complements of eating utensils and cultic paraphernalia raised questions about a cult of the dead.

With an increasing accumulation of data there also emerged refined methods for the investigation and typological classification of these two phenomena. Hand in hand with the material remains there appeared significant new inscriptional evidence. While written texts from all periods continue to be studied and published, there is no question but that the evidence from ancient Palestine and its immediate neighbors has created the greatest interest. Above all, those ninth/eighth-century BC inscriptions from the northern Sinai site of Kuntillet ʿAjrud, commonly understood as mentioning "Yahweh and his Asherah" (where Asherah is understood as a goddess), have provided what is arguably the major

1. That is, the canon of Judaism and the Old Testament of Protestant Christianity. Such a variety of competing parties has been identified in the Hebrew Bible. See, e.g., the study of Zevit (2001) and the reconstruction of Hanson (1987).

2. The terms Scylla and Charybdis originate in the *Odyssey* and describe two dangers that Odysseus and his crew had to sail between in order to pass on safely to their homes. Interestingly, the terms also recall the periods of time—whether the Trojan Wars of the thirteenth and twelfth centuries BC or the eighth-century BC age of the poet Homer—when some of the most important influences in Israelite religion developed.

Chronological Divisions for the Ancient Near East	
Early Bronze Age (EB)	c. 3300–2000 BC
Middle Bronze Age (MB)	c. 2000–1550 BC
Middle Bronze Age IIA	c. 1850–1750 BC
Middle Bronze Age IIB	c. 1750–1650 BC
Middle Bronze Age IIC	c. 1650–1550 BC
Late Bronze Age (LB)	c. 1550–1200 BC
Late Bronze Age IA	c. 1550–1450 BC
Late Bronze Age IB	c. 1450–1400 BC
Late Bronze Age IIA	c. 1400–1300 BC
Late Bronze Age IIB (LBIII)	c. 1300–1200 BC
Iron Age	c. 1200–586 BC
Iron IA	c. 1200–1100 BC
Iron IB	c. 1100–1000 BC
Iron IIA	c. 1000–900 BC
Iron IIB	c. 900–700 BC
Iron IIC	c. 700–586 BC
Neo-Babylonian	586–539 BC
Persian	539–332 BC
Hellenistic	332–53 BC

Note: I recognize and am pleased to affirm the legitimacy of the usage of BCE in place of BC and of CE in place of AD. Here I have chosen to use the traditional and widely recognized rubrics without regard to any philosophical or otherwise ideological agenda.

catalyst for a revolution in our understanding of the beliefs of Israelites during their monarchy (c. 1000–586 BC). The inscriptions that mention this blessing, while not limited to this Sinai caravansary (a sort of ancient hotel) or cult center, constitute the centerpiece of discussion about the role of a goddess or cult symbol and its relationship to Yahweh.[3] It is, in fact, no longer possible to accept a simple division between those who worshiped Yahweh as a single and unique deity, on the one hand, and those who served Baal and a pantheon of deities, on the other. Yahweh has now become a member of the pantheon of Iron Age Palestine.[4]

3. The identification of Kuntillet 'Ajrud in terms of its function as a caravansary or a cult center is disputed. See the discussion below.

4. For the purposes of this work, the Iron Age may be divided into Iron Age I from c. 1200–1000 BC and Iron Age II from c. 1000–586 BC (the time of the Babylonian destruction of Judah and Jerusalem). Baal, the name of the chief god of Canaan, is often mentioned in the Old Testament. The general West Semitic term, *ba'al*, actually means "lord," and can refer to any master or lord, not merely a divine one. As suggested in the famous contest with Elijah on Mount Carmel (1 Kings 18) and elsewhere, Baal was often

A third and final factor in the emergence of interest in the study of Israelite religion has been the methodological and cultural impact of a cluster of philosophies and worldviews that may be grouped under the general term of postmodernism. Its wide-scale rejection of traditional authoritarian forms and acceptance of particular types of pluralism has driven the discipline and its interpretation of the extrabiblical evidence in a specific direction. Thus scholars of Israelite religion in the past generation have directed their research away from assumptions of a single authoritarian faith with a single deity. Rather than seeing the "Yahweh and (his) Asherah" material at Kuntillet ʿAjrud and elsewhere as an aberration in a predominantly Yahwistic society, the majority of scholars find more inviting and inherently more probable the presence of multiple religions existing side by side in ancient Israel. These religions remained continually in a state of flux and transformation as they were affected by political, economic, and cultural forces from outside and from within the society. At Kuntillet ʿAjrud, then, Yahweh had a wife named Asherah and he had children, all of whom were members of the divine council that was worshiped in ancient Israel. Given this prevalence of multiple deities, the student of the Hebrew Scriptures must penetrate behind such erudite sources as the Deuteronomist and priestly redactors to find evidence of this religious pluralism (on these "redactors," see below).

How then should the question of the influence of postmodernism and prevailing philosophies on the study of Israelite religion be considered? Some have sought to examine it directly in terms of the philosophical rationale itself.[5] That task, however essential it might be, lies beyond the scope of this study. Others would emphasize again the role of biblical theology as a legitimate enterprise.[6] This too holds much promise but is not the direction of the present work. Rather, this study proposes to reexamine the extrabiblical and biblical evidence for the religions of the southern Levant in the Iron Age (c. 1200–586 BC) and to locate features that might be distinctive in terms of the religions of Israelites and Judeans. If it succeeds at all, it will at best serve as an initial body of data that can be used for the study of Israelite religion. It will not directly answer questions concerning the influence of philosophies upon

---

identified with the thunderstorm as the god who brought rain and fertility to the earth. Although an important god already at Ugarit (see chapter 4) and elsewhere in Canaan and Phoenicia, the term could also refer to the chief male spirit of a region. This is the case, for example, with Baal of Peor in Numbers 25. For this reason the term could also occur in the plural, as in *the baals*.

5. See, for example, the critical views of Dever (2001; 2003; 2005).

6. See the essays of Ollenburger (2004) in *Old Testament Theology: Flowering and Future*.

the current models, but will rather address both what is customary and what remains anomalous on the landscape of this ancient religion. In the end it will argue that, while there existed a bewildering variety of religious beliefs and practices in the relatively tiny states that were Israel and Judah, this does not exclude, in terms of logic or of evidence, the possibility of a single core of beliefs among some that extended back, perhaps far back, into Israel's preexilic past.[7]

Definitions

Religion

Up to this point I have begged the question of the definition of my terms, particularly the word "religion." This having so far been a brief review of current trends, it has not been necessary to define this term. However, the selection of evidence that will proceed henceforth must force a consideration of this basic question. And it must be considered in the light of archaeology and epigraphy as well as the biblical sources, rather than merely as an abstract theological construct. A working definition of religion for the purpose of this study is *the service and worship of the divine or supernatural through a system of attitudes, beliefs, and practices*.[8] This dictionary definition is intended as a heuristic device to enable discussion to proceed.

Two major problems arise for such a definition in the context of the study of Israelite religion. First, there is the question of the relationship between Israelite religion and biblical theology. This problem is unique to the subject of Israelite religion. A study of religion elsewhere in the world or at another time would not consider this issue. Here it must be addressed. Israelite religion developed out of the study of biblical

7. The exile is traditionally defined as that period of time beginning with the Babylonian conquest of Jerusalem in 587/586 BC and extending to Cyrus's conquest of the Neo-Babylonian empire (539 BC) and the beginning of the return of the Jewish deportees to rebuild Jerusalem two years later. The preexilic period includes the era of the rule of the kings of Judah and, earlier, of the northern kingdom of Israel.

8. This definition is based on that of *Webster's New Collegiate Dictionary*, 7th ed. Ziony Zevit (2001, 15) has also provided a definition (following R. R. Cavanagh [1978, 16–19]): "Israelite religions are the varied, symbolic expressions of, and appropriate responses to the deities and powers that groups of communities deliberately affirmed as being of unrestricted value to them within their worldview."

In terms of the application of this definition to the study of Israelite religion, Zevit (2001, 24–27) adds the need for objectivity, a phenomenological method that seeks to interpret the meaning of the data through its observation, and the mastery of the primary sources with an ongoing critical evaluation of the methods behind them. For other definitions, see chapter 2.

theology. In what is traditionally understood as the essay that distinguished biblical theology from dogmatic theology, Johann P. Gabler (2004, 506) observed in 1787, "biblical theology itself remains the same, namely in that it deals only with those things which holy men perceived about matters pertinent to religion, and is not made to accommodate our point of view."

In light of Israelite religion, one might add that biblical theology would not accommodate the points of view of many of the ancient Israelites. There is a recognizable distinction between biblical theology on the one hand, which emphasizes the ideals that the biblical writers thought should constitute Israel's religious beliefs and practices, and the study of Israelite religion on the other, which considers what ancient Israel actually did believe and do in matters of religion. The latter is how we will understand the term in our study. Although there can be significant overlap in the content of the two, in the final analysis the study of Israelite religion examines the biblical texts for evidence of beliefs and practices that diverge from those the texts advocate. In doing so it is necessary to supplement this material with extrabiblical sources, both written and archaeological. These assist in balancing the polemics of the biblical writers and they can provide a greater depth and illumination to their study. Furthermore, this material allows those who practiced religion an opportunity to "speak" for themselves through their own inscriptions and archaeological evidence. This is essential to understanding the whole picture, or as much of it as is available. Nevertheless, complete separation of theology from religion remains impossible.

The use of extrabiblical evidence points to the second problem or limitation that arises from my definition of religion: the sources for the study of the subject. A vast diversity of material can be grouped into many different categories to describe Israelite religion. Within the ancient boundaries of Israel, there is the evidence of material culture related to religion. On a wider geographic scale, we find written inscriptions both within the confines of ancient Israel and in the neighboring regions. Also, there are the lengthier texts from Ugarit, Emar, and other archives of the second millennium BC. In addition, later Jewish sources—such as the intertestamental texts, the Dead Sea Scrolls, Josephus, and others—contain significant insights into the religious practices of ancient Israel. One may also consult the Christian and Greco-Roman writers who were aware of earlier, and who observed contemporary, practices of the neighbors of Israel and their heirs, such as the Phoenician and Punic cultures. Not only are the materials vast, there is contention at times over how any single item should be interpreted. If this work is to serve the purpose of a survey, it must remain selective, discussing as concisely as possible almost every datum examined and interpreted.

When addressing interpretive issues that are central to scholarly debate (and this centrality itself is a controversial matter), as for example the interpretation of the blessings in the Kuntillet ʿAjrud inscriptions, I will survey the various views and defend my position. At other times, however, I can do little more than note that there is an issue and provide the reader with relevant bibliographic sources.

Then there is the Hebrew Bible itself. While preserving a variety of genres, each with many allusions to religious life, the questions about how to interpret these in their contexts are compounded by the issues of the tradition history and literary development of the biblical text. When were the religious texts written and to what extent do they reflect reality in the period they purport to describe—or in any period? These problems are unique to the biblical text although there are at times similar questions about some of the later extrabiblical sources. More needs to be said about this question than a book on Israelite religion can address. Nevertheless, it will be the concern of this study to introduce and to discuss both the major interpretive approaches and the questions that arise concerning them. These will be noted as the discussion progresses.

Methodologically, synthesizing the witnesses of a variety of texts and material cultures remains problematic. Neither texts nor artifacts from a particular period and site are necessarily more objective than the other in any interpretation, and this is all the more true when we impose religious questions on one hand and use controversial biblical texts on the other.[9] Nevertheless, an attempt must be made to address both types of evidence in order to evaluate the religious horizon with all the available data. The method used to connect the two must include the proper controls, otherwise it is difficult to plausibly integrate the biblical and archaeological dimensions. The biblical evidence must be addressed on its own terms, as must the preponderance of archaeological evidence. This will also allow each to speak for itself. However, since this study considers questions of the varieties of religion in ancient Israel, intentionally avoiding some questions that may be better addressed by a biblical theological method, the extrabiblical evidence will set much of the agenda for the use of evidence from the biblical text. At the same time I am aware that the biblical and nonbiblical evidence must also address each other, and all the more so for materials from the later Israelite period, given the broader agreement that exists as to the dating of the sources of the traditions behind the biblical texts.

Thus I am conscious of the problems in the comparative method. Assembling textual and/or archaeological evidence of similarities be-

9. See the discussions of Davis (2004) and of Zevit (2004) for a history of methodological and interpretive issues in "biblical archaeology."

tween cultures or even different sources from the same culture does not guarantee any necessary relationship between the religious beliefs or practices that the similarities suggest. Instead, it is necessary to identify those "configurations of traits" that may reveal discontinuities such as the distinctiveness of Israel's God, both in its own context and in comparison with surrounding cultures.[10] While this may appear to detract from the stated importance placed on the extrabiblical sources, it does not because such sources may form part of the traits of ancient Israelite religion, especially where they are close in time and place to this culture.

Israelite

In addition to a definition of religion, it is also appropriate to consider the significance of "Israelite" in Israelite religion. Spatial and temporal parameters form the strictures here. Spatially, ancient Israel is centered in the highlands of Canaan to the west of the Jordan River, with the possibility of an extension eastward of that water. Near the beginning of the Iron Age, in the last decade of the thirteenth century (c. 1210 BC), the victory stele of Pharaoh Merneptah records Israel as a people group alongside a list of three fortified cities: Ashkelon, Gezer, and Yanoam. Assuming a location of Yanoam to the east of Pella in the north of modern Jordan and a geographical proximity among Israel and its three neighboring cities, then thirteenth-century Israel's location could be somewhere in Palestine or immediately east of the Jordan River. Because Israel is not mentioned in Egyptian records previous to Merneptah, who was one of the last pharaohs of the era to wage war in Asia, it is reasonable to assume that Israel formed a new group on the scene of Western Asia.[11] This, combined with the sudden appearance in the highlands of Palestine of more than three hundred village sites at the beginning of the twelfth century, provides a positive correlation for the identification of Israel with some or most of these settlements in highland Canaan, west of the Jordan River.[12] A distinctive cultural connection between these settlements and those Iron Age I (c. 1200–c. 1000 BC) settlements to the east of the Jordan River and Dead Sea also may suggest Israel's habitation

10. See the discussion of Machinist (1991) on the awareness of biblical teaching concerning Israel's God as distinctive in comparison with surrounding cultures. On the broader issues of conceptual similarities and dissimilarities with Egypt and Mesopotamia, see Walton (2006).

11. Contrast this with the aforementioned fortresses of Ashkelon, Gezer, and Yanoam, all of which are mentioned centuries earlier in campaigns by pharaohs of Egypt's New Kingdom period. See Aḥituv (1984, 69, 101, 198).

12. Cf. the classic work of Finkelstein (1988). This author later changed his view of early Israel somewhat. Cf. Finkelstein (1996b).

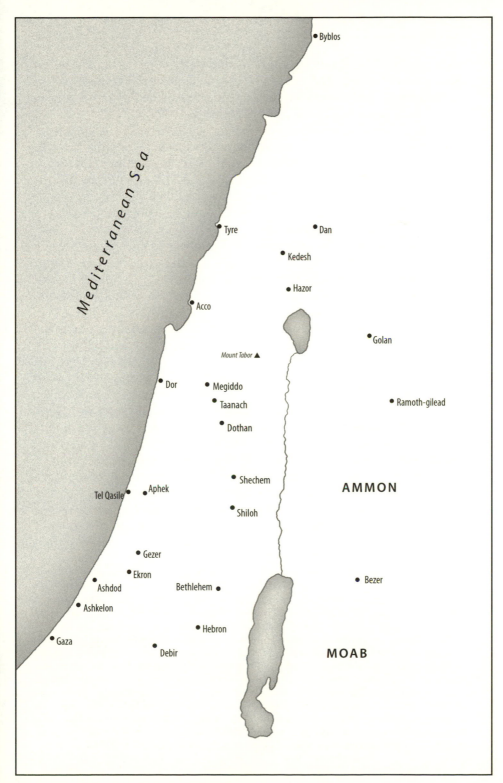

Fig. 1. Map of Southern Canaan and neighbors

of this region. The dramatic demographic shift of the highlands settlement pattern, joined with the initial appearance of the name Israel in the final decades of Egypt's New Kingdom presence in Canaan, suggests a significant historical marker at c. 1200 BC.

The question of ethnicity cannot be answered here. The definition of Israel in Iron Age I will remain a geographical one rather than an ethnic one. This is because it is difficult to determine an ethnic difference between the Israelites of the highlands of Palestine and other groups (Canaanites, Amorites, etc.) that may have inhabited the same region.[13] Without biblical evidence these highland and Transjordanian cultures cannot be further defined as Israelite, Canaanite, or whatever. However, despite evidence for cultural continuity with the preceding Late Bronze Age (c. 1550–c. 1200 BC) and an awareness of a mixture of people groups in this region, religious distinctions may yet emerge. Their connection with later, more clearly defined territories of Israel and Judah may assist in identifying what was Israelite even in Iron Age I.

At the other end of the period, the invasions of the Babylonian army led by Nebuchadnezzar culminate in the events of 587 and 586 BC. Of particular interest for this study is the period before the latter part of the seventh century. After this there is more general agreement as to the emergence of a distinctive monotheistic belief fostered by Josiah, the king of Jerusalem in the late seventh century, and his allies. Nevertheless, numerous biblical and non-Israelite texts attest to a variety of religious beliefs and practices that remained in the area. By 586 BC the spatial coordinates of Israel, including both the earlier northern kingdom of Israel as well as the southern kingdom of Judah, had been recognized extrabiblically in the Moabite, Aramean, and Assyrian accounts of battles and conquests in this area.[14] They may have reached as far north as Dan and as far south as the area west of the Dead Sea. Their eastern borders at times reached beyond the Jordan River into territories disputed

13. Cf. Judg. 2:9–12 and Bloch-Smith (2003). Bloch-Smith's attempt to associate cultural distinctives with Israel over against the Philistines uses boundary distinctions in a method not unlike that applied here. Among the many discussions of ethnicity and ancient people groups, see Grosby (2002, 13–68). He does not associate "national identity" with Israel before the united monarchy. Alternatively, see Dever (2001) for an attempt to identify specific cultural forms that distinguish the Canaanites from Israelites in the Iron Age I. See especially the wide range of studies in Brett (1996) and the study of Sparks (1998).

14. In general, Moabite territory lay to the east of Judah and the Dead Sea. Aramean territories could be found north of Israel. Assyrian campaigns emerged from that power's heartland along the Tigris River in modern-day Iraq. The ninth-century Tel Dan stele, written in Aramaic, and the Moabite stele from about the same period, attest to both the northern kingdom of Israel and the southern kingdom of Judah, the house of Omri and the house of David, respectively. See Lemaire (2004). For a summary of the Neo-Assyrian records and their references to kings of Israel and Judah, see Lambert (2004).

with Moab and Ammon. The western borders tended to be defined by the strength of lowland rivals such as Philistia and its cities, as well as city states such as Ekron, Dor, Acco, and even Tyre when it extended its influence southward.

Outline of This Book

As already noted, the purpose of this work is to survey the major elements that constitute the study of ancient Israelite religion and the approaches that have been used to study them. With a definition of religion that involves communication with the divine or supernatural through a system of attitudes, beliefs, and practices, it is possible to look at that specific practice of religion as found in ancient Israel according to the geographical and chronological boundaries discussed in the preceding section. Chapters 2 and 3 will review the study of religion to consider important methodological controls that both good and bad aspects of the history of this discipline have illustrated. Chapter 3 will also consider the use of biblical criticism in understanding the text of the Old Testament, especially the Pentateuch. The weaknesses and strengths of various theories will be examined to provide some guidance for the controlled use of this important but debated and at times confusing literature. This study of the history of scholarly reflection will seek to demonstrate, first, the absence of universal principles in defining how religion functions in societies, and second, the way in which the contemporary worldview has a profound effect on the interpretation of the Bible and other sources for our knowledge of ancient Israelite religion.

Chapters 4 and 5 will consider what is known of the religious background of Palestine before the coming of the people known as Israel. A consideration of the archaeology and textual evidence found in important sites in Syria, Egypt, Palestine, and Jordan will enable us to identify elements of Israelite religion that are either in continuity with or distinct from the pre-Israelite past. Political, economic, ecological, and sexual factors all played important roles in the diverse religious practices of this region in the third and second millennia BC. In the succeeding chapters this will be compared with biblical texts that have a claim to reflecting some of the earliest traditions of ancient Israel. In chapters 6 and 7 we will probe the ancient stories and names of Genesis 1–11 to learn what religious realities may lay behind their texts. We will consider the role of the ancestral figures, the patriarchs and matriarchs of Genesis 12–50, and how their religious descriptions compare with the practices of the early extrabiblical evidence for religion in Syria, Palestine, and Egypt. Archaeology and texts will also be consulted in the examination of the religious practices of covenant, law, cult, pilgrimage, and others as found in the remaining literature of the Pentateuch. Further, the questions of the Israelite god Yahweh and his origins will be investigated. Here too we will consider the important question of how what is known of Yahweh compares and contrasts with other major deities of the linguistic and cultural world of ancient Israel.

In chapter 8 we will consider the biblical traditions behind the formative period of Israel as a people who first emerge in villages in the highlands of central Palestine. The nature of society and its religious expressions will then be contrasted with the cult as it emerged under David and Solomon, who represent an entirely different expression of worship, one in much greater continuity with the surrounding cultures. This will prepare us for a detailed study of the period from the death of Solomon (c. 931 BC) to the destruction of his temple (c. 586 BC) in chapters 9 and 10.

This study will necessarily include an examination of the degree of diversity in religious expression as it may be seen in the poetic, prophetic, and narrative literature of the Bible as well as in the material culture in Palestine and the remaining texts, inscriptions, iconography, and personal names. A review of the evidence will enable the student of religion to appreciate the variety of religious practices and beliefs of this period. At the same time threads of continuity will be observed, both in what the Bible officially condemns and in what it regards as orthodox. Observations in chapter 11 on the exilic and postexilic periods will allow for final conclusions in chapter 12 on the construction and definition of religion in ancient Israel. The task is a long and complex one, but it provides the essential background for appreciating the diversity of expression of religion that emerged in ancient Israel and on which the biblical authors drew to construct their own understanding and interpretation of Israelite religious expression and faith.

Summary

Our working definition of *religion* is understood to be the service and worship of the divine or supernatural through a system of attitudes, beliefs, and practices. The study of ancient Israelite religion relies on drawing a distinction between theology, which emphasizes what the Bible suggests should be believed, and religion, which is more concerned with what ancient Israelites actually did believe. While there is some overlap between religion and theology, the focus of religion should be on the material culture and extrabiblical inscriptions as much as on the biblical text itself. The particular people studied will be those who occupied the ancient land traditionally ascribed to the political kingdoms of Israel and Judah from c. 1200 BC to c. 586 BC. In particular, emphasis will be placed on those who identified themselves as Israelites. The outline of the remainder of the book was given, demonstrating our intention to follow a roughly chronological scheme. The biblical texts and traditions will be integrated into this picture, evaluating continuities and distinctive discontinuities with the surrounding culture and their religious expressions.

2

Approaches to the Study of Religion

Early Theorists

Any discussion of the recent history of the study of Israelite religion must recognize the role of its earlier history. In his 1787 lecture noted earlier, Gabler (2004, 500) showed a tendency to relate religion and theology while preserving their varying emphases. Indeed, this forerunner of biblical theology cited his predecessors in distinguishing theology and religion, insofar as religion appears concerned with general Christian dogma and ethics whereas theology deals with erudite discussions of these matters. Even though his definition of religion may have been different from that used in the modern study of practices in ancient Israel, it remains true that beginning with Gabler's era and for perhaps a century afterward there was no clear distinction between Old Testament theology and Israelite religion. Part of this has to do with the dominant influence of Christian theology in the published discussions dealing with issues of Israelite religion.

Another important reason for the inclusion of Israelite religion within Old Testament theology lay with the general absence of a separate discipline of "religion." It would not emerge until the nineteenth century with the appearance of the disciplines of sociology and anthropology. These social sciences themselves were in some measure dependent on the

1859 publication of Charles Darwin's *Origin of the Species*. The method adopted by these disciplines interpreted natural phenomena by means of a rational and explanatory model built upon the occurrence of absolute laws empirically derived from systematic observations. For better or for worse the substance of this method, combined with a Hegelian philosophy of dialectic processes, appealed to thinkers who saw the possibility of applying this to the study of human society and culture. In the days of colonial expansion throughout the world, those privileged to occupy the centers of power in Western Europe were uniquely positioned to receive, collect, and evaluate descriptions of cultures and human activities from around the world.[1]

Karl Marx (1818–1883) represents the first and arguably the most influential of those thinkers who addressed the study of religion in light of the "modern" world of the nineteenth century. Marx assumed that all of human endeavor could be explained in economic terms. He understood that the manner in which people satisfied their needs for food, clothing, shelter, and the other material necessities should be the starting point for any analysis of society, culture, and religion. His theories are well known, especially those concerning the fundamental value of human labor and his view that all of history must be seen as an ongoing struggle between the bourgeoisie, who own the means of production, and the proletariat, who are dependent on, and therefore virtually enslaved to, the bourgeoisie. According to Marx, this struggle will evolve until the proletariat revolts and overthrows the bourgeoisie once and for all. After that a golden age of communism will result in which the working class will rule and the will of the workers will be law.

In Marx's vision, religion has no value.[2] It is nothing more than a kind of drug or opiate that lures the proletariat into a willingness to submit to the demands of the bourgeoisie. Such obedience to the status quo promises not material goods in this life but happiness after death. Thus religion distracts the proletariat from their ordained mission according to the immutable laws of Marx's economic theory. They become lulled into a sense of submission to the bourgeoisie and forget the call to rise and revolt against the existing order. For this reason, religion is a passing phase that should disappear with the rise of the communist states. This is the one theory of those studied here that has actually been imposed on many of the existing nations of the world. Its fallacy as a political system became clear with the widespread collapse of communism in 1989. Nevertheless, the view that society should be analyzed

1. Some of what follows is drawn from Pals (1996). I am grateful to Theodore J. Lewis for directing me to this useful work.
2. See K. Marx (2002); Marx and Engels (2002).

primarily as a class struggle and that religion should be understood as a secondary product of more fundamental materialist and economic realities has in some circles become a popular way of looking at the history and religion of ancient Israel. Indeed, the attempt to account in Marxist terms for all that was known of the history and culture of Indian and Chinese society (and later that of the ancient Near East) generated the theory of the Asiatic variant (or the Asiatic mode of production) as an alternative to the second of the five ages (the Slave-holding Age) in which Marxist historical development is understood.[3] As with the theories of Marx, the fallacy of reducing realities such as religion to a single factor, in this case to the material, should be noted. Given the complexity of human society and the many influences on human activity, both individual and collective, this reduction cannot begin to explain fully the life and religion of ancient Israel.[4] However, there can be no doubt that economic concerns did play a role in the development of religious activities in ancient Israel. The larger question has to do with the manner in which ancient Israel addressed these concerns. The evidence and its interpretation are disputed by modern interpreters.

Friedrich Max Müller (1823–1900) was another early scholar who insisted that religion be studied dispassionately, without reference to personal convictions.[5] Müller emphasized the manner in which language evolved so that words designating forces in nature later became used as divine names and applied to various deities in Classical myths. From a different and more productive perspective, Edward Burnett Tylor (1832–1917; cf. Tylor [1903]) analyzed the role of religion, which he defined as "belief in spiritual beings." He argued that the earliest beliefs of humanity affirmed spiritual forces to be at work in nature. These could be manipulated, it was believed, by rites and practices that imitated those forces. This constituted a form of sympathetic magic. Religion emerged as people recognized that these spirits, which animated the world, could be personified apart from the objects or forces where they were found and thus receive appeals in a personal manner. The result was the emergence of various deities who populated ancient mythologies. This was a higher and more evolved form of thought as it no longer assumed a direct cause and effect relationship such as magic had. Instead, the appeals could be accepted or rejected by the deities and this matched more closely perceived human experience.

3. Cf. Gelb (1979) for a summary and critique of this discussion, along with a comprehensive bibliography.
4. See, for example, an appreciation of the multiple models for understanding the emergence of early Israel in Canaan, as surveyed in Hess (1999a).
5. F. M. Müller (1975a; 1975b; 1975c; 1975d).

More famous among these nineteenth- and early twentieth-century theorists was James George Frazer (1854–1941). His multivolume *Golden Bough*[6] brought together a vast assortment of data from cultures around the world, tracing how common practices and beliefs could be found and understood by looking at all these cultures together. Frazer's work of comparative anthropology followed the theories of Tylor in examining beliefs in spiritual beings and seeking to understand the worldwide process of religion as a common development from animism through polytheism and reaching to a belief in one or a common higher spirit. Frazer shared many ideas with William Robertson Smith (1846–1894), who studied totemism in religions and sought to apply it to early Israelite beliefs and practices. Some of the more important aspects of totemism included beliefs that involved a single totem or deity representing each of the major clans and tribes of a group. There were prohibitions on marriage within the clan or family (endogamy) and requirements for marriage within the larger tribal group (exogamy). Restrictions were also placed on eating the animal represented by the tribal or clan totem, except at special feasts.[7]

The scholars represented above have been called intellectualists. They found the center of their study in the intellect and in the understanding of the ancient individuals who invented specific religious beliefs. This focus on the individual has been criticized as not sufficiently appreciating the role of cult and community in the development and definition of religion. Others saw problems with the evolutionary assumptions behind many of the explanations. Why was it assumed that all religions must proceed along the same path, from polytheism to belief in a single spirit? Some of the more "primitive" religions believed in a single spirit, whereas more technologically advanced groups believed in many deities. In fact, this becomes true in ancient Egyptian religion, where the closest approach to monotheism appeared in the fourteenth century BC. Yet this was overthrown and followed by more than a millennium of polytheism. Perhaps most problematic of all were the presuppositions behind the comparative anthropology that was used by Tylor, W. R. Smith, and especially Frazer. One simply cannot assume that, because two or more cultures somewhere in the world perform a similar ritual, any feature of those rituals could be compared in a meaningful manner. Without a full appreciation of the larger context in which rituals and other activities were carried out, their significance cannot be measured and any comparison between groups and religions is meaningless.

Frazer was not the only student of religion to collect and classify human data related to religion. William James (1842–1910), an American

6. Frazer (1911–15).
7. W. R. Smith (1894).

psychologist and philosopher, is another example of this approach.[8] Considered a key representative of the philosophy of pragmatism, James sought to describe the varieties of religious experience, particularly Western experience. In collecting his data, he showed how the richness of the fabric of religion could not be reduced to the official dogmas and formulations of religious professionals and their organizations. Instead, to understand religion one needed to appreciate its complexities and the diversity that is as rich as the communities and personalities who subscribe to religion and seek to appreciate it. James's contribution to the topic became important to the study of Israelite religion because it demonstrated the need to recognize the diversity of religious practices, beliefs, and especially experiences that the people studied may have followed. One practical result of James's work is that descriptions of religion must sometimes take on the characteristics of a list of features because there is no easily ascertained model that can or should do justice to all the various data. James also provides a background for an appreciation of religion from other than the mythological, doctrinal, and cultic perspectives. It is truly part of the human experience whether individually, in the family, in the village, in the clan, in the city, or in the state.

A slightly later contemporary of Tylor, Frazer, and James was another investigator of the human mind, the founder of psychoanalysis, Sigmund Freud (1856–1939). He applied his theories of personality development to the study of religion, especially the Jewish and Christian religions, in three books: *Totem and Taboo: Some Points of Agreement between the Mental Lives of Savages and Neurotics* (1913); *The Future of an Illusion* (1927); and *Moses and Monotheism* (1939). It was Freud's contention that his psychoanalytical reconstruction of the development of the stages of male growth could be applied to the human race and its understanding of religion. He initially combined theories of totemism with this perspective to create an understanding that in the earliest history of humanity, in a primeval family, the sons were jealous of the father for his sexual possession of their mother. They rose up and murdered their father in order to possess their mother. This resulted in guilt among the sons who repressed it through the development of the totem, an animal that symbolized their now honored father and thus could not be eaten except at special ceremonies reverencing him. Religion becomes a collective means to deal with this neurosis. It also develops as a projection of the unconscious desires of what one experienced in childhood and continues to seek, that is, a loving father who is all-powerful and able to take care of one in this life and beyond. Religion therefore should be discarded as

8. James (1902).

something useful to humans in an earlier evolutionary phase but now no longer necessary and not part of the scientific world.

For Israelite religion, Freud argued that Moses was an Egyptian follower of the monotheistic pharaoh Akhenaten (see p. 73). Moses found in the oppressed Israelites ready listeners to his monotheistic views. He led them out of Egypt, but they eventually rejected his simpler and purer religion in favor of a Yahwism learned in the desert. They killed Moses. However, the prophets and other later Israelites would attempt to revive and honor this figure whom the earlier Israelites had attempted to repress. Thus Moses became a kind of neurosis in the collective memory of early Israel but reemerged later in their history, as do all neuroses in the experience of individuals.

The speculative nature of these theories, which lack historical data to support them, need not be repeated here. It is sufficient to observe that the application of Freud's method of psychoanalysis to the fields of religion and history has no rational justification. Further, Freud's method can conceivably be applied only to religions where there is a deity who can be understood as a father, and, in the case of Moses, a single founder who occupies that role. Yet it is clear that many religions of the world do not possess such elements. Finally, we may observe the strong antipathy that Freud exhibited toward the objects of his study. One of his most influential disciples, Carl Jung (1875–1961), took a more positive view of religion as beneficial to humanity.[9] Yet Jung as well largely understood religion through psychoanalysis. In this case Jung identified archetypal forms of the collective unconscious that emerged in the articulation of various religions and beliefs. Religion remained subsumed as a product of the human mind, in a sense not far removed from the intellectualist approaches of Tylor and Frazer. Nevertheless, the influence of Freud and his disciples has been profound. Recently it has reemerged in the readings of suspicion advocated by Derrida and in his consequent deconstructionism of texts. Freud's act of questioning all human behavior and his observations that what is important is what lies beneath the surface became methods of investigation in the study of the humanities in general. As will be seen, this has had a profound influence on the work of the analysis of biblical and other religious documents that affect the interpretation of Israelite religion.

Émile Durkheim (1858–1917), whose *The Elementary Forms of Religious Life* appeared just before World War I, represents a different emphasis than those thinkers of the previous generation. He focused on the role of society in the study of religion in a manner that earlier scholars had not done. For Durkheim, religion was not defined in the

---

9. Jung (1938).

first instance by beliefs of individuals. Instead, it was determined by a distinction between the sacred and the profane. The sacred represented those significant aspects of the society that it practiced together. The profane represented the private concerns of people that were addressed outside the public and social order. Thus, instead of finding an intellectual basis for religion in beliefs, Durkheim identified a social order to religion in cultic acts. The acts of worship, mourning, and other rituals were themselves not the product of religious doctrines but rather lay at the center of what religion was. It was what the people did together. Therefore, religion took on a character that some have seen as primarily functional.[10] Religion was a manifestation of society and therefore integral to it. Unlike Freud, who saw religion as a neurosis that must be abandoned, Durkheim understood it as a social function of the people and thus a healthy and necessary part of the society. In this manner, even the rituals surrounding death could be understood primarily as social. The mourning and remembrance activities provided the society with a means of dealing with the loss of its membership and a way to regroup and to continue. The souls of individuals were in fact the distribution of the religion of the group to each member. Thus everyone shared in the experiences. Who they were when they participated in this manner could be described as their soul. The soul or spirit lived on after their death just as the social order continued.

Durkheim also emphasized the in-depth study of a culture as opposed to the superficial comparisons of religious activities between cultures. In this he provided the background both for an appreciation of the religion of ancient Israel as it was described in the biblical text and other sources, and an appreciation of that religious practice as it was so presented. This stood in contrast to some critical analyses that sought to explain what lay behind the biblical ritual texts. Durkheim's chief weakness was the tendency to reduce all religion and its values to a function of society. In this, he overlooked the individual worshiper on the one hand and the worshiper's experience on the other, as well as the use of rituals and practices that serve other than purely social purposes.

It is perhaps only natural that there should have been some reaction to the theories of religion that viewed it as a secondary effect created by more significant causes that lay elsewhere. Could there be a view of religion that accounted for the diversity of forms without looking first to another discipline? In 1917 the German theologian Rudolf Otto (1869–1937) published *Das Heilige*, translated into English as *The Knowledge of the Holy*. At a time when the reality of sacred experience was being called into question by a burgeoning secularism, Otto argued that religion was

10. Mayes (1989).

focused on an encounter with the terrifying and yet fascinating presence of the divine. This presence, when experienced, was far stronger than anything else in this world. While it could not easily be rendered into a definition, its effect was to make everything and everyone else, including the observer, as of no consequence. It was rather the encounter with and the experience of the "Holy" that mattered. Otto described the Holy as a confrontation with the numinous, a supernatural quality not of this world. Otto's ideas were largely the product of his own experience with Christianity, complemented by travels to India and the study of Hinduism.

Recent Directions

There is no doubt that the Romanian born Mircea Eliade (1907–1986) was influenced by the work of Otto. He too traveled to India and studied there, as well as in Europe, before taking up a professorship at the University of Chicago. Eliade's concern was to study and appreciate the element of the sacred that existed in religions throughout time and around the world. One of his first works on this topic, *Patterns in Comparative Religion* (1958), explored the world of symbols. Built on nature, the world's religions draw on many common symbols with which to understand and to elaborate the cosmos in which they thrive. These natural symbols, whether the rain, the moon, stones, vegetation, or other forms, are believed to contain power. The symbol may itself become personified and stories or myths grow up around it to describe its activities in human terms. These symbols may link together and become patterns that occur in history and in the cycle of time (such as the year) with the result that different symbols take on different levels of importance. The entire configuration may change from generation to generation. While it is normal for symbols to become increasingly important with the passing of time, they do not always become so. Various circumstances may cause symbols to lose their significance and to submerge for a time. They can also reappear and once again take on a special meaning.

In the same year Eliade also published *The Myth of the Eternal Return: Or, Cosmos and History*. This volume understood that all archaic forms of religion sought to return the believers back to the original state of creation, when the world was pure and unsullied. This ideal was thus the point of rituals and activities. It also was the expression of the whole view of time. The real world held little appeal as it was a constant struggle for life and existence. Much better was the sense of a return to the ideal, a time and place in which everything was special and of lasting value. History itself has no meaning or value and death could end everything. Much preferred was the focus on the mythological world and on the festivals (or whatever events) that celebrated the return to the point of creation when the divine touched the real world. This view was challenged by the advent of Israel's religion and then Judaism and Christianity. In these faiths, history was not something to escape, but rather something through which the divine chose to reveal supernatural power and to work miracles on behalf of the people. Thus history took on a significance that it did not have elsewhere. In this volume Eliade criticizes modern ways of looking at the world. Judaism and Christianity laid the foundation for modern perspectives by pushing nature into the background and separating it from God. Modern views have gone a step further and removed God altogether. All that is left is nature. For Eliade, however, this solution does not provide meaning and value to life. Compared with older religions or with Judaism and Christianity, it is not better and a good deal worse.

An important contribution was Eliade's volume, *The Sacred and the Profane* (1959). In this work he defined the sacred as that element of life among peoples living close to nature that provided meaning and worth to their existence. It did so not, as Durkheim argued, by bringing them together into a social group, but by calling out from individuals and groups an encounter with the divine. This divine presence is an irreducible experience of power and therefore of the sacred. All of life for such people is oriented around the world of their gods and goddesses. That is to say, the spiritual beings provide models through myths and rituals that enable the believers to orient their lives meaningfully. Thus all actions in the society and in the individual's life take on significance as they reenact or follow the patterns set by the myths and subsequent rituals. Life has significance as it is oriented toward the sacred.

There are difficulties with Eliade's approach. He tends to avoid incorporating a symbol's content into its definition. He also tends to imitate Frazer at points. Like Frazer, there is the impression that Eliade draws from many different cultures to identify his symbols, and that he makes these identifications without a deep study of the cultures and the full meaning of the symbols within them. Thus it is not always clear that the symbols are truly universal in significance, as opposed to having very different significations in different cultures. Nevertheless, it is important to see the significance of Eliade for the study of Israelite religion. First, his emphasis on the study of religion in a nonreductionist way is a key guide to our analysis. Religion must be studied in its own right; it cannot and should not be reduced to a function of economics or sociology. This is true of the variety of religions in ancient Israel. Second, it is important to be aware of the role of symbols and forms in religions that may share meanings. Although it needs to be established on a case-by-case basis, it will become evident that Israel borrowed many archetypes, forms, and at times whole patterns from existing religions. Nevertheless, it may have adapted and changed these forms in its own application and use of them, a point that Eliade already anticipated in his observations about the distinctive role of Judaism and Christianity and their ultimate origins in ancient Israel.

E. E. Evans-Pritchard (1902–1973) occupied the professorship of social anthropology at Oxford University. His contributions to the study of religion emerge from his firsthand, detailed study of the ethnography of African tribal cultures. In particular he lived first among the Azande and then among the Nuer peoples, spending several years with each. Learning their languages and living in their cultures, Evans-Pritchard was thus able to achieve much more of an insider's view of the culture of each of these tribes than any of his predecessors. Indeed, this approach had been suggested by the French philosopher L. Lévy-Bruhl (1857–1939), who argued against the commonly held view that tribal or "primitive" peoples are immature in their thought and thus indulge in magic and other irrational customs (1922). To this Evans-Pritchard (1937) added the ideas of society first considered by Durkheim and then developed by the British anthropologist A. R. Radcliffe-Brown. According to this view of society, it is impossible to compare and contrast customs between people groups where the customs have been lifted out of their context in the original culture. Instead, it is necessary to understand how such customs work within the group itself. Thus there is an emphasis on the total cultural context of rituals, beliefs, and other practices. When Evans-Pritchard studied the Azande he found that they understood witchcraft as a physical element in some of the members of their tribe. This element was the cause of serious illness and other misfortunes in the tribe. Through rituals and omen-like tests, the possessor of the witchcraft could be identified. Yet this was only part of a complex set of rites and practices. Evans-Pritchard was able to explain the witchcraft in a rational manner, so that it was not seen as an alternative to modern science, but as complementary, dealing with spheres of reality that science did not address. When Evans-Pritchard (1956) turned his attention to the Nuer, he was studying a tribal culture that lived not very far from the Azande. Yet, unlike the Azande, they had virtually no involvement in witchcraft. Their pantheon included "above gods" or sky gods, the "below spirits" or earth deities, and other lesser spirits. The sky gods were both one and many, so that the essence of the supreme god was also manifest in the forms of the various gods. They could possess people and make them ill or make them charismatic leaders in battle. The earth gods were less powerful and therefore less respected. They were the totem animals of various clans. However, unlike the views of earlier theorists such as Tylor,

W. R. Smith, and Freud, totemism was not the key to understanding the most important elements of the Nuer religion. It was secondary, of less importance than the sky gods. Still lower on the scale of religious power and importance were those diviners and possessors of fetishes who could affect individuals for good or ill.

Among the Nuer, the chief sky god was in charge of maintaining the moral order. When customs were not followed, especially in the case of intentional transgressions, sins were committed that required individual sacrifices. For example, every Nuer boy receives his own ox as a gift. Sacrifice for a major fault, however, may require him to slaughter this ox as a gift to the god and as the bearer of his sin. The ox, whose life is closest to a Nuer tribesman, becomes a substitute for the man. The man's heartfelt sincerity is of key importance in this case for the effectiveness of the ritual itself. While this sacrifice is personal and a time of intense emotion, other community sacrifices at special occasions (marriages, funerals, etc.) are times when the participants display the whole gamut of emotions, from elation and happiness to boredom. Group events are thus neither Otto's dramatic encounter with the numinous, the wholly other, nor are they Durkheim's expression of the sacred only through acts of the society as a whole. Again, when Evans-Pritchard investigated the Nuer view of death, he found that the people went through the appropriate rituals for their dead. However, they did so, not to maintain some sort of connection with them, but to send them off and to separate their spirits from the life of the living Nuer. The tribe was not concerned about the afterlife but focused on the physical world around them.

The effect of Evans-Pritchard's study of these and other cultures was profound for the study of religion. His was the first serious attempt to study tribal cultures in depth. His careful and thorough research from within the society led him to severely criticize many of the theorists of religion who had preceded him (1965). Their theories were abstracted from data collected from around the world. Had they studied just one culture in depth, as Evans-Pritchard did, they would have learned how inadequate their assumptions were about religion among tribal peoples. Further, for Evans-Pritchard there could be no simple division between rational modern society and "pre-logical primitives" of other cultures. Evans-Pritchard demonstrated that within the system of understanding observed by the tribal peoples, their lives were rationally ordered. Indeed, modern societies preserved many irrational activities, especially from the perspective of people such as the Nuer. It may have been Evans-Pritchard's own faith commitment of Roman Catholicism that led him to suggest the importance of viewing a society and its religion from within, and not from a supposed disinterested position of unbelief, as the best means to understand it.

There are many aspects of Evans-Pritchard's work that have proven important for the study of Israelite religion. The importance of morality, the role of sacrifice (see especially the work of Mary Douglas discussed on pp. 182–89), the need to identify how the religious forms relate to one another in a given society, and the appreciation of the culture and its religion without placing value judgments on it are just a few. It is true that this anthropologist did not provide us with a general theory of religion, as his predecessors attempted, but by remaining close to the actual practice of religion among tribal peoples, he was able to provide an accurate rendition of the religious beliefs and practices of some peoples. Such an approach also demonstrates the important role of anthropology and sociology as descriptive sciences, rather than as predictive ones.

Clifford Geertz (1926–2006) remains one of the most influential anthropologists in the world. His contribution to the study of religion begins with his appreciation of the sociologist Max Weber (1864–1920). Weber's *Ancient Judaism* (1952) was a significant sociological study in its own right.[11] His designation of Jews as a pariah people, by which he meant that they were ritually distinct from others around them, was compounded by a theory of competing groups of people (classes, castes, etc.) within a society. Thus the social order was much more complex than two or three differentiated groups or individuals (such as a king). Further, the Israelite god Yahweh was sovereign over the social order of Israel as defined by the covenant. The prophets illustrated the class conflict, denouncing not only the king, but also the priesthood, the wealthy, the nobles and aristocracy, and the wise, according to the values that these charismatic figures represented.

While influenced by Marx and others, a key concern of Weber was the need to understand the meaning or significance behind the action of a people.[12] Why do they do what they do and how is it understood? Geertz answered these questions, arguing that the value of studying a society is realized when the significance of what is done in the society is explained. He found this to be particularly true of the religion of the society. Like Evans-Pritchard, Geertz moved from the armchair scholarship and theories of earlier thinkers and lived in several societies for extended periods of time so that he could study and understand them. The cultural system of a society has become the key for Geertz. This set of values, beliefs, and practices informs the social system that is apparent in the daily life of the people and in all their activities. In its turn, this influences the individuals who make up the society in terms of what they think and do. At the same time, the individuals influence

11. See Weber (1946; 1952).
12. Pals (1996, 239).

the overall society and culture. There is a complex web of interactions in terms of beliefs and practices that are constantly in play to create the living culture of the society. Therefore Geertz (1973, 90) provides a sociological definition of religion:

> a system of symbols which acts to establish powerful, pervasive, and long-lasting moods and motivations in men by formulating conceptions of a general order of existence and clothing these conceptions with such an aura of factuality that the moods and motivations seem uniquely realistic.

As the archaeologist Colin Renfrew observes (1985, 12), this is such a vague definition that it could as easily be applied as a sociological definition of a monetary economy. More important, Geertz studied two Islamic societies, one in Morocco and the other in Indonesia. His research led him to see differences in the two groups based on many elements of their history and culture. On the one hand, Moroccan Islam tended to focus on the warrior saint as an ideal figure. This was a person who could claim lineage from the prophet and who was also inspired by a charisma (*baraka*) that enabled the individual to have a kind of double confirmation. On the other hand, the Indonesian society of Java had as its heritage an Islam where the legendary first convert realized his faith without ever seeing the Qur'an. Here the emphasis was on his role as a member of the ruling class and his focus on personal meditation and on public displays of ceremonies and theater from which all classes could benefit. This difference between an active and heritage-based Islam of moral piety, and a religion of ceremony and inward meditation, was compromised in the nineteenth century as new and more text-based movements of Islam emerged from the Middle East and spread across the Islamic world. In this manner Geertz describes the two types of religion and their significant elements as part of the greater society and culture. Such concerns dominate the definition and approach of this scholar.

While there have been criticisms of Geertz's analysis of underlying religious motivations, he has done a great deal to articulate a detailed study of the cultures and their religions. At the same time he has avoided, more than any of the other scholars reviewed here, the tendency to generalize between cultures. For Geertz, culture and religion cannot be predicted. Instead, they must be appreciated and understood as distinctive in each society that is examined. The emphasis is on the particular elements, the individual personalities, and the whole web of cultural influences that render each society and its religious expressions unique. In terms of the study of ancient Israelite religion, this emphasis on distinctive elements as well as the importance of appreciating the whole gamut of cultural interrelationships must become part of the picture and explanation.

Ninian Smart (born 1927), a philosopher of cross-cultural religions, examined the context of religions within the larger category of worldview.[13] Emphasizing the wide diversity of worldviews and the religions that they represent as well as the changes that take place in different times and cultures, Smart outlines seven broad categories in which religions may be studied and compared: practical and ritual, experiential and emotional, narrative or mythic, doctrinal and philosophical, ethical and legal, social and institutional, and material (1989, 9–21). While there is overlap between some of these categories, the model nevertheless provides a useful heuristic device for identifying the variety of elements in any religion, including Israelite.[14]

Recent contributions in religion may include, among others, the definition of Richard K. Fenn (2001a, 6): "a way of tying together multiple experiences and memories of the sacred into a single system of belief and practice." Fenn (2001b, 176) maintains that religions have their origins in attempts to deal with the irrevocable loss of death. In this respect, the rites associated with death reveal that belief in an afterlife forms a nearly universal response to death.[15] Nevertheless, the many responses to death in various cultures also reflect the multiplicity of religions in the world. The unpredictable nature of these religions remains an important point in any attempt to identify the constitution of ancient Israelite religion in its variant forms.

The social sciences also touch on the area of archaeology and the question of the identification and analysis of religion through artifacts preserved in the cultic assemblages and other isolated materials. Colin Renfrew's discussion of the identification of cultic materials remains an important point of departure.[16] Looking at evidence of public cult in a prehistoric context, Renfrew affirms the importance of symbols as a means to identify religious items and to compare them with other materials bearing the same symbolism. His analysis of cultic figurines and the distinction between votive and votary objects, on the one hand, and representations of deities on the other, suggest that positioning, size, gestures, and general context all play a role in classifying the images with which one is dealing. The recognition of ritual space and the identification of this liminal position between the natural and the supernatural suggests a place and activities that arrest the viewers' attention and bring them into a position of awe, that allow for sacrifice,

13. Smart (1960; 1969; 1983).

14. Beginning with Smart's categories, Niditch (1997, 4–7) reduced them to four for her study of Israelite religion: experiential, mythical, ritual, and ethical.

15. Robben (2004).

16. Renfrew (1985). Zevit (2001, 82–83) cites Renfrew's lists of characteristics and questions at length.

offering, and other participatory rites, and that somehow symbolize the transcendent and its mystery.

John Holladay (1987, 270–99) moves well beyond the helpful but general postulates of Renfrew to identify explicit features of location within the population centers of monarchic Israel when distinguishing what he refers to as nonconformist shrines, conformist regional shrines, and conformist state cult centers (temples). Following Holladay, "cult centers" may be "characterized by the clustering of artifacts or other features generally considered indicative of patterned religious activity on the part of population groups above the household level." A "sanctuary" may be defined as "a larger, multicomponent or presumably multi-component structure generally incorporating exterior space (courtyard or temenos) into the overall design." "Sanctuaries dominate and define their neighbourhoods." Finally, a "shrine" is understood as "smaller and simpler than a sanctuary, ideally being a unitary structure such as a single room or a cult room with attached storerooms."

Holladay applies a typology of sanctuaries and divides them into two groups, "nonconformist" and "establishment." The nonconformist sanctuaries include those whose architecture and position reflect usage away from centrist or state-sponsored cult. They include such examples as Jerusalem Cave 1 and Samaria Cave E 207 from the period of the divided monarchy. All are outside the fortified cities that they are near and all contain many vessels suggesting eating and drinking activities. Some extramural cult areas may have been connected with tombs and funerary purposes.

The study of the social sciences has provided many insights into the investigation of religion. Some of these insights have already been noted and will be used in the following analysis of Israelite religion. Carter (1996) has collected a number of useful essays illustrating specific ways in which social science essays have contributed to the study of the Hebrew Bible. In his introduction, after discussing many examples of social science applications and footnoting critics, he addresses general criticisms of the field. On the last page of his discussion, he advocates a self-critical and rigorous methodology. This is indeed essential, for there are many examples of contradictory explanations of religious phenomena, even among the contributors to the volume that Carter introduces. Thus, as will be noted in the discussion on Levitical laws, Mary Douglas (1966) relates the ban on pork consumption in ancient Israel to religious reasons. On the other hand, Marvin Harris (1996) relates this phenomenon to deforestation and ecological factors where Israel settled. However, Harris's explanation was challenged and effectively refuted by zoo-archaeological studies undertaken by Paula Wapnish and Brian Hesse. They found plenty of forests of the type in which pigs thrive in the highlands of Canaan, where early Israel settled. These forests were numerous from before Israel's settlement c. 1200 BC until well after it took place.[17] Nor is this the only example where attempts to use the social sciences have not always led to helpful results. It is enough to review the critiques already discussed with respect to many of the major thinkers of the past. More troubling is the insistence on the ongoing application of preconceived hypotheses after the facts have disproved the assumptions.

A rather clear and modern example is provided by Bernice Martin. Much of mainstream theology and sociology saw the liberation theology movement of the latter part of the twentieth century as the main source of hope for the self-esteem of the economically oppressed and discriminated men and especially women of Latin America. Yet the overwhelming majority of Latin Americans were never convinced of this. Instead, Martin (2001, 57) observes, many turned to Pentecostalism in which the same goals were realized:

> They have been "empowered" by a "regressive," "fundamentalist" Christian movement whose theological rawness and lack of intellectual sophistication causes problems and embarrassment to enlightened Western observers, including those in the mainline denominations of the developing world whose young are defecting in droves to this do-it-yourself movement of the vibrant margins or are "Pentecostalizing" parts of those established institutions themselves.

Yet this well-known fact has apparently gone largely unreported. Martin writes (2001, 57–58):

> Thus we have a series of problems to address: the long failure of social scientists in general to identify the phenomenal growth of evangelicalism in the developing world as a fact; the hostility it inspired when it could no longer be ignored; the failure of precisely those scholars most concerned with religion to recognize the movement as a significant social development; and the failure of those scholars most concerned with gender and family, including feminists, to address the Pentecostal gender paradox.

This "gender paradox" refers to the fact that despite the absence of females in overt, leadership roles among the Pentecostal groups, the worshipers and devotees are predominantly female. These females find, according to the studies done, the moral and social equivalent of an accepting family that they seek in their religious faith (Martin [2001, 62]):

17. For the original study, see Hesse (1986). Cf. Stager (1991b, 31); Hess (1999a, 510).

There is a special irony in the Latin American case since many left-leaning development specialists, both in sociology and anthropology, notwithstanding the colonial nature of Latin American Catholicism, had placed their hopes on the success of liberation theology (which was, after all, the project of Western intellectuals like themselves) as the anticapitalist "option for the poor." The popular success of Pentecostalism and the failure of liberation theology to take off among the masses was not easy to accept.

What remains important from this easily verified example is the problematic nature of explanatory theories that emerge in the West to analyze and provide models for the understanding of any society, even a contemporary one. How much more cautious should we be with the application of such models to explain ancient societies and religions. The particular nature of this example, where assumptions about the disenfranchisement and empowerment of women and their reactions in given religions are proved fallacious, anticipates some of the issues that will be raised over gender participation in Israelite religions of the monarchy.

Summary

This review of the study of religion included particular emphases on backgrounds to the anthropological and sociological studies of religion. The result of the anthropological and sociological approaches to religion was to emphasize the great diversity of religious expressions in human cultures. It becomes apparent that the proper study of religion among any group must recognize our inability to predict which rituals will be used or the meaning and significance of them. Although certain periods of transition that are shared by all human beings, especially birth and death, create an almost universal interest in questions traditionally associated with religion, the manner in which these questions are expressed and answered will vary from people to people, from family to family, and at times from individual to individual.

3

Previous Study of Israelite Religion

Early Studies of Israelite Religion

Although he was not a student of Israelite religion, Johann P. Gabler's (1753–1826) inaugural lecture in 1787 at the University of Altdorf forms a necessary background to the development of the discipline. The translated title of his lecture, "An Oration on the Proper Distinction between Biblical and Dogmatic Theology and the Specific Objectives of Each," illustrates his concern to extract the study of ancient Israelite (and early Christian, in the case of the New Testament) religion and theology and to present these as a discipline separate from dogmatic or systematic theology.[1] By so doing, Gabler liberated the study of the concepts and teachings of the Hebrew Bible from the accretions of doctrine as taught in the Christian church, something the Reformation itself had originally sought to do. His own studies led him to describe the development of

1. See Sandys-Wunsch and Eldredge (1980); Gabler (2004).

Israelite and early Christian religion and theology in historical stages, laying the foundation for the later emergence of Israelite religion as a historical discipline.[2]

Nevertheless, the significance of those early biblical studies for Israelite religion lay not so much in biblical theology as in higher criticism. Wilhelm M. L. de Wette (1780–1849) exemplified scholars of Israelite religion in the early nineteenth century whose works remained closely wedded to categories of dogmatic theology. Like Eliade later, de Wette (1815) focused on religious symbols. However, he saw them as a means of identifying universals in the historical development of Israelite religion. As did many of his successors, de Wette identified the religion of the postexilic period (c. 539–332 BC) as degenerate Judaism, removed from the earlier and better forms of Israelite faith seen in Moses, the Prophets, and the Psalms.[3] Johann G. Herder (1744–1803) had already argued (1782–1783) for the importance of the historical study of Israel's theology and religion. However, his work implied a development in the study of this subject that de Wette had not seen. It was Wilhelm Vatke (1806–1882) who in one of his earliest publications (1835) argued that all Israelite religion was not already contained in the figure of Moses. Applying to Israel Hegel's dialectical understanding of history, he argued for a three-stage development of the spirit of history based on the antitheses of nature vs. spirit, myth vs. history, slavery vs. freedom, exterior vs. interior, magic/cult vs. ethical, and unconscious vs. conscious, as follows:

1. Paganism comprised of nature religion with magic, cult, and idolatry;
2. Prophetic religion, with the climax in the eighth century, marked by the spiritual and ethical emphasis on individuals and their freedom;
3. Legalism in the priestly and Deuteronomistic sources,[4] where idolatry no longer exists but the ethical ideals of the prophets are stultified and marred.[5]

2. See Hartlich and Sachs (1952, 46); Ollenburger (2004, 4).
3. Albertz (1994, 3–4).
4. Vatke understood the Deuteronomist(ic) sources to be primarily the narratives in Deuteronomy, Joshua, Judges, Samuel, and Kings. The later priestly materials are found in Leviticus and elsewhere in the legal collections of Exodus through Deuteronomy. They form a basis for the postexilic activities and views as described in books such as Malachi, Ezra, and Nehemiah (not to mention the importance of the priests in Ezekiel, Haggai, and Zechariah).
5. Cf. Cross (2004, 9; 2005, 43).

As Cross notes, the freeing of the study of Israelite religion from dogmatic theology did not result in objectivity. Instead, Vatke substituted one master for another, Hegelian philosophy in place of dogma. Also, he did not study Israel in its own right but rather as a background to the appearance of Christianity. In doing so, he overlooked the apocalyptic literature of the Hebrew Bible and the intertestamental literature and emphasized only the legalism of the priestly materials.

Julius Wellhausen

More than any other scholar of the past, Julius Wellhausen (1844–1918) has affected both the critical study of the Hebrew Bible and our understanding of Israelite religion in terms of its historical development from the beginnings of the monarchy until the period after the return from the Babylonian exile. In 1878 Wellhausen published his *Prolegomena zur Geschichte Israels*, which was quickly translated into English as *Prolegomena to the History of Ancient Israel*. The effect of this book was to popularize a method of criticism of the Pentateuch that had begun in 1753 when the French physician Jean Astruc published anonymously his theory that the first two chapters of Genesis came from two different sources (Astruc 1753). During the century following Astruc, a variety of scholars, including notables such as Goethe, refined this hypothesis as it applies to the Pentateuch. By 1866 Karl Heinrich Graf was able to summarize the work of this form of criticism in terms of four original documents or sources from which the Pentateuch is essentially derived.

With the four documents situated in their accepted sequence, it was Wellhausen's contribution to explain the whole in a clear presentation. The happy match of the philosophy behind this theory with the prevailing philosophy of that age and the ease with which it could be understood and applied led to its near universal acceptance in the Western academic world of Hebrew Bible research. The particular importance of this theory for the study of ancient Israelite religion lay in its rejection of the possibility that the Pentateuch had any significant origins at the beginning of Israel's history as a nation, that is, during the time of Moses. Instead, the work was understood to have been composed in various parts, each of which reflected religious attitudes and concerns of the time and place from which it derived. Thus the historical knowledge provided by the Pentateuch was not that of its description of earliest Israel and its journey through the desert south of Palestine. Instead, it revealed the religious and political concerns of various groups of Israelites at different times during the period of the monarchy and later. This has had a significant impact on the study of Israelite religion and its sources in the biblical text, so much so that virtually no scholarly commentary on any of the Pentateuchal books can be written even in the present without taking into account this reconstruction. Thus it is essential to present the Documentary Hypothesis, to evaluate it, and to assess its significance for the study of Israelite religion, a task that requires a sizable excursus.

Excursus

THE DOCUMENTARY HYPOTHESIS AND ITS EVALUATION

As already noted, the Documentary Hypothesis presupposes that different written documents lay behind the five books that comprise the Pentateuch. These documents are thought to be the best model available to explain the following characteristics in the Pentateuch. First, there are the doublets such as the two creation stories found in Genesis 1 and 2, and the interweaving of two identifiable flood stories in Genesis 6–9. Second, there is the usage of different divine names, such as Elohim as the name for God in Genesis 1. Further, the language of the prose clearly suggests Yahweh Elohim as that name in Genesis 2 (vv. 4 and following). Although there are many terms used to identify Israel's God in the Hebrew Bible, Yahweh and Elohim are dominant throughout the texts. Most often they occur separately, as Elohim does in Genesis 1. However, they may also be found together as Yahweh Elohim. For more general observations concerning the language of the prose texts in the Pentateuch, see the last two paragraphs of this section (pp. 58–59). Third, there is the presence of different theologies or theological emphases. For example, many of the Abram narratives suggest that this ancestor figure had direct communication with God. However, other texts presume an intermediary such as a priest. Applying these characteristics as criteria, four source documents emerge from the Pentateuchal text, according to the Documentary Hypothesis. These documents were composed at various times in Israel's history before the Hellenistic period. The earliest consists of what is predominantly a narrative, called the J document. It is named in this manner because in German the divine name Yahweh is spelled with an initial J: "Jahweh." The J document forms a continuous narrative from creation to Moses' death.[6] A theological emphasis of the

---

6. Was J a woman? This point was first raised by Friedman (1987), who observed that, while the authors of P and D would probably have been priests and therefore men in Israel, the author of J could have been a woman. Bloom (1990) has argued that indeed this is the case. However, Friedman (1991) has severely criticized Bloom's book. He argues that

J document is the possibility of an immediate relationship with God without intermediaries. The covenant name Yahweh frequently occurs, hence the name of the source. According to the classic documentary understanding, J was written in the early Jerusalemite court of the tenth or ninth century BC.[7] It may date as early as the time of David (early tenth century). Its purpose was to demonstrate legitimacy to the house of David by showing how it was intended by God to rule Jerusalem and God's people from the beginning.

The second source in chronological sequence is the E document, so named due to its predominant use of the name "Elohim." Though a narrative like J, it is not preserved as a continuous narrative. The E material found in the Pentateuch is fragmentary. E preserves the prophetic traditions of the northern kingdom of Israel, that is, that part of the kingdom of ancient Israel that broke away from Jerusalem and Judah at Solomon's death (traditionally c. 931 BC) and remained independent until its fall to Assyria, c. 722 BC. It was written down in the mid-eighth century BC, perhaps during the prosperous reign of Jeroboam II.

The D document is so named because of its connection with Deuteronomy. Second Kings 22–23 recounts how, early in the reign of Josiah in Jerusalem, a copy of the law scroll was discovered while cleaning out and repairing the temple. The content of this scroll prompted Josiah to inaugurate his great reforms. It was de Wette who first suggested that this law book may be related to what we know as Deuteronomy. De Wette and others who followed him suggested that the text of Deuteronomy was written at the time of Josiah and, whether or not it was actually planted and subsequently discovered in the temple, it became a public justification for the reforms that were carried forward by Josiah's party, known as the Deuteronomists. The text of D is primarily the legal code of Deuteronomy, but is also evidenced by editorial materials elsewhere throughout the rest of the Pentateuch. Its theology includes emphases on how all of life is under God's control, the kingdom of God, the importance of the central sanctuary (presumably the temple in Jerusalem, although it is significant that

---

Bloom has not accurately identified the sections of the Pentateuch as J that scholars would today so identify. He also points out that Bloom does not understand biblical Hebrew and so many of his translations are inaccurate, misleading, or wrong. Finally, Friedman notes that any attempt to demonstrate that the author of J was a woman must come to terms with such characteristically J passages as Gen. 3:16 that do not seem to portray women in a positive light. However, this itself is a matter of dispute. See Hess (2004a).

7. Van Seters (1983a; 1992) seeks a later date on the basis of comparative literature. Berge (1990) denies the value of this and retains a 950 BC date. Cf. also Coote and Ord (1989).

the biblical text never makes that identification), and the importance of God's election of Israel.[8]

The latest of the documents is the P source, so named because it is ascribed to the priesthood of Israel. This source was dated to the postexilic period by Wellhausen and others. In 586 BC Jerusalem fell to Babylonian invaders. In 539 Babylon fell to the Persian invaders. The Persian emperor Cyrus allowed various peoples displaced by the Babylonians to return to their homelands and to rebuild their temples. The resultant Jewish community in Jerusalem came to be led by priests. In the late sixth or the fifth century, the P source was written and added to the Pentateuch. Its contents and concerns reflect the values of the priests of Jerusalem. Therefore Israel's history was structured according to genealogies, which were the primary concern in determining who was a priest, who was a Jew, and who was not. Priestly and cultic laws were grouped together with the P document.

P's theology placed an emphasis on Sabbath observance, on circumcision, on the revelation of the law to Israel at Mount Sinai, and on the Tent or tabernacle where God dwelt with Israel and met with them. As a work composed by the priests, it served to provide divine legitimacy for rebuilding the community around the temple after the exile.

Much of the scholarship of the Hebrew Bible and especially of the Pentateuch since 1878 has been dominated by the Documentary Hypothesis. Various changes and refinements have been made to Wellhausen's original theory. For example, there are those who wish to emphasize that the documents are best understood as a series of redactions or editorial revisions made throughout the period of the monarchy and what follows it. Other scholars have argued for the combination of J and E into a single document (referred to as JE). Some have suggested that P should be dated in the preexilic period, as early as the eighth century BC.[9] Meanwhile, others have moved the J source into the exilic period after 586 BC and argued its purpose was to introduce the later history of Joshua through Kings.[10] Despite the variations, the impact of this source theory has been powerful and longlasting. Some scholars have insisted that this is the fundamental starting point for the study of the Bible and that those who do not accept this model are not competent to work as Bible scholars. Richard Friedman is an example of just such a scholar who criticizes those who take an alternative view of the formation of the Pentateuch and thus of Israelite religion (1987; 1991; 1996; 1998; 2003).

8. Thus God has chosen Israel out of all the nations of the world to be God's special people. See Weinfeld (1991; 1996).

9. Knohl (1995); Milgrom (2000a; 2000b); Hess (2002c).

10. Joshua–Kings is referred to as the Deuteronomistic History. For this redating, see Van Seters (1992; 1994).

Nevertheless, despite the dominance of this theory in Western universities and divinity schools, there have always been scholars who have challenged the Documentary Hypothesis. The mid-twentieth-century Jewish biblical scholar, Umberto Cassuto, published critical evaluations of the theory and did not use it in his own commentaries on the Pentateuch (1961a; 1961b). Throughout the twentieth century various Protestant evangelical scholars opposed the Documentary Hypothesis on various literary bases.[11] Friedman, however, defends aspects of the Documentary Hypothesis and insists that any appropriate critique of Wellhausen's theory must take into account the numerous and different strands of argument that tie it together. Any evaluation of this influential theory must consider multiple accounts.[12]

A number of issues need to be considered in addressing the Documentary Hypothesis. The first problem with the Documentary Hypothesis concerns the lack of empirical evidence. There is no biblical text discovered in any manuscript that preserves the kind of distinctions that appear in the sources proposed by this theory. The earliest clear copy of a biblical text is that of the Ketef Hinnom silver strips (see figure 32 on p. 280). Discovered in 1979 in a tomb dated c. 600 BC and located southwest of the City of David, these two small silver scrolls, perhaps used as amulets, preserve quotations from Numbers 6:24–26, Aaron's priestly blessing, as well as possibly another text from Deuteronomy. However, the traditional documentary dating of P is postexilic (after 539 BC). Nevertheless, the scrolls themselves come from a preexilic context and the paleography (shape of the letters) may indicate an even earlier date, specifically to the mid-seventh century BC.[13] Although this is hardly conclusive for the whole of the priestly source, it is of interest that the

11. See, e.g., Young (1956); Archer (1964); Harrison (1969).

12. See Friedman (1996).

13. Although scholars have tried to argue that this is an example of an earlier tradition incorporated into P, the excavator G. Barkay (1992, 177) suggests that the blessing in the biblical text is earlier and the two forms of this blessing that occur at Ketef Hinnom are later. He also observes other P terms appearing on the silver strips, such as the word for "redeemer" (*g'l*, p. 179). This supplements the linguistic arguments of Hurvitz for a preexilic dating of P. Hurvitz's (1988) linguistic arguments for a preexilic date for P have been challenged by Blenkinsopp (1995a), who correctly notes that differences in language usage do not prove what Hurvitz and others, such as Y. Kaufmann (1960), try to demonstrate. Waaler (2002, 49–51) also argues that Deut. 7:9 is found on the first amulet as a "quotation" in which seventeen of the twenty letters are identical to the text in Deuteronomy (the first three are different). Although his attempt to date the amulet to 725–650 BC is not certain (but see his paleographical arguments, pp. 33–48), his observations that the matres lectiones (Hebrew letters used to represent vowels) of the text of the amulet matches those in the Masoretic Text is significant. Thus these silver scrolls are best understood as written copies of the biblical text that suggest a standardized and recognized text that could be drawn on, perhaps by priests of the Jerusalem temple.

only extant preexilic inscription preserves a text that the Documentary Hypothesis dates to the postexilic period.

While there is no such textual evidence for the Pentateuch, Tigay has collected evidence for the editorial development of a work such as the Gilgamesh Epic, and for the conflation of different sources in the Dead Sea Scrolls and in Tatian's *Diatessaron* of the four gospels.[14] However, none of these texts attempts to integrate entirely different types or genres of materials and weave them together into a composite whole, as is claimed of the Pentateuch. Indeed, the closest example of a combination of narrative, divine instruction, and some sanctions may be in the annals of ancient Near Eastern kings, especially in the Assyrian annals from the late second and early first millennia BC.[15] Thus the presence of multiple documents existing over many generations and being written as a single text at a date far removed from the earliest composition is neither proven nor necessary, nor are the parallels cited as close as the composite narratives such as the Neo-Assyrian annals that were originally written in that form without demonstrable antecedent sources far removed in time from the texts we now have.

A second issue with the Documentary Hypothesis is the active program of reordering and redating the documents that many scholars have undertaken. Although the theory has always been subject to the addition of sources (the L or Laity source being but one example), it was not until the latter part of the twentieth century that reordering began on a larger scale. Yehezkel Kaufmann (1955; 1960) argued for a preexilic P in the middle of the eighth century, and many more scholars have followed him, for example, Hurvitz (1988), Haran (1981), Knohl (1995), Peckham (1993), and Weinfeld (2004). Knohl (1995), and Milgrom (1991; 2000a; 2000b), date P before the eighth century when a group known as the Holiness School edited it.[16] Zevit (1995) argues it could date from the late tenth century. Wenham (1987; 1991) places P before J. Rendtorff (1986; 1990) and Wenham identify J and E as originally one document. Van Seters (1983a; 1992; 1994) has argued for a later date for J, while Berge (1990) defends an earlier monarchical date. Blum (1990) argues for the union of two compositions, a D-composition that is later and influenced by an

14. See Tigay (1975; 1982; and his edited 1985 volume); Friedman (1996).

15. The Assyrian royal annals were composed as complex narratives in their first edition (Tertel 1994). Thus it is not impossible for documents containing various types of literature to exist early in the first millennium BC. The structure of ancient legal and reform texts combines narrative (story), law (list), and sanctions, just as in the Pentateuch (Watts 1995). Further, Lemche's argument (1998, 223–24) that "the prose form, which in the Pentateuch covers several different genres of literature," was first developed by the Greeks in the sixth and fifth centuries BC is simply not the case when one examines the evidence of legal texts from the second millennium BC.

16. See Levine (2003) for a review of scholarship.

earlier D, and a P-composition. Blenkinsopp (1992; 1995a) eliminates a continuous J source, ascribing some of the segments to D. Ska (1998) denies the existence of J and E, preferring to see these as a postexilic linking of discrete preexilic traditions. Gnuse (2000) moves E to the seventh century. Rendtorff (1986; 1990; 1993a; 1993b) argued that the application of Gunkel's form criticism (see pp. 59–60) to source criticism created problems that proponents such as Noth had not noted. He has suggested a fragmentary hypothesis that has been developed by Blum (1984; 1990), Albertz (1992), and Carr (1996). The concern here is that such widespread reordering of documents within the hypothesis destroys the neatly unified interpretation of the text as advanced by its earlier advocates.

Third, the advent of computers allowed for some statistical studies to be undertaken. Andersen and Forbes, in their analyses of spelling patterns,[17] concluded that the Pentateuch has a statistically consistent style of spelling, without many vowel letters, that contrasted with the other books of the Hebrew Bible. They described this style as old-fashioned in comparison with the rest of the Bible. Although no such study has been received without criticism, this study has withstood the objections of its critics who raise questions about the antiquity of the material contained within the Pentateuch.[18] Beyond statistics, the Pentateuch preserves anomalous grammatical features that occur across the source divides but are found much less frequently in the other parts of the Hebrew Bible.[19] These observations isolate the Pentateuch and resist a

17. Andersen and Forbes (1986); Forbes (1992, 20).

18. The random nature of the use of vowel letters throughout the Masoretic Text has been argued by James Barr, who has proved to be the most severe critic of this study (Barr 1988). Nevertheless, his arguments do not succeed in overturning the methodological soundness of the analysis (Forbes 1992, 204). Other research has not endured as well. Radday and Shore's (1985) study of the authorship of Genesis used dozens of grammatical and syntactical features to tag each of the words studied from that book. Their conclusion, based on a computer analysis of all the data, argued that the Documentary Hypothesis was invalid insofar as the analysis failed to indicate distinctive styles for each of the putative documents. J and E are indistinguishable. J, E, and P are all more closely related to one another than the differences in style suggested by the genre divisions between Gen. 2–11, 12–36, and 37–49. Some, such as Abela (1987), continued to use their work. However, Forbes himself (1992, 199–200) has severely criticized the method of Radday and Shore from numerous angles. For example, the assignment of texts in Genesis to various sources created source divisions that were unrecognizable, i.e., at least 30 percent at variance with those found in Eissfeldt's divisions. Further, a check of the data and the categories at random points leads to evidence of some confusion and inaccuracy. Finally, Forbes is not persuaded that multiplying categories of syntactic tagging has increased the accuracy of the conclusion. Statistical methods continued to be employed and debated. Thus Houk (2002) attempted to use syllable counts of Hebrew words to argue for sources in Genesis, whereas O'Keefe (2005) demonstrated that the statistics did not prove what Houk claimed.

19. For example, the epicene (without distinctive gender marking) spelling of the third person singular independent pronoun. See Hess (2005a).

simple division of it into literary sources. Insofar as they demonstrate stylistic and grammatical evidence that is normally ascribed to earlier periods, they suggest a successful preservation of authentic materials.

A fourth area has to do with the literary evidence, especially the presence of doublets, that was used from the very beginning to argue for the use of multiple sources. However, doublets such as those found in Genesis 1–2 and 6–9 may not be separate sources but rather literary techniques for making specific points.[20] They may also serve theological or ideological purposes.[21] For example, Genesis 1–2 preserves two creation stories: the first chapter is general in its description of the whole cosmos; the second chapter focuses on the specific creation of the man and his world. For Wenham, Genesis 6–9 forms a large chiastic structure (a palistrophe) with its literary and theological center at 8:1. Further, other texts such as the ancient Near Eastern creation-related myth of Enki and Ninmah seem to preserve a double story, similar to Genesis 1–2.[22]

A different kind of "doublet" has been identified in Leviticus 23:34–36 and 39–41, at the end of a ritual calendar that describes the festivals of Israel over six or seven months of the calendar year. Both passages announce a festival on the same days of the year, called the Feast of Tabernacles in the first passage and a festival to the Lord in the second. It is almost universally agreed that vv. 39–41 constitute a later editorial addition to the calendar that ended at v. 38. The six-month cultic calendar from thirteenth century BC Emar (Emar 446, the only half-year

20. Cf. Wenham (1978); Alter (1981); Hess (1990b); Reis (2001). There may also be theological development and nuancing in repetitions. Cf. e.g. Biddle's (1990) discussion of the accounts of the "endangered ancestress" in Gen. 12, 20, and 26 as developments of 12:1–3, the promise to bless and curse other nations depending on how they treat the family of Abram: Gen. 12 expressing Yahweh's wrath on those who harm the chosen; Gen. 20 showing the ancestor as intercessor for nations and as an example of how the nations may respond; and Gen. 26 showing how nations may bring either cursing or blessing on themselves. Another example is the stylistic repetition of Exod. 2:23–25 in 6:2–5 as observed by Moore (1994) in his review of L. Schmidt's (1993) reassertion of classic arguments for P. Repetition does not demonstrate literary strata.

21. Cf. Childs (1986), who considers only the final canonical form of the text. Rendtorff (1993a, 41–43) has observed how the work of Noth and von Rad, in shifting focus from the internal literary issues and problems of Wellhausen and Gunkel to organizing structures of the books as a whole, prepared the way for the new emphasis on the final form of the text. It is, of course, true that the early source critics began with the text in its "final form" (see Barton [2000]). However, modern literary methods were not available to them. Literary/rhetorical purposes within the present context suggest that the reverse may be true for so-called etiologies. Van Dyk (1990) suggests that, instead of explaining the name or custom (the traditional understanding of an etiology), the referred-to name or custom may serve to "verify" the story or to add interest value to it by making it immediately relevant.

22. See Kikawada (1983).

calendar in the West Semitic[23] world apart from the biblical calendars) also describes two festivals for different deities, Dagan and Shaggar, on the fifteenth day of the first (autumn) month. Beginning on lines 8 and 45 of the tablet virtually the same festival is described for these two deities. Thus in both Leviticus 23 and the Emar text, "the differences in various details are matched by parallel periods of time when the feasts are celebrated, by similar general actions during the holy days, and by an association or even identification of the festivals with one another." If in the Emar text we do not have a second source or later editorial addition just because there is a parallel or doublet text, the same may be said for the Bible and Leviticus 23.[24] Of course, this does not argue that the biblical passage at the end of Leviticus 23 is not an editorial addition. It simply says that past arguments based on the "doublet" nature of the passage can no longer be used to prove that the addition was made later.

Fifth, one may question the assumption that the P document was a postexilic composition with postexilic sources. Not all traditions should be dated so late. For example, the practice of anointing the priests with blood and oil (Exod. 29 and Lev. 8) was formerly considered postexilic. Scholars thought that the ritual of anointing had been applied only to kings. In the postexilic period the citizens of Jerusalem and Judea had no king of their own. The arguments assumed that the high priest substituted for a king. Therefore, the anointing ritual was copied from the acts done to royalty to recognize the authority of the postexilic priesthood, as head of the postexilic community in and around Jerusalem. However, a recently published text from Emar describes an installation ritual for the priestess of the storm deity in which the priestess was anointed with blood and oil. These are the only two West Semitic installation rituals in the ancient world where priestly figures are anointed with oil.[25] Thus,

23. West Semitic is a linguistic term: it represents a language family of which Hebrew is an example. Like the languages, the cultures where these languages are spoken are related in other ways. Although this is generally true of all Semitic languages, it remains especially true of those known as West Semitic. For examples of these cultures and languages in the third and second millennia BC, see chapter 4. In the first millennium BC, they include, in addition to Israel and Judah, the surrounding lands of Philistia, Edom, Moab, Ammon, Aram, Phoenicia, and, later, Carthage and other sites around the Mediterranean where Punic was spoken.

24. For the quotation see Hess (2004b, 246; cf. forthcoming b). For the translation of the text see Fleming (1997, 436–39). For discussion of the Emar text (number 446) see Fleming (2000b, especially pp. 103–4 and 153–57). See further on pp. 118–22 below.

25. See Fleming (1998); Klingbeil (2000); Hess (2005a). See also the addition of a torch to the ceremony on the final day of the installation as the priestess goes to meet the god and live in the temple. Compare this with the "strange fire" that Nadab and Abihu offer in Lev. 10:1–2. Were they participating in a West Semitic ritual that involved the honor-

whatever reasonable, critical grounds may have existed for assuming a postexilic origin for the rite of anointing a priest with oil to compensate for the loss of the king in Jerusalem must now be revised. This does not "prove" that the priestly anointing ritual of Leviticus 8–9 must date to the end of the Late Bronze Age (1550–1200 BC); it proves only that assumptions of a postexilic origin for this element of tradition within P can no longer be accepted prima facie.

Add this evidence to the already mentioned presence of ritual calendar frameworks of six months or more with detailed seven-day ceremonies and other rites and lists of sacrifices—with no mention of a significant royal role (cf. Lev. 23 and Num. 28–29). All this evidence relates more closely to Emar texts than to later texts.[26] The resulting picture casts doubt not only on the assumptions behind various aspects of the P material but also on the assumption that the Ugaritic material—discussed in chapter 4—is the closest available extrabiblical parallel to Israelite religion.

A sixth point is more controversial. It has been argued that Deuteronomy occurs in the form of a treaty document, or covenant.[27] The biblical concept of covenant or bĕrît has a claim to antiquity in the world of ancient Israel.[28] The same is true of the ancient Near Eastern treaty. Some eighty or ninety examples of treaties made between 2400 and 650 BC are preserved.[29] These divide into two groups: those treaties made with the Hittites between c. 1400 and c. 1200 BC, and those from the regions dominated by the Neo-Assyrian Empire between the ninth and seventh centuries BC.[30] Such treaties between states served to define their

---

ing of other deities, as the torch was so used in the priestly installation ritual at Emar (Hess 2002b)?

26. This suggests, by the way, that the calendar should not be seen as the direct descendant of earlier Israelite ritual calendars (after Exod. 23:14–19; 34:18–26; and Deut. 16), but rather as the conveyer of separate and authentic earlier elements (Fleming [1999a; 1999b; 2000a; 2000b]; Hess [2004b]).

27. Lohfink (1995) has applied speech act theory to argue that Deut. 26–29 intentionally presented the picture of Moses in Moab giving a covenant in the form of a treaty between God and Israel.

28. Contrary to implications that have been read from the work of Nicholson (1986) and others, the word for covenant (br[y]t) does appear in West Semitic contexts of the second millennium BC in socioeconomic, religious, and treaty contexts in Egypt, at Alalakh and at Ugarit. Zevit (2001, 645n64) observes that at least some of the Deuteronomic laws are best understood as antecedent to seventh-century Josiah, because there are no reports that Josiah, an otherwise strong king, ever chastised anyone (individual or group) in accordance with the legislation for which he is supposed to have been responsible.

29. Kitchen (2003, 283–98) and earlier, Propp (1999, 569).

30. The Hittites described here were the dominant power of ancient Anatolia until c. 1200. Controversy surrounds the question of whether this Hittite empire can be identified with any of the Hittite peoples mentioned in the Bible. The Assyrians were centered around the Tigris River in what is today eastern Iraq.

Fig. 2. Part of Hattusas, capital of the Hittite empire (Courtesy of Richard S. Hess)

relationships. There were two types of treaties. The first type became known as the parity treaty because it was made between two powers of equal strength. The second type was the suzerain-vassal treaty, so-called because it was dictated by a state of superior power to a subject nation or state. The treaties of the Hittites were all written before the final collapse and disappearance of this empire in the early decades of the twelfth century BC.[31] Of special interest for our purposes is the form of the Hittite suzerain-vassal treaty. It consisted of the following elements:[32]

1. The *Title*, which introduces the king; for example, "Thus says the Sun, Muwattallis, the Great King, King of Hatti [the Hittites], beloved of the weather god, son of Mursilis, the Great King, the hero." Another purpose for the title was the official identification of the document as a decree of the Great King.
2. The *Historical Narrative* recounts previous relations between the Hittites and the vassal kingdom. It serves to motivate the vassal to faithfulness to his Hittite overlord.[33]

31. A branch of the ruling family continued in Carchemish, a city in what is today southern Turkey. Aspects of Hittite culture continued in the Neo-Hittite states of the first millennium BC. However, neither the Hittite language (as it is commonly known) nor this treaty form survived the collapse of the second-millennium empire.

32. For the first to identify a common structure, see Korošec (1931).

33. Ascribing to these texts "a transparent apologetic agenda: to display the Hittite protagonist in the best possible light," Lemche (1998, 159) denies their historiographical

3. The *Stipulations* take the form of case and apodictic laws and serve to effect the vassal's submission and support.[34] They include provisions that the vassal leader should visit the Hittite court regularly, furnish military aid, report plots, pay tribute, and extradite fugitives. One treaty also has a passage devoted to sexual morality. The Hittites took on few obligations to their vassals.
4. The *Document Clause* provided both for preservation of the text in a sacred place and for periodic public reading of the text. This clause is rare in treaties.
5. The *Witnesses*, usually a list of gods, witnessed the oath of the vassal accepting this treaty. Both the gods of the Hittites and the gods of the vassals were invoked as witnesses.
6. The *Curses and Blessings* are the punishments and rewards for disobedience and obedience. The curses are larger in number and more colorful than the blessings.

Parts 1, 3, and 6 always appear in the Hittite treaties. Part 2 occurs in twenty-two out of the twenty-four suzerain-vassal Hittite treaties. The other two treaties are fragmented where part 2 would be expected, but the remains suggest that part 2 was in them as well. Part 5, the Witnesses, occurs in twenty of the twenty-four treaties. Part 4, as noted, is rare. Other than Part 4, this is the customary construction of the treaties. In first-millennium BC treaties of the Neo-Assyrian empire, the curses become much more important. The historical narrative and the blessings disappear.[35]

An analysis of the structure of Deuteronomy reveals that it contains all elements of the Hittite suzerain-vassal treaty:[36]

Treaty	Deuteronomy
1. Title/Preamble	1:1–5 or 6 (God as speaker)
2. Historical Prologue	1:6–3:29
3a. Basic Commands	4–11

---

value. Yet if these were merely fantasies concocted by the Hittites (or "sweeping generalizations of quasi-historical reflection") they would not serve their purpose. The vassal would easily recognize the lies (since the history referred to is that of both overlord and vassal) and not be motivated to obey.

34. Case law, common in modern jurisprudence, envisions a particular case or circumstance and then pronounces on it. Apodictic law tends to contain only the pronouncement and does not envision a specific situation. Thus "Do not murder" is apodictic.

35. Comments such as those of Lemche (1998, 76) overlook this key difference and assume that, because treaties are found among the seventh-century BC Assyrians, there is no legitimacy to the second-millennium BC parallel with the Hittite treaties.

36. Cf. Kitchen (1989a, 124–25). The application of ancient Near Eastern treaty structure to biblical covenant originated with Mendenhall (1954).

Treaty	Deuteronomy
3b. Detailed Laws	12–26
4a. Deposit of Text	31:24–26
4b. Public Reading	31:10–13
5. Witnesses	31:19, 26, 28
6a. Blessings	28:1–14
6b. Curses	28:15–68

The biblical covenant has been understood as a combination of both treaty and law. Ancient Near Eastern law collections of the third and second millennia BC (Ur-Nammu, Lipit-Ishtar, Eshnunna, Hammurabi)—but not any that occur later—placed the blessings and curses in the same order as Deuteronomy but not as in the Hittite treaties.

Despite the difference in forms, interest in preserving an eighth- or seventh-century date for the composition of the work has inclined those scholars who do recognize a treaty structure toward a comparison with Neo-Assyrian treaties.[37]

By itself, the distinctive structure of Deuteronomy, comparable only with second-millennium BC treaties and law codes, says nothing about possible later editing and additions, not to mention the updating of the language. However, the form preserved in its first twenty-eight chapters does call into question theories that Deuteronomy was composed wholly in the eighth and seventh centuries BC.

As noted above, the Hebrew term for covenant also had antecedents in the second millennium BC. The same is true of the idea of a relationship with a deity. This occurs in the second-millennium BC West Semitic cultures of Emar, Mari, and elsewhere.[38] Already one finds a verbal approach to the chief deity and a relationship between the deity and the whole community.[39] However, it is not as developed as in Deuteronomy nor is the suzerain-vassal treaty form applied.

Seventh and last, the reader is referred to the new literary studies of the latter half of the twentieth century. These represent the strongest and most widely agreed-upon consensus challenging the older theories. As well as any other, Norman Whybray (1987) challenged the assumptions behind the formation of the Pentateuch according to the Documentary

37. Cf. Frankena (1965); Weinfeld (1972b); McCarthy (1972; 1978); Kalluveettil (1982). Steymans (1995a; 1995b) has particularly emphasized the connections between the curses and blessings of Deut. 28 and similarities found in various sources of the Neo-Assyrian king Esarhaddon. For those less optimistic about a connection with treaty structure, see Perlitt (1969); Nicholson (1986).

38. See Lewis (1996, 405–10) and Fleming (1999c, 30–31) for evidence beyond the West Semitic world.

39. See Fleming (1999c, 29–30).

Hypothesis. Among his observations, three are noted here.[40] First, the P and E documents lack sufficiently large samples to render significant conclusions. This is particularly true of E and may be one of the reasons it has sometimes been joined with J. Second, there is the problem of "a self-fulfilling prophecy" in which documents are found by application of criteria that have been created to find the documents. Whybray was neither the first nor last scholar to note this problem and it should not be ignored by the theory's proponents.[41] The circular nature of the argument consists in the history of Israel being laid out as envisioned by Wellhausen and others who then select and define the documents in such a manner as to confirm what they have created. Third, the application of the same criteria without the presumption of multiple documents yields different results. For example, Rolf Rendtorff (1986; 1990) shifted to a kind of "supplementary hypothesis" in which the emphasis is on the progressive edition of literary layers.

It is important to note that these questions concerning the Documentary Hypothesis do not thereby demonstrate a second-millennium BC composition of the Pentateuch. It is clear that the overall language of the prose texts of the Pentateuch conforms to the style of the monarchic period of Israel and Judah (c. 1000–586 BC), whatever distinctive grammatical features may occur. Long noted have been the glosses that suggest later editing and development of the text.[42] Despite the presence of early grammatical forms that distinguish the Pentateuch from other biblical literature,[43] there remains the overall impression that in its present form it was composed in the Classical Hebrew of the first half of the first millennium BC. It is not the purpose of this project to ascertain the degree of editing. Rather it is enough to observe that the old consensus on the development of Israel's religion can no longer be assumed. Instead, each type of literature in the Pentateuch may preserve traditions of greater antiquity than commonly asserted. The degree to which such elements are authentic can be determined only on a case-by-case basis, using the comparative evidence available and studying carefully the Hebrew text itself. This is not to suggest that every textual or archaeological parallel that can be found guarantees the dating. It does suggest, however,

40. Whybray's attempt to argue for a postexilic author relies heavily on Van Seters's attempts to "late date" the material in the Pentateuch, which rest on dubious historical comparisons with late Babylonian and Greek sources. See, for example, the discussions on the Genesis ancestors and my critique of his comparison of the Table of Nations in Gen. 10 with the Greek "Catalogue of Women" (Hess 1989b).

41. See Cross (2004, 10; 2005, 44).

42. E.g., there is the mention of the Chaldeans, a people of the first millennium BC, in Gen. 11:28, 31; 15:7.

43. See the third area of problems associated with the Documentary Hypothesis on p. 51.

that assumptions about dating that are based on questionable literary theories should be evaluated on the basis of relevant comparative and other evidence.

The abiding value of the Documentary Hypothesis is in the manner in which various types of Pentateuchal literature have been identified: the literature that considers the priesthood and its cult (P); the literature that emphasizes the covenant for Israel and describes its relationship with God as one of divine obligation and reciprocity (D); those elements that suggest God's role to be one of both direct confrontation with individuals and also one of work behind the scenes of human history (J); and those sections that emphasize the role of the prophets in proclaiming the message of God to the people (E). Whether or not these are different religions, they certainly represent different emphases and may reflect the presence of special groups who identified with each method of religious expression.

Religion History, Tradition History, and Orality

In the nineteenth century, the translation of ancient Near Eastern scripts and languages, such as Akkadian and Egyptian, as well as the interest in the archaeology of Bible lands, led to a new emphasis on the comparison between the literature of the ancient Near East and that of the Bible. The integration of this comparative method into biblical scholarship began with the comparison by George Smith of the Genesis flood story and that found in the Mesopotamian Gilgamesh Epic.[44] Additional comparisons were made with the Babylonian creation story, called *Enuma Elish*, as well as other ancient Near Eastern texts deemed relevant to Genesis 1–11 and other parts of the Bible.[45] In some cases these comparisons yielded seemingly valid parallels. Thus Hermann Gunkel (1862–1932) and Wolf Wilhelm Graf von Baudissin (1847–1926) attempted to study Israelite religion as it emerged from the Mesopotamian and Mediterranean influences of Babylonian and Phoenician myths.[46] Gunkel argued that Israelite religion provided evidence of shared traditions between the biblical world and the cuneiform-writing societies of ancient Mesopotamia. These traditions, understood most often as oral (rather than written), were passed down by word of mouth and occasionally written in the form of narratives or stories. They were understood by Gunkel and his successors as cumulative, that is, they gathered more

44. Mesopotamia, whose name is the Greek for "the land between the [Tigris and Euphrates] rivers," is found today in Iraq and some of Syria.

45. See Hess (1994c) for a review of the history of comparative studies of Gen. 1–11.

46. Cf. e.g., Baudissin (1911); Gunkel (1902).

and more elaboration as time went on and the stories were retold.[47] These could be found in the Hebrew Bible where they sometimes appeared as foreign elements disconnected from the surrounding text. In other cases, traditions that were integral to the biblical text of a book such as Genesis could be found by determining the smallest identifiable unit of the text and then tracing its development.[48] The scholars who used this methodology often accepted the Documentary Hypothesis and other literary critical theories. However, they sought to penetrate behind the written text to the origins of ideas and themes that influenced and became part of later Israelite religion.

Albrecht Alt (1883–1956), a student of Gunkel, extended Gunkel's tradition-historical method into other areas of ancient Israelite religion and history. He found in the cult a focal point for the collection and growth of traditions. Thus, for example, his analysis of the ancestral traditions in Genesis 12–36 (and other texts) led him to conclude that a number of tribes, each with its own deity named after an ancestor, and a number of geographical centers in Canaan, each with its own distinct El-god, were merged into the worship of the single deity Yahweh.[49] Alt also discerned other characteristics of Israel's religion, such as etiologies, which were attempts to account for sacred names or practices whose origins had been lost or forgotten. Etiologies gave them explanations suitable to their contemporary religious significance.

The theory of traditions assumes a clustering of key themes that gradually accumulated more traditions, somewhat like a snowball rolling down a hill gathering more and more snow. Martin Noth (1902–1968), working in this area, identified five such traditions as key to the background of the Pentateuch and Joshua: the exodus from Egypt; the entrance into the arable land of Palestine; the promise to the ancestors (cf. Gen. 12:1–3); the wilderness wanderings; and the revelation at Mount Sinai.[50] Gerhard von Rad (1901–1971) simplified the number of tradition complexes to two, the Exodus/conquest and the events and revelation associated with Mount Sinai.[51] Such study of traditions remains an integral part of the identification of history and religion in the Hebrew Bible. Fundamental to the assumptions of these scholars is that the various texts of the Bible can be understood only in terms of a historical development wherein original writings have undergone additions and other editorial processes that

47. See Knight (1975) for a useful summary of the study of tradition history in ancient Israel.
48. See Gunkel (1895; 1901; 1902; 1903; 1905) for the development of his thought and specific application to the traditions he identified in Genesis and Psalms.
49. See Alt (1989) and further discussion below.
50. See Noth (1972).
51. See, e.g., von Rad (1972).

have cumulatively altered their form and content to meet the political, theological, and other concerns of later bearers of the traditions.

The study of biblical traditions developed in various places, for example in the Myth and Ritual School found in Great Britain and Scandinavia.[52] This particular expression was fostered by a view of myth within the context of rituals, by the ancient Babylonian and other texts that described a New Year's Festival, and by a particular view of anthropology that argued for the diffusion of practices throughout a region and beyond.[53] Although differing among themselves in many particulars, some scholars following this approach dated comparatively late the actual writing of the biblical books. Scholars such as A. S. Kapelrud, Sigmund Mowinckel, and Helmer Ringgren developed an approach that identified a pattern of myth and ritual that could be found in Israel and throughout the ancient world. Constitutive elements were common in Babylon and Israel, for example, although they might occur in different combinations or forms. At the heart of this pattern to the cult lay the royal cult, often construed with the ascription of divine status to the king. Ringgren's own study of Israelite religion (1966), however, found a great deal more confidence in the preexilic and even premonarchic accounts of the Bible than did some of his predecessors.

This approach preferred to see oral tradition as having a dominant role. Indeed, it appeared to enjoy significant stimulus with the study of Serbo-Croatian bards who were able to memorize and recite lengthy poems without mistake. Comparisons were made with the *Iliad* and *Odyssey* of Homer in terms of oral transmission and of the accuracy of what was passed on for centuries. The relationship of all this to the ancient Near East and to the Bible was stimulated by the 1929 discovery of poetic myths about Baal and other "Canaanite" deities mentioned in the Bible, dating from the thirteenth century BC and found at the city of Ugarit near the Mediterranean coast of Syria. This gave further support to the view that lengthy poetic myths of the origins of Mediterranean and West Semitic peoples could have been orally preserved and passed along for centuries before being written down into the texts that we now have. In particular, the Ugaritic myths were studied by scholars such as Cyrus Gordon, William F. Albright, and Frank Moore Cross, who found in them themes and motifs that recur in biblical poetry.[54] For example, Ugaritic parallels are used to argue the development of the role of Israel's deity, Yahweh, as a warrior.

52. See a more complete discussion in Knight (1975).
53. See Rogerson (1974, esp. p. 67); Talmon (1978, 327).
54. See the extensive review of the study of Ugaritic in M. Smith (2001b). See also Cross (1973).

The emergence of a greater interest in folklore and other studies precipitated a renewed appreciation of the oral nature of much of the earlier materials in the Hebrew Bible. Susan Niditch (1996) argued that various forms preserved in the written text betray oral origins. This could be seen in the preservation of formulas and repetitions and in the many references to writing in the Bible that suggest it was viewed as magical in quality, the words possessing a special power by being written. Niditch found this in Exodus 17; Numbers 17; Joshua 8 and 24; Deuteronomy 6; Isaiah 8; Ezekiel 37; and Daniel 5. Niditch argues that the earlier and originally oral contents of the Bible were gradually replaced by texts, intentionally composed as literate works of art.[55] Even the appearance of extrabiblical texts from ancient Palestine does not disprove the fundamentally oral nature of the society. These inscriptions were either originally oral statements that were written later (such as letters), or, in the case of monumental inscriptions (such as the Tel Dan stele or the Moabite stele), they were set up to impress an illiterate populace.

Orality did play an important role in ancient Israel. However, these studies tend too readily to impute oral cultural features to many texts.[56] Many of these are examples of rhetoric, and occur in written as well as oral literature. Further, assumptions about low percentage figures for literacy are highly speculative. There is evidence of a large and diverse collection of extant Hebrew and other inscriptions from in and around Palestine that date from Israel's first appearance in the land (and earlier) until after the destruction of Jerusalem by the Babylonians in 587/586 BC.[57] This has been further supported by the 2005 discovery of a tenth-century BC abecedary in the Judean hill country site of Tel Zayit, south of Jerusalem. Written in a distinctive Hebrew script, the abecedary establishes the presence of people learning to read and write in the villages of ancient Judah at a time most associate with the period of the United

55. Later texts such as Jeremiah and Chronicles express a literate mentality and write earlier history from this perspective; whereas, texts such as Deut. 6; 17; 2 Kings 23; Jer. 36; and Neh. 8 demonstrate strong oral culture skills (e.g., memorization) and the need to explain things to a largely illiterate audience.

56. For example, the Izbet Sartah abecedary may be magical but there is nothing to indicate this. Rather, the crude writing suggests a text for learning how to write. Cf. also the abecedary from Tel Zayit below.

57. For example, many ancient Near Eastern treaties required the vassal king to copy and read them. How do the Karatepe, Tell Fakhariyeh, and other bilingual inscriptions relate to the theory that these monumental inscriptions served a purely iconic purpose? If they were only for the purpose of impressing an illiterate population, why go to the trouble of writing the text in two languages and two scripts? For further critique and additional problems, see the important reviews of Millard (1998b) and Schniedewind (2000). See also Hess (2002a) for a summary of the written evidence from Iron Age Palestine.

Monarchy.[58] Schniedewind (2004) affirms the complex biblical awareness of the movement from oral to written traditions and the formation
of the idea of a canon. Carr (2005), on the basis of literacy studies in
comparative Classical and ancient Near Eastern societies, suggests that
a purpose of the development of writing may have to do with the cultural
education of people and the promotion of memorization, a concern not
unknown in the Hebrew Bible (Deut. 6:4–9).

At the same time, the continued publication of thousands of cuneiform texts from the eighteenth-century BC north Syrian site of Mari
has revealed new and previously unrecognized understandings of the
background out of which the ancestral traditions of Genesis may have
emerged. Fleming (2004) cites a number of correspondences from these
texts, providing specific connections with Benjamin and others.[59] Van
Seters (1983a) had denied the validity of comparing the pastoralist ancestors with archives from an urban source such as Mari.[60] That is to say,
the comparison was considered inappropriate because Abraham, Isaac,
and Jacob appear as herders and nomads, whereas Mari was a city. However, it is now known that Mari's king, Zimri-Lim, was also chief of the
northern coalition of tribes around Mari, the *Binu Sim'al*. Thus he ruled
both the urban center and the tribes, and he did so with two separate
organizations. The tribes were herders and nomads, and thus fall into
a similar social category as the ancestors in Genesis 12–36.

Thus the roles of both oral and written traditions remain important
in the study of the biblical texts. Further, their historical development
and editing are considerations that must be addressed any time a text is
cited. Nevertheless, the diversity of opinion on almost every question of
every text threatens to render the biblical text unusable. I will attempt
to use comparative evidence, where appropriate, in the identification
of relevant texts that can be ascribed to a particular time in Israel's his-

58. The excavations were conducted under the direction of Ron Tappy. Initial study of
the orthography of the inscription was made by P. Kyle McCarter Jr. See Hess (2006).

59. At eighteenth-century BC Mari there were two tribal federations, the *Binu Sim'al*
and the *Binu Yamina*. The *Binu Yamina*, who lay to the "right" or south ("yamina"),
wandered in (but did not control) territories almost as far south as Palestine. A key
sacred center of this group was Harran. Interestingly, Israelite Benjamin was a tribe
whose ancestor was one of the sons of Rachel and Jacob. The other son was Joseph,
whose own sons, Manasseh and Ephraim, formed two tribes that settled to the north
of Benjamin, thereby positioning Benjamin to the "right"—or south—of these fraternal
tribes. Further, Jacob, father of Benjamin, was associated with the ancestral home of
the same city, Harran. Of course, Harran was also the starting point of Abram in his
journey to Canaan (Gen. 12).

The genealogies of Abram connect the ancestor not only with Israel, but also the inland
tribal groups of Edom, Moab, and Ammon. Like the tribal coalition of the *Binu Yamina*
(and the *Binu Sim'al*), these tribal groups occupy inland areas.

60. Cf. also Thompson (1974).

tory. Overall, it seems best to maintain an open mind about the dating of ancient Israelite traditions.

Mid-Twentieth-Century Directions

The Israeli scholar and biblical historian, Yehezkel Kaufmann (1955; 1960) labored on Israel's history and concluded, primarily from the biblical record, that the distinction between Canaanite image worship and Israelite aniconic monotheism was early and radical. His distinctive approach preserved an appreciation of the unique contribution that the Israelites made as outsiders coming into the land of promise.

Like Alt before him, the German scholar Georg Fohrer (1968) distinguished between the nomadic clan religion of the immigrating Israelites and the settled religion of the Canaanite inhabitants of the land and its population centers. However, he also emphasized four effects of both societies that changed and developed the religion. First among these was the Mosaic religion of Yahweh. In addition, the advent of the kingship, of prophecy, and of Deuteronomistic theology all had an impact on religion. Fohrer is an excellent example of that distinctively European approach that emphasizes the history of ideas.

In America, the dominant voice of William F. Albright contended for an early Mosaic monotheism that fixed the fundamentals of Israelite religion at the nation's beginning.[61] David Noel Freedman and Frank Moore Cross, who were students of Albright's, would recognize the importance of key early poetic texts in the Pentateuch, Psalms, and elsewhere.[62] Such archaic literature as Exodus 15, Judges 5, and Psalm 68 provided glimpses into premonarchic Israel and its belief in Yahweh as a warrior who comes from the southern mountains to lead his people to victory. G. Ernest Wright also employed a methodology that separated the religion of Israel from that of the surrounding peoples in the land. The theology of the Old Testament tied into the religion of Israel with the identification and confession of the mighty acts of God in the nation's history.

Cross's *Canaanite Myth and Hebrew Epic: Essays in the History of the Religion of Israel* appeared in 1973. The essays in this text dealt with a variety of topics. Of note was the systematic application of the Baal cycle and other Ugaritic myth sources as a template against which to compare early narratives and poetry in the Bible and their tradition history. In many ways this text served as a programmatic outline for Cross's

61. Albright (1953; 1957; 1968).
62. Cf. also Zoebel (1965; 1993); and Niditch (1997; discussed below on pp. 72–73).

students and others who built on his analyses.[63] Beyond this, the work reviewed and developed a comprehensive interpretation of Israelite religion as a distinctive but identifiable development from Late Bronze Age antecedents through the Iron Age (1200–586 BC) and into the postexilic Persian period (539–332 BC). The study provided both for an appreciation of Israelite religion as a living and evolving phenomenon and an awareness of its early appearance and development. In comparison with Wright, Kaufmann, Albright, and others, this approach represented a dramatic departure. Instead of a radical contrast between Israel and its neighbors, Cross argued that the religion developed from previous forms and ideas in Ugaritic and Canaanite cult and myth. This understanding paved the way for immense changes in the field that were to appear in the following decades.

The American school, as represented by Albright, Cross, Freedman, and others, grounded their understanding of Israelite religion in the relationship of the biblical text to the archaeology and extrabiblical texts of ancient Palestine and the ancient Near East in general. This was an optimistic era in which scholars felt that they could positively correlate with the biblical texts distinctive aspects in ancient Near Eastern texts from as early as the Middle Bronze Age (c. 2000–c. 1550 BC). Albright, along with other historians and archaeologists such as Roland de Vaux, Benjamin Mazar, Cyrus Gordon, Nelson Glueck, and Dame Kathleen Kenyon, to mention but a few, sought to situate even the earliest of the biblical periods (e.g., the ancestors in Gen. 12–36) in the textual world of West Semitic archives and excavations. This positive assessment is nowhere more present than in Albright's own works on Israelite history, archaeology, and religion, which in their time were standard textbooks for American students in their respective fields.[64] Albright's positive correlation of the Old Testament record to the archaeological evidence (textual and material) for the ancestors of Genesis 12–36 was seriously challenged by Thompson (1974) and Van Seters (1975). Their negative evaluation of biblical historiography would not be the last word, however. Much more consequential has been the manner in which, despite its debt to a figure such as Albright, study of Israelite history and religion during the past three decades has ignored his work as well as that of many others of that generation. One can look through bibliographies in many major works on Israelite religion and see no mention of key works by Albright and like-minded scholars of his generation. The reason for this lies in the new evidence and new methodologies that emerged in the last quarter of the twentieth century.

63. Cf. e.g., Miller, Hanson, and McBride (1987).
64. See Albright (1949; 1953; 1957); and his last major work before his death (1968).

The Last Thirty Years

In 1978 Rainer Albertz published his study, *Persönliche Frömmigkeit und Offizielle Religion: Religionsinterner Pluralismus in Israel und Babylon*. This work was based on a fundamental distinction between personal or popular religion and state religion. This distinction opened the door to the important realization that diverse and perhaps contradictory religious beliefs and practices occur in the same state and at the same time. There are many levels on which religion and religious expression take place. The result has been a different way of looking at Israelite religion. Scholars recognized that Israel need not have had a single religion, nor even two competing religions, but that they could have had many religious practices and beliefs that changed over time. Albertz's *Religionsgeschichte Israels in alttestamentlicher Zeit* appeared in 1992 and was translated into English in 1994 as *A History of Israelite Religion in the Old Testament Period*. Following a traditional literary critical approach and building on the research of Noth (and of Alt for the Genesis narratives), Albertz presented a historical perspective of the development of Israelite religion. Albertz used his distinction between popular (or better, family or local) and state religion as a method for the historical and critical study of the religious beliefs of Israel. His approach combines skepticism of any reliable ancestral or exodus texts preserved in the Bible with acceptance of traditional source critical approaches.

The past three decades of research in Israelite religion have also been influenced by three other significant developments. First, the already-mentioned studies critical of the ancestors or "patriarchs" of Genesis 12–36 spawned an entire school of thought, centered at the University of Copenhagen, that doubted all historical texts in the Bible, especially calling into question any identifiable, historical memory of the second millennium BC in the Hebrew Bible. Although this did not become the dominant view, its influence has been such that discussions of Israelite history no longer assume the presence of authentic recollections in the Old Testament. The burden of proof, certainly for the second millennium BC and often for the first millennium BC, has shifted to those who argue a historical source.[65] The skepticism of the early Israelite period has led to a reevaluation of the origins of Israelite religion, calling into question all assumptions concerning the beliefs of the premonarchic period. Second, research into Israelite religion has been for the most part separated from the traditional theological disciplines. The desire to tie this study to theology in some manner, which was characteristic of much

---

65. See for example the essays in Day (2004b).

earlier research, has given way to the examination of religious questions within the context of archaeology, history, and other social sciences. This gave a priority to the material and textual evidence outside the Bible as a potential source of neutral and unbiased information. Without the assumptions of theological relevance for the subject, the biblical text becomes far less valuable, a source of ideology and "tendenz" rather than an explicit account of ancient religion. Third, there has been the discovery of new evidence, both textual and archaeological, that has led to a different understanding of ancient Israel and of its beliefs than had previously been supposed. It is this evidence, along with the methods of the social sciences, that has profoundly changed the discipline.

An example of this may be found in the discovery and publication of the Kuntillet ʿAjrud texts, found in northern Sinai and dated c. 800 BC. These texts appear to mention Yahweh in conjunction with the West Semitic goddess Asherah. This has led to a reconsideration of Israelite religion in terms of its surrounding context (both earlier than and contemporary to the states of Israel and Judah). The religion of ancient Israel could no longer be divided into those who worshiped only Yahweh and those who rejected Yahweh and worshiped other deities. Instead, Israelites could and did honor both Yahweh and other deities at the same time and in the same place.

There are too many examples of this new direction and such an abundance of authors that judicious consideration of even the most important would require its own volume. The study here will briefly examine a sampling in order to appreciate the direction of the field and the contribution of some of the most interesting and significant writers.

Tryggve N. D. Mettinger is a Swedish scholar whose publications have examined specific aspects of the religion of Israel. His earlier work (1976) addressed concerns of divine legitimacy and presence in kingship in Israel, a theme not unrelated to the Myth and Ritual School. His 1988 study of the divine names of God represented a view that accentuated the differences between Israel's deity and those of the surrounding cultures. It suggested a primarily theological approach to the analysis of the ancient names of God as presented by the Hebrew Bible. More controversial was Mettinger's (1995) analysis of the lack of divine images in the Israelite faith. Mettinger determined that this phenomenon, usually identified as aniconism, had precedents in the desert south of Israel, as well as in surrounding (Mesopotamian and Egyptian), contemporary (Phoenician), and later (Punic, Nabatean, and Arabian) cultures. In his 2001 study of the role of dying and rising deities in the ancient Near Eastern and Mediterranean worlds, Mettinger examines fundamental questions about the differences among many of these cultures and their deities. The value of this study in the general field of ancient Israelite religion was that it recognized the importance of the sociological approaches of Evans-Pritchard, Geertz, and other field studies, which emphasized the importance of treating each culture separately and not making generalizations from one people group to another. The work of Mettinger epitomizes this approach as he traces similarities but also catalogs differences in the available evidence on the treatment of dying and rising deities over several millennia and continents. This approach represents an ideal, one that is not always attained in the study of long dead cultures due to the absence of sufficient and clear evidence of cultic practices and beliefs.

The study of Semitic cultures, particularly that of Ugarit, has had an impact on the analysis of the Israelite cult. The comparative study of Israel's cult, and particularly of the sacrifices of the Pentateuch, has been the concern of scholars such as Baruch Levine. Levine's approach has been philologically oriented. For example, he has compared the types of sacrifices at Ugarit and in Akkadian ritual texts from Mesopotamia with those having similar or cognate names in the Hebrew Bible. He has done the same with entire ritual texts and with particular expressions in order to ascertain both similarities and differences between their usage in the Bible and in these earlier sources.[66]

Jacob Milgrom has also studied the ancient Near Eastern, Second Temple, and Rabbinic sources in his analysis of the cultic texts of Leviticus and elsewhere in the Pentateuch.[67] He gives special consideration to anthropological categories, propounded by scholars such as Mary Douglas and others, in analyzing holiness and impurity along with life and death as key poles for interpreting the biblical descriptions of the sacrifices and cult.[68] As already noted, his conclusions challenge both the postexilic date for the Priestly source (P) and the sequence of the Holiness Code (Lev. 17–26) and the sacrificial texts.

Another scholar whose focus has been on cults is Menahem Haran, who has published largely in modern Hebrew. His distinctions between the tabernacle and temples of the Bible, on the one hand, and the "high places" (bāmôt, singular bāmāh) on the other, as well as his arguments for a more precise delineation between archaeological finds and cult items (such as altars, for example) described in the Bible, have been influential in the understanding of religious cult in ancient Israel.[69] From a differ-

66. See Levine (1963; 1965; 1974; 1993a); and his synthetic commentaries (1989; 1993b; 2000).
67. The Second Temple period is generally understood to be the period from the rebuilding of the temple described in Zechariah c. 517 BC, until the Roman destruction of it in AD 70.
68. See Milgrom (1991; 2000a; 2000b); and my review in Hess (2002c).
69. See Haran (1993; 1995).

ent perspective, Moshe Weinfeld, also an Israeli scholar, examined the Deuteronomistic Law and History. His theological analyses of the material in Deuteronomy, including studies of its covenant terminology and of its teaching on social justice, emphasized the contextual background of the ancient Near East.[70] This included study of the second- and first-millennia BC treaties as well as a wide variety of royal and monumental sources. Further research examined the background of Joshua in light of foundation texts of the Mediterranean world as well as the ancient Near East.[71] The effect has been to provide form critical studies based in the attested context of the ancient world.

A different dimension of Israelite religion may be seen in the work of a scholar such as Moshe Greenberg. Along with his emphasis on the prophet Ezekiel and the religion of the exilic and postexilic periods, Greenberg's study of extemporaneous prayer in the Hebrew Bible (1983b; 1997) gives evidence of an appreciation of the internal aspect of the faith of Israelites in general. Perhaps even more significant is Greenberg's argument (1997) that these prayers of ancient Israel do not give evidence of an evolution in popular beliefs over the centuries. This represents a contrary view on the religion of Israel in which faith is not necessarily given to profound changes during the period of the monarchy and later. Using primarily extrabiblical sources, Jeffrey Tigay addressed a different dimension of Israelite religion, similarly asserting the lack of change. His studies of the extrabiblical Hebrew inscriptions—and especially of the personal names of the inhabitants of the northern kingdom of Israel and of the southern kingdom of Judah—argued that the evidence points to the widespread worship of a single deity. The works of Greenberg and Tigay remain a strong contrast to the prevailing view that assumes a development in ancient Israel from polytheism to the worship of a single deity, beginning in the time of the divided monarchy (c. 931–c. 586 BC).

Recent decades of research have witnessed an increasing interest in gender studies that have various levels of correlation with Israelite religion. Carol L. Meyers looked at women's roles from anthropological and archaeological perspectives, with application to biblical texts such as Genesis 3 and to the roles of women in the cult.[72] One may also mention Tikva Frymer-Kensky, who examines these questions from the perspective of ancient Near Eastern texts; Phyllis Bird, as a scholar of traditional critical approaches and modern gender studies who discusses the roles of men and women in the cult; and scholars such as Phyllis

70. See Weinfeld (1970; 1972a; 1972b; 1995; 1996). Like Milgrom, Weinfeld (1991) also published his ideas in the form of a detailed scholarly commentary.
71. See Weinfeld (1993) and, for Second Temple Judaism, Weinfeld (2005).
72. See C. Meyers (1988; 2002; 2005).

Trible and Cheryl Exum, whose studies of biblical narratives touch on the role of women in the cult.[73] There are also examples of many specialized subjects, of which the study of the goddess Asherah by scholars such as Urs Winter (1983), Judith M. Hadley (2000), and William Dever (2005) is one example.

Liberation and two-thirds–world readings have also addressed the question of Israelite religion in a variety of ways. Norman Gottwald's 1979 groundbreaking analysis of the emergence of Israel in Canaan at the beginning of the Iron Age (c. 1200 BC) presented a Marxist reading of the socioeconomic conditions of the inhabitants of the surrounding cities of Canaan, their revolt against their masters, and their arrival in the hills of Palestine where they formed egalitarian communities. His understanding of an "exodus group" from Egypt who arrived in the hill country at this time allowed Gottwald to argue that they transformed the society of these "revolting peasants" into one characterized by communal and equal living. This small group of outsiders could have brought with them the belief in a single deity, Yahweh.[74] The result was a religious faith that catalyzed the oppressed and poor of the land. Such an interpretation has been criticized for its selective use of biblical texts and for the absence of evidence that Israel was ever egalitarian, an especially problematic view in light of the pictures of leadership and the warfare ideology that permeate Joshua and Judges. In contrast to Gottwald, M. Daniel Carroll R. has examined the world of eighth-century BC Israel as presented in the text of Amos.[75] He exemplifies an attempt to analyze the material using philosophies and methods that take into account the poor of Latin America and elsewhere. The result is the beginning of a different picture of Amos and his society, one that emphasizes the injustice and sin of the society as part of a false picture of reality created by the leadership. Yahweh is personally involved in the prophetic indictment of Israel.

Karel van der Toorn developed the distinction between family and state religion and also took into account the comparative Semitic texts in his 1996 study *Family Religion in Babylonia, Syria, and Israel: Continuity and Changes in the Forms of Religious Life*. According to van der Toorn, with the rise of the Israelite state, there emerged both a national religion and a family religion, the latter centered on the ancestor cult. The prophetic reaction to the politics of the northern kingdom, followed by its collapse (c. 722 BC), led to the loss of belief in the state deity as well as a diaspora

73. See Frymer-Kensky (1992; 2002); Bird (1997a; 1997b); Trible (1978; 1984); Exum (1993).
74. See especially Gottwald (1989).
75. See Carroll (1992) for his sociological analysis and application to the two-thirds world.

that cut families off from their ancestral burial places. In this context the Deuteronomists flourished and were able to promote belief in the sole deity, Yahweh, who allowed for both family devotion as well as a faith that would survive the destruction of the temple and of Jerusalem. This is an intriguing thesis that need not be proved in every detail for it to provide elements of a possible interpretation of popular religious life in ancient Israel. For such scholars monotheism and even monolatry were late in their appearance in Israel, where polytheism that matched neighboring cultures was predominant for most of the Iron Age.

Others, however, have not been so quick to abandon the early development of monotheism in Israel. As already noted, Tigay (1986) surveyed the extrabiblical Hebrew inscriptions, and especially the personal names, in order to argue for exclusive worship of Yahweh in the monarchy. This relatively brief monograph remains a key source for some of the strongest arguments that the overwhelming majority of inscriptions, if one includes seals and seal impressions (called bullae) that bear almost exclusively personal names, know only of Yahweh as the deity who is worshiped in the southern kingdom of Judah and in the northern kingdom of Israel.

Turning to ancient Israelite personal names in the Bible, Johannes de Moor (1990a; 1990b) argued for the presence of Yahweh worship in the earliest period (before 1000 BC). He followed the earlier onomastic studies of Tigay and others in objecting to any argument for large-scale redaction of the biblical record of personal names in favor of a monotheistic perspective. His objection is supported by the presence of only a small number of polytheistic names in the Bible. That is to say, if later Israel wished to obscure an earlier age of universal polytheism, one would expect it to eliminate all biblical names of Israelites that could be interpreted as owing allegiance to another god or goddess. But this is not the case. Thus personal names with El are more popular than Yahweh names before the ninth century, but both deities were identified in Israel before David.[76]

Robert Gnuse (1997) sought to survey the views of the question of Israel's origins and especially the place of religion in the history of Israel from c. 1200 BC until the postexilic period. Gnuse used a model of evolutionary development with intermittent revolutionary changes. According to Gnuse, monotheism is best understood as a development from

---

76. De Moor does not consider the possibility that El could be a generic term for a deity such as Yahweh. For criticisms of some of the derivations of Yahweh in extrabiblical sources, see Hess (1991a). De Moor (1997) acknowledges my criticism but continues to affirm his identifications of Yahweh and of Moses as made earlier. For support of the preservation of authentic personal names from before the monarchy (pre-1000 BC) see Hess (2003a; 2004c).

a polytheism that remained committed to the existence of other deities right into the exilic period (after 587 BC). It was only with the writings of Deutero-Isaiah in the postexilic period that monotheism emerged as a clear belief among the Israelite peoples. A great part of Gnuse's argument appears to rest on the assumption that sometime in the mid-first millennium BC (eighth to sixth centuries) there was a revolution across the known world from India to Greece that brought about the acceptance of monotheism in Israel. This understanding carries forward the "Axial Age" theory in which this period of time was crucial for the emergence of modern concepts and theories.[77] This, plus the crucible of the exile, led Israel to a higher and better understanding of its faith, an ethical monotheism. While there are some reservations, particularly in terms of Gnuse's methodology, there seems to be inconsistency in Gnuse's skepticism toward early Israelite worship of a single god. While he attempts to create a variety of ties with first-millennium beliefs and ideas, he too readily dismisses those of the second millennium. By his own admission, Pharaoh Akhenaten's fourteenth-century BC cult of the Aten was one of the earliest moves toward monotheism.[78] Yet he discredits any association between that cult and early Israel. Further, evidence for the worship of only one god as found in the personal names of Israelites in the Old Testament period, both in the Bible and in extrabiblical inscriptions, creates a problem for Gnuse's theory. His attempt to develop Albertz's argument that the names reflect only family piety and not the religion of society is not convincing. It is a false dichotomy to assume that these two elements of religion are separate and isolated. It is one thing to talk about the emphasis on national deities in surrounding cultures (Ammonites, Moabites, etc.) but something else to demonstrate that this is virtually the only deity named in their personal names, as is the case in late monarchic Judah (and to a lesser extent Israel). The latter is unique to Judah and it is incorrect to ignore or downplay this significant distinction in order to force the evidence into a particular interpretation.[79]

Susan Niditch (1997) provides a sociological study of Israelite religion based on a critical reading of biblical texts. This reading reflects the Albright tradition as maintained through the influence of scholars such as Cross and Freedman, who accept that early and even premonarchic legal texts and poetry can be found in the Hebrew Bible. Niditch uses categories of religious experience ultimately derived from Ninian Smart as the outline for the book: experiential, mythical, ethical, ritual.[80] Niditch's most provocative observations appear in her study of ritual as-

77. See, for example, Machinist (1986).
78. See more on this below.
79. See further argument and evidence in Hess (forthcoming a).
80. See Smart (1960; 1969; 1983; 1989) and discussion above.

pects of Israelite religion. She finds in the Passover narrative (Exod. 12) the transition from slavery to freedom remembered in a festival whose description is reduced to the basics. The Day of Atonement (Lev. 16) stresses the key role of the high priest. The trial of the woman suspected of adultery (Num. 5) is filled with symbols of the woman's sexuality (barley) and powerlessness (the uncovering of her hair). However, the brevity of Niditch's work does not allow for a more detailed discussion of the understanding of Israelite religion that the (extrabiblical) textual, onomastic, iconographic, and archaeological evidence suggest in earlier and contemporary periods.

Also in 1997 there appeared a collection of essays edited by Hershel Shanks and Jack Meinhardt, *Aspects of Monotheism: How God Is One*. While the study of Israelite religion has given rise to many collections of essays, this one is of special interest as it constitutes a dialogue between scholars of differing views who are leaders in the disciplines of Egyptology, Assyriology, and biblical studies. The first study is Redford's analysis of the religious reforms introduced to fourteenth-century BC Egypt by the pharaoh Akhenaten. Redford considers the contribution of his own excavations to understanding this movement, known as the Amarna revolution. It was, in its time, a disenfranchisement of other gods and their temples in Egypt and the acknowledgment of a single deity, the Aten, as the one who was worshiped by the royal family and others throughout Egypt. According to Redford, Akhenaten was a monotheist who displayed characteristic intolerance of other deities and privileged his own god as the sole creator deity and alone worthy of worship. However, Redford discounts any connection with Moses and the emergence of monotheism in the religion of Israel. Redford's presentation is the only one in the book that has no documentation or footnotes. Therefore, his assertions are presented without substantiation of a sort that is necessary for evaluation.

William Dever provides an important survey of extrabiblical archaeological (and some textual) evidence of religion in Iron Age Israel between 1200 and 586 BC. His study is a valuable survey of the field from the perspective of Syro-Palestinian archaeology. It argues the importance of the extrabiblical evidence for understanding the popular religion of Israel. Dever focuses on a variety of items that have been excavated and associated with Israelite religion but do not appear in the Old Testament. Dozens of terra cotta offering stands and small horned altars have been excavated west of the Jordan but none are mentioned in the Bible. Again, the evidence for the prominence of Asherah, both in the hundreds of figurines and in the inscriptions that suggest her association with Yahweh, indicate the importance of this goddess that is only hinted at in the Bible. Dever (2005) continues his study of the subject, seeking to argue that the religion of Israelite women was ignored or misunderstood by male biblical writers. This form of religious expression can best be identified by the archaeological remains. Dever again argues that the figurines represent the goddess Asherah. Therefore, this deity was concerned with the fertility of women and with their general prosperity. However, much of this remains speculative and is similar to the contemporary "paradox" that exists between the liberation theology that theologians touted as the best way to address inequities for Latin American women, and their actual preference for Pentecostalism.[81] Modern theories about what women (or men) should and should not believe do not necessarily reflect actual behavior.

P. Kyle McCarter's essay in the Shanks and Meinhardt volume begins by setting the reforms of Hezekiah and Josiah, two "monotheistic" reforming kings in eighth- and seventh-century BC Jerusalem, in the context of the reform of the seventh-century pharaoh Shabaka, who also discovered an ancient text and attempted to base reforms on it. He surveys archaeological evidence such as Hezekiah's wall, the Kuntillet ʿAjrud inscriptions and sanctuary, and Mesopotamian texts that suggest a movement toward a single deity in interaction with biblical texts. However, his contention that other nations surrounding Israel and Judah were similar in their worship of a single national deity does not stand up to the evidence. First, by McCarter's own admission he must exclude the Phoenician states since they clearly worshiped multiple deities. Second, his evidence for nations east and south of Judah does not hold up under close scrutiny. For one thing, the Ammonite corpus shows examples of many different divine names within its onomastic collection, unlike the personal names (biblical and extrabiblical) in Judah and even Israel. The fact is that the evidence from nations such as Edom is ambiguous and open to various interpretations, as Dever suggests.

Keel and Uehlinger's volume (1992; English translation 1998) was hailed as the most important work available on Israelite religion. Its value can be found in its summary of all the extrabiblical evidence available to the authors in terms of ancient Palestinian cultic practices. No other publication has cataloged and produced a century-by-century survey of the representational art of ancient Palestine with a full awareness of the dominant forms and motifs, and how these develop and change. By focusing on the evidence and avoiding extensive biblical interpretations and correlations, Keel and Uehlinger succeed in providing a useful volume for anyone interested in the subject. I will summarize the particulars of their evidence as it relates to the content of succeeding chapters.

81. Cf. B. Martin (2001) and the discussion in chapter 2 on sociological studies of religion.

Patrick J. Miller Jr. (2000) provides a thorough, contemporary summary of the major areas of research that touch on the question of the beliefs and practices of ancient Israel. Of particular importance are the essays covering the teaching role of the priests, the intercessory and healing roles of the prophet, and the checks placed on royal power. Less convincing is Miller's acceptance of the royal participation in an enthronement of Yahweh festival at the time of the Feast of Tabernacles, an interpretation similar to Mowinckel.

John Day (2000) provides a useful guide for understanding many of the major deities mentioned in the Old Testament. Day relies heavily on the evidence from the texts found at Ugarit. Day demonstrates persuasively that Yahweh's origins are not the same as El's of Ugarit. Asherah is shown to be the consort of El at Ugarit. Her connection with Baal in the Bible is not as a description of the chief divine couple, according to Day, but rather a biblical polemic to condemn both deities. The biblical writers appropriate Baal imagery from Ugarit, including the god's appearance as a dying and living deity. In particular Hosea takes this imagery and uses it for his own purposes in his indictment of the northern kingdom. Astarte and Anat, wives of Baal at Ugarit, become deities of minimal description during Israel's monarchy, although Day finds continuing traces of them in some rhetorical wordplay. Day reasonably identifies Astarte with the Queen of Heaven, mentioned in Jeremiah 7:18; 44:17–19, 45. The sun and moon are both deities that are rejected by the biblical authors. Day reviews the solar evidence relevant to Samson, his places of sojourn, and his experiences. A lengthy section on Isaiah 14 and the imagery of Lucifer there is set in both a historical and mythological context. In the former, Nebuchadnezzar is the Lucifer figure, whereas the mythological context goes back to the Baal epic and the description of Athtar's failed attempt to take over the god's throne. Mot and Resheph, who both appear in the Bible as common nouns (death and pestilence), have various levels of personification in biblical texts, from echoes of mythic themes to more apparent manifestations of these figures. Day seeks to answer the argument of Tigay that the dominant Yahwistic elements in the personal names from ancient Israel demonstrate monotheism throughout the monarchy. While Day is correct that the presence of Yahwistic names does not prove widespread monotheism (pp. 226–28), he is incorrect to minimize the significance of this data. It is a significant counterbalance to other evidence. Neither Israel nor Judah were monolithic in either monotheism or polytheism.

Mark S. Smith (1990a; revised 2003) represents a unique synthesis of virtually all the relevant textual (biblical and otherwise) and much of the archaeological evidence. Smith argues that there are three major tendencies in the history of Israelite religion. There is the convergence of the characteristics of deities such as El, Baal, and Asherah into those of Yahweh. There is the divergence of the figures of Baal and Asherah from Yahweh. Finally, there is the role of the monarchy in the acceptance of various deities and images associated with Yahweh as well as later rejection of these under Josiah. Smith then turns his attention toward the evidence for various deities during the period of the Judges, that is, Iron Age I (c. 1200–c. 1000 BC), which was largely a time that saw the convergence of deities such as El and Yahweh. Poetic texts such as Exodus 15, Deuteronomy 32, and Psalm 82 preserve the belief of this period where El was still the chief deity and Yahweh (like Baal in the Ugaritic literature) was a subordinate. References to the goddess Asherah and to ʾăšērîm in the Bible do not prove that this goddess was recognized in Iron Age Israel. They are either generic references to female deities (in the case of the plural form), references to a cult image of Yahweh, or a kind of resurrection of the goddess by the later Deuteronomists (monotheistic theologians from the time of Josiah in the late seventh century BC, and later) who write this deity's name back into the history of Israel in an attempt to demonstrate its monarchical apostasy. Baal was a clear threat from the ninth century onward as the account of Ahab and Jezebel's attempt to introduce the Tyrian form of this deity (Baal Shamem) demonstrates (1 Kings 18). Their ill-fated endeavor led to a prophetic revolt and intolerance for the god. Nevertheless, various characteristics such as those of the storm and storm cloud were adopted and applied to Yahweh. As noted, Asherah was reduced to a cult symbol of Yahweh. However, the female characteristics of Yahweh and some background to the personification of Wisdom (e.g., Prov. 3) owe their origins to Asherah. The sun deity was subsumed by Yahweh, who took on its characteristics. The actual symbol of the sun in the form of the winged sun disk became a later symbol of the Judean monarchy. The cult of the dead was largely tolerated, except possibly for necromancy, until the eighth century or later, when the prophetic literature begins to condemn it.

Mark S. Smith (2001a) continues his study and analysis of Ugaritic texts and their relation to the interpretation of the biblical text. Smith creates a model for the analysis of West Semitic religion as found in the Bible and at Ugarit. Central to this contribution is the picture of the Ugaritic pantheon as a family, similar to Ugarit's royal family. In this family El and his consort, Asherah, occupy the first and highest level of the hierarchy. On the second level is the family of the supreme couple, the seventy sons of Asherah (Athirat in Ugaritic texts). This family receives support and service by the remaining two lower levels of the pantheon. These are occupied by craft specialists and other messengers and domestic servants. Smith suggests that this royal family model formed the basis for early Israel's pantheon. He rejects early belief in a single deity by ancient Israel. He prefers to understand early biblical poems (Num. 23, 24; Deut. 32; Judg. 5; and Ps. 82) as indicating that Yahweh was a second-level deity subservient to El. Only later did Yahweh become identified with El and achieve first-level status in the pantheon. Even during the ninth and eighth centuries BC, biblical prophets such as Elijah, Hosea, and Amos did not exclude the possibility of multiple deities among other nations, although they condemned Israel for worshiping deities other than Yahweh. It was sociological factors such as the decline in the importance of the family lineage-based society and the emergence of supranational powers such as Assyria and Babylonia in the seventh and sixth centuries that led to the emergence of a belief in only one deity. Especially the latter drove the writer of Isaiah 40–55 to employ rhetorical techniques that contrasted the efforts needed to manufacture idols with the power of Yahweh as the creator of all.

Smith appropriately questions the old model of Frazer about dying and rising gods. Discussion about early monotheism centers around the prohibition of other gods and images in the Decalogue. Although there are allusions to some matters such as the relation of divinity and royalty in the biblical text, there is little direct biblical evidence for the Ugaritic pantheon model of a divine family that Smith proposes. In fact, even in such matters as the royal connection, there are many examples in what the Bible regards as early Israelite religion where cult and worship do not involve the king at all. Indeed, here Emar and its archive can provide balance. At Emar the emphasis on a pantheon is far less prominent than at Ugarit. In fact, the entire religious picture is considerably different than Ugarit and in many ways closer to biblical Israel, both sociologically and in matters of cult practice.

Ziony Zevit (2001) has produced a comprehensive review and assessment of the archaeological and textual sources for the religion of ancient Israel. His book is methodologically rigorous and the most complete inventory of the relevant data on the history of ancient Israelite religion yet available. Zevit makes a conscious effort to provide a typological framework in order to categorize the diversity of evidence. For the author, as for the writers of the Old Testament, the Israelites as a whole and in smaller groups worshiped a variety of deities whose identity and myths are in some cases known and in other cases unknown. In his review of the various cult places where Israelites of the Iron Age worshiped, the archaeological evidence allows Zevit to propose examples where the presence of two cult stands, two altars, and/or pairs of other religious implements suggest the worship of two deities. Examples of this and of some cases where three or more deities were worshiped suggest polytheism in many of the urban centers throughout northern and southern Israel.

However, there are examples of cult sites whose singleness might suggest a single deity. Preeminent among these is the early Iron Age site on Mount Ebal (c. 250–1150 BC) that Zevit identifies as a bona fide cult site where Israelites worshiped. Its unique nature can now be set in a context of excavated Iron Age cult sites that, particularly in the northern kingdom, demonstrate that singularity was the norm rather than the exception.[82]

Zevit's discussion of the inscriptional evidence allows him to reexamine the inscriptions traditionally cited in a survey of Israelite religion. His is one of the few works on religion to publish a full examination of the paleography, morphology, and interpretation of a host of inscriptions previously available only in part or not at all. Texts from Khirbet Beit Lei, Khirbet el-Qom, Kuntillet ʿAjrud, En Gedi, and elsewhere come under Zevit's close examination (all discussed below in chapter 10). As will be argued, I believe that he is correct to see the blessings from Kuntillet ʿAjrud as evidence for the worship of two deities, Yahweh and Asherah. Yet while his analyses demonstrate a wide diversity of religions that accepted Asherah and Baal along with Yahweh, the selection is curiously edited. No similar focus is given to the silver amulets from Ketef Hinnom or the Yahwistic blessings in the introductory formulae of the Arad and Lachish letters. All these support a stronger acceptance of Yahweh as uniquely (or alone) worshiped by some. While it is true that the primary focus of Zevit's study is the various religions of Israel, other than the monotheism of Josiah, his conclusions about the widespread worship of multiple deities remain one-sided because the inscriptional data representing a unique emphasis on Yahweh is not fully considered. The same seems true of the study of Israelite onomastica. In fact, there is a difference in the percentages of Yahwistic personal names versus other theophoric names among Israelites and the relative percentages of names from neighboring countries that use their national deity when compared with those theophoric names that explicitly mention other deities. Thus while every count of Yahwistic names in Israel results in a number and percentage that far exceeds all other personal names with explicit divine names as an element, the ratios in Ammon and surrounding countries are the reverse.[83] It is therefore not in accord with the evidence to imply that Israelite onomastica indicate no significant tendencies toward the worship of a single deity. Nevertheless, Zevit's analysis of the biblical texts relevant to his enterprise suggests widespread polytheism throughout

82. M. Smith (2004) criticizes Zevit for an inappropriate emphasis on discontinuity between the Iron Age Israelites and their predecessors. This important review highlights issues concerning the full appreciation of the antecedent cultures, archaeologically and especially with reference to the Bronze Age West Semitic cuneiform archives such as those at Ugarit, Mari, and Emar.

83. See Hess (forthcoming a).

the nation at all periods until the centralization of Josiah (c. 622 BC), reemerging all the stronger after that single event.

Alongside the already-mentioned works of Zevit and Dever, there have appeared many studies related to the material culture of ancient Israel and its relevance to the interpretation of the religion of the land. An outstanding example of the use of archaeological research is Dever himself. He and many of his students have contributed important monographs and research articles on many aspects of the research. In 1995, Dever published a major review and critique of studies of Israelite religion. He demonstrated the lack of proper and comprehensive use of the material cultural findings in study after study of the subject. Although Zevit's study has corrected that lack for English readers, the challenge of the archaeological evidence remains an essential factor in any analysis of Israelite religion. Thus much of this study is incorporated into my analysis.

One way of looking at Israel's religion is through the lens of ritual, the practices and activities that comprise a significant part both of religion and of areas of life not necessarily to be considered as religious. Indeed, Gerald Klingbeil (forthcoming) surveys the study of this in the more general area of religious studies and then focuses in the specific area of the Bible, examining both the history of this study and also its role in the Bible itself. Ritual does more than mirror social order and religious beliefs. It also creates a reality in which the participants are brought to a new level of understanding.

This survey of some major recent works reveals that controversies in the discussion of Israelite religion remain and that there is no solution on the horizon. Included among these, but by no means limited to them, are the questions of the emergence of belief in a single deity, the earliest appearance of Yahweh, the place of the Pentateuchal sources and especially Genesis in the discussion of Israel's religion, the role of Asherah, the place of religious evidence from Israelite personal names and other inscriptions, the treatment of the dead and belief in an afterlife, and the use of anthropological and other models in the analysis of these questions. The purpose of the present study will be to identify the major sources relevant to questions of Israelite religion in the biblical and extrabiblical texts, and in the archaeology of Israel. Rather than a final answer to the questions, this work seeks to provide a beginning point for the reader in the detailed but key questions of early Israelite religions.

Summary

Traditional biblical scholarship has demonstrated both the strengths and weaknesses of older theological and philosophical perspectives.

Interest in the religious practices of the Old Testament has existed for a long time in the Western world. Further, literary analyses have demonstrated streams of literature in the Pentateuch and elsewhere that reflect different, though not necessarily contradictory, emphases. Thus some are concerned with personal communion with God and with its continuation from generation to generation in the tribes and nation. Other streams focus on the priesthood, the cult, and the issues of cleanness and sacrifice that surround it. Finally, there are those that emphasize the relation with God as defined through covenant and its specific stipulations. On the negative side, however, is the conviction that these literary elements could be precisely delineated, even splitting sentences and phrases into distinct written sources, and that they could be dated as arising at specific points in Israel's history. This has not gone without challenge and remains the most controversial part of the critical theories of the traditional scholarship.

Recent studies in the religion of Israel have demonstrated the diversity of the sources in the textual and material culture that can and need to be used in constructing as full a picture as possible. At the same time, the many issues addressed and the ongoing disagreements about interpretation emphasize that no single method has demonstrated its competence for the interpretation of the field and that the gaps in the data create gaps in our knowledge. More questions exist now than a generation ago. Perhaps the most generally agreed upon result of the many publications within recent decades has been the sense that the picture of religion in ancient Israel is far more complex than had once been supposed. It is not a question of two or three views of religion that different groups followed, but of a diversity of religious beliefs that changed from region to region and from generation to generation. Great syntheses and sweeping generalizations no longer hold.

Therefore we need to begin again and to examine the evidence that has accrued. Setting aside the assumption that we must find a comprehensive synthesis, we can perhaps better appreciate the diversity of texts and artifacts and the manner in which they address diverse expressions of religious faith. We can also examine and appreciate the great amount of work that has already been done by scholars in this field. I will continue to refer to and interact with earlier research and interpretations. Based on the reasonable assumption that in some sense people understand their own religious beliefs in light of those who preceded them, whether to follow, change, or reject what went before, I now turn to the period preceding ancient Israel as defined here. I consider the Bronze Age West Semitic and related cultures.

4

Pre-Israelite West Semitic Religion

Syria and Egypt

The background to the religious practices of Israel during the monarchy of the first millennium BC lies in previous millennia. In particular, it should be located in the West Semitic world of which Israel was a part, as defined by language and region. This chapter will consider the major sources of written and material Bronze Age evidence from areas of importance *outside* Palestine. Chapter 5 will consider specifically the areas of Palestine and Jordan. An important part of this background can be found in the texts from neighboring cultures, especially those major urban centers located in modern northern Syria. During the third millennium, the Early Bronze Age (c. 3300–2000 BC) reveals little in the way of writing except for the city of Ebla, whose texts date from the twenty-fourth century BC. During the Middle Bronze Age (c. 2000–1550 BC), the archives of Mari, another north Syrian city, reveal much about religion in this early period. In the Late Bronze Age (c. 1550–1200 BC), the archives of Amarna, Ugarit, and Emar provide relevant background information concerning the religious life of Israel's predecessors. There is a great deal of archaeological evidence from each of these centers, and others, that might be noted.[1] In the second millennium BC, cult centers in and around Palestine flourished. Some of these continued into Israel's existence during the Iron Age (c. 1200–586 BC). These will be surveyed and briefly discussed. Not all the relevant materials from these cities and cultural sources can be surveyed here. Rather, many items of a textual and especially archaeological relevance will be placed in context in the later surveys of biblical texts, where they may more directly address issues of interpretation there.

Early Bronze Age Archives—Ebla

We begin, then, with the north Syrian site of Ebla, whose archive was discovered in 1975. Although most of the thousands of tablets remain to be published, and though many aspects of the language itself are debated, some matters of the religious life have come to light.[2] For example, in the texts the names of various deities have been identified. These include: the "god of the fathers," Admu, earth mother Adamma (cf. the biblical name Adam), storm god Ada, Adaru "strength," Gabadu "effulgence" (cf. Hebrew *kābōd*, "glory"), god of Amana (Baal Hammon?), Ashtar (Ishtar), Baal?, Balikh (double river), Dagan (divinized Euphrates), lord of gods, Dabir, Gamish (Chemosh?), Hazi (Ugaritic Mt. *Ṣpn*, Hebrew Zaphon), Kakkab "star," Resheph, Samiu (heavens?), and the

1. Note that clay tablets of cuneiform script form the primary source of written records discussed here from the third and second millennia BC. Except for the Ugaritic language with its cuneiform alphabet, most of the texts are written in the Akkadian language, the common language of writing during this period in the ancient Near East.
    2. See the discussions in Pomponio and Xella (1997) and in M. Smith (1999).

sun goddess.[3] The deity *zi-mi-nu/na* may be associated with the *šmn* of Ugarit who has been related to Phoenician Eshmun.[4] Many of these gods and goddesses anticipate deities known to Israel and its neighbors more than fifteen hundred years later. The significance of such a list indicates the conservative and enduring nature of various aspects of what comes to be called Canaanite (or, more broadly, West Semitic) religion.

At Ebla we also have the first attested occurrence of the West Semitic term *nabi'utum*, which has been identified with the meaning "prophet."[5] Compare the biblical *nābî'*, "prophet." In addition, there is probably here an early reference to the well-known *marzēaḥ* festival of Ugarit and the later Iron Age period in a reference to women receiving garments "on the day of the *mar-za-u* in the month of *Man* (May)."[6] At Ebla, lists of deceased who receive offerings include a cuneiform sign indicating divinity in front of the royal names. This may suggest a belief that these deceased ancestors were deified.[7]

Middle Bronze Age Archives

Mari

ARCHAEOLOGY AND ARCHITECTURE

The north Syrian city of Mari, located at the bend of the Euphrates River and dating from the eighteenth century BC, reveals archaeological evidence of temples. The temple of Dagan was uncovered west of the palace. It contained some three hundred rooms. The temple's proximity to the palace resembles the configuration at the site of Alalakh in Syria to the west. Its many rooms are not unlike those of the palace at Knossos in Crete.

Other material evidence for religion includes an interesting seal that depicts an aged El-type deity enthroned on a mountain between two streams and flanked by two vegetation goddesses emerging from the waters. A warlike figure thrusts a spear into the waters. If it is indeed

---

3. See further on the citations of the (H)ada (Hadad, Addu) deity and his role in Eblaite society in Schwemer (2001, 11–91).

4. Mettinger (2001, 163).

5. Kitchen (2003, 384).

6. *Materiali epigrafici di Ebla* 2.46 rev. I:1–3; cf. Johnston (2002, 181).

7. B. Schmidt (1994, 15–20) believes that the form may refer to the personal gods of each of the kings, e.g., "the god of king X." He argues that in the king list from Lagash, a city contemporary with Ebla, the deceased who receive offerings are not deified because the names are not preceded by this particular sign, a divine determinative sign that indicates divinity.

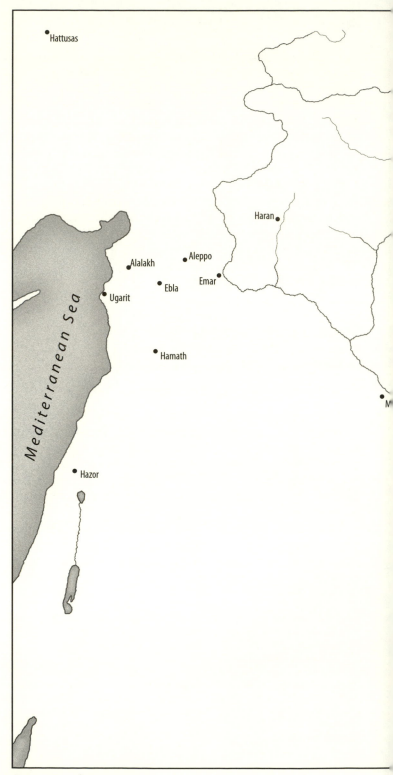

Fig. 3. Map of Mesopotamia

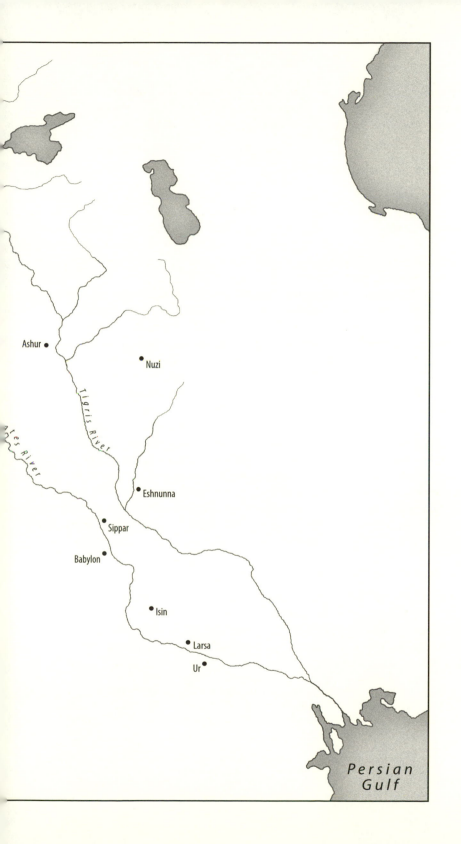

El in his abode, then perhaps Baal is the one who pierces the waters (Yamm, "Sea"). The same theme occurs in the Ugaritic Baal cycle.[8]

For significant connections between Mari and the Bible regarding the tabernacle, see pp. 203–5.

MYTHIC ELEMENTS

Better known are the hundreds of letters discovered at Mari, most of which contain the correspondence of King Zimri-Lim during the final years of his reign as a relatively independent sovereign.[9] Several of these refer to deities and heroic figures, many of whom become well known in later West Semitic myths. One letter contains a prophecy from the storm god Addu that connects the storm god's victory over the sea with kingship: Thus speaks the storm god Addu to the king of Mari: "I restored you [Zimri-Lim] to your father's throne. I gave you the weapon(s) with which I fought against the Sea."[10] As with the seal that was mentioned above, the theme of the storm god at battle with the personified and divinized Sea lies deep in the mytho-religious traditions of the West Semitic Bronze Age (c. 3300–1200 BC). Half a millennium later, a god list from Ugarit (*KTU* 1.47; for *KTU*, see Dietrich, Loretz and Sanmartín [1995]) connects the storm god Addu (or [H]adad) with Baal, and the sea god Yamm with Tamtum (Tiamat), whose name at Mari is here translated as "Sea." Yamm is also divinized at Emar and given offerings. Schwemer observes evidence for the storm deity Addu in letters that mention Addu's gifts and offerings, prayers, cult stone, and the securing of kingship.[11] The deity is mentioned in contexts with Shamash, Dagan, Enlil, Iturmer, and Anu. Furthermore, numerous personal names are constructed with the determinative (dIŠKUR) for Addu. The deity also appears in a similar manner at Old Babylonian Alalakh and surrounding areas.[12]

DYING AND RISING GODS

Another letter from one Yaminite king[13] to another in northeastern Syria suggests an awareness of the "dying and rising god" motif that is so prominent in the ancient Near East and in the Mediterranean world of the first millennium BC. The myth, in which the god Dumuzi spends half the year in the underworld and half the year in the world above ground

8. Vanel (1965, 73–74); Keel (1978, fig. 42; 1986, 309); M. Smith (2003, 40).
9. See Heimpel (2003) for a useful translation of many of the letters into English.
10. The text is A 1968. Cf. Nissinen (2003, 21–22); M. Smith (2003, 94).
11. Schwemer (2001, 277–304).
12. Ibid., 211–37.
13. The Mari texts record two tribal confederations, the *Binu-Yamina* and the *Binu-Sim'al*. This king belonged to the former tribal confederation.

The Message of Adad

Say to my lord: Nur-Sin speaks as follows: Abiya, the prophet of Adad who is lord of Aleppo, came here and said,

"Adad said:

'I gave all the land to Yahdun-Lim. With my weapons, I did not [need to] ask for an opponent, but he abandoned me. So I gave Shamshi-Adad the land I had previously given to him (Yahdun-Lim). As for Shamshi-Adad . . . Let me put you back on your ancestral throne. I gave you the weapons with which I attacked Sea. I anointed you with the oil of my awe-inspiring brightness. No one will be able to stand against you.

Listen to this one matter. If anyone cries out for judgment and says, I am wronged. Stay and decide their case. Give a fair answer. This is what I want from you. When you march out to war, don't do so without an oracle. If I stand forth in my oracle, then march to war. If not, don't march out the gate.'"

The prophet said this to me. So I have sent the hair of the prophet and his fringe to my lord.

Mari A 1968; eighteenth century BC from Mari. Translation by author; see Nissinen (2003, 21–22) for the transliteration, another translation, and commentary.

(giving fertility to the land), is known in the earliest mythological texts from third-millennium BC Sumerian and Akkadian cultures in what is today Iraq. A Dumuzi myth of death and living again is suggested in a remarkable text from a letter at Mari:[14]

> As for me, look at me. Not yet [?] . . . I escaped from death, and from the midst of Ahuna [I escaped] ten times during uprising[s]. Why, now, [am I not] like Dumuzi? They kill him [*idakkūšu*] at the [time of] counting the year [*munût šattim*]. [In the spring(?),] he always comes back [*it-ta-na-a(r)*] to the temple of Annunitum.

Text A.512.7–15 suggests that a substitution was offered at the time of Dumuzi's entrance into the temple:

> On the day I conveyed this letter to my lord, the *pudûm* [expiation] of my Lord was offered in the temple of Annunitum of Shehrum. I have had Dumuzi enter in the temple of Annunitum in Mari.

Dumuzi's association with Annunitum (a manifestation of the goddess Ishtar at Mari) and his death and return are described in these

---

14. Mettinger (2001, 201), using a translation by Daniel Fleming of A.1146.39–44. The myth of Dumuzi, associated as it is with the annual vegetation cycle, first appears in the world's earliest literature, in the Sumerian texts. See Jacobsen (1976).

passages. These celebrations of his return to life and the associations of Dumuzi with grain gods (Ningishzida and possibly Damu) present Dumuzi's return as a means to explain the reawakening of plant life.[15] Dumuzi was known in this fashion in the West Semitic world of eighteenth-century BC Mari, more than a thousand years before women are pictured mourning for him, under the name of Tammuz, in the temple in Jerusalem (Ezek. 8:14).

RITUAL TEXTS

Other types of texts at Mari include the rituals.[16] Among them are texts that describe the festivals of various deities, others that describe the lunar cycle, and still others that detail a variety of rituals: for the consecration of divine statues, for different life passages (birth, marriage, interment), for purification, for exorcism and sorcery, for ordeals and the conclusion of contracts, and for the army. Both gods and kings are included among the recipients. The two major festivals are the *kispum* and the Feast of Ishtar. The Feast of Ishtar occurred at the end of the seventh month (the month of Dagan in October) and lasted until the tenth month (Belet-biri in December).[17] The *kispum* was a funerary meal with sacrifices for the dead.[18] It anticipates *kispum* rituals that continued in the West Semitic world into the first millennium BC.

TREATIES

Another source for the official religion of Mari is found in the descriptions of treaty-making activities. Anticipating Leviticus 11, the division of clean and unclean animals may be implied in several Mari treaty accounts. On occasions when officials of Mari performed a treaty-making ritual with other nations, these groups brought animals such as a puppy, a goat, and a young bull or calf. None of these were acceptable to the Mari officials, who would sacrifice only the foal of a she-ass in the ritual.[19]

15. Mettinger (2001, 204).

16. See Lafont (1999).

17. During the reign of Zimri-Lim there was an occasion where the Feast of Ishtar took place during months 10–12.

18. *Kispum* offerings are given to the statues of dead kings. B. Schmidt (1994, 43) argues that the *kispum* is an adaptation of a preexisting Sumerian mortuary rite. Although food is offered to Sargon's and Naram-Sin's statues, neither of these names are preceded by the divine determinative. Their primary purpose was to legitimate the present king by connecting his dynasty to that of earlier kings. While this is possible, there is no way of knowing for certain the status given to the dead kings. However, offerings are normally made to creatures capable of receiving them.

19. Malamat (1995).

PROPHECIES

One of the most significant discoveries in the religion of Mari has to do with prophetic texts. More than sixty tablets report messages from prophets.[20] Among these a band of prophets inquired into omens for the king's well-being and advised the king on this. Other topics include victory and salvation for the king, prediction of illness and death, demand for justice toward one's subjects, and the need for faithfulness to the deity or the requirement to be judged by the deity.[21] At Mari the chief deity, the storm god Addu, promised blessings for obedience and made threats for disobedience. More than one oracle could be written down and sent. Thus there emerged an early form of a collection of oracles, along with provision of the historical context. This anticipated the later collections of prophetic oracles in the biblical books of the prophets.

The Hebrew word *nābî* "prophet" is attested at Mari in the eighteenth century BC, and it seems to have been in the lexicon even earlier at Ebla. Hans Barstad (1993) finds special concerns among the Mari prophets with war and the defeat of the enemy. Oracles against foreign nations, so common in the Old Testament prophetic books, are also found at Mari. Mention is made of the writing of the prophecies. Prophecy thus predates Israel, even as it continues in societies contemporary with Israel's existence. Of course, this is attested in the Bible with a figure like Balaam, a prophet from the north who is contemporary with Israel's first generation (Num. 22–24). Daniel Fleming argues that the prophets of Mari and Emar (thirteenth century BC), who use the term for "prophet" cognate to the Hebrew word *nābî*, derive that term from the practice of naming or invoking the gods for assistance.[22] Thus these prophets are intercessors just as the Old Testament prophets were.[23]

Fleming (1995, 145) observes that the prophet at Mari was associated with the West Semitic Hanean people. Related cultic officiants (*munabbiātu*) of the goddess *Išhara* used names derived from the Akkadian (not West Semitic) word, *nabû*, also meaning "to name," that is, to invoke ancestral and protective deities. Compare the Syrian general Naaman who expects

20. Nissinen (2003) published fifty of the texts with an additional fifteen that in some way relate to prophets.
21. Kitchen (2003, 384–85, 391).
22. See Fleming (1993). Huehnergard (1999) challenges this, observing that it is unlikely that the Hebrew form would have an active sense. Instead, he prefers the traditional understanding of a passive form, rendering it "the one called (by God)," and finds no relationship with Emar *munabbiātu*. However, the forms are close in spelling and appearance and Huehnergard's arguments rest entirely on the difficulty of finding a Hebrew *qātil* form that is active, a relatively weak argument given the other similarities.
23. R. P. Gordon (1995, 83–86) wonders whether there is anything distinctive about biblical prophets and can identify only the God that they served as distinctive.

Elisha, a *nābî'*, to *call on* the name of his deity (2 Kings 5:11). Hutton (1995) asks whether biblical prophecy is best understood as containing magic power in the words of the speakers or whether it is merely street theater, designed to represent the message to the people. He relates the oracles of judgment to curses in the ancient Near East. Using speech act theory Hutton concludes that there is some force in the message but that it is not a magical word. Instead, it is accepted social convention of the power of the speakers in their role as prophets (or whatever) that gives the message power and the words force. While there may be substance to Hutton's argument, the widely accepted origins of the prophetic word in the sphere of the divine gave it a unique authority, whether at Mari or in later Israel.

André Lemaire (1999) summarizes research on the West Semitic prophets and prophecies. He notes that there exist fifty-seven specific messages from Mari prophets but that this prophecy was unknown in Babylon, occurring only in the West (at Mari). Its forms resemble the prophetic actions and words of Samuel, Saul, and Ezekiel. Like Jeremiah, prophecies can be reorganized and edited along thematic lines. At Mari this was done during the lifetime of the author of the prophecies.

In contrast to the Mari prophecy texts, Neo-Assyrian prophecies "predict" only a series of rulers, their lengths of reigns, and good or bad events associated with them. They date to the seventh century BC, from the time of the Neo-Assyrian kings Esarhaddon and Ashurbanipal, and are generally messages from the goddess Ishtar. As at Mari, Neo-Assyrian tablets of considerable size could contain collections of oracles by a variety of prophets and prophetesses.[24] In this manner the tradition of the twelve Minor Prophets in the Old Testament may be understood as having been collected and written on a single scroll.

Egypt

In Egypt as well in the early part of the second millennium there are examples of prophecies and the development of mythologies that may have had an affect on later West Semitic religious beliefs. The Instruction of Merikare from about 2000 BC includes texts where the author twice mentions prophecies from before his time. This concept of future prediction also occurs in the rubric, "what the ancestors foretold," as found in the Admonitions of Ipuwer.

Of the many Egyptian deities, Osiris had one of the most profound influences on the West Semitic world and its heritage. The major sources are attested as early as the third-millennium BC Pyramid Texts and recur

24. Kitchen (2003, 389, 391).

in the second-millennium Great Hymn to Osiris and later in Plutarch's (c. 100 AD) *De Iside et Osiride*.[25] At Abydos there took place the Great Procession where a statue of the god went forth from his temple, stayed overnight in a necropolis, and returned to his temple the next day amid great celebration. In or near December there was another festival, comprising a funeral for Osiris followed a week later by the erection of a Djed pillar symbolizing resurrection. Associated with these events are "Osiris gardens" where sprouting grain symbolized resurrection. The idea of a resurrected god occurs in litanies in the Pyramid Texts. There Osiris is repeatedly called on to "raise yourself." In the myths, however, Osiris does not himself function as a dying and rising god. He does not return from the dead. Osiris remains in the netherworld where he rises and lives again. He comes alive on earth in the form of his son, Horus.

Finally, a survey of early second-millennium Egypt and its potential for religious influence on West Semites and the Israelite people should include the site of Tell el-Dab'a in the eastern Nile Delta. This city has been identified with the Hyksos capital of Avaris.[26] Through the Middle Bronze Age it was a fortified city whose material culture was closer in style to Canaanite than to Egyptian. In the Middle Bronze IIB (c. 1750–c. 1550 BC) layers, dating to the eighteenth century BC, a Canaanite-style temple with a long axis was discovered. It was divided into three rooms with a recessed niche—the most holy place—in the rear wall of the third room. At a size of 70 by 105 feet, it is the largest Canaanite temple ever discovered. Seventy feet from the main entrance was a sacrificial altar and a location for one or two trees. The acorns on the altar suggest that the remaining tree pits originally contained evergreen oaks transplanted from Canaan as sacred trees.[27] The altar, the niche, the three-roomed sanctuary, and the trees all form antecedents to later temples, sacred trees, and other cultic practices in ancient Israel and its neighbors.

Late Bronze Age Archives

Egypt

Egyptian religious practices that can be related to later West Semitic forms are found in the second half of the second millennium. The Cairo Hymn to Amun in Egypt (c. 1500/1400 BC) portrays Amun as the

25. Mettinger (2001, 167–68).
26. This is described by the excavator in Bietak (1996). The Hyksos were a group of West Semitic leaders who reigned in the Nile Delta region from c. 1750 BC to c. 1550 BC.
27. Bietak (1996, 36–40); Alpert-Nakhai (2001, 100); Stager (2003, 34).

sole deity before he created the other deities. Much closer to the belief in a single,
unique god is the teaching of Akhenaten.
For this fourteenth-century BC pharaoh,
the worship of Aten alone was necessary.
His family, who lived in their newly built
capital (modern Tell el-Amarna), joined
him in the worship of Aten. Although this
theology was promoted, it never seems
to have replaced the worship of other
deities throughout Egypt in general. A
counterrevolution led to the abandonment of Amarna and the return of the
royal family to Thebes. Subsequently, in
the fourteenth and thirteenth centuries
Egyptian theologians considered Amun as
the one god and all other deities as manifestations. In one popular Egyptian story
of the time (Apophis and Seqenenre), the
Hyksos are imagined to have worshiped
Seth alone.[28]

Fig. 4. Amarna Tablet (Courtesy
of Chris Miller)

Prophecy also continued, not only in
Egypt but also in cities along the Levan-
tine coast. In the eleventh century BC the Egyptian Wenamun visited
the city of Byblos and its royal court. He wished to obtain timber for
the sacred bark boat of the god Amon. At Byblos, a member of the court
became possessed during a religious rite and ecstatically ordered that
they should listen to Wenamun:[29]

> Now when he offered to his gods, the god (Amon) seized a great seer from
> among his great seers, and he caused him to be in an ecstatic state, and he
> said to him: "Bring up the god! Bring the messenger who bears him! It is
> Amon who has sent him. He is the one who has caused that he come."

Also discovered in Egypt at the site of Amarna are more than three
hundred pieces of royal correspondence between the pharaoh and the
princes of towns throughout Canaan. Most of these affirm loyalty to
the pharaoh and request his military assistance against enemies. Dating from the middle of the fourteenth century BC, this correspondence
provides the earliest substantial written evidence from many of the
towns that the Bible associated with Israel in the subsequent centuries.

28. Kitchen (2003, 331). Seth is a deity associated with the West Semitic god Baal.
29. Kitchen (2003, 388); translation by Robert K. Ritner in Nissinen (2003, 220).

For the most part this correspondence from Canaan includes reference only to the storm god, called either Hadad or Baal, and to the sun god.[30] The former is mentioned only six times in letters from northern Canaan, while the latter is the title consistently applied to pharaoh. Why are no other deities mentioned when a variety of deities are found in the correspondence from other countries, including Egypt, and also from Byblos (farther to the north)? Four reasons present themselves as possibilities. First, the Canaanite rulers' subservience to pharaoh prevented them from invoking their own non-Egyptian deities. Second, the pharaoh himself is ascribed deity and thus there may have been a reluctance to allow any other god or goddess to rival him. Third, the local priesthoods may not have been involved in the politics as represented in these letters. Finally, we may also imagine that in the smaller and mostly inland population centers of this region fewer deities were named and worshiped than at an international trading center and much larger coastal city such as Ugarit (see below). This also explains the relatively few names for gods and goddesses among the traditions preserved from early Israel in Canaan, as found for example in Joshua, Judges, and 1 and 2 Samuel.

Even so, there are a number of deities' names in inscriptions of Middle Bronze Age and Late Bronze Age Canaan. A fifteenth-century BC cuneiform letter from Taanach mentions Baal as a deity. A twelfth-century BC inscription, found at Qubur el-Walayadah, located about six miles southeast of Gaza, contains a personal name with the divine name El (*'y'l* "Where is El?"). *Ba'al* occurs in a brief inscription from Bronze Age Lachish, as does *'l'b* "the god of the father," and *b'lt* "lady."[31] The Semitic name of the goddess *'lt* (*'Elat?*) appears in a thirteenth-century BC inscription from the same site.[32]

Byblos, a city whose ruins may still be seen on the Mediterranean coast of Lebanon, presents something of a different case. More Amarna letters originated from the leader of Byblos than any other single source. In them there is a preponderance of references to the deity, "the Lady of Byblos."[33] However, twice there are references to a male deity, once as "my living

30. Hess (1986). On the attestations of Baal and Hadad/Addu at Amarna and Ugarit, see Schwemer (2001, 502–48). He also discusses connections with the Hurrian deity Teššub as well as the evidence from Alalakh Level IV and Hattusas (pp. 443–502). The names of Baal, Hadad, and Teššub were all represented by a single cuneiform determinative and sign, dIŠKUR, which makes it impossible to determine which name is intended in most cases.

31. See M. Smith (2003, 29); Puech (1986–87). On these expressions see further the discussion here regarding Ebla and Ugarit. "God of the fathers" is attested at Ebla and in the ritual texts from Ugarit.

32. See discussion of Bronze Age Lachish in chapter 5, pp. 134–35.

33. In fact, she is mentioned forty-two times. See Hess (1986, 151).

god" and another as "my DA.MU."[34] This may be a male counterpart of
the Lady of Byblos. Tryggve Mettinger relates this to a deity known as
Damu.[35] By the tenth century BC, as suggested by inscriptions in and
near Byblos,[36] has Damu become known as Baal of Byblos and as "lord,"
an epithet spelled exactly the same as the divine name Adon (found, e.g.,
in Josh. 3:11)? Mettinger argues that DA.MU was a logographic writing
that represented the god Adon.[37] He notes the connection of Damu and
Dumuzi in some Sumerian hymns, and the role of Damu as a dying and
rising vegetation deity (identified with the Sumerian deity Ningishzida).
He finds a possible syncretism already in the early second-millennium Old
Babylonian period, and argues that the association of Damu and Dumuzi
is in "good harmony" with the evidence.[38] If so, this explains the association of grain with Dumuzi, who otherwise appears in the early myths
only as a shepherd. Further, third-millennium BC (and later) pyramid
texts from Egypt identify a deity in the hinterland of Byblos as "the Living
One." This appellation could fit Baal and it might anticipate the dying
and rising Adonis known in Byblos during Phoenician times.[39] These
connections share a certain quality of speculation but they exemplify
both the frustratingly sparse nature of the evidence and the intriguing
possibilities of diverse attestations and their connections.

In Israel itself, the town of Shechem may have had a pantheon similar
to other Canaanite cities. In one of the fourteenth-century BC Amarna
letters from Labaya, Shechem's leader, he mentions "my god" in relation
to his father. In EA 252 lines 28–31 there are two parallel lines that suggest this connection, framed by a promise to guard those who attacked
what belonged to Labaya:

> I will indeed guard
>> the men who captured the town and my god,
>> the plunderers of my father.
> And I will indeed guard them!

34. The two letters are EA 129.51 and EA 84.35. The tablet identification follows a system devised by Knudtzon whose 1915 publication of the Amarna cuneiform texts remains
a standard to this day. It was supplemented by Anson Rainey (1978) with Amarna texts
identified and published subsequent to Knudtzon's edition. The "EA" is an abbreviation
for El-Amarna text. The first number identifies the tablet, and the number after the period
or full stop is the line of the cuneiform text on that particular tablet.

35. Mettinger (2001, 137–45).

36. These include the Yehimilk inscription and a broken text discovered a few miles
from Byblos.

37. Logograms are written signs where each sign normally represents a word or
concept. Here the two signs, despite being pronounced differently than Adon, together
represent that divine name.

38. Mettinger (2001, 185, 212).

39. See chapter 9, pp. 258–59.

> ### Letter from the Leader of Shechem to the Pharaoh about His Ancestral God
>
> Address the king my lord:
>
> A message from Labaya, your servant:
>
> I fall at the feet of the king, my lord. You wrote to me, "Protect the men who captured the town." But how can I protect the men? The town was captured during a battle. While I was swearing peace, an officer was swearing with me. Then the town and my god were captured. I have been slandered before the king my lord. Now, when an ant is swatted, does it not fight back, and bite the hand of the man who swats it? How then can I show fear nowadays? Another town of mine will be seized! Now, you may go on to say, "Fall under them so that they might attack you." I would do this. Indeed, I will guard the men who captured the town and my god, the plunderers of my father. I will indeed guard them!
>
> EA 252; c. 1350 BC from Amarna. Translation by author, modified from Hess (1993b).

Could this suggest veneration of an ancestral deity?[40] If so, it is the earliest extrabiblical and textual indication of ancestor reverence or worship in what would become Israel itself. Figurines and cuneiform texts discovered at Shechem suggest tentatively that the Baal berith, "lord of the covenant," mentioned in Judges was an epithet of a god El Berit who functioned as a divine witness of treaties and covenants made on behalf of the city throughout the Late Bronze Age and into the early Iron Age.[41]

Ugarit

North of Byblos lay the site of Ugarit on the Mediterranean coast of Syria. Ugarit has been excavated since 1929.[42] The excavations have revealed a vast metropolis of the Late Bronze Age. The site has also yielded many hundreds of alphabetic and syllabic cuneiform texts from the thirteenth century BC, including many with religious significance.[43] Although Ugarit was situated near Canaan, it did not identify itself or the inhabitants of its kingdom as Canaanite. Nevertheless it was West Semitic in language and culture and its texts contain mythological and cultic information that is closely related to that of Canaan. Cautions against equating Ugaritic religion with Canaanite religion in the Bible

40. Hess (1993, 102).
41. See Judg. 8:33; 9:4 and Lewis (1996).
42. For a summary of the archaeological excavations and their results, see Yon (2003).
43. Del Olmo Lete (1999a); Wyatt (1999).

must be made. However, there remains a common West Semitic heritage to Ugarit and the Bible.[44]

Archaeology

The site of Ugarit (modern Ras Shamra) includes two main temples on the acropolis. Although disputed by some, this temple identification is based on stelae naming Baal and Dagan that were found in or near them. It is thought that the western temple belongs to Baal and the eastern one belongs to Dagan, although it should be noted that Dagan does not otherwise appear to play a significant role at the site or in the texts. Each temple had a courtyard, a vestibule in front of the sanctuary approached by a large staircase, and an inner room with a stone platform.[45] The sea was visible from the Baal temple. Stone anchors discovered there attest to a marine association to the temple and to Baal.[46] In particular, Baal Zaphon was associated with Mount Zaphon to the north of Ugarit and identified with a ship and with maritime activities.[47] The name of this mountain is remembered in Psalm 48:2 [Heb. 3] where it is compared with Mount Zion. Literally, "Mount Zion the farthest reaches of Zaphon," (*har ṣîyôn yarkĕtê ṣāpôn*).

A comprehensive picture of the archaeology of the religion at Ugarit is not possible in a volume devoted to the study of Israelite religion. Suffice it to say that the temple architecture and many of the small finds such as stelae, ivories, cult stands, votive anchors, ceremonial adzeheads, and other objects found in the "rhyton sanctuary" and at other locations at Ugarit anticipate the same sort of cultic paraphernalia found in Iron Age Israel of the monarchic period.

Mythology of Gods and Goddesses

In addition to the archaeological data already mentioned, the majority of sources for the study of religion at Ugarit occur in a variety of texts. Best known are the mythological tablets. Myths include those concerning Baal (who builds a house or temple), Aqhat (where the king Danilu seeks a son, Aqhat), and Keret (where Keret seeks a son).[48] Comparing

---

44. So M. Smith (2001a, 15–16), contra Grabbe (1994).

45. Curtis (1999, 14); Kitchen (2003, 403).

46. Yon (1997, 260); Alpert-Nakhai (2001, 124). Baal's battle with Yamm, the Sea, occurs in the Baal cycle in the Ugaritic mythological texts.

47. Brody (1998, 9–19) refers to *KTU* 1.16 I 6–9, to 1.16 II 44–47 and to the thirteenth-century BC Egyptian Papyrus Sallier IV.

48. The elements that constitute myth are disputed. Thus M. Smith (2001a, 23) argues that if the Baal epic is a myth then biblical narratives about the storm god Yahweh are mythic. It may be better to view "myths" at Ugarit as narrative stories that deal with the interactions of multiple deities.

the story of Keret with the above temples, it is significant to note that King Keret is commanded to wash himself, take offerings, ascend to the top of the tower, go up to the crest of the wall, lift his hands to heaven, and sacrifice to his father Bull El.[49]

In addition to myths, there are myth and ritual texts (as for example the account of the birth of the gracious gods [*KTU* 1.23]), god lists, ritual instructions (first of the wine [New Year's?] festival; and the description of a deity visiting a royal palace, perhaps in a royal procession),[50] personal name lists (with divine names forming part of the personal names), correspondence (with divine blessings), and omen and magic texts.

Del Olmo Lete finds that statistically, in terms of their occurrences in various literary genres, the principal gods of the cultic-sacrificial pantheon of Ugarit as based on those receiving the most offerings are:[51]

1. *il*[52] (El)	7. *'ttr* (Athtar)	13. *'ttrt* (Ashtart)
2. *b'l/hdd* (Baal and Addu)	8. *tkmn wšnm*	14. *ušhry*
3. *'nt* (Anat)	9. *špš* (Shapshu)	15. *atrt* (Asherah)
4. *ršp* (Reshep)	10. *šlm* (Shalim)	16. *pdry*
5. *yrh* (Yarih)	11. *inš ilm*	17. *arsy*
6. *ktr*	12. *b'lt bhtm*	

By one count, there are 240 divine names and epithets found at Ugarit, with influences from Amorite, Hurrian, Hittite, and Sumero-Akkadian sources (though none from Egypt).[53] As is apparent from the chart above, some of the more important deities who also are often mentioned in the Bible are described here.

El is the chief Ugaritic god and he resembles the biblical Yahweh in that he is described as an aged, wise creator possessing a court (called the "sons of God") and a dwelling at the source of rivers.[54] No other god begets gods except El. However, El is not the same as Yahweh. John Day

49. Cf. 2 Kings 3:27; and roof altars of 2 Kings 23:12; Kitchen (2003, 403). Similar scenes on the tops of the besieged city of Ashkelon, on the southern Mediterranean coast of Israel, occur on an Egyptian relief dated to the end of the thirteenth century BC that describes a campaign of Pharaoh Merneptah against the city.

50. *KTU* 1.43; Kitchen (2003, 404).

51. Del Olmo Lete (1999a, 71).

52. Del Olmo Lete equates *il* with Dagan. However, Day (2000, 89) denies this equation, noting that the names of Dagan and El never occur together in poetic parallelism and that the two deities are distinguished from each other in the offering lists.

53. Del Olmo Lete (1999a, 78).

54. As much as any other text, Deut. 32:6–7 applies traits of Ugaritic El to Yahweh. Cf. Eden as the dwelling of El in Day (2000, 29–32). For the court of the "sons" of God or Elohim/El, see 1 Kings 22; Job 1–2; Ps. 82; Isa. 6; and possible allusions in texts such as Gen. 1:26 and 11:7.

points out that Yahweh's fierce anger and storm theophany preclude a simple identification with wholly benevolent El.[55] El was amalgamated with Yahweh, as can be seen in his aged status, his wisdom, his role as creator and healer, his appearance in visions and dreams, his leadership of the divine assembly, and his qualities of mercy and compassion.[56] El may well have been the high god in the first half of the second millennium who was overtaken in importance by Addu (Hadad) the weather god during the middle of the millennium.[57]

Athirat, biblical Asherah,[58] is El's consort at Ugarit but she becomes Baal's consort in the Bible.[59] Is this a deliberate polemic by the biblical writers?[60] Her identification with biblical Asherah is supported by the role of Ugarit's Athirat as mother of the gods at Ugarit and the Bible's Asherah as mentioned alongside the host of heaven, which may be compared to the sons of God.[61] Asherah appears in the Bible in 1 Kings 18 and elsewhere.[62] Following the lead of other scholars, attempts have been made to banish the goddess from the Bible by arguing that the deity was written back

55. See Day (2000, 113–14). A theophany is a divine appearance as in Deut. 33:2 and Judg. 5:4–5. Cf. the discussion of theophanies and early occurrences of Yahweh in chapter 6.

56. For El/Yahweh's aged appearance, see *KTU* 1.3 V 2, 24–25; 1.4 IV 24; Job 36:26; Ps. 102:24 [Heb. 25]; and Dan. 7:9. For his wisdom, see *KTU* 1.4 V 65; and Ezek. 28:2–5. On his role as creator, see *KTU* 1.16 V–VI; Gen. 14:19, 22; and 1 Sam. 1:1 where the name Elkanah, meaning "El has created," may be associated with the Hittite Elkunirsa (an abbreviated form of "El Creator of Earth") myth. For El/Yahweh as healer, see Gen. 20:17; Num. 12:13; 2 Kings 20:5, 8; and Ps. 107:20. His appearance in visions and dreams and his leadership of the divine assembly occurs in *KTU* 1.14 II 7, 11; Ps. 82:1; and Isa. 14:13, which may be compared with *KTU* 1.10 I 3–4. For El/Yahweh's qualities of mercy and compassion, see Exod. 34:6 and Ps. 103:8. See Day (2000, 17–21, 24–26); M. Smith (2003, 39, 41); Greenfield (1987, 554). Kottsieper (1998) has argued that El was originally an Aramean deity. However, the evidence for this has been challenged by Maier and Tropper (1998).

57. Kitchen (2003, 332).

58. The etymology is related to Semitic, *'tr*, "place," "holy place." Cf. the association of Athirat with Qudshu (*KTU* 1.16 I 11, 22), which also means "sanctuary." See Day (2000, 61–62).

59. Bernhardt (1967). Cf. the title of the goddess *qnyt 'ilm*, "Creatress of the gods."

60. Cf. Day (2000, 48).

61. 2 Kings 17:16; Job 38:7; Day (2000, 47).

62. There is question as to the authenticity of this reference, occurring only in v. 19. It is recognized as an addition in Origen's edition of the LXX. There is no text supporting Asherah at Tyre (M. Smith [2003, 110, 126–27]; but see Zevit [2001, 652]). Indeed, Smith finds no evidence for Asherah in Israel before the second half of the monarchy. M. Smith (2003, 108–9) records occurrences in narratives (Judg. 3:7; 6:25–30); law (Exod. 34:13; Deut. 7:5; 12:3; 16:21); and prophecy (Isa. 17:8; 27:9; Jer. 17:2; Mic. 5:14 [Heb. 13]) where "asherah" and "asherim" appear as a cult symbol and cultic items. With Olyan (1988, 3–19), Smith observes that Asherah was accepted outside the recognized cult (1 Kings 14:23; 2 Kings 17:10, 16; Jer. 17:2) as well as inside the cult of Samaria (1 Kings 16:33; 2 Kings 13:6) and Jerusalem (2 Kings 21:7; 23:6; 2 Chron. 24:18).

into the text by the Deuteronomists.[63] However, this defeats their purpose since these scribes sought to eliminate other deities as possible rivals to Yahweh.[64] Others have found Asherah in the Bible where she is not explicitly mentioned. For example, Whitt (1992) has argued that Yahweh's wife, whom he divorces in Hosea 2, is Asherah. However, J. Schmitt (1995, 123) has noted the improbability of this: "one wonders about the effectiveness of a prophet whose god is intolerant of any other deity yet is a god who recognizes a goddess and sends her away." Israel, and no one else, remains the explicit wife of Yahweh in this and other biblical texts. Athirat at Ugarit has the epithet *ym* ("Sea") that associates her with this body of water and with the god Yamm who embodies its power.

The deities Athirat/Asherah and Astarte, distinct in some contexts, are sometimes identified with each other. Thus the names interchange in the Bible and in West Semitic culture.[65] Astarte's epithet, "name of Baal," suggests that Astarte is the consort of Baal.[66] Pardee identifies Astarte in a Ugaritic poetic text where she appears (with her Ugaritic name *'ttrt*) in parallel with *lb'* ("lion[ness]"), demonstrating an association of the goddess with feline imagery.[67]

Baal is associated with the sky. He is the main character in the largest of the Ugaritic myths, a lengthy "cycle" of poetic narratives. In the story, Baal (a) battles the Sea (Yamm) and wins [*KTU* 1.2], (b) builds his temple/palace [*KTU* 1.3–4], and (c) loses to Death (Mot).[68] Then he appears alive, back from the dead.[69] Each of these events, as described in the Baal cycle, contains significant parallels with biblical phrases, themes, and ideas. Thus Baal's conflict with Yamm compares with Yahweh's conflict with the sea

---

63. M. Smith (1990a). In the second edition (2003) of this book, Smith seems more reserved.

64. See Hess (1992b), Dever (1995, 44), and Day (2000, 42–47), all of whom accept Asherah as an Iron Age goddess.

65. Stern (2001a, 23).

66. For the epithet, see *KTU* 1.16 VI 56 (for *KTU*, see Donner and Röllig 1973–1979); KAI 14:18; *PE* 1.10.31 (Eusebius, *Praeparatio evangelica*, as cited in Attridge and Oden 1981). Cf. M. Smith (2001a, 74); Cross (1973); McCarter (1987); Olyan (1988).

67. Pardee (2005), referring to the text Ras ibn Hani 98/02.

68. Johnston (2002, 29–30) notes that there is no textual connection between this event and Baal's construction of a window in his palace. Therefore he argues that Jer. 9:21 and the picture of death entering one's house through the windows is a reflection of a common belief about the power and personification of death, but is not related to this event in the Baal cycle.

69. M. Smith (1998; 2001a, 120–22) prefers to associate Baal with the Hittite gods who disappear, but do not die. However, Baal is clearly associated with death and "later" in the narrative is alive. Legitimate concerns over the imposition of an anthropological category, such as dying and rising gods, must be balanced against the textual evidence. Smith's denial of Baal as a dying and rising god seems forced. Day (2000, 117), who follows Mettinger (2001), argues that the theme of death and life is essential to the myth.

(Hebrew *yam*). His victory over the sea, like that of Baal, is associated with his kingship and with creation.[70]

Baal follows his victory with the construction of his house or temple. Yahweh's temple is described subsequent to his victory at the sea (Exod. 15:17–18). Baal dwells on Mount Zaphon, a mountain of "utmost heights" similar to the abode of Yahweh in Psalm 48:2 [Heb. 3] and Isaiah 14:13. Baal's death may be compared to the mourning for Hadad (another name for Baal) in Zechariah 12:11. Baal's slumber in the ninth-century BC taunt by Elijah (1 Kings 18:27) may also refer to his death. There is also the eighth-century BC polemic of Hosea that Israel died because of Baal but will be resurrected (Hosea 13:1). While some of the imagery of Hosea 5 and 6, and 13 and 14, may be taken over from the dying and rising fertility god Baal,[71] the death of Baal in the Ugaritic mythology may reflect something distinctive to Ugaritic society and especially its royalty.[72] However, Baal's subordination to the chief god El and his apparent death in the underworld are not compatible with Yahweh.[73] As a dying and returning god, Baal at Ugarit evolves from a generic storm god to one who descends to the netherworld and comes back. This development of Baal's role was aided by his absorption of themes from Dumuzi, the dying and rising vegetation deity from Mesopotamia.[74]

Anat may be the consort of Baal, at least according to some texts.[75] There was also a Ben Anath, son of *mrś* and father of Zakarbaal, who belonged to the dynasty of Amurru and whose name appears on several arrowheads from eleventh-century BC Beqaʿ, inland in Lebanon.[76] Alternatively, Ben Anath may refer to an honorific military title or to a class of warriors.[77] At Ugarit, Anat can appear as an unattached female with an uncontrollable passion and intensity.[78] Anat occurs later in Phoenician and also in Egyptian Aramaic (including late fifth-century BC Elephantine), but not in monarchic Israelite texts other than in place names, such as Jeremiah's hometown of Anathoth. For some scholars, Anat's wars (*KTU* 1.3 II 3–30) suggest similarities with Yahweh's wars:

70. For kingship see Pss. 29:10; 74:12–15; 93:1–4. For creation see Pss. 74:12–17; 89:9–12 [Heb. 10–13]; 104:5–9; Job 38:8–11.

71. Day (2000, 117–22).

72. Cf. M. Smith (2001a, 100), who argues that this symbolizes that the dynasty at Ugarit is vulnerable.

73. Day (2000, 15).

74. Mettinger (2001, 209).

75. Cf. also Astarte as discussed above.

76. McCarter (1996, 40).

77. For the military title, see Day (2000, 134). For the warrior class compare the biblical judge Shamgar ben Anat and the physician in the court of Ramesses III, named Bin-Anath. Cf. Kitchen (2003, 216).

78. M. Smith (2001a, 56).

a mountain venue, potentially universal scope, heaps of corpses and skulls, a metaphor of a harvest, feeding on captives, drinking the blood of the defeated, wading in blood, drunkenness, and laughter.[79] In Egypt, Anat and Astarte are described as a shield to Ramesses III, a pharaoh in the twelfth century BC.

Shapshu is the sun goddess. Hebrew shemesh (šemeš) "sun" is both masculine and feminine in gender. At Ugarit, the sun goddess Shapshu serves as El's special messenger.[80] In Psalm 84:9–11 Yahweh is a sun and a shield. As with the sun, the verb zr' "rise" is also applied to Yahweh (Deut. 33:2; Isa. 60:1). Israelite personal names contain elements such as šḥr "dawn" and n(w)r "light."[81] Solar worship and its accoutrements are criticized in Ezekiel 8:16; 2 Kings 23:5, 11; and Job 31:26–28. The combination of storm and solar imagery as applied to Yahweh occurs in Ezekiel 43:2 and Psalm 50:1–3.[82] For the sun and kingship see 2 Samuel 23:3–4 and Psalm 72:1–6. These form a verbal picture of the winged sun disk that comes to symbolize the Judean monarchy in the iconography of seals and seal impressions in the late eighth century BC and later.

Mot is the underworld god of the dead who is described as strong and as swallowing the dead with his throat.[83] The similar Hebrew word for "death" (mwt) is also described as strong in the Bible (Song 8:6).[84] Like Mot, Sheol as the place of the dead is pictured as swallowing its victims (Isa. 5:14; Hab. 2:5).

Resheph is god of plague and pestilence. His arrows bring plague and pestilence and he is equated at Ugarit with the plague god Nergal.[85] Compare Habakkuk 3:5 and Psalm 78:50 where pestilence and plague (rešep) accompany Yahweh.

Molech is an underworld deity (Isa. 57:9). On the basis of the word mlk in Phoenician texts, Eissfeldt argued that this was a sacrifice, often a human sacrifice. Heider (1985) and Day (1989) have persuasively ar-

---

79. See M. Smith (2003, 101–7) for this and for the following lists of references. For the mountain see Pss. 2:6; 48:1–8; 110; Joel 3:9–14 [Heb. 4:9–14]; Zech. 14:4–5. For a universality see Isa. 59:15–19. For many dead bodies see Isa. 34:2–3. For the skulls see Deut. 32:42. The harvest picture occurs in Joel 3:13 [Heb. 4:13]; cf. Rev. 14:14–20. For feeding on captives and drinking their (own) blood see Isa. 49:26; Zech. 9:15 (LXX); and Num. 23:24. For moving through blood and bathing in it see Pss. 58:10; 68:23. Drunkenness with blood occurs in Deut. 32:42 and Isa. 63:3–6. For the laughter of battle see Ps. 2:4.

80. KTU 1.6 VI; M. Smith (2001a, 61).

81. J. Glen Taylor (1993; 1994); M. Smith (2003, 149).

82. M. Smith (2003, 152).

83. KTU 1.6 V 17–22.

84. Day (2000, 188) notes that the parallel phrase in the Ugaritic mythic poetic text, "Baal is strong," lived on in the Cypriot god Baal-Az and the name of a later Cypriot king, Azbaal. See Johnston (2002, 30n24).

85. Day (2000, 198); KTU 1.47.27; 1.118.26. Cf. also Job 5:7; Song 8:6–7.

gued for the existence of a deity, Molech, as attested in the Bible. An eighth-century inscription from Incirli, Turkey, seems to mention Molech. Zuckerman and Kaufman write of it: "Of particular importance . . . is the detailed discussion of the use of *mulk*-sacrifices of sheep, horses, and—if we read correctly—first-born humans in the process of war, and the gods' reactions to those sacrifices." [86] *Mlk*-sacrifices were offered to *b'lhmn* (Baal Hamon) and *tnt* (Tanit) in the western Mediterranean at Hadrametum, Constantine, Guelma, and Malta.[87] The offering of children to an underworld deity was remembered in Classical times. Diodorus Siculus (*Library of History* XX 14.4–7) notes that Kronos received child sacrifices at Carthage. Cretans sent their firstborn to be sacrificed at Delphi (Plutarch, *Theseus* 16). The story of the Minotaur with the head of a bull may have this tradition of human sacrifice behind it. Youths were sent to their deaths in Crete. Precincts for child sacrifice have been found at Carthage, Sicily, and Sardinia. In the fourth and third centuries BC, Carthage's precinct contained about 20,000 urns of which 88 percent contained child sacrifices, a number that had increased from earlier times. Despite some scholarly rebuttal, the presence of evidence for child sacrifice is substantial.[88] Both the Pozo Moro monument from Iron Age Spain (c. 1200–600 BC) and the depiction of Pharaoh Merneptah's 1209 BC siege of Ashkelon, located along the Mediterranean coast in southern Israel, may portray this phenomenon.

Dagan, although not possessing any significant role in the religious texts of Ugarit, does occupy an important status as lord of the grain at thirteenth-century BC Emar.[89] He is also mentioned in the Bible as a god worshiped by the Philistines and he appears in the place name, Beth-Dagan (also Beth-Dagon), at sites in Judah and in Asher.

Isaiah 14:12–15, along with Ezekiel 28:12–19 and Job 15:7–8, alludes to a story whose roots or themes may lie in Baal mythology in which Athtar seeks but fails to occupy Baal's throne.[90] This episode occurs in the Baal cycle at the point where Baal has been killed by Mot and his throne sits empty. When Athtar tries to sit on the throne, however, his feet do not reach the floor and so he cannot occupy it. Its application to historical kings in the prophetic texts indicts them for hubris.

86. Zuckerman and Kaufman (1998).
87. KAI 61A.3–4; 98.1–2; 99.1–2; 103.1–2; 107.1–4; 109.1–2; 110.1; 167.1–2.
88. M. Smith (2003, 173–74); Stager and Wolff (1984); for Pozo Moro see pp. 326–27.
89. Cf. Day (2000, 89). This now greatly illuminates the usage of *dgn* as grain in the Keret epic and the equation of Dagan with grain by Philo of Byblos. The significance of Dagan at Emar further substantiates the much earlier evidence from a twenty-fourth-century BC inscription, which placed the god's rulership in the Upper Euphrates and parts of Syria. See Day (2000, 86–89).
90. Day (2000, 166–84). Day finds this myth passed along through Jebusite Jerusalem. The reference to Zaphon as the holy mountain becomes identified with Jerusalem.

Astarte, along with Anat, was a consort of Baal. According to 1 Samuel 31:10, Saul's armor was deposited in a temple of Ashtaroth.[91] Otherwise, Ashtaroth occurs with Baal(s) in the Bible in early historical traditions (Judg. 10:6; 1 Sam. 7:4; 12:10).

In the god lists there is a god named *šmn* who may be Eshmun.[92] He is associated with the Baal gods but distinguished from Baal.[93]

A useful perspective on the organization of these and the other deities at Ugarit is provided by Mark Smith.[94] He argues that there are four tiers of deities: the highest level occupied by El and his consort Athirat/Asherah; the second level by their children, the divine assembly or "the seventy sons of Athirat";[95] the third level by craftsmen and trader deities such as Kothar-wa-Hasis; and the fourth level by minor deities such as messenger gods. He compares these with the strata of Ugaritic society and with the biblical Yahweh ruling in his heavenly court in 1 Kings 22:19–23, Isaiah 6, and Daniel 7.[96] On the basis of the extrabiblical evidence as well as indications of Asherah worship in the Jerusalem temple (2 Kings 17:16), Smith argues that Asherah was Yahweh's consort. Using Psalm 82 and the Septuagint of Deuteronomy 32:8–9, Smith and Day conclude that Yahweh was at some time assigned to be chief deity in the pantheon and that the other gods were a second tier of divinity. In this scenario, originally El, not Yahweh, was chief deity.[97] Only with the collapse of the first and second tiers in Israelite religion did Yahweh become identified with El. The remaining deities were demoted to the status of "angels." Smith suggests that the first two levels are systematized as a family.[98] On the lower two levels, the gatekeepers and messengers are male while the domestic servants are female. The divine family is modeled on the royal household. Yahweh in the Bible may also have been the head of a divine family, although the present text of the Bible recognizes no additional family or middle "tiers."

91. However, it is a temple of Anat that has been discovered at the site. This has led Day (2000, 135) to suggest that Ashtaroth may in this case mean "goddesses" in general, rather than a particular goddess.

92. If so, the name omits the initial aleph, rendered here as "E." It would be understood as a prothetic vowel, which eases pronunciation by removing the consonant cluster from the beginning of the word.

93. Mettinger (2001, 163).

94. M. Smith (2001a, 45–46; cf. 2005 for temples mediating divine attributes to worshipers). See also the summary above, on pp. 76–77.

95. See M. Smith (2001a, 55, 157) for the significance of the number 70 in West Semitic myth and polity. See also the discussion below on Gen. 1–11 regarding Enoch and Lamech.

96. See Day (2000, 22–24); M. Smith (2001a, 47–53).

97. Cf. Ps. 82; M. Smith (2001a, 155–57).

98. M. Smith (2001a, 54–55, 59–61).

Indeed, the view that this was ever a biblical model is without evidence. It rather appears to be an example of a well-developed polytheism. At Ugarit the family model provided a conceptual unity of polytheism.[99] In the Bible, texts such as Isaiah 9:6 [Heb. 5] and Psalms 45:6 [Heb. 7] associate divine titles with Davidic royalty.[100] This may suggest that the model was known from other cultures and that it was also used as a basis for court society at Ugarit. However, it does not seem to have enjoyed acceptance in the attested religion of Israel.[101] Nor was it the case that the society of Israel was modeled on that of a much larger and more cosmopolitan coastal city such as Ugarit. If any of the Late Bronze Age city-state archives have a society that may be compared to Israel's, it is the inland West Semitic city of Emar, as described below.

RITUALS[102]

Ritual texts have their own vocabulary at Ugarit, as in the Bible and throughout the ancient Near East. Baruch Levine (1993a) compares Israelite burnt offerings ('ōlâ) and peace or fellowship offerings (šĕlāmîm) with Ugaritic and Akkadian sacrifices of similar names. At Ugarit these two sacrifices were the two basic types where officiants and people ate of the victim.[103] The former, the burnt offering (šrp), was used to attract the deity to the temple, while the latter (šlmm) functioned as a gift of greeting that the worshiper presented in the courtyard of the temple. Similarly, the first offering in Leviticus (1:3–17) is the burnt offering. Perhaps it introduced the worshiper and God, although the text suggests a variety of other functions, including atonement. The fellowship offering (Lev. 3; 7:11–21) is an offering of gratitude to God. The comparison of Ugaritic with biblical sacrifices requires caution. For example, the two Ugaritic sacrifices often occur together. However, the first is not the equivalent of the biblical burnt offering since it is not entirely consumed. Both officiants and offerers ate from these sacrifices. The burnt offering may be closer to the Ugaritic ur(m).

Day and Smith summarize other names for sacrifices at Ugarit that also appear in Hebrew, including zebaḥ "sacrifice" (Ugaritic ḏbḥ), zebaḥ hayyāmîm (the annual offering), neder (offering of a vow), minḥâ (tribute offering), kālîl (burnt offering), and tĕnûpâ "elevation offering" (Ugaritic

99. M. Smith (2001a, 77–79).
100. Ibid., 159–60.
101. On the subject of Israelite kingship, see the discussion in chapter 8.
102. For the texts in English translation and their analysis, see Pardee (2002); del Olmo Lete (1999a); Merlo and Xella (1999). For editions of ritual texts, see Pardee (2000). Arnaud (2001) provides editions of more recently excavated texts.
103. Del Olmo Lete (1995, 44).

The Baal Cycle: Baal and Yamm

The word had not yet left his mouth,
From his lips the matter,
And she gave forth her voice,
"May he sink beneath the throne of Prince
    Yamm."

Kothar-wa-Hasis responds:
"Indeed I address you, Prince Baal,
I repeat, O Cloudrider.

Now, your enemy, O Baal,
Now, your enemy you smite,
Now, you destroy your adversary.

Take your eternal rule,
Your everlasting sovereignty."

Kothar forms the maces,
And he proclaims their names.
"You shall have the name Yagarrish.
Yagarrish, drive out Yamm.
Drive out Yamm from his chair.
Nahar from the throne of his sovereignty.

May you leap from the hand of Baal,
Like a bird of prey from his fingers.
Hit the shoulder of Prince Yamm,
Between the hands of Judge River."

The mace leaps from the hand of Baal,
Like a bird of prey from his fingers.

It hits the shoulder of Prince Yamm,
Between the hands of Judge River.

Yamm is strong, he does not fall,
His joints do not buckle,
His form does not break up.

Kothar forms the maces,
And he proclaims their names.
"You shall have the name Ayyamurru,
Ayyamurru, remove Yamm,
Remove Yamm from his chair,
Nahar from the throne of his sovereignty.

May you leap from the hand of Baal,
Like a bird of prey from his fingers.
Hit the skull of Prince Yamm,
Between the eyes of Judge River,
May Yamm collapse and fall to the
    ground."

The mace leaps from the hand of Baal,
Like a bird of prey from his fingers.
It hits the skull of Prince Yamm,
Between the eyes of Judge River,
Yamm collapses and falls to the ground.
His joints buckle,
And his form breaks up.

Baal drags and sets upon Yamm,
He finishes off Judge River.

KTU 1.2 IV lines 6–27; Fourteenth/Thirteenth Century BC from Ugarit. Translation by author. See Mark S. Smith, "The Baal Cycle," pp. 81–180 in *Ugaritic Narrative Poetry*. Edited by S. B. Parker. Vol. 9 of SBL Writings from the Ancient World. Atlanta: Scholars Press, 1997. See pp. 102–4 for transliteration, another translation, and notes.

šnpt, although the nature of the sacrifice described by this term at Ugarit is not clear).[104]

The liturgies of the Ugaritic texts were arranged according to time, space, and type of rite.[105] Sacrificial liturgies most often include a list of offerings specifying the divine recipients. They sometimes provide details about where the offering is given and when it is given.[106]

The biblical tradition has assigned a theological significance to the sacrifices. Foremost among these is that of atonement. Studies of the Ugaritic texts have also led to suggestions of theological significance there. De Moor and Sanders (1991) have argued that evidence from Ugaritic texts demonstrates that Canaanite culture preserved ideas about personal, moral, and religious guilt for sin. Expiation could be obtained from the divine world through animal sacrifices. They cite one text in particular that defines the offering of animals such as a ram and a he-ass. Part of the ritual involves the recitation of sins and includes the following:[107]

> whether your sin:
> be it in your anger,
> be it in your impatience,
> be it in some turpitude that you should commit;
> whether you sin:
> as concerns the sacrifices
> or as concerns the _t_ʿ-sacrifice.
> The sacrifice, it is sacrificed,
> the _t_ʿ-sacrifice, it is offered,
> the slaughtering is done.
> May it be borne to the father of the sons of 'Ilu.

This text comes from the ritual of atonement at Ugarit. *KTU* 1.40 (with duplicates) repeats this passage six times with minor variations as different sacrifices are made. Wyatt (1998, 342) likens this ritual to the

104. Day (1994, 52); M. Smith (2003, 23). Cf. del Olmo Lete (1995, 45). Selman (1995) notes that neither the Mesopotamian nor Ugaritic rituals had as their stated purposes fellowship with the deities nor was there an equivalent to the Passover. He also maintains that there is no parallel to the concern for atonement (p. 101). However, these views must all be questioned. See the analyses of Levine (above) and of de Moor and Sanders, as well as Kaufman in the following paragraphs.

105. Del Olmo Lete (1999a).

106. Ibid., 87.

107. The translation is from Pardee (2002, 81–83). The text is Ras Shamra 1.002 = *KTU* 1.40. Cf. de Moor and Sanders (1991, 284–87) and Wyatt (1998, 344–45) for other translations. Cf. also Pardee and Bordreuil (1992, 709). It must be emphasized that translations of such texts from Ugarit contain unusual and sometimes unclear words in the description of rituals and their meaning.

Day of Atonement (Lev. 16) in Israel and observes that it offers a rare glimpse into ethical concerns at Ugarit.

Del Olmo Lete (1999a, 157–58) notes that three categories of sin are discussed, of which the second and third are mentioned in the above quote. The first type refers to following the customs or mores of other peoples and mentions what appear to be seven people groups (Qaṭian, Didmian, Hurrian, Hittite, Alashian, ĠBR, and QRZBL), similar to what are traditionally the seven nations of Canaan that Israel must completely remove from the promised land.[108] The second type of sin involves personal morality: anger, impatience,[109] and immorality. The third group involves cultic sins.

Funeral liturgies are known in the mythological texts, with lamentation, rites, and curse formulas for disturbing the dead. Such rites and lamentations are modeled in the following excerpt from a mythological text:[110]

> Then the Kindly One, *Ilu*, the Benign,
>   came down from the throne, sat on the footstool,
>   and leaving the footstool, sat on the ground;
> he sprinkled ash of affliction on his head,
>   dust of humiliation on his skull,
>   for clothing he covered himself with a ritual tunic;
> (his) skin with a stone (knife) he gashed,
>   the two tresses with a razor,
>   he lacerated (his) cheeks and chin;
> harrowed the bone of his arm,
>   ploughed like a garden his chest,
>   like a valley harrowed his back.
> He raised his voice and exclaimed:
>   "*Ba'lu* is dead! What will happen to the people?
>   The son of *Dagānu*! What will happen to the multitude?
>   After *Ba'lu* I shall go down to the 'earth.'"

Cutting one's hair and lacerating oneself are forbidden in the Bible as mourning rituals (Lev. 19:27–28, 21:5), although it did take place as a sign of mourning.[111]

---

108. A list of seven occurs in Deut. 7:1; Josh. 3:10; and 24:11.

109. Del Olmo Lete (1999a) renders this as cowardliness: *qṣrt npš*. Kitchen (2003, 405) notes that impatience was linked with sin in Israel as well.

110. Cf. *KTU* 1.5 VI 11–25; 1.6 I 2–8 (del Olmo Lete [1999a, 161–62]).

111. Deut. 14:1; Isa. 22:2; Jer. 16:6; 41:5; 47:5; cf. Johnston (2002, 48). In 1 Kings 18:28, the prophets of Baal also lacerate themselves in an attempt to gain the god's attention and favor. Deut. 14:1–5 decries the cutting of one's flesh and the tonsure for the dead. B. Schmidt (1994, 166–78) argues that the cutting of one's flesh was designed to blur the distinction between the living and the dead. The Deuteronomists viewed only these mourning rites

Kings, when they died, became *rpum*, associated with the biblical Rephaim.[112] At Ugarit, *rpum* and the *mlkm* are terms for the dead. There probably was no widespread mortuary cult but there certainly was a connection with the dead.[113] For the dead kings at least, there are maintenance offerings and rituals.[114]

Ilib "god of the fathers" is a term that appears at Ugarit and is thought by many to refer to divinized ancestors. Others identify these with deities who are personal and family gods. This is based on the corresponding use of this term in Mesopotamian texts, as well as its comparison with Hurrian usage in cultic texts and god lists.[115] The evidence seems to come from *KTU* 1.116 lines 10ff., where the Hurrian term for a type of deity appears in conjunction with "the gods of the fathers," and introduces a list of deities to whom sacrifices are made. Nevertheless, these could just as easily be ancestors recognized as deities. A Ugaritic king list (*KTU* 1.113), similar to the already mentioned king list from Ebla, precedes the royal names of dead kings with *il* "god," probably indicating that the kings had become divine.[116]

Prayers

KTU 1.119 provides the only example of a prayer to Baal. It appears at the end of the ritual tablet Ras Shamra 24.266, where the king performs a sequence of rituals in the month of *Iba'latu* (December/January, immediately following the winter solstice). The prayer begins on the verso, line 27. The top of the verso is broken but what remains of it here will be cited (lines 20–35), following the translation of Pardee:[117]

> . . .
> On the fourth day: birds.
> On the fifth day: birds and a liver and a ram as a burnt offering for
>   *Ba'lu* of Ugarit in the temple.
> On the seventh day: you shall bring the purifiers near.

---

as illegitimate, because they blurred the distinction between the living and the dead in the exilic and postexilic world, where such distinctions were important.

112. For the biblical and Phoenician usage of this term, see chapter 9, "Excursus: Religion of Phoenicia," pp. 294–95.

113. See Pardee (2000; 2002); Lewis (2002, 198–203). According to some, these are divinized and immortal heroes who can and do extend blessing upon the faithful citizens of Ugarit and act as their protective spirits. See del Olmo Lete (1999a, 168–69) for this. See Pitard (1999) for the problematic nature of all interpretations of this term.

114. In Akkadian these are *kispum* rituals.

115. B. Schmidt (1994, 53–59).

116. Contrast B. Schmidt, who argues that here also the reference is to the personal gods of the kings.

117. Pardee (2002, 52–53, 149–50). See also the translation of Wyatt (1998, 420–22).

> When the sun sets, the king will be free (of further cultic
>   obligations).
> Behold the oil of well-being of *Ba'lu*, libation-offering for the
>   benefit of the *Malakūma*, of the best quality.
> When a strong foe attacks your gate, a warrior your walls,
> You shall lift your eyes to *Ba'lu* and say:
> O *Ba'lu*, if you drive the strong one from our gate, the warrior
>   from our walls,
> A bull, O *Ba'lu*, we shall sanctify,
> a vow, O *Ba'lu*, we shall fulfill;
> a firstborn, O *Ba'lu*, we shall sanctify,
> a *ḥtp*-offering, O *Ba'lu*, we shall fulfill,
> a feast, O *Ba'lu*, we shall offer;
> To the sanctuary, O *Ba'lu*, we shall ascend,
> that path, O *Ba'lu*, we shall take.
> And *Ba'lu* will hear your prayer:
> He will drive the strong foe from your gate,
> the warrior from your walls.

Del Olmo Lete (1999a, 306) comments on this text:

> This cultic Ugaritic prayer, which has all the meaning of an "oracle of salva-
> tion" and, more specifically, is testimony to a "salvation history" in which *Ba'lu*
> appears no longer as the god of fertility but as lord of history and its transfor-
> mations, shows us one religious activity of the Canaanite world, i.e., prayer,
> which undoubtedly was more common than the extant texts suggest.

KTU 1.123 (Ras Shamra 24.271) is a prayer in which the petitioner
appeals to a variety of deities for well-being (*šlm*).
   KTU 1.124 (Ras Shamra 24.272) is a consultation on behalf of a sick
child of the king. The king consults Ditanu the founder of the dynasty and
is given instructions as to what to do so that the child will recover.[118]

DIVINATION

Divination at Ugarit is found in texts that describe its many forms:
royal necromancy, extispicy, astrology (but only one such text, *KTU*
1.163), teratomancy, incantations (especially against snakebites and
demons), and magical prescriptions for illnesses.[119]

118. See del Olmo Lete (1999a, 310–15), who compares 1 Samuel 28 and Saul's consultation of Samuel, the one responsible for the dynasties of both Saul and David, concerning his
own problem. However, Philip Johnston, in a private communication (April 12, 2007), suggests 2 Samuel 12 and the story there of David's sick child may be a closer comparison.
   119. See del Olmo Lete (1999a, 345–88); Spronk (1999, who also deals with prayer);
Xella (1999). The teratomancy material is partly parallel to the *šumma izbu* series found
in Akkadian and Mesopotamian omen texts.

MARZĒAḤ

Although mention of this event may be found earlier, the *marzēaḥ* festival appears in more detail at Ugarit. Philip Johnston (2002, 182) likens the *marzēaḥ* at Ugarit to Masonic Lodges or Rotary clubs. It was an assembly comprising members from a higher economic class who celebrated a festival with a banquet in honor of a specific deity such as

---

Ritual for Admittance of the King into the Underworld

The text concerning the sacrifice for the Shades:

You have called for the Rephaim of the earth.

You have called for the clan of the Di[danites(?)].

Call for ULKN, the Repha.

Call for TRMN, the Repha.

Call for SDN-w-RD[N, the Repha.]

Call for TR.'LLMN, [the Repha.]

Call for the Rephaim of old.

You have called for the Rephaim of the earth.

You have called for the clan of the Dida[nites(?)].

Call for king Ammishtamru.

Call for king Niqmaddu, as well.

Weep, O Seat of Niqmaddu.

May his footstool weep.

May the royal table weep in front of it.

Let it swallow its tears.

Desolation and desolation of desolations.

Give your heat, O Shapshu,

Give your heat, O Great Light.

High above Shapshu cries out:

After your lord, from the throne,

After your lord, to the earth, descend.

To the earth, descend. Go beneath the dust,

Beneath SDN-w-RDN,

Beneath TR'LLMN,

Beneath the Rephaim of old,

Beneath king Ammishtamru,

Beneath king Niqmaddu, as well.

Once and (offer?) a noble sacrifice,

Twice and (offer?) a noble sacrifice,

Three times and (offer?) a noble sacrifice,

Four times and (offer?) a noble sacrifice,

Five times and (offer?) a noble sacrifice,

Six times and (offer?) a noble sacrifice,

Seven times and (offer?) a noble sacrifice,

Present a bird of well-being,

Well-being for Ammurapi and well-being for his household,

Well-being for Tharriyelli and well-being for her household,

Well-being for Ugarit and well-being for its gates.

KTU 1.161 lines 1–34; c. 1200 BC from Ugarit. Translation by author; see Pardee (2002, 85–88, 113–15) for the transliteration, another translation, and notes on the text. For additional translation and notes, see also Baruch A. Levine, Jean-Michel de Tarragon, and Anne Robertson, The Patrons of the Ugaritic Dynasty (*KTU* 1.161) (1.105). Pages 357–58 in *Canonical Compositions from the Biblical World*. Vol. I of The Context of Scripture. Edited by W. W. Hallo and K. L. Younger Jr. Leiden: Brill, 1997.

Anat.[120] It had legal sanction, met in cities and villages, met for drinking, could involve substantial money including the leasing of houses and vineyards, possessed a defined membership, continued for generations, and could have a patron deity.[121] No text specifies a cultic or funerary connection. However, in the Ugaritic myths the god El holds a *marzēaḥ*, which includes a drinking banquet, until he collapses in drunkenness (*KTU* 1.114 15). Rephaim texts mention the *mrz'*, a variant of the customary spelling of *mrzḥ*, where either El or Dan'el invites the Rephaim to "my *marzēaḥ*" as well as "my house" and "my palace."[122]

An important ritual text (*KTU* 1.161) mentions the Rephaim (*rpum*) and the dead king (*mlk*). The text is associated with Ugarit's king Ammurapi, who performs a ritual on behalf of kings who preceded him. As with other such king lists of the ancient Near East, the connection with deceased predecessors on the throne is a means of establishing legitimacy for the king.[123]

CULTIC FUNCTIONARIES

The cultic functionaries[124] included a variety of titled figures who were also found with similar names in the Bible. The priest occurs at Ugarit (*KTU* 4.29 1; 4.38 1; 4.68 72) and in the Bible (*kōhēn*, 2 Kings 10:19). The servants who work at the temple and cultic sites at Ugarit are the *ytnm* (*KTU* 4.93 1) and in Israel they are the *nĕtûnîm/nĕtînîm*.[125] Those dedicated to the temple and its deity include the *qādēš* in both Israel and Ugarit.[126] The Ugaritic "chief of priests" (*rb khnm*, *KTU* 1.6 VI 55–56) may correspond

---

120. B. Schmidt (1994, 62–66).

121. Cf. *KTU* 1.114; 3.9; 4.399; 4.642. Cf. the Akkadian texts Ras Shamra 14.16; 15.70; 15.88; 18.01.

122. Cf. *KTU* 1.21 II 1, 5, 9.

123. B. Schmidt (1994, 100–20) argues that this text has nothing to do with an ancestor cult. However, the combination of a ritual and a list of the deceased dynasty of Ugarit seem to suggest a connection between the two. For the later biblical and inscriptional evidence on the Rephaim, see chapter 9, "Excursus: Religion of Phoenicia," p. 294. For the use of king lists to establish legitimacy, see Hess (1989b).

124. M. Smith (2003, 23–24).

125. *Nĕtûnîm*—Num. 3:9; 8:19. *Nĕtînîm*—1 Chron. 9:2; Ezra 2:43, 58, 70; 7:7; 8:17 (Qere; Kethib *nĕtûnîm*), 20; Neh. 3:26, 31; 7:46, 60, 72; 10:29; 11:3, 21.

126. Deut. 23:18 [Heb. 18]; 1 Kings 14:24; 15:12; 22:47; 2 Kings 23:7; Job 36:14; *KTU* 1.112 21; 4.29 3; 4.36; 4.38 2; 4.68 73. There are many theories about the roles of these figures at Ugarit and in the Israelite cults. Gruber (1986) suggests that biblical *qĕdēšâ* refers to a (secular) prostitute whereas Ugaritic and Akkadian cognates refer to cultic functionaries whose roles do not include sexual activities. Bird (1997b) argues that there was no male prostitution, such as the masculine *qādēš* may imply. Day (2004a) convincingly argues for both male prostitutes and cultic prostitution as described in the Bible, though he observes the difficulty of drawing any conclusions from the limited use of the terms at Ugarit. Cf. chapter 10 and the excursus "Sacred Prostitution," pp. 332–35.

to the biblical high priest.[127] The holy site of the tent of meeting formed a sanctuary for both cultures.[128]

Emar

Emar was a city that flourished in the fourteenth and thirteenth centuries BC in northern Syria.[129] It was controlled by the Hittite empire from the time of Mursilis II in the late fourteenth century but the personal names of the citizens reflect strong West Semitic and Hurrian cultural influences and probable ethnicities. The inland location and pastoral economy of the site, as well as its cultural and chronological proximity to earliest Israel, suggest that the two cultures could have influenced each other. Unlike Ugarit, where many of the mythologies and religious texts were written in an alphabetic script whose consonantal alphabet preserves no vowels,[130] the unique collection of West Semitic religious texts from Emar are written in Akkadian, sometimes in multiple copies. These syllabic texts preserve full vocalization. Despite the difficulty of reading the script, more is known for certain about the religious vocabulary in Akkadian than that in Ugaritic. This is because of the thousands of religious texts in the ancient Near East that are written in Akkadian.

TEXTS

There are a number of texts from Emar that date from the thirteenth century BC that describe rituals and festivals.[131] These texts are not mythological but cultic. They resemble ritual texts from ancient Israel, especially those in Leviticus 8–10 and 23. Despite the much greater number of religious texts from Ugarit, those found at Emar provide a closer connection in terms of purpose and content to cultic texts that are found in the Pentateuch.[132] This is an extremely important point

127. *hakkōhēn haggādōl* (Lev. 21:10; Num. 35:25, 28; Josh. 20:6; 2 Kings 12:11 [Heb. 11]; 22:4, 8; Neh. 3:1, 20; 13:28; 2 Chron. 34:9; Hag. 1:2, 12, 14; 2:2, 4; Zech. 3:1, 8; 6:11).

128. *'ōhel mô'ēd*—Exod. 27:21; *KTU* 1.4 IV 20–26.

129. For the archaeology of the site, see Beyer (1980; 1982); Margueron (1982; 1995); Pitard (1996).

130. The exception here is of course the aleph signs that represent three different vowels.

131. For the major text editions, see Arnaud (1985a; 1985b; 1986; 1987; 1991). For other editions and English translations of key texts, see Fleming (1992; 1997; 2000b).

132. See Hess (1996a, 75) for an attempt to "compare a selection of cuneiform archives from [Ugarit, Emar, and Alalakh, which] are close to one another both chronologically and geographically." That this was the purpose, using text genres defined by Van Soldt (1991), and that it was not to examine the Alalakh IV archives "in terms of their archaeological findspots" should be kept in mind in light of later attempts to critique the work for not doing

that has not been fully appreciated. It provides a third perspective, in addition to Ugarit and Israel, that is both contemporary and nearby. From this viewpoint one can better evaluate the proposed similarities between Ugarit and Israel. The net effect is to cast doubt on common assumptions about what earliest Israel should have believed and been like. For example, the absence at Emar of many of the Ugaritic mythologies may call into question facile connections between Israelite terms and phrases and those of fully developed mythologies. If they are not found at Emar, perhaps they were not known in Israel either, and perhaps the entire picture of early Israel's beliefs should be approached more cautiously. At the least, the Emar evidence suggests a greater diversity in West Semitic emphases and practices in the thirteenth century BC than was formerly recognized. Perhaps the greater similarity between the Emar and biblical cultic texts also implies that logically we should begin with Emar before turning to Ugarit, and recognize the former's priority in comparative religious discussions. Because the Emar texts have not been sufficiently appreciated in terms of their evaluation as part of an overview of the religious practices of Israel, it is worthwhile to examine them at length.[133]

Before proceeding it is important to observe that the storm god Baal was the chief deity at Emar. This fact is attested both by the following texts and by the temple of Baal at Emar and his cult there, as well as the presence of Baal (and the corresponding Hurrian storm deity, *Teššub*) in many personal names.[134]

EMAR 369

Emar 369[135] describes the installation of the high priestess of the storm god at Emar. In this ritual the priestess is anointed with oil just as Aaron and the priests are also anointed in Leviticus 8. These are the only two installation rituals in the ancient world where priestly figures are anointed with oil.[136] There is also an atypical use of a torch on the final day of the installation, when the priestess goes to meet the god and live in the temple. Compare this with the "strange fire" that Nadab and

---

what it was *not* designed to accomplish (von Dassow [2005, 5]). At Ugarit, both private and palace archives preserve religious texts, whereas at Emar what would commonly be designated as religious texts have been largely confined to the temple archives.

133. A complete edition, translation, and philological commentary of all the texts studied here may be found in Fleming (2000b).

134. Schwemer (2001, 548–73).

135. The number refers to a specific text, following the numbering system of the cuneiform tablets from Emar in the *editio princeps* of Arnaud (1985a; 1985b; 1986; 1987; 1991).

136. See Fleming (1998); Klingbeil (2000).

Abihu offer in Leviticus 10:1–2. Were they participating in a West Semitic ritual that involved the honoring of other deities?[137] Thus the anointing text demonstrates the antiquity of obscure elements of the priestly installation rituals of Leviticus 8–10, which bear witness to authentic West Semitic practices in use as early as the Late Bronze Age, but not attested outside the Bible in the first millennium BC.

EMAR 373

Emar's *zukru* festival compares with the spring festivals of Passover and Unleavened Bread, as well as other ritual festivals in West Semitic religion of the second millennium BC. There are at least six important points of comparison.

First, both are referred to by the Semitic verbal root *zkr,* "to speak, remember, invoke" as *zukru* (Emar) and *zikkārōn* (Hebrew, Exod. 12:14; Lev. 23:24). The *zukru* festival is an invocation to the gods with a spoken component no longer preserved. Fleming compares this to Hebrew *tōdâ* "giving thanks" and to the biblical Hebrew *'azkārâ,* an offering that remembers God and produces a "fragrance for the direct point of contact between the giver and God."[138]

Second, both *zukru* and Passover festivals require the roasting of a lamb.

Third, in both festivals twilight is a critical time.

Fourth, at Emar this festival constitutes a seven-day sequence in which the climactic event happens on the "powerful" seventh day.[139] Compare Mari's seven-day ritual in Dagan's temple. At Ugarit, Baal's precious metals for his palace are placed in the fire for seven days in order to refine them. Keret goes to *Udm* and besieges that city for seven days. Dan'el serves Baal and the birth goddesses for two seven-day cycles. Like the biblical feast of Passover and Unleavened Bread, *zukru* also occurs on the fifteenth day of the first month and lasts for a seven-day cycle in which the first and last days are the most important in terms of activities.

Fifth, all the gods are brought out of the city for the *zukru* festival, and the populace, who also come out for the *zukru* festival, is provided with bread and drink. These compare with the banquet of Israel's elders with God in Exodus 24:9–11 and David's festival of bringing the ark into Jerusalem and giving food to the people as part of a celebration.[140] Pass-

137. See Hess (2002a).
138. Fleming (2000b, 123–24 [124n326]). The Hebrew word is especially associated with the grain offering of Lev. 2:2, 9, 16.
139. Ibid., 74–75.
140. 2 Sam. 6:17–19; cf. Fleming (2000b, 78).

The Consecration of the High Priestess of the Storm God at Emar

The ritual tablet of the high priestess of Emar's storm god.

When Emar's citizens raise the high priestess for the storm god, they take lots from NINURTA's temple and they seize them before the storm god. The daughter of any Emar citizen may be designated. On that day they take good oil from both the palace and from NINKUR's temple. They place it on her head. Then they offer a sheep, a jar, and a portion of wine. They give the diviner a shekel of silver. To NINURTA's temple they return eight dried loaves and one standard vessel, along with the lots. At the time of the shaving ritual's consecration, they consecrate all the pantheon of Emar by means of bread and beer.

On the second day there is the shaving of the high priestess. An ox and six sheep go to the temple of the storm god. The divine weapon and the priestess walk behind them while the singers walk in front of them. They reach the temple of the storm god and there at the gate of the courtyard they shave the high priestess . . . they make an act of veneration before the storm god. Her father bears the divine weapon as an offering on her behalf. When they finish the great veneration, they give the diviner a shekel of silver. They offer an ox and six sheep to the storm god. They place in front of the gods the ceremonial piece of beef and the ceremonial piece of lamb. They also place in front of the gods seven ration loaves, seven dried loaves, and two dried loaves with fruit. They fill wine goblets. The royal officials who make the consecration, the heralds, seven, and seven hamasha'u(?) men eat and drink at the storm god's temple. The men of the consecration each receive one ration loaf and one standard serving of barley beer.

The family leader cuts up a sheep at his house. He cooks it while they arrange four tables each with three ration loaves at the gate of the storm god's temple at the apartment of the high priestess. One table is for the former high priestess. One table is for the high priestess of the town of Shumu. One table is for the lady in charge of security. One table is for the king of Emar. One table is for the king of the town of Shatappu. On each of them they place the lamb meat and a dried loaf containing fruit. They take to each a container of barley beer and a container for receiving the barley beer. To the pantheon of Emar they offer to each one ration loaf, one portion of barley beer, thick bread, cedar oil, and fruit. They divide these among the deities.

Before evening they take the good oil from NINKUR's temple and from the palace. At the gate of the storm god the diviner pours it on the head of the high priestess. The men responsible for the consecration leave the storm god's temple. They then bring her into her family home.

Emar 369 lines 1–21 (days one and two); thirteenth century BC from Emar. Translation by author; see Fleming (1992, 10–14) for the transliteration, another translation, and commentary.

over was also celebrated with special bread and with drink. In addition, it took place as a festival apart from royalty and priesthood. The focus of the celebration was on the family.[141]

The sixth and final point of comparison considers the antiquity of the *zukru* festival. The mention of the *zukru* at eighteenth-century BC Mari suggests that this ritual was older and more widespread than thirteenth-century BC Emar. It seems to have involved the chief god of the region where it was practiced.[142] The memorial festivals of Passover and Unleavened Bread may thus have West Semitic antecedents. Thus the Passover and Feast of Unleavened Bread have similarities with the *zukru* festival at Emar and elsewhere. The similarities in matters of some detail are unlikely to have been coincidental. These imply that the two were not originally separate but, as at Emar, comprised a single unified festival. See the discussion in chapter 7 (pp. 181–82) for the critical arguments over the separate origins of the Passover and Feast of Unleavened Bread in nomadic and settled societies, respectively. These early sociological analyses fail when confronted with the study of actual societies, in this case of Emar. Thus the arguments and methods of Evans-Pritchard, Geertz, and other sociologists of religion who insist on the need to examine the societies themselves, and not to make generalizations about what tribes and cultures are "supposed to do," find ready application to the analysis of ancient Israel. Where they can be tested, the generalizations are proved wrong.

Although unrelated to the Passover itself, other elements of the *zukru* festival assist in understanding the role of particular biblical phenomena. The *sikkānu* stones play a key role in the ritual of installing the high priestess of the storm god Baal and have parallels with Hittite and Hebrew standing stones. They resemble the Hebrew *maṣṣēbâ* (plural *maṣṣēbôt*) and the Hittite *ḫuwaši* stones. Individual *sikkānu* stones are associated with specific deities. The high priestess (NIN.DINGIR) is anointed and then she anoints the stone representing *Ḥebat*, the storm-god's divine consort. On the night following the enthronement of the *maš'artu* priestess, a *sikkānu* stone is set up on the roof and presented with offerings. In the Hittite *ḫuwaši* festival, a stone stele outside the city is visited by the divine image during festivals. Small models of the stone, made of precious metals, are placed in urban sanctuaries. There may be more than two stones.[143] Oil and blood are rubbed on

141. Although Exod. 23:14–17; 34:18–23; and Deut. 16 command all Israelite males to participate, Deut. 16:11 and 14 suggest that everyone was involved.

142. Fleming (2000b, 98–99). For the *zukrum* at Mari, see Nissinen (2003, 17–21) and the translation of text A. 1121 + A. 2731.

143. Fleming (2000b, 82–85). Cf. also the ten upright stones at the high place of Gezer as noted below.

The *Zukru* Festival

On the second day, on the 15th (of the month) or Shaggar-day, they enact (the festival). They lead forth Dagan lord of the firstborn, NINURTA, Shashabetu of NINURTA's temple, Belet-ekalli (the divine lady of the palace), the moon and the sun of the palace, the pantheon and the Shashabiyanatu deities. They lead them to the Gate of the Standing Stones . . . of the king, ten lambs of the town [go] before Dagan.

They offer to Dagan . . . a ration of barley bread, a container, a flagon of the king's wine . . . a container from the temple. For the populace there are . . . a beer jar of the temple. They offer to Shashabetu: . . . two lambs from the town, a beer jar, a flagon of the king's wine, a ration of barley bread, a container from the temple. They offer to Belet-ekalli, and the moon and the sun of the palace, royal lambs, three larger measures and three rations of barley bread, three jars, and three containers of royal wine.

When they have eaten and drunk, they anoint the standing stones with oil and blood. Before evening, they transport the gods back to the town. They enact the smaller consecration at the Great Battle Gate. For the pantheon they burn a ewe along (presenting) with a jar and two pair of royal barley bread. . . .

On the seventh day, Dagan, the pantheon, and the Shashabiyanatu deities emerge. His (Dagan's) face is covered. They give the rituals for the gods as on the previous day. The meats, breads, and everything that they have eaten from the previous days they lift up and they . . . in return. Nothing will go up to the town. At the fire . . . they uncover the face of Dagan. Dagan's wagon passes . . . [standing stone]s. He [goe]s to NINURTA. . . . They perform the rituals as on the previous day.

Emar 373 lines 41–60, 202–9 (days one and seven); thirteenth century BC from Emar. Translation by author; see Fleming (2000b) for the transliteration, another translation, and commentary.

---

the stones. Oil is used in anointing stones elsewhere and may represent purity and pleasure. Fleming suggests concerning the ritual: "The stones are anointed in preparation for the moment of meeting, so that the god himself will inhabit not only the statue but the stones."[144] This is the case in Hittite rituals and Fleming suggests it may also occur at the Emar *zukru*. The only other example of anointing with both blood and oil is found in the installation of the priests in Leviticus 8:30.[145] Compare the biblical references to the use of standing stones. See chapter 7 below.

Finally, it may be noted that, in preparatory rites and during the journey to the stones of the *zukru* festival, Dagan's face was covered.

---

144. Fleming (2000b, 86–87). The use of blood in anointing stones is unique before pre-Islamic Arabic practice.

145. Fleming (1998, 410).

This hid his glory, something that was revealed only at the center of the *zukru* and only to the stones; not to people.[146] This recalls the hiding of the glory of Moses' face and its revelation in Exodus 34, as well as the veil in the tabernacle that covered the presence of God.

EMAR 446

Another example of an important ritual text from thirteenth-century BC Emar is Emar 446, a ritual calendar.[147] In the ancient Near East, the "new year" is never called that. Instead, it is the "head of the year." Mesopotamia, Anatolia, and Israel may have recognized two "heads" to their year: one in the spring and the other in the autumn when the seasons changed. The position of the *zukru* festival during autumn in the month at the head of the year corresponds to other ancient Near Eastern "New Year's festivals," and to the Jewish Rosh Hashanah.[148]

This festival calendar at Emar is unique among any and all known cuneiform texts. However, it may be compared to the Pentateuch ritual calendars, especially Leviticus 23.[149] Following are ten comparisons: the first through sixth cover diverse areas of form; the rest cover content.

First, cultic ritual texts from Emar and Ugarit were written in the third person. Leviticus 23 preserves some third-person narrative in at least seventeen of the forty-one verses that constitute the multimonth calendar of Leviticus 23:4–44.[150]

Second, Emar 446 covers six months of the year. Although there are seven months inclusive from Nisan until Tishri, the Israelite ritual calendar also reflects this interest in one half of the year. In both, the spring and autumn provide the beginning and ending points.

Third, both calendars use the name of the month as the primary means of identifying the month and of organizing the text.

Fourth, for the first and last months, Leviticus 23 identifies the ritual actions that occurred by introducing each one with a phrase that includes the preposition *b-* (with the sense of "in" or "on"), the number of the day, and the word for "month" (vv. 5, 6, 24, 27, 34, and 39). This parallels most of the rituals on the Emar calendar, as it does other Akkadian and Ugaritic ritual calendars.[151] In fact, in Emar 446

---

146. Fleming (2000b, 92–93).
147. See Fleming (1999a; 1999c; 2000b); Hess (2004b).
148. Fleming (2000b, 126–32).
149. See Hess (2004b). The other Pentateuchal ritual calendars are found in Exod. 23:10–19; 34:18–26; Num. 28–29; and Deut. 16.
150. Verses 4a, 5, 8b, 9, 11, 13, 14b, 17b, 20, 21b, 23, 26, 27a, 29–30, 33–35a, 37b, 43–44.
151. Farley (1974, 186).

many cultic actions were defined by their position in a given month. For example, the biblical Feast of Weeks that occurs in the middle of the calendar resembles the description of the Emar festivals during the month of Anna. In both cases, these are intermediate, occurring between the major festivals at the beginning and the end of the calendar. In both cases, specifics as to the particular day of the month are missing. Therefore, it seems unlikely that a single standard formula can be identified for introducing calendar festivals. The Emar calendar demonstrates that such variation by itself does not prove a later editorial innovation.

Fifth, numerous rituals occur in the first month of the Emar calendar. Several of these occurred on the fifteenth day of the month.[152] Lines 8 and 45 of Emar 446 specify this day as the setting for the two rituals that follow. In both rituals the deities' images were brought forth and there were processions. In both sheep were slaughtered (lines 9–10 and 46). Although the deities are different and the details of the rituals are different, this grouping of festivals on the same day may be compared with the Feast of Booths/Tabernacles as described in Leviticus 23:34–36, 39–43. Both descriptions begin with the same specific date, the fifteenth day of the seventh month. Both descriptions outline a "festival" (Hebrew *ḥag*) emphasizing the first and eighth days as times of rest. However, all the other details are different. The term, "feast of booths" (*ḥag hassukkōt*), occurs only in v. 34. In verse 39 the festival is designated the "feast of Yahweh" (*ḥag yhwh*). The first description emphasizes doing no work and presenting "fire offerings" to Yahweh. The second description emphasizes resting, the gathering of branches, living in booths, and the remembering of Yahweh's deliverance from Egypt. Were it not for discussion of this feast elsewhere in the Bible, it could be argued that these are two different feasts that occur simultaneously. The same is true for the Emar text. In both ritual calendars, the differences in various details are matched by parallel periods of time when the feasts were celebrated and by similar general actions during the holy days. In addition to a remarkable parallel of form for these festivals at Emar and Israel, the similarity suggests that a second description of a ritual occurring on the same day or days as the first, and positioned soon after the first description in a text, does not by itself indicate that it is an editorial addition.[153] Rather, this practice is now known and attested in more than one multi-month West Semitic ritual calendar.

152. See also the discussion of this comparison in chapter 3 in the excursus on the Documentary Hypothesis, pp. 52–53.
153. See Hess (2004b, 246) for a list of commentators who accept this phenomenon in Lev. 23:33–43 as sufficient reason for an editorial insertion.

Sixth, Emar 446 describes a number of feasts in its calendar. Some of these are mentioned in a single line. Others are much longer. For example, one feast of the deity NINURTA during the first month occupies at least nineteen lines (22–40) of text and perhaps more. The same is true of the rituals described in Leviticus 23. The Feast of Trumpets is described in nineteen Hebrew words (vv. 24b–25). However, the description of the Feast of Weeks occupies verses 10–22 and contains 197 words. Again, the size of a ritual description in such a calendar cannot be used to determine its origin as an editorial addition.

The seventh point of comparison notes that both the Emar and the biblical calendars focus on feasts that emphasize grains, whether the planting of them, as at Emar, or their harvest, as found in Israel. At Emar this is clear with respect to Dagan, the first deity to have received offerings in the first month. He was "Lord of the Seed." Emar's ritual to prepare for the sowing of the fields in the autumn corresponds to the springtime of Israel with its harvest festivals and focus on the grain in the form of unleavened bread and grain offerings.

Eighth, in Emar 446 the ritual for the storm god seems to have occurred in the early spring (lines 107–110), just as the ritual for the Passover took place in the spring in Israel (e.g., Lev. 23:5–8). Although little is known about the storm god at Emar, it is clear that the evidence from Ugarit and the Bible associate this deity with Baal in his roles as warrior and as one who provides for the fertility of the land and the bringing forth of a rich harvest. The biblical Passover's position in the spring also associates the roles of Israel's God with a warrior who fought against Egypt and delivered Israel from there and with the one who had given the harvest and blessings of the land to Israel. The historical element does not occur in the Emar calendar, but the emphasis on agricultural concerns does.

In light of the agricultural emphasis in both calendars, it is important to recognize that this is integrated with specific dates for the various festivals. Thus the Emar calendar contradicts the view commonly expressed regarding Leviticus 23 that such fixation of dates renders the calendar independent from an original connection to an agricultural cycle and thus betrays a late development in the evolution of the cultic calendar.[154] To the contrary, at both Emar and in Israel the specific dates are correlated not only with days during the month, but also with seasonal events.

As a ninth point of comparison, I first note that some argue for the nomadic origin of the Passover because the biblical festival uses a lamb roasted with fire, and at the same time argue for a settled origin for the

154. Gerstenberger (1996, 338).

subsequent Feast of Unleavened Bread because the bread must have been the product of a settled economy. Neither of the two joined festivals mention an altar or a priest. Emar 446 describes festivals in which lambs are burnt (line 92; a bird is burnt at line 99), breads of various types are used (lines 21, 51, 78), and there is the absence of an altar or priest. In fact, an altar is never mentioned and a "diviner" appears to function in place of a priest. Yet this festival takes place on behalf of people who are settled and appear to live in an urban environment. Thus theories about the nomadic origins of various aspects of the Passover remain speculative.

The tenth and last point of comparison addresses the Feast of the Firstfruits that appears in Leviticus 23:9–22, which is described twice. The first description is in vv. 9–14. There are three components of this festival: the priest elevates a sheaf of grain before Yahweh (v. 11); a lamb, grain (i.e., flour), and wine are offered to Yahweh (vv. 12–13); and the harvest must not be consumed until the offering is made (v. 14).

Compare this with the concluding lines for one of the festivals described in the first month in Emar 446, lines 50–57. The offerings were for Dagan, chief deity in the region and here described as "Lord of the Seed" (*be-el NUMUN.MEŠ*). The offerings took place before the planting of the seed and concerned its success, just as the Feast of the Firstfruits took place before consuming the grain harvest. Similar to the elevating of the sheaf in Israel, at Emar there was also an initial rite involving the cult leader and grain. In this case the diviner threw seed onto the ground.[155] Mutton, bread, and drink are involved in the rite.[156] Some of this was offered to Dagan, though the text is broken here. Finally, the ritual concludes with a warning that the planting of grain must not begin until these sacrifices are performed.[157]

Although the Israelite festival of Passover and Unleavened Bread and the Emar grain festival concern two different seasons, they both focus on grain. They both begin with a ritual involving that grain, whether throwing it on the ground or waving a sheaf of the harvest. They both involve mutton, drink, and bread. They both conclude with a warning not to proceed to the next stage, whether planting the seed or eating the harvest, until the ritual is completed.

Whatever the dating of the final form of Leviticus 23 as we now have it and whatever concerns may have shaped it over time, this multilevel collection of similarities in form and content between Emar 446 and Leviticus 23 demonstrates a heritage of the cultic calendar and rituals

155. Line 51, LÚ MÁŠ.ŠU.GÍD.GÍD *i-na KI i-na-di.*
156. Lines 51b–52, NINDA *x iš-tu* É DINGIR(?) *ka₄-sà-tu₄* UZU ZAG GAB.
157. Lines 56b–57, *a-di ku-ba-di₄ ú-ga-ma-ru ma-am-ma e-ri-ši ú-ul! u-ṣi.*

of Leviticus that predates the first millennium BC. Indeed, this type of text and some of its special days with their rituals have a heritage that reaches back to the Late Bronze Age.

Thus the Emar rituals provide a new dimension to the West Semitic religious world of the Late Bronze Age. They differ from the contributions of the Middle Bronze Age Mari prophetic texts and from the Late Bronze Age Ugaritic mythologies in that these describe actual ritual performances that were undertaken for the welfare of the people of Emar. However, unlike the Ugaritic ritual texts that often focus on the variety of deities and the specifics of the offerings to each one, those at Emar are concerned more about the performance of the human participants to achieve a goal, whether its purpose is to install a priestess or to celebrate a feast so as to achieve fruitfulness for the sowing of crops. These distinctives at Emar indicate a much closer comparison of form and content with the ritual texts of the Bible, especially Leviticus. Not only does the cumulative weight of comparative evidence link these two traditions—and they are after all the only two possessing many similarities of genre—it also casts doubt on assumptions about the relatively late dating of these biblical texts. Whenever their final form may have appeared, it is clear that many of the religious practices contained therein possess a demonstrable tradition that reaches back before the formation of Israel and into the Bronze Age. Once again we see how justified are the critical methodologies of sociologists and anthropologists of religion, who emphasize the study and appreciation of each culture for its own value, and who refuse to make facile generalizations about how tribes and other people groups might be expected to perform rituals.

Summary

From as early as written records appear in West Semitic cultures, beginning with Ebla in the twenty-fourth century BC, there is evidence of the names of deities that the Israelites later knew and worshiped in the first millennium BC. From eighteenth-century BC Mari and from Late Bronze Age Ugarit and Emar, there appear long-room temple structures, along with standing stones, altars, images, offering bowls, and other cultic forms that anticipate first-millennium BC worship forms. At the same time the Mari texts demonstrate the institutionalized roles of prophets, priests, and other religious functionaries that provide background for ancient Israel. Along with the names of various deities known later, the mythic themes of a vegetation-related Dumuzi who annually returns from death, and of the battle of the chief god with the Sea, all these are found early in the second millennium BC.

At Ugarit details of myths concerning Baal, El, Asherah, and Anat, and the development of earlier myth themes provide the most comprehensive background to the biblical worldview's knowledge and use of myth. Atonement rituals, intercessory prayers, divination, *marzēaḥ* festivals, and other forms anticipate ancient Israel's world of religious expression. Emar presents a thirteenth-century BC collection of texts that describes in detail rituals of priestly installation and of festivals celebrated through the cultic year. The effect of this is to provide a previously unknown textual background for many of the Levitical texts that serve the same function in Israel's priestly traditions.

5

Pre-Israelite West Semitic Religion

Palestine and Jordan

In the second millennium BC, cult centers in Palestine and Jordan flourished. Some of these extended into Israel's floruit during the Iron Age (c. 1200–586 BC). These will be surveyed and briefly discussed. However, not all the relevant materials from these cities and cultural sources will be surveyed in this chapter. Rather, many items of textual and (especially) archaeological relevance will be discussed later in the context of surveys of biblical texts, where they more directly address issues of interpretation.

Bronze Age West Semitic Cult Sites in North Israel

The archaeological evidence for Palestine during the period before Israel became a recognized people group is especially important to review because it provides an understanding of the degree to which Israelite practices resembled those of the previous generations in the land. The Middle Bronze Age[1] (c. 2000–c. 1550 BC) and the Late Bronze Age (c. 1550–c. 1200 BC) remains are presented together in order to provide a sense of any development that might be present. In the following list of sites, those with significant cultic remains or those with a special interest were chosen. The review will generally begin with the northern sites and move southward, although sites within a region will be taken into account and grouped together.

Hazor

Tel Hazor, north of the Sea of Galilee, is the largest archaeological site of Bronze and Iron Age Palestine. The upper tell or acropolis and the lower tell together comprise more than 170 acres. The lower city dates from the first century of Middle Bronze IIB (c. 1750–c. 1550 BC). The director of excavations in the 1990s, Amnon Ben-Tor (1997, 3), notes the connections between Hazor and similar fortifications and temples in Syria and at Tel Dan. In Area A on the acropolis, perhaps as early as c. 1650–c. 1550 BC, there was found a single-room temple with a *bāmâ* or raised area at the back (western) wall. A two-room temple in the lower city also had a niche in its back wall. As some point before its destruction in Late Bronze IA (c. 1550–c. 1450 BC) a basalt orthostat entrance was added. Ben-Tor compares this temple with the *migdōl* or fortress temple discovered to the south at Shechem.[2]

---

1. The beginning of the Middle Bronze Age and the possibility of the existence of an Intermediate Bronze Age between the Early Bronze and the Middle Bronze Age are matters of controversy, thus dating schemes vary.

2. Ben-Tor (1993a, 604).

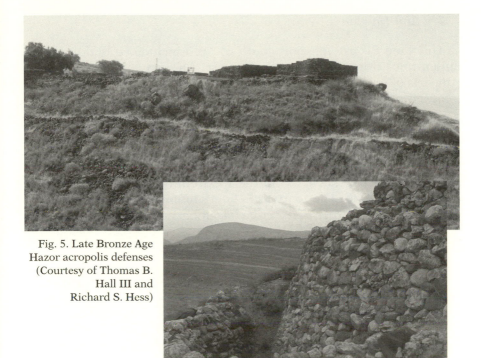

Fig. 5. Late Bronze Age
Hazor acropolis defenses
(Courtesy of Thomas B.
Hall III and
Richard S. Hess)

Stratum XIV was violently destroyed at the end of the fourteenth century BC, perhaps by Pharaoh Seti I. Hazor possessed multiple places of worship in the Late Bronze Age. In Area H, at the northern end of the lower tell, the Middle Bronze Age temple that was flanked by two rooms (similar to the temple at Alalakh in Syria) was divided into three parts after the fourteenth-century BC Basalt orthostats appeared, including one with a lion figure. There were also bowls and offering tables. A sculpture with its head severed was found lying in an ash pit in the "most holy" room. Elsewhere in the lower city at Area C, there was found a temple with ten basalt stelae, one of which exhibited two lifted hands under an upturned crescent, symbolizing the moon deity. Here too was found a crouching lion portrayed on an orthostat, a decapitated seated figure holding a cup (the head was found nearby), a pottery mask, and a bronze "standard."[3]

The long temple on the acropolis was rebuilt and lined with orthostats. This temple went out of use after the fifteenth century but other shrines were found nearby.[4]

3. Ben-Tor (1997, 3).
4. Alpert-Nakhai (2001, 101–2, 126–33) connects the temple with the ruling family and attributes their loss of power to the rise of Egyptian power and influence. The ongoing role of the other acropolis temple and the multiple worship centers would then indicate

Tell Abu Hawam

This Late Bronze Age port south of Acco included a building with an entrance oriented toward the sunrise. The structure had external supports of four columns. Also found was a bronze statue with a seated male figure wearing a hat.[5]

Tel Nami

South of Abu Hawam was the port of Tel Nami. It included a courtyard sanctuary with benches at the northern extremity of the mound dated to c. 1400–c. 1200 BC. The courtyard's floor contained broken pieces of a ceramic incense burner, and a large basalt basin on a basalt pedestal.[6]

Tel Mevorakh

South of Tel Nami and a few miles inland, Tel Mevorakh had three cult centers through the Late Bronze Age. The first one, oriented east-west and abutting a Middle Bronze Age earthwork, resembled one of the Hazor temples and the Fosse temple at Lachish. It had a stone libation bowl with two depressions on its upper surface. It was lined with offering benches and had a raised altar and bowls. The sequence of sanctuaries had many other vessels as well as jewelry, two bronze cymbals, a bronze dagger, and cylinder seals. A bronze snake figurine was discovered, not unlike that found at Timna in the Negev.[7]

Megiddo

A small Middle Bronze IIA (c. 1850–c. 1750 BC, Stratum XIII) cult room (4040C) and high place (D, later F) were discovered in Megiddo along with an altar, stelae, seven-cup vessels, a silver crescent, and female figurines. Two bovine figurines come from the tombs.[8] Among the cult sites from this city, temple 2048, dated to the Middle Bronze Age period, stands out for its continuity and size. It was a fortress temple built on a platform with two chambers flanking the entrance. These were built into two towers. Decorated vessels, a bronze snake, two clay liver models, and animal bones were found there as well. Temple 2048 lost its

---

the vitality of other groups and perhaps the city's autonomy from direct Egyptian control. While possible, this remains speculative.

5. Bilensi (1985).
6. Artzy (1991, 197).
7. Stern (1977). On the snake at Timna see the discussion in chapter 7, pp. 202–3.
8. May and Engberg (1935, 34).

Fig. 6. Third-millennium BC Early Bronze Age altar at Megiddo (Courtesy of Richard S. Hess)

niche, which was replaced by a bench in which three Middle Kingdom statues were buried (mid-thirteenth century BC). In the twelfth century BC (Stratum VIIA) the niche reappeared.[9]

Nahariya

Most of the finds came from a heap outside a rectangular temple and date to Middle Bronze IIB. These included offering stands, bowls, seven-cup vessels, and animal figurines. Similar forms were located beneath a *bāmâ* or circular stone structure of the same period, along with silver plaques and a stone mold of a nude female figurine with horns projecting from her head.[10]

Tell Kitan

Seven and a half miles north of Beth Shan, on a hill overlooking the spot where the Nahal Tavor joins the Jordan River, there was an Middle Bronze IIB cult center, originally a small room with two pillars flanking the entrance and in the courtyard a row of eight standing stones in front

9. Aharoni (1993, 1006–12); Ussishkin (1997, 463–64).
10. Dothan (1993, 1090–92).

Fig. 7. Late Bronze Age Beth Shan behind Roman Scythopolis (Courtesy of Richard S. Hess)

with two larger standing stones behind the row. In the middle of the eight, and slightly taller, was a stone statue carved in the form of a nude goddess whose hands were cupped around her breasts. Later in the same period a new temple was built without harming the earlier one. Ash pits with animal bones, four crude stone figurines, a basalt slab, and four basalt bases (for standing stones) were found. The Late Bronze I temple was erected where the earlier temples stood before they were destroyed. It contained a hall and two side rooms, with many ritual vessels, some silver pendants, and a single bronze knife.[11]

Beth Shan

Five successive temples were constructed on the site beginning with the earliest at the start of the Late Bronze Age (c. 1550 BC) and continuing after 1200 BC. The earliest temple's plan included three parts, with the central and inner rooms lined with benches along their walls. In the following phase a larger area was added with several structures built around a central courtyard. The precinct is unique in plan. The Mekal stele was found here. It contains a small stone cultic scene with a dedication from an Egyptian official to the memory of his father. The scene on the stele includes a seated god in Canaanite dress. South of

11. Eisenberg (1993).

the sanctuary another building contained a basalt orthostat with the scene of a lion and a dog (or lionness) on it. In the thirteenth century BC another temple was built on a north-south axis. Its main hall was supported by two pillars and its inner sanctuary was raised several feet above the floor. A foundation deposit there included dozens of cylinder seals displaying northern Syrian influence.[12]

Tell el-Far'ah North

At this site, seven miles northeast of Shechem, a Middle Bronze Age (c. 1550 BC) underground chamber, or "cella" was found. At a size of about fifteen by ten feet, it was lined with slabs and bones of suckling pigs. This has been compared to a similar underground cella to the north at Alalakh. A cult site at the gate was also found.[13]

Bronze Age West Semitic Cult Sites in Jordan

Pella

The Middle Bronze II and Late Bronze Ages saw burials within the walls that may have been beneath domestic floors and contained funnels for food and drink.[14] Compare those at Ugarit in Syria and those much closer at Edrei and Ashtaroth in northern Jordan. There is also evidence of an "Egyptian governor's residence" and a cult site there. This confirms the cosmopolitan nature of the site, also seen in the smaller finds, in the Amarna letters written to the pharaoh from the site, and in the discovery of written texts, as yet undeciphered.

Tell el-Hayyat

In the Jordan Valley, three miles southwest of Pella and east of the Jordan River, lay this site, unfortified and comprising just over one acre in area. It contained a temple that was rectilinear in plan and extended over several phases during the Middle Bronze Age. The temple housed a raised mudbrick altar, a bench, a stone altar, and a group of standing stones. Sheep and goat bones and cooking pots in the temple and its courtyard suggest meat offerings. The interior walls and floor were painted red. Bones of sheep and goats were in the majority (63 percent);

12. A. Mazar (1997a, 306).
13. De Miroschedji (1993, 438).
14. Bourke (1997).

21 percent of bones were those of pigs. The site appears to have been peacefully abandoned during the sixteenth century BC.[15]

Tell Deir 'Alla

This site is located east of the Jordan River, near to where the Jabbok meets the Jordan. On the north slope of the site, a sanctuary was found dating from the beginning of the Late Bronze Age (c. 1550 BC). The main room of the sanctuary included thick walls, some four to five bricks wide. Two pottery shrines were found as well as an Egyptian faience vase with the cartouche of the Egyptian queen Tawesret (c. 1200 BC). Storerooms to the west contained, among other things, Mycenean pottery and twelve clay tablets. Three of these had writing on them in the form of an undeciphered script. Situated on an artificial terrace and above the surrounding structures, this sanctuary would have been built as a regional center of worship and as part of an international place of contact, especially with Egypt. Perhaps this was the seat of Egypt's control of the Gilead region east of the Jordan River.[16]

Tell Tsafut

South of Tell Deir 'Alla in the east-west Baq'ah Valley, Tell Tsafut was located. At this site a red plastered room from the Late Bronze Age was found. In the room was found a bronze seated deity wearing a flat crown and gold wrappings around his arms. There were also heads of female figurines.[17]

Amman

A thirteenth-century BC site at Amman, Jordan, yielded the burned bones of infants, taken as evidence of child sacrifice.[18]

Bronze Age West Semitic Cult Sites in Central Israel

Shechem

Inside Shechem, c. 1650–1540 BC, there was a fortress temple with walls about seventeen feet thick and with two large towers flanking the

15. Falconer and Magness-Gardiner (1993).
16. Van der Kooij (1993, 339–40).
17. See Wimmer (1997).
18. Hennessy (1985). Cf. Judg. 11; 2 Kings 3:27; 16:3 (= 2 Chron. 28:3); 21:6 (= 2 Chron. 33:6); Philo of Byblos (*PE* 1.10.44 = 4.6.11). See also pp. 136, 257–58, 262.

Fig. 8. Late Bronze Age Shechem fortress temple (Courtesy of Richard S. Hess)

entrance. Two standing stones also stood on either side of the entrance. About a century later, c. 1550–1450 BC, a new fortress temple containing an altar and a large standing stone was built over the old temple. The stone altar and standing stone were buried and covered with a plastered floor in the Iron Age I (c. 1200–c. 1000 BC). A bronze figure of a Canaanite god was also found.[19]

As noted above, an Amarna letter from Shechem appears to identify the ruler's father (ancestor) as "my god" (*i-li*).[20] On the slopes of Mount Gerazim, about one-fifth of a mile from Shechem, a stone pillar and the foundation for an altar were found in a courtyard. The central chamber had rooms built around it.

Shiloh

This site preserved Middle Bronze IIB storerooms with jars, bowls, cultic stands, and a vessel in the form of a bull. Jewelry included a silver pendant with the image of an Anatolian deity. In the Late Bronze Age neither sanctuary nor settlement was found. Only one area was found with any indication of occupation; it contained animal bones, pottery, and a female figurine.[21]

19. Campbell (1993, 1349–52).
20. Cf. Hess (1993b) and chapter 4, pp. 94–95.
21. Finkelstein (1993). See further discussion in chapter 8, on pp. 221–22.

Fig. 9. Standing stones at Gezer (Courtesy of Richard S. Hess)

Jerusalem

North of the present-day Damascus Gate, in and around the grounds of the *École Biblique*, were found more than a century ago a fragment of an Egyptian stele mentioning Osiris, an Egyptian offering table, two alabaster vessels, a small stone statuette of a seated figure, and fragments of Egyptian lotus capitals. Near the end of the thirteenth century BC, an Egyptian temple stood here along what must have been the road from Jerusalem to the central hill country.[22]

Gezer

Excavations to levels dating from c. 1650 BC revealed ten large standing stones at the high place. There was a basin to the west of the stones. The area around was plastered and surrounded by a low wall, probably to mark off the sacred area. There were burned animal bones.[23]

Lachish

At the base of the tell there was a succession of three temples known as "fosse temples" (because of their location in the pit or fosse of the tell)

22. Barkay (1990; 1996; 2000); Alpert-Nakhai (2001, 151–52). Today the location is situated along the Nablus road.
23. Dever (1993, 500–501); Alpert-Nakhai (2001, 94–95, 105).

in the Late Bronze Age. The first fosse temple (c. 1550–c. 1450 BC) was a modest structure with a hall and two siderooms. In subsequent phases, the size of the main hall was doubled and additional rooms around it were added. Among the finds there was an ivory pyxis with scenes portraying various wild animals.

On the tell was a temple with a long hall oriented east to west. The hall led to a stone staircase with three stone column bases to its left and a plastered installation on the right. The stair led to the raised inner room of the sanctuary. Among the many Egyptian items, there was a gold plaque of a nude female, perhaps a goddess, who was holding large lotus-like plants and standing on the back of a horse. This Canaanite-Egyptian form has been identified by some as Astarte but this is not certain. In addition, a graffito of a deity in the

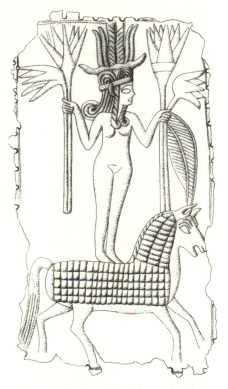

Fig. 10. Lachish goddess plaque (© The Israel Museum, Jerusalem)

temple also attests to a Canaanite purpose for the sacred place, alongside the Egyptian temple architecture.[24]

A thirteenth-century BC inscription on a ewer from the fosse temple may contain a reference to the goddess Elat, "Mattan. An offering [to] my [la]dy Elat."[25] The last two terms are means of referring to Asherah at Ugarit, especially the final term.[26] Both the ewer and the tenth-century BC Taanach cult stand have a tree flanked by twin animals that are feeding. Hestrin (1987b) sees a connection between this figure in Palestine and the goddess Asherah. The name of Reshef, god of plague, was also found on the ewer and the drawings appear to depict the god.[27]

24. Ussishkin (1993a, 898–905). In addition to Lachish, Egypto-Canaanite temples are found at Gaza, Ashkelon, Ashdod, Aphek, and Jerusalem in the Late Bronze Age.

25. M. Smith (2003, 28–29). The text is read as *mtn . šy [l rb]ty 'lt*. For more on the ewer and the interpretation of this inscription see chapter 8, p. 238.

26. Ibid., cf. *KTU* 1.4[1.1 IV] 14; 3.5 45 = 1.3 V 37; 4.1 8 = 1.4 I 7; 4.4[1.4 IV] 49; 6.1 [1.61] 40; 15.3[1.15 III] 26; 14.4 198, 202 = 1.14 IV 35, 39.

27. Puech (1986–87, 22–24).

Ashkelon

From the end of the Middle Bronze Age (c. 1650–c. 1550 BC), a small shrine room was found at the entrance to the fortified city. In this room was discovered a small bronze calf figurine whose head and feet were coated with silver. Beside the calf was a pot with a hole carved in it as though the calf might use the hollowed clay form as a shelter. See further discussion in chapter 6, "The Golden Calf."

A plaque discovered at Megiddo and dating from c. 1200 BC mentions an Egyptian temple at Ashkelon. More significant is the presence of an Egyptian relief at Medinet Habu that portrays Pharaoh Merneptah's siege of the city c. 1209 BC. This relief depicts citizens of Ashkelon within their besieged walls raising incense burners to their deities and lifting up smaller figures, perhaps children who are about to be hurled to their deaths or in some other manner to be sacrificed for the salvation of their city.

Bronze Age West Semitic Cult Sites in South Israel

Hebron

A cuneiform economic text was discovered at Tell er-Rumeidah, the site of ancient Hebron. Dating from the seventeenth or sixteenth century BC, it contains Hurrian and Amorite personal names, makes reference to sheep and he-goat offerings, and describes a king, perhaps at Hebron.[28] This text suggests that even in what may appear to be an isolated site such as Hebron there was nevertheless present a multicultural population of Hurrians and West Semitic Amorites. Its description of offerings from flocks and herds of sheep and goats suggests a pastoral people and the blood sacrifices are comparable to those found elsewhere in the West Semitic world. Like the Egyptian Execration texts of about the same period, kings govern cities. Finally, the presence of cuneiform-trained scribes in Hebron suggests that writing was known and used for administrative and religious purposes in Middle Bronze Age southern Palestine. From this same period fragments of administrative and other texts have been discovered at Hazor. These link it with the Amorite cultures to the north, especially Mari, on the basis of script, grammar, names, and forms.[29]

28. See Anbar and Na'aman (1986–87).
29. Cf. Malamat (1989); Ben-Tor (1992); Horowitz and Shaffer (1992a; 1992b; 1992c); Hess (2003b).

Tel Haror

Located twelve and a half miles west of Beersheba, Tel Haror was a large Middle Bronze IIB city in the northern Negev with a room and a courtyard extending more than thirty feet on all sides. Both contained niches and offering benches that were covered with ash, animal bones, and vessels. The bones were 62 percent sheep and goats, 28 percent fowl, and 5 percent dogs. A courtyard pit included a red-painted arm that belonged to a large statue. These pits also included seven-spouted lamps, whole bird and puppy skeletons, vessels with snakes, bulls in relief, and Cypriote wares.[30]

Iconography and Bronze Age Religion in Southern Canaan

Keel and Uehlinger have studied numerous seals used to understand the Middle Bronze IIB period.[31] They see the dominant animal motifs as caprids, representing prosperity and fertility, and as lions, representing virility and potency. Naked goddesses form a major motif. This is rare at other times and places and suggests an importance of erotic sexuality during this period. Also distinctive is the appearance of male and female worshipers and couples. This "equality of the sexes" is not so apparent in later art where the female often disappears. Although unfashioned standing stones are found at Gezer and elsewhere, images of the deities and humans, as well as the sacred trees and rituals, suggest a high degree of sexuality that came to characterize the popular understanding of biblical religion as "Canaanite religion." However, it is more prominent in art of this period than at later times. The calf image at Ashkelon had not yet been discovered when Keel and Uehlinger wrote their study. This also may demonstrate the presence of warrior deities in principal Palestinian cities in the early second millennium BC. If so, it balances the eroticism of the glyptic art. The predominance of the fertility images in Palestine in the Middle Bronze Age recalls the concern of Abraham, Isaac, and Jacob and their wives for children, and their turning to God for the fulfillment of that desire.

The Late Bronze Age was a time of Egyptian influence in terms of culture and religion.[32] Deities and worshipers are predominantly male. At Hazor, temple materials include lion orthostats and a stele representing the moon god of Haran (from northern Syria). From Megiddo come pear-shaped gold leaf pendants of nude goddess figures. Inexpensive

---

30. Oren (1993, 580–81).
31. Keel and Uehlinger (1998).
32. Ibid., 49–108.

Fig. 11. Megiddo ivory with image of chariot and prince on throne (Courtesy of the Oriental Institute of the University of Chicago)

terra cotta figures of nude females also appear at this time. An enthroned youthful deity with a blossom in gold leaf may be a weather god. Other metal figures portray Baal and Reshef, which replace the goddess images. Military themes, symbolized by the appearance of the chariot on the Megiddo ivory and elsewhere, replace the erotic emphasis of Middle Bronze IIB. On the same ivory a victorious prince sits on a throne while one female attendant hands him a towel and another plays a lyre. Thus the female status has been lowered from equal partnership to servanthood. At Lachish the "qudshu type" (Egyptian-influenced) nude goddess appears with shoulder-length hair and holding lotus blossoms. On one gold leaf piece she stands on an armored horse as she does on a clay model from Beth Shan. Elsewhere at Beth Shan she appears as mistress of the city. Is this the warrior goddess Anat? These are motifs of war and warriors rather than sexuality. At Lachish and elsewhere the palmetto tree flanked by caprids is a familiar motif. In some representations the tree is replaced by a pubic triangle, reflecting the association of the tree with a goddess and fertility. Among male deities the roles of Seth and Baal are combined into one warrior god in a number of pictorial representations at Lachish. Keel and Uehlinger suggest that the sexual role of the female deity is gradually replaced by a warrior role. In addition, the female deity terra cotta forms (never male terra cotta forms) suggest a privatization of this form of worship, and with it perhaps a popularization.

Summary

On both sides of the Jordan River, the early part of the Middle Bronze Age (c. 1800–1650 BC) was characterized by nonurban and rural cult sites that reflected the interests of local and regional tribal groups. In the last century of the Middle Bronze Age (c. 1650–c. 1550 BC) the picture changed as the region became urbanized in a manner resembling Syria's urbanization. Cities developed multiple temples, including special fortress temples in sites in the Jordan Valley. City gate sanctuaries flourished at Ashkelon and Tell el-Far'ah North.[33]

Middle Bronze IIB Palestine has a few fragments of textual evidence of the contemporary religious beliefs. Texts from Hazor, Megiddo, and Hebron, as well as related art from these and other sites, identify deities and suggest religious practices tied in with local concerns and with human, agricultural, and livestock fertility. Albright and others dated the ancestral figures and traditions of some of Genesis 12–36 to this period.[34] Although this has been severely attacked and often dismissed, there do remain some similarities. It is possible that some of these traditions contain elements that reach back to the middle of the second millennium BC.[35]

Late Bronze IA (c. 1550–c. 1450 BC) saw a continuation of the late Middle Bronze Age cult centers. In Late Bronze IIA (c. 1400–c. 1300 BC) and Late Bronze IIB (c. 1300–c. 1200 BC) the Egyptians exercised more control over the region (after Pharaoh Tuthmosis III's victories in the region). By this time (and as early as Late Bronze IB, c. 1450–c. 1400 BC) most sites had become urban. Hazor retained more self-government and independence from Egypt as suggested by its Amarna letters and its material remains. The main temple was now found in a new area. This was the orthostat temple with its Hittite and northern influence. Elsewhere, by Late Bronze IIA, general prosperity provided for enlarging or further building. By Late Bronze IIB the number of cult sites had doubled over the previous periods. Temples with both Egyptian and Canaanite features were seen in Jerusalem, Lachish, Beth Shan, and all along the coastal plain. As suggested by the temples in Egypt, these were centers for the collection of agricultural and other taxes from the local lands under their control. In general, the evidence suggests the maintenance continually of West Semitic dynasties in cities along the coast and sporadically inland, though more so around the Jezreel Valley. Northern culture, influenced by the Hurrian and Hittite kingdoms, penetrated into the Huleh basin and the Jordan Valley. From there it spread westward, mixing with the

33. Alpert-Nakhai (2001, 107–15).
34. See especially Albright (1957).
35. The attacks were made by Thompson (1974) and Van Seters (1975). McCarter (1999) more recently dismisses any validity to these traditions. For a contrary view see Hess, Satterthwaite, and Wenham (1993). See also the arguments above in chapter 3, in the sections on "Julius Wellhausen" (p. 45) and "Religion History, Tradition History, and Orality" (p. 59). There I indicate that radical dismissal of the existence of second-millennium traditions in the Bible is without warrant. See the discussion of the personal names in Gen. 1–11 below in chapters 6 and 7 for further evidence of possible Bronze Age sources. Finally, the Tell er-Rumeidah tablet at what was ancient Hebron demonstrates the possibility of written records in this region during the same time that the figures and events of Gen. 12–26 may have existed and occurred.

Egyptian influence in areas such as the Jezreel Valley as far as the Acco plain. This view, already suggested by the historical records from Egypt, Ugarit, Alalakh, Hattusas, and the smaller cuneiform finds in Palestine, is confirmed by the material culture as revealed in the religious artifacts and architecture. It is further supported by the remaining archaeological picture of Palestine and by the personal names. The latter show a preponderance of northern names (i.e., Hurrian, Anatolian, and Indo-Aryan languages) in the mainly inland areas noted. The coastal areas, except Acco, were dominated exclusively by leaders with West Semitic names.[36] To a greater or lesser extent Late Bronze Age religion and culture in Palestine were largely colored by the imperial interests that dominated different regions of the land.

In Egyptian texts of the Late Bronze Age the divine name Yahweh may appear as a place name in the southern desert.[37] However, it is in Palestine where a variety of deities are represented in personal names of the fourteenth century BC. Among these the presence of Asherah is most frequently attested as part of the name borne by the leader of Amurru. Indeed, it is attested more often in texts in this form than it ever was in the Middle Bronze Age.[38] Divine names by themselves are unusual although the equation of the pharaoh with the sun god is common.[39] Thus there is no diminution of the worship and respect given to deities. As already noted, an Amarna text from Shechem mentions a personal god of the leader of that city and seems to associate it with his father, leading to the conclusion that a form of ancestral worship may have been active in Palestine at this time.[40]

The focus on military images in the Late Bronze Age and the role of female warriors recalls the biblical picture in Judges 4–5 of Deborah as warrior (cf. also Miriam, Achsah, and other women such as Jephthah's daughter and the Levite's concubine who are associated with war) as well as the emphasis on warfare in traditions from the exodus through Joshua's "conquest" and the period of the judges. It is to this biblical witness and its traditions that we now turn.

36. For a general discussion of the personal names in the Amarna correspondence and their correlation with the archaeological evidence in this matter, see Hess (1989a). For a linguistic analysis of the Amarna names, see Hess (1993a). The value of this name analysis for reconstructing historical theories about the cultural influence from the north is discussed in Hess (1997). The names from sources other than the Amarna texts are studied in Hess (2003b).

37. See Hess (1991a) and chapter 6, p. 159.

38. Hess (1996b).

39. Hess (1986).

40. Hess (1993b).

6

Narrative and Legal Strands
of the Pentateuch

The Pentateuch is filled with information about Israelite religion. It is impossible to ignore this when discussing the subject. Unfortunately, it has also proven impossible to arrive at a consensus when examining the contents of this important collection of writings. The Documentary Hypothesis was discussed in detail in the excursus in chapter 3. I am unable to subscribe to the hypothesis in its details for the reasons presented there. I do not feel that one can with any sort of "scientific" certainty identify the time when the texts that comprise the Pentateuch as we now have them were written. The prose sections seem to constitute a compilation from the time of the monarchy, that is, the first half of the first millennium BC.

I agree with those who date some of the poetry into the second millennium BC. Further, as observed in the excursus of chapter 3 and in some of the discussions of West Semitic archives and sites in chapters 4 and 5, the traditions and various writings contain religious and cultic practices attested elsewhere in the second millennium BC but not in the first. The dating assigned to the origins of many of these records might be based on the proximity in geography and chronology to extrabiblical records or material items that most closely resemble their biblical correspondents. Now I have no difficulty in finding early examples of these from each of the three major collections of literature in the Pentateuch: the narratives and prophetic materials (largely J and E), the priestly and cultic materials (mostly P), and the covenant along with the law of Deuteronomy and related materials (much of D). Thus the division (between chapters 6 and 7) of the discussion of Pentateuchal literature into these three groupings is an attempt to acknowledge these literary threads that largely comprise the Pentateuch without prejudicing the dating, authorship, or origins of the material, or its having passed through both oral and literary stages before reaching its present form. However, my emphasis on extrabiblical connections with these literary threads allows for suggestions as to when and where specific literary pieces may have originated.

A work of this size and scope cannot provide a comprehensive overview of everything religious in the Pentateuch or in its major literary strands. I have selected certain items for discussion according to my assessment of their importance for answering current questions about Israelite religion. This includes the literary threads' meaningful connections to extrabiblical material that sheds light on Israelite religion. Informed readers may have preferred to include other materials and exclude some that I have included. I am keenly aware that the selection of this material is to some extent a personal one. Accordingly, I assert the author's prerogative to make the selection and to suggest that this is intended to be a representation of the religious concerns found in the Pentateuch.

Before going further in this chapter, I encourage the reader to review chapter 3 and particularly the section titled "Religion History, Tradition History, and Orality," and the excursus on the Documentary Hypothesis. These provide the necessary background and are assumed in what follows.

Religious Aspects of the Narrative Strands

Creation

The narrative strands normally begin with the creation account that is found starting at Genesis 2:4b. Key in Genesis 2 and 3 is the role of the Garden of Eden as a prototypical sanctuary for ancient Israel, and the issues surrounding the eating of the fruit and God's subsequent judgments on the world and the human race. More of this will be explored in chapter 8 on the United Monarchy (p. 000). Many of these items have already appeared or will appear later in this study in the context of larger considerations relevant to the subject.[1]

Cain's Line (Gen. 4:17–26)

Important to the understanding of Israelite religion are the theophoric elements in personal names in Genesis 1–11. Personal names, especially in the genealogies, form a significant part of the overall structuring of Genesis 1–11 and reflect religious beliefs. Thus the personal names become a significant part of the background of Israelite religion, especially if it is possible to determine something about the origins of these name collections. Most name collections are associated with the priestly literature of the Pentateuch whose interest lies in preserving family lines to determine who was Israelite or Jewish and who was not. Thus, personal names in the line of Cain, having nothing directly to do with the family line from Adam to Abram, are instead often associated with the narrative strands. I will systematically examine each personal name of Genesis 1–11 in terms of its etymology and the extent to which it may indicate cultural and, especially, religious preferences.

Although the etymology of Cain's name is not certain, it has been associated with the South Arabic root for "smith," which has the same spelling. That Cain has connections with the south is further supported by his apparent association with the metalworking smiths from the wilderness, the Kenites. This association appears in an oracle of Balaam (Num. 24:21–22), although the context is not easy to interpret. However, Cain's name may also be associated with the similarly spelled Hebrew word for "song" (*qînâ*). In either case, the suggestion is one of a figure who participates in technological and cultural advances.

The names and descriptions of many of Cain's descendants continue this theme of cultural innovation.[2] Cain's building of a city ties in with his son Enoch. The Enoch of Cain's line, distinct from the Enoch of Genesis 5, may originally have been tied to the Sumerian UNU(G), the name for the city of Uruk.[3]

If this is the case, then the association of Irad with the ancient Sumerian city of Eridu gains greater weight and supports the overall conclu-

1. See also discussion in relevant articles in Hess and Tsumura (1994).
2. Cf. Hess (1993c, 37–57).
3. Skinner (1930, 117).

sion that the early part of the line of Cain was associated with two of the earliest cities known in Mesopotamia, both in archaeological excavations and in literature of the region.[4]

The next two names, Mehujael and Methushael, may refer to religious beliefs that emerged in their culture. The first name means "El (or) the god enlivens" while the second is probably a description of a devotee of an underworld deity (literally, "man" [or devotee] of El [the god] *š'l*, where in the latter option the root is identical to that for Sheol, the place of the dead). This deity has perhaps now been identified at thirteenth-century BC Emar where the name is read as Shuwala and associated with the Mesopotamian god of the underworld, Nergal.[5] The word for "man" in Methushael is *mutu*. This term is common in West Semitic personal names of the second millennium BC but rare, if at all known, in names from the first millennium BC.

Lamech has no known etymology. However, it serves a pivotal point in the genealogy both in the line of Cain and in that of Seth.[6]

If Adah is understood as meaning "ornament" (in the sense of jewelry) and Zillah is associated with the meaning "musical cymbal," we find suggestion of the introduction of visual and musical arts.

Jabal is associated with the nomadic culture of tent dwellers. His second role has been disputed on the basis of the Hebrew word *miqneh*, which has two possible meanings. If the word means "livestock," it could support a nomadic life. If it means "possessions," it might suggest an urban, materialistic culture.

Jubal is explicitly associated with stringed and wind musical instruments, and Tubal-Cain with the work of a metal smith. The name Naamah may refer to loveliness or to music, depending on which of two West Semitic roots are used as derivatives.

Many of these names have associations with the second millennium BC or earlier, either through the names of Sumerian cities such as Uruk and Eridu, or through elements that do not occur later in personal names. Examples of these include Methushael and the first part of Tubal-Cain, which may refer to the Hurrian word for "smith." While it is true that the root behind Cain (and the second part of Tubal-Cain) occurs only in

4. The phonological objection, that the initial ayin of the name in Genesis would not reflect a Sumerian phoneme (see Davila [1995, 210]) is not convincing if there was an intentional attempt by the author of Genesis to play on the similar sounding word for "city" in Hebrew, *îr*, spelled with an initial ayin. See Hess (1993a, 40–41).

5. Cf. Hess (forthcoming c) and Johnston (2002, 78–79), citing Emar text 385 line 23 and 388 lines 6 and 57 in Arnaud (1986). See also de Moor (1990b, 239) and Korpel (1990, 348). For the identification of Shuwaliya with the Hurrian deity Shuwaliyat (= Akkadian Ninurta) see Tsukimoto (1989, 9).

6. Cf. Hess (1991b).

names from the first millennium BC and later, it is also true that there are no South Arabic inscriptions from before the first millennium BC. Because this element occurs outside the Bible only in South Arabian names, it is likely that this root occurs earlier in names from that region but that these names are not attested in written inscriptions because such inscriptions do not exist. Elements of other names that appear in this genealogy are attested in the second millennium. Thus, where it is possible to evaluate these personal names in terms of existing collections of names from outside the Bible, they reflect the earlier second-millennium BC onomastic world (and perhaps earlier than that).[7]

Both the etymologies of the personal names and the descriptions of the lives of the descendants suggest the development of culture and civilization, urban and possibly nomadic, which contains within its elements worship of unknown or underworld deities and murderous violence (cf. the poem of Lamech). In its narrative context, the picture is one of religious and moral degeneration in the midst of civilized life.

The context describes this degeneration as the outcome of the self-will of Cain and his own inability to seek God for the forgiveness of his sin, both the sin of anger and the sin of fratricide. The continuation of Cain's line represents humanity in general in its pursuit of all the aspects of "modern, civilized" life. However, it is a life that has separated itself from God and therefore one that leads to the corruption already seen and further developed in Genesis 6:1–4. Finally, it brings the judgment of God and the need to destroy the world.

Cain's line has been compared with that of Mesopotamian king lists that claim to record kings from before the flood. Some of these lists are associated with particular counselors or sages (*apkallu*), each of whom served a particular antediluvian king, and who performed feats similar to those described in Genesis 4. Thus there is one counselor for each generation, comprising a line as in Genesis 4.[8] The associations of the names and their etymologies with the oldest of cities and second-millennium BC deities and onomastic terms contextualize this list in the second millennium BC.

This provides the background for the apparently mythological fragment of Genesis 6:1–4 that describes the union of the "sons of God" and the "daughters of 'the '*ādām*.'" There is much debate about the background of this story and its meaning and context here in Genesis. No clear parallel exists, although a fall from heaven, as preserved in the mythology behind the imagery of Isaiah 14 and elsewhere, is not an

7. See further in Hess (1992a; 1993c; forthcoming c).
8. See Hallo (1991, 176).

uncommon motif within other stories.9 In the context of Genesis 1–11 this is best understood as the same tradition, one in which entities from the world of the eternal, the world of God, chose physical union with mortal women. Following Genesis 4 and 5 it portrays a further degeneration of humanity already suggested by Cain's line and contrasts with the righteousness of Seth's line and especially with Noah. The Nephilim, literally "fallen ones," are those great and sometimes giant heroes of renown who have fallen in battle. Elsewhere they are equated with the early giants in Canaan, when Israel first settles there. In all cases, they are not an ethnic group but a class or type of people found in many societies and ethnicities.10

Table of Nations (Gen. 10)

Genesis 10 has been called the Table of Nations because it lists most of the peoples of the known world when it was written.[11] This group is divided and presented in the style of a segmented genealogy, one that has been divided into different branches. We find here a list distinct from the other genealogies in Genesis and unlike anything else in the ancient Near East. This is true for two reasons: the Table of Nations is segmented and names of people groups appear much more frequently than personal names (Nimrod and the line of Shem are the only clear personal names). While much scholarly discussion goes on about some of the less familiar names,[12] the importance of this list lies in its attestation of a common source for all of humanity. What is certain is that none of the names have been shown to belong to a mythological people. Everyone named existed somewhere. As such they are all real people who have a common ancestor in Noah. They therefore belong together as equal in creation and in the sight of God. None has any claim to superiority over another. This is all the more true in light of the cursing of Canaan in Genesis 9.[13] It is as if the Table of Nations demonstrates that

9. See Hendel (2004) and his full discussion and bibliography. For Isa. 14:12–13 see Albani (2004).

10. See Hess (1992a) "Nephilim." For further on the biblical and Phoenician usage of this term, see chapter 9, "Excursus: Religion of Phoenicia," pp. 294–95. See also chapter 4, p. 104.

11. Many source critics recognize in Gen. 10 a composite construction made of both narrative and priestly strands, i.e., J and P sources. The priestly strands are sometimes identified with vv. 1–7, 20, 22–24, and 31–32.

12. Cf. Horowitz (1990) for a comparison with the seventh-century BC Babylonian world map. Horowitz argues that "islands of nations" in verse 5 includes all regions that the Israelites would have traveled over water to reach, including coastlands.

13. See Bergsma and Hahn (2005) for a review of the interpretations of this difficult passage. They suggest that Ham's sin was the rape of his mother that led to the birth of Canaan.

the curse of Canaan, while affecting the Canaanites, has no permanent affect on the nations of the world. Genesis 10 is a divine testimony that implicitly opposes any racial discrimination or bigotry.

By some counts seventy nations are mentioned. Deuteronomy 32:8 mentions how God apportioned the nations. Later Judaism assumes seventy guardian angels for the seventy nations. John Day relates this to the seventy sons of Athirat (Asherah) and presumably El, the chief deities in the pantheon at Ugarit. He compares Psalm 82 and finds here an allusion to the heavenly court, in which God ruled over the spirits chosen to rule the seventy nations mentioned in this chapter.[14]

Tradition Studies

Tradition history study asks the question: How do the stories of Genesis come to us from an early period? Is anything recoverable of a period before or close to the time of Israel's emergence in Canaan? For background and evaluation of this approach to biblical studies in general, see chapter 3, Religion History, Tradition History, and Orality.

Herman Gunkel inaugurated much of form criticism and tradition studies at the time of the translation and publication of the Babylonian creation story *Enuma Elish* and other myths in the decades before 1900. Gunkel argued that mythic motifs and core pieces of material were passed down orally and adapted into the early stories of Semitic peoples, including Israel and the Bible. For this reason he felt that he could find motifs common to Babylonian and biblical texts.

In the first half of the twentieth century Gunkel was followed by Albrecht Alt and then by his student Martin Noth. When they examined Genesis 12–50, they noted that different names for God were applied at different places and that the ancestors each had a different place in Palestine where they spent most of their time. To explain these phenomena the traditio-historical approach (also known as tradition history) was developed. In this understanding, Israel's ancestor stories began as oral short stories and gradually evolved into large, connected accounts. Before they were ever written down, small, oral units were built into bigger ones as Israel's predecessors told stories and passed them down from one generation to the next. For Alt, the religion of the ancestors was tied together with the "god of the fathers" of the Amorites.[15] Its origins were to be found in tribal contexts. Thus the different names of God such as "Fear of Isaac" (Gen. 31:42) and "Mighty One of Jacob" (Gen. 49:24; Ps. 132:2, 5) were not epithets of a single deity. Instead,

14. Day (1994, 38–39).
15. For this and what follows see Alt (1989), first published in 1929.

they represented different gods, each originating as the eponym of a tribal ancestor and (in large measure) each associated with a different tribe. Only at a later time did the stories of the different tribal ancestors, originally unrelated, merge into a single line of Abram, Isaac, and Jacob.

Alt also identified the divine names compounded with El as originating in the urban cult centers. Thus El-Elyon in Jerusalem (Gen. 14:18–22), El-Olam in Beersheba (Gen. 21:33), El-Bethel at Bethel (Gen. 35:7), and El-Berit at Shechem (Judg. 9:46) were sanctuary deities. Alt argued that these El gods therefore represented the worship of the indigenous inhabitants whereas the tribal deities represented those of the various Israelite tribes. The two coalesced into the Yahwist movement and all the deities were subordinated to Yahweh as manifestations of the one God. Having posited this development of Israel's concept of the deity, scholars then attempted to "attach" these oral traditions to the traditional written "sources" of Genesis.[16]

The term "god of the fathers," possibly occurring at twenty-fourth-century BC Ebla as a deity, is also found early in the Old Assyrian archives from Kanesh c. 1900 BC.[17] Witness formulae include "May Ashur and the God of your father be witness" and "May Ashur and Ilabrat, the God of our father be witness," where Il-abrat may be a similar structure to the name El-Shaddai (El-Bethel or El-Olam). It also occurs among the Amorites and at thirteenth-century BC Ugarit (*ilib*). Some of the recent discussions have substantially followed Alt.[18] On one hand, van der Toorn argues that "god of the fathers" refers to the deified father himself.[19] Akkadian and Hurrian parallels suggest that the words "god" and "father" are juxtaposed so as to produce an epexegetical genitive, "the god who is the father." On the other hand, Schmidt, on the basis of evidence at Ugarit, examines the use of the term in god lists and cultic texts, both in Ugaritic and Hurrian.[20] He concludes that it functions more like a title than an individual deity and suggests that it be understood as "the gods of the fathers" known from Mesopotamian sources, that is, members of the pantheon, especially personal or family deities.

---

16. For example, on the basis of distinctive elements in the E strand of the Jacob narratives, including different divine names and Jacob's portrayal as the founder of a new cult at Bethel, Weisman (1992) argues for the E strand of Jacob as older than Abraham or Isaac material and pre-Yahwistic in its religion. Cf. also Jaroš (1974), who identified the E source as containing material characteristic of "Canaanite" religion.

17. See Ebla in chapter 4 and Kitchen (2003, 330).

18. McCarter (1999, rev. Hendel) incorporates Alt's view into an analysis of "The Patriarchal Age" in his history of Israel.

19. Van der Toorn (1996a).

20. B. Schmidt (1994, 53–59).

Perhaps the interpretation that best conforms to both the extrabiblical and biblical evidence is that of Miller.[21] Among Abram and his family, El Shaddai (later identified as Yahweh) was the family or clan deity. There is no suggestion that this was a deified ancestor of the family because the name never appears in the genealogies. He is the God of Abraham (Gen. 24:27) who provides "protection and guidance for the family as well as the blessings of fertility and continuity of life."

Elohim, the most common noun for "God" in the Old Testament appears to be a plural (byform?) of El but is used as a singular noun (i.e., with singular verbs and adjectives) to identify the God of Israel. Burnett's study follows some customary wisdom in identifying the term as an abstract plural with concretizing force.[22] It originated in the northern kingdom of Israel as a description of the polytheistic pantheon of gods that were worshiped there and came to be applied to Yahweh, God of Israel, as the single national deity. While this argument involves a wonderful linkage of a variety of biblical texts, like so many of the theories about the development of the divine names that are applied to Israel's God, it remains speculative.[23]

Ancestral Religion

One may identify a list of distinctive features of the religion depicted in Genesis 12–50, especially in contrast to the Mosaic Yahwism of Exodus through Deuteronomy (and the remainder of the Old Testament that appeals to these books).[24]

First, it is open and inclusive. Everyone relates to the same God and there is no discussion of a plurality of deities. God speaks to all, whether the pharaoh of Egypt, Abimelech, or Abraham.

Second, there is an absence of antagonism between the ancestors and the religious practices of the Canaanites. In Genesis 12–50 one reads nothing about the destruction of the altars of other gods or of their images, nor does one learn of contests between Yahweh and the other gods and goddesses.

Third, in Genesis, Abram and his descendants worship in a manner that includes mention of trees and pillars (where Abram placed altars), but not of prescribed places of worship or of Sabbath or food laws. Further, circumcision is practiced on Ishmael as well as those in the line of Israel.

21. P. Miller (2000, 63).
22. Burnett (2001) maintains the term originally described a pantheon of deities that early in Israel was applied to one god.
23. For further information on this method see the review and critique of Niditch's work on pp. 72–73.
24. See especially the list of Moberly (1992a, 84–87).

Fourth, this religion lacks prophets and priests. One might say that the priests are the leaders of their households.

Fifth, Abram and his offspring live as sojourners and they live peacefully with their neighbors, the Canaanites and Amorites. Their role in the promised land is not to purify it of any or all of those already occupying it.

Sixth, moral obedience is not prominent. Perhaps this is not surprising because there are no legal collections before the giving of Torah at Mount Sinai in Exodus 19–40.

Seventh, holiness as an exclusive characteristic is not emphasized. People are not driven out from Abram's family because of moral failures, but only because of personal rivalries, as with Hagar and Ishmael.

Eighth, there is an importance placed on the family and its continuation for the sake of God's promise. In the ancient Near East and particularly West Semitic religion, the head of the family was the key to the religion. It was essential for him to have an heir to carry on the family. The leader of each generation would continue to "feed" and care for the aged and deceased.[25]

Ninth, the name Elohim is more fundamental than Yahweh here, but the reverse is true outside of Genesis 12–50.[26] Further, neither Baal nor any other deities are mentioned in Genesis 12–50.

Tenth, Jerusalem played no significant role. It is not explicitly designated as the site of any events in Genesis. If Salem in Genesis 14:18 or Moriah in Genesis 22:2 are associated with Jerusalem, then significant traditions are associated with the place. However, neither the site of Abraham's sacrifice of his son nor the place of Melchizedek's kingship can be established with certainty.

In light of these distinctions, Walter Moberly makes an important observation regarding the origins of the religious practice as depicted in Genesis 12–50:[27]

> If . . . patriarchal religion corresponds to some kind of historical reality, then presumably this is either some form of a genuinely ancient, pre-Yahwistic religion or something that was an "unorthodox" strand within Yahwistic religion (e.g., prior to Josiah's reform). The difficulty with the latter suggestion is precisely the complete lack of that holiness and exclusiveness which is one of the most fundamental characteristics of Yahwism.

It is not unreasonable to assume, therefore, that the depiction of religion in Genesis 12–50 may indeed have a claim to origins in part

25. See van der Toorn (1996a).
26. Kitchen (2003, 332).
27. Moberly (1992a, 84–87).

from the period prior to the emergence of Israel as a national Yahweh-worshiping community.

In terms of the implications of this for the religion of "pre-Israel," Dale Patrick observes how the absence of other deities is a picture painted, with incidental exceptions, right up to the time of the promulgation of the Ten Commandments in Exodus 20.[28] He suggests that the assumption here is that the people cannot be held guilty of breaking a law that has not yet been given. Since the law prohibiting the worship of other deities does not occur before Exodus 20, the presence of other deities and their worship is not addressed earlier.

Moberly sets aside the extrabiblical historical issues and asks questions about the function of the ancestral narratives in the context of the Pentateuch.[29] In doing so, he seeks an alternative route to that proposed by source criticism and provides a rationale for the record of the religious practices of Genesis 12–50 in anticipation of Exodus through Deuteronomy. Thus Abraham is the man of faith who awaits the fulfillment of God's promises. Isaac's role stresses the continuity with Abraham, even appearing in similar narratives (cf. Gen. 12, 20, and 26). Jacob, a trickster, finds God at work in his life as well, with divine promises. He also parallels Moses in a number of ways, especially during his days in the wilderness before confronting the pharaoh. Joseph models the successful believer in a foreign environment.

Genesis 49

Although there are many texts in these chapters that merit further study in terms of their religious significance, a final note considers the poem of Genesis 49. This is one of several examples of poems in the Pentateuch and books such as Judges that some suggest contain examples of early poems or poetic fragments, dating from before the monarchy. Others include Exodus 15, Judges 5, and perhaps Deuteronomy 33.[30] Among the possible early reflections of Israelite religion in this chapter from Genesis, Mark Smith finds in verses 24–26 a collection of epithets applied originally to the Ugaritic El and subsequently taken over by Yahweh. Especially important is the last phrase of verse 25, *birkōt šādayim wārāham*, "the blessings of 'Breasts-and-Womb.'" This translation leads Smith to argue that these are epithets of Asherah at Ugarit and therefore this is a reference to the Bronze Age goddess.[31] Yahweh is thereby given

28. Patrick (1995).
29. Moberly (1992b).
30. See Zoebel (1965; 1993 and bibliography there).
31. M. Smith (2003, 48–52). Smith cites the translation of Bruce Vawter.

the attributes applied to Asherah, the consort of El. While this is possible, it is not proven. Rather, it is disputed by other scholars, who point out that in this Genesis poem the attributes of Asherah are not strictly epithets. Smith is correct that these expressions are also used of the goddess Anat at Ugarit. Thus they reflect a personification of the unique powers/abilities/attributes of the female as might be expected to apply to chief female deities. Interestingly, the term "Breasts-and-Womb" is never so used as an attribute of either goddess. Rather, in various texts these attributes are applied individually. They represent the powers of fertility and reproduction. In the poems of Genesis 49 it is not surprising that they are ascribed to the God of Israel, who is understood as Creator and Sustainer of everything.

As in Deuteronomy 33:26–27 and Psalm 18:13–15 (= 2 Sam. 22:14–16), so in Genesis 49, imagery that occurs in Ugaritic myths where it is applied to El and Baal is here applied to Yahweh.[32] However, the model need not be syncretism or convergence, contrary to what has been suggested elsewhere. Rather, we see a transformational model in which the God of Israel—who in the canonical sequence (Exodus following Genesis) will shortly be individualized by his redemptive role in the exodus and his unique bestowal of the detailed covenant of Sinai—is seen as transforming expressions used in other religions and cultural media and applying them (or having them applied) in new ways to his own revelation of himself. Here perhaps there is also direct assimilation so that this deity is praised as possessor of other divine attributes that neighboring gods might have been thought to possess. Finally, there will also come at times direct confrontation and rejection. Psalm 82 and other texts suggest that, rather than assimilating the characteristics of neighboring deities, Yahweh overthrows them.

Plagues

Exodus opens with Israel having grown to a nation in Egypt, where it faced oppression by pharaohs who did not know Joseph and the salvation he provided for Egypt (Gen. 37–50). There is much that could be recounted concerning the birth of Moses, his escape from death as an infant, his upbringing in the house of pharaoh, his flight to Midian, and his return to Egypt to deliver the people of Israel. The appearance of God and the revelation of the divine Yahweh are discussed below in the section on Sinai under "Theophany." A major religious event remembered at this time was the exodus. Leading up to that event were the plagues of Exodus 7–12. These events are divided between the Narrative

32. M. Smith (2003, 56).

Fig. 12. Temple of Amon-Re at Karnak (Courtesy of Richard S. Hess)

Strands and the Priestly and Cultic Strands. They may be included here as primarily narrative.

Though the plagues narrative of Exodus 7–12 does not directly polemicize against the Egyptian deities, the author(s) of this account indirectly challenged the religion of ancient Egypt. This was true for each of the plagues. From the beginning, God is portrayed as challenging the Egyptians and their pride. Even their ability to control the snake was brought under divine control (Exod. 7:8–12). The first plague (Exod. 7:15–25) involved changing the Nile river to blood. The Nile was deified by the Egyptians as Hapi and was their lifegiver.[33] Red was the color of Hapi's enemy and murderer, Seth. The second plague (Exod. 8:1–14) involved frogs. Heqat, who appeared with a frog's head, controlled the multiplication of frogs. These amphibians symbolized abundance and prosperity.[34] The third and fourth plagues (Exod. 8:16–24) brought gnats and flies (mosquitoes?), which may have been connected with Kheprer, the flying beetle and god of resurrection. The fifth plague (Exod. 9:1–7) brought a pestilence on domesticated animals. This may have been identified with cults such as Apis, and with

33. Hoffmeier refers to Hort (1957; 1958), who argued that this red color could come from flagellates originating in Lake Tana, in Ethiopia, at the time of the flooding of the Nile in September. The effects of this infestation would lead to the subsequent five plagues. See Hoffmeier (1997, 146–53) and also Currid (1997, 109–13), Kitchen (2003, 253), and Humphreys (2003) for discussion of the plagues.

34. Hort notes that frogs can come into Egypt at the end of the Nile's flood. For the symbolism, see Kitchen (2003, 253).

other deities such as Re and Ptah, who were personified as bulls.[35] The sixth plague (Exod. 9:8–12) brought boils or smallpox. This would have challenged Egyptian healer deities, Sekhmet or Amon-Re.[36] The seventh plague (Exod. 9:13–35) brought hail. Egyptian deities involved here include Nut (sky), Shu (supports sky), and Tefnut (moisture). Plague eight (Exod. 10:1–20) brought locusts. Senehem was the divine protector against pests. The Tanis stele mentions a group of gods as protectors against pests.

The ninth plague (Exod. 10:21–29) brought darkness throughout Egypt. This was a direct challenge to Amon-Re, chief deity of Egypt and the personification of the sun.[37] Pharaoh was the "son of Re" and virtually all of Egyptian life, belief, and culture was guided by the sun. The tenth plague (Exod. 11–12), the death of the firstborn, was a direct challenge to pharaoh who as a god of Egypt should control the life of his own son, also a god.

Exodus Event

The escape of Israelite slaves from Egypt, together with the defeat of the Egyptian army at the Red (traditionally Reed) Sea, represents the single most significant theological event in Israel's memory. As with other major events of historical significance, such as the Israelite defeat of the Hazor alliance in Judges 4–5, a prose account of the event (Exod. 14) is followed by a poetic rendition (Exod. 15). Like the account of the "new creation" brought about by the flood waters in Genesis 6–9, which itself hearkens back to Genesis 1:2, the parting of the Red Sea anticipates the creation of the new people of Israel.[38]

That the exodus reflects a historical event, however large or small, is suggested both by the details of the narrative that set well in the context of Egypt of the thirteenth century BC,[39] and by the generally recognized oddity of the account as a foundation story of a people's history. If there had been no oppression and exodus, why would any Israelite author invent such an origin for her/his people? If Israel was indigenous to Canaan and never came from Egypt, how did this story come to form the beginning of the nation's epic?[40]

35. This anthrax could have been spread by frogs (Hort 1957; 1958).
36. This infection could have been spread by the flies (Hort 1957; 1958).
37. Hoffmeier (1997, 148) suggests a khamsin sandstorm in the spring.
38. Currid (1997, 114–17).
39. See the report of slaves who attempted to escape from Egypt as recorded in the thirteenth-century BC Papyrus Anastasi V, 19:2–20:6. See further details in Kitchen (2003, 245–65) and G. Davies (2004).
40. See Sarna (1999, rev. Shanks). Shanks (2001) mentions these points, observing that there are three aspects to the biblical story of the exodus: miracles, details, and the

The story of the exodus, repeated again and again in Israel's Scriptures, represents the key historic act of redemption that formed a unique contribution to the religious identity of this people. Although Ugaritic and other ancient Near Eastern sources contain a triumph of the chief god over the divine Sea, there is no parallel to this anywhere in the ancient Near Eastern sources. The exodus tradition represents a distinctive contribution of Israel's faith not found elsewhere in ancient Near Eastern religious traditions. As early as the exodus tradition and Yahweh's association with it, Israel's God becomes known by this historic act of redemption. In this manner, the miraculous association with the exodus event and God's defeat of the most powerful army known become the means by which Israel recognizes its identity and the basis for its own response of covenantal faithfulness to this deity.

Sinai

In addition to the exodus tradition, Mark Smith (2003, 25) finds in Yahweh's southern sanctuary in Sinai (or other mountains) a feature of Israelite religion that has no precedent in Canaanite religion. Here consideration will be given to two aspects of the Sinai tradition: the Golden Calf and the appearance of God in theophany. Matters of law and covenant at Sinai will be discussed later in this chapter in the section on "Law and the Decalogue."

THE GOLDEN CALF

In the city of Ashkelon, which lies on the coast of southern Palestine, excavations uncovered a massive wall and glacis combined structure that was built during the Middle Bronze IIB (c. 1750–c. 1550 BC) period, when Ashkelon was still Canaanite (not yet Philistine).[41] The north gate to the city of this time was approached by a steep ascent. Near the base of this ascent a small "sanctuary" was discovered in which was found

---

general point that Semitic peoples escaped from slavery in Egypt and made their way to Canaan. The first, miracles, is a matter of faith. Archaeology does not prove them, nor does it disprove them. The second is a matter of interpretation. Details may be misunderstood by later readers and translators, and it is important to be as careful as possible in understanding what the Bible claims and does not claim. Nevertheless, the bulk of the detail, at least as understood here, is a possibility. The third area, the general view of an escape, has precedent as seen in the evidence cited above. An Egyptologist such as Redford (1992, 257–64) denies any relation between the biblical account of the Israelite exodus and any event of the second millennium BC. He prefers to date the origins of the story much later in the first millennium. In this he is contradicted by Kitchen (1993; 1994; 2000a) and his own student Hoffmeier (1997), who lay out detailed connections of factual congruence between second-millennium Egyptian sources and the biblical account in Exodus.

41. See also Stager (1991a).

Fig. 13. Tel Ashkelon (Courtesy of Richard S. Hess)

a ceramic model shrine in which a 14 ounce, 4" × 4.5" bronze model of a horned calf was found. Traces reveal that the calf was covered with a thick overleaf of pure silver. It would have stood on a small platform and been exhibited as emerging from an "entrance" at the base of the shrine. In Ugaritic mythology and in Canaanite iconography, the calf was associated with Baal.[42] Later, Jeroboam I constructed golden calves at Bethel and Ai, which he associated with the worship of Yahweh. Construction of silver images and the worship of calf images is condemned by Hosea (13:1–2).

Of special interest is Aaron's construction of the calf image recorded in Exodus 32. In Exodus 32:24 Aaron claims that the calf virtually generated itself, having come forth from the fire. This compares to the "opening of the mouth" rituals surrounding the manufacture of Mesopotamian images. The texts regard the image to have been made in heaven as divine from the beginning. The priests and their rituals do not make it divine. It is made so by the gods of heaven.[43] Calf worship here and throughout the Old Testament is not a fertility rite but instead describes a military figure

42. As Fleming (1999b) notes, the association of El with the calf has no parallels in the Bronze Age. El's identity as divine parent and chief deity, like that of Hittite and Mesopotamian counterparts, is never associated with a calf, only with a bull. Day (2000, 34–39) makes no distinction between the calf images of Aaron and Jeroboam, and El's portrayal as a bull.

43. Walker and Dick (2001); Hurowitz (2003).

who leads the people into battle. As Janzen shows, the words here used to describe eating, drinking, and playing are used in contexts elsewhere of joyful celebrations at military victories.[44] This certainly fits the narratives of the exodus and wilderness wanderings, which are frequently characterized by military threats from Israel's enemies.

Exodus 32:20 and the actions of burning, grinding, and strewing the idol have been compared to a similar series of actions

Fig. 14. Middle Bronze Age silver and bronze calf from Ashkelon (Courtesy of the Israel Antiquities Authority)

performed in mythological texts from Ugarit.[45] Anat burns the god of death, Mot, with fire. She grinds him and scatters him about on a field. It is argued that this is an image of "total destruction," perhaps a stereotypical description inserted here despite the physical difficulty of actually burning and grinding gold. In fact, the example of the silver calf from Ashkelon suggests that the image may have been (partly?) coated with the metal. Most of the image might have been made of a material susceptible to such an operation. The subsequent drinking of the waters has been likened to the ordeal of the woman suspected of adultery in Numbers 5:11–31. In these and other ancient Near Eastern ordeals, the curses of the oath that the people swear (cf. Exod. 24) will have an effect on them if they have violated their covenant.[46]

THEOPHANY

In light of the discovery of a calf at Ashkelon and of Janzen's identification of Exodus with military ritual, it seems appropriate to understand

44. See the discussion by Janzen (1990).
45. *KTU* 1.6 II 30–37. Loewenstamm (1967; 1975).
46. Cf. Weinfeld (1991, 413). Frankel (1994) emends the Exodus text. According to him the original text depicted the Israelites drinking water mixed with fragments of the tablets of the covenant rather than with the idol fragments. However, there is no need for such an emendation that has no textual support. The fragments of the calf would exemplify breaking the covenant. Furthermore, it was necessary for Moses to destroy the calf and for him to demonstrate to the people in a vivid manner the horror of idolatry.

Fig. 15. Jebel
Musa, pos-
sible site of
Mount Sinai
(Courtesy of
Richard S.
Hess)

the condemned ritual at Mount Sinai as an attempt by Aaron to portray or invoke a deity, perhaps Yahweh, as coming forth from a southern mountain or mountainous land such as Sinai, Kadesh, or Teman, in order to lead his people on to military victory. Perhaps the calf was intended as an alternative to God on the mountain, where the Israelites had lost patience in their wait for him to lead them.[47] As in Exodus 32 where the calf is at the base of the mountain, so at Ashkelon the calf image is at the base of the city. In both cases the image is one of the figure protecting the mountain/city and its people by positioning itself at the entry to the mountain/city. Compare the border sanctuaries of Dan and Bethel, where Jeroboam I set up calf images for the northern kingdom of Israel, and also sanctuaries such as Arad and perhaps Beersheba at the southern borders of Judah.[48] However, the tiny size of the Ashkelon image strains credulity as a military image. Perhaps this is a small model of a larger image that existed.

Other texts describe the dramatic appearance of Yahweh and his act of leading his people to military victory. See, for example, Deuteronomy 33:2; Judges 5:4–5; Habakkuk 3:3–4; and Yahweh of Teman in the Kuntillet ʿAjrud inscription from c. 800 BC. These encounters, described in what most accept as some of the oldest poetry (and writing) in the Bible, detail how God appears suddenly to his people to wage war on their behalf. Other theophanies are less warlike but no less frightening

47. The view that this image was a pedestal for a deity to alight and ride upon runs contrary to the biblical statement of Exod. 32:5 and of the Jeroboam parallel in 1 Kings 12:28. See Day (2000, 40). For questions about allusions to ordeals in the Psalms, cf. Johnston (2005).

48. See also Schunck (1971).

or life changing. Some occur in Genesis 28:10–17; 32:24–30; Exodus 3–4; 19–20; 24:15–18; Joshua 5:13–15; 1 Kings 18:36–40; 19:9–14; Isaiah 6; Jeremiah 1; and Ezekiel 1.[49]

Some scholars see here the origins of the worship of Yahweh in the southern desert of what are today the regions of the Sinai and the Negev. In the topographical list of Pharaoh Amenophis III (c. 1395–1358 BC) is found the expression *tȝ šȝsw yhw*, which can be interpreted, "the Shosu-land of Yahweh" or "Yhw in the land of the Shasu." Shosu/Shasu was an Egyptian term for groups of nomadic peoples who were located in the desert areas east of Egypt. If this is to be interpreted as the name of a place or people in the area of Seir (Edom) and the southern desert, rather than to the north, then the biblical theophanies mentioned above, the associations in Exodus of Yahweh worship with Midianites and with Sinai, and the revelation of Yahweh in Exodus 3 and 6 may be related.[50] This does not necessarily relate the Egyptian term to Israelites (although that is possible). It simply argues that Yahweh was known and worshiped in the deserts south of Canaan in the fourteenth century BC.[51] However, there are those who question the identification of this place name with Yahweh.[52] Even so, Smith is correct in affirming the early identification of Yahweh with sources in the southern desert (Judg. 1:16; 4:11; 5:4–6, 24). He suggests that the desert origins parallel those of the Ugaritic god Athtar (rather than Baal), who is both a warrior deity and a precipitation-producing deity associated with inland desert sites. He notes that Numbers 23:8, 22 and 24:8 associate the god of the exodus with El, and argues that El should be distinguished from Yahweh.[53]

Although the study of the characteristics of the God of Israel is a topic proper to Old Testament theology, it is important to see certain aspects

---

49. See Savran (2005).

50. The southern origin is supported by Görg (1976); Mettinger (1988, 24–28); Axelsson (1987, 58–61). For the northern view, see Astour (1979); de Moor (1990b, 111–12).

51. Van der Toorn (1993) traces Yahweh's origins outside Canaan to Edom and Midian. Following Axelsson, he argues that the earliest biblical texts demonstrate that, despite southern desert origins, Yahweh first appeared in the hill country of Israel rather than Judah. Van der Toorn follows Edelman and Blenkinsopp in arguing that the Gibeonites were originally Edomites. He concludes that the Gibeonites introduced Yahweh to Israel through Saul. This last point is least convincing although the Gibeonites may have known of Yahweh before Israel's appearance. Additional attempts have been made to locate the divine name Yahweh in a Ugaritic myth (spelled as *yw*), in a personal name from a fourteenth-century BC (Amarna) text from Tyre, or in the personal name of a contemporary text from far to the north of Palestine (de Moor [1990b; 1997]). Due to the fragmentary nature of all these texts and the possibility of other interpretations, none can be regarded as certain or even probable. Cf. Hess (1991a). Even the Egyptian geographic name discussed above cannot be asserted without doubt as containing the name of God.

52. M. Smith (2001a, 276).

53. Ibid., 145–47.

of Yahweh that are evident from extrabiblical and biblical sources. For example, Yahweh, like El, is gracious and compassionate.[54] This is evident in Exodus 34:6–7, a key text in the analysis of God's character. The first set of characteristics enumerated is "merciful and gracious." The gracious (Hebrew root *ḥnn*) character of God is found in seventh/sixth century BC inscriptions from Khirbet Beit Lei and the Jerusalem amulet, as well as throughout the Bible.[55]

The fact that Yahweh allows no images of himself is unusual in comparison with other ancient Near Eastern deities. This aniconic character is stated in the Ten Commandments (Exod. 20:3–6; Deut. 5:7–10) and attested by the invisible enthronement of Yahweh upon the Ark of the Covenant and between the cherubim in the sanctuary.[56] For the use of standing stones (*maṣṣēbôt*), see p. 198. Challenges to this message include the golden calf of Exodus 32 and the bulls that Jeroboam I erected at Dan and Bethel.[57]

Yahweh's role as warrior is found early and consistently in the history of Israel. In addition to the poems of Exodus 15 and Judges 5, where Yahweh fights battles on behalf of Israel against Egypt and the Canaanites, he battles alone against the Philistine deities (1 Sam. 5:1–5) and later will fight against Israel itself when it violates God's covenant.[58]

As in these examples, there occurs a pattern in the Baal cycle and other mythologies of the West Semitic world: the march of the divine warrior; the convulsing of nature; the return of the divine warrior to his holy mountain and the assumption of kingship; and the utterance of the thunder or voice of the warrior with the provision of rain to fertilize the earth.[59] Among the

54. See further in chapter 4, pp. 97–98.

55. P. Miller (2000, 12–13).

56. Kitchen (2003, 280) compares the gilded box of the Ark with four libation vessels from Tutankhamun's tomb of the fourteenth century BC. It also had four rings and poles to carry it. Further at the Deir el-Bahri temple of Queen Hatshepsut (c. 1470 BC), a scene of a festival procession shows an empty lion throne with a fan symbolizing the deity.

Cullican (1968, 82–83) and Stockton (1974–75, 9; cf. Zevit [2001, 329]) note that from the thirteenth until the second century BC in Syria an empty sphinx throne indicated a sky god, especially with reference to Baal Shamem. Cullican cites the glyptic evidence of cylinder seals and Stockton refers to the following description of Hierapolis from Lucian's *De Syria dea*, 34: "In the body of the temple . . . there stands . . . a throne for the Sun god; but there is no image upon the throne for the effigies of the Sun and Moon are not exhibited . . . not from a prohibition, but because the Sun and the Moon are plain for all to see."

57. 1 Kings 12:25–33; P. Miller (2000, 15–23).

58. E.g., Amos 5:18–20; Isa. 10; P. Miller (2000, 7–9).

59. Cross (1973, 151–63). Cf. M. Smith (2003, 80) and the texts *KTU* 1.4 VII 29–35, 1.101 1–4, and EA 147.13–15, where the theophany and Baal's role as warrior are explicitly connected. In the Bible these are joined in Ps. 18:6–19 (= 2 Sam. 22:7–20); 68:7–10. For the connection between storm deity and Yahweh as warrior, see Ps. 29; 1 Kings 19; 2 Esdras 13:1–4. The storm always moves eastward from the Mediterranean.

enemies that Yahweh fights are: Yam "Sea,"[60] Rahab,[61] the seven-headed dragon Leviathan,[62] and Mot "Death."[63] Isaiah 51:9–11 joins Rahab with dragon (tannin) and "Sea" (Yam).

As for the mountain, Zaphon "the north" in Ugaritic imagery was Jebel el-Aqraʿ. Its Hittite name was Ḫazzi. Its Classical identification was Mons Cassius, where Zeus and Typhon fought. The divine warrior has an association with Mount Zion/Zaphon.[64]

Yahweh's voice, his power to give rain, and its association with the temple occur in many biblical texts.[65] Joel 3:9–18 [Heb. 4:9–18] associates various aspects of the divine mountain and Yahweh's voice.[66] This imagery anticipated another key characteristic of Israel's God: his role as king. Exodus 15:18 anticipates many of the psalms when it concludes praise of God's victory with the confession, "Yahweh will reign forever and ever." To convey this kingly theme, Israel borrowed the mythological motifs of Baal's victory over Yamm ("Sea") and the consequent establishment of his kingship as a medium to establish Yahweh's kingship in relation to the greatest military power of the day, Egypt.[67] As with Baal and others, this establishment of kingship entails first rulership over the divine assembly, which in the myths is made up of gods. In the accounts of Yahweh, it is made up of angelic beings (1 Kings 22; Job 2; Ps. 82; Isa. 6) who act in accordance with Yahweh's will. Unlike the mythologies there is no disagreement in the divine assembly of Israel's God. All obey God alone. More than any other text, Psalm 82 demonstrates the absolute dominion of Yahweh over all the assembly, so that he can and does depose the ones given authority to rule over various nations of the world.

60. Job 7:12; Pss. 65:7 [Heb. 8]; 74:13; 89:9 [Heb. 10]; Prov. 8:29; Isa. 51:10; Jer. 5:22; cf. *KTU* 1.2 IV.

61. Ps. 89:9–10 [Heb. 10–11].

62. Job 3:8; 41:1 [Heb. 40:25]; Pss. 74:14; 104:26; Isa. 27:1; Ezek. 32:2; Rev. 13:1; 2 Esdras 6:49.

63. Ps. 18:5–6 [Heb. 6–7] (= 2 Sam. 22:6–7); Isa. 25:8; 28:15, 18; Hosea 13:14; Hab. 2:5; Rev. 21:4; Odes Sol. 15:9; 29:4.

64. Ps. 48:2 [Heb. 3]; Isa. 14:13; 31:4; 66:18–21; Joel 3:9–17, 19–21 [Heb. 4:9–17, 19–21]; Zech. 14:4; 2 Esdras 13:35; so M. Smith (2003, 89) for texts that connect battle imagery with Jerusalem or Mount Zion.

65. Jer. 3:3; 5:24; 10:13; 14:4; 51:16; Amos 1:2; 4:7; Hag. 1:7–11; Zech. 10:1; Mal. 3:10.

66. M. Smith (2003, 90–91).

67. Cf. P. Miller (2000, 10). See the Mari letter (A 1968) that connects the storm god's (Adad's) victory over the sea with kingship in chapter 4, p. 87. Thus the storm god Adad to the king of Mari: "When you [Zimri-Lim] sat on the throne of your father, I gave you the weapon(s) with which I fought against the Sea (*tamtum*)." See M. Smith (2003, 94). A god list from Ugarit (*KTU* 1.47) connects Adad with Baal, and Yamm with Tamtum (Tiamat). Yamm is also divinized at Emar and given offerings.

Although the kingship of Yahweh was affirmed in the earliest records of Israel as a nation, this was an extension of the role of Yahweh as the family god, the God of the fathers for the whole family or nation of Israel. Its application to David is seen in Psalm 2 and Psalm 89:19–37 [Heb. 20–38].[68]

Religious Aspects of the Covenant and Deuteronomic Law

Covenant Making

The first mention of the term "covenant" in the Hebrew Bible is in Genesis 9:9–17, which describes the covenant between God and Noah after the flood of the preceding chapters. This is one of three major covenants in the Pentateuch, the others being the one made with Abram and his successors in Genesis 12:1–3 and the following chapters, and the covenant between God and the nation of Israel on Mount Sinai. In their literary contexts, these covenants each emphasize a different mediator: Noah, Abraham, and Moses respectively. They each reveal God by a different name: Elohim, El Shaddai, Yahweh. They also each contain a different sign: rainbow, circumcision (Gen. 15), and Sabbath.[69]

The covenant of Genesis 12:1–3 is repeated many times as a promise to Abram and to his descendants. Of greatest interest in terms of comparative West Semitic religions is the covenant-making act of Genesis 15, especially verses 9–17. Here God made a covenant by instructing Abram to cut certain animals into two pieces. After this, God made a promise to Abram and then, in the form of a smoking firepot, he alone passed between the pieces. Thus God took an oath by his very life that he would fulfill his promises. The act of killing animals as part of a treaty ceremony is attested in the Middle Bronze Age (c. 2000–c. 1550 BC) at Mari for the purposes of a treaty and at Alalakh as part of a land grant.[70] The use of treaty forms in covenant making in order to describe a new relationship with a deity is not unknown at Mari and possibly also at Emar.[71] Nevertheless, it is not as developed and refined as in Genesis and especially in Deuteronomy.[72]

68. Cf. v. 25 [Heb. 26] where Sea and River(s) are titles of God's antagonists; M. Smith (2003, 92). Cf. also the Babylonian Marduk and his defeat of Tiamat in *Enuma Elish*.

69. I thank Theodore Lewis for this observation.

70. See summary and bibliography in Hess (1994f; 2002d). The particular form of oath taking in this context in Gen. 15 is closer to the Middle Bronze Age examples from Mari and Alalakh than it is to Jer. 34 and the covenant ceremony there.

71. See Fleming (1999c, 30–31) and Lewis (1996, 405–10) for this and other evidence beyond the West Semitic world.

72. For further study of the covenant in Deuteronomy, see the last part of this section, "Treaty and Covenant."

Law and the Decalogue

There are many laws in the Pentateuch that are relevant to religious practice. Some of the cultic laws have been examined in the above section, chapter 4, especially under the Late Bronze Age (c. 1550–c. 1200 BC) archives at Emar. However, some of the most important distinctives of Israelite religion occur in the Decalogue (Exod. 20; Deut. 5). The laws regarding the worship of no other god, the prohibition of images, and the observance of the Sabbath play a key role in distinguishing Israel from its neighbors.[73]

The question of the dating of the Decalogue is a vexed one. Some scholars find it to be a postexilic (after 539 BC) production that sought to summarize the law.[74] This may be possible but there is no empirical evidence on which to demonstrate either an earlier or later dating of the work. Internal evidence, such as the relationship of the second half of the Decalogue (in its Masoretic Text form) to the structure of Deuteronomy 12–26 and its location in Deuteronomy before those laws and in Exodus before the Book of the Covenant may imply that the more detailed laws are expansive and derivative, but this also cannot be demonstrated beyond all doubt.[75] Nevertheless, the contents of the Decalogue formed an essential part of Israelite belief at the time of their composition, and this implies a long-standing constituent of central beliefs of their religion.

Exodus 20:3 (Deut. 5:7) prohibits the worship of any god other than Yahweh, or the placement of "any other god before me." This seems to be categorical and exclusive of competing deities among the nations that Israel was to drive out, as well as among those with whom they may live peacefully. This implies an allegiance to the nation of Israel and to its covenant, as opposed to an alliance with any other nation and its god(s). Yahweh is not just first but alone worthy of devotion. The unique reality of Yahweh lies behind the Shemaʿ: Hear O Israel Yahweh our God Yahweh alone (or "is one"). This statement in Deuteronomy 6:4 may itself have become a slogan, used by Israelites who supported exclusive devotion to Yahweh.[76]

The larger question for the religion of Israel is when this law emerged in the nation. The law itself does not require a philosophical monotheism, but rather demands that only Yahweh be recognized as deity by his follow-

73. The prohibition of the misuse of the divine name, while of key importance, is a common concern in neighboring religions.

74. So, for example, Friedman (1987, 251); Van Seters (1994, 247–52); Himbaza (2004); and Aaron (2006).

75. For the structure of Deut. 12–26, see Kaufman (1987). For the structure of the Decalogue in relation to that of the Book of the Covenant, see Hess (1980).

76. See Block (2004).

Fig. 16. Tel Bethsaida (Courtesy of Richard S. Hess)

ers. The idea of the worship of a single deity has a significant precedent in the Amarna revolution in Egypt of the mid-fourteenth century BC. The royal family appears to have recognized only one deity, the divine Aten. At least one Egyptian text suggests that one of the kings of the Hyksos, the West Semitic rulers of Egypt before 1550 BC, worshiped Seth (= Baal) alone.[77] Thus the idea of the worship of a single deity need not have been original to Egypt, but may have been borrowed from earlier West Semitic peoples. In any case, the sun disk Aten, who was worshiped as god alone by Pharaoh Akhenaten in the fourteenth century BC, had parallels with the later revelation of Yahweh. He is pictured and described with a face, heart, mouth, and limbs. He is referred to as father and Akhenaten is his son. This pharaoh banned the Egyptian word for (multiple) gods.[78] Indeed, there is no evidence in early Israel that the elimination of other spiritual beings was carried so far. Rather in early poetry, such as Exodus 15:11, the incomparability of Yahweh is affirmed.

Attempts to find the worship of a single god in the Babylonian exaltation of Marduk or in some of the Ugaritic texts[79] have not been success-

77. Cf. Papyrus Sallier 1; Propp (1999, 540).
78. Propp (1999, 544–46).
79. Cf. de Moor (1990b; 1997). The same is true of the other surrounding cultures as discussed in the essays in Porter (1997). See Hess (1991a) for a more complete assessment.

ful. However, the principle of the high god El's possessing a name that itself encompasses the entire divinity of Ugarit insofar as it functions as a generic term for "god" suggests a West Semitic context in which the worship of a single deity could emerge.[80]

Nevertheless, the Egyptian model provides a Late Bronze Age antecedent that renders possible a similar view of Israel's God, especially in light of the close association between Egypt and earliest Israel in the biblical traditions. This analogy renders the command in the Decalogue as possible and plausible. There is no extrabiblical evidence to support it in early Israel but neither is there any to demonstrate that early Israel worshiped a chief god other than Yahweh. James Hoffmeier (2005, 181–92) summarizes evidence for the literary unity of Exodus 20–24 and its formal comparison with second millennium BC Hittite vassal treaties. What little evidence exists supports the observation of Judges 2:10–13, that early Israel consistently ignored this injunction and sought to worship other deities.

Exodus 20:4–6 (Deut. 5:8–10) prohibits the construction of images of deities, especially of Israel's God. It is closely tied with the preceding prohibition. The reason may be found in Deuteronomy 4:15–20 (v. 15, "You saw no form on the day Yahweh spoke to you at Horeb from the midst of the fire"). No rival human witness is acceptable, nor any attempt to transform the worship of the living God into an attachment to a particular object, institution, or routine. The imageless nature of the worship of Yahweh has also been compared with Pharaoh Akhenaten's Amarna revolution. However, this religion did use and display an image of the sun disk itself as well as the rays that emanated from it. The same is true of the Iron Age cult center at the gate of Tel Bethsaida, north of the Sea of Galilee. Here the moon cult is represented by a crescent shape.[81] Perhaps closer in type are the unworked standing stones, stelae, or maṣṣēbôt of the Negev and adjacent Sinai area, as discussed above.[82] Yet, insofar as these stones represent deities, they function as images. A better representation may lie in the Taanach cult stand from the tenth century BC and the possible imageless representation of Yahweh there. See discussion in chapter 8, "The United Monarchy." Note also the lack of male images in Israel in most of the

80. Cf. Propp (1999, 566–67).
81. See discussion of this religion in Theuer (2000).
82. See the thorough review and discussion in Mettinger (1995). As he notes, similar stelae occur in Phoenicia and in Palestine at sites such as Hazor and Gezer, although they sometimes have figures carved on them. See further Lewis's critique of Mettinger (1998). Note however the comment of Mettinger (1995, 17): "Israelite aniconism seems to be as old as the Solomonic temple and may antedate it by centuries."

iconography of the monarchy.[83] Although the evidence is negative, it is difficult to argue otherwise when the absence of images is the point to be demonstrated. As noted, this aniconism remains throughout the period of Israel's history.

Exodus 20:8–11 (Deut. 5:12–15) commands observance of the Sabbath (Heb. *šabbāt*), a word whose etymology is related to a root meaning "to cease." Nevertheless, the sanctifying of the Sabbath carries with it a positive function as well, "to make holy." In the Exodus Decalogue the rationale presented is that of God's rest on the seventh day of creation. This makes the Sabbath observance a reflection of the created order. In Deuteronomy the reason for the Sabbath is attached to God's deliverance of Israel from Egypt. In the Dead Sea Scroll fragments, one text conflates the Deuteronomy and Exodus rationales.[84] The many other manuscripts that we have of Deuteronomy and Exodus have not conflated these reasons but have preserved them separately.

The Sabbath as the setting aside of one day out of every seven to worship God was considered unique to ancient Israel. See the discussion in chapter 4 under Emar, where the West Semitic *zukru* festival has a seven-day period of observance. However, this is not the same as a special observance every week. In Egypt, a "week" was ten days long (Hoffmeier 2005, 173). In Mesopotamia, the Akkadian *šappatu* identified the fifteenth day of each lunar month. However, it remains unclear that this had any religious significance or relationship to the Israelite Sabbath. A cuneiform text relating to rituals at the temple of the sun god of Sippar in Babylonia mentions liturgical activities to be carried on at the temple on the eighth and fifteenth days of every month as well as possibly on the first day. This provides the closest similarity to a Sabbath outside of the Bible.[85] However, it differs from the biblical Sabbath that occurred every seven days and, rather than a time of special temple rites, remained a day of rest especially for the worker and the slave.[86] The biblical Sabbath is connected with the sanctification

83. M. Smith (2001a, 151) observes that W. F. Albright affirmed this as proof of monotheism. However, without refuting this contention, Smith concludes that Albright "took such great historical and textual leaps." It is not clear why Smith asserts this. See Lewis (1998, 42–43) for a review of some apparent male images that seem to be non-Israelite rather than forms of Israelite Yahweh.

84. Cf. 4QDtn; Eshel (1991).

85. Cf. Maul (1999) who has published this cultic calendar from the eighth to sixth century BC. It derives from the temple of the sun god at Sippar, one of the oldest and most important temples in Babylonia. It orders special songs and activities for deities on the first, eighth, and fifteenth (and also on the twentieth day—a special day for the sun god) days of each lunar month.

86. In Deuteronomy, an additional phrase (v. 14) mandates rest for Israel's slaves. Beyond this we learn that Sabbath sanctification includes remembering that Israel itself

of time, just as sacrifice is related to the sanctification of the world. In each case part of the whole is given back to the Creator in recognition of his prior ownership. This is the key idea behind this law. Shea argues that Sargon's account of the conquest of Judean Gath in 712 BC preserves the earliest extrabiblical mention of the Sabbath when it notes that the city was entered *ina 7-šu*, "on its seventh day." This is possible but the text may be interpreted other than as an indication of a Sabbath observance. If it is so read, however, it would be the earliest extrabiblical reference to the Sabbath.[87]

Treaty and Covenant

The form of certain biblical covenants is related to the ancient Near Eastern treaty form. Therefore, to understand the biblical covenant it is necessary to study the ancient Near Eastern treaty. In the ancient Near East, when two countries sought to have peace, they would draw up a treaty. Treaties between parties of equal power are called parity treaties. Treaties between unequal parties are called vassal treaties because the weaker country became a vassal to the stronger country. Although the forms of these two types of treaties are similar, there are some differences. The reader is encouraged to review the discussion of the vassal treaty structure and Deuteronomy as outlined in the sixth point critiquing the Documentary Hypothesis in the excursus in chapter 3. There it is argued that the overall structure of Deuteronomy preserves in a distinctive manner that of the Hittite suzerain-vassal treaty of the thirteenth century BC.

The concept of the covenant as a relationship between God and people and as designated by the West Semitic word *br(y)t* occurs already in thirteenth-century BC Egypt and in the title of a contemporary Hurrian hymn from Ugarit: God of the covenant.[88] Thus this term was widely known and used in the ancient Near East of the Late Bronze Age.

A comparison with the Hittite vassal treaty structure may also address theological issues in the understanding of the Sinai covenant itself. For example, does disobedience bring an end to the covenant? This is not a contract that effects eternal alienation because of one breach. The covenant ends through persistent disobedience that mocks the commitment at the heart of the covenant. Even then, such cases are not definitive.

---

was once in servitude and that Yahweh delivered Israel from servitude in Egypt. Thus after commands prohibiting improper worship of Israel's God, Deuteronomy allows for a particular type of worship, one that remembers God's deliverance and seeks to provide for those who are still in slavery.

87. See Shea (1994).

88. See Propp (1999, 569); Kitchen (2003, 283–98).

The Great Kings of the Hittites emphasized their mercy, their renewal of favor to a perjured vassal. However, no treaty was unbreakable. This was true even of land grants, defined by some as unconditional, but in fact containing clauses that state that disobedience brings an end to the grant.[89] Nevertheless, mercy was present. Mercy could also be expected from Israel's God. God held out hope for forgiveness. This occurs in a cult that allowed for repentance, forgiveness, and the restoration of relationship with God.

The nature of the covenant emphasized the importance of personal responsibility. Such a personal nature to the covenant, coupled with individual responsibility, led directly to Jeremiah's hope of a new covenant written on the hearts of people (Jer. 31:31–34).

Further, there are terms whose usage in treaties parallels their appearance in the biblical covenants. Perhaps best known is the biblical term (here a verb) for "love," *'āhēb*. In treaties this describes that which is owed to an overlord: to be faithful, to be dedicated in service, to be ready to die for the overlord. The treaty established a family-like relationship that involved love and obedience as one.[90] Note, however, that Nicholson (1986) and others have criticized this understanding. They properly point out that this terminology also belongs to everyday life and is not unique to covenants. Further, Ackerman (2002) sees love in the treaty context as normally coming from the member of superior status in a relationship rather than inferior status. Lapsley (2003) concludes that an emotional component is essential to the understanding of love in Deuteronomy. Nevertheless, the importance of mutual commitment and loyalty in the context of love remains as a foundation of the relationship as understood in the Bible as well as the treaty. Likewise, the term for "servant," *'ebed*, describes one who owes exclusive loyalty to the overlord (Deut. 9:27). "To know someone," *yāda'*, is to recognize them as overlord (Deut. 7:9; 11:2) or as vassal (Deut. 13:3). The description of a "special people," *sĕgullâ*, describes a special relationship, not based on natural ties but on election. This could include a wife's relation to a husband, a king's relation to a deity, and a vassal's relationship to an overlord (Deut. 7:6).

The covenant that God made with Abram in Genesis 12 and repeated in the following chapters exemplifies a promissory covenant.[91] Abram acted faithfully toward God, but God made the covenant as a gracious act without any previous agreement. This covenant had no legal demands

89. See Knoppers (1996, 686).
90. See Deut. 6:5 and Moran (1963).
91. This occurs in the covenant with David in 2 Sam. 7. However, Eslinger (1994) disputes that this is an unconditional covenant, seeing it firmly embedded in the Sinai covenant.

on the part of Abram. It was a promise kept solely on the basis of God's word, a word given in grace and maintained in grace. For this reason, some have compared this covenant with grants of lands and privileges that kings gave to loyal supporters in the ancient world.[92] However, there is no standard form for such grants nor are the grants without conditions.[93] In nearly all cases where the full text of the grant is recorded (whether Hittite, Ugaritic, or Akkadian), there is either an implicit or often an explicit demand of the king for loyalty and specific acts of service. The same, of course, is true for both Abram and David. They and their successors were called to loyal faithfulness.[94]

Summary

This chapter has examined materials in and related to the Pentateuch. Building on the analysis of chapter 3 and particularly the section on "Religion History, Tradition History, and Orality," and the excursus on the Documentary Hypothesis, it was considered best to examine here the major streams of narrative and covenant literature, and in the subsequent chapter the priestly literature. Although these streams interweave and include materials not usually identified with them, this approach provides a review of many of the major religious emphases found in or relevant to the first five books of the Bible. Thus the narrative strands early on describe the great inclusiveness of the Table of Nations in Genesis 10 and continue this theme in the religion of the ancestors found in Genesis 12–50. The story shifts in Exodus to a battle for Israel's survival against Egypt and its deities, and then against Israel's own propensities to reject the warrior Yahweh from the southern desert in favor of the golden calf.

The covenant and Deuteronomic law witnessed to the adaptation and transformation of religious rites. This could include the significance of killing animals, now not only for vows associated with secular land grants but also for the covenant between God and Abraham in Genesis 15. The distinctive laws of worshiping Yahweh alone are preceded by Pharoah Akhenaten's worship of Aten in fourteenth-century Egypt. The prohibition of images of the deity reminds one of the absence of formed images in the Negev and Sinai. A seventh day Sabbath-like observance may be found at a temple in Sippar. However, in every case these antecedents and parallels have been altered and transformed in the biblical traditions

92. Cf. Weinfeld (1970; 1972b).
93. Cf. Knoppers (1996).
94. For Abram, cf., e.g., Gen. 12:1; 17:1; 22:1–19.

according to the theology of the writers and editors.[95] However, all are transformed in the Decalogue and the legal stipulations of the Book of the Covenant and in subsequent legal collections. These were summarized in the treaty-turned-covenant of Deuteronomy where the means by which the seriousness of a permanent relationship between Yahweh and Israel was defined by transforming this international medium of defining secular relationships. It remains to consider the significance of the priestly and cultic literature in the strands of the Pentateuch.

95. See pp. 91–92, 163–67, 197–202.

7

Priestly and Cultic Strands
of the Pentateuch

Creation

The role of Genesis 1:1–2:4a in the priestly strands of the Pentateuch is usually defined in light of its emphasis on the importance of the Sabbath as well as the distinction between the sky, waters, and dry ground for creation. These are considered of special interest to the priests, as for example, the discussion of clean and unclean animals below indicates. Genesis 1:2 presents God's spirit hovering over the waters of the deep and may reflect themes of the battle between the storm god and the sea, as described above in the section on the mythological texts at Mari and Ugarit. In Genesis 1, however, there is no explicit statement of this theme.[1] If anything, there is a reservation about affirming such myths. To the contrary, many find here an antipolytheistic religious polemic. For example, the absence of the words for "sun" and "moon" in the account of their creation may reflect a reluctance to name these deities (Gen. 1:14–18) who were worshiped in the ancient West Semitic world, and even in Palestine, as suggested by the place names Beth Shemesh (house/temple of the sun [deity]) and Jericho ([shrine of the] moon [deity]).[2] Further examples of such polemic may occur in the commands to "be fruitful and multiply," as applied to animals (1:22) and people (1:28). This can be understood as a direct assault on any attempt to ascribe reproductive power to a god or goddess (Baal or Asherah) insofar as the power to reproduce is explicitly given by Israel's God to creatures. They do not need to obtain it from other deities. They already possess it.[3]

Personal Names

The Name of God (Gen. 4:26)

Although Yahweh and Elohim are both used throughout Genesis as names of God, there has been much discussion asking by what name God was known to those who lived before the revelation of Exodus 6. This discussion revolves around the interpretation of Genesis 4:26.

The comment attached to Enosh in 4:26 describes his generation as a time of confessing the name of Yahweh in prayer. This raises a problem with Exodus 6:3 which the NIV translates, "I appeared to Abraham, to Isaac, and to Jacob as God Almighty [= El Shaddai], but by my name the LORD [= Yahweh] I did not make myself known to them." Does this contradict Genesis 4:26? This issue raises basic questions about the

---

1. See Tsumura (2005).

2. On this see also M. Smith (2001a, 38). Genesis 1 minimizes both the cosmic waters of v. 2 and the sea monsters as divine enemies (despite their prevalence as deities in surrounding cultures), and suppresses the divinity of the greater and lesser lights, the sun and the moon. Although the term "great light" for the sun appears in Ugaritic, in Gen. 1 these are not deities.

3. See Bird (1981, repr. in Hess and Tsumura [1994]).

religion of those who worshiped God before Moses. Several solutions have been proposed.[4]

For source critics Genesis 4:26 is assigned to the JE or the narrative source, while Exodus 6:3 is related to the P or priestly source. Using source criticism, it is possible to explain the origins of the two contradictory claims. The assumption is that JE is earlier and P updates the story of Moses so that the revelation of God's divine name occurs there. From P's perspective, all the occurrences in JE in Genesis are anachronistic. To those who are not convinced of the dating of these sources, there appears to be a contradiction in which P has retained uses of the divine name that are said to occur before the name was actually revealed.

Others understand that something special was made known in Exodus 6 that was not revealed earlier.[5] It is implicit in the name Yahweh, but not equal to that name. This could include the practice of worship itself, a special revelation of the deity, or his being made known in the events of the exodus and Sinai.[6] Warning (2001) has studied the occurrences of El Shaddai in Genesis and Exodus. The divine name occurs seven times and the seventh is in Exodus 6:3. He concludes that this is a summary and concluding statement that reviews the previous occurrences and now, with the revelation of God's name, anticipates a new revelation of God.

Some translate the second half of Exodus 6:3 as a question, "and did I not make myself known to them by my name Yahweh?" This is an example of affirmation by exclamatory negation and would resolve the issue.[7] But what is not made clear is how it fits into the context of Exodus 6.

Another view is that Yahweh's name was first revealed in Moses' day but then was retrojected back into the earlier periods by an author who discerned here and there a special manifestation of God's personal character.[8] This is the understanding of Moberly.[9] For him, Exodus 6:3 should be interpreted in a way that means that the name of Yahweh was unknown to the Genesis ancestors. El Shaddai was the name that God used, a name connected with divine promises of blessing and especially with promises of descendants.[10] Genesis often uses the generic name for God, Elohim, which is consistent with the open and inclusive religious

---

4. Hess (1992a), "Enosh."

5. Houtman (1993a, 101–2).

6. See Westermann (1984, 340–41) for the first option, Speiser (1964, 37–38) for the second, and Seitz (1998, 235–47) for the third option.

7. W. J. Martin (1955, 18–19); Driver (1973, 109).

8. Wenham (1980, 182–83, 188).

9. Moberly (1992a; 1992b).

10. Although the LXX and Vulgate translate Shaddai as "almighty" and the rabbinic literature understands the term as "who suffices," the best translation is to relate it to Akkadian *šadû*, "mountain," and translate it as El, the mountain one. This is better than "breast," which defies the masculine nature of El, and preferred to Hebrew *śādeh*, "field,"

perspective of the Genesis ancestors. Yahweh's name was written into the ancestral accounts as part of the theological reflection and appropriation of these accounts, especially those of Abraham in whose stories Yahweh appears most frequently.

In a careful linguistic analysis of the statements in Exodus 6:3, Garr (1992) has argued that El Shaddai is part of the revelation of God while Yahweh is expressed as the full revelation of the one who is God. God appears in Genesis as El Shaddai in his promises to the Genesis ancestors.[11] Of these, the promise of increase in number has already begun to be fulfilled (Gen. 47:27; Exod. 1:7) but that of land and a new relationship await fulfillment. Yahweh appears in Genesis 17 and 21. When God promises the covenant of a relationship in Genesis 17:7, he does so as El Shaddai and the verbal forms expressed unrealized situations. When this promise is remembered in Exodus 6:4, it is as Yahweh and the verbal forms describe a certain event, which will now be fulfilled (Exod. 6:7) through Yahweh. The verb "to be known" in Exodus 6:3 implies an exclusive covenant relationship. As God keeps his promises fully, he becomes known as Yahweh in the period of Moses.

From the standpoint of the history of Yahwism, it is important to note that Exodus 6:2–3 confirms that Yahweh originally revealed himself as El, the traditional name of the chief god of the West Semitic pantheon.[12] This was evident whether he was manifest as El Shaddai, El Elyon, or another El figure. The Middle Bronze Age (c. 2000–1550 BC) origins of the name Yahweh (see below) place the identification with El in this period, traditionally associated by some with the Genesis ancestors, when Yahweh was known by these El names.

In Exodus 3:14 God identifies his name as *'ehyeh 'ăšer 'ehyeh*, "I am who I am" or "I will be who I will be." This interpretation suggests that the name, Yahweh, was possibly a verbal form based on the *hwyh* root, "to be." In the hiphil or causative form, this means "to cause to be." As *yhwh* it appears to some as a third person imperfect of either the basic or the causative stem. It has been suggested that the name is a shortened form that includes God's other name, El. Frank Moore Cross identifies the original "sentence name" as (*el*) *ḏū yahwī ṣaba'ôt*, "El who creates the hosts."[13] Alternatively, Johannes de Moor (1990b, 234–47; 1997), on the basis of *Ya/la-aḥ-wi-il* and similar names from Mari and other Amorite sources of the early second millennium BC, suggests an original *yhw-'il*, "Let El be." De Moor wants to assign the name to an early ancestor of

---

for which the sibilants do not agree. The Shaddayin in the Deir 'Alla inscription are the "mountain ones" who meet on the mountain where El resides. See Day (2000, 32–34).

11. Gen. 17:1; 28:3–4; 35:11–12.
12. P. Miller (2000, 25).
13. Cross (1973, 71), followed by P. Miller (2000, 2).

Israel, but there is no evidence for this. Cross's reconstruction is speculative although it seems possible that the name should be understood as a causative form, because Aramaic causatives of *hyh* occur.[14] Further, the complement with El is not surprising and likely reflects an attempt to identify the chief god of the West Semitic pantheon with Israel's deity. However, Tropper (2001) has pointed out the difficulties of this analysis given the general absence of divine names based on causative verbal forms with the *y*-prefix and the impossibility of explaining the vowels used to vocalize this name. For Tropper the name had two variant forms that cannot be geographically defined in the preexilic period, *Yahu* and *Yahwa*. Tropper believes that the name is based on a duplicated stem, *wah-wah*, or something similar, whose original meaning has been lost.

No single explanation emerges as convincing. However, this statement of essential being in Exodus 3:14 forms the basis for understanding Yahweh as life and as the giver of life.[15]

Seth's Line (Gen. 5)

In its context Genesis 5[16] is preceded by the line of Cain in Genesis 4. In that line the general topics of culture and civilization are introduced into the human race. We should note that Cain's line ends with Lamech and his immediate offspring. It progresses no further. This contrasts with the line of Genesis 5 where the line will continue on with Noah and his descendants. This point is brought home forcibly by the prologue to Genesis 5 in 4:25–26. There the Cainite line is specifically brought to an end with the birth of Seth, not because he is meant as a substitute for Cain but because he is the substitute for Abel whose line Cain sought to interrupt and destroy. Cain's plot is now foiled and Seth provides new hope for humanity.[17] The names of this line and the notes associated with the name bearers reflect a spiritual dimension.

Thus Adam is tied most closely with this line. Indeed, the name Adam first appears in 4:25. Before this verse in Genesis, all occurrences of the Hebrew word *'ādām* should be translated by the common noun, "man," or, in the case of 1:26–27, the generic "humanity." Thus the name means "humanity." Indeed, Adam's "grandson" Enosh also car-

---

14. Day (2000, 14) notes that Exod. 3:14 assumes a qal form of the verb.

15. Johnston (2002, 39).

16. This discussion follows Hess (1993c).

17. While I would argue for the literary unity of each of these sections, see Wallace (1990) for an example of a scholar who also recognizes the numerous literary/theological connections of 5:1 with what precedes and what follows and attempts to explain it with a "Toledot of Adam" redactor who inserts notes here and there to unite the J and P sources.

ries a name with a synonymous meaning, "humanity." In a sense this is the confession that is made at the naming of Seth, whose name is related to the word for "substitute." Enosh becomes the new Adam, the new progenitor of the line of hope. Thus with two figures at the beginning of the line whose names mean "humanity," the text proceeds to emphasize what it sees as the direction where humanity should go. Also important to see in Genesis 4:26 is the way in which the line of Genesis 5 is prefaced with a time when people began to pray. Thus the expectation is enhanced that the line of Enosh is one of special spiritual significance.

The other names begin with Kenan, which is the name Cain plus a suffix. As Adam fathered Cain in Genesis 4, so the second Adam, Enosh, fathers a Cain in the line of Genesis 5. Kenan serves to relate the two genealogies and to prepare for the contrast that follows in the names of Seth's line.

Mahalalel can be translated "praising El" or "praise of El." Jared means "to descend" and, as is the custom in ancient Near Eastern names, may be a shortened form of a name that confesses God's act of descending to bring aid. We may compare God's descent to inspect the Tower of Babel in Genesis 11:5. The same verb is used there as appears in the name Jared. Enoch probably means something to do with introducing or initiating. However, the emphasis on this figure lies with his walk with God and with his ascent to heaven.

Methuselah, in contrast to the previous names, may suggest a figure with a pagan name. It may mean "devotee of Shalach," an underworld deity, or the second half of the name may be an epithet of God with a meaning such as a "missile." This is supported by the absence of Shalach as a divine name anywhere in the Near East. If so, it suggests the meaning of a devotee of God who protects the devotee like a weapon. Such would not be an unheard-of idea, especially in light of the many, early comparisons of God as a rock in the Bible.[18] In both cases the sense of security and protection of God would be preeminent.

For Lamech, we have no etymology. However, his prophecy, given when he named Noah, confessed his belief in Yahweh who cursed the ground. In this way he contrasts with the Lamech of Genesis 4 and is not to be understood as rebellious.[19] Also Lamech's lifespan of 777 years is significant, though exactly how may no longer be clear. We can only note that seven is a number of completion that in Genesis 1 is the number of the day given over to God. As in Genesis 4, so here the bearer of

18. Gen. 49:24; Deut. 32:4, 15, 18, 30, 31; 1 Sam. 2:2; 2 Sam. 22:32, 47; 23:3.
19. Contra Horowitz (1990, 28–29), who has to go through too many linguistic gymnastics to arrive at this, even if Lamech's hoped for blessing is not realized in Noah's viticulture.

the name Lamech forms a transition in the genealogy.[20] In Cain's line, it is a transition from a linear to a segmented genealogy with brothers and sisters. In Genesis 5 the transition is from the line of Seth to Noah and his line.[21]

Thus, with the possible exception of Methuselah, each figure, through the meaning of his name or through an associated comment, suggests an emphasis on the spiritual and in some cases possibly on one who can be identified later with the God of Israel. Like the names in Cain's line, these betray early origins. Before the Hellenistic period, the personal name Adam occurs in no clearly attested example later than the thirteenth century BC at Emar. Attested as early as the twenty-fourth century at Ebla, Adam forms part of a month name and occurs as a divine name. Elements such as the root behind Jared and the first vocable in Methuselah occur almost entirely in names of the second millennium BC but are not found in West Semitic personal names of the first millennium BC. The other elements used in these personal names occur in West Semitic names found in both the second and first millennia BC.[22] As with the genealogy of Cain, this line may best be dated in large part to the second millennium BC and Middle or Late Bronze Age (c. 1550–c. 1200 BC).

Shem's Line (Gen. 11)

There are two parts to Genesis 11. The first is the Tower of Babel narrative whose primary purpose is to demonstrate the inability of humanity to make a name for themselves through any efforts of their own. They cannot reach God through building a tower just as the race of Genesis 6:1–4 could not reach God through trying to produce bigger and longer-lived offspring. The attempt of the tower builders to assault heaven, and thereby to challenge God, is a violation of the divine will that is condemned in the Bible and in ancient Near Eastern literature.[23] However, this time the divine judgment is not a flood but a dispersal of the nations as described in Genesis 10. God will make a name for the one

20. Hess (1991b).

21. Marks (1995, 25) observes that, according to the ages in the Hebrew text, Noah is the firstborn of the line after Adam's death. Lamech sees in Noah a second Adam, and in Adam's death, an expected lifting of the curse. Marks (p. 29) suggests that Noah's name, which may mean "rest," is here interpreted as "comfort," which verb (*nḥm*) also means "repentance" (Gen. 6:6). Thus the text provides a choice of comfort or repentance.

22. See the issue of Cain's name and root, found here in the name Kenan, in the discussion on p. 143. See also Hess (1993c).

23. Greenspahn (1994) refers to the Gilgamesh Epic and to various Sumerian proverbs such as: "The tallest (man) cannot reach heaven. The widest man cannot cover the mountains."

whom he chooses, and that choice is found in the line of Shem, whose name in Hebrew is the word for "name." The concern, "lest we be scattered across the earth," describes a fear for the loss of identity.[24]

As 11:2 identifies the location of Babel, so locations form an important theme in the line of Shem. This is especially apparent from the names of Serug, Nahor, and Terah. All of these may be related to similarly sounding city names in the area around Harran, the home of Abram before he began his journey to Canaan. The names of Peleg and Eber may suggest migration from one place to another. The former is identified with the root for "division," and may associate the division of early groups of people with Peleg's group moving away. The consonants of Eber are identical with the Hebrew root "to cross over." The context locates Abram's family in northern Syria around Harran.

There is a second theme running through the names of Genesis 11, one already noted with the name of Shem. It is a theme of the relationship of this line to God or at least to spiritual matters. Shelah has the same name as the second element in the name Methuselah. Whether it refers to a deity or is a divine epithet, Shelah may reflect the paganism of Abram's forefathers, something specifically said of Laban (Gen. 31:53), and of Nahor and Terah (Josh. 24:2). The name Reu means "friend." It may be a shortened form of an expression such as "friend of God" or it also may suggest a friendship with a pagan deity. The name Abram itself also carries a possible double meaning to its name, either "[my] father is the deity Ram" or "[my] father is exalted." Even in the latter case, we cannot be certain if this name refers to God or to another deity.

24. It is true that this phrase implies a refusal to carry out 1:26–28, as Turner (1990, 32) notes, but this is hardly the main reason in the text for either the building of the tower or for the judgment of God. The matter of "making a name" has an interesting parallel in the Mesopotamian myth known as the Gilgamesh Epic (Machinist [1986, 194]), which is associated with Gen. 1–11 for other reasons, as already noted. In the story itself Gilgamesh seeks to make a name by finding immortality, which he fails to do. In the prologue and epilogue to the story, Machinist observes that his "name" is made through the city wall, which the reader is invited to admire (though this itself may point to the foundation text that is normally placed underneath the wall of a new structure). Both immortality and the construction of a large structure suggest parallels with the Tower of Babel. Walton (1995) relates the tower to the Mesopotamian ziggurat and argues that the people did not sin by uniting rather than "scattering." Instead, they built a ziggurat as a ladder to heaven and thereby attempted to create their gods in human form, as deities who require such a ladder. Walton argues for a historical context for the story of the tower in the fourth millennium BC, as a failed prototype of later urbanization in the form of the third-millennium "temple cities." At the beginning of the fourth millennium, the southern Mesopotamian plain experienced a huge population increase. Its main city was at Eridu. This was followed by a dispersion of peoples from this area to other parts of the ancient Near East. Walton follows Kramer (1968) in relating the Sumerian myth of Enmerkar and the Lord of Aratta to this event. In the account the god of Eridu changes the speech of the people.

Genesis 11 thus sets the stage for the appearance of Abram, whose ancestry locates him in northern Syria and whose ancestors appear as figures worshiping different deities. Both locale and belief would change with the calling of God and Abram's response in faith. The historical roots of these names may be traced back to the early second millennium BC insofar as the personal names may be identified with places in northern Mesopotamia.

Summary of the Personal Names in Genesis 1–11

The names that are useful for analysis in terms of their etymology suggest that these genealogies, at least in part, are connected with earliest Israel's traditions. In general, the lists are best analyzed as originating in the Bronze Age of the second millennium BC in a West Semitic context.[25] One may go further and suggest a Middle Bronze origin in the Amorite region at the headwaters of the Euphrates River. If so then these lists remember a time when people worshiped various deities, including those of the underworld. The lists were at some time incorporated into their present place in Israel's sacred literature, at which point the divine elements were forgotten, muted, or changed so that, at least in terms of Abram's line in Genesis 5 and 11, there remained no divine name that could not be either an epithet, as in Methuselah, or a generic designation for "god," as for example 'ēl in Mahalalel.

Sacrifice

Israelite religion is probably considered more often in the context of sacrifice than of any other concept. The priestly and cultic literature of the Pentateuch abounds with examples of and regulations regarding sacrifice. Although some see the first biblical account of sacrifice in the provision of animal skins (Gen. 3:21) that God makes for Adam and Eve, its appearance with Cain and Abel seems actually to be the first example of an offering that is initiated by the people who make it and of the offering as freely given to God.

Some of the issues raised here may serve as an introduction to the more general topic of sacrifice in ancient Israel. For instance, the biblical text gives no explicit reason for God's preference for Abel's offering. This

25. For a complete analysis of all the personal names in Gen. 1–11 (except those of Abram's generation) see Hess (1993c). On the question of the name Cain and other occurrences of that root in Tubal-Cain and Kenan, see the discussion on p. 143.

has given rise to speculation concerning this sacrifice and the biblical understanding of sacrifice in general.[26] Some, focusing on the different occupations of the two, have found a distinction in the types of offerings given by Cain and Abel.[27] This involves the assumption that Cain represents settled farmers while Abel symbolizes the nomadic herders. Since there is no internal textual reason to suggest this was the purpose of Genesis 4, it should not be emphasized.

A second alternative makes the lack of a specific mention in the text the point of the argument. Cain and Abel were judged by divine decision that can neither be questioned nor understood.[28] This conclusion seems more a counsel of desperation than a model of exegesis. Van Wolde (1991, 29) argues that the looking and not looking of Yahweh indicates nothing about preference. But this is unlikely given the consistent usage of this biblical expression. When God "looks" at something it always suggests evaluation, usually favor (when disapproval, it is explicit).

A related view argues that God is capricious and arbitrary.[29] He is an unpredictable figure in this story, one who makes mistakes and repents. However, this argument seems problematic. In this passage of Genesis 4, a capricious deity would not provide for any redress of Abel's murder. Perhaps the interpretation reflects more the search for an ethically ambiguous figure of deity.

Nor is it likely that what was brought has anything to do with the issue. Cain's tribute is described as a *minhâ*, "offering." The word refers both to a grain offering (Gen. 4:3) and to a meat offering (Gen. 4:4). Thus it is not clear that the intent is to build upon the cursed ground of Genesis 3:17 and to reject Cain's offering because it came from the ground.[30]

The text does make a distinction between Abel's offering "from the firstborn of his flock and their fat" and Cain's offering "from the fruit of the land."[31] In offering the firstborn, Abel's act parallels that of Israelite sacrifices in which the firstborn represents both that which belongs to God as well as the entirety of the flock. By giving the firstborn and the best of the animal (i.e., the fat), Abel is understood as having given everything to God.

26. Even Hebrews 11:4 does little more than observe the offering as demonstrative of faith. For a general discussion of sacrifice, see Gane (2004).

27. Cf. Gunkel (1902, 37) and Skinner (1930, 105).

28. Cf. von Rad (1972, 104) and Westermann (1984).

29. Cf. Hendel (1991), and earlier, Freud (1927; 1939; 1961) and my discussion of Freud's views in chapter 2.

30. Cf. Spina (1992).

31. Cf. Cassuto (1961a, 206–7); Sarna (1970, 29; 1989, 32); Waltke (1986); Wenham (1987, 103–4).

We now turn to consider sacrifice as a means of access to the larger cultic system as described in the "priestly" material of the Pentateuch. First, two major approaches to the sacrificial and cultic system will be examined: the origins approach and the structuralist approach. Then consideration will be given to the literary context of the cultic presentation. The ancient Near Eastern comparisons will also be considered, as well as what might be learned from them. As outlined in the biblical texts, the cultic system presents an ideal, as does much of the law in the Pentateuch. Although this is not necessarily identical to the actual religious practice of ancient Israel, the texts do provide a means of access into Israel's religious life. The ancient Near Eastern parallels discussed here, as well as those described in chapter 4 (especially the sections on Emar and Ugarit), suggest that many of the practices in these texts have a greater antiquity than was formerly thought.

The Origins Approach

This is the traditional method by which scholars divided the Pentateuchal texts into sources. Thus the Passover in Exodus 12 was understood as made up of the following literary sources: P 12:1–20, 28, 40–51; 13:1–2; J 12:21–23, 27b, 29–34; and 37–39; D 12:24–27a and 13:3–16; E 12:35–36.[32] Behind these were the oral sources of tradition history. In this case the Passover was thought to have arisen from various pre-Israelite Canaanite (or otherwise non-Israelite) feasts.

For example, Julius Wellhausen identified a spring agricultural festival (*maṣṣōt*) as the origin of the Feast of Unleavened Bread that immediately followed Passover in the biblical calendar. The Passover itself was not associated with the Feast of Unleavened Bread until about 621 BC, at the time of the Judean king Josiah's reform.[33] For Leonard Rost, the Passover was originally a primitive sacrificial ritual of nomads. They celebrated the rite of sacrificing a lamb to their god(s) before moving on to their arable summer pastures. Roland de Vaux understood the Passover as a springtime sacrifice of a young animal prior to migration to the summer pastures. Blood was smeared on the tent posts to ward off evil spirits. Although combined relatively late, these settled and nomadic rituals predated Israel and thus the exodus itself (Martin Noth). Therefore Brevard Childs saw the Passover as pre-Israelite and only later attached to the exodus from Egypt.

This critical interpretation of the origin and development of the Passover was not without its own criticism. John Van Seters argued

32. According to Childs (1974, 184–95).
33. Cf. Wellhausen (1973). My discussion is a summary of Childs (1974, 184–95).

that the theories are speculative, lacking any evidence.[34] Supporting this, Alexander (1995) observes that wherever the Passover is mentioned in the Pentateuch, the Feast of Unleavened Bread also occurs.[35] Thus there is no literary basis for dividing the two based on supposed origins.

The discovery and study of the *zukru* festival at thirteenth-century BC Emar has shed light on the discussion. The *zukru* demonstrates that there were special festivals in the spring among West Semitic groups such as the population at Emar.[36] The *zukru* is derived from the same verbal root (*zkr*, "to remember, invoke") as that found in the biblical description of Passover in Exodus 12:14 and Leviticus 23:24. The *zukru* began on the fifteenth day of the first month and lasted seven days, just like the Passover and the Feast of Unleavened Bread. Twilight was a critical time, a lamb was roasted, and distinctive bread and herbs were eaten—just like the Passover. In this early period this was a festival of a settled people that combined the major elements of the Passover and the Feast of Unleavened Bread. Thus the interpretations of the Passover as a late combination of a nomadic festival where the meat was consumed, and of an agricultural festival where bread was eaten, have no warrant. They were both joined from the beginning and both festivals were focused on the community's great god (Dagan or Yahweh).[37]

The Structuralist Approach

A structuralist approach to sacrifice examines the significance of the act in the context of the network of contemporary symbols and understandings arising from the culture itself. In contrast to an origins approach, it considers the primary interpretation of meaning to derive from the contemporary society's usage of sacrifice within its cult, rather than

34. Cf. Van Seters (1983b).

35. This includes traditional J texts such as Exod. 34:25. He also notes that the Passover is linked with the Israelite exodus wherever it is mentioned in the Pentateuch. The debate continues. Bernard Levinson (1997) has argued that the Passover and *maṣṣōt* were two different festivals that were joined by Josiah. He centralized the Passover in the Jerusalem temple and made the *maṣṣōt* into a celebration in the homes. This is the background of Deut. 16:1–17. However, McConville (2000) has argued that Levinson's terminological distinctions cannot be sustained and that his assumption about an original division between Passover and *maṣṣōt* is not required. For McConville, Deuteronomy envisions both appearance at the central sanctuary and celebration throughout the land for these festivals. This latter serves to further limit the power of the monarchy. In response, Levinson (2000) notes that McConville does not place his "anti-monarchy posture" in a historical context.

36. See further on the discussion of Emar in chapter 4 (p. 112).

37. See Fleming (1999a; 1999c; 2000b); Hess (2004b).

from a hypothetical origin and evolution. The work of Mary Douglas is representative of this approach.[38]

Before examining sacrifice in this context it is important to consider the context of the sacred and the profane in which sacrifice takes place. The construction of the tabernacle (Exod. 25–30, 35–40), the institution of sacrifices (Lev. 1–7), the consecration of the priests (Lev. 8–10), and the great day for the eradication of impurity from the nation of Israel (Lev. 16) are all intertwined with concerns about the holiness of the people as a community before God (Exod. 24, 31–34; Lev. 11–15; 17–26). Taken together the results seem to suggest that spiritual life occurred in three concentric spheres. At the center were the priests, who had the most direct contact with God and his holiness.[39] Thus their sins required the most valuable of animal sacrifices to achieve atonement. At the next outer level were the Israelites. Although designated at one point as a nation of priests (Exod. 19:6), their daily lives were devoted to pursuits other than those of the anointed priests. Finally, at the outer fringe there were the other nations of the world. These were separate from Israel and had no sacrifice prescribed for them within the cult.

This approach of three concentric circles may also be applied to space. At the center of the world, from a sacred standpoint, was the tabernacle and the most holy place within it. Here God's presence was made manifest in a special way and the divine life resided in all its power. No one could enter the most holy place and live, except for the high priest. Even for him it was required and allowed only once a year. Around the tabernacle was the camp of Israel. Here the community could dwell. Nevertheless, God's life and presence, while not as powerfully holy as in the tabernacle, remained evident. Symbols of death, such as a corpse or those afflicted by psoriasis,[40] could not remain in the camp. Corpse contamination was a significant issue for it meant contact with the world of death. Numbers 19 describes a purification offering in a ritual to cleanse someone who has come into contact with a dead body. This required a specially prepared and sacrificed red heifer, whose ashes had to be used, along with washings on the third and seventh days.[41]

38. Douglas (1966; 1993; 1999); Sawyer (1996).

39. Lev. 4:13–21 requires that a young bull be brought as an offering. This offering is identical for a purification offering that involves the sin of the whole nation (v. 13) and is contrasted with a single goat or lamb for the purification offering of a leader (v. 22) or of the average citizen (4:27, 32).

40. "Leprosy" as used in most translations of the Bible is probably not an accurate translation for this skin disease, i.e., as Hansen's disease. The point here is that the appearance of the skin, white and flaking, resembled death. See Browne (1986).

41. See Levine (1993b, 457–79); Milgrom (1990, 157–63); Lewis (2002, 182). The latter also notes Pitard's (2002, 150–51) discussion of Ugarit and the fact that burials there took place directly beneath houses, so that there was apparently no issue with corpse

Beyond the camp of Israel was the wilderness. This remained at the opposite pole from the tabernacle. It was a place of death and chaos whereas the tabernacle symbolized order and life. Thus on the Day of Atonement the high priest confessed the sins of Israel on the head of a goat that was sent out of the camp and into the wilderness. This "scapegoat" removed the uncleanness that defiled the camp and the tabernacle and that prevented God's full presence and life from abiding with Israel. The goat took the uncleanness to a place of death.[42]

Finally, the concentric circles of sanctity also apply to the animal world, just as they do to people. At the center are the sacrificial animals. They are the ones most like Israel, taken from the nation's flocks and herds. They are limited to a few species, often with specifications regarding gender, age, and wholeness. The next outer circle contains the clean animals. These include those animals that can be eaten by the Israelites and thus they have a role to play within the community. The final group is the unclean animals. These constitute the majority of animals. They represent those with whom Israel is to have no part. They can neither be eaten nor used for any other purpose.

These three sets of the three concentric circles share many features. In a given set, each circle is analogous to its matching circles in the other sets. Thus the priests work in the tabernacle and sacrifice animals there. The Israelites live in the camp and eat clean animals there. The nations live outside Israel's community and eat unclean animals. In all three sets the inner circle is a subset of the middle group, while the outer circle is completely separate. The priests are part of the community of Israel but Israel is separate from the nations. The tabernacle is within the camp of Israel, but there is a clear boundary between the camp and the rest of the world. The sacrificial animals are also clean animals, but the unclean animals are distinct from them.

The subject of animal sacrifice raises the question of the significance of the slaughter of animals. While this is expounded in Leviticus 17 and elsewhere,[43] these biblical discussions do not consider the symbolic significance of animal sacrifice. A possible understanding is to find in the death of the animal a transition from the world of impotent mortals to the world of omnipotent deity.[44] Thus the killing and burning of the

---

contamination in this earlier West Semitic society—unlike Israel. The same sort of burial procedures may have been used at Pella. See discussion of these sites in chapter 4.

42. Johnston (2002, 44–45) suggests that in Israel this is the most comprehensive reason for the dead creating uncleanness. He also lists: the widely held association of death and uncleanness in neighboring cultures; the need to combat the cult of the dead; and the biblical connection between sin and death, from Gen. 2:16–17 onward.

43. See Hess (forthcoming b).

44. Budd (1989), following the anthropologist Edmund Leach.

animals provides a physical representation of an actual connection between the sacrificer who is mortal and the divine realm where there is no death. The animal's death enables this crossing and contact between the two worlds. While this is a possible understanding, it is important to observe that it is nowhere so described in the Bible. Instead, the repeated emphasis is on how God receives the sacrifice as a pleasing aroma.[45]

The "pleasing aroma" that the sacrifice gives to God is the common response for divine acceptance of the offering.[46] It occurs forty-three times in the Bible, primarily in Exodus, Leviticus, Numbers, and Ezekiel (and once in Gen. 8:21). It is found only in sacrificial contexts or imagery. Other gods can also receive a pleasing aroma (Ezek. 6:13; 16:19; 20:28). Occasionally it designates something other than a sacrifice. Thus the return of Israel after their deportation to other nations is a pleasing aroma (Ezek. 20:41). The aroma is not to be understood as some sort of bribe toward God. It is not that the God of Israel depends on mortals for food or that God is enticed by such sacrifices to do the bidding of the offerers. In fact, Leviticus 26:31 states that no amount of "pleasing aroma" can substitute for faithfulness nor can it prevent God's judgment for disobedience to his covenant.[47] Instead, the term is best understood as a means of signifying the offerer's desire for God's gracious acceptance of the sacrifice and its fulfillment of the purpose for which it was given.

The atoning significance of animal sacrifice reached its high point on the Day of Atonement in Leviticus 16. And it occurred within the context of two poles of meaning: disorder and nothingness outside the camp and structure and full life within the community. Two goats were chosen and were distinguished by lots.[48] As noted above, the high priest[49] sent one

45. Gen. 8:21; Exod. 29:18, 25, 41; Lev. 2:12; 3:16; 8:21, 28; 23:13; 26:31, etc.

46. See Hess (forthcoming b) comment on Lev. 1:9.

47. Cf. Ps. 50:8–15.

48. The lots here and elsewhere in the Bible in the context of the priests represent an approved means of identifying the will of God. They are most likely related to the Urim and Thummim, which are mentioned five times in the Bible: Exod. 28:30; Lev. 8:8; Deut. 33:8; Ezra 2:63; and Neh. 7:65. The Levites were to guard these instruments that were used only by priests. Urim may derive from the Hebrew word for "light," 'ûr. If so, it could signify a gem that reflects light in various ways to indicate different answers. Thummim, as vocalized, has no known etymology. The Talmud (b. Yoma 73b) related it to "perfection, faultless," using the Hebrew root tmm. If so, this might indicate a "yes" or "no" answer, i.e., where "perfect" means "yes." Van Dam (1997, 217–32) suggests that the Urim and Thummim were a single gem whose miraculous light provided confirmation to the priest's words. However, this is speculative and doesn't take into account that they were objects that could be thrown down according to 1 Sam. 14:43. See my comment on Lev. 8:8 (Hess, forthcoming b). For the comparison between the Urim and Thummim and some dice found in the cultic area of Iron Age Dan, see chapter 10, p. 302n18.

49. For the much-discussed matters of the priestly line(s), see the following section on "Priests." For the earliest period of Israel's history and the tradition of Moses in the

goat outside the community to carry the sins and defilement away from Israel and its God. The other goat was sacrificed at the altar within the camp. The blood is then sprinkled on a box, called the place of atonement and located at the most holy place in the tabernacle, in order to gain atonement or reconciliation and thereby to allow the community to return to wholeness.[50]

The first seven chapters of Leviticus list a variety of approved Israelite sacrifices, including both grain and meat sacrifices.[51] Leviticus 1 describes the "burnt offering" ('ōlâ), which is entirely consumed by the fire, so that no edible parts remain. This is one of the oldest and most ubiquitous of sacrifices.[52] It can render atonement (Lev. 1:4) by substituting the life of the animal for the sinner, however it seems primarily to

---

Pentateuch, there arises the question of Moses as a religious leader of authority. Dozeman (2000) argues that Exod. 34:29–35 is a story about two masks of Moses: his mask of "concretion" in the form of a shining face that demonstrates his cultic authority and separates him from the people by representing God's presence; and his veil (hood or strips of cloth), which is a mask of concealment that demonstrates his social and judicial authority over Israel. Moses is cultic mediator in Exod. 34:34 and Num. 7:89. The latter anticipates the transfer of this authority to the priests (Num. 8:1–4) and Levites (8:5–26) who assume the social responsibility of Mosaic authority. By Num. 7:89 the veils and the authority of Moses are transferred to the tabernacle, which is veiled (Exod. 26:31–35; 40:3, 20–21). During this period the glory of the Lord descends from Mount Sinai (Exod. 24:15–18) to the tabernacle (Exod. 40:34–38) and to the altar (Lev. 9:23–24).

50. Hendel (1989) provides another example of an anthropological approach as he applies it to the Passover lamb preparation. The roasting of the meat implies identification with the way it is prepared in Egypt, not in Israel. Hendel further argues that other Israelite sacrifices have the meat burned (for dedication to Yahweh) or boiled (for Israelite consumption). The roasting of the lamb recalls the time in Egypt and of what it meant to be there. The splashing of blood on the doorpost, like that on the altar in other sacrifices, recalls the covenant bond between the participants and God. However, as Fleming (1999a, 27) notes, a ewe is roasted at an Emar festival. It is therefore hard to see how roasting is alien to a West Semitic people like Israel. Further, the means by which the sacrificial meat was to be prepared for priestly or other consumption is not specified. Boiling occurs in the context of the sons of Eli in 1 Sam. 2:13–15, with the Nazirite law of Num. 6:19, and in the Passover of 2 Chron. 25:13. The latter would appear to run directly contrary to the argument of Hendel regarding the preparation of the Passover sacrifice. For Williamson (2005) Isa. 6:1–4 suggests broader temple access.

51. See Jenson (1992; 1995). From a different perspective, Hendel (1989) examines the "pilgrimmage [sic] model" of V. Turner, who sees participants moving through three stages in a pilgrimage: separation, marginalization, and reaggregation. Thus the Israelites escape from Egypt, they encounter Yahweh at Sinai, and then return to their ancestral homeland, the promised land. This symbolizes the transformation of the people from slaves to freed possessors of their land. It suggests a ritual that could be reenacted at any shrine. In such a rite social divisions are transcended and the people become a united identity, with a common purpose.

52. See the discussion of this sacrifice in the Ugaritic cultic literature in chapter 4, p. 104.

represent a gift to God,[53] a complete dedication. Chapter 4 describes a second offering of expiation or forgiveness. There the term "purification offering" (*ḥaṭṭā't*) may be preferred to the term "sin offering," because it seems to deal primarily with impurities and because the particular stem (*piel*) of this root implies removal of sin and impurity (Lev. 4:1–5:13). The purpose of this offering is directly related to atonement and seeks to restore fellowship with God. Associated with the purification offering is the "reparation offering" (*'āšām*), sometimes called the "guilt offering." This serves as a repayment of debt. The "fellowship offering" (*šĕlāmîm*, sometimes called a "peace offering") of Leviticus 3:1–5 includes a provision in which some of the meat is returned to the offerers. It thus can function as a communion or fellowship meal before God.[54]

Commenting on the three expiatory offerings (burnt, purification, and reparation offerings), Wenham (1979, 111) writes:

> The sacrificial system therefore presents different models or analogies to describe the effects of sin and the way of remedying them. The burnt offering uses a personal picture: of man the guilty sinner who deserves to die for his sin and of the animal dying in his place. God accepts the animal as a ransom for man. The sin [purification] offering uses a medical model: sin makes the world so dirty that God can no longer dwell there. The blood of the animal disinfects the sanctuary in order that God may continue to be present with his people. The reparation offering presents a commercial picture of sin. Sin is a debt which man incurs against God. The debt is paid through the offered animal.

The animal sacrifices required specific types of animals as detailed in their description in Leviticus 1–7. A few chapters later, in Leviticus 11 (cf. Deut. 14), the clean and unclean animals are defined. Genesis 1 suggests that the Israelite worldview understands three parts to the world: the sky, the sea, and the earth. The locomotion of animals appropriate to each sphere helps to determine whether they are clean. In general, a species whose locomotion is appropriate to that part of the world is clean. Thus birds that fly with wings, fish that swim with scales, and animals that walk with legs and hooves are clean. However, animals that do not have such characteristics of locomotion—and especially those that move back and forth between the spheres of sky, water, and land—are understood

53. The worshipers, by placing their hands on the offering, represent themselves in the victim and thus they dedicate themselves entirely to God (Wenham [1995, 79–83]). Jenson (1995) believes that it was only later that this offering became associated with atonement (Lev. 1:4; 16:24). See further, Milgrom (1991, 1042).

54. Cf. 1 Sam. 1:3–5; Wenham (1995, 84). Cf. A. Marx (2005) for sacrifice as divine life and fellowship. Cf. Modéus (2005) for the fellowship offering as a temple/cultic sacrifice in general.

as unclean. Thus lizards that move between the water and the land and ostriches who don't fly are unclean.[55] However, this does not explain all the clean/unclean distinctions. Another distinction considers carnivores that are unclean because they eat blood and therefore violate a universal prohibition.[56] There may also be a sense of wholeness and balance in animals, just as in the priesthood (Lev. 21:18–24) and in matters of social justice and dealings with one's neighbors (Lev. 24:19–20). So also sacrificial animals that have any abnormalities are considered unworthy (Lev. 22:20, 22–25).[57] The result of the exclusion of large groups of animals as unclean places large numbers of species off limits to Israel and thereby protects these animals.[58]

In ancient Israelite law the "clean" land animals, the ones that were permitted for eating and sacrifice, included the ox, the sheep, and the goat. These animals had the longest history of domestic association with the early Israelites, going back to their earliest known period, which they remembered as a time where their ancestors were pastoral nomads (Deut. 26:5). The pig, an animal normally kept by settled (nonnomadic) peoples, appeared relatively late in Israelite domestic experience and was therefore never included among the "clean" animals. The horse and the camel also were relatively late entrants in the Israelite domesticated animal scene. We may apply somewhat the same logic to the Hittite animal world. Animals such as the ox, the sheep, and the pig were kept by the Hittites and their ancestors long before the horse and mule were

55. Cf. Douglas (1966).

56. Cf. Gen. 9:4–6; Lev. 17:14; Douglas (1993).

57. Douglas (1993) connects justice and righteousness with not having too little or too much. Similar terms are used in Lev. 19:35–36 to describe equal and unequal weights and measures. Douglas suggests that some animals are forbidden because they symbolize injustice and unrighteousness, whether through their predatory nature or through their absence of right proportions or senses. Gnuse (1995) criticized this study as hypothetical and lacking in documentation for the fields in which Douglas works. However, it remains a useful heuristic model.

58. On comparable ideas of clean and unclean animals among the Hittites, see Hoffner (1997, 224). Douglas (1999) argues that the rules of Lev. 11 regarding unclean land animals actually protect these animals from being killed by Israelites and used for any purposes, whether food or clothing or anything else. The concept of uncleanness is therefore not that of disgust but closer to that of honor and shame in the Middle Ages. Killing and eating animals is only to be done on consecrated ground and with a specific group of animals that are domesticated as part of Israel's community. In addition, Houston (1993) suggests that originally meat could be eaten only after sacrifice to a god. Therefore, dogs, pigs, some scavenger birds, and other creatures that were not sacrificed to gods were considered unclean. The priestly writers absolutized this distinction and made it a mark of dedication to Yahweh. Carmichael (1995) hypothesizes that the forbidden mixtures in Deut. 22 and Lev. 19 are metaphors about intermarriages with foreigners. These theories are possible but the absence of explicit statements demonstrating their veracity means they must remain in the realm of conjecture.

introduced. Corresponding categories of sacrifice and clean versus unclean animals applied there as in Israel. At eighteenth-century BC Mari there is also evidence of the distinction between clean and unclean animals. In Mari treaties, puppies, goats, and young bulls or calves were unacceptable for sacrifices in confirming the treaties. Only the foal of a she-ass could be used.[59] Thus the animals sacrificed were those closest to Israel, most like them, and most valued by them. This may imply a substitutionary role for these sacrifices, in some sense taking the place of the Israelites themselves.

In light of the discussion on holiness, the connection between holiness and wholeness should be noted. The description of the tabernacle in Exodus 25–30 and 35–40 suggests a structure that is complete and without flaw. It must be so as a place for the holy God to meet with his people for reconciliation and for fellowship. This correspondence in holiness with the tabernacle is such that its wholeness and holiness anticipates a similar view of the human body.[60] Thus Leviticus 11–15 describes other Israelite bodies (animal but mainly human) and the issues of wholeness and holiness. The human body must also be whole in order to draw near to God in his holiness. Not only does this mean there can be no deformity, but there also must be a full integrity so that anything that compromises integrity, especially as it relates to life in the form of menstruation or loss of semen, can render one unclean. The same is true of any symbol of death, such as psoriasis of the skin. This appearance of death cannot enter the presence of God. In this sense the body symbolizes the tabernacle and the holy place where God and the person meet.[61]

Literary Context[62]

In Leviticus 1–9, the sacrifices are outlined three times, and each time in a different sequence. Anson Rainey has provided an explanation for these differences.[63] Leviticus 1:1–6:7 [Heb. 1:1–5:26] follows a

59. Cf. Malamat (1995). See further in chapter 4, p. 88.

60. The priestly anointing of Lev. 8–9 follows the details about the construction of the tabernacle and the institution of sacrifices there, because as the tabernacle is the holy center of Israel so the high priest is the holy center of Israel. He represents the nation.

61. Cf. the New Testament application of this principle in 1 Pet. 2:4–12 where Christians are built into a holy house (temple) in which the priest Christ is the chief cornerstone.

62. From a broader literary perspective than that discussed here, the whole book of Leviticus has been analyzed as a ring structure by Douglas (1993). She discerns a large chiasm through the book. There is a turning point at chapter 19, where emphasis is on equity between people. There as well is the command in 19:18, to love your neighbor as yourself.

63. Cf. Rainey (1970), building on the prescriptive/descriptive distinction of Levine (1963; 1965).

didactic order. Those producing a pleasing odor are grouped together in the first three chapters; they are the burnt offering, the grain offering, and the fellowship offering. There follows those sacrifices that concern only expiation; they are the purification offering for ritual sins and the reparation offering for social sins of such matters as fraud as well as for related sins against God. This sequence might be used for those learning the sacrifices in terms of the function(s) of each.

The second sequence is an administrative one. Leviticus 6:8–7:38 [Heb. 6:1–7:38] follows an order according to the recipients of offerings. God alone receives the burnt offering, which appears first. The cereal, purification, and reparation offerings have as their recipients both God and the priests. The last offering described is the fellowship offering. Here the division is three ways according to the recipients: God; God and priests; God, priests, and offerers. In addition, the frequency of the offerings may be considered as part of this last order. The burnt offerings are the most frequent type of offering made. They appear first.

The third and final sequence appears in Leviticus 8–9, where the priests are ordained. This is the procedural order in which the sacrifices are used for specific purposes. The purification offering occurs first and serves to remove sin and its effects from the offerer. This is a necessary prerequisite for any and all offerings that follow. The burnt offering comes next. As noted, it represents the dedication of the offerer wholly to God, setting this one apart in consecration to God. Finally, the fellowship offering celebrates the ongoing and growing relationship to God. This order recurs for other purposes in Leviticus 14–15; 2 Chronicles 29:20–36; and Ezekiel 43:18–27.[64]

Ancient Near Eastern Context

One of the reasons that lay behind the decision of nineteenth-century source criticism to date the priestly source late in the Old Testament history, as late as the postexilic period, was the complexity of the rituals described in Leviticus and elsewhere. It was thought that such complexity reflected an evolutionary development that should place it late in Israel's history. However, the discovery of many ritual texts from Egypt, Ugarit, the Hittite empire, and other ancient Near Eastern sources all demonstrated a far greater complexity of sacrificial, festival, and ritual

64. As a basic understanding of how people relate to God, it forms the background for the New Testament teaching of salvation and the Christian life as found in Romans, for example. Thus the Christian first receives forgiveness of sins as in the purification offering. Then there is the dedication of one's life to God in Christ as in the burnt offering. Finally, the Christian walks in fellowship with his or her Savior as in the fellowship offering.

activities in the Bronze Age of the second millennium BC than that re-corded in the Hebrew Bible. No doubt this in part is due to the multitude of deities worshiped in these cultures. In fact, in West Semitic cultures there seems to be a larger number of deities worshiped in the second millennium BC than in the first. This suggests that the earlier cultures contained the more complex rituals. Thus if the dating of the priestly rituals in the biblical text is related to their complexity, those texts should be assigned to an earlier date rather than a later one.

In terms of proximity to the biblical rituals, thirteenth-century BC Ugarit's sacrificial texts contain many examples of terminology similar to that found in the biblical texts. The burnt offering appears at Ugarit as 'lh (Hebrew 'ōlâ) while the fellowship offering is cognate with the Ugaritic šlm (Hebrew šĕlāmîm).[65] However, the use of the sacrifices seems to have been different, reflecting a different culture. At Ugarit the burnt offering may have been used to attract the deity to the temple while the "fellowship offering" functioned as a gift of greeting.[66] Other offerings cognate to Hebrew include Ugaritic ḏbḥ (Hebrew zebaḥ), "sacrifice," Ugaritic šnpt (Hebrew tĕnûpâ), "elevation offering," and Ugaritic trm(m)t (Hebrew tĕrûmâ), another "elevation offering."[67]

Baruch Levine (2002) has commented on the modes of sacrifice found in the Bible and in the ancient Near East. There is the presentation and display before the deity. This could involve the presentation in a courtyard outside the temple itself. It could also involve the removal of the offer-ing to be eaten by the priests. There is also the mode of the sacrifice as prepared food to be received and consumed by the deity. Finally, there is the mode of the offering on the altar itself. This altar offering was burnt before God in Israel as in other cultures.

As already noted, Ugaritic ritual texts do refer to moral and religious guilt and the possibility of sacrifice to achieve expiation from sin.[68] In the Hittite culture the use of substitution was a cultic principle. Thus Hittite rituals could transfer evil. There is also evidence in the Hittite texts of allowances to the poor for a reduction in the cost of the offering.

The reader is referred to additional ancient Near Eastern comparisons, especially those from Mari and Emar in addition to Ugarit, as already

65. Cf. Levine (1993a); del Olmo Lete (1995, 44); Kitchen (2003, 405).

66. Cf. Levine (1993a). Selman (1995) notes that neither the Mesopotamian nor Ugaritic rituals had as their stated purpose fellowship with the deities nor was there an equivalent to the Passover. He (p. 101) also maintains that there is no parallel to the concern for atonement. However, these views must all be questioned. See the discussion of sacrificial text on p. 106 and the next paragraph here.

67. Cf. Day (1994, 52) and del Olmo Lete (1995, 45). For these last two offerings as both elevation offerings, see Milgrom (1991).

68. See p. 106 on the theological significance of the rituals at Ugarit. Cf. de Moor and Sanders (1991, 284–87).

outlined in the above discussion of sacrifice and in the appropriate sections of chapter 4.

Conclusion

Hebrew sacrifice, like sacrifice in other religious traditions, is best understood by using a comparative model rather than an evolutionary one. Sacrifice and cult do not develop this way nor is their intepretation correctly understood with such a method. The structuralist model is a better one but there are limitations to its approach. By its nature, such a systemic model cannot easily be tested nor is it subject to falsification. Also, it tends to ignore matters of sin and guilt.

It is important to keep in mind the physical nature of the animal sacrifices. In our culture the blood-filled nature of animal slaughter is hidden and not experienced by most of us. In contrast, everyone who participated in the sacrifices in Israel and the surrounding nations lived with its raw physical aspects on a regular basis.[69]

Finally, there is the fundamental nature of biblical sacrifice: that which is best is freely offered to God in expression of sorrow for sin or joy for blessing. The most valuable of all created things, life as represented in the blood, is alone sufficient payment for the seriousness of sin. The sacrificed life of an animal is alone worthy of dining with God in joy for divine blessing.[70]

69. Cf. the following translation of a fragment of a sheep sacrifice from the early second millennium BC (the Old Babylonian period; Foxvog [1989, 169], following the Sumerian):

Fell the sheep! Cut off the head of the sheep! Let the blood vessels (of the neck) drip! The sheep—the leg blood should be done. The sheep—the blood vessels should be done. Roast the hooves (!) and the tail! Pull out the shoulder and rib cuts! Roast the shoulder cut! Place it on the table! Wash the large omentum in water! Arrange it on the table! Inspect their intestines! Pull out the intestines! Separate out the intestines! Pull out the connective tissue (?)! Clear the feces from the colon and wash it in water! Inspect the liver (?)! Pull out the ligament(s) of the heart(?)! Cut up the flesh! Cut up the flesh! [the remainder is broken]

Although this is not a description of an Israelite sacrifice, it could be (with the exception of the omen inspection). It is one of the few such descriptions preserved for us that depicts the killing and dismemberment of a sacrificial animal.

70. In Judaism and Christianity this understanding of sacrifice remained. For example, fasting was not a confession that God hated food or that food was evil. Rather, it gratefully acknowledged the value of food but set it aside on the Day of Atonement (this is the historically attested understanding of the expression "to deny yourselves" in Lev. 16:31). This was something done before God in recognition that sacrifice of one's food could symbolize the earnestness of sorrow for sin by foregoing that which was good and delightful for a person. The symbolic nature of ritual is emphasized by David P. Wright (1994, 402–3). He notes that it is an attempt to control areas of reality that appear no

Priests

In terms of sacrifices, the role of priests, especially the high priest, is described in the section above. As an "office," priesthood in the Pentateuch and the Old Testament may be briefly summarized here. The first priest mentioned in the Bible is Melchizedek, a figure who is not Israelite and who appears in a stylistically unique text among the Abraham narratives, in Genesis 14:18–20. His role there was to bless Abram by El-Elyon, "god/El most high," and to provide the victor in battle with bread and wine. If Salem is associated with Jerusalem then Melchizedek may foreshadow the Jerusalem priesthood. However, his separation from Abram's offspring and especially those of Aaron and the Levites also anticipates the possible incursion into the priesthood of Aaron by the descendants of Moses or even those of a pre-Israelite priesthood. The latter usually refers to the Jebusite priesthood in Jerusalem.

Before the covenant of the law at Mount Sinai and the subsequent installation of priests (Lev. 8–9), Noah, Abram, and the successive leaders of his family built altars, made sacrifices, and functioned in the role of priests.[71] In Leviticus, in addition to presiding over the sacrifices, the priests are given the responsibility of distinguishing between what is clean and unclean and of teaching the people of Israel about the Torah ("law" or "instruction"; Lev. 10:10–11). In Deuteronomy, the priests were grouped together with the tribe of Levi who more generally were given the task of assisting the priests in their roles.[72] In addition to responsibilities of distinguishing uncleannesses in people (Deut. 24:8), they also instructed Israel in the Torah of God and assisted in judgments (Deut. 17:8–13; 31:9–13; 33:8–10). Some view the grouping of the priests with Levi as Deuteronomy's identification of the privileges and responsibilities of the priests with the whole tribe of Levi.[73] Others see in Deuteronomy's expression *hakkōhănîm halěvîyīm*, "the priests, the Levites" (e.g., 18:1) simply an understanding of the priests as Levites.

In Judges 17–18, on their way to the northern Israelite city of Dan, the tribe of Dan encountered a Levite. They offered him the opportunity to function as their priest and he accepted. This role, illicit in the view of the later writers or editors of the book, is sometimes seen as an "anticipation" of the establishment of illicit cult centers and priests in

---

longer under control. For this purpose, analogy and symbolism "allows the unknown, unexpressible, or overwhelming to be concretized, comprehended, grasped, and, as a result, brought conceptually under one's power."

71. Cf. Gen. 8:20; 12:7–8; 13:18; 22:9, 13; 26:25; 33:20; 35:1, 3, 7.

72. The Levites are mentioned only once in Leviticus, with reference to the towns of refuge in Lev. 25:32–34.

73. Cf. Emerton (1962); Grabbe (1995, 42–43).

Dan, Bethel, and elsewhere by the first king of the breakaway northern kingdom of Israel, Jeroboam I (1 Kings 12:28–33). However, the indictment of the author of this passage in 1 Kings explicitly states that Jeroboam appointed priests "even though they were not Levites" (v. 31). The assumption that the Levite here was a descendant of Moses and thus a "Mushite" priest rather than a descendant of Aaron, rests on the view that the name of Moses in the Levite's genealogy of Judges 18:30 was altered to that of Manneseh by the addition of the Hebrew letter "n" in the name. One would like to see additional evidence.

In 1 and 2 Samuel, Samuel appears as a successor to Eli the priest, as someone who sacrifices and functions as a priest, although he is not there designated explicitly as a *kōhēn* or priest. According to the first verse in these books, Samuel is not a Levite, at least not through his father's line. His father is a member of the tribe of Ephraim. More discussion arises regarding the role of Zadok who, alongside Abiathar, functioned as priest during the reign of David. Second Samuel 8:17 identifies Zadok as the son of Ahitub who elsewhere is connected as the grandson of Eli (1 Sam. 14:3). However, it is argued that, despite the additional priestly connection in 1 Chronicles 6:8, the verse in 2 Samuel is corrupt. Attempts have been made then to argue that Zadok is in fact a priest from the old Jebusite line in Jerusalem. Even Melchizedek of Genesis 14:18 is enlisted since the second part of his name is constructed with the Semitic root *ṣdq*, identical to the root behind the name Zadok. This is then understood as the name of a god who was worshiped in Jerusalem. All this is possible. Second Samuel 8:17 may be corrupt, especially with reference to the part of the verse that mentions Abiathar, where the genealogy seems to be reversed. However, there is no textual evidence for corruption with respect to Zadok. His lack of further introduction in this verse is hardly surprising as it is part of a list of officials serving with David, wherein no one is given any further introduction.[74] Zadok's son is recorded as high priest for Solomon (1 Kings 4:2). It seems as though a significant line of Zadokite priests continued to function during the monarchy. At least they are remembered by Ezekiel the prophet, who envisions the future restoration of the temple to include exclusively priests of Zadok at God's altar (Ezek. 40:46; 43:19; 44:15). After the exile the name of this priest occurs in priestly genealogies (Ezra 7:2; Neh. 11:11).

During the period of the divided kingdom or divided monarchy, c. 931–586 BC, the priests played key roles as representatives of official religion for good or for bad. In the northern kingdom, Jeroboam I's priests are generally regarded in a negative sense and forthrightly in opposition to Hosea (4:4–6; 5:1–2; 6:9; 10:5) and Amos (7:10–17), eighth-century BC

74. This argument against the lineage of Zadok is made by Grabbe (1995, 44).

prophets in the northern kingdom. In the south the good priest Jehoiada rescued the last surviving member of the line of David, Joash, from the murderous Athaliah, and then staged a coup to do away with the queen and place Joash on the throne (2 Kings 11–12; 2 Chron. 23–24). His gathering of resources for the renovation of the temple in Jerusalem is an act of piety that defines the persona of a righteous leader throughout the ancient Near East. Elsewhere the prophets Isaiah and Jeremiah condemn the priests as corrupt spiritual leaders.[75]

The postexilic period was a time when the priests continued to be chastised for corruption (Mal. 1:6; 2:1). However, as in the preexilic era, one priest might have been dedicated to God for a particular purpose. Thus the high priest Joshua, c. 520 BC, became a figure of hope for renewal and restoration (Zech. 3:1–9; 6:11). Indeed, the prophets looked forward to a future age of a greatly expanded and blessed priesthood (Isa. 61:6; 66:21), one that would be pure and faithful to God (Ezek. 44:15, 28; 48:11).

Blood

Genesis 9:3–6 prohibits the consumption of blood and the act of murder. In both cases the reason for this prohibition lies with the blood of animals and humans. The life of the creature is understood to be in the blood. Life is a divine gift and of such value that no amount of goods can purchase it. It is for this reason that capital punishment is stipulated for murder. The only way to repay the taking of one life is by taking another life.

In sacrifices and offerings blood was used as a means to atone for sin and to purify an object. Thus it could prepare the altar for an offering (Lev. 1:5, 11, 15; 3:2, 8, 13; 7:2; 8:19, 24; 9:12; 17:6) and serve to atone for sin at that altar (Lev. 4:5–7, 16–18, 25, 30, 34; 5:9—these descriptions also function for purification). In addition to preparing the holy place for sacrifice, blood could be placed on people to purify them as new members of the covenant (Exod. 24:8). It could also be placed on houses for a similar purpose (Lev. 14:48–53).[76] The application of the blood to Aaron's right ear lobe, thumb, and big toe, when he was ordained as priest (Lev. 8:23–24; cf. 14:14–18, 25–28), may have served a similar function. Jacob Milgrom reasonably suggests that the blood was applied to the extremities to achieve purification and protection against evil at the outer and most vulnerable areas of the body.[77] The further anointing

75. Cf. Isa. 28:7; Jer. 1:18; 2:8; 5:31; 6:13; 8:10.
76. Cf. Milgrom (1991, 881); for blood's role in status, identity, and boundaries see Gilders (2004).
77. Cf. Milgrom (1991, 529); Gorman (1990, 135); Hess (forthcoming b).

of the priest with both oil and blood (Lev. 8:30) may have climaxed and sealed the relationship between the priest and God.[78]

Blood for the forgiveness of sins took on a key role in the Day of Atonement as described in Leviticus 16. There the high priest performed an annual purification rite for all the sins of Israel so that, as the whole nation participated, they would be forgiven and the uncleanness that separates them from God would be removed. Blood was used for the purification offering of the high priest (vv. 11, 14) and for the purification offering of the sanctuary and of all Israel (vv. 15–19).

The proper handling of the blood required that one sacrifice correctly on an altar. Leviticus 17:3–9 precludes giving sacrifice to other deities but it also presumes that all animal sacrifice must be performed at an altar. Some see this as a prohibition against all slaughtering of animals, so that it is all required to take place at an altar. But this contradicts Deuteronomy 12:15–16, 20–27 and the permission to kill nonsacrificial animals for food away from an altar. Leviticus 17 deals with sacrifices and so it is natural to understand the verb as referring to sacrifices, rather than any sort of common butchering.[79] In 1 Samuel 14:32–35 Saul's army, famished from lack of food, butchered and ate meat "over" (Hebrew *'al*) the blood. Milgrom (2000a, 17–22) suggests that this implies that the blood was poured on the ground as an offering to other non-Yahweh deities. Saul's makeshift altar for butchering would have ended this practice. Thus 1 Samuel does not violate an overall harmony between diverse legal collections and sources that together suggest a prohibition on eating animals sacrificed anywhere other than at an approved altar. However, no text explicitly precludes the eating of animal meat butchered elsewhere so long as it is not done in the context of a sacrifice to other deities.

Leviticus 17:11 grounds the prohibition concerning the eating of blood on the fact that the blood represents the "life" of the creature. The word for "life" is the Hebrew *nepeš*. The *nepeš* represents the vitality of the person. In Genesis 2:7 the man became a living *nepeš* when God combined flesh made from dust and spirit from the divine breath. In texts such as Isaiah 5:14 and Psalm 105:18 the *nepeš* represents the throat or neck that is connected to the mouth and through which the basic needs of life, air, and sustenance flow into the body. In Proverbs 16:26 a worker works because his *nepeš* drives him on. Here it has the sense of the person's desire to live; see also Deuteronomy 23:24. In Exodus 23:9 the *nepeš* describes the life situation of the Israelites who knew what it

78. Cf. Hartley (1992, 114).
79. See Snaith (1975); Levine (1989, 113); Noordtzij (1982, 174–75); Hartley (1992, 270–71); Hess (forthcoming b).

was like to be slaves in Egypt. While Leviticus 17:11 may refer to the *nepeš* as the life that is in the blood, verse 10 uses the term as a pronoun to describe the *nepeš* who eats blood, that is, anyone.[80] Thus the *nepeš* describes that element of the person that chooses life, seeking it and experiencing it. It is the vitality of the human person or of the animal. In itself it is not sufficient, but the *nepeš* is always needy and desiring. It leaves the physical body at death and thus brings about the disintegration of the physical person.

Thus the blood is understood as possessing that life force that can both preserve from death and also cleanse from sin in the purification and other expiatory offerings. It symbolizes and represents the *nepeš*.[81]

Wanderings through the Negev

The Pentateuch and particularly Numbers outlines how the generation of Israel that came out of Egypt and stood before God at Mount Sinai also wandered and died in the Negev. The Negev described here includes the region circumscribed by a line running from the southeast corner eastward to the southern tip of the Dead Sea and southward along the Arabah to the northern tip of the Gulf of Aqaba. From there it proceeds northwest to the southeastern corner of the Mediterranean Sea. The drier climate that prevailed at the end of the third millennium BC and the minimal erosion that resulted meant that many religious sites experienced a minimum of alteration, even where their use continued. Therefore the religious sites reflect practices that may not have been in use only in the Negev but also elsewhere among the peoples whom the Israelites encountered. There are three generic types of religious sites: *maṣṣēbôt*, open shrines, and crenelations. In addition, the "Hathor temple" stands out as a unique site that reflects both the religious practice of the region and elements of interest in the study of the biblical tabernacle. This leads to comparative observations on the tabernacle and the vocabulary used to describe it. Although some of the Pentateuchal texts related to many of these archaeological phenomena are located in narrative strands traditionally assigned to J and E, it was considered better to group the relevant material into a single distinctively archaeological section and to present it here as part of the priestly and cultic material.

---

80. This use of *nepeš* as a pronoun is not uncommon and may also explain the use of the term *nepeš mēt*, literally "dead person" or "corpse," in Lev. 21:11 and Num. 6:6. See Lewis (2002).

81. See Hartley (1992, 273–78); Flüglister (1977); Kiuchi (1987); Hess (forthcoming b).

Maṣṣēbôt (Standing Stones)

In the southern Negev and eastern Sinai some 142 sites with *maṣṣēbôt* have been found.[82] For Avner, *maṣṣēbôt* are more than simply standing stones. They often represent deities.[83] In the Uvda Valley alone many sites have been documented. They first appear as early as c. 10,000 BC. They continue in use until the seventh century AD and, according to some witnesses, right up to the twentieth century. A single stone may be used or there may be more standing in a row or in a collection. Groups of seven and nine are common, though they can number close to one hundred. Some are incorporated into tombs. Tent camps could have *maṣṣēbôt* behind the tents. These groups are similar to collections of deities represented in sculpture elsewhere in the ancient Near East. Sometimes they face east with offering tables in front. They are often near an ancient road. West of the *maṣṣēbôt* is the open court. In one case (site 151) a partially restored set of *maṣṣēbôt* were located. Originally, only eight of several dozen were found standing. In the middle of the circle of stones was an ash spot. The uncalibrated carbon 14 dating placed the age of the site at about 7,600 years. Other *maṣṣēbôt* may have been used to mark tombs.[84]

What is unusual about these stones is that they were not carved in any way and thus, unlike other cultures, do not attempt to present the deities in an anthropomorphic or pictorial manner. Mettinger suggests that in this sort of West Semitic context we have early evidence for the imageless nature of Israelite worship as demonstrated in the Ten Commandments.[85] However, as Hurowitz notes, there is a difference between unshaped stones that represent deities and the empty "seat" of the Ark of the Covenant that represents the place where God chooses to dwell.[86] Although both may be termed aniconism, the representation of God by any object was deemed illegitimate as it bound God to a particular object. However, the idea of the "empty seat" implied divine freedom to dwell among his people.

These stones are located in the desert and normally face east. They can represent ancestral spirits. The latter can be found in the Ugaritic Tale of Aqhat where Danel desires a descendant who will set up a stele for his memory.[87] An example of stones that represent deities can be

---

82. Cf. Avner (2001, 31). An earlier form of the discussion that follows appeared in Hess (1994f). For greater detail regarding the archaeology of the Sinai desert and the Negev, and of Israel's sojourn here, see Hoffmeier (2005).

83. Cf. Avner (1984; 1993); DeFord (1997).

84. Cf. Avner (1993, 167).

85. Cf. Mettinger (1995).

86. Cf. Hurowitz (1997); Exod. 37:1–5; 40:3–5, 20–21 (and Deuteronomy; cf. Wilson [2005]). See arguments for aniconism in Mettinger (1995) but also the important criticisms of Lewis (1998).

87. See Avner (2001, 33).

Fig. 17. Standing stones from Uvda Valley (Courtesy of Richard S. Hess)

found with Jacob at Bethel in Genesis 28:22, but this is clearly portrayed as a memorial stele rather than a representation of a deity. The eighth-century BC Aramaic Sefire inscriptions identify as the "house of god" the stone pillars on which they are written. Avner identifies narrow tall stones with male gods and shorter stones with goddesses. From this perspective the *maṣṣēbôt* that occur in pairs usually have the male on the right and the female on the left. Avner cites many examples of this relationship in ancient Near Eastern art as well as Song of Songs 2:6 and 8:3. He cites a variety of biblical texts, both negative (Lev. 26:1; Deut. 7:5; 1 Kings 14:22–23; 2 Kings 3:2; and Jer. 43:13) and positive (Josh. 24:25–27; Isa. 19:19–20).[88]

Further examples of memorial purposes for standing stones occur with the Late Bronze Age Egyptian stele of Mekal at Beth Shan, described in chapter 5 above. Standing stones from this time inscribed as victory stelae also occur at Megiddo. In the ninth century BC, the Aramaic stele at Tel Dan and the Moabite stele from east of the Dead Sea both describe victories over Israel. Standing stones erected outside the city walls and intended to represent deities are mentioned in Hittite and Akkadian texts. See the discussion of both in chapter 4 under Emar

---

88. Avner (2001, 35–36, 40). M. Smith (2003, 167–68) notes how Absalom set up a funerary stele (2 Sam. 18:18).

Fig. 18. Structures marking
burials in the Sinai peninsula
(Courtesy of Richard S. Hess)

373. Elsewhere, as outlined in chapter 4, these stones occur in Bronze and Iron Age cult centers within towns and cities in sanctuaries and at the gates to the cities.[89]

Open Sanctuaries

Open sanctuaries have been found in the southern Negev as well as in Palestine at En Gedi. They are simply a line or low wall of stones that mark off a space used for religious purposes. The most common types are rectangular in shape and, in twenty-one cases, they occur in pairs. The line of stones is normally a double line but sometimes it may be a single or a triple line. The four corners often face cardinal points on the compass. The cell, which is a marked-off section of the sanctuary, can cut one corner and stand on a north-south axis. This way the small *maṣṣēbôt* can face east. In one example, the central *maṣṣēbâ* may have an offering table in front and a pendant beside it. The court area may also have small stones in it. Are these representations of ancestors left by families, are they deities, or are they both (or neither)? There are also three storage pits and a lower pit whose uncalibrated carbon 14 date is 6640 BC. Nearby and to the east are small stones placed in the sand configured as animals, probably leopards. These all face east, have large eyes, and two have a smaller animal on top of a larger one. Are these gods or does the artwork serve another purpose? It is impossible to know for certain.

Rock Cut Crenelations

These lines appear on the top of hills and are found all over the ancient Near East. The crenelations or "teeth" are always found beside

89. For additional discussion of the biblical evidence and a survey of the appearance of these stones in Phoenicia and in Israel, see chapter 10, p. 302.

Fig. 19. Negev open sanctuary (Courtesy of Richard S. Hess)

ancient roads. They are simply piles of stones built in layers. The inside is regularly blackened by libations. They are often built to mark a tomb or an otherwise holy place. These cairns sometimes served as altars or as sacred monuments. One often finds paths leading to them. Crenelations can date from some seven thousand years ago, on the basis of carbon 14 dating and the flints found beside them.

Burials can be marked by these piles of stones. They often contain the remains of honored individuals. By their nature burials may be the

Fig. 20. Negev rock cut crenelations (Courtesy of Richard S. Hess)

sole remaining physical evidence of a tribe or people group. In the Sinai peninsula, artificial rock formations that resemble houses appear in clusters. Individuals were buried beneath the structures, with remains dating back some four or five millennia.

Hathor Temple

Separate from these other religious remains is a temple in the Timna Valley, referred to as the Hathor temple because of its relationship to the Egyptian deity Hathor. The first architectural form here may have been a Canaanite high place containing a large stone with a circular depression, a ditch on the side, and *maṣṣēbôt*. There was also an offering table and the area was paved with red sandstone. Six *maṣṣēbôt* and a basin were found on the west side of the temple. Then sometime during the twelfth century BC the Egyptian presence appeared. The occupying power did not destroy the local forms but adapted them. They created a sanctuary here, adapting the local god to Hathor. This phase probably dates from around the time of Pharaoh Ramesses III, as may be observed by a drawing and inscription on the vertical cliff that rises behind and above the site and by Papyrus Harris's mention of Atiqa as a place of copper for Ramesses III. The copper mines in the Timnah Valley fit this reference, as few other places do.[90] The Egyptians added a building structure and a stone pavement in front. A wall surrounding the sanctuary was built and later a small cell was added on the right side. "Midianite" ware was also found here. Two stone-lined holes were found along with large quantities of red and yellow cloth. The cloth gives evidence that the holy place was covered by cloth as a tent shrine.[91] In addition, a copper image of a snake was found. Some scholars associate this sanctuary with the Midianites and with the origins of the worship of Yahweh.[92] While such conclusions are speculative, the tent sanctuary clearly has parallels with the biblical tabernacle that Israel used in the wilderness and continued to use to house the ark until the temple was constructed. The Egyptian royal war tent provides additional background to the protocol of the tent as a place where God would be king among his people who marched in the wilderness. The Hathor temple example indicates that this also had religious connotations.[93]

90. Cf. also the Wadi Feinan in the region east of the Arabah (in modern Jordan) north of the Timna Valley and south of the Dead Sea. This was also a copper mining site in ancient Edom with clear evidence of habitation reaching back to the tenth century BC.
91. Set up by Egyptians, used by "Midianites"? See Kitchen (2003, 279).
92. Cf. Staubli (1991, 231).
93. The objection is sometimes made that, because of the Egyptian control of Timna in the thirteenth century BC, it would have been impossible for Israel to pass by the area unhindered. Cf. Rothenberg (1972b, 63–64); Ahlström (1993, 417–18). However, Timna

Fig. 21. Hathor Temple (Courtesy of Richard S. Hess)

A bronze serpent, similar to the image discovered at Late Bronze Age Tell Mevorakh (see chapter 5) far to the north, was uncovered here. Dated to the thirteenth century BC, it reminds the Bible reader of the bronze serpent lifted up in the desert by Moses

Fig. 22. Timna Valley (Courtesy of Richard S. Hess)

to provide healing for those Israelites who were perishing from the snakebites of the "burning ones" or *śĕrāpîm* (Num. 21:6–9).

The Tabernacle: Biblical, Egyptian, and West Semitic Contexts

The biblical tabernacle was about 15 feet by 45 feet.[94] The material over the frame was, from inside to outside: colored cloth with cherubim

---

could have been an outpost of Egyptian control, just as many regions of Palestine and Syria were so administered. Thus it would have been possible for other groups to pass by the area without incident, as long as they did not challenge the exploitation of the resources.

94. Cf. Kitchen (2003, 275–76).

figures; goat hair; red dyed rams' skins; and leather worked or adorned in a special way (*taḥaš*). The area around it was about 100 by 75 feet. Six wagons with two oxen each transported the whole tabernacle (Num. 7:3–8).

The size and orientation may be compared to the Egyptian royal war tent used by Ramesses II at the battle of Qadesh (c. 1275 BC). At Abu Simbel a relief of Ramesses II's Egyptian camp provides comparisons with the tabernacle: a rectangular courtyard within the larger rectangular camp; a rectangular reception tent parallel to the holy place; and the adjacent square pharaoh's chamber with two winged deities (Horus) flanking the pharaoh's cartouche, similar to the holy of holies and the two cherubim. Egypt's army camped with one of its four divisions on each of the four sides of the tent. The personal temples of Ramesses II or III could be 200 by 600 feet, huge in comparison to the biblical tabernacle.[95] These rectangular architectural forms ceased after 1200 BC. The tabernacle's features have also been compared with the wooden structures protecting the dead pharaoh's sarcophagus in the New Kingdom, including the thirteenth-century BC tomb-chapel of Ipuy. One can find there decorated, gold-overlaid, and linen-covered wooden frames and solid structures that resemble the construction techniques of the account in Exodus 25–40.[96]

Fleming (2000) has argued that texts from eighteenth-century BC Mari and thirteenth-century BC Ugarit also provide West Semitic antecedents to the biblical tabernacle.[97] In one Mari text (M.6873) a large tent or "covering" (Akkadian *ḫurpatum*) is described as supported by ten wooden frames (Akkadian *qersum* = Hebrew *qereš* in Exod. 26:15 *et passim* totaling some fifty-one occurrences). It required forty-three individuals to carry it. The setting up of these tent frames takes place on a special day of sacrifice when the gods apparently congregate at the tent, for they then depart from there to their own temples. In another text (*FM* III, 4:ii:7–14), divine images were placed within the frames and given an animal (ass) sacrifice.[98]

At Ugarit the term *qrš* is used to describe the shelter of the chief god El (*KTU* 1.4 IV 24) just as a term related to the tent or covering (Akkadian *ḫurpatum* = Ugaritic *'rpt*) describes the "cloud" where Baal lives (*KTU* 1.4 VII 19) and the Hebrew *'ărāpel*, the "dark cloud" of Yahweh's special

95. See additional examples of Egyptian tabernacles and decorations in Kitchen (2003, 276–79); Holman (2000). Detailed comparisons with Egyptian forms, as well as linguistic derivations, are summarized for the architecture of the tabernacle, its contents, and the priestly attire by Hoffmeier (2005: 209–22).

96. Cf. Kitchen (1993; 2000b).

97. Cf. Fleming (2000a); cf. M. Smith (2001a, 142).

98. Cf. Kitchen (2003, 277).

glory (Exod. 20:21; Deut. 4:11; 1 Kings 8:12–13). Thus the tabernacle has many connections with second millennium BC tent shrines and cannot be understood as a later creation artificially designed to (pretend to) anticipate the temple.[99] Kitchen (2003, 277) contrasts this with Assyria and Babylonia where there is no cultic use of tents in the first millennium BC and where Assyrian camps were round or oval (rather than rectangular).

The building of the tabernacle and of the temple show similar features: divine command, transmission of the command, preparations, the work with a description of what is accomplished, dedication/inauguration, blessing/rejoicing, and the divine response.[100] Similar to the account of the tabernacle construction in the Bible are the accounts of the Sumerian Gudea (third millennium BC), Samsu-iluna of Babylon (c. 1700), the Ugaritic Baal myth (thirteenth century BC), and Tiglath-pileser I of Assyria (c. 1100).[101]

Conclusion

Like the narrative strands, the priestly story also begins with creation, although this time it focuses on the Sabbath, the genealogies, and the orderliness of the world in the boundaries assigned to the sky, the water, and the dry ground. The etymologies of the personal names in the genealogies of Genesis 1–11 point to an early second-millennium north-Syrian context in which the early family that was to become Israel worshiped other deities. Israel is called on to use a simplified sacrificial system as a means of relating to Yahweh, whether through first fruit and fellowship offerings that actualized its belief that Yahweh created all and sought to enjoy life with his people, or through the purification, reparation, and burnt offerings that provided reconciliation after the relationship had been compromised because of sin. The role of the priests provides the means of access to Yahweh through administration of the sacrificial system, and as the teachers of God's Torah or instruction to the people. Blood is the physical manifestation of that "life" or *nepeš* that every person and animal possesses as a gift from Yahweh of absolute value.

The religious practices found in the accounts of the wilderness wanderings have great antiquity and continue into the modern age, with Bedouin reverence or worship given to standing stones as late as the

---

99. Cf. Fritz (1977). See further Cross (2005). Note that Keret offers sacrifices to gods in a tent (Kitchen [2003, 277]).

100. Cf. especially Exod. 25–40 and 1 Kings 5–9.

101. See Kitchen (2003, 282); Hurowitz (1985).

twentieth century AD. What is the significance of all this for a study of Israelite religion? Given the pervasiveness and endurance of these practices, the following points may be noted.

First, Israel did not have to wait until it entered Canaan to encounter a religious environment. If any of Israel did indeed spend time in the desert, they certainly encountered much in the way of religious life.

Second, these practices should not be seen merely as importations from the more "civilized" city-states of the Phoenicians and others. On the contrary, the custom of constructing an altar of uncut stones, mentioned in Exodus 20, would be most unusual among urban populations of Canaan. However, the use of unworked stone was quite common in the southern Negev.

Third, defining areas for worship and rituals was native to the land. Indeed, the presence of sacred spaces was not unknown in the Israelite cult. The mapping out of space around the tabernacle or around the sacred mountain and the designation of it as sacred are found in the accounts of Israel at Sinai and of the tabernacle worship while in the wilderness.

Fourth, the *maṣṣēbôt* as erected stones of special religious significance were common throughout the ancient Near East, and have remained a custom until the present. The use of special pillars, designated in the Solomonic temple as Joachin and Boaz, became a part of the official cult of Israel's worship. The use of special standing stones or piles of stones (as in the crenelations) as special markers, may be compared with the construction of such memorials as those erected at the crossing of the Jordan River and at the covenant renewal ceremony at Shechem, both recorded in Joshua.[102]

Fifth, we may also observe the number and density of cultic sites in this area, far in excess of anything found in the cultivated regions of Canaan to the south. To what extent does this reflect a religious influence of the desert on the cultivated land? We may compare the many biblical traditions of Moses, Elijah, and the New Testament John and Jesus, as well as the desert fathers and mothers, all of whom drew inspiration from their desert experiences.

Sixth, the tombs on ridges beside crenelations attest to the importance of certain burials and of marking the site. A burial mound in the Judean desert at the Valley of Achor was raised for Achan (Josh. 7:26). Here Achan's name is associated with what may have been the older name of the valley, Achor, meaning "destruction, disaster."[103] Such an association of a burial with an already established tradition is not unique to the Bible. Indeed, on the lower Golan plateau, east of the Sea of Galilee,

102. Cf. Josh. 4; 8:30–35; 24.
103. For this association in the biblical text, see Hess (1994a).

there was discovered a "Stonehenge" type of monument called Rogem Hiri. Although this was built and used in the third millennium BC, in the middle of it was a cairn with a burial that dated to the mid- to late second millennium BC.[104]

Seventh, as for the Hathor temple, the presence of a tent sanctuary and the use of a votive copper snake are reflected in the biblical accounts of Israel's wilderness wanderings with the tent sanctuary of the tabernacle and the use of a copper or bronze snake to ward off the plague (Num. 21:4–9).

Finally, we should note the biblical observations of a desert that was far from empty, but contained many sites that could be identified in the itineraries in Numbers, as well as many peoples, including the Amalekites and the Edomites. Of interest are the Kenites (Judg. 4:11; 1 Sam. 15:6; 27:10; 30:29) whose association with metal working may be deduced from their itinerant lifestyle and from the South Arabic etymology of the root behind their name, "metal smith" (*qyn*). This cannot help but bring to mind the southern Negev, with cult sites and copper mines and refineries. There is also increasing evidence for Iron Age copper mines east of the Arabah in lowland Edom.[105]

Thus Israel's journey through the desert is one filled with religious practices and rites that the people either imitated or transformed. Thus standing stones or *maṣṣēbôt* could serve as images of deities but they could also serve to commemorate great events or to honor victories or vows. Antecedents to the tabernacle can be found at Mari, Ugarit, Egypt, and at the "Midianite" and Egyptian "Hathor temple" in the Timna Valley. Nevertheless, as with the sacrificial system and special holidays, the accoutrements found in the desert also could be used by the nation as a means to express its unique relationship with Yahweh.

Having considered this foundational material, largely undated or archaic, it is now possible to focus our attention on the biblical and archaeological context of early Israel and the United Monarchy of Saul, David, and Solomon.

104. Cf. Mizrachi (1992).
105. Cf. Levy and Najjar (2006).

8

Early Israel and the United Monarchy

This chapter will consider the religious life suggested by the early "historical" books of the Old Testament and by the archaeological evidence that existed during the period identified as Iron Age I (c. 1200–c. 1000 BC). Here we have the first extrabiblical evidence, both textual and (with a previously unattested clarity) material, for the existence of the people known as Israel. We also have some of the earliest texts in the Bible that are believed to reflect the reality of an ancient Israel. Issues surrounding the religion of this period are crucial: first, for appreciating the emergence of Israel from the Late Bronze Age (c. 1550–c. 1200 BC) civilizations and religions; second, for understanding the role that the period plays as a means of preparing for the first-millennium BC states of the northern and southern kingdoms (Israel and Judah); third, for understanding the manner in which Israel worshiped its chief deity, Yahweh; and fourth, for appreciating how they preserve an understanding of this period as formative for their worship centers, especially the temple in Jerusalem.

Israel at the Beginning

The issue of the origins of Israel is primarily a historical one. However, it raises important questions about the religion of Israel in terms of the appropriation of the people's faith in Yahweh and the nature of those spiritual realities that brought the nation together as "Israel" and enabled it to join in a community. The theories regarding Israel's origins in Canaan have been explored elsewhere.[1] It will serve the purpose of this study to review briefly the major theories and to summarize some of the conclusions.

Archaeological and other social science disciplines have attempted to identify the origin of the Israelites once they settled in Canaan. This has resulted in five theories, each of which reflects the age in which it was formulated.[2] They can be broadly grouped into two categories, according to whether the Israelites originally came from outside Canaan or from within Canaan. According to the first two theories, they came from outside Canaan. According to the latter three, Israel originated from within Canaan.

The first theory is the oldest, often referred to as the conquest. According to this view, the first twelve chapters of Joshua interpret Israel's appearance in Canaan as one involving the defeat and conquest of Canaanite cities. Some of the archaeological evidence from major sites, such as the thirteenth-century BC destruction layer at Hazor, does seem to point to such an interpretation.[3] However, the absence of destruction layers elsewhere has led most archaeologists to abandon this as a

---

1. See Hess (1999a). Other studies such as Dever (2003) and Killebrew (2005, 149–96) provide useful updates and perspectives. However, the revolution that has emerged as a result of the surveys of the Palestinian highlands as published in a preliminary fashion by Finkelstein (1988) were the last major item of new information to have input into the discussion.

2. On the nature of archaeology as driven by theories and especially by the current popular fads in philosophy and social sciences methodologies, see Trigger (1998).

3. Cf. Yadin (1985).

dominant theory. This is true despite the explicit statement in Joshua 11:13 that Israel burnt none of the mounds on which cities stood except that of Hazor. Thus one might not expect to find archaeological levels of burning and destruction elsewhere at this time.

The perceived problems with the absence of violent destruction levels at many sites led Albrecht Alt earlier in the twentieth century to propose a second theory regarding Israel. He suggested that Israel's origin is to be found in wandering seminomadic clans from east of the Jordan River who peacefully entered the land, settling in the hilly country that was unoccupied. Brought together into a loosely knit association by a group of Yahweh worshipers from the desert, and perhaps ultimately from Egypt, this larger group populated the hill country and eventually grew strong enough to band together and to gain dominance over the rest of the land during the period of the monarchy. The major problem with this theory is the absence of an accounting for battles and wars that are recorded not only in the biblical traditions but also in the thirteenth-century BC Egyptian Merneptah Stele and in the archaeological burn layers of Hazor, Lachish, and Bethel.

Most of the more recent theories have been built on the assumption that there never was an exodus or at least that the primary group of people who identified themselves as Israel in later generations did not originate in a migration from outside biblical Israel but from within that land. There are variations. A third theory, the peasant revolt hypothesis, allows for a small group coming from outside and changing the religion of the existing Canaanites in the land.[4] Others advocate that there was no Israel until the eighth century BC and therefore the people of highland Canaan in the thirteenth and twelfth centuries BC would not have recognized themselves as Israelites. In all the remaining theories the primary group that later became Israel was indigenous to the land.

The impetus for this approach comes from the changing archaeological interpretation during the past two decades. When any new cultural element appears in a land, the archaeological assumption is that the presence of this people will be detectable through the appearance of new forms of material culture. For a long time, archaeologists identified the coming of Israel with the appearance of specific types of private houses, particular types of storage jars, a special means of storing water at the archaeological sites in Canaan, and a new form of agricultural activity. The house was the four-room house. The jar was the collared-ring pithos. The water storage method was the plaster-lined cistern. The agricultural method involved the building of terraces. However, evidence

4. Cf. Gottwald (1979).

for these types of cultural features has now been found in earlier strata of archaeological sites as well.

A fourth theory found the origin of the Israelites among the semi-nomads who roamed the hill country of Palestine with their flocks. This view developed as a result of the evidence from archaeological surveys of the hill country carried forward in the past forty years. The results indicate a dramatic shift in demography in this region where the Bible portrays many of the Israelite stories in Judges, Ruth, and 1 and 2 Samuel. Before c. 1200 BC the region contained only a few fortified cities. After 1200 BC the region was dominated by the appearance of about three hundred villages. This is the major archaeological evidence for the appearance of a new people in this region. However, according to this fourth theory these people did not come from outside of the hill country. Instead, they were there all along. Before 1200 BC they were made up of nomadic groups who had no permanent settlement. After that date they settled down and changed their lifestyles to farming and agriculture.

The major difficulty with this view and the previous one is the existence of evidence for cultural influence from outside Canaan. This is especially true of the evidence of cultural influence from north of Canaan that was present at this time, and both earlier and later, in and around the hill country of Palestine. While cultural influence does not "prove" immigration, it certainly allows for it and often there is some exchange of population in the process.

A fifth model addresses the general environmental and political factors of the era. Hopkins (1993, 209–10) credits both Egyptian taxation and difficult environmental factors as reasons for the transition to nomadic pastoralism at the beginning of the Late Bronze Age. In ancient times, these nomadic groups were called Shasu[5] by the Egyptians. Hopkins makes comparisons with a similar phenomenon in Ottoman Iraq, observing that more than half of the population responded with a shift to pastoralism. Similar motives are credited with the ending of the Late Bronze Age and the appearance of Israel. Coote and Whitelam (1987) advocate this perspective. It is also found in Stiebing (1989, 186–87), who summarizes:[6]

> It was the growing frequency of *drought*—and the crop failures and hunger
> it brought with it—that set in motion the internal strife, *warfare, plague,*

5. On the Shasu, see p. 159.

6. Here and in Stiebing (1994) he surveys the evidence from across Europe, the Mediterranean, and the Middle East to demonstrate a climatic drying and reduction in population. Whitelam (1994, 81) also cites the studies of Desborough to demonstrate that the Late Bronze Age decline of Mycenaean palace centers led to settlement shifts in highland and other remote areas.

piracy, destruction of cities, decline in population, inflation, and *population movements.* . . . The widespread drought might very well have been largely responsible not only for the destruction of most of the Canaanite cities, but also for the creation in Canaan of detached groups of seminomads, refugee peasant farmers, and occasional bands of brigands who, together with a small contingent of escaped slaves from Egypt, would join to form the Israelite tribes.

Thomas L. Thompson (1992) has proposed a further development of this hypothesis. He understands the shifts in settlement patterns in the hill country in terms of their broad chronological and geographic context, as stimulated by ecological factors. Chronologically, the shift from the Middle Bronze Age to the Late Bronze Age (c. 1550 BC), like the earlier Early Bronze IV to Middle Bronze I shift (c. 2000 BC), saw a decrease in population centers in terms of their number and size. This was caused by a drier climate. Such a drier climate existed throughout the Late Bronze Age. However, things got even worse in terms of drought in Iron Age I. Throughout the Mediterranean region there is evidence that this period saw a 20 percent decrease in rainfall and a rise in temperature of two or three degrees centigrade. This brought about the further reduction of population centers, and their impoverishment and abandonment with no political or social structure to support the larger sites. The destruction by fire, which some sites periodically experienced, may have been the result of internal tensions that led to strife, destruction, and abandonment. The villages that appeared were settled in various regions of Palestine where interrelated agricultural specializations and dependencies allowed for the emergence of what Thompson defines as Mediterranean economies. Thus the change in settlement patterns in the hill country was an entirely internal matter, caused by ecological forces and reactions to them by inhabitants.

Several problems should be noted with this analysis. First, Thompson (1992, 235) puts the number of Iron Age I hill country occupants at ten thousand. Finkelstein and Silberman (2001, 115) place it at forty-five thousand. William Dever, on the basis of the discovery of about three hundred sites in the hill country, places it at seventy-five thousand.[7] If the latter number is correct, Thompson's thesis of no involvement from outside Palestine and the minimal resedentarization of pastoral groups cannot be correct. There are too many people in comparison with the fewer Late Bronze Age population centers.[8] They must come from somewhere else.

7. Cf. Dever in Shanks, et al. (1992, 43). Dever (2001, 110) specifies as follows: twelve thousand c. 1200 BC; fifty-five thousand in the twelfth century; and seventy-five thousand in the eleventh century.

8. Zevit (2001, 91) is emphatic about the problems with assuming a large hill country nomadic population in the Late Bronze Age. Seeing it as an argument from silence and a

Second, as noted above there is the refusal to recognize the presence of outsiders in Palestine at this time. Thompson minimizes the data that do not fit his model, but it is clear that people from the north were present and very possibly people from elsewhere.[9] Note that Rainey (1994b) and others suggest that a decline in rainfall and subsequent decline in food production led to a reduction in the Canaanite urban population that resulted in pastoralist movement to the hill country where they settled and produced their own food. Rainey follows the hypothesis of the peaceful immigration model but incorporates more recent data.

Third, there is uncertainty regarding the increased drought at the end of the Late Bronze Age. Van der Steen (1996, 65) notes that there is no evidence for a drop in the level of the Dead Sea at this time, which would be expected were there a drought in the area. Merling (1997, 99) observes that this makes Thompson's model the weakest one since it is so dependent on the factor of a change in the climate, which cannot yet be conclusively proven.

Fourth, there is a tendency toward an ecological or economic determinism. If one looks at the problem through economic "lenses," one will find only economic solutions.[10] This is not a complete explanation of the history nor can it be used to discount the biblical record simply because the Bible chooses to focus on values other than economic factors.

Can anything be concluded based on these different models? Despite various strengths and weaknesses, there is no reason at present to reject outright any of these models. Aspects of each of them may well have been true. For one thing, the tradition of conquest is too strongly present in the biblical text to argue for a complete fabrication. Recent research has demonstrated that Joshua 9–12, in its form, structure, and themes, is identical to other historical/ideological conquest accounts found among the Hittites, Egyptians, and Assyrians,[11] and, in terms of its episodic accounts, parallels the West Semitic conquest accounts from north Syria as detailed by the leader of the north Syrian site of Mayarzana in the

---

failure to engage with the dimorphic society model (in which herders and sedentary peoples are mutually dependent on one another), he notes that herders would have found their best areas on the coastal plain rather than in the hill country. Yet pastoralists are mentioned in contemporary Egyptian records as inhabiting the area south of Gaza but not the coastal plain or the hill country. Finally, there are no archaeological traces of seminomadism from this period unlike those that occur from other periods in the region.

9. Cf. Whitelam (1994, 80), who cites evidence for the urban elite of Palestine as having been part of a "world economy."

10. This criticism can also be applied to the attempt of Drews (1993) to trace the end of the Bronze Age to the introduction of a new type of infantry javelin into warfare, and to Muth (1997), who attributes the emergence of Israel to the appearance of iron tools (and subsequent increase in food production) in Iron Age I.

11. Cf. Younger (1990, 197–237).

fourteenth-century BC Amarna letters.[12] Thus there are no grounds to see these chapters as a theological interpretation of a class revolt[13] or as anything other than an authentic (albeit certainly biased) memory of wars that Israel undertook against its neighbors and in which it received what it believed to be divine aid to obtain success. The same appears to be true for the people groups that Israel encountered. Hostetter (1996, 149–50) has argued that these also represent a strong and early memory that confirms Israel as substantially comprised of a people entering the land from outside and encountering groups that were alien to them.

Second, other elements from both outside and within Canaan became attached to the people of Israel. In Joshua 6 and 9 respectively, this occurs with Rahab and with the Gibeonites. However, this is not the dominant motif and there is not substantial evidence for some sort of egalitarian source to these texts.[14] Indeed, Lawson Younger's careful comparison (1990) with other ancient Near Eastern sources leads him to conclude:

> The historical narrative in which Joshua 9–12 is cast utilizes a common transmission code observable in numerous ancient Near Eastern conquest accounts, employing the same ideology. Since the ideology which lies behind the text of Joshua is one like that underlying other ancient Near Eastern conquest accounts—namely, imperialistic—then "egalitarian, peasant" Israel is employing a transmission code (a "communicative mode") which is self-contradictory.

Thus to accept all the models to at least some degree is not simply to opt for a middle-of-the-road position but to affirm the diversity of human motivations and social action involved in the process of becoming a people. For example, Zevit suggests a combination of settlement by infiltration and settlement by conquest.[15] This probably explains the majority of settlements in Iron Age I.

Such an interpretation preserves an understanding of the conquest. As already observed this has a strong tradition in the variety of literatures preserved in the Old Testament. This in itself raises a fundamental

12. These letters are EA 185 and EA 186. Cf. Hess (1999b). Parker (1997, 132–33) is correct that the style of Josh. 10 is different from that of Mesha and the Tel Dan stele. However, what Parker describes as "too monotonous" and "too restricted" is exactly the same as the style of the conquest accounts in the second-millennium Mayarzana correspondence and in the ancient Near Eastern conquest accounts already mentioned.

13. So Brueggemann (1986).

14. As argued by Gottwald (1989) and Brueggemann (1986).

15. Cf. Zevit (2001, 111n44). He uses this as a hypothesis to explain the fact that some Late Bronze Age sites continued into Iron I without interruption while others were destroyed and many new sites developed. For the data see Ji (1995, 129–38).

question as to the interpretation of biblical historical accounts. This is true despite the problems that remain, such as the absence of archaeological evidence at Jericho and other sites. To raise these issues is not necessarily to question the reality of a conquest. This question was addressed by the Assyriologist William W. Hallo (1990, 193–94) in his 1989 presidential address to the American Oriental Society. Hallo argued that:

> The biblical record must be, for this purpose, scrutinized like other historiographical traditions of the ancient Near East, neither exempted from the standards demanded of those other traditions, nor subjected to severer ones than they are. . . . Unless one rearranges the biblical evidence, like Séan Warner, or utilizes it eclectically as Norman K. Gottwald has essentially done with his reinterpretation, one can hardly deny the reality of a conquest from abroad, implying a previous period of wanderings, a dramatic escape from the prior place of residence and an oppression there that prompted the escape.

Cult Sites and Sacrifice

Mount Ebal

At 3,100 feet, Mount Ebal is the highest mountain in Samaria. Mount Gerizim, its counterpart, is 2,900 feet in height. Nine and one-third miles to the west is Samaria, where Ahab and his successors later ruled the northern kingdom. Ebal and Gerizim are geologically similar, with the same terra rosa from the Eocene period. They form the sides to the valley of Shechem that lies between them. To the east lies the Valley of Beth-Dagan and the Wadi Farah road. Twenty-three miles east can be found Tell el-Far'ah North, identified with ancient Tirzah, an early capital of the northern kingdom. This wadi passage connects the Jordan Valley to the central hill country.

On Mount Gerizim to the south of Mount Ebal, the early settlement dates to the seventh century BC. At the top is a church from the time of Justinian. A pine forest lies to the east. On a lower peak is Khirbet er-Ras, a site with a temple to Apollo and a stairway. On another peak of Gerizim the Samaritans settled with their cultic rituals. Their main buildings date as early as the Persian period, although archaeologists have yet to locate the rival Samaritan temple.[16] Adam Zertal led the Israeli survey of this region. On Mount Ebal he found nothing from the Bronze or Iron Ages, except for a single installation. The site occurs

16. Anderson (1991).

Fig. 23. Mount Ebal site (Courtesy of Ralph Hawkins)

some feet away from the ridge that forms the third highest peak on the mountain. Located on this lower peak, it is dated between c. 1250 and 1150 BC.[17]

The site is surrounded by two concentric enclosure walls. No building was found in the outer court. There is an inner enclosure wall at the higher northern part of the peak. There are three steps at the entrance to this area. Although sites from the Persian, Roman, and later periods have been found at Mount Ebal, the mountain contains no other sites from the Bronze or Iron Ages. This is the only site where pottery belonged to the thirteenth through the middle of the twelfth centuries BC alone. Two levels were found. The earlier level is dated by two Egyptian scarabs. These were found to belong to the second half of the thirteenth century BC.[18]

The area has reasonably good acoustics and is the only place identified on Mount Ebal where it is possible for thousands of people to gather and view what is going on.

If this site were to contain an altar, there are a number of interesting parallels with biblical texts. The first one considers the animals "sacrificed" here. Following Zertal's description, excavations revealed a central complex. In this central complex were found two layers of ash with some 2,800 bones. The bones included sheep, goats, cattle, fallow deer, hedgehogs, doe, porcupine, and lizards. West of the "altar" were two courtyards. The major concentration of animal bones was found at the "altar." The upper, later layer is mainly that of cattle bones. The bones are burnt, possibly indicating cult sacrifice. The bones have cut marks.

17. For this and what follows, cf. Zertal (1985; 1986; 1986–87).
18. Weinstein (1997, 88–89) argues that this is insufficient evidence to date this structure. He prefers a twelfth-century BC date but does not explain why.

Fig. 24. Mount Ebal "ramp" and "altar" (Courtesy of Richard S. Hess)

Of some eleven other sites from the same time period in the region of
Israel (mostly in the lowlands and plains), analysis revealed bones of dogs
and donkeys elsewhere, but not here. Mount Ebal is the only site where
only the bones of edible animals were found. Bones of gazelle and pigs
were found elsewhere but not here. This is in accord with the biblical
dietary laws. However, a large percentage of bones of fallow deer were
found, which does not adhere to the animals used for sacrifice. Even so,
several species of fallow deer exist and some are permitted for eating
(Deut. 14:5), if not for sacrifice. Horwitz (1986–87, 187) suggests we have
here "a pastoral economy based primarily on caprovine herding and to
a lesser extent cattle. In addition, the high proportion of hunted animals
(fallow deer) supports the hypothesis of a nomadic or seminomadic
society." The area was not a place of food production. No sickle blades
were found, unlike other contemporary domestic sites.

If we follow Zertal in identifying the site as an altar, then its construction has a number of correlations with aspects of altars described in the
Pentateuch. The earlier thirteenth-century BC level included a round installation with ashes and bones found at the center of the twelfth-century
BC altar, in addition to the customary fill of earth and stones. Leviticus
6:3–4 requires that ashes be placed in a ritually pure site. At the east side
of the "altar" was found a chalice-shaped container made of rock from
the other side of the Jordan River. About 1200 BC, with no indication
of a violent disruption or break, apparently the same people who had
been visiting the site built a larger "altar." This level of occupation lasted

for about fifty years, according to pottery, and then it was abandoned without any indication of what happened. No figurines were found.

The north courtyard contains what Zertal (1986–87) has described as a "ramp" going up to the "altar." Exodus 20:26 forbids the construction of steps on an altar so that no priest would expose himself when he used the steps. A ramp fulfilled this purpose. A veranda around the top of the "altar" has also been identified.[19] Was it used to sprinkle blood on the four corners of the altar?

The pottery suggests a connection with the local region and perhaps with the area east of the Jordan River. Although the type of pottery in dominance changes between the two occupation levels and there are three times as much pottery in the later phase, the material culture does not otherwise appear different. Twenty percent of the pottery found is distinct to the area occupied by the Israelite tribe of Manasseh. It appears at the beginning of the thirteenth century BC and disappears at the end of the twelfth century BC. The abandonment could be related to the beginning of the Israelite settlement at Shiloh, where the Bible records the establishment of a sanctuary by Israel after entering the land. The presence of this pottery in Transjordan at sites such as Tell Deir ʿAlla is slightly earlier. Thus an east to west movement of the people using this pottery has been argued by Zertal.[20]

Is this actually an altar similar to that of Joshua as described in Joshua 8:30–35? This interpretation has been disputed.[21] It has been suggested that this is merely an early farmhouse and agricultural installation, the beginnings of a settlement.[22] Or perhaps it is a watchtower. The excavator, Adam Zertal, disputes these interpretations, however.[23] The rough stones for the "altar," the context of an area capable of handling a large public gathering, the "kosher" animal bones found in the area, the lack of any sizable wall that could be used for defense, the lack of particular sickle blades and other farming implements, and the position of the structure away from the peak of the ridge where it would be if it were a watchtower, may all suggest a cultic installation. This is not, however, to suggest that it is the altar of Joshua. Nor does it seem to be an altar at

19. Zevit (2001, 303) considers this to be a *yĕsōd* as was required for certain blood sacrifices. Traditionally this has been interpreted as the base of the altar (cf. NIV).

20. Zertal (1991a, 32–34; 1996; 1998) refers to the distribution of three types of cooking pots. However, Dever (Shanks et al. [1992, 51]) disputes this as impossible to demonstrate from an archaeological standpoint. Nevertheless, ongoing publication of the ceramic data continue to support this (Zevit [2001, 102–3]). The analysis of the genealogical data of Chronicles (Galil [1983, xxiii–xxiv]) correlates well with the presence of an early Israel east of the Jordan River.

21. Cf. Dever in Shanks et al. (1992, 33–34); Dever (2003, 89–90).

22. Cf. Ahlström (1993, 366).

23. Cf. Zertal (1985; 1986; 1986–87).

all, at least not the usual type of altar. There is no evidence of the sorts of things often found at altars: cult figurines, votive offerings, and *maṣṣēbôt*. But then the biblical texts argue that such was not allowed.[24] Is it cultic? According to Grabbe (2002, 85) the evidence from the site "demonstrates nothing." Against Grabbe, Bloch-Smith and Alpert-Nakhai describe the site as an atypical cultic site for Iron Age I Manasseh sites insofar as it is isolated on a hilltop and distant from any extensive agricultural land.[25] Thus it does not fit into the typology of surrounding sites in the region from the same period. They suggest the earlier altar may have been Canaanite and the later structure was built on by the Israelites. However, the absence of Canaanite cultic paraphernalia makes a Canaanite altar difficult to identify there. Further, the continuity of culture between the phases suggests the same people who occupied the earlier one may also have used the later one.

The site on Mount Ebal remains anomalous. Perhaps for this reason some wish to remove any cultic association from it. By so doing, its obvious discontinuity with the earlier cults of the surrounding areas does not require explanation.

However, no other interpretation of the site commends itself. It seems not to be well positioned for a watchtower. This would make more sense if the structure were moved a distance of some feet to the peak of the ridge itself. The farmhouse identification requires one to explain the absence of horse, donkey, pig, and gazelle bones. As Zevit (2001, 200) observes: "The skewed distribution of bones supports a nondomestic interpretation of the site." He also observes that the pottery, both in terms of types and distribution over the site, point toward a site where at least some of the animals may have been killed for cultic purposes. Typologically, although the site is unique, the altar resembles that of the later Israelite sanctuary in the fort at Arad. Both were built of an outer shell of uncut stones with an inner fill of dirt, stones, and (at Mount Ebal) ash. This altar construction distinguishes them from other forms of Canaanite altars and those in surrounding cultures. The continuity of the Ebal altar for animal sacrifice with one built centuries later at Arad implies a tradition of altar construction that was unique and ongoing in the religious life of ancient Israel. Finally, the single structure may imply a single deity as the focus of worship. If this site on Mount Ebal is an altar, then the absence of images, the particular animals sacrificed, the

24. Zertal (1995, 273) concludes that the cultic nature of the site has been generally accepted and that no convincing alternative for it has been successful. His own analysis of contemporary and later fortresses in the region concludes that they are not like the Mount Ebal site.

25. Cf. Bloch-Smith and Alpert-Nakhai (1999, 71, 77). The region occupied by the Israelite tribe of Manasseh west of the Jordan River includes the area of Mount Ebal.

possible connection with a later Israelite cult site, and the single altar provide a distinctive collection of elements that set it apart from other Canaanite evidence. Beyond this, the identification of this site remains an open question that cannot be settled at present.

Shiloh

Shiloh (Tell Seilun) is a pre-Israelite cult center, a Middle Bronze Age shrine, and a Late Bronze Age site occupied by a pastoral population.[26] Finkelstein identified Late Bronze Age Shiloh as a cult center without links to any permanent settlement. The animal bones found with the offering vessels are

Fig. 25. Site of Khirbet Seilun, identified with biblical Shiloh (Courtesy of Richard S. Hess)

mainly sheep and goats with a few cattle bones. This is more suggestive of a nomadic pastoral economy than of a settled economy.[27]

Noth suggested that the Shiloh sanctuary was intertribal, though he was influenced by his amphictyony hypothesis.[28] Orlinsky (1962), de Geus (1976), Mayes (1974), and de Vaux (1978) argued that it was local. The archaeological and settlement evidence suggests that in the first half of the eleventh century BC, when occupation at Shiloh peaked, settlement was only beginning in the Upper Galilee, Beersheba Valley, and, to a certain extent, in the Judean hills. The plain of Issachar was uninhabited. Shiloh therefore was not a center for distant groups. However, the "well-developed architecture and the hints of very advanced planning"[29] suggest a sphere of influence beyond the region of Ephraim (where the site was located) to Benjamin and Manasseh. Thus this may well have been an intertribal sanctuary site as suggested in 1 Samuel. Although the sanctuary at the top of the site is missing, the pillared buildings of Area C formed part of the sanctuary complex. Vessels with animal reliefs were found there.

26. Cf. Finkelstein (1988). For the Bronze Age site see the discussion under the list of sites at the end of chapter 5, p. 133.

27. The ratio of sheep/goats to cattle is 94 to 6.

28. This refers to the now discredited amphictyony hypothesis argued that the Israelite central sanctuary with a twelve-tribe league following the model of the Classical Greek league of twelve cities.

29. Finkelstein (1985).

Shiloh precedes the sanctuary of Bethel. Eighty-five to ninety percent of the central hill country Iron Age I sites are in the territories of Ephraim and Manasseh. Only later, at the end of the eleventh century BC, did settlement expand to "gain momentum" in Benjamin, Judah, and the Beersheba Valley.

Why was Shiloh the location of an early cult center? A Middle Bronze II cult site existed but no Late Bronze Age city with indigenous inhabitants. The region around Shiloh represents a dense Israelite settlement area with a sparse Canaanite population. It flourished from the second half of the twelfth century BC to the first half of the eleventh century BC, when it was destroyed, presumably by the Philistines.[30] Its size was two and two-thirds acres, comparable to large villages such as Ai. Note that the cult site has not been found for the Middle Bronze, Late Bronze, and Iron I occupations. Some have suggested that it was located on the summit and destroyed in subsequent occupations. Also, it may have not existed as a permanent structure with identifiable remains. As a cult center between c. 1150 and c. 1050 BC, its location may reflect the development and change of occupation in the hill country. Conceivably, the site may have become more central to the settlement at this point than the Ebal site. Thus the center of habitation moved south.

Gilgal at Khirbet ed-Dawwara?

From the second half of the eleventh century until c. 900 BC in Benjamin, the most densely settled area of the hill country, and in the desert fringe to the east of the cultivated area, modern Khirbet ed-Dawwara, there is the earliest example of "full-scale Israelite fortification" with casemate-like rooms adjacent to the perimeter wall.[31] Given its remote eastern location, its lack of customary domestic implements for such a site, and its having commenced occupation after the destruction of Shiloh, is this both a fort against the Philistines and the cult center of the Gilgal of Samuel and Saul?[32] Israel Finkelstein argues the former and only suggests the latter, observing that such a conclusion requires this Gilgal to be different from the one in the Jordan Valley (i.e., the Gilgal of Joshua) and that, without further evidence, it could also be Beth-aven or simply an unnamed site. However, only thirty-six animal bone fragments were found. They included the remains of sheep, goats, cattle, dogs, and deer (Sadeh 1990).[33]

30. Cf. the story of the Philistine defeat of the Israelites in 1 Sam. 4.
31. Cf. Finkelstein (1990, 197).
32. Cf. its mention in 1 Sam. 7:16; 10:8; 11:14–15; 13:4, 7–8, 12, 15; 15:12, 21, 33.
33. Ahlström (1993, 438–39) suggests the site could have been a base on the border between Ephraim and Benjamin from which Saul extended his military control over the Jordan Valley and Transjordan.

Other Biblical Cult Centers

The Bible records additional cult centers at Mizpah (Judg. 20:1–3, 8–10, 21:1, 5, 8; 1 Sam. 7:5–11; 10:17–24); Hebron (2 Sam. 5:3; 15:7); Bethlehem (Judg. 19:18); Nob (1 Sam. 21:1–10 [Heb. 2–11]; 22:16–19); and Gibeath of Saul (2 Sam. 21:9).[34]

On a national level the biblical text indicates that the tribes of Israel united around the covenant with their God.[35] They celebrated three feasts in the course of the year: Unleavened Bread in spring, Weeks at the beginning of summer, and Tabernacles in autumn. The last feast achieved special prominence as the Feast of Yahweh (Lev. 23:39), where the booths or "tabernacles" were perhaps associated with temporary dwellings where farmers lived at the time of the harvest.[36] As suggested by their connection with the cultic calendar tradition already found at thirteenth-century BC Emar, the Passover (Exod. 12) and other festivals also appeared early and helped to stimulate the memory of Israel's deliverance from Egypt.[37]

Animal Bones and Human Diet in the Hill Country

Given the prominence of sheep and goat bones at the sites of Ebal, Shiloh, and Khirbet ed-Dawwara in the twelfth century BC and later, the relationship of this diet to the Bible and its contrast to surrounding cultures is observed in a cogent paragraph by Ashkelon's excavator:[38]

> Our staff zoo-archaeologists, Dr. Paula Wapnish and Professor Brian Hesse of the University of Alabama in Birmingham, have begun to document a rather dramatic shift in domesticated species at the end of the Late Bronze Age and the beginning of the Iron Age (12th century BC). The shift is from sheep and goats to pigs and cattle. This shift occurred at Ashkelon and other coastal sites, but not in the central highland villages of the same period dominated by Israelites—settlements like Ai, Raddana, and Ebal. From a strictly ecological perspective, this seems surprising. The oak-pine-and-terebinth woodlands that dominated the central hill country of Canaan, where the earliest Israelite settlements of about 1200 BC are to be found, are ideally suited for pig production, especially because of the shade and acorns. One reason why such a hog-acorn economy did not thrive in the early Israelite environment must ultimately be rooted in very early religious

34. See Zevit (2001, 255).
35. See the section in chapter 6 on "Treaty and Covenant" on pp. 167–69.
36. So P. Miller (2000, 84); although Lev. 23:42 associates it with the Exodus from Egypt. On the antiquity of this part of the cultic calendar see the discussion on p. 118.
37. Ibid.
38. Stager (1991a, 31). Cf. Hesse (1986).

taboos that forbade the consumption of pork. If so, these findings would nullify the hypothesis of anthropologist Marvin Harris that "kosher" rules can be explained primarily by ecological considerations. These findings would also contradict those scholars who argue for a much later date for the introduction of these dietary restrictions.

Thus another explanation must be found for this diet. Wapnish (1993, 429) follows the comment of Hecker regarding Amarna, a site in Egypt where pork was a food associated with the urban poor. Thus one would expect to find it in urban environments but not in the highland villages. Indeed, Finkelstein (1996a, 206) notes that Iron I sites where pig bones occur include "Philistine" (Ashkelon, Miqne, Timnah-Batash) and transjordanian (Hesban) locations, but not hill country ones (Ebal, Shiloh, Raddana). The Bible suggests that the biblical law prohibiting consumption of pork has an antiquity associated with earliest Israel, that is, during the Early Iron Age. This would have been the time that the hill country of Palestine was least urban and most village-centered. Therefore, the biblical date of the appearance of the law must be early in order to coincide with the archaeological data.[39] Some scholars feel that a pork-free diet also helps to establish Israelite ethnic boundaries.

Death and Human Sacrifice?

The vow of Jephthah and the sacrifice of his daughter occur in Judges 11:30–40. He promised to sacrifice the first creature who came to meet him on his return. This turned out to be his daughter. He fulfilled his vow to sacrifice her as a burnt offering. Such a sacrifice would have been understood as a human sacrifice, not as a devotion of his daughter to a life dedicated to work or her commitment to the Israelite tabernacle (or some other cult center). The statement that this sacrifice was made to Yahweh does not suggest that this was the ideal either then or later. However, it does imply that people such as Jephthah did not see a contradiction between human sacrifice and worship of Yahweh. If this text contains traditions reaching back to Iron Age I, then it may suggest the presence of human sacrifice at this time in Transjordan. If so, this

39. Cf. Finkelstein and Silberman (2001, 119–20). Zevit (2001, 100) considers presence or absence of pig bones to be a second-order datum because the number of sites providing them is statistically insignificant and because the argument arises from the *absence* of evidence. However, it should be remembered that this is true of virtually all Iron Age I hill sites (as opposed to virtually all coastal sites in Canaan where this evidence has been reviewed) and that the presence of pig bones at "nonhill country" sites of Palestine in Iron Age I is a positive datum. While technically an argument from silence, the "silence" is "broken" in such a manner as to form a "gastrobar" that matches other evidence for settlement at this time.

could occur in continuity with the earlier Egyptian relief of Ashkelon, which may depict child sacrifice there at the end of the thirteenth century BC.[40] It also anticipates the more widespread evidence for human sacrifice in the first millennium BC as detailed in chapter 9.

Although significant both earlier and later, there is an absence of tombs in the Iron Age I hill country. It may be that this absence is reflective of the abandonment of more elaborate and socially elite burials as occurred in the Late Bronze Age. If so, this further supports the emergence of a simple, egalitarian society in the hill country that rejected earlier conventions.[41] Compare also the absence of temples already mentioned.[42]

The United Monarchy

Although there has been debate on the existence of the United Monarchy, studies have defended a significant archaeological presence in Jerusalem in the tenth century BC as well as both the attestation of the name of David as early as the tenth century and the geopolitical possibility of a mini-empire at the same time.[43] Excavations in 2005 by Eilat Mazar (2006) at the City of David and south of the Temple Mount have revealed a late eleventh-century BC wall running from west to east across the top of the ancient town. Built on bedrock and containing Phoenician pottery from the time of David, this wall could suggest a large palace of the sort that would be found only at the center of a significant kingdom of that era. If these early indications prove well-founded then new evidence will exist for a small empire during the days of David and Solomon.

This section will consider the literary traditions of religious significance that may be traced to the United Monarchy. Consideration will then be given to the archaeological evidence and textual traditions tied to Jerusalem and especially to the temple.

Kingship and Saul

Judges remembers some of the earliest leadership in Israel to have been by "judges." The term, deriving from the West Semitic root *ṭpṭ*, is

40. See chapter 4, p. 102, and chapter 5, p. 136.
41. Faust (2004).
42. Cf. chapter 6.
43. For the archaeology, see Cahill (2003; 2004). For the textual evidence of a tenth-century BC David and the possibility of a small "empire," see Kitchen (2002; 2003, 93, 99–100, 452–53).

found in earlier societies such as that of eighteenth-century BC Mari. There it is used of an office of leadership as much as and more than that of a judicial figure. Its usage in the biblical Judges occurs as a charismatically appointed office, that is, one established and controlled by Yahweh rather than one that was hereditary. This appears to be unique in the ancient Near East. While judicial functions are described, most of the narratives deal with situations where a divinely appointed leader, with or without the assistance of fellow Israelites, delivers oppressed tribes by killing the enemy. From a religious standpoint this might seem ideal because it allows God's selection to determine who becomes a judge. However, Judges exhibits a pattern of appointments to this office that become increasingly deviant from the divine will and gradually spirals out of control in terms of their own lives and effectiveness.[44] At the end of the book there is a civil war in which nearly the entire tribe of Benjamin is wiped out. At no time does a judge unite all the tribes of Israel and the one case of a judge, Gideon, founding a dynasty ends in tragedy and ruin.

The people demand a permanent leader: a king instead of a judge. This is met with resistance by the prophet Samuel. He perceives the nation as rejecting him although Yahweh's revelation insists that they are rejecting the deity (1 Sam. 8:7). The choice of Saul emphasizes that of a *nāgîd* or "leader" rather than a *melek* or "king."[45] Nevertheless, his function as a permanent military leader led Saul to assume the trappings of kingship and the Bible does ascribe the title of king to him.[46] In particular 1 Samuel 11:5 suggests that the increased pressure of the Philistines and other enemies brought about Saul's role as a permanent king. Saul's subsequent rejection as king, a fact announced by Samuel, occurs in the context of two separate actions: rather than wait for Samuel, he performed a sacrifice and thus usurped Samuel's role (1 Sam. 13:4–15); and he did not fully exterminate the hated Amalekite enemy (1 Sam. 15). Nevertheless, David and Solomon at times sacrificed and acted with an authority that superseded any priest. Yet they were not condemned for this. Diana Edelman (1991) asserts that the story of 1 Samuel 15 looks for Saul to follow God's guidance despite public opinion, private misgivings, or the attraction of political motives. His failure in this regard becomes the author of Samuel's reason for Saul's rejection. Mark George comments on 1 Samuel 13, noting that David is a man after Yahweh's own heart because of his continual practice of enquiring of Yahweh and then

44. Cf. B. Webb (1987); Exum (1990).
45. Cf. 1 Sam. 9:16 where Yahweh describes Saul in this manner. See also 1 Sam. 10:1 where Samuel uses the term when he anoints Saul as leader. For 1 Sam. and Saul, see Long (1989).
46. Cf. e.g., 1 Sam. 12:1–2, 13–14; 13:1; 15:1.

declaring his trust in Yahweh, actions that stand in contrast to Saul's particular concern for cultic observance and failure to inquire continually of Yahweh.[47] In the end, Saul and his son and successor, Jonathan, are killed by the Philistine enemy. This is connected with his consultation of a medium the night before the battle (1 Sam. 28). The presence of spiritual channelers suggests the presence of a belief in contact and consultation with the dead that, despite attempts to outlaw it (including Saul's own prohibition), remained a popular form of devotion that continued into the monarchical period.

2 Samuel 7 and David

The rise of David and his dynasty represent a distinctive and permanent set of rulers who are portrayed in the Hebrew Bible as receiving their rulership as a covenantal gift from Yahweh. Nowhere is this more clearly stated than in 2 Samuel 7. This text is widely assumed to be a late addition retrojected back into the traditions of the dynasty's founder. However, ancient Near Eastern parallels with second-millennium BC Hittite sources provide evidence for the antiquity of many of the ideas and expressions.

Moshe Weinfeld compares the Abrahamic and Davidic covenants with neo-Assyrian land grants and especially with the earlier Late Bronze Age (c. 1500–c. 1200 BC) Hittite grants in which the most prominent items bestowed by the Hittite king on Syrian vassals were land and the right of the reigning sovereign to preserve his dynasty.[48] There are several ways that Hittite treaties bear ideas similar to those found in 2 Samuel 7 and the divine covenant in which God promises David an eternal dynasty. For one thing, compare the divine promise of 2 Samuel 7:14–15 to the treaty between the Hittite king and Ulmi-Teshub: "If one of your descendants sins the king will prosecute him at his court. Then when he is found guilty . . . if he deserves death he will die. But nobody will take away from the descendant of Ulmi-Teshub either his house or his land in order to give it to a descendant of somebody else."[49]

Compare the divine adoption of sonship in 2 Samuel 7:14 (and in the Psalms)[50] with the bilingual testament of Hittite king Hattusili I, "Behold,

---

47. Cf. George (2002, 457).

48. Cf. Weinfeld (1993, 236–47).

49. Laato (1997) has studied early second-millennium BC Mari and Eshnunna texts, as well as those from later periods, concluding that ideas such as the promise of an eternal dynasty were known and used before and after the time of David. The identification of this vocabulary as Deuteronomistic is not proven nor can it be used to date the prophecy.

50. An example is found in Ps. 45:6 [Heb. 7] where the king is addressed as "your throne, O God, will last forever." Although it is possible to understand this line as "your divine

I declared for you the young Labarna: He shall sit on the throne. I, the king called him my son." Thus the concept of sonship has nothing to do with a mythology where a god "adopts" a human king into divinity as his son.[51] Instead, it is part of the legitimating process in which the king establishes a dynasty. Nuzi adoption contracts also call someone a son in order to establish the rights and privileges of the one chosen. Other verbal parallels with ancient Near Eastern documents of various types can be found. Gary Knoppers (1996) successfully challenges the argument that 2 Samuel 7 must be based solely on a land grant document in terms of structure and verbal parallelism. The biblical documents draw from a variety of sources according to their own needs and purposes.

In addition to 2 Samuel 7, written history and psalms reflect God's chosen king and city. These perhaps were written for the elite, the literate members of the court.[52] However, there was also an increasing number of Israelites who would either hear the stories read and psalms sung by Levites or other court representatives, or would themselves be able to read.[53]

Nor is the distinctive role of the king in Ugaritic literature the only legitimate comparison with the biblical texts that discuss David and the period of the monarchy. Many similarities have already been noted in the discussion of Ugarit in chapter 4. Many of the psalms of the Bible, often connected with David and his lineage, reveal a degree of similarity on multiple levels of correspondence. The closest parallels with the psalms as well as other Hebrew poetry can be found in the Ugaritic poetic texts. Thus at Ugarit Baal is a Cloud Rider just like Yahweh rides the clouds in Psalm 104:3.[54] There are parallels with expressions and cadences as applied to Baal and to Yahweh:[55]

---

throne" or to see it interpolated into the psalm in a postexilic context where such kingship is ascribed to God alone, the simplest understanding remains that this psalm of a royal wedding ascribes a divine aspect to the royal bridegroom. It was upon such texts that the Myth and Ritual School (see the discussion of this school of thought in chapter 3, p. 61) established the view that ancient Israel regarded and celebrated its king in Jerusalem as a deity. However, the Hittites and the royalty at Ugarit received such ascriptions and yet it is clear that the living kings of both were not worshiped as divine through cultic activities or other means. Thus it is best to understand the unique role of the king in Jerusalem as one possessing a special relationship to God without any necessary bestowal of divinity.

51. This was the view of some biblical scholars in the past. See the preceding note.

52. Cf. Liverani (1990); Machinist (1976).

53. Cf. Hess (2002b).

54. *KTU* 1.1 IV 8. De Moor (1971, 98) and Day (2000, 92) note that *Be-'-li-ra-kab-bi* "Baal of the chariot," is known from Samal and that Ramesses II compared himself with Baal when he rode his chariot. Elsewhere in Ugaritic literature *rkb* means "ride" or "mount." Ps. 68:4 [Heb. 5] refers to Yahweh as a rider through the deserts, reading *rōkēb bāʾărābōt*, following Day (2000, 92–93), in accordance with the wilderness and Sinai traditions.

55. For music at Ugarit see Koitabashi (1998).

KTU 1.2 IV 9–10 has "As for your enemy, O Baal, as for your enemy, you'll smite (him), you'll destroy your adversary."

Psalm 92:9 has "For surely your enemies, O LORD, surely your enemies will perish; all evildoers will be scattered."

If the psalms contain repeated instances of prayers to Yahweh, *KTU* 1.119 provides the best and perhaps the only example of a lengthy prayer to Baal, occurring at the end of a ritual tablet.[56]

Additional themes found earlier in Ugaritic mythology recur in the Psalms and in the poetic literature. For example, Psalm 29 deals with Yahweh's conflict with the sea. Other biblical poems address conflict with the dragon. In Psalm 74:13 the *tannînîm* or dragon has multiple heads.[57]

The Ark, Jerusalem, and the Temple

There are two types of presentations of the temple in Jerusalem, pictorial and literary. The pictorial begins with 2 Samuel 6:12–23. There religious processions of the ark into Jerusalem are accompanied by David's ritualistic dance. In the view of some this personifies the victory of God over enemies. The description resembles actions performed in the Ugaritic texts' explanation of Baal's defeat of his enemies and his distribution of food to all people (a divine banquet also found in Ugaritic texts).[58] More generally, the intense music and dancing may function to call Yahweh's attention to David and to look favorably on his action.[59]

The pictorial description also focused on Solomon's construction of the temple that united all the people in the work of its construction, and in rendering Jerusalem and its God as the recognized center of the greatest empire with the greatest God who lived in the greatest temple.[60] Its description is that of long-room Syrian temples known earlier in various Palestinian sites such as Bronze Age Hazor.[61] Many temples in

56. See chapter 4, pp. 108–9.
57. See further on these and other themes in chapter 4, p. 96. Day (2000, 98–107) holds that the Leviathan and Behemoth, as described in Job 40–41, designate mythical rather than zoological creatures.
58. Seow (1989, 7–8) understands 2 Sam. 5–6 within the context of "a religio-political drama celebrating the victory of YHWH as the divine warrior of Canaanite mythology and his consequent accession as king."
59. David Wright (2002) regards the dancing as erotic.
60. Cf. C. Meyers (1987); also Strange (1991, 24–29), but Strange's attempts to ascribe here a divine kingship to Solomon are speculative.
61. For others see the list in chapter 5, p. 126.

and around contemporary Syria also possessed this form. For a long time Tell Taʿyinat in modern Turkey was thought to have the closest example of a temple like that of Solomon's. The Tell Taʿyinat temple was located adjacent to the palace on its site, just as is described in Jerusalem for Solomon's temple.[62] More recently, an even closer parallel has been identified at ʿAin Dara in northern Syria. There the tenth-century BC temple possesses three rooms, two pillars at the entrance, and features such as recessed and latticed windows. Later a multistory set of rooms was built around three sides of the temple.[63] It is actually larger than Solomon's temple. Footsteps, each three feet long, were carved into the entrance steps and the portal to suggest a huge deity.[64]

Peter Machinist (1976) notes how these items were used as a justification of the Israelite appropriation of Canaanite culture. Psalm 29 appropriates attributes to Yahweh that had been given to Baal.[65] The building projects in the Canaanite center of Jerusalem and especially the construction of the temple on the basis of Canaanite forms were all arguments that Yahweh had conquered the Canaanite deities. Machinist compares a similar situation in Mesopotamia a century or two earlier in which literature and architecture were used by Assyria to demonstrate its conquest and appropriation of Babylon and its culture.

The literary presentation of the temple focuses on 1 Kings 5–9 and its description of the temple's construction and dedication. Victor Hurowitz (1992) compares temple building accounts from ancient Mesopotamia, from Ugarit, and from the Bible. Five elements occur in all the accounts: (1) a reason to build or restore a temple that includes a divine command or consent; (2) preparations for the construction; (3) description of the construction process and of the result; (4) dedication of the structure; (5) prayers for blessings on the temple and its builder; and sometimes (6) conditional curses and blessings to the future ruler who will be called on to rebuild or restore the temple. Each of these categories is applied to the appropriate section of 1 Kings 5–9, and the structures of both are found to be identical. The description that most closely resembles 1 Kings 5–9 is that of the twelfth- and eleventh-century BC Assyrian king Tiglath-pileser I.[66]

62. King and Stager (2001, 335–36), who also note that the later Philistine temple at Ekron follows this "West Semitic" model.

63. Monson (1999; 2000).

64. Cf. Baal's size, throne, palace, and "hand" (*KTU* 1.101 1–3; 1.6 I 59–61; 1.4 VI 56–57; 1.23 33–35; as collected by M. Smith [2001a, 84]).

65. See further in chapter 4, p. 97.

66. The same comparisons can be made with the building of the second temple in Zech. 4:6–10. Cf. Laato (1994). Van Seters (1997, 55) disputes the parallels as general and vague. However, he does not provide the sort of detailed examination that Hurowitz (1992) undertakes, both in terms of the varieties of literature and of the study of the texts

Additional parallels with 1 Kings 5–9 may be found in other Mesopotamian and Ugaritic literature. Assyrian texts describing the return of the god to its temple resemble the bringing of the ark to the temple in 1 Kings 8:1–11. Mesopotamian instructions for builders, receipts, didactic school texts, and the descriptions of temple vessels and buildings all have parallels in 1 Kings 5–9. Phoenician and Aramaic building inscriptions contain date formulae similar to that which occurs in the construction of the temple. The naming of the temple's master builder (here Hiram) also appears in the Ugaritic Baal epic, in *Enuma Elish* Tablet V, and in Mesopotamian grant documents.

Formally, Solomon's prayer of dedication in 1 Kings 8 may resemble other prayers of dedication by Assyrian and Babylonian rulers. In all these, concerns for dynastic stability and the answering of prayers predominate. However, with the Mesopotamian rulers it is assumed that the deity will answer because of the new home that is built for it. In 1 Kings, the temple is not assumed to be a "home" for the deity. In the context of what is designated Deuteronomistic theology, Solomon appeals to the word of God, in the forms of the divine promise to David and of the covenant made with all of Israel. Thus an ancient Near Eastern form is followed but its content is transformed by a wholly unique biblical theology.

Such a literary context raises interesting questions about the composition of these chapters. Did the author make use of royal administrative records and other temple inscriptions? Roger Tomes (1996) distinguishes form (temple building account) from motivation and sees for the latter the threatened destruction of the temple at the beginning of the sixth century BC. However, because the overall form seems to have been followed so closely, most or all of this text, just like other such accounts, may have been a temple building description written at the time of its construction in the international court of Solomon's day. Donald Wiseman (1993, 42) suggests that the official annals of Solomon's reign would have preserved this type of description, as found elsewhere in ancient Near Eastern royal annals.

Ziony Zevit (2001, 340–43) observes that the temple was enveloped on three sides by a three-storied chambered building.[67] The temple includes a façade entrance, called an *'ūlām*, a holy place or antechamber for only the priests, called a *hēkāl*, and a most holy cubicle, known as *děbīr*. The antechamber and a distinct holy of holies are found in pre-

themselves. Nevertheless, he is accurate in his observation that, when it comes to the written text, the perspective is not that of the king but of the historian. Thus, whatever the sources, they have been modified to fit into their present context.

67. See the above example of ʿAin Dara where evidence for such structures existed. For this structure attached to the temple building itself, cf. 1 Kings 6:5, 10.

Israelite Canaan at sites such as at Hazor and Lachish.[68] Model shrines also reflect both antechambers and most holy places.[69]

Hurowitz (1994, 37) discusses the architecture of Solomon's temple in light of what is known about other ancient Near Eastern temples and palaces. He concludes that the temple of Solomon was decorated with floral patterns in symbolism of the garden that often surrounded temples and palaces, that the pillars Yachin and Boaz represented the trees of life and knowledge as in the Garden of Eden, that the lion and cattle decorations symbolized the peaceful coexistence of wild and tame animals, that the cedar wood represented the Lebanon mountains where deity was often said to reside, and that the locations of divine palaces by a sea and at the confluence of rivers were represented by the bronze sea and the water basins.[70] William Dever concurs, adding the following to the list of similarities with contemporary temples: a long-room temple pattern, ashlar masonry, wooden beams alternating with stone at every third course, carved wooden panels placed over the masonry, and decorations of cherubs, lions, and palm trees. Note Dever's comment (2001, 145): "We now have direct Bronze and Iron Age parallels for *every single feature* of the 'Solomonic temple' as described in the Hebrew Bible; and the best parallels come from, and only from, the Canaanite-Phoenician world of the 15th–9th centuries."

Additional Evidence of Cultic Materials from Iron Age I (c. 1200–c. 1000 BC)

Cultural Background of Iron Age I Palestinian Highlands

As noted in the first section of this chapter, there are grounds for identifying many of the Iron Age I villages, of which about three hundred have been discovered in the highlands of Palestine, with early Israel. There are estimates of between 40,000 and 75,000 people living west of the Jordan River in the central highlands.[71] The culture of these villages can be identified.[72] The sites themselves are small and oval-shaped villages. The use of coarse pots and silos reveals a simple lifestyle. There

68. See chapter 5, p. 126.
69. See further in chapter 10, p. 307.
70. Hurowitz (1994, 33) suggests that the pictures of animals were intended as depictions of God's power and dominion over creation. The cherubim represented his retinue and guard. For the copper stands in the courtyard of the temple as cult stands, see King and Stager (2001, 341). God's presence is immediate in Ezek. 40–48 and replaces the ark. Cf. Joyce (2005).
71. Cf. Bloch-Smith and Alpert-Nakhai (1999, 77).
72. Cf. Finkelstein (1988; 1988–89).

Fig. 26. Palestinian highlands (Courtesy of Richard S. Hess)

is no evidence of monumental building or centralized authority. There was no king in Israel.[73]

Alphabetic writing did exist at this time. This is different from the Late Bronze Age when the script was cuneiform and the language was Akkadian. Akkadian was the common language of trade and diplomacy used throughout the eastern Mediterranean and the Middle East. Lipiński (1993b, 322) notes that this change in writing in Palestine came about with the "extinction of the tradition of cuneiform writing used in Canaan in the Late Bronze Age mainly for purposes of international correspondence. Local needs were obviously satisfied by the alphabetic script." The fact that few historical records remain from this period has to do with the shift from more permanent clay tablets to perishable papyrus and animal skin. Already in the twelfth century BC, examples of inscriptions in southern Canaan include the Khirbet Raddana jar handle with the name of Ahilud on it.[74] From a slightly later period an abecedary was found at Izbet-Sartah, a site probably identified with the Israelite village of Ebenezer. This text, like the tenth-century BC Gezer calendar and the abecedary from Tel Zayit, is an exercise of someone who was

73. Cf. Dever (2001, 113).
74. Cf. Bloch-Smith and Alpert-Nakhai (1999, 73), with photo. In fact, the list of recovered inscriptions demonstrates reading and writing throughout all the regions of settled Israel, both rural and urban, in every century after this. See Hess (2002c).

Fig. 27. Bull from Early
Iron Age site east of
Dothan (Courtesy of
the Israel Antiquities
Authority)

learning how to write.[75] Dever (2001, 203) observes, "We may assume that writing, and even what we may call 'functional' literacy, was reasonably widespread by the 10th century, and certainly by the 9th century."

Initial settlement began in the Lower Galilee at this time. The Nazareth hills and the Beit Netofa Valley, found in the tribal allotments of Zebulun and Naphtali, were among the first to be settled, according to the occupational evidence.[76] Eastern lower Galilee was not settled prior to the tenth century BC.

With rare exceptions, there are no shrines or temples in the village culture of the Iron Age I highlands in contrast to the proliferation of such in the fortified cities of the Late Bronze Age. This suggests a change from the traditional religious worship of the preceding period to a "simple, aniconic, noninstitutionalized cult."[77] In addition, the absence of pig bones suggests an ethnic marker for people for whom eating pork is taboo.

75. Izbet-Sartah is located west of the hill country, near Aphek and just overlooking the coastal plain. It has been identified with the Ebenezer of 1 Sam. 4:1; 5:1; 7:12. It is disputed whether this site is Israelite in an ethnic sense, and whether the writing can be called Hebrew as opposed to a "pre-Hebrew" script. Cf. Ahlström (1993, 353–56). However, as has been noted, what is Israelite and what is not Israelite cannot easily be distinguished from the material culture. Further, to dispute that a script is Hebrew, because it is too early, is meaningless unless one can say with certainty when the Hebrew script began and how widely it was distributed. Tel Zayit is a site of eight acres southwest of Jerusalem and eighteen miles east of Ashkelon. The script has been generally identified as an example of one in the transition period from a generally Phoenician script to one that is specifically Hebrew. See Hess 2006; Tappy et al., 2006.

76. Cf. Gal (1991; 1992); Zertal (1991a; 1991b). Movement of settlement from the eastern to the western slopes of the central hill country led to increased specialization and population pressure that brought encounters with Philistines of the coastal plain and competition for resources (Finkelstein 1995). Contrast Dever (2003).

77. Dever (2001, 113–14).

Additional Iron Age I Cultic Sites

The Iron I period includes the emergence of several hundred villages in the highlands of Palestine and the areas east of the Jordan during the first part of the twelfth century. At least some of the inhabitants of these villages may be identified as recently settled Israel, as suggested above. The unusual aspect of these villages, in terms of religion, is the manner in which they minimize objects related to worship. Using the traditional means to identify cult centers, the early Iron Age cult sites are virtually free of any of the expected objects or architecture that customarily identify religious centers. There are almost no figurines nor are there any distinctive altars or temple/shrine architecture. Unlike the large fortress temple at Shechem, for example, village sites at Dan, Ai, Khirbet Raddana (although not much of a cultic nature was found here), Tell Irbid, and Tell es-Sa'idiyeh contain evidence of simple cultic structures that stood among domestic structures. One finds at these sites an occasional standing stone, offering bench, or distinctive vessel.[78]

This contrasts with Late Bronze Age (c. 1550–c. 1200 BC) evidence from occupied sites of the same hill country region.[79] These sites are often characterized as larger population centers, whereas those highland settlements of the Iron Age I period were villages. The finds at these village sites have revealed few distinctions in terms of any specialized architectural constructions or any prestige objects such as jewelry or cult items. The people of this society simply did not manufacture or use the same sorts of objects for worship as the evidence of their settled

78. Cf. Biran (1993, 326); Joseph Callaway (1993, 44–45); James Callaway (1993); Lenzen (1997, 181); Tubb (1993, 1298); Alpert-Nakhai (2001, 170–76). Alpert-Nakhai also includes Tell el-'Umeiri. However, this site has the largest defensive system in Palestine in the Early Iron Age. Cf. Geraty (1997). Villages at Hazor and Megiddo also contained more elaborate remains, but these may have included forms from the Bronze Age, as did sites such as Dan. Cf. Ussishkin (1997, 464); Yadin (1993, 600–602). Tel Qiri, located near what may have been regarded as the ancient sacred area of Mt. Carmel and close to the Canaanite passes into the Megiddo Plain, contained materials that may reflect its having been situated adjacent to important international trade routes. The unfortified nature of the settlement and the remains that attest to a wealthy group of inhabitants suggest a security that was not available to previous periods. Its cultic repertoire from the end of the eleventh century is more elaborate and includes a building, an incense burner, and the remains of sacrifices in the form of foreleg bones of goat and sheep. See Ben-Tor (1993b, 1228–29).

79. In fact, Alpert-Nakhai (2001, 120, 136–52) identifies seven sites west of the Jordan and four sites east of the Jordan that she argues lie within the region of early Israel or immediately adjacent to it. Excavations at these sites have revealed distinctive architecture or cultic objects that suggest religious activities. She lists Beth Shean, Shechem, Aphek, Shiloh, Gezer, and Jerusalem west of the Jordan, and Pella, Tell Abu al-Kharaz, Tell Deir 'Alla, and Tel Safut east of the river. See further the list of sites at the end of chapter 5 and the discussion of many of these there.

predecessors suggests. Some sites such as Shechem and Shiloh continue to exhibit special cultic buildings and objects into the Iron Age I. Others such as Tell el-ʿUmeiri developed defenses with cultic installations. However, the highland villages of Iron Age I did not follow this pattern. In addition to the questionable Ebal site and what remains at Shiloh, already discussed, the following paragraphs list the major finds of cult sites and possible cultic implements in the region.

The first is the aptly named Bull site located four miles east of Dothan. The open site on top of the hill was used for the cultic purposes of the local village with a bronze bull figurine, a *maṣṣēbâ*, a small temenos wall surrounding an open-air paved area, and perhaps an additional cult object. The figurine has been identified as a zebu bull because of its northern style. Late Bronze Age Hazor has five such figurines and Ugarit has examples as well. Forms of this type of bull appear with the Sea Peoples on the relief at Medinet Habu.[80] It is about seven inches long and five inches high. The bull figurine has been likened to the Middle Bronze Age Ashkelon object, but that image is more like a calf than a bull. In light of the form, some suggest that the image may represent either a weather god or El.[81] Others see in the image a figure of Baal like the one destroyed by Gideon in Judges 6.[82] One may compare the (village) altar to Baal in Judges 6:25–26 and Gideon's later ephod, as well as the ephod, *tĕrāpîm*, and image of Judges 17:4–5.[83] At the Bull site, the *maṣṣēbâ* has a flat stone in front of it.[84] It may or may not have been Israelite.[85] Although the Bull site occurs within the area of the early Iron Age villages in the hill country, it appears to be unique. The small size of the cultic site and the immediate surrounding area do not support a view that this was a center for many worshipers. Rather, it appears to have been local to the nearby village or villages. Further, given the comparisons already noted, there remains nothing distinctive about this site. Finally, there is a question about the dating, so that some would reassign it to the Middle Bronze Age.[86]

80. Cf. Zevit (2001, 178–79). See discussion of comparisons in A. Mazar (1982).

81. Cf. Keel and Uehlinger (1998, 118). Early on Yahweh appears as an El figure. See Dever (2001, 175).

82. Cf. Bloch-Smith and Alpert-Nakhai (1999, 76–77).

83. See Callaway and Miller (1999, 86).

84. A similar arrangement in an Iron Age I domestic setting at Tell el-ʿUmeiri has been identified by L. G. Herr, and one with multiple *maṣṣēbôt* is attested at Dan (Zevit [2001, 178n94]).

85. Cf. Zevit (2001, 180, 250–51). He compares both the Bull site and Mount Ebal with Minoan peak sanctuaries that served cult purposes from 1900 to 1600 BC and continued on mainland Greece until the eighth century. They were visible from villages and within a few hours' walk, serving a local region. Compare also the high places of Iron Age II in Isa. 57:7; 65:7; Hosea 4:13.

86. Cf. Finkelstein (1998).

Hazor was a village in the eleventh century BC. A jar was found at the site of Hazor with bronze votive objects. Also found there were incense stands, arrowheads, and four standing stones bordering a paved area. There was also a statue of a male figure with a cone hat and a weapon in his left hand.[87] A goddess with serpents was found on a silver-plated bronze standard at Hazor stelae temple C.[88]

Dan did not have a sanctuary but a small room with a chalice, a krater, and a clay model shrine. Megiddo, in residential area CC, yielded ceramic cult stands, zoomorphic vessels, a kernos, and a bird bowl. Tell el-Wawiyat, a small single-period site in the Beit Netofah Valley, yielded a jar stand, a column base, a tabun (oven), and a tripod basalt bowl.[89]

Khirbet Raddana, a highlands village, contained two houses with offering stands, stone-paved platforms, and an interesting kernos krater with bullhead spouts that may suggest Hittite influence. Tel Qiri, on the Carmel slopes, contained a standing stone and a stone basin as well as many chalices and a figurine of the Egyptian god Ptah-Sokar.[90]

The Shechem fortress temple has been identified with the temple of Baal-berith/El-berith of Judges 9.[91] Canaanite worship at a temple at Shechem focused on El/Baal-Berith (Judg. 9:4) who was worshiped beyond Shechem according to Judges 8:33.[92] El-Berith in Judges 9:46 might be a more general use of "El" as "god," who in this case would be identified with Baal. The temple of El/Baal-berith was destroyed by Abimelech (Judg. 9). It can be identified with the Late Bronze Age fortress temple identified at Shechem which was destroyed about 1100 BC.[93] In the Bible this is the first appearance of so large a religious structure.[94] Shechem may have had a pantheon, similar to other Canaanite cities. As already noted, in the fourteenth-century BC Amarna letters, the leader mentions "my god" in relation to his father. This may describe the worship or veneration of an ancestral spirit.[95] Figurines and cuneiform texts from Shechem suggest tentatively that the term Baal-berith, "lord of the covenant," was an epithet of the god El berit who functioned as a divine witness of treaties and covenants made on behalf of the city.[96]

87. Cf. Yadin (1993).
88. Cf. Kitchen (2003, 408).
89. Cf. Biran (1993); Ussishkin (1997); Alpert-Nakhai (2001, 172–73).
90. Cf. Yadin (1993); Alpert-Nakhai (2001, 174).
91. Temple 2b of Temenos 9/Stratum XI.
92. See Day (2000, 69).
93. Stager (1999; 2003).
94. Followed by the Philistine temples; Kitchen (2003, 402).
95. See Hess (1993b, 102).
96. Cf. Lewis (1996). For further discussion concerning the complex and ancient tradition history surrounding Shechem and its relation to early Israel (warlike in Gen. 34; peaceful in Josh. 24:25–26), see M. Smith (2003, 42).

There is mention of a Dagan temple at Philistine Ashdod in 1 Samuel 5:1–7. Jonathan Maccabaeus burnt a temple of Dagan at Ashdod in the second century BC.[97] First Chronicles 10:10 mentions a Dagan temple at Beth Shan.[98] Dagan appears in the place name of Beth-Dagan (also Beth-Dagon), the name of two sites located in Judah and Asher.

The ewer (two feet high and decorated in red paint) from c. 1220 BC at the Canaanite "fosse" temple at Lachish appears with depictions of ibexes flanking a tree. Hestrin (1987b) has identified these as symbolic of Asherah, a goddess also portrayed south in Egypt and north at Ugarit. The text probably reads "Mattan. An offering [to] my [la]dy Elat."[99] Alongside were a dozen scepters and two ivory pomegranates. Found at a thirteenth-century BC temple, in an area some seventy-five feet by forty-five feet, it possessed an entrance to the north near buildings used by a priest(?) and lit by slot windows or a clerestory and a white plaster mud-brick altar. Further, there is a gold plaque portraying a nude crowned goddess holding lotuses. Bones of sacrificial animals (sheep and goats as well as birds and fish) showed a predominance of interest in the right foreleg.[100]

At Ai, there is a room in the Israelite village with benches along its sides and a channel. Objects include a fenestrated stand (on the bench), an unfenestrated stand (on the floor), and an animal figurine.

East of the Jordan River, the site of Tell el-ʿUmeiri contained what has been identified as a standing stone against an inner casemate wall. Tell es-Saʿidiyeh, in the level subsequent to its destruction in Late Bronze IIB, had an eleventh-century BC building consisting of two rooms with a plastered offering bench and a niche at the rear wall. Tell Irbid, a walled site from the Late Bronze Age into Iron Age I, contained a room with an incense burner, goblets, lamps, and a basalt stand.[101]

In summary, with the exception of the continuing fortress sanctuary at Shechem, the other cult centers, including the Bull site (and Mount Ebal, if it is a sanctuary), tended to be small and simple, often open-air or built among other domestic dwellings. In this manner they contrasted with those of the Late Bronze Age.[102] In Iron Age I no female deities are found in the pictorial art, except in the cheap terra cotta figurines. These suggest the role of the goddess in personal veneration for everyday needs

97. See 1 Macc. 10:83–84; 11:4; Day (2000, 86).
98. Day (2000) regards this as "hardly . . . an early tradition."
99. M. Smith (2003, 28–29). See further on Lachish and the ewer in chapter 5 on pp. 134–35.
100. So Kitchen (2003, 406–8); cf. Lev. 7:32–34 on the subject of the right foreleg.
101. Cf. Alpert-Nakhai (2001, 175).
102. Ibid., 176.

of women. Images of deities, including Amun, Baal-Seth, and Reshef, are masculine, dominant, and triumphant.[103]

Cultic Sites of the Tenth Century BC

Much of the United Monarchy extends into the tenth century BC. At this time the site of Dan included a large rectangular platform made of ashlars, with two storage buildings, one with two large Aegean-style pithoi (jars) and a third with a snake decoration.[104] Seven-spouted lamps, an Astarte figurine, a four-horned altar, and an incense stand added to the repertoire. Food was prepared in the vicinity as pots and bowls suggest. The sacred area included a complex of rooms, identified as the liškă, with a sacrificial altar.[105] There was a basin with grooved slabs to channel liquids into two jars, and four green faience figurines.

At Hazor in Room 3283 there was a stone, six and a half feet in height and shaped like a banana (a maṣṣēbâ?). A room was lined with benches along the three walls of the raised platform. There was also the base of an incense stand, an axe head and other bronze objects, and a seated cone-head figurine. Like the slightly earlier Bull site, the bronzes lay in a deposit before the stone. Rituals toward the maṣṣēbâ were directed southward.[106]

Taanach of the tenth century BC yielded no shrine. However, offering stands were found, as were an olive press, a mold for making female figurines, and some knuckle bones (astragli) used for divination.[107] For the offering stands, see chapter 10 under the section "Iconography."

At Tell el-Hammah, at the southern entrance to the Beth Shan Valley, in the tenth century BC in room 406 there were found a zoomorphic vessel, the remaining upper half of a female plaque figurine, and a multi-handled krater with animals in relief.[108]

Tel Rehov, south of Beth Shan, was an important Jordan Valley center in the tenth century BC. The open-air sanctuary in the lower city included an altar of unworked stone on top of a mud-brick plat-

103. See Keel and Uehlinger (1998, 109–31).
104. Cf. Dan's description of a serpent in Gen. 49:17. Zevit (2001, 180–85) suggests that in antiquity the Huleh basin was a marshland with Dan on high ground. The city became associated with boats (Judg. 5:17) and with the anchors found at the cult site as votive offerings. The marshland of the Huleh basin was crossed by these boats. Others connect the Judges reference to Dan's remaining in ships with the tribe hiring themselves out to work on board Phoenician vessels.
105. For the liškă, see 1 Sam. 9:22; 1 Chron. 9:26. This seems to be a set of rooms associated with the high place.
106. Cf. Zevit (2001, 202–5).
107. Cf. Dever (2001, 178); Kitchen (2003, 410).
108. Cf. Cahill and Tarler (1993).

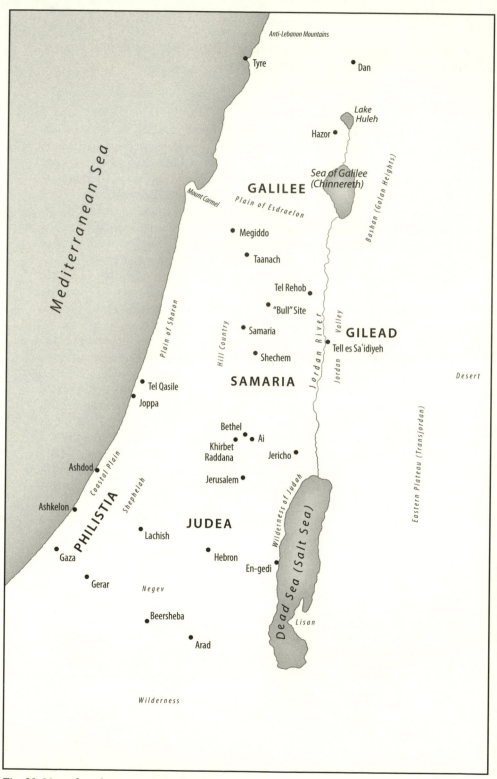

Fig. 28. Map of tenth-century BC cultic sites

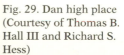

Fig. 29. Dan high place
(Courtesy of Thomas B.
Hall III and Richard S.
Hess)

form, four unhewn standing stones like those at Tel Dan, a ceramic cult stand similar to those at Pella, an animal figurine, and two female figurines.[109]

At Tell Qasile, during the United Monarchy, temple 118 was surrounded on three sides by a plastered courtyard. It served as a public center. A round stone altar, evidence of columns, a raised platform, and cult vessels with animal forms were found.[110]

At Tell Mazar, mound A is near the tell itself, about two miles north of Tell Deir 'Alla and two miles east of the Jordan River in the Jordan Valley. There were three rooms and benches for offerings mainly along the northern and western walls. The vessels included two chalices, a cult stand, storage jars, kraters, and bowls. Mound A is dated to the tenth century BC.[111]

At Lachish, cult room 49 contained benches, an altar, four clay stands, and other cultic implements, including fourteen bowls. The altar had no collar. No figurines were found. Two pairs of juxtaposed

109. Cf. Mazar and Camp (2000).
110. Cf. A. Mazar (1993, 1209–12).
111. Cf. De Groot (1993, 989).

stands were excavated. These resemble the ones found at Megiddo and Hazor.[112]

On the site where the later and more impressive temples of Arad would be built, there was what may have been a sacred enclosure.[113] Sometime before the destruction of the fortress Stratum XI, probably by the time of Pharoah Shishak's invasion in 926 BC, a temple was built in the northeastern corner of the fort. The paved courtyard, with a central sacrificial altar, led through an opening in its western wall to a broadroom (north-south axis) with benches on the west side and on the south side. This in turn led through an opening in the broadroom's western wall to a small niche (about four feet square) via three raised steps. The niche has a low platform in its northwest corner and two stelae, one of which had fallen on the platform, as well as two small altars without horns in front of the stelae. Traces of animal fat suggest foods were offered. They could have been purification offerings according to Leviticus. However, the biblical text required an altar with horns.

Iron Age I Place and Personal Names, Especially in Early Israel

The place names and the personal names preserved from Iron Age I reveal the designations of at least five deities that were known in Palestine at this time.

Several place names occur in a form composed of Baal plus a name: Baal-Shalishah (2 Kings 4:42); Baal-Perazim (2 Sam. 5:20); and Baal-Tamar (Judg. 20:33).[114] They may have been cult centers for the worship of local clans. It is not clear whether the deity worshiped was Baal or whether it was actually Yahweh who took the epithet or the name of Baal. The word "baal" can refer to the god by that name and also to a common noun meaning "lord, master."[115] And the uncertainty extends to Jonathan's sons Eshbaal and Meribaal, and to David's son Beeliada.[116] Although the same may by true for Gideon's other name, Jerubbaal, "Let Baal contend," or less likely "May Baal give increase,"[117] it is not so explained in the story of Judges 6–7. Rather Jerubbaal appears

112. See Zevit (2001, 213–17, 311–12), who suggests that perhaps one major and two minor deities were worshiped.

113. Ibid., 158.

114. See P. Miller (2000, 66).

115. Cf. Hosea 2:16 [Heb. 18]. The eighth-century BC prophet uses these terms with reference to Yahweh.

116. Thus, contra M. Smith (2003, 46), this should not be used as evidence of the worship of Baal in Saul's family.

117. Cf. Day (2000, 72).

as an appeal to let Baal defend himself when Gideon tears down his altar.[118]

Astarte occurs in the place names Ashtaroth and Ashteroth-Karnaim. It may also appear in the expression of Deuteronomy 7:13; 28:4, 18, 51, rendered as "the young of your flock." This latter refers to Astarte's role as a fertility goddess.[119]

The divine sun appears in names such as Samson and Beth-Shemesh.[120] It is personified in Psalm 19:6 [Heb. 7].[121] Samson may be a solar hero.[122] His name is derived from the Hebrew word for sun and he is associated with places such as Beth-Shemesh. There is also the association of the sun with a strong man in Psalm 19:4–5 [Heb. 5–6], and the contrast with Delilah, whose name sounds like the Hebrew word for night (laylâ).

The moon deity, Yeraḥ, appears in place names such as Beth-yeraḥ and Jericho.[123] It also occurs at thirteenth-century BC Hazor where a statue of a deity occurs with a crescent on its chest and a stele was found with hands raised to a crescent. A later stele from the site associated

118. Cf. M. Smith (2003, 43), who argues that this narrative hides the origin of the name in a context of Baal worshipers. He compares the similar name of the Amarna Age Byblian leader, Rib-Adda. While it is clear from the account that some of the townspeople worshiped Baal, the origin and meaning behind any personal name may have various explanations. The rationale for giving the name to Rib-Adda does not need to be identical to that for Jerubbaal. Nevertheless, one may suspect that in the time of the Judges Baal worship may lie behind the name, while its reinterpretation may have signaled a change in Jerubbaal's practice. In this manner, the name Gideon, as "the hewer," could have been applied to the figure by himself and by later Yahwistic bearers of this tradition.

119. See Day (2000, 128–32, 165), who describes the "Sheger," which appears in the second half of these verses and is rendered "and the young of your sheep," as a deity.

120. Day (2000, 152) identifies this site (Josh. 15:10) with Ir-Shemesh (Josh. 19:41) and Har-heres (Judg. 1:35). Day also notes En-Shemesh (Josh. 15:7; 18:17) in Judah and Timnath-serah (Josh. 19:50; 24:30) in Ephraim. He also notes Shamash-Edom in Thutmose III's fifteenth-century BC Palestinian town list.

121. Elsewhere, sun worship may be identified with Yahweh in texts such as 1 Kings 8:12; 2 Kings 23:5, 11; and Ezek. 8:16. The latter three references are noted in Day (2000, 156) as placing sun worship in the Jerusalem temple. Job 38:7 identifies the sun as part of the host of heaven or of the sons of God. These texts are supported by the identification of sun imagery with Yahweh in personal names, by pictures of the sun in iconography of the Judean kingdom, and by other artistic representations from in and around Palestine. See J. Glen Taylor (1993; 1994; 1996). However, the evidence is subject to alternative interpretation, and it is not certain what the "identification" of Yahweh with sun worship means. Was Yahweh worshiped as a form of the sun deity or believed to possess all the attributes that other people ascribed to the sun deity? However it is understood, the collected data presents a significant case for some sort of relationship between Yahweh and sun imagery.

122. Cf. Day (2000, 161–62).

123. Ibid., 163.

with Bethsaida was found there, possibly related to the moon cult.[124] Lunar worship is mentioned in Deuteronomy 4:19; 17:3; 2 Kings 23:5; Jeremiah 8:2; and Job 31:26.

The goddess Anat is known as Baal's consort and as a goddess of war in the Ugaritic myths. She appears in the Bible only in personal (Shamgar ben Anath) and place names (Anathoth, Beth-Anath, Beth-Anoth).[125] Arrowheads reputedly from near Bethlehem include names that refer to Anat (Ben Anat) and the servant of the "lioness" (Abdilabi'at).[126]

Summary

The beginning of the chapter surveyed the theories regarding Israel's appearance in the land and concluded that each perspective has something to contribute and that none is totally without merit. Nevertheless, there is evidence for a significant and influential element of early Israel to have entered the land from outside. The identification of the structure on Mount Ebal from c. 1200 BC remains controversial. Nevertheless, there remains the need to accommodate all the evidence, and the interpretation of an altar at this site cannot be discounted a priori.

Among evidence of religious practices at this time, there is a ban on pork among the early Israelites and possibly also the Canaanites, and the possibility of human sacrifice as suggested by the Ashkelon relief from c. 1210 BC and by the acts of Jephthah in Judges 11.

Kingship is treated with some ambiguity in the Bible as to its ultimate value. Nevertheless, the institution of the practice in eleventh-century BC Israel supports the belief that it was designed to enable Israel to achieve a self-identity and thus oppose the nations around it. Although there are perhaps hints in the Bible, there is no ongoing evidence for human kingship to have been recognized as divine. Expressions of God's covenant with David and similarities of the temple descriptions with known archaeological and textual data from around the tenth century render plausible an eleventh-century context for the institution of kingship.

The diverse catalogs of archaeological evidence provide a sense of the simple cult and culture of highland Palestine during the Iron Age I. Despite the surrounding sophistication of the cities that survived the Late Bronze Age, there remained a contrast in the more "egalitarian" villages.

124. A personal name, *a-bi-eraḫ*(30), occurs on a Middle Bronze Age administrative tablet found at Hazor. The name means "The lunar deity is (my) father."
125. Cf. Walls (1992); Day (2000, 132–33).
126. Cf. Hess (2004c).

Finally, we might suggest that the advent of kingship led to an abandonment of the egalitarian ideals of the highland culture and the embracing of a new form of government for Israel. The largely aniconic and simple nature of Israelite faith in the highland settlements changed under the influence of a more sophisticated monarchy that incorporated examples of polytheistic worship.

Written Sources for the Divided Monarchy

As has been the approach in the previous chapters, the focus here will be on an examination of the relevant sources to learn what may be known of the practices of peoples in ancient Israel during the period between c. 931 and 586 BC. Although some of the biblical and extrabiblical sources lie beyond this time period, they contain authentic memories of the earlier period and these will be used to supplement the contemporary sources.

Literary: Bible

Kings of Ancient Israel

The Bible relates that after the death of Solomon the kingdom was divided into two parts. In the south, the tribe of Judah and the tribe of Benjamin allied. These two preserved the ruling dynasty of David at Jerusalem. In the north, a new king arose and led the remaining tribal territories. His name was Jeroboam I (c. 931/30–c. 911/10 BC).[1] He instituted cultic practices of the north, celebrating the Feast of Booths (?) in the eighth month, a month removed from Judah's celebration of it in the seventh month. Jeroboam I also instituted the worship of gold calves at the northern and southern borders of his kingdom, Dan and Bethel (1 Kings 12:28–32). The Iron Age I (c. 1200–c. 1000 BC) Bull site in the north (see chapter 8) indicates a wider usage of this type of cult than previously thought. Contemporary Assyrian, Aramaic, and Phoenician documents further confirm that kings could appoint and dismiss priests, establish cultic calendars, and build temples and shrines.[2] Jeroboam's son, Nadab, and most northern kings followed his cultic practices. Perhaps the frequently referenced written sources for Kings and Chronicles were similar to other ancient Near Eastern chronicles, in which were recorded pious acts of rededication of shrines and continuing patronage, along with innovative religious acts of kings.[3]

1. This and the following dates for the kings of Judah and Israel follow Kitchen (2003, 30–32). Though there is much controversy on this matter of dating, the basic premises of E. Thiele and later scholars like Kitchen and Rainey (Rainey and Notley [2006, 172–74]) regarding differences between the dating systems used by the northern and southern kingdoms and as found in the books of the Kings remain valid. Here these dates are intended as useful markers for comparing the times and reigns of different kings and the religious activities associated with them.

2. Zevit (2001, 449–57).

3. E.g., Ahab's construction of a temple and altar for Baal in 1 Kings 16:30–33. Written sources in Kings and Chronicles include references to the law of Moses (1 Kings 2:3; 2 Kings 14:15; 1 Chron. 16:40; 2 Chron. 23:18; 25:4; 30:5, 18; 31:3; 35:12); the annals of Solomon (1 Kings 11:41); the annals of the Kings of Israel (1 Kings 14:19; 15:31; 16:5, 14, 20, 27; 22:39; 2 Kings 1:18; 10:34; 13:8, 12; 14:28; 15:11, 15, 21, 26, 31; 2 Chron. 33:18); the annals of the Kings of Judah (1 Kings 14:29; 15:7, 23; 22:45 [Heb. 46]; 2 Kings 8:23; 12:19 [Heb. 20]; 14:18; 15:6, 36; 16:19; 20:20; 21:17, 25; 23:28; 24:5); the records of Samuel the seer, the records of Nathan the prophet, and the records of Gad the seer (1 Chron. 29:29); the records of Nathan the prophet, the prophecy of Ahijah the Shilonite, and the

Fig. 30. The Black Obelisk of Shalmaneser III, possibly portraying Jehu in obeisance to Shalmaneser (Courtesy of James Hoffmeier)

During Ahab's reign, Hiel of Bethel laid the foundations of Jericho and brought about the death of his youngest and oldest sons (1 Kings 16:34). While this may relate to Joshua's curse (Josh. 6:26), it may also be related to foundation sacrifices (including human sacrifices), placed at the gate of a new town to ward off evil.[4]

Figures such as Ahab (c. 875/74–c. 853 BC) and Ahaziah (c. 853–c. 852 BC; 1 Kings 22:51–52 [Heb. 53–54]) may have been mentioned in the context of Baal worship by the sources referenced in Kings and Chronicles, but other kings did not worship Baal and were not so mentioned. The more perfunctory acts of continuing the cult of Jeroboam I could be done by kings at the capitals of either Tirzah or Shechem and did not require more than the royal assent. Thus Zimri (c. 886/85 BC), who reigned for only a week, was able to participate in them and received notice by the author of Kings in the annals that he cited (1 Kings 16:15). Therefore,

visions of Iddo the seer (2 Chron. 9:29); the records of Shemaiah the prophet and of Iddo the seer (2 Chron. 12:15); the "midrash" on the prophet Iddo (2 Chron. 13:22); the book of the Kings of Judah and Israel (2 Chron. 16:11; 25:26; 27:7; 28:26; "Israel and Judah" reversed in 2 Chron. 35:27; 36:8); the annals of Jehu (2 Chron. 20:34); the "midrash" on the book of the Kings (2 Chron. 24:27); the vision of Isaiah (2 Chron. 32:32); the records of the seers (2 Chron. 33:19); what is written by David and Solomon (2 Chron. 35:4); and the laments of Jeremiah (2 Chron. 35:25). See Hess (2005b).

4. Johnston (2002, 37).

while Zevit ascribes these Deuteronomistic notes[5] to a historical source (which may have recorded them in a positive manner), he notes that Israelite religion was "a matter dependent only nominally on the king."[6] Support from the cultic leadership was one of several sources from which the northern kings drew their legitimacy.

During Ahab's reign a minority worshiped Baal exclusively while another minority worshiped Yahweh exclusively. First Kings 19:18 and 2 Kings 10:18–23 indicate that Baal was worshiped by bowing and kissing, and by priests wearing special clothes. When Jehu (c. 841–c. 814/13 BC) extirpated the cult, he did not touch the asherah that Ahab had built (2 Kings 13:6).[7] Popular sympathy may have regarded Asherah as separate from Baal and more acceptable, even to Yahweh worship.[8] In line with Kuntillet ʿAjrud and other inscriptions (see below) Yahweh and Asherah were the chief deities and they were partners. If Ahab believed this it may explain why he did not place the asherah in the temple of Baal (1 Kings 16:32–33). Asherah was Yahweh's consort. Jehu's destruction of the temple left the asherah symbol unaffected. In the north in the eighth century BC the presence of Baal names as well as the extrabiblical personal name ʿglyw, "Yahweh is a calf" (or "calf of Yahweh")[9] testify, along with Kings, Amos, and Hosea, to the continuing presence of various divinities and images.[10]

In the south there is much more detail about illicit cultic institutions. Here the kings achieved legitimacy independent of the cult and dominated it. In addition to the temple to Yahweh, Solomon set up high places or *bāmôt* to Astarte of Sidon, Chemosh of Moab, and Milkom of Ammon (1 Kings 11:5–7; 2 Kings 23:13). They were maintained for three centuries (except during Hezekiah's rule) until destroyed by Josiah.

5. "Deuteronomist" refers to the scribe who edited the historical books of Joshua, Judges, Samuel, and Kings in the time of Josiah. These works share a common theological perspective—"Deuteronomistic"—related to the evaluation of kings and people according to their belief in one deity, Yahweh, and their exclusive worship of him and rejection of all other religious beliefs, practices, and images.

6. Zevit (2001, 457). For the development of kingship in Israel and its relationship to religion and the cult, see p. 225.

7. The use of the term "asherah," as spelled here without capitalization implies a reference to the image rather than necessarily to the goddess. It could also refer to the goddess associated with the image but that is a matter of scholarly debate. See the discussion below regarding the Kuntillet ʿAjrud inscriptions.

8. Zevit (2001, 466).

9. M. Smith (2003, 83); Hess (forthcoming a).

10. M. Smith (2003, 84) also cites the associations of Yahweh (as Horus-Yaho) with the bull image in Amherst Papyrus 63 of the Hellenistic period. As with the discussion of Baal/baal in personal names of the previous century, these might not refer to the divine name Baal, but rather to an epithet "lord" that could refer to Yahweh. See chapter 8.

In 1 Kings 14:22–24 the suggestion is that Judeans set up "high places" with *maṣṣēbôt* and *'ăšērîm* "on every high hill and under every leafy tree."[11] Zevit, who suggests that these were located outside the cities, notes that 2 Chronicles 11:13–17 mentions that Jeroboam I did not support many of the priests and Levites there, so they moved south.[12] The mention of the so-called high places or *bāmôt* may suggest that this is where they took up residence. The invasion of Pharaoh Shishak in Rehoboam's fifth year (926 BC) is juxtaposed to this idolatry as a punishment for Rehoboam's failure to deal with these assaults (1 Kings 14:25–28).

Asa of the southern kingdom (c. 912/11–c. 871/70 BC) followed David in removing the *qĕdēšîm* (cultic personnel), the *gillulîm* (round images; 1 Kings 15:12; see next section), and the *mipleṣet*, an image set up by his mother.[13] He did not remove the *bāmôt* and made votive offerings at the temple (1 Kings 15:9–15). He also imprisoned Hanani, the seer, and persecuted others (2 Chron. 16:7–10). That he was able to expel (rather than put to death) the *qĕdēšîm* suggests that they may not have been Judahites.[14] As at Ugarit they may have been musicians or poets recounting the ancient myths of Canaan. Some, however, continued (1 Kings 22:47) and may have connected with the rural cults. Precious objects were gathered into Jerusalem from the *bāmôt* (where they had been dedicated) in 1 Kings 15:16–19.

Jehoshaphat (c. 871/70–c. 849/48 BC) continued Asa's religious policy by avoiding the *bāmôt*. He drove out the *qĕdēšîm* (1 Kings 22:46 [Heb. 47]).

Jehoshaphat's son Jehoram (c. 849/48–c. 842 BC) married Ahab's daughter Athaliah (c. 841–c. 835 BC), who would succeed him to the throne of Judah. Jehoram "walked in the ways of the kings of Israel" like Ahab (2 Kings 8:18). At Ekron, the old Philistine city, the Bible may indicate that the Baal worshiped at this time was named Baal-zebul. If so, then in 2 Kings 1:2, 3, 6, and 16, the writer changed the name of Baal-zebul, meaning prince Baal, into the more derogatory Baal-zebub, meaning Baal or lord of flies.[15]

With the coup against Athaliah and the restoration of the Judean monarchy in the person of young Joash (c. 835–c. 796/95 BC), two covenants were made (2 Kings 11:17), one between Yahweh and the king and his people, and the other between King Joash and the people. A Baal temple in Jerusalem was pulled down and its one priest, Mattan, was killed (11:18).

---

11. *'Ăšērîm* is the plural of "asherah." See above note on asherah. *Maṣṣēbôt* is likewise the plural of *maṣṣēbâ*, the standing stones.

12. Zevit (2001, 461n48).

13. For *gillulîm* "round images"; 1 Kings 15:12; see next section below. For *mipleṣet*, see 1 Kings 15:13; 2 Chron. 15:16.

14. Zevit (2001, 462–63); cf. Deut. 23:18–19, which forbids Israelites from practicing it.

15. Day (2000, 69, 79–81).

The following kings, J(eh)oash (c. 835–c. 796/95 BC), Amaziah (c. 796/95–c. 776/75 BC), Uzziah or Azariah (c. 776/75–c. 736/35 BC), and Jotham (c. 750–735/730 BC), did what was right before Yahweh.[16]

Ahaz (c. 735/34 or 731/30–c. 715 BC) son of Jotham, like Jehoram, "walked in the ways of the kings of Israel." He introduced a new altar, removed the *yām* or large water basin, and made changes to the temple architecture and laver stands (2 Kings 16:10–18). The result may suggest that this was not an Assyrian innovation only (this has been suggested based on Ahaz's alliance with that empire [2 Kings 16:7–9]), but may have been influenced by West Semitic mythology. Such myths differed from the accounts about Yahweh (Exod. 15) and emphasized instead the conflict between Baal and Yamm found at Ugarit.[17] The text, however, condemns it as a foreign intrusion. Second Chronicles 28:24–25 indicates that Ahaz built *bāmôt* in the cities of Judah. He also passed his son through the fire, very possibly an indication of human sacrifice.[18] Leviticus 20:2–5 suggests that human sacrifice took place at the temple and therefore forbids it.

Hezekiah (c. 715–c. 687/86 BC), son of Ahaz, took away the *bāmôt* and destroyed *maṣṣēbôt*, *ăšērîm*, and the Nehushtan serpent that was worshiped.[19]

Manasseh (c. 687/86–c. 642 BC), son of Hezekiah, rebuilt the *bāmôt* for Yahweh in cities (including some at a city gate in Jerusalem), erected altars for Baal, established the Asherah cult with her image in the temple of Yahweh, provided a place for women to sew garments for her image,[20]

16. Cf. 2 Kings 12:2–3 [Heb. 3–4]; 14:3–4; 15:3–4, 34–35.

17. Yam(m) was the divine Sea whose battle with Baal is recorded in the Baal cycle from Ugarit and already mentioned in an eighteenth-century BC Mari letter. See chapter 4, "Mythology of Gods and Goddesses," pp. 99–100. Exodus 15 may use mythopoetic themes regarding Yahweh's defeat of the Egyptian army through his control of the waters of the Reed Sea. However, it differs from the battle between Baal and Yamm in that the Sea is not regarded as a divine enemy.

18. Zevit (2001, 467, 469) suggests that the absence of a connection between the Baal temple and Athaliah implies that it was constructed under a king such as Jehoram. He also maintains that the act of passing a child through the fire was not a human sacrifice but the "scorching" of the child who then lived. However, as Lev. 18:21 and 20:1–4 affirm, it was associated with Molech, not with Yahwism. Further, its divination aspect, whether part of Molech worship or reflecting other traditions, is attested in Deut. 18:14–19. None of these texts suggest anything other than human sacrifice and this is the most natural way of understanding anything, whether a person or a city, that is consigned to the flames. Cf. Hess (forthcoming b).

19. Cf. Fried (2002, 437, 444–50), who finds the four cult centers at Lachish, Arad, Beersheba, and Tel Halif destroyed by Sennacherib and never rebuilt. See below for more detailed discussion. Her critique of the Hezekiah texts depends on the royal destruction of high places throughout the kingdom.

20. M. Smith (2003, 113–14) suggests that the term *pesel hā'ăšērâ* (2 Kings 21:7) may imply a more elaborate version of the symbol. He compares the clothes to those that hung on cult statues in Mesopotamia and Ugarit.

caused his son to pass through the fire, and practiced various divination techniques.[21] Related to this is Deuteronomy 18:11, part of a list of forbidden mantic offices.[22] This text resembles Leviticus 19:31 in that both include mediums and wizards in their prohibitions. The terms *'ôbôt* and *yiddĕ'ōnîm* also appear in Isaiah 8:19; 19:3; 29:4; and 1 Samuel 28:3, 7–9 (see below) as possible examples of early usages of these names for divination and mantic specialists. In the Isaiah texts, however, they are not the offices but the shades, "ghosts and familiar spirits."[23]

Josiah (c. 640–609 BC), son of Manasseh, undid all that Manasseh had done and extended his reforms even to the removal of Solomonic *bāmôt* in Jerusalem at the Mount of Olives (2 Kings 22–23).[24] To the extent that he controlled parts of the north, he reversed all the cultic innovations introduced by Jeroboam I (2 Kings 23:15–19). The foreign cultic figures (*kĕmārîm*) were forced to stop their activities, the Judahite priests were permitted to continue to serve only in a limited way in Jerusalem, and the northern Israelite priests were put to death at their altars (2 Kings 23:5–9, 20). An earlier refurbishing project by Joash (2 Kings 12:14–16) was continued by Josiah on a grander scale, drawing income away from the Jerusalem priests. It did not survive Josiah.[25]

Josiah's sons and successors, Jehoahaz (609 BC) and Jehoiakim (609–598 BC), reversed their father's practices (2 Kings 23:32, 37) that had become unpopular. The kings who reigned after Josiah may have

---

21. 2 Kings 21:2–7; 23:4–10; Zevit (2001, 472–73).

22. The similarity of vv. 10–12 with 2 Kings 21:6 and the account of the sins of Manasseh leads B. Schmidt (1994) to conclude that these practices were not Canaanite in origin but were late Mesopotamian practices that were written into the text by the Deuteronomist. One does not need to accept this reconstruction to appreciate the significance of these legal texts for the activities of Manasseh.

23. The question of the meaning of *'ôb* has been taken up once again by Johnston (2002, 161–66). He refers to Hoffner (1967), who suggested a cognate with a term found in Hittite, Hurrian, and Akkadian, meaning a "pit" used for contact with the dead. Tropper (1989, 312–16) agrees with many who connect it with *'āb*, "father" and thus ancestor spirits. Van der Toorn (1993) suggests a connection with *ilib*, the ancient Near Eastern deity from Ugarit and elsewhere that is often associated with divinized ancestors. However, Johnston notes that none of the biblical texts requires a meaning associated with ancestors. Nevertheless, the possibility remains.

24. As with her treatment of Hezekiah, Fried (2002, 437, 450–60) considers 2 Kings 23:8 to define Josiah's destruction of the *bāmôt* as extending to the whole of Judah. However, a close reading of the text suggests that the *bāmôt* in general were desecrated, not necessarily destroyed. The text indicates that he tore down only the "*bāmôt* of the gates—at the entrance to the Gate of Joshua, the city governor, which is on the left of the city gate." Thus Fried's assertion that there were no seventh-century *bāmôt* in any of the Judean sites excavated does not contradict the text, although it is not clear that her own analysis of the stratigraphy and remains at these sites is always persuasive (e.g., Lachish).

25. Zevit (2001, 475–76).

despoiled the temple for the support of their kingdom. In particular, this involved the paying of tribute to the king of Egypt (2 Kings 23:33–35).

Prophets of Ancient Israel

Representing both institutional and noninstitutional religion throughout the history of Israel's monarchy, the prophets and their prophecies had a profound affect on religious life.[26] Judges 4:9 (fulfilled in vv. 17–22) may suggest that this idea occurred very early in Israel's history.[27] This view that the divine will to some extent controlled human events was found outside Israel.[28] Stories about early mantic prophets included that of Nathan, who might have formed a model for defining expectations regarding later prophets.[29] Elsewhere in the historic books, prophetic activities could affect all classes of society within Israel. Elijah and Elisha were early-ninth-century BC prophets whose work is recorded in texts extending from 1 Kings 18 through 2 Kings 13. Although Elijah was portrayed as a loner, Elisha had a group of followers at Gilgal (2 Kings 4:38; 5:22; 6:1). He also appeared and lived for a while at Dothan (6:13) and at Mount Carmel (2 Kings 4:25). Prophets could lead celebrations and initiate sacrifices on special days (2 Kings 4:23; 1 Sam. 16:2–5). They used music to achieve ecstasy (1 Sam. 10:5; 2 Kings 3:15; 1 Chron. 25:1). Others might call out the god's name, dance, and lacerate themselves either dressed or naked. They could heal and provide food (1 Kings 17:9–16), curse enemies (2 Kings 2:23–24), command natural phenomena (1 Sam. 12:18), and intercede (1 Sam. 7:5). They could address kings but their influence in national policy does not appear to have been decisive in most cases. From the ninth century, 1 Kings 18:20–40 describes the famous story of Elijah versus the prophets of Baal.[30] First Kings 18:13 and 22:6 suggest that there must have been several hundred Yahweh prophets aside from Elijah. Zevit correctly understands the prophets (he calls them "prophet-priests") of Asherah (1 Kings 18:19) to have

26. Cf. Blenkinsopp (1995b, 115–65); Grabbe (1995, 66–118); Zevit (2001, 481–86). Zevit lists some fifty-eight references to prophecies and their fulfillment (often both) in the Deuteronomistic History.

27. Others see here and elsewhere the editorial insertion of a later Deuteronomistic theologian.

28. Zevit (2001, 488) cites examples of divine intervention perceived by the royalty and common people among the Neo-Assyrians.

29. Ibid., 495–99.

30. Ninth- and eighth-century prophets such as Elijah, Hosea, and Amos oppose the cults of other Israelite gods but, according to M. Smith (2001a, 163), they don't address foreign gods even in their own territory. This explains the putative absence of belief in only one god at this time. However, Barton (2005) argues cogently that Amos directly criticized Israel's official cult.

been original to the text. Thus they were also present in the confrontation with Elijah.[31] In light of the inscriptional evidence suggesting that some believed that Yahweh had a consort, the Asherah prophets would have awaited the result of the contest to see which deity was served by the goddess. However, there is no indication in the present biblical text that Elijah tolerated Asherah. Rather, his battle was with the imported national deity from Tyre, Baal. The contest did not directly address the goddess.

Although the prophetic books and individual pericopes from them are much discussed as to their dating, it is generally agreed that these texts, especially in their polemics, reflect known practices of some people at certain times in ancient Israel. In the prophetic books, prophets receive visions (Isa. 6), perform symbolic and magical acts (Isa. 20:1–6), announce death to those opposing them (Jer. 28:16–17), predict the future (Isa. 41:21–29), and are persecuted (Jer. 20:1–2). Some of the prophets also warn and indict the wealthy (Isa. 5:8–10) and their display (Isa. 3:16–24), drunken carousers (Isa. 5:11–13; 56:12), authorities (Isa. 10:1–4), the king (Jer. 13:18), hypocrites (Isa. 1:10–20), priests and their cults (Isa. 28:7–13), the inhabitants of cities and lands (Isa. 29:1–10), and the people in general (Jer. 5).[32] The prophetic texts especially, but also other biblical sources as well, include many items, people, and practices that reflect the diversity of religious beliefs in ancient Israel.[33]

Hosea was written to the northern kingdom of Israel in the middle of the eighth century BC. There was much confusion in the north regarding Yahweh. Perhaps Yahweh was a manifestation of Baal as a national deity distinguished from the local baals. Offerings were made on certain days and offerers invoked a particular deity (Hosea 2:13–17 [Heb. 15–19]). Invoking the name determined the recipient of the offering. The designations "my baal" and the "days of the baalim" suggest festivals to Baal in which his name was proclaimed.[34] The prophet indicted Israel, for example, Hosea 4:10–14 (cf. 6:10), over sexual activity that did not increase their numbers. Men participated alongside female officiants.

31. Zevit (2001, 503); contrast M. Smith (2003, 126–30), and see discussion on Asherah on p. 283, as well as the discussion of Smith's position on pp. 75–77.

32. As noted above, for more on the role of prophets and their function, see Blenkinsopp (1995b, 115–65) and Grabbe (1995, 66–118). Zevit suggests that the concern for social justice did not play a prominent role in half or more of the prophetic books, nor did they often suggest remedies (Isa. 58:6–8 being an exception). See Zevit (2001, 506–10).

33. Cryer (1994) suggests that, other than astrology, the Bible implies that all practices of Mesopotamian divination were present in Israel. Deuteronomistic and Priestly laws restricted divination to being practiced only by the religious leaders.

34. Cf. Deut. 17:3 for presumed knowledge of rites for the worship of other gods; cf. Zevit (2001, 609). NIV renders "my baal" as "my master," and "days of Baalim" as "the days [she burned incense] to the Baals."

The females functioned as prostitutes. The difference between the *zōnâ* and the *qĕdēšâ*, two activities of the female participants, is not clear.

Calf images were a concern to Hosea. In Hosea 8:4–6, the *ʿăṣabbîm* "images," especially the calf image(s), were made of gold and silver. In Hosea 10:5–8 the deity at Beth Aven was connected with a calf image worshiped by Samaria (the northern kingdom). The departure of the calf image as a vassal's tribute to Assyria was a delight to the priests but mourned by the people who feared the departure of their protector. Beth Aven, located near Bethel, could mean either House of Strength or House of Iniquity, a wordplay that was not lost on the prophet. Hosea 13:1–2 recounts Ephraim's guilt, that is, that of the northern kingdom of Israel who worshiped other gods. The reference there to death on account of Baal refers to the incident during the wilderness wanderings of Israel at Baal Peor (cf. Hosea 9:10), though it may also contain memories of the Baal myth from Ugarit.[35] Baal as a silver image and other engraved figures or dedicatory inscriptions are described in Hosea 13. Kissing calves was a means of adoration, as was human sacrifice.[36]

Amos also addressed the diverse religious practices of the northern kingdom of Israel in the middle part of the eighth century BC. In Amos 2:7b–8 he describes a situation of multiple altars for various deities. At each altar a woman is available for sex to all who visit, both father and son. These activities were sanctioned and considered beneficial by the participants.[37] In Amos 5:26 astral deities are mentioned as "the star of your god(s)."

Amos 6:3–7 occurs between two speeches about military defeat and destruction. The festival described here is a *marzēaḥ* that may have been designed to ward off such defeat (an apotropaic ritual) with a quorum of ten men (vv. 9–10) reclining, eating meats, singing, playing a lyre, drinking wine by the bowl, and anointing themselves with oil. Although the term *marzēaḥ* does not occur in this text, all the events described fit well into the context of a *marzēaḥ* festival.[38] Mark Smith (2003, 170) argues that the *marzēaḥ* is not condemned, only its use to exploit the poor. See also Jeremiah 16:5–9.

Micah writes a decade or two later than Amos in the eighth century BC. Although focusing on the southern kingdom of Judah, Micah 1:6–7 addressed the northern kingdom. The cult in the city of Samaria included:

35. See chapter 4, p. 96. For this text as an ironic twist on the death and resurrection of Baal in the Baal cycle, see Day (2000, 120). He argues that Baal's death is related to Israel's death or destruction. The only resurrection hope for Israel, however, is its repentance.

36. See the discussion of the gold calf of Exod. 32, and the Ashkelon calf image (Fig. 15) in chapter 6.

37. Cf. the continuation of this in Ezek. 16.

38. Cf. King (1988). See chapter 4, p. 110.

pĕsîlîm or sculpted images; *'etnan zōnâ* or "prostitute fees," perhaps of cooked food; and *'ăṣabbîm* or small portable images of guardian deities that could accompany the people into battle or on festival days. In Micah 5:10–14 [Heb. 9–13], the prophet speaks of a future time when the people of God will no longer have witchcraft, images, and asherah poles on which to rely. Micah 6:6–7, along with Ezekiel 16:20–21, 36; 23:37–39, indicates the ongoing practice of child sacrifice in Israel, as Psalm 106:37 suggests its practice before the monarchy.[39] Indeed, other texts in the prophets may suggest infant sacrifice. Isaiah records traditions contemporary with Micah but also reflecting later practices. For example, there is what might be described as singing and flute playing during a nighttime procession, and the act of lighting a fire on a tophet or fire pit (Isa. 30:27–33). Could this be related to chthonic (underworld) deities? Plutarch mentions Carthaginian offerings of children to Kronos with the music of flutes and drums to hide the cries.[40] Some find human sacrifice in this depiction.[41] However, a close reading of the text finds no explicit mention of any sacrifice. Isaiah 28:15 and 18 may suggest a ceremony for protection from death at the Assyrian invasion of 722 BC. If so, the terms Lie and Deceit (*kāzāb* and *šeqer*), would reflect underworld deities.[42] Jeremiah 19:4–6 describes the passing of sons through fire, the renaming of Ben Hinnom Valley as the Valley of Slaughter, and the shedding of innocent blood.[43] Jeremiah 32:35 identifies the same act of "passing" sons and daughters to Molech in the Ben Hinnom Valley. Yahweh's denial (19:5; 32:35) that he ever commanded burnt offerings or child sacrifice at *bāmôt* suggests that some believed that he willed this. Indeed, Ezekiel 20:25–26 suggests that Yahweh gave this law. This text is often presented as an alternative tradition about Israel in the wilderness in which God commanded his people to sacrifice their firstborn. However, the traditions that existed by the time of Ezekiel suggest that the command to offer the firstborn sons, which was given in Egypt (Exod. 13:1–2), was then adjusted at Sinai and redefined as the dedication of the Levites for service to the Lord (Num. 3:44–45).[44]

39. See earlier evidence in chapter 4, p. 101. See also chapter 5, "Amman," p. 132, and "Ashkelon," p. 136. For additional evidence of Phoenician child sacrifice, see chapter 10, p. 326.

40. Cf. Plutarch, *De Superstitione* 13. On Phoenician and Punic archaeological evidence for infant sacrifice, see p. 293.

41. Cf. Mosca (1975); M. Smith (2003, 172).

42. Cf. the first Arslan Tash amulet. However, the biblical evidence is not sufficiently clear to be specific about how the "covenant with death" functions in terms of religious belief or practice.

43. The name of this valley forms the background to the Gehenna of the New Testament.

44. Block (1997, 638–41) takes a different approach, arguing that this statement is a rhetorical flourish of Ezekiel that refers to God's judgment against Israel in the wilderness so that a whole generation died.

Further references to the offering of children in this manner occur in Ezekiel 20:28–31; 23:37–39. Zevit believes that the children were already dead and that the fire ritual is funerary.[45] He argues that this was done by the Sepharvaim in 2 Kings 17:31. Those buried in the tophets at Carthage and elsewhere were premature, stillborn, and very young infants. However, the osteological evidence as well as the implications of the type of burials suggests infant sacrifice. Human sacrifice seems to have existed in Phoenicia and Israel at least until the middle of the first millennium BC.

Gardens were dedicated to deities (Isa. 1:29) as in Egypt and Mesopotamia. In the summer women might plant Phoenician gardens of Adonis that represented the power of fertility (Isa. 17:10–11). This was connected with the Greek god Adonis, whose name derives from the West Semitic *ʾādōn(î)* "(my) lord." Adonis represented Eshmun, Reshep, and Melqart in Phoenician, and Baal, Baal Hamon, Baal Shamem, and Eshmun in Punic. The epithet for Adonis was *nʿmn*, "the pleasant one," as here in Isaiah. He was worshiped on roofs as was common in West Semitic rites. He was also the partner of the goddess at Byblos.[46] The symbolism of Adonis gardens in the Mediterranean and their connection with sterility is attested in Classical and Roman times, and may be suggested as early as this text from Isaiah.[47] Through the first half of the first millennium AD both Origen and Jerome referred to Adonis as Venus's lover who was bewailed in the summer, in June and July. They identified him with Tammuz of Ezekiel 8:14, and noted that the wailing ritual was done at a grove in Bethlehem.[48] They also mentioned the celebration for the resurrection of this god and connected it with vegetation. Interestingly, these early Christian writers made no reference to any influence of the resurrection belief as coming from Christianity. The second-century AD writer Lucian (*De Syria dea*) observed the rites to Adonis in Byblos where he was mourned one day (because the boar killed him) and then on the next day was proclaimed as alive and sent into the air. The women shaved their heads, and those who didn't had to prostitute themselves to foreigners and give the proceeds to Aphrodite.[49] Lucian suggested that the Egyptian Osiris, rather than Adonis, lay behind these rites. In fact,

45. Cf. Zevit (2001, 550–52).

46. See Mettinger (2001, 125–28).

47. Ibid., 146–48. Mettinger also (p. 211) identifies this goddess with Astarte on the basis of a fourth-century BC inscription. Small plantings of seeds in the summer before the regular sowing continued in Christian celebrations of the midsummer Feast of St. John.

48. This took place from the second century until the beginning of the fourth century AD, between the reigns of the emperors Hadrian and Constantine.

49. Cf. the section on "Sacred Prostitution" on p. 332, and the similarity of this practice to that mentioned by Herodotus for the Ishtar cult in Babylon.

the Dumuzi myth was behind all these, a myth wherein a deity goes to the underworld and returns with the annual cycle of vegetation. Mettinger argues that this myth was already known in thirteenth-century BC Ugarit in the form of Baal.[50]

Various types of images were worshiped in the gardens and elsewhere (Isa. 2:6–11). People prostrated themselves before images of silver, gold, and other materials.[51] Isaiah 2:6 associates prognosticators with the east. People sought out specialists in necromancy to predict the future (Isa. 8:19–20; 28:14). Isaiah 14 represents mythopoetic elements that may already be found in the mythology of Ugarit.[52] Isaiah 28:7–22 describes rhetorically the act of making a covenant with the netherworld. The text may deal with Hezekiah's closure of the "high places" (*bāmôt*) and their use as a means of access to oracles of Yahweh.[53] The *'ĕlōhîm*, often translated "God" or "gods," can also be rendered as "spirits (of the dead)."

Texts that are even more difficult to interpret, and very likely later, appear in the final chapters of Isaiah, often referred to as Trito-Isaiah. In Isaiah 57:5–13 an array of religious rituals are mentioned: idols under trees, killing children in wadis, libations and grain offerings, sacrifices on mountaintops, a cult about a "covenant" in the home, oil divination (oleomancy) from the underworld god Molech, collections of idols, and prostrations to the underworld.[54] In Isaiah 57:8, rituals of *zikkārōn* (NIV "pagan symbols," literally "memorial") and *yād* (NIV "nakedness," literally "hand") are unclear. Lewis and Ackerman argue that vv. 5b–6 deal with child sacrifice rituals, whereas verses 3–5a and 7–8 indict fertility rites.[55] Verse 13 criticizes image worship in general. In vv. 5–6 the term

50. Cf. Mettinger (2001, 148–54). He observes the tendency to mourn the Mediterranean Adonis but notes how little information exists about the Levantine Adonis. All connect their death and resurrection with the seasons and mark annual celebrations around July. Osiris is distinguished from Adonis at Byblos as late as Lucian. However, in Alexandria in Egypt the emphasis on a chthonic (underworld) Adonis was no doubt influenced by the Osiris cult, with a similar bilocation (being both above the ground and in the underworld) as in the Osiris myth. Cf. Mettinger (2001, 179), referring to Theocritus.

51. Cf. Isa. 2:19–21; 30:22; Jer. 8:19. The reference to going into rocks may indicate worship within caves, although it more probably suggests the search for refuge.

52. See chapter 4, p. 96.

53. Cf. Isa. 2:19–21; Zevit (2001, 660). B. Schmidt (1994, 144–65, 287) views Isa. 8:19–9:1; 19:3; 28:1–22; and 29:4 as products of a late post-Deuteronomistic redactor who characterized the period of Ahaz as having been influenced by the Mesopotamian practice of necromancy. This was part of a strategy to condemn all Israel at this time and thus to justify the destruction of Jerusalem. However, a belief in contact with the underworld and necromancy was already present at Ugarit and in texts such as these and 1 Sam. 28:7–20. See Lewis (2002, 198–202).

54. For the last point, compare 1 Sam. 28:14 and Saul's first putting his nose to the ground and then prostrating himself before the shade of Samuel.

55. Cf. Lewis (1987) and Ackerman (1992).

for "smooth stones" (NIV) could perhaps refer to the dead.[56] However, the term *ḥallĕqê* is literally "smooth things of [a ravine]" and thus is indefinite as to its referent. Because the verse goes on to indict the worshipers for directing their offerings toward these "smooth things," they are probably to be understood as objects of idolatry. In verse 9, *mlk* may well refer to Molech, god of the underworld, rather than *melek*, the Hebrew word for "king."[57] Molech was an appropriate object for oil and perfume, and the reference to Sheol, "the grave," at the end of the verse appears to clinch this identification. In that case verse 6 condemns the cult of the dead and verse 9 criticizes human sacrifice. Elsewhere, Lewis attempts to draw out allusions referring to the cult of the dead.[58] But is this actually the case? Isaiah 57:5–13 concerns fertility rituals (so Ackerman), and verses 5 and 8 with their emphasis on lust, beds, and looking on the nakedness of others support such a conclusion. Therefore, Johnston argues that a reference in verses 5–8 to a cult of the dead is speculative.[59] A fertility ritual would not promote the cult of the dead. Verse 9, however, does refer to Molech, the god of the underworld, and in this context the verse could at least imply that this scene describes a religious practice that involved the world of the dead.

In Isaiah 65:3–5a, 7, 11, and 66:17, ritually purified participants enter gardens for animal and incense offerings.[60] They present pig's blood and eat pork and three-day-old meat (*piggūl*). They also offer incense and pour libations.[61] The deities Gad and Meni are honored. Pigs are associated with the cult of Adonis/Naaman/Baal, who was killed by a pig in some myths. *Lĕbēnîm* (NIV "altars of brick") in verse 3 may be incense stands or altars of unfired clay in the shape of a brick.[62] These practices describe a religious culture that may concern chthonic (underworld) forces and fertility deities.

Isaiah 66:3 describes a series of ritual acts that include slaughtering a bull, offering a lamb, making a grain offering, and offering incense. This is contrasted with killing a man, breaking the neck of a dog, presenting pig's blood, and bending the knee. Zevit (2001) suggests that the second

56. Cf. Irwin (1967).
57. This would require a change of the vowels written into the Hebrew text by the Masoretes in the seventh to ninth centuries AD, but not a change of the original consonants.
58. Cf. Lewis (1987; 1989).
59. Cf. Johnston (2002, 175–78).
60. However, there is no clear evidence in these texts of such a practice in caves; contra Zevit (2001).
61. Again, there is an association with spending the night. However, nothing in the text associates their activities with a cave. For B. Schmidt (1994), this then describes an incubation ritual which, although innocent by itself, is condemned when associated with necromancy.
62. Cf. Ackerman (1992, 169–73).

group of actions are condemned rituals. However, they may simply be actions that are regarded as not pleasing to God and contrary to his will.[63] Whether or not "the *bōšet*" (NIV "shameful gods") of Jeremiah 3:24 refers to Baal, this deity was "fed" animals sacrificed from the flocks and herds as well as children of both sexes.[64]

In the middle of the "scroll" of Isaiah, Deutero-Isaiah (chapters 40–55) preserves materials that fit well in the context of the Babylonian deportation or exile (586–539 BC). Thus foreign gods and goddesses are mentioned. The Babylonian deities Bel and Nebo tumble and fall in Isaiah 46:1–7. In Isaiah 48:5 Israel's God explains that he foretold all that has come to pass, something that the images that Israelites worship did not do. The Bible recounts parodies of image making that portray them as ineffective.[65] In Isaiah 44:12–17 living trees, stripped and formed into blocks of wood, had drawn on them an outline of a shape made with a compass. Their builders formed a carved image and used the scraps of wood to cook a communion meal of bread and meat. These included prostration and formulas seeking salvation similar to nocturnal Babylonian and Egyptian ceremonies for their cult images. Unlike Mesopotamian rituals, neither is a temple worker mentioned nor are temple precincts used. There is no opening of the mouth ritual, or washing or bathing. Fire, rather than water, empowers.[66]

Numerous rituals appear in Jeremiah in the years before the final Babylonian destruction of the first Jerusalem temple in 586 BC. The texts of Jeremiah 2:8, 11, 18, 20b, 23a, and 3:6b–7a, 13 identify prophets as leaders of the people who prophesy by Baal and participate in idolatrous cults. The people follow them with adultery and prostitution under spreading trees on high hills. Yet they deny that their actions involve the worship of other deities.

Jeremiah 7:9–11 appears to include rituals to Baal and other deities in a list of sins that worshipers at the temple of Yahweh would commit and feel no danger for having done so. They were either reported by the worshipers directly to Yahweh as a means of salvation, or they reported

63. Cf. Hittite rituals that use humans, swine, and canines (*Keilschrifturkunden aus Boghazköi* 17.28 IV 45–46).

64. In Jer. 5:7–9 the "prostitute's house" (*bêt zōnâ*) may be a metaphor for a shrine or temple dedicated to another deity because it is used here in the context of idolatry. Nevertheless, the lusty horses suggest sexual activity (Hess [1992c]). Zevit (2001, 540) identifies the mention of horses with a particular gait and dance the men performed before the women, but this goes beyond the evidence in this text. Apparently, the men addressed the women with a shout.

65. Cf. Isa. 40:18–20; 41:6–7; 44:12–17; 46:1–7; Jer. 10:2–15.

66. Thus Zevit (2001) may be correct in seeing here a preexilic oracle of Isaiah. For a more complete discussion of the opening of the mouth ritual and comparisons with the biblical texts, see Hurowitz (2003).

their rescue to Yahwist worshipers in the temple. It is difficult to distinguish between those deities indigenous to ancient Israel and those imported, such as the already-mentioned Baal who was associated with Tyre in 1 Kings 18. In Jeremiah 2:27–28 the people worship male and female deities, Baal and Asherah, while turning their back on Yahweh worship.[67] Here, however, it is not fertility but salvation that the worshipers seek. In Jeremiah 7:30–32 Judahites placed *šiqqûṣêhem* "their despicable things" in the temple (whatever they were) and built *bāmôt* for the tophet in the Hinnom Valley, to the west of Jerusalem.[68] This fire pit could include a mass grave. The fact that Yahweh denies commanding the Israelites to burn their children, and to build the *bāmôt*, suggests that some who practiced these activities believed that he had so commanded. Jeremiah 8:1–2 describes a "desperate ritual" of removing the bones of religious and other leaders and spreading them on the ground before the host of heaven.[69] This will have no effect and the bones will become mulch. In Jerusalem people burned incense on altars to Baal (2 Kings 23:5; Jer. 7:9; 11:17).

Jeremiah 7:17–18 and 44:3, 15–19 describe a domestic (family) cult to the Queen of Heaven, possibly identified with Astarte.[70] The *kawwānîm*, "sweet cakes," are cognate to the Akkadian *kamānu*, baked in ashes or on charcoal and used in the Ishtar cult.[71] Women, as primary officiants, made cakes, poured libations, and burned incense to the Queen of Heaven. Men offered incense and poured libations. They promised the Queen of Heaven that if she saved them they would renew her cult, and they would continue to do so when they moved to Egypt. She was a cosmic goddess who could be propitiated by offerings.

Jeremiah 16:5–9 describes the *marzēaḥ*, a feast that began much earlier (see chapter 4) and continued into late antiquity (see above Amos 6:3–7). It was a banquet or feast attested throughout the West Semitic world. It could be celebrated to mark events in the course of life such as marrying and burying, but it could also take place for other reasons. Assuming the Septuagint (Greek translation) of verse 7, then the "bread" is broken for the dead. Retaining the Masoretic (Hebrew) Text, then it is "bread" for comfort. If the rites of this festival served an apotropaic purpose (to ward off evil or sin), then Jeremiah would have been forbid-

67. Normally the wooden tree or object would refer to Asherah and the stone to Baal. M. Smith (2003, 116) follows others who see the roles of wood as mother and stone as father reversed here.

68. Cf. Isa. 30:33.

69. Cf. Zevit (2001, 543).

70. Astarte was the only West Semitic goddess bearing this title during the Iron Age, though M. Smith (2003, 127) also allows for Ishtar or a combination of the two.

71. Cf. Held (1982, 77); Jer. 44:19.

den to enter because such rites would not prevent the judgment God planned for Israel.[72]

Rooftop rituals occurred at Ugarit and at Ashkelon in the Merneptah relief of the siege of 1209 BC (see pp. 102, 136, 224–25) where the Canaanite citizens of Ashkelon appear to raise their hands and to burn incense in burners to their deities. In Israel rooftop rituals were also enacted, according to Jeremiah 19:12–13 and 32:29. Here incense was offered to astral deities and libations to other divinities. Compare a Syrian model of a figure with an incense burner and two animals on the roof of a two-story tower, c. 1000 BC.[73]

The exilic text of Ezekiel 8:3–17 describes Ezekiel's tour of the abominations in the Jerusalem temple precincts at the time of the destruction of the temple. It is a passage full of textual difficulties. It suggests the (re)introduction of cultic activities into the temple after Josiah's unexpected death in 609 BC. In verse 3 there is the statue of a seated figure and a seat (*môšab sēmel*). In vv. 7–12 there is an enclosed dark chamber with figurines (*gillûlîm*) and smoking censers. The figures on the walls could reflect many of the animals and other images found on contemporary seals.[74] The Tammuz ritual (v. 14) involved wailing in the dry summer for the coming of the autumn rains. It was associated with the dying and reappearance or resurrection of Dumuzi (= Tammuz), Baal, and Adonis, discussed above with reference to the gardens. Verses 16–17 describe bowing to the sun in worship, an act of sun worship clearly attested in Palestine and Jerusalem as early as the fourteenth century BC, when princes prostrated themselves seven times before the pharaoh as the divine sun deity. Were these purification rites celebrated in the autumn on the sixth day of the sixth month (8:1) in August/September in preparation for the seventh month with its biblical rituals? No priests, sacrifices, or offerings are mentioned. It seems therefore that nonpriestly groups used the temple at this time.

Ezekiel 13:17–21 describes the use of nets and breadcrumbs to trap birds. This has parallels in Egyptian myth. Zevit (2001, 562) suggests that the act, performed by women, gave them control of the life force so that some might live longer at the expense of others.

---

72. For B. Schmidt (1994, 249), the association with funerary matters is an isolated example or a later redaction of the book. However, as Lewis (2002, 179–80) shows, these actions are well attested in the Bible as mourning rites. Johnston (2002, 184–85) argues that associations with the dead, other than their explicit connections here with mourning and funerary rites, go beyond the evidence.

73. Cf. Bretschneider (1991, pl. 58 no. 55, 216–17).

74. The list of Zevit (2001, 559) includes uraeus, beetles, locusts, fish, falcons, doves, cocks, lions, deer, bovids, horse, griffins, and human-like figures.

Ezekiel 14:3–4, 7–8 mentions the "idols," *gillûlîm*, a term used else-where for dung balls and figurines. The prophet states that the people focused on these even as they inquired from prophets of Yahweh. They also sacrificed their children to these (Ezek. 23:37–39). The phrases "in their hearts" or "on their heart" may suggest that the idolatry was a state of mind or it may imply they wore figurines around their necks, on their arms, or on their garments.[75]

Ezekiel 16:15–21, 36, part of a complex allegory that describes Is-rael's failure in its past, also suggests various rituals. Here valuable materials, perhaps from the temple, were used in non-Yahweh cults at *bāmôt*, where images of male deities (perhaps phallic images; *ṣalmê zākār*, literally "male images") were worshiped. Offerings of food-stuffs were burnt as a pleasing odor.[76] Children were also offered as sacrifices in some cults. In Ezekiel 43:7–9 offerings to and veneration of royal ancestors are described, along with an activity described as prostitution.[77]

Other objects associated with religious worship include altars, *'ăšērîm*, and sacred pillars.[78] Habakkuk 2:18–20 uses the terms "dumb" and "silent" to describe images. This may suggest that worshipers believed that they could be addressed. Speaking to tree and stone and assuming revelation from them suggests divination.

Zephaniah, a prophet who flourished c. 520 BC, mentions the *kĕmārîm* in Zephaniah 1:4–9, and the regular priests who worshiped Baal, the astral deities (with prostrations on the roofs), and perhaps Molech. Avoiding the thresholds seems to have been a custom associated with certain foreign deities (1 Sam. 5:5).

Psalmic texts also reveal the religions of Israel, but not nearly as explicitly or as frequently.[79] From Egypt a section of Papyrus Amherst 63 contains a hymn to Horus that has verbal and sequential parallels to Psalm 20:1–10. This manuscript, dated to about the second century BC, is in Aramaic but betrays a Canaanite origin. Zevit considers a connection between Horus and Baal or Baal Shamen. Psalms 42–83

75. Cf. Song 8:6a; Hess (2005c, 237–38). See Hallo (1993) for Mesopotamia. See Barkay (1992) for Egypt and Judah.

76. Zevit (2001, 565) notes that these included honey, a substance banned in the temple cult (Lev. 2:11).

77. Block (1998, 583–85). Johnston (2002, 178–81) argues, in agreement with com-parative studies of this term, that *peger* here refers to offerings or sacrifices, and not stelae. For an alternative view, see B. Schmidt (1994, 245–66).

78. As noted above, there is some dispute as to what *'ăšērîm* actually were. Generally, they may be regarded as wooden poles symbolizing a goddess such as Asherah and called in the Bible by the name of *'ăšērîm*. For further on the question of Asherah/asherah, see pp. 283–89. Cf. Isa. 17:8; 27:9; Jer. 17:1–3.

79. Zevit (2001, 669–85).

comprise what is called "the Elohistic Psalter." Some of these psalms have Elohim where elsewhere Yahweh appears.[80] Thus Psalms 14 and 53 are almost identical except for the name used of God in 14:2, 4, 7 and 53:3, 5, 7. The same may be true of Psalm 40:14–18 and Psalm 70. The collection includes smaller groups of Korahite (42–49), Davidic (51–65, 68–70), and Asaphite (50, 73–83) psalms. The psalms of the Asaphites of the north and the Korahites of the south (and north) have been dated on linguistic grounds to the ninth to sixth centuries BC.[81] The Elohistic Psalter collection may have originated during or after Hezekiah's time (c. 700 BC).

Death and Resurrection

Johnston notes that Psalm 16:10, "For you do not give me up to Sheol, or let your faithful one see the Pit," suggests that here the psalmist feels "instinctively" that Sheol is an unfitting fate for Yahweh's faithful one and that therefore he holds out hope for continual communion in the presence of Yahweh as suggested in Psalm 16:11.[82] Here the door is opened in a small way for a distinction between the righteous and the wicked beyond death. Further, Johnston notes Psalm 49:15: "But God will redeem my life from the grave (Sheol); he will surely take me to himself." This verse in its context, where it contrasts with the fate of those who trust in themselves (Ps. 49:13–14), suggests an even greater distinction between the righteous and the wicked. Johnston suggests that other texts, such as Proverbs 15:24 and Job 19:25–27, may also rea-

---

80. While Elohim replaces Yahweh in the psalms cited above, Zevit (2001, 681–84) argues that Elohim replaces names of other deities in the other psalms. Specific Psalms include: Pss. 42–43 refer to the headwaters of Banias and Dan and a deity there; Ps. 68 refers to a theophany (vv. 8–9), Elohim bring(s) fertility and snow and Shadday scattered the kings (vv. 8–15), Elohim ascended Mount Bashan with chariots and soldiers and took the mountains of Sinai, Bashan, and Zalmon (vv. 16–19). Cf. also Kuntillet ʿAjrud and Deir ʿAlla texts. Using additional texts, Zevit concludes that, along with Yahweh, deities such as Adonay, Asherah, Baal, Baalat, El, Molech, Mot, and Yam competed in north Israelite myths for control of peoples, lands, and the universe. Zevit (2001, 684–85) finds "overt mythology and mythological allusions" in Gen. 1:27; 6:1–4; Exod. 4:22–23 (cf. Hosea 11:1; Jer. 3:19; 31:7–9, 20), 22–28; Isa. 25:6–8 (the little apocalypse); 27:1; Pss. 2:7; 18:14–16; 29:1–10; 65:8; 74:12–17; 89:10–11, 26; 93:1–5; 104:6–11; Job 3:8; 9:8, 13; 26:11–13; 38:8–11; 40:25–32. In the case of the Asaph psalms that are also from north Israel, these preserve myths and songs from shrines in Issachar, Asher, Naphtali, and northern Bashan. References to northern kingdom sites were changed to Jerusalem and related southern sites. However, even if one accepts the widespread borrowing of earlier, mythic terms and phrases, it does not prove that the resultant psalms resembled the Canaanite/Israelite songs. They might contain only expressions reworked into entirely new forms, themes, and content.

81. Cf. Hurvitz (1972).

82. Cf. Johnston (1995; 2002, 201–4).

sonably refer to a postmortem existence that lies other than in Sheol.[83] However, it may be better to understand Sheol as a general reference for the place of the dead underground and that all go there, with the exception of a chosen few.[84] The Bible may suggest a diversity of views regarding Sheol, some seeing it as a destination with separate "regions" for righteous and unrighteous.[85] Sheol in general is the lowest spot in contrast to the heights of the heavens.[86] Its gates or bars cannot be broken.[87] Personified as a creature with a great appetite but receiving poor food, it might well have represented in some minds a kind of underworld deity.[88] This latter point, however, is nowhere made explicit in the biblical text.

Various texts speak of national resurrection (Ezek. 37) or of some undefined life beyond death for Yahweh's servant (Isa. 53). Individual resurrection is suggested by Isaiah 26:19 (written in the context of vv. 14 and 19b that refer to individual dead): "But your dead will live; their bodies will rise. You who dwell in the dust, wake up and shout for joy. Your dew is like the dew of the morning; the earth will give birth to her dead," and by Daniel 12:2: "Multitudes who sleep in the dust of the earth will awake: some to everlasting life, others to shame and everlasting contempt."[89] The rarity of these texts in the Old Testament suggests that individual life after death was either of little interest to the authors or that it was a gradual and late development in Israelite theology.

The Bible records many examples of family religion and personal piety during the monarchy and at other times.[90] The oldest living male of the family, the *dōd*, led the family cult (Amos 6:10). There could be annual sacrifices and feasts, as with David's family.[91] The Passover is an example of a family celebration (Exod. 12), as was Purim later (Esther 9:20–28). Other events included the observance of the Sabbath, the practice of

83. Cf. Johnston (2002, 207–14).

84. So Enoch (Gen 5:24) and Elijah (2 Kings 2:11), and the later tradition concerning the assumption of Moses. On Sheol, see also the discussion in chapter 6 regarding the personal name Methushael. For Sheol as an underground location, see comment above on Isa. 57:5–13.

85. See the criticism of Lewis (2002, 187–89), answered by Johnston (2002, 201, 217).

86. Cf. Deut. 32:22; Isa. 7:11; Amos 9:2.

87. Cf. Isa. 38:10; Pss. 9:13 [Heb. 14]; 107:18; Job 38:17; Jon. 2:6 [Heb. 7]; etc.

88. Lewis (2002, 184–85). Cf. Isa. 5:14; Hab. 2:5; Prov. 27:20; like Mot at Ugarit (*KTU* 1.5 I 19–20; 5.2 2–4); Isa. 14:9; Hosea 13:14. For the background of Sheol as a deity cf. Hess (forthcoming c).

89. See Johnston (2002, 218–30). Levenson (1993; 2002; 2006) argues that for most of the Old Testament no physical resurrection was attested. Instead, the concept was understood in terms of a long life with many progeny to carry on one's name.

90. See P. Miller (2000, 67–76).

91. Cf. 1 Sam. 1:18; 9:22; 20:6, 28–29. The meal was perhaps eaten in the sanctuary in a special room, called a *liškâ*. See p. 239.

circumcision on the newborn male (Gen. 17:23–27; Exod. 4:24–26), the naming of children, and the use of prayers, laments, blessings, and curses. Less orthodox family practices included the use of female figurines that may have been thought to aid in human fertility.[92] There were also the offerings at the family tomb. If some sort of religious shrine existed at the entrance to the house, perhaps Deuteronomy 6:4–9 was intended to replace it with the word of God. Children, success, and health were values of family religion, rather than sin and forgiveness.

The Bible mentions *těrāpîm* as unrelated to Yahweh worship. Perhaps *těrāpîm* were used for fertility (e.g., Michal in 1 Sam. 19:13, 16). Van der Toorn (1990; 1994a; 2002) has argued that *těrāpîm* are figures of some sort and they may have represented fertility or a cult of dead ancestors. For several reasons, however, the connection with dead ancestors is not so persuasive, as Johnston (2002, 188) has noted.[93] First, in parallel with *'ělōhîm*, *těrāpîm* are more likely to mean "gods" than "the dead." Second, consultation of *těrāpîm* does not prove they were ancestors. Third, Josiah's abolition of mediums and *těrāpîm* was in response to a ban on consulting the dead (Deut. 18:11; 2 Kings 23:24), but many other practices are mentioned and so the equation of *těrāpîm* with the dead is arbitrary. Fourth, the Septuagint uses multiple translations for *těrāpîm* and so cannot serve as proof of one translation. Finally, at Assyria, Nuzi, and Emar none of van der Toorn's texts equate household gods with the dead or their spirits. Nevertheless, the consistent and widespread connection between *těrāpîm* and ancestors in Israel, and significant parallels outside Israel in West Semitic contexts, support van der Toorn's position and at least suggest that these images were associated with ancestors.

Johnston discusses the role of deities associated with the dead and the cult of the dead. He notes that Song 8:6 alludes to death as strong, recalling the power of the Mot ("Death," here *māwet*) to destroy Baal (2002, 71–81). It also mentions *rešep* (Resheph?) in the plural as the "flashes" of fire. Resheph is the god of pestilence at Ugarit and elsewhere. However, neither figure is explicitly treated as a deity in the text. Regarding Deuteronomy 26:14, Johnston (2002, 170) suggests that food was indeed placed in the grave as an aid for the journey to the underworld. He accepts the possibility of a diversity of views regarding the significance of this evidence. Johnston notes the following later references in the intertestamental literature. Gifts are placed before them just as before the dead (Ep Jer. 27). Tobit encourages his readers to place their bread on the grave of the righteous, but to give none to sinners (Tobit 4:17). Sirach endorses the view that good things poured out upon a mouth

92. See chapter 10, pp. 308–10.
93. Cf. van der Toorn (1990).

that is closed are like offerings of food placed upon a grave (Sir. 30:18). Once again it is important to accept that there were a variety of beliefs regarding the dead and especially one's deceased family. Over many centuries and in different parts of Israel, among different families, there is no reason to doubt that views regarding the deceased members of one's family varied, as did the significance ascribed to various practices, such as the placement of food at the tombs.

First Samuel 28:3–25 is understood by B. Schmidt (1994, 205–20) as a late "intrusion" in the description of the battle with the Philistines. Yet the whole text need not be regarded so.[94] The use of divination is attested by the Neo-Assyrian kings Esarhaddon and Ashurbanipal before battles, as well as by Greeks and Romans. Schmidt argues that this is the earliest Mesopotamian evidence for the practice of necromancy (disputing interpretations that discern it in earlier texts). In both Mesopotamia and 1 Samuel 28, only the one who performed the recitations and preparations could see the ghost, who would be conjured at dawn after a night of preparation. Hutter (1983) and Johnston (2002, 145–46, 157) see the woman's words as a formula for conjuring up 'ĕlōhîm) or "spirits" and successfully achieving necromancy. This explains the plural, "I see spirits rising," when only Samuel seems to appear. The site of the event, En-Dor ('ên dôr), has been interpreted as "Spring of the (former) generations," "Spring of the oracular sanctuary," and other meanings associated with contact with the dead. Note that the reader's awareness, from verses 7–9, of Saul's expulsion of 'ōbôt and yiddĕ'ōnîm from the land is intimately tied in with the whole narrative and explains the reactions of the woman and many of Saul himself.[95] Indeed, the whole text may be a rhetorical denunciation of Saul in such a manner as to contrast necromancy with guidance from Yahweh.[96] Therefore, it is unlikely that this is a later Deuteronomistic insertion into a tale that was so popular that it had to remain in the narrative. Instead, this suggests that contact with the dead existed in Israel and among its neighbors as early as one can trace the matter.

Literary: Classical Sources

Many sources have been noted already in conjunction with individual figures such as Adonis. Of the various classical literary sources that more fully address West Semitic religion, Josephus and Lucian's *De Syria dea*

94. Cf. Arnold (2004).
95. Johnston (2002, 154–58).
96. Cf. Arnold (2004).

contain some materials related to Iron Age religious practices in Israel. More important, the resources of Eusebius are significant.

Eusebius cites Philo of Byblos, a first-century AD source, in his discussion of ancient Canaanite religions and cosmogonies.[97] In the citation, Philo draws upon records of Sanchuniathon, a priest from many centuries earlier. However, some hold that the text is actually a Hellenistic creation of the third, second, or first century BC. Dating the source to the Hellenistic period is based on the following points: the lack of any otherwise known ancient source behind it, the view that gods were dead humans given special honors, emphasis on the origins of culture, and the influence of Greek myth.[98] Nevertheless, the second, third, and fourth points may be disputed. Neither they nor the first point render the later date certain.

Practices mentioned in this text include the worship of the dead and the use of '*ăšērîm* and *maṣṣēbôt*. The following text discusses some of these practices:[99]

> The most ancient of the barbarians, and especially Phoenicians and Egyptians, from whom the rest of mankind received their traditions, considered as greatest gods those men who had made discoveries valuable for life's necessities or those who had in some way benefited their nations. Since they considered these men as benefactors and sources of many blessings, they worshiped them as gods even after they had passed on. They built temples and also consecrated steles and staves in their name. The Phoenicians paid great honor to them and instituted magnificent feasts for them. They assigned names chosen especially from those of their kings to the cosmic elements to some of the recognized deities.

Onomastic

Personal Names

Personal names can reveal something of the popular faith of the people. Seals and impressions (bullae) from the Iron Age give evidence of perhaps close to two thousand personal names, and the number is increasing with new evidence coming to light. What is unusual for Judah and Israel is the near absence of personal names compounded with divine names of deities other than Yahweh or the generic term for "god" ('*ēl*). More than 46 percent of all Israelite and Judahite names are Yahwistic

97. Cf. Attridge and Oden (1981, 29, 37, 41, 43).
98. Ibid., 7–9.
99. Ibid., 31–33.

names, about 6 percent are *'ēl* names, and about 1 percent are personal names compounded with all other divine names that are clearly not epithets.[100] Before the monarchy there is no extrabiblical evidence for names compounded with "Yahweh" or its abbreviated form.[101] Van der Toorn (1996b) hypothesizes that at an earlier time the worship of Yahweh was restricted to a minority population (and later grew to a national religion).[102] Others note an "onomastic lag" between the introduction of a deity and the use of that deity in personal names.[103] However, no explanation is certain.

In terms of the public use of personal names in society, Israel and Judah were Yahwistic worshiping communities. The major exception was the northern kingdom at the capital of Samaria in the early eighth century BC, where a number of personal names in the ostraca found there use Baal. Even here, however, it is a minority of names. Further, the *b'l* element may simply refer to the common noun "lord," an epithet of any deity, including Yahweh.[104] To Yahweh were ascribed the many characteristics of other deities found in personal names. For example, *Sheharya*, "Yahweh is dawn,"[105] ascribes a characteristic to the God of Israel that at Ugarit is given status as a separate deity, *Shahar* (*šḥr*) or Dawn.

The situation is different outside of Israel, both in Canaan before the arrival of the Israelites and in the Phoenician and Aramaic names contemporary with Israel. In all cases, other divine names occur in the personal names.[106] In Late Bronze Age Canaan of the fourteenth century

---

100. Tigay (1986) identified 557 Yahwistic personal names, 44 *'ēl* names, and a handful of Baal names. Cf. Millard (1998b); M. Smith (2003, 35).

101. Lemaire notes that the suggestion that an Iron Age I arrowhead has a personal name compounded with YHWH has been disputed as to its reading (personal communication, 7/2003). De Moor (1990b) theorizes that Yahweh occurs at Ugarit and in an Amarna letter, whether as part of personal names or separately. See my evaluation of this interpretation in Hess (1991a).

102. That Yahweh worship was in the minority in early Israel is a testimony to the syncretism described in Judg. 2:9–11, although it is not clear that van der Toorn would date the introduction of the idea of a single deity so early.

103. Cf. Tigay (1986, 17).

104. In Hess (forthcoming a), I calculate that 15 percent of names in the Samaria ostraca contain a non-Yahweh element if one assumes that all the Baal names refer to the god Baal. If one interprets them as referring to a common noun "lord" and identifying Yahweh or no deity, then the percentage drops to 12.66 percent.

105. Cf. J. Glen Taylor (1993, 90).

106. Day (2000, 227–28) argues against the view of Tigay (1986; 1987) that this demonstrates the worship of a single deity in monarchic Israel. While the extreme position of total monotheism can hardly be demonstrated (from neither the Bible nor the extrabiblical inscriptions) the Yahwistic element of the personal names is significant. Day presents four arguments: 1) Yahwistic names imply not that Yahweh was the only deity but that he was the most important deity; 2) many names could be traditional; 3) Tigay's evidence is limited to late monarchic Judah; 4) the statistical ratio of the number of Yahwistic names

BC, Baal and Asherah occur in names: Baal by itself (Baalumme) or with a predicate nominative (Balumehr—"Baal is a warrior"), and Asherah in the form of "servant of Asherah" (Abdi-Ashirti).[107] In Phoenician and Punic names, Anat, Baal, Eshmun, and Melqart occur as deities, by themselves and compounded with other elements.[108]

From the time of the monarchy, seals naming people with Yahwistic names (and so presumably Yahweh worshipers) are given titles such as "the priest" and "priest of Dor."[109] This supports the presence of a priesthood in Israelite worship of Yahweh and perhaps the presence of some such cult at Dor.

Zevit (2001, 586–609) presents a different view of the Israelite personal names with divine name elements. He notes that the Yahweh names are the largest class of Israelite names, dominant from the United Monarchy until the exile. Yahweh is never depicted as an animal nor is he ever referred to as "Prince" (*zbl*) or "treasure" (*nks*). This is based on the 2,202 names that Zadok (1988, 397–459) counts. Zevit (2001, 608n95) estimates that less than 20 percent of Israelites bore non-Yahwistic names. Other deities that were worshiped include: Canaanite Anat, Yam, Mot, and Reshep (but not Asherah!); and the Egyptian *'mwn* (Amon), *ḥwr* (Horus), *bs* (Bes in *bsy*, Ezra 2:49), and *'s* (Isis). Given that Yahwistic names appear from the time of the United Monarchy, it is clear that the spread of Yahwism is pre-Davidic. Many in David's administration bore Yahwistic names.[110] If the majority of Israelites were Yahwistic, the multiple cult centers suggest no single or centralized means of worshiping. Generally following Pardee (1988, 132), Zevit (2001, 608) argues that Yahwistic names indicate little about cultic affiliation. First Kings 19:18 reports seven thousand who had not worshiped Baal, this out of a total population of the ninth-century BC northerners of perhaps half a million, is less than 5 percent. On the other hand, exclusive Baal worshipers of the north in the ninth century

---

compared to the number of "pagan" names is lower than suggested. Several responses to these points may be made: 1) "importance" is not relevant because it does not challenge the data nor does it prove the alternative; 2) whether the names are traditional or not, the frequency proves that people preferred Yahwistic names (Pardee [1988] makes the point that in other archives such as Ugarit, the ratio of deities in personal names to those in other types of literature varies significantly); 3) Tigay's evidence included all onomastic data available at that time, although a preponderance originates in late monarchic Judean contexts, the large amount of onomastic data recovered in the decade since Tigay wrote has not changed these percentages and conclusions; and 4) the error is not identified in detail by Day so it is difficult to evaluate the validity of this argument. The scholars cited in this section do not seem to agree with his observation. See Hess (forthcoming a).

107. Cf. Hess (1993a, 235–36).
108. Cf. Benz (1972, 233–34).
109. See Stern (2001b, 25).
110. Cf. Zevit (2001, 607).

could fill the temple of Baal, and that could be at most a few thousand.[111] Within Israel there was a minority who chose the names of other deities for their children, but in general the non-Yahwistic names seem to have been used by parents with Yahwistic names and vice versa.[112] This suggests random choices for at least one minority group.

Lemaire (1994a, 135–45) notes that this is similar to the names appearing in inscriptions of Transjordanian and Aramaean peoples. They all contain a limited number of deities, less than in the names from the empires of Mesopotamia or Egypt. Although Zevit endorses this conclusion, his own analysis of the Ammonite onomastica tells a different story.[113] The chief deity, Milkom, occurs in only nine names.[114] *'l* occurs 150 times, lending credence to the view that this is a generic term for "god," whether in Ammon or Israel. Other deities and their frequencies include: *b'l*—two; *gd*—three; *yh/yhw*—three; *mwt*—one; *mr*—one.[115] In contrast to Israel, where Yahwistic names have a huge dominance compared with all those compounded with other deities, in Ammon the evidence is the opposite. The Ammonite personal names composed of other deities outnumber those with Milkom.[116]

Van der Toorn (1994b) has observed the theophoric elements in Hebrew personal names. Elements such as *'āb* ("father"), *'āḥ* ("brother"), and *'am* ("uncle"; "people") have been understood as references to living family members. Noth (1928) suggested that they refer to a god (hence the term, theophoric). Van der Toorn suggests that they are divinized ancestors. Although Johnston (2002, 190) sees this as a strong argument, and although the theophoric elements could refer to divinized ancestors, there is simply no evidence that can support this conclusively. Analysis of personal names is notoriously difficult and open to a variety of interpretations. It would seem that the ancestral connection is more likely when these kinship terms began to be used. It remains a possible explanation of the later names but these may also have become terms that were used without a specific referent in the mind of the name giver.

111. Cf. 2 Kings 10:19–21; Zevit (2001, 649–50).
112. Cf. Zevit (2001, 649).
113. Ibid., 651n75. For these purposes Zevit relies on the work of Aufrecht (1989, 356–76), a collection of Ammonite inscriptions including all available data from seals and bullae.
114. Zevit notes this fact but does not attempt to explain it.
115. As in Israel, goddesses such as Asherah receive little or no mention.
116. See Hess (forthcoming a). Aufrecht (1999) suggests the view that El was the chief deity in Ammon and therefore these references are not to a generic term for a deity but rather to a god named El similar to the chief deity of the Ugaritic pantheon. However, no textual evidence outside the onomastica supports this. Further, the consistent usage of *'l* as a generic term for deity in Israelite texts places the burden of proof on the attempt to assert that El was recognized as a deity in Ammon.

Johnston (2002, 31) discusses personal (and place) names associated with death (Hebrew *mwt*), such as Ahimoth (1 Chron. 6:25 [Heb. 10]) "Death is (my) brother," Azmawet (1 Chron. 8:36) "Death is strong," and others. These are examples of name forms that can take divine names in the position of "Death," for example, Ahijah, "Yahweh is (my) brother." However, they can also take nondivine adjectives and epithets in that position, also: Ahiezer, "Help/Aid is (my) brother," Ahinadab, "Willing is (my) brother," Ahinoam, "Pleasant/Beautiful is (my) brother." Thus regarding the deity "Death" (*mwt*), the evidence from the personal names in Israel remains ambiguous unless either the term can be shown to be a divine name elsewhere in the Old Testament or in other Israelite writings, or the form of the name always contains a divine name at this point. Since that is not the case with the personal names containing "Death," it is not possible to conclude from these names that Death or *Mwt* was worshiped as a god in ancient Israel.

A challenge to the use of personal names in the study of Israelite religion has come from Joseph Callaway (1999). Using biblical and archaeological evidence, he attempts to argue that the personal names on Israelite seals and bullae describe an elite, urban population that was dominated by the reforms of Josiah. It does not reflect the larger rural population. However, none of this is convincing. First, there is much more evidence of writing in ancient Israel than Callaway's sources suggest.[117] From the eleventh-century BC abecedary in the village of Izbet-Sartah (and now a tenth-century BC abecedary at the Judean site of Tel Zayit) to the multiple attestations of writing from villages and rural areas in every century of the Iron Age, there is no indication that seals with written names were unavailable to nonurban individuals. Further, the number of published seals and bullae has more than doubled since Callaway published, and there is a wide range of writing styles on these seals, reflecting both the elite and their professional scribes as well as those who were neither professional nor artistic.[118] To attribute all seals and sources of personal names to Judah's urban elite is speculation. Second, Callaway ignores the neighboring cultures where the evidence for the personal names exists at the same time on similar sources of seals and bullae, and yet reveals a completely different set of data in terms of references to foreign deities (as noted above). In this regard, a major pillar of Callaway's argument rests on what he calls standardization, in which personal names of a whole nation, or at least the elite, are changed to follow the policy of the

117. Sources such as Jamieson-Drake (1991); contrast Millard (1995); Hess (2002b).

118. Callaway refers to Tigay (1986). See Demsky and Bar-Ilan (1988, 15); Avigad (1986, 121); Schniedewind (2000, 328).

capital. If this is the case in Jerusalem, there is no evidence for it. There are no contemporary examples. More important, one would expect to see examples of names changing from non-Yahwistic forms to Yahwistic forms between generations. This does not exist in any consistent manner. Nor can it be argued that all the seals and bullae must come from after Josiah, that is, after 650 BC. Paleography does not support this claim.[119]

Place Names

Of the 502 place names in the Bible, none are Yahwistic. Toponyms with *b'l* are found in the time of ancient Israel (e.g., Kiriath Baal, Baal Tamar, Baal Perazim, Baal Hazor), yet they are unattested in Canaanite toponyms from Egyptian sources during the Middle and Late Bronze Ages (c. 2000–1200 BC). The most reasonable explanation seems to be that they were introduced about the time that Israel appeared in Canaan (c. 1200 BC) or later. In the south, in Judah and Simeon in particular, some eight place names have a form of the element, Baal/ba'al. This leads Zevit (2001, 606, 649) to conclude that Baal worship was more prevalent than might be supposed on the basis of biblical evidence alone. Baal was a popular deity in the towns.

Epigraphic[120]

There are a few religious texts among the inscriptions from neighboring states that were contemporary with Israel during the divided monarchy. In Philistia, inscriptions have now identified the deities Baal, Asherah, Qudshu, Anat, and Ptgyh, as attested at Tel Miqne Ekron.[121] The first, occurring on an inscription dated c. 700 BC ("For Baal and for Padi"), reminds one of the deity Baal "Zebub," the city deity of Ekron according to 2 Kings 1:2–3.[122]

119. See further Hess (forthcoming a).
120. See texts and discussions in Dobbs-Allsopp et al. (2005); Donner and Röllig (1973–79); Gibson (1971–82); G. Davies (1991); Hess (1992c); Smelik (1991).
121. See Gitin (2003). For further on Ptgyh, Demsky (1997, 1–5; 1998, 53–58) reads *ptnyh* = Greek *pōtnia*, "lady, mistress, queen," to describe Athena, Artemis, and females in general. Here Demsky equates it with Asherah, as do Gitin, Dothan, and Naveh (1997, 12) who note that the name appears elsewhere at Tel Miqne on a jar inscription. Both the problem with reading a *nun* and the issue of a redundancy in the inscription ("his lady, his lady") raise questions about this interpretation. Schäfer-Lichtenberger (1998, 64–76) identifies *ptgyh*, Ekron's principal deity, with Pytho at Delphi, which was the Mycenaean shrine of Gaia before Apollo became the dominant deity. Thus she reads this as Pythogayah.
122. See Gitin and Cogan (1999), as well as earlier discussion on p. 251.

Mesha, the King of Moab, and His Dedication to His God, Chemosh

I am Mesha, son of Chemosh[yat], king of Moab, the Dibonite. My father ruled over Moab thirty years, and I ruled after my father. I made this high place for Chemosh at Qarḥoh—a high pl[ace of sal]vation—because he delivered me from all the kings, and because he showed me (victory) over all my enemies.

Omri ruled over Israel. He oppressed Moab for a long time, because Chemosh was angry at his land. His son succeeded him. He also said, "I will oppress Moab!" In my days he said. . . . I saw (victory) over him and his household. Israel has utterly perished forever. Omri has possessed all the land of Madeba. He had already resided there during his time and half his son's time, forty years. But Chemosh restored it in my days.

I built Ba'alme'on. I put in it the reservoir/canal.

I built Qiryaten.

The people of Gad had settled in the land of 'Aṭarot from of old, and the king of Israel had fortified 'Aṭarot for them. Nevertheless, I fought against the town, and seized it. I killed all the people from the city, as a satisfaction (offering) for Chemosh and Moab. I brought back from there the hearth(?) of (its) dwd(?). I dragged it before Chemosh in Qiryat. I settled in it the men of Sharon and those of Maḥarat.

Then Chemosh said to me: "Go, seize Nebo from Israel." So I went by night. I fought against it from the break of dawn until noon. I seized it. I killed all: 7,000 warriors, foreign men, women (warriors?), foreign women, and "wombs" (slave women?). I devoted it to Ashtar Chemosh. I took from there the altar hearth of Yahweh. I dragged them before Chemosh.

The king of Israel fortified Yahaz. He resided there when he fought against me. Chemosh drove him out before me. I took 200 men from Moab, all its leaders. I went up against Yahaz. I seized it in order to add (it) to Dibon.

I repaired Qarḥoh, the wall of the park and the walls of the acropolis. I repaired the gates. I repaired its towers. I repaired the palace. I made the retaining wall for the spring inside the town. There was no cistern inside the city, in Qarḥoh. So I said to all the people: "Make yourselves each a cistern in his house." I cut the channels for Qarḥoh by using Israelite prisoners.

I repaired Aroer.

I made highways at Arnon . . .

I repaired Beth-Bamoth because it was destroyed.

I repaired Bezer because it was ruins. To do this I used fifty Dibonite men because all Dibon was obedient.

I ruled over hundreds in the towns that I annexed to the land.

I built . . . ba and Beth-Diblaten and Beth-Ba'alme'on. There I made . . . the sheep of the land.

Regarding Ḥoronaim, the house of David resided in it. . . . Chemosh said to me:

"Go down, fight against Ḥoronaim." So I went down . . . and Chemosh [rest]ored it in my days . . .

Mesha Stele; c. 850–810 BC from Madeba in Moab. Translation by author who thanks K. Lawson Younger Jr. for his suggestions. For transliteration, see Donner and Röllig (1973–1979; KAI 181) and see also Lemaire (1994b; 1994c).

There is mention of national deities in monumental inscriptions, such as Chemosh, the god of Moab, in the ninth-century BC Mesha stele. The same stele also mentions Yahweh as god of Israel and notes a cult object in a Transjordanian Israelite town in the mid-ninth century.[123] The following represent the most important religious inscriptions concerning ancient Israelite religion during the monarchy. Following the name of the inscription a translation will be presented unless the text is longer than a few lines. In that case, I will summarize its relevant content. Where there is debate regarding the translation, I will provide alternatives and discuss issues. I will note the provenance, context, and date of the inscription and discuss its significance for the religion of Israel.

Deir 'Alla Plasters

Deir 'Alla is an ancient cult site located in the Jordan Valley. Plaster fragments containing writing have been found in what may have been a cult center. This site may be dated to the late ninth century BC. The ink writing presents a text in a distinctive dialect of Aramaic, influenced by the Canaanite dialects of the area. As reconstructed from the plaster fragments, it describes a seer named Balaam son of Beor. Balaam had a vision that has been understood as a picture of the natural world turned upside down.[124] The name of the god El appears. Of interest for the question of religious distinctives is the mention of the Shaddayin, who appear as a divine council responsible for the supernatural effects. The term Shaddayin occurs only at this Transjordan site, although it may be related to a divine name found especially in Genesis, El Shaddai.[125] Could this refer to God as lord of the Shaddayin? Another prophecy text occurs at about the same time and farther to the north. In c. 800 BC, Zakkur of Hamath sought divine assistance through seers and diviners according to his Aramaic inscription.[126]

Jerusalem Pomegranate

Some date the paleography of the Jerusalem pomegranate to this same period, although with only a few letters the date is difficult to ascertain. Although unprovenanced, this small ivory pomegranate probably functioned as the head of a scepter. Several of the letters for "house/temple" and "Yahweh" are missing. Nevertheless, the most likely reconstruction

123. See Lemaire (1994c).

124. Cf. Hackett (1980, 29–30). Cf. Numbers 22–24 for Balaam in the Bible.

125. For the former, see M. Smith (2003, 58). For the latter, see Engle (1979, 55, 62) and Hestrin (1987b, 221–22). Cf. also Hadley (2000, 196–205); Holland (1977); Kletter (2001); and LaRocca-Pitts (2001, 161–204).

126. Cf. Kitchen (2003, 388–89).

allows a translation, "Belonging to the tem[ple of Yahw]eh, holy to the priests."[127] This translation implies a temple and priesthood related to Yahweh in Israel.

Halpern has proposed an alternative interpretation. He read a personal name in the gap, perhaps Ahijah. This would then refer to a priestly line, the "house" of Ahijah, where "house" refers to the lineage or family.[128] However, it is more likely that a cultic object would contain the name of the divine dedicatee rather than the name of the family that owns it. The name of a deity on presumably cultic objects occurs at Tel Miqne (cf. below, under the discussion of the Kuntillet 'Ajrud texts) and elsewhere in the ancient Near East. The personal name of the owner on such an object, without the name of the deity, would be less likely.

"The house of Yahweh" also appears on an ostracon from the collection of Shlomo Moussaieff that mentions a gift of three shekels to that sanctuary. It occurs as well on an Arad ostracon. However, Stern (2001b, 25) suggests that all these could refer to other sanctuaries in Judah. Perhaps this is true, although it seems likely that the ostraca might refer to the place name where the sanctuary was located. The pomegranate seems to be an artistic and precious object such as would be found in the capital city and the chief sanctuary, rather than at cult places outside Jerusalem.

Recent study of both the pomegranate and the "three shekels ostracon" has led some to challenge their authenticity, primarily Yuval Goren and his team of geologists and other scientists.[129] They challenge both the writing and the patina (or coat) as modern.

However, the epigrapher, Robert Deutsch, writes concerning the claim of forgery that many of the later "embellishments" reflect customary handling of items at the Israel Museum at the time of its acquisition.[130] A point by point refutation of Goren's published analysis has been written by Lemaire (2006), with a discussion of the patina residue by Rosenfeld and Ilani (2006).

If true, these points raise serious questions about the method of Goren and the team. It certainly demonstrates the ease with which challenges can be made to authentic artifacts and the need to be cautious about accepting such assertions. Nevertheless, the few letters that remain on the object make it very difficult to distinguish between an authentic object and a skilled forgery. Further, the absence of any ivory pomegranate from a clearly stratified Iron Age context in this region creates

127. Cf. Lemaire (1981); Hess (1992c, 34–37; 1996b, 215–17).

128. Halpern's view appears in private correspondence in a letter that is reported in an anonymous article (Anonymous [1992]).

129. See Goren, Aḥituv, et al. (2005); Goren, Ayalon, et al. (2005).

130. See http://biblical-studies.blogspot.com/2005/07/short-note-on-recent-forgeries.

Fig. 31. Ein Gedi (Courtesy of Richard S. Hess and Thomas B. Hall III)

additional questions as to whether such an object existed at that time. It seems best to leave the question open for the present.

Ein Gedi Cave

Zevit (2001, 351–59) suggests two possible translations of this text:

1. . . . cursed is the one who will damage/deface/wipe out
2. and will act with vengeance against her/raise her up/reckon. . . .
3. Blessed is YHWH
4. Blessed among the nation[s] . . . he will reign. . . .
5.
6. Blessed is ʾDNY
7.
8. cursed

or

1. . . . cursed is Ashur. May he obliterate him
2. and act with vengeance against him . . .
3. Blessed is YHWH
4. Blessed among the nation[s] . . . May he reign
5.
6. May 'DNY be blessed . . .
7. cursed

The text was discovered written on a cave wall located on the cliffs overlooking Ein Gedi on the western side of the Dead Sea. This is a celebratory inscription, dating to c. 700 BC and perhaps related to the victory over Sennacherib. Yahweh is mentioned in parallel with Adonai, either as another deity or more likely (given the use of this term in contemporary Hebrew) as an epithet of Yahweh, meaning "lord." Yahweh is blessed and described as a ruler, perhaps over many nations. Ashur, the god of Assyria or the nation of Assyria itself, is cursed. Someone, presumably Yahweh, is called upon to destroy Ashur.

Ketef Hinnom Silver Strips

This translation of the best known part of the silver strips is based on the blessing of Aaron in Numbers 6:24–26. The text of Numbers 6:24–26 is given below with the phrases on the strips in bold:

> **The Lord bless you**
> > **and keep you;**
> **the Lord make his face shine upon you**
> > and be gracious to you;
> the Lord turn his face toward you
> > **and give you peace.**[131]

The silver strips were discovered in a cave burial at Ketef Hinnom, a site southwest of the City of David in Jerusalem. These two silver strips were found rolled up and formed part of the burial assembly. When unrolled, it was found that the texts contained biblical text. Both the pottery from the caves and the paleography of the writing on the strips suggest a date at the end of the Judean monarchy, c. 600 BC. The strips formed the earliest attestation of biblical texts. Waaler (2002) has highlighted several important features about these two texts and their

131. Cf. Hess (1992c, 37–40). Cohen (1993) compares the additional writing on the strips with comparable expressions in Akkadian and Hebrew. He finds them to be stylistic variants of the same idea represented by the phrases "make his face shine upon you" and "turn his face toward you." The former means to cause to rejoice and the latter means to show special favor toward.

reference to Numbers 6. Although written by
two different hands, they preserve vowel letters identical to those found in the Masoretic
Text of Numbers. This makes it unlikely that
they were written down from oral dictation
or that they come from entirely different
sources. Also, the first strip appears to have
what may be a "quotation" of Deuteronomy
7:9, a second Pentateuchal text. However, the
words are also found in Nehemiah 1:5 and
Daniel 9:4.[132] This suggests a copying of well-
established texts at the time the silver strips
were composed.[133]

Renz's attempt to assign a postexilic date
to the texts has been disputed by Barkay and
colleagues.[134] They note that the archaeological
context confirms a preexilic date toward the
end of the seventh century BC. The paleography suggests that the inscription was written
in the middle of the seventh century. In the first
strip, they restore "the rebuker of the Evil" in
lines 3–4 (*hg'r b[r]'*). This provides an emphasis
on the apotropaic function of the silver strips,
and leads to a conclusion supporting the commonly accepted function of the strips as amulets. The tomb inscriptions from Phoenician
and Aramaic tombs as well as the inscriptions

Fig. 32. Ketef Hinnom silver
strip (Courtesy of the Israel
Antiquities Authority)

accompanying the c. 700 BC Tomb of the Royal Steward in Jerusalem
and the Khirbet el-Qom tomb (see below) all contain warnings and curses
directed toward those who would rob the tomb or disturb the body's rest.
It may be that these amulets served a similar purpose.[135] Finally, Barkay
and colleagues note the family context of this use of the Aaronic blessing,
unique in its early appearances.

Khirbet Beit Lei

Khirbet Beit Lei is a burial cave five miles east of Lachish. Lemaire
(1977) and Zevit (2001, 405–37) date the inscriptions c. 700 BC, but Cross

132. Cf. Barkay et al. (2003; 2004, 68).
133. This remains true whether or not one accepts Waaler's attempt to date the paleography of the strips earlier (725–650 BC) than the traditional dates.
134. Cf. Renz (1995, 1:447–56) and Barkay et al. (2004).
135. See Lewis (2002, 180–81).

(1970) dates it no earlier than 600 BC. Zevit identifies a series of eight "stops" that one encounters while passing through the cave:[136]

Stop 1 is a drawing interpreted as the mound of Lachish with the palace-fort in the center. The associated inscription reads "Curser."[137]

Stop 2 is a drawing of a standing lyre player. Is this Asherah? See the lyre player portrayed at Kuntillet 'Ajrud below.

Stop 3 is an inscription, "He/They/You cursed him" or "his curser."[138]

Stop 4 is a drawing of a human figure with hands raised in supplication.

Stop 5 contains the two main inscriptions opposite the entrance. Two alternative readings and translations have been proposed:

> Upper inscription, first proposal:[139]
> 1. "Yahweh (is) the God of the whole earth; the moun-
> 2. tains of Judah belong to him, to the God of Jerusalem."
>
> Lower inscription:
> 3. "The (Mount of) Moriah you have favored, the dwelling of Yah, Yahweh."
>
> Upper inscription, second proposal:[140]
> 1. "Yahweh, my god, exposed/laid bare his land
> 2. A terror he led for his own sake to Jerusalem."[141]
>
> Lower inscription
> 3. "The source smote the hand. Absolve (from culpability) the hand, Yahweh."

For Zevit, Jeremiah's (2:13; 17:13) use of "source" as a metaphor for Yahweh is a reflex of an earlier usage.[142]

Stop 6 is a drawing of a person with raised hands.

Stop 7 includes two inscriptions:

136. Cross dates stop 3 at 587 BC.
137. The Hebrew is *'wrr*.
138. The Hebrew is *'rrhw*.
139. Following Naveh (1963), the Hebrew text is: 1. *yhwh 'lhy . kl h'rṣ h* 2. *ry yhd lw l'lhy yršlm* 3. *hmwryh 'th ḥnnt nwh yh yhwh*.
140. Following Zevit (2001, 421–27), 1. *yhwh 'lhy glh 'rṣh* 2. *'rṣ yhd lw 'l yršlm* 3. *hmqr yd hyh nqh yd yhwh*.
141. Zevit observes that the term *'arîṣ* "terror" occurs in Isa. 29:20; 49:25; Jer. 20:11; Ps. 37:35. As for *yhd*, from the root, *hdh*, "he led," it may occur as a biblical hapax (occurring only once) in Isa. 11:8.
142. Cf. Zevit (2001, 426). Compare also Jer. 30:10–11a from a later period for a negative response and Isa. 41:8–15 for a positive one.

Fig. 33. Lachish gate area where ostraca were found (Courtesy of Richard S. Hess)

The upper one:[143] "Save. Destruction."

The lower one:[144]
1. "Cursed (be/is)
2. (who) he will sing (in) time to come (or tomorrow?)."

Stop 8 is a drawing of two boats, including one with a figure (a deity?) in it. The two boats may include one without a figure who may represent Yahweh and the other with a figure who may be a second deity or a human. This may relate to Deuteronomy 28:68: Yahweh will send you back in ships to Egypt.

Miqneyahu Seal

This eighth-century BC seal is translated "Belonging to Miqneyahu, servant of Yahweh."[145] The seal provides evidence for an active cult of Yahweh in which figures such as Miqneyahu could serve as officiants. See also seals with inscriptions of "priest" and "priest of Dor" above under "Personal Names."

143. The Hebrew text is *hwš hwh*.
144. The Hebrew text is 1. *' 'rr h?* 2. *y šr mḥrt?*
145. The Hebrew text is *lmqnyhw 'bd yhwh*. Cf. G. Davies (1991, 100, 172); Avigad and Sass (1997, #27).

Letter about the Temple of Yahweh

To my lord, Eliyashib:

    May Yahweh give regard for your well-being. Now give Shemaryahu. . . . Give the Qerosite.
. . . Regarding what you commanded me, he is well. He resides at the temple of Yahweh.

Arad 18; c. 600 BC from Arad. Translation by author; see A. Lemaire, *Inscriptions hébraïques.*
Volume 1. *Les ostraca.* Littératures anciennes du Proche-Orient 9. Paris: Les Éditions du Cerf,
1977, pp. 145–253; Yohanan Aharoni, *Arad Inscriptions.* Judean Desert Studies. Jerusalem:
Israel Exploration Society, 1981, texts 1–3, 18; Johannes Renz, *Die Althebräischen Inschriften.*
3 volumes: *Teil 1. Text und Kommentar, Teil 2. Zusammenfassende Erörterungen, Paläographie
und Glossar, Band III. Texte und Tafeln.* Darmstadt: Wissenschaftliche Buchgesellschaft,
1995, volume 1, pp. 347–63, 382–84; F. W. Dobbs-Allsopp, J. J. M. Roberts, C. L. Seow, and
R. E. Whitaker, *Hebrew Inscriptions. Texts from the Biblical Period of the Monarchy with
Concordance.* New Haven: Yale University Press, 2005, pp. 37–41.

Yahweh Blessings on Ostraca from Lachish and Arad

Ostraca from Lachish and Arad contain dozens of messages sent
between military officials at these two sites and elsewhere. The relevant
correspondence dates from the final decades or (at Lachish) months
of the independent kingdom of Judah. The ostraca are a formal correspondence in a desperate situation. Both groups normally include, as
part of their formulaic expressions, the wish for Yahweh's blessing. One
ostracon from Lachish also mentions a *nb'*, "prophet," whose message
is summarized in a single command, "Beware."[146]

Kuntillet 'Ajrud Texts

A collection of inscriptions from c. 800 BC were discovered at the northern Sinai site of Kuntillet 'Ajrud.[147] Commonly understood as mentioning
"Yahweh and his Asherah," the texts have provided what is arguably the
major catalyst for a revolution in our understanding of the beliefs of the
Israelites during the monarchy. The inscriptions that mention this blessing,
while not limited to what is either a Sinai caravansary or a cult center (see
below), provide the centerpiece for discussion of the role of a goddess or
cult symbol and its relationship to Yahweh. It is, in fact, no longer possible
to accept a simple division between those who worshiped Yahweh as a
single and unique deity, on the one hand, and those who served Baal and a
pantheon of deities, on the other. As a result of the finds at Kuntillet 'Ajrud,
Yahweh has become a member of the pantheon of Iron Age Palestine.

146. The Hebrew word is *hšmr*.
147. The dating is on the basis of radiocarbon; Shanks (1996a, 12).

The discovery of these inscriptions in the excavations of the desert site has provoked a large literature debating their interpretation and their significance for Israelite religion.[148] Some of the texts appear on the walls of a structure excavated in 1975–76 at Kuntillet ʿAjrud. Others are found on ceramic jars at the site. On the basis of an absence of cultic objects, Judith Hadley (1993) argued that the structure is probably not a cult center but rather a caravansary, an early "hotel" for travelers across the northern Sinai desert. However, Zevit argues that the benches (like many cult centers with large pithoi), the earthquake architecture (as at the high place at Dan), the ink on plaster writing (Deir ʿAlla), and the natural temenos (sacred enclosure) wall affected by the steep edges of the hills surrounding the site[149] all point to a cultic installation. Nevertheless, the absence of altars, incense burners, and maṣṣēbôt, as well as the casual style of the script, continue to confirm the view that this is a caravansary.[150] One jar alone had written on it several inscriptions along with drawings of figures best identified as Bes figures. Bes was an Egyptian deity whose images functioned as a kind of good luck charm. They can be found throughout the ancient Near East and the Mediterranean world.

In the eyes of some scholars, this is the most significant set of texts yet discovered for understanding Israelite religion. These important inscriptions mention Yahweh and Asherah as deities invoked in the pronouncement of blessings on various people. El and Baal are also mentioned in a single poem. However, the interpretation of these texts bristles with problems. Elsewhere, I (1992c; 1996b) have argued that the mention of Asherah, in conjunction with Yahweh, is not a cult symbol nor is "his Asherah" the best translation. Instead, it is preferable to render the goddess's name as Asheratah, in accordance with the spelling and reading of her name everywhere outside the Bible for more than a thousand years. The tradition of reading and pronouncing this name as Asherah is one that derives directly from the Bible. In the translations below, for the sake of accuracy, I will render the goddess's name as "Asheratah." However, I will continue to use "Asherah" in the text of this study, since it is the most commonly accepted way of spelling the name of the goddess.

148. For some of the earlier discussion see Meshel (1978a; 1978b; 1979); Gilula (1978–79); Naveh (1979); Block (1979, 65–66); Catastini (1982); Emerton (1982); Angerstorfer (1982); Lemaire (1984); Weinfeld (1984); Dever (1984); Day, (1986); W. Maier (1986); Tigay (1986; 1987); Coogan (1987); Freedman (1987); Hadley (1987; 1989, 159–73); McCarter (1987); M. Smith (1987; 1990a); Koch (1988); Olyan (1988, 23–37); Dietrich and Loretz (1992); H.-P. Müller (1992); Hess (1992c); Wiggins (1993); Merlo (1994).

149. Cf. Zevit (2001, 370–71, 374–75n47). In his view, the sheer clifflike nature of the site would make it difficult for travelers to reach the place with their animals.

150. Fried (2002, 448); Rainey (2002, 547); Kitchen (2003, 413). On the basis of parallels at Horvat Uza and Sakkara, Rainey suggests that the blessings are practice formulas for beginning a business letter.

It is not certain who wrote these inscriptions. In particular, some have thought that the texts that mention Baal and El were composed by non-Israelites. The texts associate these deities with war and with theophanies. If they are Israelite, and this is increasingly thought likely,[151] they indicate either (1) Baal, like El, should be identified with Yahweh; or (2) there was a rival cult that accepted Baal as a martial deity. The most frequently mentioned deity, the only one associated with Asherah, and the one who appears in the blessings formulae, is Yahweh. His name is associated with two place names that occur as Yahweh of the Teman (*htmn*) and Yahweh of Samaria (*šmrn*). The Teman was a desert region to the south of Judah, while Samaria was either the capital of the northern kingdom of Israel or, possibly, the nation of Israel itself.

Although best identified as a caravansary with some cultic associations in my view, this site yields the following distinctives in terms of its religious inscriptions: (1) Yahweh as a deity associated both with the state of Israel and with a region outside of Israel and Judah, in the southern desert; (2) Yahweh as a male deity with a female consort, Asherah, a goddess also associated with El, the chief deity in thirteenth-century BC mythological texts from Ugarit; and (3) Yahweh and Asherah as powerful deities capable of blessing others.

The following inscriptions were identified on wall plaster and on large jars.[152]

A. This is an inscription on the north side of the door between the bench room and the courtyard:[153]

1. "And in the shining forth of El at the he[ads of the mountains
2. And the mountains will melt [like wax beneath him
3. And the knolls will be crushed [in Mount Bashan
4. and six on [
5. to bless Baal on the day of w[ar
6. to the name of El on the day of w[ar"

B. This is an inscription from the west wall of the bench room:[154]

151. Cf. M. Smith (2003, 73).
152. See Zevit (2001, 372–405) for the following discussion here. His work is one of the few to examine all the inscriptions systematically.
153. The text of the inscription is: 1. *bzrḥ . 'l . br['šy hrm* 2. *wymsn hrm[kdng tḥth* 3. *wydkn . gbnm[bhr bšn* 4. *wšdš . 'ly[* 5. *lbrk . b'l . bym mlḥ[mh* 6. *lšm[.] 'l . bym mlḥ[mh.*
154. The text of the inscription is: 1. *t]'rk . ymm wyšb'w[. wy]tnw . l[y]hwh[.]tymn . wl[] 'šrt[* 2. *]hyṭb . yhwh . hty[mn].*

1. "[l]engthen their days and they will be filled, [and they] will give to
2.] do good, Yahweh (of) the Te[man]"

C. This is an inscription from pithos A overwriting Bes figurines:[155]

1. "Said [ ] the ?: "Say to Yehal['el] and to Yossah and to [PN . . . I b]lessed you
2. to Yahweh of Shomron and to Asheratah."

D. This inscription from jar B appears alongside five people in a row and a sixth one above the five. They face left and gesture as though praying. It is written to the right of the procession:[156]

1. "Said 2. Amaryo: 3. "Say to my lord: 4. Are you peace? 5. I blessed you to Yah 6. weh Teman 7. and to Asheratah. May he bl 8. ess and may he guard you 9. and may he be with my 10. lord . . . 11. like . . .""

E. Inscriptions from jar B include some that are close to the procession. There are six names. Three have theophoric suffixes, *-yw*, that are customary with northern Israelite names. Another is *mṣry*, perhaps referring to someone associated with Egypt.[157] These six may be the six figures represented pictorially on the pithos. Samaria and Teman include the most northern and southern areas of Yahweh's dominion.[158] However, they may also indicate two regions especially identified with Yahweh by the visitors to this site.

F. This is an inscription from pithos B partially covering the procession.[159]

1.] "for/to Yahweh (of) the Teman and to Asheratah[
2. all that he asks from a man who acts compassionately he[?], and YHW will give him according to his heart."

155. Zevit (2001, 391–92) interprets this as a request to inform three or more individuals that someone has blessed them. The text of the inscription is: 1. *'mr . '[.]hm°k . 'mr . lyhl[.] wlyw'šh . wl[(23 spaces).b]rkt . 'tkm* 2. *lyhwh . šmrn . wl'šrth.*
156. The text is: 1. *'mr* 2. *'mryw '* 3. *mr l . 'dn[y* 4. *hšlm . 't* 5. *brktk l[y* 6. *hwh tmn* 7. *wl'šrth . yb* 8. *rk . wyšmrk* 9. *wyhy 'm . 'dn* 10. *y[?]* 11. *k[?].*
157. Zevit (2001, 398) notes an ostracon and two bullae from Judah with this name.
158. Ibid., 650.
159. The inscription reads: 1. *] lyhwh htmn . wl'šrth* 2. *kl 'šr . yš'l . ḥnn h'[?] wntn lh yhw[klbbh.* For *Yhwh htmn*, compare Yhwh *ḥṣb'wt* in Amos 9:5. For "a man who acts compassionately," cf. Exod. 22:26. For "he will give him according to his heart," cf. Ps. 20:4–5.

The inscriptions include blessings upon the reader by Yahweh of Teman and Yahweh of Samaria. Another can be translated, "I bless you by Yahweh of Samaria and A/asheratah."

Who or what is A/asheratah in these inscriptions? Four options have been suggested:

a. a symbol of Yahweh
b. personal name of the goddess Asherah
c. a symbol of Asherah
d. personal name of the goddess Asherah/Asheratah

That Asherah is a symbol of Yahweh is not impossible. However, it is unknown in Israel for Yahweh to have a cult symbol.[160] Keel and Uehlinger (1992) propose a cult symbol subordinated to Yahweh. In this interpretation the Asherah symbol is no goddess. As developed by Miller, Asherah became a symbol of Yahweh who expresses his presence, a kind of hypostasis that possesses no gender but only the presence of God.[161] With Hadley, he sees in her an anticipation of Lady Wisdom in Proverbs and the development of the Law as a personification of God.[162] However, this view suffers from several problems.

M. Smith (1991; 2003, 126–28) argues that the references that associate Asherah with Baal (Judg. 3:7; 1 Kings 18:19; 2 Kings 23:4) must all be discounted as late editorials and glosses by the Deuteronomists.[163] But why would the Deuteronomists defeat their own purposes of monotheism by rehabilitating a forgotten goddess? Nor is the text's failure to mention Asherah in Jehu's reform of 2 Kings 9–10 proof that this deity/hypostasis was acceptable to the Yahwist Jehu. Rather, the emphasis on Baal includes all the deities in his pantheon, such as Asherah, and only occasionally did the biblical writers feel the need to specify them and give them the "honor" of naming them.

A second problem arises with a twelfth-century BC Babylonian text, in which the names of many gods are subsumed under one deity, Marduk, who is chief god of Babylon. However, Marduk's wife's name is missing.[164] This is no oversight but a demonstration of the fact that the female goddess was never assimilated into the male deity, even in such a

160. For the biblical references to the biblical asherah as something that can be cut, planted, and otherwise treated as a tree or a wooden pole, see Reed (1949). M. Smith (2003, 112) also refers to the citations of *m. 'Abod. Zar.* 3:5, 7, which describe the asherah as a planted tree with an idol.

161. Cf. P. Miller (2000, 29–40).

162. See Prov. 3:18; and Hadley (2000).

163. Smith suggests that Judg. 2:13; 3:7; 1 Sam. 7:4 and 12:10 all use the terms baals and asherahs to refer to foreign gods and goddesses in general. This is possible.

164. Cf. Lambert (1975).

polytheistic context. This evidence argues against the view that Asherah was or became a hypostasis of Yahweh.[165]

There is evidence for the continuous presence of Asherah in the West Semitic pantheon from c. 2000 BC on into the Persian period without any textual suggestion of her becoming a hypostasis of a chief male deity.[166] And nowhere in the Ugaritic texts, the Old Testament, or elsewhere is Asherah associated with wisdom.[167]

The view that this is the personal name of the goddess Asherah implies that Yahweh had a consort. Most scholars conclude that this is the correct analysis.[168] Most accept the addition of an -*h* suffix in the inscription as a third personal pronominal suffix, "his Asherah."[169] However, no personal name ever has a pronominal suffix attached to it in Classical Hebrew. Nevertheless, other West Semitic languages do provide occasional examples of this phenomenon.

If this is a symbol of the goddess, as in the form of a wooden pole, it would be acceptable grammatically and would be supported by other attestations in the Bible. Thus Yahweh has a consort. At least one or two writers of this graffiti (from Samaria) had a view of their god that allowed for other deities, a perspective reflected as well in the prophets.

My view assumes that this is the personal name of the goddess. In this scenario, the final -*h* consonant in the inscription's spelling of the name could be a second feminine ending (Zevit [2001]) or a vowel letter reflecting a final *a* vowel (Angerstorfer [1982]). In the latter case, the name is not Asherah but Asheratah. This is the preferred explanation, based as it is on comparative forms in Iron Age names of southern Palestine and on all other West Semitic occurrences of the deity's name from the second millennium and the Iron Age epigraphy of the first millennium BC.[170] Asherah, spelled as it is in the Bible (*'ăšērâ*), is never found in extrabiblical texts of the monarchy in Israel. At Khirbet el-Qom (see below) and on ostraca from seventh-century BC Tell

165. Contra P. Miller (2000, 30).

166. Cf. Hess (1996b). See also Day (2000, 42–47), who recognizes that she appears in parallel to the deity Baal in 2 Kings 23:4 (and Baals in Judg. 2:13; 3:7; 10:6; 1 Sam. 7:3, 4; 12:10); that the graven image (*pesel*) of Asherah most probably refers to a deity and not to an image of a deity (2 Kings 21:7), as is true of the "horrid thing" (*mipleṣet*) made for Asherah (1 Kings 15:13 = 2 Chron. 15:16). However, Day agrees that by the time of the Chronicler (sixth to fourth centuries BC) there was probably no clear understanding of the deity.

167. See Day (2000, 67).

168. Cf. Dever (1984; 1999); Weinfeld (1984, 122); Friedman (1987); Dietrich and Loretz (1992); Xella (1995); Binger (1997); and Rainey (1998).

169. E.g., Binger (1995); Dever (1999, 14*); Day (2000, 49–52).

170. Cf. Hess (1996b).

Miqne (= Ekron) the spelling *'šrt(h)* is always found.[171] Thus I think the deity was Asheratah, identical to the Asherah of the Bible, only spelled slightly differently.[172]

Khirbet el-Qom Blessing

Khirbet el-Qom, a site eight miles west of Hebron, also yielded an inscription from a time period near that of Kuntillet 'Ajrud. Some have interpreted them all in the same way, as evidence of a consort for Yahweh. Thus there is evidence for polytheism with Yahweh in Judah. Dever observes that line three has been deliberately overwritten and suggests that in the eighth century BC someone found it a theological problem to produce this blessing.[173] But this is not the only possible reason for the tracings.

Zevit has restudied this inscription and produced the following translation:[174]

1. "Uryahu, the prosperous, his inscription ([or] an inscription)
2. I blessed Uryahu to Yahweh
3. to wit, from his enemies . . . for the sake of Asheratah save him
4. . . . by Abiyahu
5. . . . ?? and to Asheratah
6. . . . A[sh]eratah"

The title "prosperous" appears in Micah 6:12 and Psalm 45:12 [Heb. 13]; 112:3. A personal name followed by a definite article and a title is found on seventh-century BC inscriptions from the City of David. Zevit argues that Uriyahu was a devotee of Asherah and had problems, perhaps an illness, that his enemies claimed were hopeless.[175] Abiyahu interceded to Yahweh for Uriyahu and pleaded that he deliver Uriyahu for the sake of the goddess Asherah, that is, she was worthy of a favor from Yahweh. Zevit compares an Old Babylonian (seventeenth-century BC) royal prayer and notes that Yahweh is the object of appeals in the Psalms for the sake of his loving loyalty (*ḥesed*, Ps. 6:4 [Heb. 5]), goodness (Ps. 25:7), and name (Pss. 106:8; 109:21). The drawing of the hand beside the inscription is, according to this theory, the left hand of Uriyahu that was extended to grasp the supporting hand of Yahweh

---

171. Cf. Gitin (1993, 250).
172. Cf. the evidence collected in Hess (1996b). Cf. also Hess (1992c, 19–31).
173. Cf. Dever (1999, 10).
174. Cf. Zevit (2001, 359–70). The inscription is: 1. *'ryhw h'šr ktbh* 2. *brkt 'ryhw lyhwh* 3. *wmmṣrryyh/r hlš'rttrhhwš'lh* 4. *l'byhw* 5. . . . *d/r/b'g/?wll'šrth* 6. . . . . . . *'??rth*.
175. Cf. Pss. 3:2–3; 42:4, 11; Hess (1996b); Zevit (2001, 368–69, 650).

or perhaps of Abiyahu.[176] An alternative view sees the hand as part of a warning or attempt to ward off the concern of anyone wishing to disturb the corpse, as with the Ketef Hinnom amulet, discussed above. In this theory, the blessing of Uriyahu before Yahweh and Asherah expedites salvation, while the drawing of the hand wards off any evil or disturbance.[177]

Summary

The inscriptional materials attested in ancient Israel and describing the period between c. 931 and c. 586 BC reflect a diversity of beliefs that lie somewhere between two extremes. On the one hand, there is the position of the Bible and its prophets in which Yahweh and Yahweh alone should be worshiped and confessed. On the other hand, there are the various beliefs in multiple deities including Baal, Asherah, and Yahweh. The following chapter provides a description of the noninscriptional material from the same period. See the summary there for an integration of the great variety of cultural material, written and nonwritten, into a synthesis of diversity in Iron Age II Israel.

Excursus

RELIGION OF PHOENICIA

As with ancient Israel, so there is evidence for religious beliefs and practices among Israel's neighbors. This work is concerned primarily with Israelite religion and therefore the religions of the surrounding peoples of the Iron Age are not considered except as they come into direct contact with Israelite religion. However, it is useful to examine Phoenician religion. This multiform set of religions provides a parallel to the religions of ancient Israel and enables us to see another descendant of the second-millennium Bronze Age religious traditions of Canaan that flourished contemporaneously with Israelite religions. Clifford (1990), whose discussion is useful for understanding Phoenician religion, posits that, due to the fragmented nature of the Phoenician city-states, there is no reason to assume complete uniformity

176. Cf. Hess (1992c, 31–34).
177. Cf. Puech (1992, 128); Lewis (2002, 182). See the above discussion of the Ketef Hinnom plaques for further examples of this concern.

of religious persuasion. Instead, he traces some elements that are common throughout the region and others that are distinct during the period of Phoenician activity, 1200–332 BC. Note that the name, Phoenicia, is a Greek term used to describe roughly the same ethnic groups and geographical area as those defined by the earlier Semitic term, Canaan.

Common Elements

The evidence from Classical Greek and Roman authors, as well as other sources, attests to at least seven elements that are common to several Phoenician cities. First, gods conducted business in assemblies in a manner similar to human meetings. The assemblies were subordinate to certain individual gods. Second, divine names, such as *baʿal* and *ʾēl*, could be both names and titles. Gods were often associated with places or natural wonders (mountains, springs, stars). Some gods had interchangeable functions with different names for Egyptian, Greek, and Latin equivalents. Third, dying and rising gods are common. Eshmun appears at Sidon (= Greek Asclepios), Adonis at Byblos, and Melqart at Tyre (= Greek Heracles/Hercules). Melqart, meaning "king of the city," probably denotes an underworld deity whose cult appears in the tenth century BC.

While such deities are well known, the specific attributes and myths differ significantly from one city and era to another. Sidonian Eshmun's name was interpreted by Damascius (fifth century AD) as either from the Semitic word for first (the first element, Esh) or as from the word for eight (the name, shmoun, without the initial "e") or as oil (*šemen*, see below). The derivation from "eight" is suggested because he was the eighth son of Sydyk. However, some interpretations have perferred an etymology from "oil" (*šemen*). The myth that the writer Damascius relates describes how a goddess "rekindled the life" of Eshmoun. The connection with the Greek Asclepios and healing derives from the etymology of the name from "oil," a substance regularly used in healing.[178] Egyptian hieratic transcriptions of West Semitic magical texts from the second millennium BC included a reference to Eshmun and possibly to Astarte, his spouse at Sidon. At Ugarit there was a god named *šmn* who may be Eshmun.[179] He was associated with the Baal gods but distinguished from Baal. Although Eshmun may have been a dying and rising deity, this is not stated before the time of Damascius and must be inferred from his

178. Cf. Lipiński (1973).
179. This is formed without the augmented aleph "E" at the beginning.

possible connection with the same themes of the neighboring Sidonian Herakles/Melqart.[180]

In his monograph on this topic, Tryggve Mettinger (2001, 83–111) noted that like Baal at Ugarit, Melqart of Tyre (i.e., the Greek Herakles) may have been a dying and rising god. The tradition that Hiram of Tyre, contemporary of Solomon, began the "awakening of Melqart" festival is found in Josephus and his sources. Evidence for the official title of a religious figure who "raises/resurrects the god" comes from the fourth century BC and later. On a fifth-century BC Sidonian vase there appeared a series of scenes that describe how a figure that can be identified as Melqart/Herakles was burnt to death and later resurrected. This association with death by fire is found in allusions in various myths and even an observed human sacrifice by Tertullian in second-century AD North Africa. The Pyrgi inscription describes the burial of a god whom Mettinger takes to be Melqart, but this should not be seen as mythically in conflict with the idea of a death in flames. It has been thought that the incineration motif might have been introduced as new burial techniques came to dominate the Mediterranean, with cremation replacing the more popular practice of burials in the Late Bronze Age (as at Ugarit for example).

In the latter half of the first millennium BC, there was mention of Osiris in connection with Herakles at Tyre, Cyprus, Malta, and Gades (Spain).[181] Osiris represents yet another dying and rising deity, originally associated with Egypt but developed into various manifestations around the Mediterranean world.

A fourth common element is the symposium. This event, identified as a *marzēaḥ*, appears in three relevant Phoenician and Punic inscriptions from fourth-century BC Sidon, from third-century BC Marseilles, and in a first-century BC inscription from Piraeus near Athens. There is a Sidonian bronze bowl dedicated to the *marzēaḥ* of Shamash. The Marseilles text refers to the *marzēaḥ* of the gods. The Athens text honors a leading citizen with a crown and stele on the fourth day of the *marzēaḥ*. Clifford argues: "The three texts show that the symposia were held for a god in a particular temple, and that the ceremonies were marked by drinking, memorial offerings, and sacrifice; they involved appropriation of funds and were celebrated annually by local associations of merchants."[182] The ninth-century BC banquet scene on a Phoenician bowl from Salamis, on the island of Cyprus, suggests a *marzēaḥ* with musicians, a dancer, drink-

180. Cf. Mettinger (2001, 155–65).
181. Ibid., 180–82.
182. Cf. Clifford (1990, 58).

ing, carrying wine, and sexual intercourse.[183] In the following centuries, Nabatean and Palmyrene inscriptions associated the *marzēaḥ* with dead kings and gods, and with priests of Bel. The Talmud and the sixth-century AD Madeba map in Jordan identify Baal-Peor with the *marzēaḥ* and relate these to the Mayumas festivals in Mediterranean cities that Roman rulers sometimes banned due to their licentiousness.[184] The evidence from Ugarit, the Bible,[185] and that cited here suggest that the *marzēaḥ* was a banquet that possibly involved a funerary feast.[186]

Fifth, some twenty thousand urns with infant and animal bones cremated and buried in the tophet (sanctuary) at Carthage during a period of six hundred years attest to infant sacrifice. Other cemeteries have children's bones that included both cremated and inhumed examples. The data suggests that such sacrifices were used for purposes of population control, as animal substitution decreased with an increase in population at Carthage. Tophets in ten places around the Mediterranean (North Africa, Sicily, and Sardinia) have been found to contain bones of cremated children and votive stone stelae.[187] Textually, the use of the term *mlk* in Phoenician and Punic texts was thought to refer to sacrifice,[188] but more likely describes the deity who receives child sacrifices, Molek/Molech in the Old Testament.[189] This deity already appears as Maliku at Ebla, Mari, and Ugarit. Maliku is associated in Akkadian texts with the Mesopotamian Nergal, god of the underworld.[190]

A sixth common element is found in stories concerning the creation of the world or cosmogonies. Compare the phrase "El, creator of the earth" that appears in two Phoenician inscriptions (eighth and second centuries BC) and in Philo (of Alexandria) at the turn of the era. The term occurs earlier in the name of Samuel's father, Elkanah, and still earlier in the title of the Hittite Hurrian myth, Elkunirsa. Philo reports several cosmogonies.[191]

183. Cf. King and Stager (2001, 356–57), with drawing. A sixth-century BC Moabite text assigned a *marzēaḥ* along with millstones and a house to a Sara, while at the same time warning Yisha to stay away. See Bordreuil and Pardee (1990); Johnston (2002, 182).

184. Cf. Pope (1972, 191–92); Johnston (2002, 183). Ps. 106:28 connects Baal-Peor with a cult of the dead.

185. See discussion earlier in this chapter, especially under "Prophets of Ancient Israel," concerning Jer. 16:5–9; Amos 6:3–7; Mic. 6:6–7; Ezek. 16:20–21, 36; 23:37–39; and Ps. 106:37. For Ugarit, see chapter 4.

186. Cf. M. Smith (1994, 140–44); Johnston (2002, 184).

187. See Brown (1991); King and Stager (2001, 360–61).

188. Cf. Eissfeldt (1935).

189. This term came from the Semitic root meaning "to be king," and developed into a divine name.

190. See Heider (1985); Day (1989); Johnston (2002, 36); Lewis (2002, 185).

191. See also the cosmogony of Philo of Byblos, described above in this chapter on p. 269.

Seventh are the Rephaim. The term "Rephaim" refers to the shades of the dead in the Old Testament. It occurs some twenty-seven times in the Hebrew Bible,[192] where it can refer to legendary giants.[193] The Phoenician and Punic texts use this term as a name for shades of the dead.[194] The root of the name is *rp'*. It means "to heal," and this may be the origin of the term. At Ugarit, the designation *rpu* (*KTU* 1.108) describes a deity associated with Ashtaroth and Edrei, places elsewhere related to the underworld and Molech, and the home of the last of the Rephaim in the Bible.[195] At Ugarit, the transjordanian site of Ashtoreth was the seat of the god Mlk (*KTU* 1.100 41 and 1.107 42). In the Old Testament Molech was located in Hinnom, a valley connected to the valley of the Rephaim.[196] Smith follows the revocalizing of "doctors" (*rōpĕ'îm*) to "*rĕpā'îm*" (i.e., the Rephaim or "dead ancestors") in 2 Chronicles 16:12 to designate those whom Asa consulted for his diseased feet.[197] Asa's action is understood as turning away from Yahweh.

Johnston (2002, 128–29) describes the biblical Rephaim as lifeless. In Isaiah 14:9–10 they are awakened to greet the king who joins them. At that point they confess weakness. Unlike the Ugaritic Rpum, those in the Bible are never connected to a patron or a founder.[198] The term seems to have originated in reference to ancient warriors, perhaps especially though not exclusively associated with the Argob region near the modern border of Jordan and Syria. It was applied at Ugarit to deified ancestors and heroes (e.g., Dan'el, *KTU* 1.17–19) who could travel on chariots and celebrate a banquet (*KTU* 1.20–22), witness a marriage (Keret's), and bless Ugarit and individuals with health and fertility (*KTU* 1.82; 1.161).[199] In

192. Cf. Isa. 14:9; 26:14, 19; Ps. 88:10 [Heb. 11]; Job 26:5; Prov. 2:18; 9:18; 21:16.

193. Cf. Gen. 14:5; 15:20; Deut. 2:11, 20; 3:11; Josh. 12:4; 17:15. Cf. also the discussion in chapter 7, p. 175.

194. See *KTU* 1.100 41; 1.107 17 for Molech; and KAI 13:7–8; 14:8–9; 117:1 for the Rephaim. Day (2000, 217–19) cites both 1 Sam. 28:13 and Isa. 8:19 as evidence of some sort of "divinization of the dead."

195. Cf. Josh. 12:4; 13:12, 31; Num. 21:33; Deut. 1:4; 3:1. M. Smith (2003, 179n69) notes a subterranean complex that was discovered at Edrei (Dera') in Transjordan. This complex has been likened to tombs such as those found beneath houses at Ugarit. It may provide further evidence of a connection between the dynasty and culture of Ugarit and, with Ashtaroth, these locations in Transjordan near the modern border between Syria and Jordan. See further in chapter 4, p. 104.

196. Cf. 2 Kings 23:10; Josh. 18:16; Day (2000, 218–25).

197. Cf. M. Smith (2003, 168–69).

198. Johnston notes that dead Rephaim are never named. While alive, Rephaim such as Og are named. See Deut. 3:11 and Josh. 12:4; 13:12; and others in 1 Chron. 20:4 (as descendants of the Rephaim). If Smith's emendation of 2 Chron. 16:12 (above) is accepted, then Rephaim are also consulted. However, Johnston argues against this change since it lacks textual support.

199. Cf. Johnston (2002, 134–42).

Phoenician, the term (as *rp'm*) appears on the sixth- and fifth-centuries BC sarcophagi of two Sidonian kings, cursing those who disturb their tombs. In their imprecations, the kings state that, if disturbed, the interlopers will have no resting place with the *rp'm*. In Neo-Punic texts of the first century AD at El Amruni, a dedication to the divine *rp'm* is rendered in Latin as DMRS, an abbreviation meaning "to the sacred spirits." In the Bible, however, this term was reinterpreted from the perspective that the dead are generally weak, without life or vitality.

Elements Specific to a City

In addition to the above observations regarding dying and rising gods, the following distinctives have been noted. At Tyre, Melqart was the chief god. The name, Melqart, may be translated "king of the city." By tradition, Hiram, who was associated with David and Solomon, became the first to celebrate the "awakening" festival, suggesting a dying and rising of the deity.[200] The ninth-century BC stele of Bir-Hadad shows a god with a battle-axe and a conical hat like Baal. Perhaps Melqart was initially a hypostasis of the Phoenician king and later patron and founder of the city with its dye and trading industries. Scholars have variously identified the Baal of Tyre in the Elijah narratives with Baal Shamem, a deity mentioned on the Esarhaddon treaty and identified as Haddu (Ugaritic *Ba'lu*, though other identities have been proposed), with Baal Lebanon (mentioned in an eighth-century BC Phoenician inscription at Limassol), and with Baal Hermon. In a seventh-century BC treaty between Baal of Tyre and Esarhaddon, Bayt-il heads the Tyrian list of deities. El remains the best option for this deity. Perhaps El is patriarch and head of the assembly, while Melqart is head of the dynasty, similar to the mythology that may have applied at Ugarit. Several third- and second-century BC inscriptions mention Milk-Astart, perhaps a "consort of Ashtart" or "Milk of the city Ashtart." Also mentioned in the Esarhaddon treaty is Baal Malage (Ugaritic Kotharu?), Baal Saphon, Melqart, Eshmun, and Ashtart (as war goddess).

At Sidon, inscriptions refer to temples that have been dedicated to Ashtart, Eshmun (dying and rising god at Sidon), Ashtart Face of Baal, and Baal of Sidon.

At Byblos two temples from the second millennium BC were dedicated to Reshep and Ba'alat. Ba'alat was "mistress" or "sovereign" of Byblos. She continued into the first millennium BC and became associated with

---

200. So Josephus quoting the Tyrian annals in *Contra Apionem* I. 118–119; *Jewish Antiquities* VIII. 146. Cf. Clifford (1990, 59).

portrayals of the Egyptian Hathor, and with the second-century AD epithet, "Byblian Aphrodite."

At Carthage, in a second-century BC treaty with Hamilcar and Philip of Macedon, triads of deities are mentioned. The first triad is Baʿal Hamon, Tanit, and Reshep. Clifford denies a common triad for all the Phoenician cities but notes how the deities in these cities often appeared in triads.[201]

---

201. Clifford's own recognition of the scarcity of evidence challenges the theory proposed by Niehr (1990). Niehr argues that the Bible portrays Yahweh as the "high god" who presides over a heavenly council, lives on a holy mountain, creates heaven and earth, and assimilates the roles of the sun deity. Niehr likens Yahweh's portrayal in the Bible to Baalshamem in the Aramaic and Phoenician sources. Thus the influence of Baalshamem, not Deuteronomistic theology, explains Yahweh. The paucity of extrabiblical evidence, however, cannot bear the weight of this thesis.

10

Archaeological Sources for the Divided Monarchy

Cult

Cult Centers

Following Holladay's classification scheme (see chapter 2), Jerusalem Cave 1 is understood as a nonconformist sanctuary. The site is an artificial cave on the eastern slope of the City of David and outside the walls. It dates from the late eighth and seventh centuries BC. It contains many animal figurines, horse-and-rider figurines, pillar figurines, and a variety of other cultic objects.[1] Samaria Cave E 207 was located four-tenths of a mile southeast of the city gate of Samaria and contained pottery and cult objects similar to those from Jerusalem Cave 1. Other nonconformist cult centers include a cult area with figurines at Tell en-Nasbeh (Cave 193) and a center at Tell Beit Mirsim (Courtyard NW 32–12).

West of Jerusalem nineteen or twenty tumuli have been found. These have been related to the twenty-one kings in Jerusalem between David and Zedekiah. They have been understood as centers for a mourning ceremony at the time of each king's demise.[2] The city also yielded some 250 rock cut caves and bench tombs with Hathor-style headrests.[3] They

1. Cf. Holladay (1987). The final publication of this cave by Eshel and Prag (1995) appeared after Holladay's article. Eshel and Prag caution against assuming too much since less than 5 percent of the artifacts are distinctively cultic, a distribution known from many domestic sites in Iron Age Palestine. Conflicting reports (Shanks [1996c]) render arguments about the use of this cave inconclusive. See also Zevit (2001, 206–10) who argues in favor of a cult site. The figurines—21 horse-and-rider figurines, 7 birds, 38 other animals, 16 human pillar figurines, a fenestrated stand, 3 miniature couches, 2 miniature altars, a rattle, and a model shrine—were mostly intact, piled toward the back of the cave. The heads of female figurines had been intentionally removed and placed elsewhere. The cave was protected by an indirect entrance. Two niches with flat stones in front may indicate two deities who may have been worshiped here. Alpert-Nakhai (2001, 190) follows Holland (1977, 154) in seeing the site as a repository for a sanctuary. If used as a cult site, Keel and Uehlinger (1998, 348–49) suggest an underworld context with eating and drinking typical of a *marzēaḥ*.

2. Barkay (2003, 68) notes that Chronicles records the absence of a memorial mound for Jehoram (2 Chron. 21:19), which would require only twenty tumuli. A tumulus is an artificial mound, sometimes raised over a grave. However, none of these contain indications of a burial. King (1993, 141) records the comments of the surveyor and excavator, Ruth Amiran. Amiran found nineteen tumuli on summits and ridges west of Jerusalem. One she excavated measured 20 feet in height and 105 feet in diameter. Most of the tumuli were heaped up on ridges well above the level of their surroundings. Dating from the second half of the eighth century through the seventh century BC, they possessed platforms, pits, and a place for burning. Cooking or sacrifice could take place. Barkay (1994; 2003) notes similarities with Iron Age tumuli in Central Anatolia and Salamis, Cyprus, where they often contain royal burials. Zevit (2001, 210–13) argues that more than one excavated tumulus contained a platform that could be viewed by people standing within a walled area. The construction suggests a one-time usage. Jeremiah 34:5 records "burnings" of kings of Judah that took place after their death and burial (cf. 2 Chron. 16:14; 21:19). The presence of a pit may suggest chthonic sacrifices to underworld deities or to the dead. Zevit (2001, 303–5) notes that the eastern side of the tumulus had an elliptical platform on which was a pit lined with slabs and approached by a ramp. Here chthonic rituals may have been performed, where the pit functioned as a pyre or a place for the presentation of offerings. Barkay (2003, 66, 68) excavated tumulus 4, which, due to the presence of *lĕmelek* jar handles, he identified with Hezekiah's funeral fire (*lĕmelek*, "to the king," is an inscription used on administrative jars during the time of Hezekiah).

3. The headrests were located at the Church of St. Stephen on the Nablus Road north of the Old City of Jerusalem. Cf. King and Stager (2001, 368). See Hadley (2000) and Dever

are dated between the tenth and seventh centuries BC. For the silver strips or good luck charms (amulets) with Numbers 6:24–27 and Deuteronomy 7:9 scratched on them, see the discussion in chapter 9 under "Ketef Hinnom Silver Strips." Are these texts evidence of reforms by Josiah?[4]

Following this are summaries of the "establishment" shrines at Megiddo (Locus 2081), Lachish (Stratum V Building 49), possibly Beer-sheba (where only an altar remains), and the sanctuaries at Dan and at Arad.[5]

Excavations at Megiddo's level from the tenth century BC yielded a household shrine and room 2081 with cult vessels and two four-horned limestone incense altars.[6] A large and a small horned altar stood side by side, and a large and a small stand were positioned on the shelf and on the floor respectively. Perhaps these suggest the worship of two deities. A small portion of burnt grain was found on the floor before the large altar.[7] On the north wall of 2081 a door led to a narrow room paved with stone and flanked at its entrance by two standing stones. Elsewhere on the site, horns from one or two large altars were found. Three small altars were found in a corner and other cult objects elsewhere. However, not all of this is necessarily cultic. Except for the two altars and two stands, Kitchen describes the rest as "domestic clutter."[8] Nevertheless, it remains likely that this material is typologically similar with other items found in cultic sites elsewhere. A room at the south end of a larger structure (Schumacher Shrine 338) was a broad room, with two "stelae" equidistant from the far sides of the room and four other stone columns on the same longitudinal axis. Zevit suggests that the "stelae" were likely support pillars in the room.[9] The remaining four columns may have served either to represent images or as a place for offerings. A bronze seated male figurine was also found, as were horned and round stone altars that stood in the courtyard.[10]

(2001, 180) for identification of this Barbie-style (also called omega-style) hairdo with the Egyptian goddess Qudshu who is identified with the Canaanite Asherah.

4. Cf. Kitchen (2003, 419).

5. Except for the cult center at Arad, J. Glen Taylor (1993, 69–79) finds no certain evidence for a solar alignment of the structure. Even in the case of Arad, the structure's context within an east-west oriented fort may suggest other explanations for its orientation. On the altars see Rainey (1994a).

6. Cf. Shiloh (1993, 1015–19); Dever (2001, 176). Stratum VA-IVBa includes this locus 2081. Zevit (2001, 232–33) dates it to early in the reign of Jeroboam I and before Shishak (931–926 BC).

7. Cf. Lev. 6:16; Zevit (2001, 220–25, 312–13).

8. Cf. Kitchen (2003, 410) and Bloch-Smith (2005) for questions about the standing stones.

9. Cf. Zevit (2001, 230).

10. Cf. Shiloh (1993, 1015–19); Alpert-Nakhai (2001, 177).

Fig. 34. Judean captives from Sennacherib's relief of the capture of Lachish (© Copyright the Trustees of the British Museum)

Inscribed with scenes of Lachish (Tell ed-Duweir), Sennacherib's dramatic reliefs of the capture and destruction of Lachish in 701 BC portray incense burners removed from the site. Although no Iron Age sanctuary has been identified on the tell, the evidence from the reliefs suggests cultic activity and also a cult center that was destroyed at the end of the eighth century BC.[11] Cult room 49 of Stratum V (tenth century BC) yielded a limestone four-horned incense altar and a basalt standing stone. The remains suggest animal sacrifices and the sharing of sacred meals. The room has a low bench along the walls, similar to the Canaanite bench temple of Tel Mevorakh. It differed from the preceding Late Bronze Age temples at Lachish in that it was simpler and had no refuse pits.[12]

Beersheba, possibly also a regional center, had a horned altar of ashlar stones that was dismantled perhaps during Hezekiah's reforms, although others date its reuse in walls to the early eighth century BC,

11. Cf. Fried (2002, 445).
12. Cf. Alpert-Nakhai (2001, 178–79).

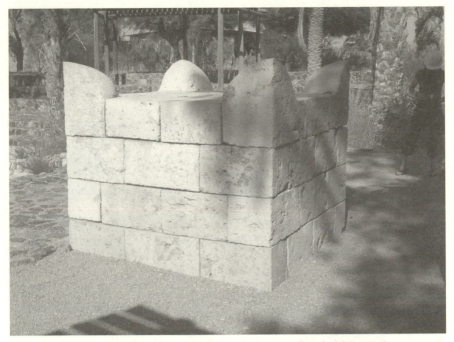

Fig. 35. Beersheba reconstructed horned altar (Courtesy of Richard S. Hess)

well before Hezekiah.[13] It also had a large two-handled eighth-century pot inscribed with *qdš*, "holy," and set apart for cultic usage.[14] Zevit reconstructs the altar at a much smaller height than Exodus 27:1, and smaller than others reconstruct it.[15] He observes that, although dressed stones formed the sides, the interior and top would have consisted of earth. The site includes two rooms (room 25 and building 430) for domestic purposes (ninth and eighth centuries BC) with a lamp, an incense burner, a female figurine, and a model couch. These may have to do with fertility and giving birth, thus there is the the presence of what may be a birthing stool.

Dan is by far the largest Iron Age Israelite cult site, a "state sanctuary" comparable with similar sanctuaries in Phoenicia (cf. Tell Taʿyinat). At the "high place" on Tel Dan there is a large podium with a monumental flight of stairs (from the south) and an adjoining three-room sanctuary (biblical *liškâ*) with a stone altar, ash pit, and three iron shovels

13. Fried (2002, 447–48), referring to Gadegaard (1978), contends that the altar may have cracked when attempts were made to light a fire on it sufficient to consume a sacrificial animal.

14. Cf. Dever (2001, 181).

15. Cf. Zevit (2001, 173–74).

for ashes.[16] A large horn, some twenty inches high, may reflect a huge altar on the platform, or that the platform itself was an altar with horns at its corners.[17] King and Stager compare this monumental structure with the "mountain of El" in Ezekiel 43. The Ezekiel altar is of a size similar to the one at Dan's high place, about twenty feet square.[18] By Stratum IV (eighth century BC) the platform was large enough (62 feet by 26 feet) to hold a structure the size of the desert tabernacle that might have contained Jeroboam I's calf.[19] South of this platform were two small hornless altars with a rim and tray that could represent two lesser deities.[20] The three incense shovels and related installations may be associated with chthonic worship. In the mid-ninth century, the sanctuary was enlarged significantly. A monumental staircase was added to the south side of the platform in the early eighth century. Beneath a small limestone altar in one room was a bronze and silver scepter head. There were also three iron shovels and a sunken jar. Near the complex was a jar handle stamped with the name *ImmadiYo*, the final syllable providing a possibly shortened form of Yahweh.[21]

Fig. 36. *Maṣṣēbôt* from the outer court at Dan
(Courtesy of Richard S. Hess)

Five *maṣṣēbôt* were situated outside the city's southern entrance. Another set of five stones existed within the outer chamber of the gate. Another set was identified at the northern edge of the western wall of the same chamber with a basin beside it, perhaps for pouring libations.[22] At the upper gate another set of five stones was found, and a set of three stones occurred outside the southern gate in a niche attached to the wall. Biran associates some of these sets with the *bāmôt* of 2 Kings 23:8. In addition, altars and pottery

16. Cf. Dever (2001, 175). For the whole site and description, cf. Biran (1994).
17. Cf. Zevit (2001, 187).
18. Cf. King and Stager (2001, 328, 330). They also identify the Urim and Thummim with sacred dice, similar to the one found at the sacred area at Dan.
19. Cf. Zevit (2001, 190).
20. Ibid., 310–11.
21. Alpert-Nakhai (2001, 184–85) sees this as an indication of Yahwistic worship.
22. Cf. Zevit (2001, 191–94).

Fig. 37. Dan high place (Courtesy of Richard S. Hess)

vessels were found beside the city gate. The seven-spouted lamps and other pottery suggest that people entering the city could pay homage to the deity.

The sanctuary at Arad probably represents a regional center due to its relatively large size in relation to the rest of the fortress that makes up the site, and its central and public access within the fort. In the three-room sanctuary, there were found animal bones, a bronze image of a crouching lion, and an eighth-century ceramic offering stand. Stratum X included an altar of unworked field stones slightly north of where the earlier sacrificial altar had been in the center of the courtyard. Benches were rearranged and two shallow bowls were inscribed with "*qoph kaph*," an abbreviation of "[that which is] sacred for the priests." In Strata X and IX this cult center was in use. As a result of the analysis of Herzog these have now been dated to the eighth century BC, with a dismantling of the temple sometime in the late eighth century, perhaps during centralizing reforms brought about by Hezekiah, remembered as the reforming king of Judah.[23] As elsewhere, the dual nature of the implements found in the

23. See Herzog (1997; 2002); Dever (2005, 170–75). Dever identifies the bronze lion with the goddess Asherah. Cf. Zevit (2001, 298–300). Cf. also the view of Fried (2002,

Fig. 38. Arad cult center (Courtesy of Thomas B. Hall III)

eighth-century levels may suggest the worship of two deities. The benches
may have contained ritual objects. Those performing the rituals faced
westward. The altar of unworked stones (and without horns) occupied
the courtyard. The main outer altar had a core of earth and stones and
was faced with field stones. Its top was plastered and included a flint
slab as a place for burning. Channels directed the runoff. The step at its
southern base may have been a *yĕsôd*, often translated as "foundation" or
"base." The absence of horns would not allow for a biblical purification
offering. Kitchen, following others, observes that the ostraca found near
Arad's gate provide names linked with priestly, Levitical families: Mer-
emoth (cf. Ezra 8:33), Joshaphat, Pashhur (cf. Jer. 20:1), Besal, Korah,
sons of Gilgal.[24] These could be names from priestly families known in
Jerusalem in the sixth and fifth centuries BC.[25]

445–47), who dates Stratum IX to the period ending in the destruction of Sennacherib,
when she believes that the archaeology indicates the sanctuary was buried and not reused.
In her dating she appears to accept the revised dating of the site that places Stratum XII
in the tenth century. Cf. Zimhoni (1985, 86–87); Finkelstein (1996a); and Herzog (1997,
113–292).

24. Kitchen (2003, 416).

25. There were also Yahwistic names such as Eshiyahu and Netanyahu according to
Alpert-Nakhai (2001, 186), who, however, dates the main usage of Strata VII–VI to the
seventh century with destruction late in that century or early in the sixth.

These various cult centers do not resemble one another, unlike those of the Bronze Age described in chapter 5.[26] Later sites in the region include late seventh- or early sixth-century BC ones about six miles south of Arad at Qitmit and at Ein-Hazeva near the Arabah. These include evidence of the Edomite deity Qaus.[27]

Barrick has studied the references to the high places (*bāmôt*)[28] of Moab in the Bible, in archaeology, and in the ninth-century BC Moabite stele.[29] He finds them in towns and cities, not in the open. He and others suggest that this may be true of Israel's high places.[30] Despite the objections of Emerton, Fried has demonstrated that the Akkadian cognate allows for, and the biblical (ninety-seven times) and Moabite usages expect that the *bāmôt* are located within walled population centers.[31] Detailing the various sanctuaries in the towns around Judah and Israel, Alpert-Nakhai argues that the united monarchy placed these *bāmôt* strategically in centers that would unite local populations by practicing a single religion. First Samuel 9 and the *bāmâ* at Tel Dan suggest it could include a public building (a *liškâ* for the consumption of the sacrifice?), a sacrificial altar, and a sanctuary complex.[32] Nevertheless, Smith notes that high places are found in both urban (1 Kings 13:32; 2 Kings 23:8) and rural settings (Ezek. 6:13; Hosea 4:13).[33] In the divided monarchy, *bāmôt* were built at sites of special importance to the kings, such as Dan, Bethel, and Arad, as well as Vered Jericho, Uza, Radum, and the "stone stairs" at Meṣad-Michmash.[34] Zevit (2001, 262) regards *bāmôt* as publicly accessible areas that regularly possessed *maṣṣēbôt*.

Standing stones or *maṣṣēbôt* also continued to be used.[35] They may have symbolically represented the divine or served as receptacles for the divine presence. The small reliefs on coinage from Byblos depict them in a walled-in area, while coinage from Tyre has them erected under a

26. These, along with the sites mentioned above in chapter 5, lead Zevit (2001, 255) to suggest a maximum number of seventeen Israelite temples, although the number could be much higher.

27. Cf. Kitchen (2003, 419).

28. These are similar to the *bêt bāmôt*, though the *bêt bāmôt* are used only of non-Yahwistic centers.

29. Cf. Barrick (1991; 1996).

30. Cf. Alpert-Nakhai (1994, 25); Stern (2001b, 23–24); and Dever (1995, 47).

31. Cf. Emerton (1997); Fried (2002, 437–42).

32. However, it does not necessarily follow that every one of these items was required at all times and places in Judah for a *bāmâ* to exist.

33. Cf. M. Smith (2003, 161).

34. Cf. Stern (2001b, 23–24).

35. They appear in Phoenician as *mṣbt*, in Punic as *m(n)ṣbt*, in Aramaic as *nṣb*, and in Nabatean as *mṣb*, *nṣb*, and *nṣbt*. The terms are based on the root, *nṣb*, "to erect." For the evidence of these stones in the Negev, see p. 197.

tree. At Paphos in Cyprus they have a central place in a cultic(?) structure, and reliefs from Sidon portray their transportation in a wagon. Eighth- and seventh-century BC Sefire inscriptions refer to stones with the writing *bty 'lhy'*, "houses of gods." This relates to Philo of Alexandria's term *baitylos*, which he describes as both a divine name and a name for such stones. Alternatively, as with Pharaoh Shishaq's erection of one at Megiddo (c. 926 BC) and the Assyrian king Sargon's setting one at Ashdod (late eighth century BC), they could serve as memorial stelae. Funerary or commemorative stelae are attested at Ugarit (*KTU* 1.17 I 28; 6.13; 6.14), at Kition in Cyprus (KAI 35.1–3), at Athens (KAI 53), at Lapethos (KAI 43.6), and at a place chosen by the Aramean king Panammu for his stele (KAI 214.16, 21).[36] In the Bible, groupings occur at Mt. Sinai (Exod. 24:4) and at Beth Shemesh in Egypt (Jer. 43:13).[37] Elsewhere several appear with Jacob at Bethel (Gen. 28:10–22; 31:13), at Gilead as a boundary marker (Gen. 31:43–54), at Rachel's grave near Ephratah (Gen. 35:16–20), on the Mount of Olives where Josiah destroyed it (2 Kings 23:13–14; 2 Chron. 34:4), in "the king's valley" where Absalom erected a funerary monument for himself (2 Sam. 18:18), and at Shechem (Josh. 24:26). In the future, Israel would establish a stele for Yahweh (Isa. 19:19). The condemnations of *maṣṣēbôt* erected "under every high hill and under every green/leafy/flourishing tree" imply two different types of cult places, according to Zevit.[38]

Altars are described in the Bible in Exodus 20:22–27; 27:1–8 (38:1–7); and in Deuteronomy 12. Zevit compares Aegean altars filled with earth, ash, and rubble with that of the altar described in Exodus 27 and 38.[39] It was covered with bronze, had four horns, and was hollow (to be filled with earth or rubble). He also observes a horizontal band around the altar beneath the top,[40] and a grating, perhaps to catch coals, beneath it. The Bible relates that Solomon also constructed a bronze covered altar, filled with stones.[41] The inner altar of the tabernacle was similar to the Solomonic one. Jehoiakin's changes included elimination of the horns on the altars. There was a replacement of the small horned altar with a small table. A small wine decanter with the inscription, "belonging to Mattanyahu, wine of libation, a quarter (measure)," resembles those

36. Cf. M. Smith (2003, 168).
37. Cf. Zevit (2001, 257–59).
38. Ibid., 260–62. He also suggests that the *maṣṣēbôt* from Arad, the Bull site, Dan, and Lachish (locus 81) represented Yahweh. Another single deity center with *maṣṣēbôt* was Hazor.
39. Ibid., 288–92.
40. Ibid., 288, *karkōb*; Gitin (2002, 100), *zēr*; cf. Exod. 27:5; 30:3. Cf. *mikbār ma'ĕśeh rešet*.
41. 1 Kings 8:64; 9:25; 1 Chron. 21:29; 2 Chron. 1:5–6; 4:1.

found at Khirbet el-Qom, at Arad, and on the Jerusalem Ophel. Paleo-graphically, it has been dated to the eighth and seventh centuries BC.[42]

Model shrines represented actual shrines. They have been found at Israelite sites at Dan, Tel Rekhesh, Tirzah, and Jerusalem Cave 1. The earliest is from Dan, dating from the twelfth and eleventh centuries BC. It resembles ones from Ugarit and Deir 'Alla. The one from Tel Rekhesh also dates from Iron Age I and includes a series of clay buttons that represent the deity or the deities. At Tirzah a shrine dated to the ninth and eighth centuries BC was recovered from a pit near the city gate. There are poked holes and a crescent in the center of the fronton. The one from Jerusalem is plain and, like the others, has a very high sill for a door. More likely this was intended as a large window for light. These are miniatures of larger wayside shrines that gave the possessor access to the larger shrines from a distance. Summarizing his evidence, Zevit identifies them as the biblical *ḥammān* that could be hewed or broken (Ezek. 6:4, 6; 2 Chron. 34:4–7).[43]

In addition to Jerusalem, Samaria, Arad, Dan, Megiddo, Lachish, and Beersheba, the following have likely cultic materials.

At Hazor in the eighth century BC in house 3067a (Area B), there were objects such as human and animal figurines as well as an ivory pyxis lid showing a man at a sacred tree.[44] This may indicate religious activity but it is difficult to say anything about a cult.

Tel Kedesh, located between Taanach and Megiddo, included a building dating perhaps from the eighth century BC. It contained a four-horned, collarless limestone altar. This appears to be slight evidence for a cult.

At Tirzah (Tell el-Far'ah North), at a location eleven and a half feet inside the city gate, there was found a square installation of flat stones with a monolithic column, a pedestal, and a basin. Basins were found inside the gates at Bethsaida, Lachish, Gezer, and Ekron. They may have been used by travelers and for libations on possibly adjacent standing stones. There is also house 440 of Stratum VIIb from the beginning of the ninth century BC. This included remnants of a model shrine and an image of a body of a nursing woman. Locus 452 yielded a female figurine with a "tamborine."[45]

Kuntillet 'Ajrud, occupied c. 850–750 BC, was located thirty-one miles south of Kadesh Barnea. Of the two buildings, the larger one (forty-nine by eighty-two feet) was a hostel with a sanctuary of two rooms at its entrance. The offerings found on the plastered benches and side repositories, along with the inscriptions (discussed above), indicate a diversity of religious expressions.

---

42. Cf. Zevit (2001, 297–98). The text is *lmtnyhw. yyn. nsk. rb't.*
43. Ibid., 328–40.
44. Cf. Willett (1999, 205); Alpert-Nakhai (2001, 189); Dever (2005).
45. See Zevit (2001, 238–41).

Domestic Cult Materials

Domestic materials may be defined as "religious" on the basis of a typology of the same sorts of materials as those found elsewhere in the ancient Near East in cultic contexts. These include items such as female figurines, horse-and-rider figurines, other anthropomorphic and zoomorphic vessels, model furniture and chariot wheels, rattles, lamps, cup-and-saucer vessels, and limestone altars.[46]

There are dozens of terra-cotta offering stands from the twelfth to the seventh centuries BC, and forty or more limestone altars from the tenth to the sixth centuries in Israel and Judah. These items are not explicitly mentioned in the Bible, although both continue Bronze Age forms.[47] Plain stands may be primarily associated with domestic contexts, rather than public cult centers. At Ai, the Jerusalem cave, and Hazor, a fenestrated stand is paired with a plain stand, which could indicate the worship of two deities.[48]

Both incense altars and female figurines in domestic shrines at Tel Masos, Tell el-Far'ah North, Beersheba, and Tell Halif focus on women and, in the view of some, provide a cult to Asherah.[49] Pritchard had identified some seven types of female figurines from Palestine, whereas M. Tadmor identified eight groups: ones with extended arms and sometimes holding objects, those holding their breasts, those standing with their arms along their sides, those lying with their arms along their sides, those with pierced ears or hands crossed in front of their breasts, those holding disks or tambourines, those either pregnant or holding a child, and those in the round including ones with a serpent.[50]

In Judah during the period between the fall of the northern kingdom (c. 722 BC) and the southern state's own destruction by Babylon (586 BC), there was a dominance of the pillar-based female figurines (the second type listed by Tadmor—those holding their breasts). Some have suggested that the base may represent a tree, which is a symbol of the goddess Asherah.[51] However, there are no distinctive marks to indicate

46. Hägg (1993) observes that human and animal figurines in Bronze Age Aegean cult sanctuaries were votive offerings left by worshipers. Cf. J. Glen Taylor (1993, 58–66).

47. See Dever (2001, 188).

48. Zevit (2001, 314–16).

49. Willett (1999, 101–65); Alpert-Nakhai (2001, 191).

50. Cf. Pritchard (1934); Tadmor (1981; 1982; 1996).

51. See the example of the Late Bronze Age Lachish ewer and related finds associated with Qudshu in Egypt. For her identification with Asherah, see Hadley (1989; 2000), Holladay (1987), and Hestrin (1987b). Dever (1996, 36; 2001, 193) notes that these figurines are more "chaste" than their earlier Canaanite and Israelite counterparts. They emphasize only the breasts rather than the lower part of the body. From both Israel and Judah archaeologists have identified more than two thousand female figurines.

Fig. 39. Pillar-based Judean female figurines (Courtesy of the Israel Antiquities Authority)

any kind of flora, nor is there reason to suspect that this is anything other than a mass-produced method of standing the figurines upright. They also possessed large breasts and a head. The head was made from a separate mold, though a variation has the head as a crudely pinched piece of clay. Virtually unique to Judah, some 822 have been identified from the period of the monarchy within the traditional territory of the southern kingdom of Judah.[52] Of these, 405 were found in Jerusalem. The clay mixture suggests a composition of Jerusalem clay.[53] They were originally painted with white, black, and red colors. The eyes and hair received prominence. Zevit suggests that the figures represented multiple deities rather than Asherah alone. Perhaps they were related to goddesses seated on thrones, bearing children, offering divine milk, playing lyre and tambourine (or holding a sun disk), holding a dove, or those deities pictured with images of lions and serpents. At Tell en-Nasbeh all but one of the 120 figurine fragments found were broken, usually at the neck. This suggests an intentional fracture perhaps as a means of sending a message to those who would worship or otherwise identify with

52. Byrne (2004, 139) suggests that this constitutes 96 percent of the total of 854 female figurines that have been found. See also Johnston (2003).
53. Stern (2001b, 27).

the figurine.[54] Kitchen (2003, 418–19) argues that one cannot be sure about the identity of the figurines and that they may be nothing more than good luck charms. However, he does believe that the 350 found in Jerusalem Cave 1 are evidence of the cultic reforms of Josiah, which implies an image associated with a deity.[55]

The pillar-based figurines are connected with the priority and prestige that was given to motherhood, with the dangers that women faced in achieving this status, and also with the concern to nurse and successfully raise children.[56] In Judean areas, they disappear after the Babylonian destruction of Jerusalem, 586 BC. The mass production of this large a number, with nearly half found in the capital city of Jerusalem and with almost all of the remainder exclusive to the territory of Judah, points to a state-sponsored project. As Byrne (2004) notes, it is not at all necessary for such objects to be limited to cult sites in order for the state to sanction them. Religious objects that occur in domestic contexts, as well, may have been created and encouraged by the state. Nor is there anything in the features of the objects that can successfully distinguish between female deities and humans. Their resemblance to earlier figures and figurines, some of which were inscribed on gold or silver plaques, is undoubted. The same is true of female forms from neighboring and contemporary regions. However, this does not require an identical purpose for all such figurines whose use extended over a period of more than half a millennium. Furthermore, most of the other figurines display female genitalia, something that none of the Judean forms do, despite their prominent breasts. Byrne (2004) compares these forms to Aztec figurines that are understood as emphasizing the role of motherhood. It seems that these figurines served a similar purpose: to encourage or assist in the role of reproduction and motherhood. Thus the large breasts might suggest lactation after birth. The figurines provided a visible means of maintaining and enhancing a population that was threatened with destruction by Sennacherib's campaign in 701 BC and by subsequent and ongoing pressure from the Assyrian (and later Babylonian) state in the seventh century BC. Others have argued that these figurines represent the goddess Asherah and provided women with access to a religion that was denied them in the official temple cult.[57]

---

54. Zevit (2001, 271–72). Kletter (1996) disputes this, arguing that the more fragile nature of the figurines would render them more likely to break than the accompanying pottery. Tappy (1998) rightly questions this position as a weak argument. However, Kletter (1996, 56) notes further that: (1) there is no sign of deliberate breakage, (2) these breakings follow those of similar forms dropped from a height, (3) they are often in a context with other broken items, and (4) they are not hostile in appearance. Ultimately none of this is decisive.

55. Cf. Kitchen (2003, 418–19).

56. Cf. van der Toorn (1994b, 77–92); Dever (1996).

57. See Dever (2005).

These interpretations must be balanced by the discussion of the "Approaches to the Study of Religion" in chapter 2. One can compare similar religious figurines from the other side of the planet and from different times and cultures only with the greatest of caution. Because similar (to the observer) female figurines served a particular purpose among the Aztecs of the past centuries does not in itself demonstrate anything about how these figurines were used in ancient Judah. At most it provides one hypothesis that must be tested by all that can be known about the cultural context. The view that these figurines provided women in Iron Age Judah with religious access that was otherwise denied to them in the Jerusalem temple cult is an interpretation nowhere supported by any data from that time or by traditions (within or outside the Bible) extending back to that period. It is rather an interpretation imposed by a twenty-first-century Western academic perspective. Insofar as this is true, it recalls the review in chapter 2 of the attempts of liberation theology in Latin America to "free" women (and men) with a politically correct and academically "approved" agenda that ultimately failed. If sheer numbers are any indication, women found more "freedom" to be who they wished to be in the Pentecostal religious movements that have swept the continent of South America in the past decades. All this shows that ascribing to people values and motivations of our contemporary society and using those to define models for the interpretation of artifacts within expected systems of cultural behavior have not proven successful in cultures that we understand far better than those of ancient Israel and its neighbors.

Although it is impossible to say with certainty, the cheaper terra cotta forms, as well as the state sponsorship and mass production, suggest depictions of humans rather than goddesses. Both the dominance of Yahwistic personal names and the biblically attested reforms of Hezekiah and Josiah argue against divine images. However, the apparently intentional breaking of these images and the biblically attested polytheism of Manasseh argue in favor of these images as divine representations. Nevertheless, as noted in the section on seals below, the complete absence of any representation of a deity other than Yahweh in the iconography is a strong argument in favor of these images not being divine insofar as they were state-supported. In that case, any intentional destruction of them might be attributed to another cause, whether invasion from outside, some sort of popular uprising, or a change in government policy. It is possible that they had different meanings for different people, although the state sponsorship suggests a single official meaning. In terms of their purpose and function, the most likely conclusion is that the images served to promote the bearing of Judean children by Judean women at a time when both politics and economics dictated the importance of this value as expressed in texts such as Genesis 1:26–28 and 3:16.

Male figurines number only a few dozen from Judah. There are two main types, those riding and those wearing turbans. Stern (2001b, 28) suggests that the former signify warriors and the latter represent deities, perhaps Yahweh. See, however, below under "Iconography."

Hazor may provide an interesting model of popular religious sympathies. It has the best stratigraphic sequence published for any site in Palestine in this period. Hazor contains a relatively low number of religious artifacts in domestic areas until c. 750 BC (Stratum V). The number jumps from 7.33 artifacts per stratum to 36 artifacts. Is this suggestive of a sudden increase in non-Yahwistic religion? Did it lead to the messages of the prophets Amos and Hosea?[58] A similar increase in domestic cult objects appears in the south at Tell Beit Mirsim. It also occurs close to the end of the southern kingdom's existence. There it is possible to calculate a figure of 45 percent of the domestic dwellings that had identifiable cult objects.[59] These observations correlate with the results of a study of incense holders and limestone altars in private homes. The same increase in size and number occurs in Palestine in the seventh century BC. These appear first in the north and move south.[60] Close to the end of both kingdoms there is an apparent increase in domestic cult activity, perhaps reflecting a movement toward the worship of a variety of deities in such cultic contexts.

Egyptian amulets in Israelite sites include those of the deities Isis, Horus, Sekhmet (or Bastet), Ptah, and the divine eye, Udjet. The use of such images declined in the seventh century BC.[61] These data require us to see a dynamic picture of Israelite religions allowing for a variety of different and even contradictory expressions of piety within Yahwism. Significant local variations, as well as the worship and adoration of other gods and goddesses, suggest that the line between the worship of Yahweh and that of other deities was not always so sharply drawn.

Summary

Local shrines existed in the North and South during the United Monarchy. Dan was the major Israelite sanctuary of the Divided Monarchy that has been excavated. It remained different from the sanctuary at Arad, which was Judean.[62] Both sanctuaries have a central location in their cities and have a direct access approach. Both have monumental

---

58. J. Glen Taylor (1993, 37–40) studied the horse figurine from Hazor and compared this image with the horse ("Yahweh") image on the Taanach cult stand. See p. 321.

59. Cf. Holladay (1987, 275–80).

60. Cf. Zwickel (1990).

61. See Zevit (2001, 344–46).

62. King (1993, 116) distinguishes between Solomon's temple and the Arad Sanctuary. The former had its entrance on the shorter side of the rectangle and therefore was called a

altars for burnt offerings that were not found in shrines.[63] Both include sacrificial ritual, the eating of ritual meals, and aniconic features. Holladay and Zevit affirm centralized control for the sanctuaries at Dan and Arad, as well as Hazor, Lachish, and Megiddo.[64] However, the northern sites (Dan, Hazor, and Megiddo) have differences of form.

"Nonconformist" and domestic clusters are different in their emphasis on iconographic images. Cultic areas have many lamps and vessels for food preparation, eating, and drinking. So many large vessels require an explanation other than as food offerings. The presence of double altars, *maṣṣēbôt*, and other cultic items suggests that two deities were worshiped at Hazor XI (tenth century BC), Lachish cult room 49 (end of tenth century),[65] Megiddo cult corner 2081 (end of the tenth century), Arad XI (ninth century), and Dan cult room 2831 (eighth century). Kuntillet ʿAjrud, Jerusalem Cave 1, and all these sites except Dan, exhibit evidence of the veneration or worship of two deities, perhaps Yahweh and Asherah.[66]

Hierarchical state religion was aniconic, shrine-centered and sanctuary-centered worship. Indeed, much of the evidence (Megiddo Locus 2081, Building 10, and Lachish Level V Building 49) suggests the United Monarchy was more aniconic than later periods. What about the Solomonic temple? Perhaps the ivory pomegranate is "a straw in the wind," providing the only possible archaeological evidence of this "house of God," and one that has now been challenged.

According to Holladay (1987, 281–82), nonconformist and domestic cults were physically removed from the official shrines and sanctuaries,

---

long-axis temple. This is similar to second-millennium temples at Shechem and Megiddo and to the eighth-century Tell Taʿyinat (Hattina) temple in the Amuq Valley of Syria.

63. Fritz (1993, 185) observes that only two Iron Age altars have been found in Israel, at Arad and at Beersheba, and there is no evidence that either of these was used for burnt offerings. Apparently, he does not include the numerous smaller limestone altars that have been found at Arad and elsewhere. Even with these, few have remains of organic material or evidence of burning. Haran (1993; 1995) suggests that incense would have been too expensive for all but the state temple. He believes that these altars were used for grain and cake offerings and libations to the worship of the Host of Heaven and of the Queen of Heaven, imported astral cults from Assyria (contra M. Smith [2003, 127]). However, Gitin (1992, 47*), followed by King and Stager (2001, 345), suggests the incense was burnt in smaller containers on top of the altars. Certainly, the many altars in the refinery area of Ekron would have fumigated the olive oil processing installations of odor and vermin. Ibid., 347, for frankincense and myrrh as available only from trees native to Yemen (Seba) and Somaliland (Somalia and southeastern Ethiopia) but as capable of being transplanted and attested even in Jerusalem (Song 4:13–14).

64. Holladay (1987, 251, 254–57, 280–81); Zevit (2001, 656–57).

65. Kitchen (2003, 410) regards it as noncultic and domestic.

66. So Zevit (2001, 653–55), who, however, suggests that people visiting the Jerusalem site may also have worshiped chthonic deities.

probably best explained as popular phenomena, probably dependent upon traditions of folk religion stretching back into the Bronze ages, but revitalized by foreign contacts—particularly with Phoenicia (e.g., Kuntillet 'Ajrud)—during the great age of mercantile activity which immediately preceded, and probably occasioned, the Assyrian and Babylonian takeovers of the two kingdoms.

Dever catalogs the elements of this popular religion: *bāmôt* or "high places" and other shrines, images, *'ăšērîm* including sacred trees, Asherah, rites for birth and children, pilgrimages, planting and harvest festivals, *marzēaḥ* or banquets, libation and other rites for the dead, cakes for the Queen of Heaven, wailing for Tammuz, solar and astral worship, divination and sorcery, and perhaps child sacrifice.[67] He suggests that this domestic religion was uniquely the provenance of women who were excluded from the official cult.

During the twelfth and eleventh centuries BC (Iron I), village shrines and pilgrimage sites suggest simplicity of worship. The wealth located in the Shiloh cultic storage rooms was unusual and implied a specialized religious group there. The "high places" or *bāmôt* occur but their main development begins in the tenth century, the period of the United Monarchy, when they are located at key centers. They are archaeologically attested at Megiddo, Taanach, and Lachish. Alpert-Nakhai connects this with the development of priestly power. She observes the ongoing role of smaller local cult centers as well (Tel Rehov and Tel Qasile). During the later Divided Monarchy (eighth to sixth centuries BC) the "high places" continued as state-sponsored religious centers, while cult centers appeared at village sites, along trade routes, and in alternative nonconformist contexts.[68]

Iconography

We have already seen examples of iconography in the anthropomorphic and zoomorphic figurines associated with cult sites and found in domestic environments. We have also looked at the female figurines, especially those that are pillar-based. I shall consider here seals, ivories, some of the drawings from Kuntillet 'Ajrud, the Taanach cult stand with

67. Cf. Dever (2001, 196). Ackerman (1989; 1992, 8–34) identifies the Queen of Heaven with Astarte. Day (2000, 149) identifies this deity with the specifically Canaanite Astarte who is related to the heavens in the Eshmunazar inscription (KAI 14 line 16) and in the title, Aphrodite Ourania. Her temple was originally at Ashkelon (Herodotus *Histories* 1.105). The fourth-century BC Kition tariff mentions cakes being baked for a divine queen.

68. Alpert-Nakhai (2001, 192–93, 203). For Alpert-Nakhai, the high places became a key means in monarchic Israel of "forging" a nation from tribal groups.

four decorative panels, additional cult stands, stone bowls, and the Pozo Moro funerary monument.

Seals

A seal contains the personal name or some pictorial or schematic design that represented the bearer of the seal. We find many seals in ancient Israel and throughout the ancient Near East. Seals from ancient Israel date from as early as the end of the ninth century BC and increase in number through the eighth and seventh centuries BC. Most of the seals are created in the shape of round stamps rather than the more common Syrian and Mesopotamian cylinders. They form important sources for onomastic studies, since many seals with writing contain at least one personal name and sometimes a patronym. However, the artistic carvings that appear on them provide less information later in the monarchy. This is because they tend to appear on the earlier seals and to disappear on the later ones.[69] Many of the Hebrew seals have no artistic forms on them. The occurrence of seals with only inscriptions and without ornamentation is virtually unknown elsewhere. It provides further evidence of a more literate population.[70]

The decorations on seals include natural objects, animals, and trees, as well as the occasional human figure. The griffin is a popular figure. Egyptian influence appears in many ornamented seals. Theriomorphic deities, especially the protective ones, resemble artistic forms in other ancient Near Eastern cultures.[71] However, the significance of their presence in Israel remains small. They do not appear on most of the seals. This symbolism changes from one culture to another and from one age to another. Thus the absence of explicit identification and contemporary elaboration of the myths or meanings behind these forms render any analysis speculative.

Fig. 40. The Jezebel seal (Courtesy of the Israel Antiquities Authority)

Keel and Uehlinger (1998, 133–75) observe that the tenth century BC saw the gradual disappearance of anthropomorphic representations of deities. This was both an Egyptian trait and a reflection of influence

---

69. Herr (1988, 373).
70. Hestrin and Dayagi-Mendels (1979, 9–10); Grafman (1983, 134–35).
71. Keel and Schroer (1985); Schroer (1987, 421–31).

from the north, where deities were represented with their symbols. As was true earlier, the tree and lion are symbols of a goddess, whether of Asherah or Astarte is no longer clear. One recurring theme, known as the "Lord of the Ostriches," may point to a representation of Yahweh as God of the steppe and as an aggressive deity. Increasingly, female worshipers appear with tambourines. In the Bible, the description of the Solomonic temple, while sharing features with Phoenician forms, is unusual in that the bulls are given no prominent role. This is different elsewhere where they are images of the chief male deity. Instead, at the Jerusalem temple they appear as beasts of burden, bearing the bronze washing pool (2 Kings 16:17). There is no evidence that Yahweh regularly shared the temple with a female consort.

Iron Age IIB (c. 925–c. 722 BC) finds Judah with only a few pictorial representations, symbols of royalty adapted from Egypt as well as some local motifs. The northern kingdom adapted and contributed to the flourishing Phoenician artistic and religious traditions. The themes of "Lord of the Ostriches" and also "Lord of the Caprids" are found there. Neutral animals are used, deer in Israel and does in Judah (cf. Ps. 42:1 [Heb. 2]). Keel and Uehlinger suggest that these may represent the worshipers. The lion and the sun occur as images of power and strength. The roaring lion appears in Judah.[72] A few bull pictures can be found in Samaria but these and the cult of Jeroboam at Dan and Bethel are thought to be holdovers of an older tradition. A youthful figure with four wings is found at Hazor, Gezer, and elsewhere, but not in Judah proper at this time. Is this the storm god Baal? The solar disk and the lotus, associated with the sun god as symbols of regeneration, become popular Northern Kingdom images. Except along the Philistine coastal areas, there is an absence of nude female plaques. There is an almost total absence of anthropomorphic images showing a female deity, but pillar-based figurines of females begin to appear and to rise in prominence.[73]

In Iron Age IIC (c. 722–586 BC), centers of power in Palestine become foci for Assyrian cultural and religious influence. Ishtar is represented anthropomorphically on Palestinian stamp seals. The solar disk and solar themes are replaced by the lunar disk and the crescent moon, symbols of the moon god. Two trees flank symbols of a deity and represent the entrance to the deity's shrine. Thus the lampstand between the two trees of Zechariah 4:11 also represents a deity, Yahweh. In addition to the moon, the stars and the astral cults played a significant role. There also appear hundreds of pillar-based female figurines. They occur in homes and tombs, perhaps reflecting the family piety that was accorded to the

72. Keel and Uehlinger deny this as a symbol of Yahweh.
73. See Keel and Uehlinger (1998, 177–281). On these figurines, see pp. 308–12.

plaque images of the Late Bronze Age and Iron Age I.[74] In the coastal regions, but not Judah, the nude goddess continues. She is identified with Astarte by Keel and Uehlinger. The clothed goddess is Asherah. They identify the Queen of Heaven, in Jeremiah 7 and 44, as Yahweh's Asherah. Some 450 small statues of a horse and a male rider occur. Although the disk on some of the horses can be interpreted as other than a solar disk, its correlation with 2 Kings 23:11 remains attractive.[75] The horse-and-rider statues, which can appear in groups, may be connected with the host of heaven and with guardian spirits or angels. The 211 seal motifs found in the Burnt Archive in Jerusalem include only two with solar motifs, indicating the diminution of the influence of solar imagery (and Egyptian influence). The solar symbolism of the numerous rosettes in Judah may refer directly to symbols of Yahweh. Otherwise, seals from Judah lack images in Iron Age IIC. The omega-shaped ("barbie" style or Hathor style) headrests of the tombs may reflect a symbol of the earth as a womb. These forms appear in second-millennium BC Palestine as well. Thus this period saw an end to Egyptian influence, an increasingly Assyrian influence, and some evidence of the aniconic reforms such as the Bible credits to Josiah.[76]

Keel and Uehlinger note that no deities other than Yahweh had significance in the iconography of the latter part of the monarchy, as well as in the century after the fall of Jerusalem. This is in contrast to Edom, for example, where there was a goddess portrayed alongside the chief deity, Qaus. In Judah images disappear from seals.[77]

Fig. 41. Ivory sphinx (Courtesy of the Israel Antiquities Authority)

Ivories

Ivories are present throughout the period of ancient Israel's history. Archaeologists discovered a cache of ivories at Megiddo, dating from the Iron Age I. More relevant to this study is the discovery of ivories at Samaria. Archaeologists discovered five hundred fragments dating to

74. See p. 308.
75. So also Day (2000, 153); contra Keel and Uehlinger (1998, 345).
76. Cf. Keel and Uehlinger (1998, 283–372).
77. Cf. Keel and Uehlinger (1992; 1998) and Ornan (2005) for similar abstraction in Mesopotamia.

Fig. 42. Sphinx at pyramids in Egypt (Courtesy of Richard S. Hess)

the ninth or eighth centuries BC.[78] Unfortunately, they are badly broken and only partially published. Even so, the ivories do contain representations of lions, bulls, and sphinx. Egyptian motifs include images of several Egyptian deities such as Horus, Ra, Isis, and Osiris. Isis may appear in the form of her symbol, a tree. Phoenician styles include the common one of a woman appearing over a balcony and peering through a window. Their owners brought many of these ivories from outside Samaria. However, unfinished ivories also suggest the presence of artisans in Samaria. Only wealthy citizens could afford carved ivories. Thus, foreign religion and culture influenced the aristocratic class of Samaria.

One of the most common figures found on ivories and cult stands (see "Taanach Cult Stand" below) was the sphinx. This figure is a composite of a human face, lion's front quarters, bull's hindquarters, and eagle's wings. A similar combination of features is described in Ezekiel's vision of God's throne (Ezek. 1:10). This figure may be identified with the cherubim who flanked the ark of the covenant in the tabernacle and in the Jerusalem temple.[79] As symbols of the attributes of these creatures, that is, human

78. Cf. King (1988, 143–47), with a picture of an ivory sphinx on the cover of the book; Barnett (1982).
79. Cf. Exod. 25:18–22; 37:7–9; 1 Kings 6:27; E. Borowski (1995).

wisdom and animal power and speed, Elie Borowski (1995) suggests that the cherub symbolizes God's omniscience and omnipotence. Ornan (1995) notes the widespread presence of these figures throughout the first millennium BC in positions that flank and protect deities.

Kuntillet 'Ajrud Drawings

The presence of drawings at this desert site,[80] especially those that appear near inscriptions referring to Yahweh and Asherah, have generated much discussion. The figures occur on a collection of sherds from a large storage jar. There are three figures. Two on the left (from the viewer's perspective) are standing. They have bovine faces and feet, and are adorned with feathered headdresses. They stand with their arms behind their backs and are so linked to each other. Dots decorate the upper parts of their bodies. They suggest some form of apparel. The lower parts of their bodies do not have this decoration, suggesting possible nakedness. The projec-

Fig. 43. Kuntillet 'Ajrud drawings

tion between the legs of each figure may be a phallus or a tail. The third figure to the right sits and plays a lyre. The "dotted apparel" stretches the full length of the body. It also describes the hair. The figure faces to the right towards the lyre, unlike the two standing figures who face toward the front.

Can these figures be identified? Do they have any relationship to the inscription that occurs with them? Some have tied the identification of the figures to the inscription. In that case, either the two standing figures appear as representations of Yahweh and Asherah, or the lyre player represents Asherah. Arguments for these interpretations include: bull calf imagery of Yahweh in the Bible, formal similarities of the lyre player to figures elsewhere identified as Asherah, and the etymology of Asherah as one who follows her male consort (introducing a three-

---

80. For the site of Kuntillet 'Ajrud, see p. 307. For the inscriptions from this site, see chapter 9, p. 283.

dimensional perspective into the drawing).[81] However, none of these arguments can overturn the careful analysis of art historian Pirhiya Beck, who concludes that the two standing figures are both representations of Bes, the Egyptian dwarf deity who appears throughout the eastern Mediterranean in various forms.[82] The facial appearance, the nudity, the headdress, and even the accompanying lyre player are understandable on this interpretation. The artistic form is Phoenician. Then the lyre player cannot be a deity of superior rank because this musician would occupy an inferior role playing for the Bes figures.[83] Zevit (2001, 387–89, 392) argues that the Bes figures are symbols of deity that can apply to any god or goddess. In this case he suggests that the larger one signifies Yahweh without actually portraying him. Zevit identifies Asherah as the lyre player, pointing to such a portrayal of her in Ugaritic mythology.[84] However, Kitchen (2003, 415) correctly notes that Yahweh and Bes have nothing in common.

The unparalleled appearance of these types of Bes figures with Yahweh and Asherah creates doubt that there was an intentional association with the figures and the accompanying writing. Instead, it represents one more example of figures and writing found on the plastered walls and sherds throughout the caravansary. This interpretation of the figures and their lack of association with the inscription is much more understandable given the noncultic nature of the structure in which they occur. If this was a cult center of some sort, arguments relating the art and inscriptions to a single ideology or theology would be more persuasive. A priestly leadership would have directed the cult and probably represented an official or state religion, or at least a coherent religious perspective. However, an interpretation of the site as noncultic allows the iconography and the inscriptions to represent random expressions of popular piety, emanating from different times and different ethnic groups. Any such manifestation of religious belief could have passed through the site.[85] It is possible that this may have been true, at least for a short period.

81. For bull/calf imagery, see Coogan (1987, 119); McCarter (1987, 137–55). For formal comparisons with Asherah and the issues involved, see Dever (1984; 2005). For the etymology of Asherah as "one who follows after" and its association with the inscription, see Margalit (1989, 374).

82. Cf. Beck (1982, fig. 4). See also Olyan (1988, 29nn31, 32). Olyan refers to a similar conclusion that the figures are those of Bes by Stolz (1980, 168). Cf. Dever (1984). Hadley (1989, 184–85) argues that the Bes figures were intentionally placed at the entrance to the caravansary to ward off wild animals and other dangers.

83. Cf. Hadley (1989, 184, 194).

84. Cf. Nougayrol (1968, 557–58), Ras Shamra 24.245, lines 5–7.

85. Arguments for a state-controlled cult represented at Kuntillet ʿAjrud may turn out to be correct. However, the weight of evidence is not on their side at present. The inscriptions and drawings (with the lack of cultic artifacts) appear to indicate that this

On Kuntillet 'Ajrud pithos A, two ibexes flank and face a stylized tree. As noted in chapter 5, under "Iconography and Bronze Age Religion in Southern Canaan," ibexes and trees are also found on the thirteenth-century BC Lachish ewer along with the inscription, "An offering to my lady, Elat (*'lt*)." Elat means "goddess" and may refer to Asherah. Joan Taylor (1995) identifies this pictorial form with similar trees and goddesses from Phoenicia (Tanit) and Ras Shamra. She suggests that the Asherah of the Bible was a cut or pruned tree and sees a possible relationship with the later Jewish menorah.

Taanach Cult Stand

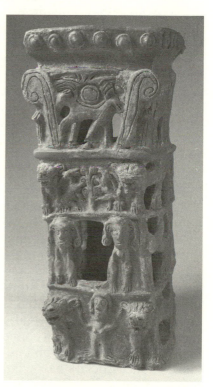

While many pictorial objects suggest religion, few provide the wealth of images found in one of the Taanach cult stands, included among the finds that are associated with the cult center there. Dated to the tenth century BC, this object provides a fascinating glimpse into something of the mythology or ideology that informed the (presumably) official cult in this city. On one of the four sides of the stand there are a series of four panels, each portraying a different scene. I will number the panels from bottom (panel 1) to top (panel 4). Panels 1 and 3 are both flanked by carvings of two lions facing the viewer. On panel 1 there is the portrait of a nude female with each arm raised toward the ear of one of the lions. Two identical creatures with four legs flank panel 2. They face the

Fig. 44. Taanach cult stand (Courtesy of the Israel Antiquities Authority)

was one of the "peripheral sites exposed to foreign influence." Cf. Tigay (1986, 29; 1987, 176). Some argue that the building in which the inscriptions and drawings were found is a government structure and that therefore the views represented must be those of the state-supported cult. Cf. Schroer (1987, 32); Koch (1988, 99). This view requires the demonstration that (1) the building was controlled by a government such as Judah or Israel, rather than a local Bedouin group; (2) that the government was capable of and interested in exerting its control in cultic matters; and (3) that the government concerned can be identified, not an easy task given the variety of places named in the inscriptions.

viewer. These creatures have human faces, however, and their bodies, which continue along the molding of the two sides of the stand, exhibit wings. They are best identified as sphinxes or griffins. Between them is an empty space void of any molding. This space shows no sign of ever having contained anything that might have broken and fallen off. The molding around the empty space is smooth and intact. Panel 3, flanked by lions, has at its center a tree. Two identical animals flank either side of the tree, each facing the tree and standing on its back legs. The animals are ibex or goats (cf. Lev. 17:7). Panel 4, at the top of this side of the stand, portrays a quadruped, drawn more simply than any of the other living creatures portrayed on the four panels. The quadruped faces to the left. Over its body there hovers a disk with wavy lines extending out from either side of it. This is a winged sun disk. Voluted columns flank this animal.

Difficulties exist with any interpretation of pictorial symbols such as those described here. Scholars who have studied the first and third panels and compared the scenes with other parallels in iconography and in West Semitic texts, have tended to agree that both the woman and the tree represent the same deity, Asherah.[86] Kitchen (2003, 410) claimed that only in Egypt is a goddess identified with lions and that is Qadishtu or Qadishtu-Astarte-Anat. However, this is no longer true. There is Ugaritic textual evidence explicitly associating Astarte with a lioness.[87] However, there may have been less separation between Asherah and Astarte in the Iron Age, so that a clear distinction between the two is not necessary or even possible. As noted in the previous section, the tree represents the tree of life, also called the Asherah, which appears in iconography at Kuntillet 'Ajrud and perhaps also in a blessing there. This analysis of the iconography on the cult stand does not depend on the direct association of a goddess such as Asherah with lions. Rather, it assumes a connection with the tree surrounded by ibex figures. Nevertheless, Egyptian, Ugaritic, and Canaanite evidence now allow for an association of Astarte with lions and with the image found here. If Astarte and Asherah are interchangeable, then either goddess might be portrayed.

If the first and third panels represent Asherah or Astarte, what do the second and fourth represent? The fourth panel displays a quadruped surmounted by a sun disk. Scholars have been inclined to identify the

86. Cf. Dever (1984, 33n24; 2005); Hestrin (1987a, 68–71); J. G. Taylor (1987, 16–18; 1988, 560). See, however, King and Stager (2001, 343), who do not accept the identification with Asherah as established. Indeed, they are correct in noting the absence of a text to demonstrate this.

87. See chapter 4, p. 99. It is not clear that it ever was true, given the Amarna-era name of a female leader in Canaan. See EA 273 and 274; Hess (1993a, 175).

animal as a calf, a natural enough deduction given the known association of the calf with Canaanite worship.[88] Associations of this animal with Baal have led Hestrin to identify the fourth panel as a representation of Baal.[89] However, J. Glen Taylor suggests that the animal portrayed in this panel is an equid. He recounts how he arranged for two animal biologists to study this image and how they came to this conclusion.[90] He also identifies this image with the reference in 2 Kings 23:11 to the horses dedicated to the sun. The Judean king Josiah destroyed them. Thus the sun disk, the equid, and the columns (representing the temple) all fit together as a Canaanite religious expression. The winged sun disk is a common motif in iconography throughout the ancient Near East.[91] Its possible association with horses also appears in figurines found in Palestine, including at Megiddo and at Jerusalem (Cave 1).[92]

Panel 2 represents two sphinxes on either side of an empty space. The lack of an indication of anything broken off the molding around that space is clear to anyone who cares to inspect the stand. J. Glen Taylor has proposed that the two sphinxes are cherubs and that this is a representation of the aniconic deity, Yahweh. King and Stager (2001, 344) argue that the cherubim themselves represent Yahweh. However, this is not clear from any biblical text or any extrabiblical text. What is clear is that no other Canaanite deity possesses an aniconic tradition. If panels 1 and 3 represent Asherah or Astarte, then panels 2 and 4 also represent the same deity. If panel 2 is a (non)representation of Yahweh, then we should expect the same of panel 4, whether it is an equid or a bovine. This Canaanite representation of Yahweh may suggest an aspect of the portrayal unique to the Northern Kingdom. If it is a bovine and the stand does date to the tenth century BC, it could suggest the portrayal of Yahweh that Jeroboam I intended. He erected images of calves at the cult centers of Dan and Bethel. If it is an equid, 2 Kings 23:11 suggests the relationship with Yahweh. The inscription at Kuntillet ʿAjrud has made an association of Yahweh with Asherah. The arguments of symmetry in the presentations, of the aniconic nature of panel 2, and of the

88. Cf. Lapp (1969a, 44); Hestrin (1987a, 67).

89. Cf. Hestrin (1986; 1987A, 75); King (1988, 107).

90. Cf. J. G. Taylor (1988, 561–66; 1993, 24–37; 1994, 55–59). This suggestion was first made by Glock (1978). It is followed by Hadley (1989, 219). Hestrin (1991, 59) argues that the absence of a mane on the representation opposes the interpretation of these animals as horses.

91. See especially Mendenhall (1973, 32–56). For the appearance of this motif in the Bible, see J. G. Taylor (1993); M. Smith (1988; 1990b).

92. May and Engberg (1935); Kenyon (1978, 76); Holland (1977); Hadley (1989, 219); J. G. Taylor (1994, 58). M. Smith (1990a, 116) also indicates that these objects were discovered at Lachish and Hazor. For the Iron Age I finds at the places mentioned, see "Cult Centers," p. 297.

evidence from Kuntillet ʿAjrud all point to an association of both panels 2 and 4 with Yahweh.[93]

The alternating pattern created by the four panels on the stand reminds one of the A-B-A'-B' parallelism found in Canaanite and biblical literature.[94] Scholars have noted the use of biblical parallelism for the purpose of emphasis.[95] The same sort of emphasis of these two deities may be taking place on this cult stand, and may reflect both their association and prominence among inhabitants of Taanach in the tenth century.

Additional Cult Stands

Archaeologists discovered another cult stand at Taanach.[96] Hadley has identified alternating rows of lions and sphinxes, although earlier scholars found only lions. This suggests deities similar to those found on the first stand mentioned above. There is also a tree flanked by ibexes and architectural features on the top tier. Although more poorly made, the motifs resemble those of the first cult stand (see p. 321). The lions and the tree may suggest that this stand also depicted Asherah or Astarte.[97]

Two cult stands were found in what is probably a tenth-century BC context at Pella in the Jordan Valley. The excavators, J. B. Hennessy, A. W. McNicoll, and T. F. Potts, have published photographs of the stands.[98] Both stands are similar in their general shape to the Taanach cult stand and others found elsewhere, which are "square" in shape and constructed with clay panels. One stand has an incised tree design on each of its preserved panels. It has horns on each of the four corners on the top, though no evidence of the burning of incense or anything else. Although poorly preserved, the second cult stand reveals two figurines

93. M. Smith (1990b, 32n16) suggests that a tradition associating the calf and Baal could have persisted at Taanach and could be represented on panel 4. This is a possibility, but my present assessment of the arguments favors J. G. Taylor's identification with Yahweh. Smith does not address the question of the identification of panel 2. Hadley (1989, 220–21) accepts the identification with Yahweh and observes that neither the Ugaritic literature nor the Bible provide substantial identification of Asherah with Baal, the one other god whom scholars have found here. Cf. Zevit (2001, 324) who believes that Yahweh and Asherah are represented (maximally; minimally he suggests two unidentified deities).

94. Cf. Watson (1986, 114–22).

95. Cf. Kugel (1981, 51); Alter (1985).

96. Cf. Sellin (1904, 75–76); Lapp (1969b, 16–17); Glock (1978, 1143–44); Hadley (1989, 221–22).

97. Cf. Hestrin (1988, 117). Zevit (2001, 325) creatively suggests that these stands represent different views of a shrine with the top register pointing toward the inner sanctum.

98. Cf. Potts (1984); Potts, Colledge, and Edwards (1985); Hadley (1989, 213–16). Cult stands have also been found at Megiddo, Beth Shan, Ai, and Ashdod. See summary and bibliography in Hestrin (1987a, 67).

on one of the lower panels. They are nude females. One figure with its head preserved has a Hathor-style headdress. The other figurine's stand, in the shape of an animal's (perhaps a lion's) head, is preserved. The lion's head and the Hathor-style headdress lead Hadley to identify the nude figurines with Asherah. No horns appear on the top of this second stand but at least one corner had attached a human, perhaps female, head looking inward toward the top tray, perhaps used for sacrifices.

If these two cult stands describe a single theme, the one could have depicted the tree symbol of Asherah or Astarte while the other could have emphasized Asherah or Astarte in female form. Pella in the tenth century may not have been an Israelite city but this is not certain. In any case, it had a Canaanite legacy. The two cult stands seem to portray Asherah in the same way as the Taanach cult stands. Note also the horns on the cult stand. If these are not Israelite stands, then perhaps the Israelites borrowed this feature. Pella contains the earliest archaeological evidence for these horns. This suggests a non-Israelite origin.

Cult stands from Megiddo portray the shape of buildings with windows but no doors. Compare Baal's house where death entered through windows but not doors.[99] The picture is one in which the deities enter through windows, not doors, while the temple functionaries use the doors.[100]

A tenth-century BC ditch (*favissa*) near biblical Jabneh (Tel Yavné) yielded more than sixty ceramic "crates," described as "mostly parts of cult stands."[101] The ceramic finds were accidentally unearthed by a bulldozer and include many varieties of creatures and human figures decorating the "ceramic crates," some of which could have been house shrines. The site and the region was Philistine in the tenth century and so this interesting and important find describes artistic and cultural forms among one of Israel's neighbors.

Stone Bowls

Archaeologists have found more than a hundred bowls made of steatite and of other materials throughout the Near East. The majority occur in Syria-Palestine.[102] Appearing between the ninth and seventh centuries BC, these bowls exhibit incised designs of palm trees and human heads, as well as lions' heads and paws. Cultic connections and the images of lions and trees have led Ruth Hestrin to relate them to Asherah. She connects

99. *KTU* 1.4 V 126–27 and VI 8–9 (cf. also Jer. 9:20).
100. Cf. Zevit (2001, 325–28).
101. Kletter and Ziffer (2003, 46*). I thank Raz Kletter for permission to view this amazing collection of anthropomorphic and zoomorphic objects at the Israel Antiquities Authority in Jerusalem. I thank Sam Wolff for arranging the visit on May 21, 2006.
102. Cf. Hestrin (1988, 115–17).

the hands with those of the pillar figurines. There the female figures hold their breasts "offering nourishment and life." Again, the connection with Asherah is made. However, it could as easily be argued that the goddess represented here is Astarte. Indeed, as noted in chapter 4, this is to date the only West Semitic goddess that has explicit textual association with a lion.[103] As with the iconography on the Taanach cult stand, the distinction between Asherah and Astarte may have been blurred.

Pozo Moro Funerary Monument

In southeastern Spain a funerary monument was discovered. It was dated c. 400 BC and provides interesting evidence for the discussion of human sacrifice. Kempinski (1995) summarized the structure of this monument and its clear Punic and Phoenician heritage. One of the two sculpted carvings that are preserved from the monument shows a picture of a seated monster about to swallow the contents of a bowl. In the bowl is what appears to be a human figure. In addition, attendants have placed meat and other food dishes on two offering tables before the seated figure. Kempinski identifies this figure with Mot and interprets this image as that of the deity of the underworld receiving human and animal sacrifice.[104] Additional evidence for human sacrifice comes from the high place at Punic Carthage, which reveals thousands of infant burials in what appear to be sacrificial urns, similar to those used for sacrificed animals.[105]

Did Israel practice human sacrifice? Some argue that Genesis 22, where God commands Abraham to sacrifice Isaac, and Micah 6:6–8, where the prophet builds up to a crescendo of human sacrifice as opposed to the more desirable spiritual values, suggest that the Israelites did.[106] While the people may indeed have sacrificed to Molech, there is no evidence from the biblical text that it was ever approved in the Yahwism of Moses or the prophets. Genesis 22 explicitly forbids the sacrifice of Isaac and offers a substitute animal. Indeed, the chapter is introduced with a warning that this was a test rather than God's will that somehow

---

103. See chapter 4, p. 99.

104. See also Heider (1985) for a similar argument. Kempinski goes on to identify Egyptian motifs of life and creation from other sculpted fragments of this monument. On this basis he argues that the builders of the Pozo Moro monument held to a belief that their sacrifices for the dead would have a redeeming quality and that they could be connected with a resurrection. However, this is not explicit from the monument and its carvings.

105. See "Excursus: Religion of Phoenicia" on p. 290. See earlier evidence regarding Molech in chapter 4, pp. 101–2. See also chapter 5 regarding "Amman," p. 132, and "Ashkelon," p. 136.

106. Cf. Mosca (1975); Levenson (1993).

changes by the end of the chapter.[107] Micah 6 never states that God expects or requires human sacrifice. To the contrary, his requirements are stated explicitly in that section but human sacrifice is not one of them.[108]

Burials and Funerary Cults

Archaeology

Tombs from the period of the monarchy have been discovered throughout Palestine. They are common in Jerusalem, with concentrations east of the City of David in the modern village of Silwan and north of the Old City of Jerusalem. The latter includes the site of Gordon's Calvary. Like the adjacent tombs at St. Stephen's Church, the tomb of Gordon's Calvary (and those of Silwan) are characteristically marked by benches, on which the body was placed, and by the distinctive Hathor or "barbie" style headrests. Josephus identified the tombs north of the city as belonging to the later kings of Judah. Those from Silwan are probably from the eighth and seventh centuries BC.[109] Two possible tombs in the City of David itself have been identified as those of David and Solomon, but nothing remains. The bench tomb form is the predominant style of tomb throughout the Iron Age Judean highlands. However, those in the lowlands and the area of the northern kingdom are simple or cist graves, insofar as they can be found. This has led Bloch-Smith (1992b) to distinguish between Israelite (highland) and Canaanite (lowland) burials.

Recent Scholarship

Several studies have appeared that discuss the presence of a funerary cult in the Semitic world of the ancient Near East and especially among the West Semites.[110] In general, burial was considered essential in ancient Israel. Ecclesiastes 6:3 compares a stillborn child favorably

107. See also Johnston (2002, 37).
108. For additional discussion on biblical prophetic texts and others that address human sacrifice, see chapter 9, p. 256.
109. Cf. Ussishkin (1993b) and Shanks (1994) for the discussion here.
110. Cf. Bloch-Smith (1992a; 1992b); Lewis (1989); M. Smith and Bloch-Smith (1988); Spronk (1986); Tropper (1989). In this regard, Schmidt (1994, 7–10) makes some useful distinctions. The ancestor cult focuses on dead predecessors while the cult of the dead looks at the dead in general. Veneration of the dead assumes that the dead continue on in some capacity that allows them to influence deities on behalf of the living. Worship of the dead requires more than the gratitude and care that veneration assumes. The living must secure the favor of the dead through offerings of various sorts. Ancestor worship is a subclass of the worship of the dead. However, the care for and feeding of the dead may

to an unburied man, and Deuteronomy 21:22–23 commands that even an executed criminal should be buried the same day. Cremation was not practiced in ancient Israel.[111]

Bloch-Smith's examination of the 850 excavated and published Late Bronze and Iron Age burials in the southern Levant has led her to conclude that every one of these burials provides evidence of feeding the dead.[112] When she adds this evidence to that already collected for Samaria E 207,[113] she concludes that some form of veneration of the dead existed throughout ancient Israel, similar to the evidence that is found among Israel's neighbors. This emphasizes the importance of family religious practices and their identity in contrast to or as a complement of the state cult.[114] Family tombs in the Bible and in the archaeological record witness to the ownership of the land by the family, both living and deceased, forever. The archaeological evidence suggests that, despite reforms mentioned during the reigns of Hezekiah and Josiah, there was no change in the popular view of treatment of the dead.[115]

Smith has noted that the practices of feeding, consulting, and mourning the dead were known at Ugarit and continued in Israel.[116] Lewis (1989, 120–22) proposes that the command to take care of (*piqdû-nā'*) Jezebel's body (2 Kings 9:34–37) involves the fulfillment of appropriate funerary rites. However, Johnston (2002, 193) finds no other evidence for such a use of this Hebrew expression. Necromancy alone may have been criticized before 750 BC (1 Sam. 28:3; cf. Isa. 8:16–20 [vv. 20b–22 are secondary but continue the criticism]; 29:4; Lev. 19:26; Deut. 18:9–22; Ps. 106:28; all of which may be later including the Samuel gloss, according to Smith). Even so, Manasseh permitted necromancy (2 Kings 21:6).

However, Johnston (1994) has denied this as a valid interpretation of the archaeological evidence. He claims that there is no evidence for "continued sustenance of the dead" from the archaeological or bibli-

---

assume that the dead are weak and unable to influence the living. Thus death and ancestor cults are different from commemoration of the dead.

111. Cf. Johnston (2002, 51–57).

112. Cf. Bloch-Smith (1992b).

113. Possibly also Jerusalem Cave 1, although Eshel and Prag (1995) dispute a cultic interpretation, but see Shanks (1996c). For these sites see pp. 297 and 307.

114. Ackerman (1992) and Albertz (1992) follow scholars like Blum (1984) in assuming the radical distinction between popular or family religion and state cult. This distinction is challenged by Loretz (1992a and 1992b).

115. Cf. Bloch-Smith (1992b, 224). However, Cooper and Goldstein (1993, 294) are not correct in their argument that stelae or *maṣṣēbôt* were originally associated only with graves of venerated ancestors. This is clear from the archaeological evidence from the Negev where such stelae are found in contexts separate from burials. See p. 198.

116. Cf. M. Smith (2003, 162–71), who finds criticisms to feeding and consulting the dead in Deut. 26:14 and Isa. 8:19. See Pitard (2002, 151–55) and earlier work cited there.

cal records. He follows Cooley (1983, 52) who writes concerning Late Bronze Age tombs that food and drink were provided for the journey to the underworld and that this journey was assumed to have been completed when only the bones remained. These were removed into an ossuary. Johnston (2002, 62) applies this interpretation to the Judean tombs. In fact, he notes that most of the burial sites that have been discussed, where they possessed vessels with food remains, lie outside the central highlands, for example, those at Beth Shemesh and Lachish. The population in these sites was mixed at best, and hardly 100 percent Judean. Even at the site of Aitun, no food has been recorded in the vessels. Therefore, it is not clear that any custom of feeding the dead was practiced in the Judean highlands.[117] Given the diversity of evidence in religious expression, it is not possible to conclude that there was an absolute distinction in this practice and that no Israelites would have been involved in these food and drink rituals associated with the dead. Nevertheless, the archaeological evidence for widespread feeding of the dead in and around Jerusalem remains to be established.

B. Schmidt (1994) argues that no worship of the dead can be deduced from the evidence. Noting that the Navajo never adopted the ancestor cult of the Pueblo, Schmidt (1994, 274) sees an analogy suggesting that the similar cults in neighboring regions around Israel do not allow us to conclude anything about ancient Israel. Further, not all Judean tombs have evidence of eating. Khirbet Beit Lei has no grave goods. Nevertheless, Schmidt's view of the absence of veneration of the dead for most of the monarchy is not without problems. Indeed, Lewis (2002, 190–99) has demonstrated that both in Egyptian letters to the dead and in Mesopotamian sources there was a clear concern to feed and take care of the dead for the services that they could render the living.[118] The dead were fed not because they were weak and powerless but because they were honored as spirits who could affect for good or evil the lives of the living. Such spirits did not have power on the level of the high gods and goddesses of Canaan, but they represented the interests of the family to which the offerer belonged. The fact that some tombs did not possess the same sort of evidence for feeding the dead demonstrates again the diversity of this practice and that it was a family and personal activity, not a state-enforced one.

117. Cf. Johnston (2002, 57–65). See also Scurlock (1997), who reviews the Mesopotamian idea that feeding the dead kept them at peace, while failing to take care of them brought out their wrath in plagues among the living. Scurlock suggests that this belief, which has parallels in other Asian and European cultures, could also have been prevalent in Israel.

118. However, see Johnston (2005) for a critical evaluation of the differences between Egyptian and West Semitic views of the afterlife.

Summary for the Divided Monarchy

Both the biblical and the extrabiblical evidence concur that Yahweh as a sole deity was present early in Iron Age II (cf. the Yahwistic dominance of theophoric elements in personal names), and that polytheism never died out, even at the end of the monarchy (cf. Ezek. 8). The following observations represent some of the major tendencies in popular Israelite religion during the monarchy.

Given the diversity of religious expression, what some have identified as popular and state religion in Judah and Israel existed on a continuum.[119]

At the one extreme was the prophetic religion of God (Yahweh) alone, superior to all Baals, covenantal, and requiring a personal and ethical as well as religious response from the people. Examples of this occur in the Old Testament prophets and historical books, in the personal names of all Judeans and most Israelites, in the Ketef Hinnom silver plaques, and perhaps in some of the worship at a cult center at Beersheba.[120] Patrick Miller (2000, 48–51) lists six features of this religion: (1) exclusive worship of Yahweh; (2) dreams, the casting of lots within the sacred assembly, and prophetic revelation as the primary means of the divine revelation of God's will; (3) sanctuary worship, initially distributed at a number of places, becoming restricted to the Jerusalem temple; (4) pilgrimage festivals to celebrate Yahweh's past works of good and his present grace; (5) morality and especially social justice; and (6) religious leadership effected by priests and prophets. The priests, kings, and prophets led this worship. The priests sought God's will (e.g., 1 Sam. 14:23–36), taught the people (Lev. 10:10–11), and performed sacrifices (Lev. 1–9; Deut. 33:8–11). The prophets received messages from God for the king (1 Sam. 10), proclaimed God's justice and covenant (Amos), and announced God's plans (1 Kings 22). The kings could of-

119. Berlinerblau (1993, 18), following the tendency to find biblical perspectives on Israelite religion to be so ideologically loaded as to be useless for a reconstruction of Iron Age Palestinian religion, defines "popular religion" as "any association of individuals living within the borders of ancient Israel who by dint of their religious beliefs, political beliefs, rituals, symbols, and so on, are denigrated by the authors of the Old Testament." This definition is not acceptable because it assumes that the religion of the Old Testament formed no part of the religious faith of Iron Age inhabitants of Palestine. Such a negative evaluation is without substance as I have sought to demonstrate by examining especially the extrabiblical evidence. Cf. also Hess (1992c).

120. At the Arad sanctuary, the presence of two incense altars and two standing stones suggests the worship of more than one deity in the eighth century. If so, then the actual dismantling of this sanctuary at the end of the eighth century may itself provide evidence of a centralization of worship and a rejection of the recognition of multiple deities. See Herzog (1997; 2002); Dever (2005, 170–75).

ficiate in cultic activities (2 Sam. 6) and lead in reforms (Hezekiah and Josiah). The power of the kings could be held in check by the critique of the prophets.[121]

At the other extreme was the imported Baal cult from Tyre, that the Bible indicates had been brought to Israel by Jezebel and to Judah by Athaliah. This confessed Baal as god and allowed no room for Yahweh. Its larger context can be found in the Ugaritic texts, in Philo of Byblos, and in the Phoenician/Canaanite temples and personal names. Both of these extremes sought death for all who opposed them.

Between these two was the official cult of the northern kingdom (and sometimes the southern kingdom), epitomized by the cult center at Dan, the Taanach cult stand, and possibly cult centers such as at Megiddo. The official cult confessed Yahweh as a national deity who would guarantee the nation's military security. Other nations could have their gods and the people could worship local Baals. These local deities were possibly manifestations of the one deity Baal rather than separate and unrelated deities.[122]

Also between the two extremes, and coincident with the national cult just described, was the popular religion found, as discussed above, in the inscriptions of Kuntillet ʿAjrud, in nonconformist cult centers with their materials for (funerary [*marzēaḥ*]?) banquets, in domestic cult figurines, in some Samarian personal names, and in Israelite place names containing "baal" where it is not clear whether "baal/lord" refers to Yahweh or to a god of the region.[123] This saw the Baals as the local, fertility deities while Yahweh was a remote national deity.

The religious practices of this last point could be divided into two subgroups: those practices and objects that were questionable but did not formally acknowledge the existence of other deities, and those that did. Included in the former were heterodox cult objects such as *maṣṣēbôt*, pillar and plaque figurines, high places, calf images erected by Jeroboam I, the Nehustan or bronze serpent, and the *ʾăšērîm* if they were cult objects of Yahweh. In addition, there were mediums used to consult with spirits of the dead (1 Sam. 28) and the cult of the dead itself, as well as the ephod of Judges 17–18. *Tĕrāpîm* or ancestor figurines, *marzēaḥ* meals associated with funerary rituals, and the various eating and drinking vessels in tombs round out the picture.[124]

121. See P. Miller (2000, 162–97).
122. Day (2000, 68) notes a similar phenomenon at Ugarit where in the pantheon list (*KTU* 1.47.5–11) the name Baal is repeated seven times, suggesting that Baal could appear in various manifestations. In the Old Testament these manifestations are defined according to particular geographic locations.
123. Cf. Dearman (1993).
124. Cf. P. Miller (2000, 51–56).

Evidence for cults that clearly recognized the presence of other deities include Jezebel's priests and the temple of Baal (2 Kings 10:18–27); the already-mentioned names compounded with Baal in the eighth-century BC Samaria ostraca (unless baal is understood as "lord" rather than a deity by that name); child sacrifice;[125] the practices recorded in Ezekiel 8 just before the Babylonian destruction of the Jerusalem temple (a room with pictures of reptiles, mourning for Tammuz, and sun worship); and the worship of the Queen of Heaven (Ishtar?) at the same time.[126]

The destruction of the Jerusalem temple, followed by the return and rebuilding, suggest a continuation of many aspects of Israelite culture. However, the Jews in the province of Yehud, who settled in and around Jerusalem, do not reveal the same degree of diversity in religious practices. Instead, their focus on the temple, on Torah, and on their own survival appears to lead to a general rejection of other cultic practices and cult objects. At the same time, in regions to the north and west of the area of Jerusalem, there continued a variety of cultic practices that did include figurines. The witness of the colony at Elephantine at the end of the fifth century may suggest a diversity of cultic activities among the Jews there or it may imply a variety of West Semitic groups in the region, including at least one who recognized the religious authority of the priesthood in Jerusalem.[127]

Excursus

SACRED PROSTITUTION

In terms of deities, many scholars have understood the popular religious theology of Baal worship as follows: Baal served as the local

125. As already noted, this can be found in the frieze of the besieged city of Ashkelon on the Merneptah panels at Karnak where larger people hold smaller people over the walls; in Moab in 2 Kings 3:27; among the Avvites in 2 Kings 17:31; in Israel in 2 Kings 16:3; 21:6; 23:10; and in the Psalms (106:37–38) and the prophets (Isa. 57:5; Jer. 19:5; 32:35). See Day (2000, 209–16).

126. See Jer. 7:18; 44:15–30; P. Miller (2000, 57–61). However, Thompson (1992, 412–13) denies that Yahweh was worshiped in Jerusalem before the Persian period. This worship originated in Samaria and came to Jerusalem when the Samarian citizens migrated to Jerusalem. These immigrants bore no relationship to the earlier population of Jerusalem and Judea in the time of the Assyrians. This view fails to take into account the abundance of preexilic inscriptions from outside the Bible, e.g., the many Yahwistic personal names (and that no other deity occurs in late Judean personal names), the Yahwistic blessings on the Arad and Lachish ostraca, the Ketef Hinnom amulet, and the Khirbet el-Qom inscription.

127. See further on p. 341.

manifestation of the male fertility deity. Baal was the lord of the rain and the thunderstorm. Asherah was the female deity. The rain provided fertility for the land.

Theologically, this envisioned the rain upon the soil as the male principle of Baal fructifying the "female" land and so rendering it fruitful. The sexual license found at the centers of Baal worship (the high places) attempted to reenact this process through something termed "cultic prostitution." Through the principle of sympathetic magic these acts between local inhabitants and cult prostitutes provided fertility for the soil.[128] John Day traces this view back to Frazer, whose emphasis on comparative practices led him to conclude the importance of fertility in the actions.[129]

This view appeals to the theological mind. It has enjoyed great popularity. It lacks only one thing: evidence. It does not appear in any biblical or extrabiblical texts. To the contrary, the prophets do not debate theology. Rather, they condemn both the worship of the false gods and the licentious activities associated with that worship. The two acts resemble one another insofar as the Israelites observed a covenantal faith with Yahweh, a covenantal faith that carried the strength of a marriage commitment. Thus adultery on the human level became a metaphor for adultery on the national and divine level.

In the Bible there are groups, qĕdēšîm and zônôt, who seem to be prostitutes. Texts such as Genesis 38:15, 21–22; Hosea 4:14; and Deuteronomy 23:17–18 associate the terms for female prostitute (zônâ) with that of a sacred female functionary (qĕdēšâ).[130] These make it clear that prostitutes functioned at the cult, even at the temple of Jerusalem. Does this support the theological interpretation as given above?

Van der Toorn (1989; 1992; 1994b, 93–110) has argued that it does not. On the associations of libertinism and Baal worship, van der Toorn writes, "Sexual excesses were part of the expected ritualised behaviour at festivals and belonged as such to the popular culture of the time. The same could be said of fraternity parties, New Year's parties, and the like in our own secular religion" (1989, 203). He argues that the qĕdēšîm and the zônôt were generally nonpriestly employees of the temple (1989, 203–5). That they sometimes served as prostitutes seems to be the case but there is no evidence that this prostitution had any sacred character to it. It was simply a means of income for the religious cult. Thus the woman of Proverbs 7 who seduces the young man was

128. For a useful summary of this view, see Winward (1976, 49–52).
129. Cf. Day (2004a, 16). See chapter 2, p. 28.
130. See Day (2004a, 3–11), who cites these texts and answers a variety of attempts to disconnect the two terms by separating the texts into original sources or raising questions about the degree to which they reflect reality in ancient Israel.

not a professional prostitute but used this as a source of income to fulfill a vow made in the temple to Yahweh (v. 14).[131] The woman was "strange" (*zārâ*) and "alien" (*nokrîyâ*), because her actions had cut her off spiritually from her family and household, through which alone the Israelite could lay claim to the inheritance that Yahweh had given to his people.[132] The man, in joining her, also risked loosing himself from his family and its inheritance of the land (cf. Prov. 2:18–22, esp. v. 22), and thus God's provision for his life.

Regarding this question, very little evidence exists in Palestine outside the Bible. However, the corresponding cultures in Mesopotamia offer plenty of data on this subject. Lambert (1992) identifies a variety of types of prostitution, from that which had no apparent association with any cult to all sorts of prostitutes associated with the cult. He observes that all prostitution was by definition sacral or sacramental because the sexual act was a natural force personified in the Mesopotamian goddess Inanna/Ishtar.[133] Some prostitutes had a distinctive dress and hairstyle. Lambert also notes that prostitution "was perhaps the only profession which allowed a woman to earn a good income outside the family."[134] Because cultic prostitution does not appear in the ancient Near Eastern law codes does not prove it did not exist. In the Neo-Assyrian tablets, from the time of the Israelite monarchy, male and female prostitutes are mentioned along with priestly figures who are all dedicated to Ishtar. Wilhelm (1990) refers to an Old Babylonian legal text that mentions prostitutes along with other temple offices. He studies the account of the Greek historian Herodotus that describes how all women in Babylonia participated in cultic prostitution at one point in their lives.[135] He (as well as Lambert)

131. Cf. also Goodfriend (1992). Garrett (1990) argues that the "brazen face" of v. 13b means that the woman is lying to ease the young man's conscience.

132. Cf. C. J. H. Wright (1990, 92–97).

133. For the identification of this goddess with West Semitic Astarte and the Queen of Heaven of Ezek. 8, see Ackerman (1992).

134. Cf. Lambert (1992, 135). The small amount of evidence for male prostitution in the ancient Near East suggests that it was rare. Homosexuality does not receive a mention in the laws of Hammurabi but its activity (only male) brings the severest of penalties in the Middle Assyrian Laws. Biblical scholars have identified the "dog" of Deut. 23:18 with male prostitutes. However, Stager (1991b) suggests that the dogs were real dogs at the sanctuary and not prostitutes. This is due to (1) the role of dogs in Greek myths, (2) Greek healing practices associating dogs and snakes in the Asclepian sanctuary at Epidaurus, (3) "dogs" among the temple personnel in the fifth-century BC Cypriote plaque, (4) the association of dogs and healing cults in Mesopotamia, and (5) the need to explain seven hundred dog burials discovered at fifth-century BC Ashkelon within the city. However, if one accepts the existence of female prostitutes there is no reason to deny that the corresponding masculine term "holy, dedicated one" *qādēš* might refer to male prostitutes in passages such as 1 Kings 15:12 and 2 Kings 23:7. See Day (2004a, 11–12, 17).

135. Cf. Wilhelm (1990).

notes that because this is a late source does not mean that it is incorrect. Wilhelm also publishes a text from Nuzi (fifteenth or fourteenth century BC) that describes how a certain woman was dedicated "to Ishtar" to work as a prostitute.[136] Day (2004a) adds later Greco-Roman writers such as Lucian, Eusebius, and others who describe prostitution as taking place in temples throughout the Mediterranean world.

There are aspects of the description in Proverbs 7 that suggest Canaanite fertility religion.[137] However, the explanation that this refers to prostitution for the purpose of repaying vows rests on an unnatural interpretation of 7:14, where the perfect verb is better rendered as "today I *have paid* my vows."[138]

The explanation that much of the prostitution that is described in the Bible is in the arena of general debauchery is attractive insofar as it provides a more "natural" understanding of the sexual activity. Perhaps the theological explanation grew popular in a generation of scholars for whom promiscuous sexual activity required a theological motivation. From the viewpoint of Western society in the present age it is no longer necessary to justify such actions or to dignify them with a theology. Perhaps we have come closer to the culture of the nation that the prophets of the Old Testament addressed. Even so, the absence of extant archaeological evidence from Palestine does not exclude the possibility of cultic prostitution there. Indeed, it seems likely that it took place, if, as other evidence suggests, there was such a practice existing in the ancient Near East and Mediterranean world before, during, and after the period of the biblical descriptions.

The biblical text suggests that Israel's cult consistently provided means by which people who were too poor to afford more expensive items for sacrifice could use cheaper materials. This is explicitly mentioned with respect to offerings distinctive to women, such as those after childbirth (Lev. 12:6–8). If women were driven into prostitution to fulfill their vows, it may not have been the fault of the sacrificial system itself. Rather the whole system of sacred prostitution, however it is to be understood exactly, seems to reflect a distortion of what we know of the legal and cultic system.

136. Ibid., 517.
137. E.g., v. 26, cf. Garrett (1990, 682).
138. Cf. Day (2004a, 7–8).

11

Exilic and Postexilic Religion

Historical and Cultural Aspects

Although the purpose of this book has been to trace the religious practices of ancient Israel until the end of the monarchy, it is important to gain some sense of the direction that it took in the period after the Babylonian destruction of Jerusalem. Therefore this brief examination provides some reflections on the history and religion of the late sixth and early fifth centuries BC, through the period traditionally ascribed to Ezra and Nehemiah.[1]

The exilic period occurs during the time when the Neo-Babylonian Empire occupied the formerly independent state of Judah, from 586 to 539 BC. There is debate regarding the degree of habitation in and around Jerusalem at this time.[2] Part of the problem has to do with the lack of archaeological evidence in the land for the remainder of the sixth century BC. Nor is there a great deal of religious evidence. Nevertheless, the biblical tradition (2 Kings 25:22–25; Jer. 40–41) is that Gedaliah was

---

1. See the surveys of this period by Williamson (1999); Briant (2002); Lipschits (2005); and the studies in Lipschits and Oeming (2006).

2. For the view that the land was largely uninhabited during the exilic period, see Stern (2001a, 303–11; 2002). For the view that it was inhabited and maintained large-scale continuity of culture with the period before 586 BC, see Barstad (1996; 2003); Blenkinsopp (2002); Oded (2003). Within postexilic Jerusalem, Ussishkin (2005) argues that large areas were inhabited, whereas Geva (2006) maintains that the circumference of walls was much smaller and thus fewer people would have filled the city.

governor for a period of time, with his seat north of Jerusalem at Mizpeh, modern Tell en-Nasbeh in Benjaminite territory. This region seems to have been undisturbed by the Babylonian invasion. There may have been the continuation of some sort of cultic activity at Bethel.[3]

In Babylon itself, there is not a great deal of clarity regarding relevant material from this short period. There is little in the way of annals for the latter part of Nebuchadnezzar II's reign or that of his successors. The religion of Judah and of Jews in Babylon is thus understood in terms of the biblical materials and of later reflections from the extrabiblical evidence of the Persian period.

The postexilic period is the period of the Persian Empire. The sources for this period and the Persian Empire in general include the Bible, Herodotus, other Greek historians, Persian and Babylonian Chronicles and other texts, and the archaeology. Although the Persian period traditionally extends from 539 BC until the conquest by Alexander the Great in 330 BC, this study will limit its focus to the first part of this period, ending with the Jerusalem visits of Ezra and Nehemiah in the mid-fifth century BC.

Cyrus seized the Median capital Ecbatana in 550 BC and conquered Lydia in a winter campaign of 547 and 546 BC. A general, Gobryas, entered Babylon in October 539 without resistance. Babylon welcomed Cyrus, who appeared a few weeks later, as a liberator. Babylon and the cities of the empire were preserved intact. The various gods that Nebuchadnezzar had collected in Babylon were returned to their cities and ancient rituals were restored. Cyrus "took the hand of Marduk" and thus became legitimate ruler of Babylon. This involved a ceremony enacted between Cyrus and the chief deity of Babylon, Marduk. His son Cambyses was installed as regent. In 538 BC Cyrus issued a royal proclamation allowing the Jews to return to Palestine and to rebuild the temple (Ezra 6:2–12). The contemporary Cyrus Cylinder records the return of the gods of many lands by Cyrus, and it requests their prayers on behalf of him and his son Cambyses. Cyrus was remembered as one who imposed a lighter yoke of taxation in comparison with his successors such as Darius I.[4] Certainty is not available regarding his commitment to Zoroastrianism, in contrast to Darius, Xerxes, and their successors.

Sheshbazzar was possibly the son of Jehoiachin and identified with the Shenazzar of 1 Chron. 3:18, had the Babylonian name *Sin-ab-uṣur*. He led the returnees who likely restored some sort of cult. Zerubbabel, possibly the nephew or brother of Sheshbazzar, succeeded him as governor

---

3. See Blenkinsopp (2003).
4. Cf. Briant (2002, 67–68).

of Palestine. Exiles continued to return (Hag. 1:3–11; 2:15–17). Bright (1981) stresses the increasing depression and subsequent syncretism that was felt by the returnees as the temple work did not progress beyond the foundations. The community felt a need for separation and holiness (Isa. 65:8–16; 66:15–17). The Persian appointment of Zerubbabel (and possibly also Sheshbazzar) indicates that the Persian government respected the Judean tradition of leadership in a "son of David."[5]

According to Herodotus, Cambyses, the successor to Cyrus and conqueror of Egypt, took his own life when he learned of a rival claimant to the throne who was impersonating his deceased brother. This occurred in 522 BC and ushered in a time of uncertainty regarding the empire and its future. Darius, an army officer with royal lineage, claimed the throne and ousted the rival. By 520 BC relative stability was restored throughout the empire.

This period of political uncertainty and instability may have aroused messianic hopes in prophets who sought to encourage the completion of temple building in Jerusalem. Haggai, perhaps in 520 BC, and Zechariah at about the same time and for some years after, exhorted the people to complete the task. The temple may have been dedicated in 515 BC. Later, Tattenai, in whose satrapy Jerusalem lay, wrote to the Persian court to determine the source of authority for building the temple. Darius confirmed that it was a royal decree and ordered Tattenai to provide the subventions to build and maintain the cult.[6] Zerubbabel is not mentioned again.

Socially the formation of new communities and their economic prosperity characterized the Neo-Babylonian and Persian periods in southern Babylonia. These included deported ethnic minorities.[7] The Jewish groups played some part in this prosperity.[8] Property owners and cult personnel composed these self-governing communities under imperial supervision.[9] Among the Jews, some cult must have persisted. This probably involved the collection and handing on of the biblical texts. Many Jews might have had little motivation to return to their land and to rebuild. However, a Late Babylonian text demonstrates that Jews in Babylonia in 498 BC did preserve Yahwistic personal names.[10]

5. Cf. Oded (1995).

6. Cf. Ezra 5:1–6:18.

7. In his survey of named individuals in Neo- and Late Babylonian legal documents, Zadok (2003, 552) identifies some 960 non-Babylonian names. This is a sizable number but it shrinks to less than 2 percent when it is realized that Zadok examined more than fifty thousand names from this time.

8. Cf. Blenkinsopp (1991, 52).

9. The temple cult played an important role in the collection and storage of taxes, both those for local administration and those that were sent on to the imperial centers of the Persian Empire. For this distinction see Schaper (1995).

10. Cf. Lambert (forthcoming).

In this text some eight personal names contain the divine name Yahweh, including one case where both a father and a son possess such names.[11] Thus in the late sixth and early fifth centuries BC Yahweh was worshiped by Jews in Babylonia.

Baal is no longer mentioned in the Bible after this time. However, Zechariah 12:11 refers to the Aramaean cult of Hadad-rimmon in the plain of Megiddo. Much later, in 168 BC Antiochus IV Epiphanes dedicated the Jerusalem temple to Zeus Olympios, a Hellenistic equivalent of Baal Shamem, possibly the same deity that was introduced by Jezebel.[12] During the period of the Maccabees in the second century BC, Josephus records that Judas destroyed the Philistine temple to Dagan in Ashdod. Niehr (2003) argues that the priestly emphasis on purity and the Deuteronomists' monotheism led to the end of a cult of royal dead, and condemnation of the practices of feeding the dead, funeral banquets, necromancy, and funeral rites. However, R. Schmitt (2003) suggests that the archaeological evidence attests to an ongoing popular religion of votive offerings that is in continuity with the Iron Age.

Miller has noted that this was a period of separation from other peoples and practices rather than proselytism; of a focus on Torah, its study and obedience at the heart of religious practice; and of the Jerusalem temple's collection of a significant percentage of all wealth created.[13]

Blenkinsopp (1991) has suggested a sociological context that the exiles and Ezra and Nehemiah formed and in which they participated. The "civic temple community" was a model suggested by Max Weber. He argued that it was the dominant reality throughout the Persian Empire, in cities stretching from Greece and Anatolia to Babylonia and Persia. The Persians regulated this society through an imperial officer who controlled the priesthood and ensured payment of tribute. Most temples possessed extensive lands. Citizens were free, land-owning males and citizenship required one's support of the cult. The community jealously guarded its privileges. The temple housed the city's treasury. A city council of elders (including priests) administered it. They decided secular and religious affairs. According to Blenkinsopp, many of these items compare favorably with the postexilic period as described in Ezra and Nehemiah.

The decisive event of the postexilic community was the rebuilding of the temple, commanded by Cyrus and paid for by the Persian administration. The initial returnees set up an altar and laid the temple foundations. Further work occurred after the Persian conquest of Egypt.

---

11. Interestingly, the Yahweh elements in the names are spelled two ways, even in the case of the father and son. The spellings are *ia-ḫu* and *ia-ma*.

12. See Day (2000, 71); M. Smith (2003, 69–70).

13. Perhaps this amounted to a third of the resources. Cf. P. Miller (2000, 98–99).

This began in the second year of Darius, c. 520 BC. Note that with the temple endowment, the Persians required that prayers be made for the royal family. However, contributions also came from the Babylonian Jewish community. Repatriates from Babylon and natives who had separated themselves (Ezra 6:21) comprised the temple community. Elders governed seventeen ancestral houses. Between eight hundred and one thousand adult males held membership in each one. They possessed their own land. There were also guilds of masons and carpenters. Nehemiah's work included a committee to ensure just collections and disbursements of the temple wealth (Neh. 13:13). Thus the Jerusalem temple resembled the "civic temple community" model, although it was unusual insofar as it apparently did not have land of its own.

Some have argued for syncretism and the worship of other deities at this time. Insofar as Isaiah 57 presents a picture of the postexilic world, it describes the worship of Molech and other deities with symbols in the home and images, child sacrifices, wine and grain offerings, and acts of prostitution in the hills and ravines (vv. 5–9). This assumes that Isaiah 57 describes a particular postexilic environment, which is not proven and in many ways resembles the preexilic picture.[14]

An alternative perspective notes the absence of the ubiquitous pillar-based figurines in the period of the second half of the sixth century BC. Although some have argued that such figurines continued, they did so only outside Jerusalem and its immediate environs, not where those returning from the exile settled. There are no figurines in postexilic Jerusalem.[15] Thus the use of these figurines, whether as good luck charms, as images of a goddess, or for some other religious purpose, appears to have stopped with those who returned from the exile.

In the late fifth-century BC Jewish mercenary colony of Elephantine in Upper Egypt there was a temple to Yahu wherein the Jerusalem priesthood gave permission for grain offerings. However, money was given to and oaths were taken before such deities as Anatyahu, Anatbethel, Eshembethel, and Herembethel. Miller (2000, 61–62) notes the nearby presence of Arameans with their temple to the Queen of Heaven and wonders whether these other divine names represent hypostatic forms of Yahweh or separate deities. Day (2000, 142–44) argues that Hosea 14:8 [Heb. 9] uses a wordplay on Anat, just as Jeremiah 48:13 refers to the deity Bethel. Thus he believes that Anat was held to be a wife of Yahweh at Elephantine and in preexilic times. However, in Hosea the tree is used to describe Yahweh, not a goddess or wisdom personified (as for example in Prov. 3:18). Therefore, the evidence is weak for an

14. See discussion under the section on biblical texts in chapter 9, p. 248.
15. Cf. Stern (1999, 254); Johnston (2003, 87).

association with either goddess Anat or Asherah.[16] The Elephantine texts also mention the ongoing institution of the *marzēaḥ* festival.[17]

Practices and views regarding burial and the dead continued from the Iron Age but also turned in new directions. Stern (1982) observes three types of burials in his examination of twenty-seven sites: (1) bench tombs as before the exile and dating to the sixth century BC; (2) cist tombs from the sixth and fifth centuries BC; and (3) shaft tombs from the fifth and fourth centuries BC. The cist tombs contain Persian and local items. The shaft tombs were similar to contemporary Phoenician and Cypriot tombs and may reflect the presence of non-Jews. Later texts suggest an ongoing role for rites associated with the dead. Ben Sira condemns feeding the dead (30:18). Tobit 4:17 may refer either to feeding the dead or to providing food for mourners. Praying to the dead is mentioned in 2 Baruch 85:12 and Pseudo-Philo 33:5. Sotah 34b attests to Caleb praying to the Genesis ancestors.[18]

Theological Directions

Traditional literary critical approaches have attempted to identify strands of biblical tradition in preexilic Judaism that continued into the postexilic period. They have then sought to cluster as much of the Old Testament literature as they can around these strands and to argue for their postexilic composition. An example of this approach is Hanson.[19] Although one may not agree with his late postexilic dates for everything he lists, his view that many of the forces and groups that were active in postexilic Judaism were present simultaneously is probably more realistic than an attempt to see each shift of emphasis in the literature as a different part of the chronological sequence. Hanson identifies four types of preexilic theological antecedents: (1) Zion theology as found in Isaiah 7–11 and the opposition of Jeremiah 7:1–15 and 26 recalled God's promise for an eternal dynasty of David; (2) prophetic theology as found in Amos, Hosea, and Jeremiah saw apostasy as leading to destruction; (3) priestly theology, found among the priests serving in Jerusalem when the cult was centralized under Josiah, emphasized the centrality of both the temple and the Zadokite priesthood and downgraded the king (Ezek. 40–48); and (4) wisdom theology, as in Proverbs,

16. Cf. M. Smith (2003, 136).
17. One letter describes how a certain Haggai is to collect the *marzēaḥ* for Ashian (Lewis [1989, 90]; Johnston [2002, 183]).
18. Cf. M. Smith (2003, 170–71).
19. Cf. Hanson (1987). For questions about conflicts in Isa. 56–66, see Middlemas (2005).

attempted to see the principles behind life and to control them, within the fear of the Lord.

The people of the postexilic period retained these perspectives. Haggai applied royalist Zion theology to Zerubbabel. Zechariah 1–8 also went in this direction. However, Rose (2003) argues that there is nothing of Zerubbabel in Haggai 2 and that Zechariah 3 and 6 depended on Jeremiah and did not reveal a messianic fervor at the time. According to Hanson, Second Isaiah followed in the prophetic tradition that saw God, not the king, as in control. Zechariah emphasized the priestly tradition, where it praised Joshua the high priest (Zech. 3:1–9; 6:11). The wisdom tradition is found in the psalms and proverbs that belong to the postexilic period.

Apocalyptic, a new form of literature, appeared in this late period.[20] Although not confined to Judaism, it became popular there. It is distinctive among texts of the Old Testament and elsewhere, insofar as its contents are consistently religious. As a type of literature, apocalyptic cannot be defined by a single set of criteria that always appear.[21] Rather, a collection of characteristics exists of which some may occur in a recognized piece of such writing. Thus the following chracteristics may be found in apocalyptic literature: a seer appeared in visionary dialogue with a heavenly counterpart; the seer remained anonymous and used an Old Testament saint's name (e.g., Enoch, Abraham, Moses, Ezra); human history was viewed negatively as well as humanity's ability to do anything good about it; there was optimism toward God's own intervention at the end of history; God's people struggle with their enemies on earth as part of a greater struggle between God and his enemy; angels and demons were involved, along with dragons, monsters, and other animals; because victory for God and his people was assured, the saints must patiently endure the difficult present. There may also be messianic expectations of both a royal figure in David's line and of a heavenly messiah as suggested in Daniel 7:13–14.[22] The function of apocalypticism was to influence behavior through a divine interpretation of the present world in light of the supernatural world and of the future eschatological salvation.[23]

The origins of this literature lay in a number of possible catalysts: a despair with existing forms caused by the destruction of Jerusalem, the return from exile and the pitiful rebuilding of the Jerusalem temple,

20. See the substantial review in Collins (1998).
21. See the review of the study by Grabbe (2003) and the response of Collins (2003).
22. For Day (2000, 106) this represents the eschatologization of the Baal myth in which the son of man in the clouds of heaven is Baal and the Ancient of Days on which his kingship is dependent is El.
23. See Collins (1979; 1987; 1998).

the end of recognized prophets and prophecy, and later, dissatisfaction with the Hasmonean theocracy.[24] Some argue that Zoroastrianism was the major influence of apocalyptic.[25] Similar features between the two include: the dualism of a struggle between good and evil, the expectation of God's sudden appearance, the resurrection and judgment of all, the destruction of the world by fire, and the final victory of God followed by a new beginning of world history.

However, there are problems with positing Zoroastrian influence as the main force behind apocalyptic. Some items are already found in what is generally believed to be preexilic elements of the Old Testament. These include dualism, God's sudden appearance, the resurrection and judgment, and the final victory of God. Further, the message of apocalyptic texts like Zechariah 9–14 and Daniel was to resist foreign influences and maintain pure Judaism. Thus while forms of expression may be imported, beliefs would have been more difficult to defend if borrowed from Persian sources. There are other sources for a belief in resurrection, especially belief in a national resurrection (Ezek. 37),[26] and the tradition of West Semitic dying and rising deities.[27]

It has been argued that apocalyptic literature has antecedents in prophecy and in wisdom literature. Hanson (1979) represents the view that apocalyptic has its origins in prophecy. This view argues that ancient Israel was faced with a crisis in the postexilic period. This crisis was one in which the Judeans no longer had an autonomous state or the right of self-determination. They felt marginalized and groups within Judaism felt an even greater disenfranchisement. This led to the rejection of traditional forms of self-expression, which they felt were inadequate to cope with the new loss of identity. Prophecy was built on existing promises of God. These promises would be demonstrated as true by God's judgment on sinners and the exaltation and well-being of the righteous. However, with the destruction of the temple it appeared that sinners were well off and that the righteous were persecuted. Therefore new forms of expression were sought. These could be found in postexilic groups that

24. Cf. R. Webb (1990).

25. See, e.g., Nel (2003).

26. Many regard Dan. 12:2 and possibly Isa. 26:19 as postexilic. These texts, especially Daniel, are generally recognized as describing a personal resurrection. See this discussion in chapter 9, p. 265.

27. Johnston (2002, 236) adds the following arguments against Persian influence: Zoroastrian judgment and heaven and hell precede resurrection rather than follow it; Zoroastrian resurrection involves forming bodies from the elements whereas in Israel there is a rising directly from the ground; Zoroastrians exposed their dead for birds to eat while in Israel exposure was a curse and abhorred; sources for Zoroastrian views of the resurrection come from a late ninth-century AD manuscript with mention of the resurrection no earlier than a fourth-century BC manuscript.

rejected the rebuilding of the temple and the existing political powers in Jerusalem in the form of the (Zadokite) priesthood. In place of this, visionary movements foretold of the restoration predicted by earlier prophets, but in a new setting. No longer would it take place in history. Instead, it would lie beyond history.

Philip Davies (1989) critiques this, noting that appeals to secret knowledge and heavenly revelation are more characteristic of groups in power who want to justify their status. Daniel does not appear to be the product of a marginal group within Judaism. Nevertheless, this does not exclude the possibility of apocalyptic arising out of a context of prophetic frustration.

The origins of apocalypticism in wisdom traditions are suggested by Davies (1989) and Collins (1987; 1998; 2003). Daniel is an interpreter of dreams. Enoch ascends and visits heaven. Both interpret visions and mysteries. In Enoch the universe is a set of symbols that interpret events on earth. Themes include judgment after death, resurrection, and a new creation of the earth. In Daniel dreams are reported and presented in a manner known elsewhere in the ancient Near East. Angels function as forces behind the history of events on earth. Hope for salvation becomes an expectation of a resurrection from the dead.

Davies (1989, 264–65) argues that Babylonian mantic methods were used throughout Jewish apocalyptic literature:[28]

> [F]or the Jewish scribe the law revealed by God to Moses took the place of the catalogues of omens which formed the canon of the Babylonian scribe. The comparison is not fanciful: the notion of the scriptures containing hidden truth which inspired study could unlock is not found only in Daniel, Qumran and the New Testament but provides the basic rationale of rabbinic exegesis. . . .
>
> The four apocalypses of Daniel, appended to a cycle of court-tales which extol the virture of the adopted Jewish mantic, draw most of their inspiration either from the tales or from mantic-scribal conventions and interests, such as the "plot" of history in the sequence of world-kingdoms (ch. 7), the hidden meaning of ancient books (ch. 9), the pseudo-predictions of political events (chs. 10–12), and ancient mythical motifs. More dramatically, the influence in Daniel's symbolism of the Babylonian mantic catalogues such as *šumma izbu* series has been demonstrated.

However, cautions are necessary, especially from the standpoint of Davies's claims. Lucas (1989) has undertaken a study of many of the specific comparisons that have been made between Babylonian myths, birth omens (*šumma izbu*), and astrological geography, on the one hand,

---

28. Mantic origins for Zech. 9–14 have also been suggested by Larkin (1994).

and the animal imagery in Daniel, on the other hand. He finds no evidence for direct borrowing from the myths and also finds problems with the astrological geography (the lack of direct correlation without inferences). It is true that bizarre images of animals could have been borrowed from the birth omens and used for their strong impact as ominous symbols. However, Lucas (1990; 2002) suggests the primary source for animal imagery was the Old Testament. Lucas also critiques the view that the "four empires" scheme found in Daniel 2 and 7 originated in Persia and that it was combined with a division of history into ten periods (cf. the ten kings of Dan. 7) first in the Hellenistic Sibylline Oracles. He argues that:

1. Four ages of the world were known at least from the time of Hesiod.
2. The four empires scheme in Daniel reflects historical experience rather than Sibylline Oracles.
3. While in Daniel 7 ten kings belong to the fourth empire, in the Sibylline Oracle 4 and Persian sources there are ten periods between the four empires.
4. The division of history into ten periods has precedents in Hebrew as well as Mesopotamian sources.

For Collins (1979), Jewish apocalyptic is not just a result of prophecy or of Babylonian influence. Jewish apocalypticism is a new creation to meet the needs of a new age. This seems possible. However, the reality of prophetic influence remains very likely within the tradition of Israelite religion as reflected in its history and in the biblical texts.

12

Conclusions

We began this study proposing to examine the constituent elements of ancient Israelite religion, understanding religion to be the service and worship of the divine or supernatural through a system of attitudes, beliefs, and practices. We sought to understand this in the light of what ancient Israelites actually believed and did, rather than what they were ideally expected to believe and do. The latter was recognized as the focus of theology rather than of Israelite religion. Ancient Israel itself we take to be those people who identified themselves as Israelites and lived between c. 1200 and 586 BC. The anthropological and sociological history of the study of religion demonstrated its diverse and unpredictable features in the many cultures of human society. The failure to identify universal rules or principles meant that each culture required examination on its own merits and according to its own understanding of religion, however difficult that might be.

Earlier critical biblical scholarship on the subject of Israelite religion certainly assisted in identifying strands of tradition and emphases of different sorts, especially in the Pentateuch. This was studied in more detail in chapters 6 and 7. Nevertheless, critical reflection on this research had raised important questions about the certainty of its results, in areas such as dating and in the delineation of specific and absolute divisions between the sources and traditions. This was further aggravated by archaeological discoveries that demonstrated difficulties with assumptions about evolutionary development of religion from simple to complex and the corollary views regarding originally distinct and simpler elements of text and practice that must have preceded the religious records of the biblical traditions themselves.

Recent scholarship in ancient Israelite religion attests to the failure of a single synthetic model and to the ongoing need for humility when approaching much of the data. We simply do not know enough about the ancient culture and the beliefs and practices to assert certainty in our analysis of the material. We remain dependent on heuristic models with their potential to become anachronistic and to demonstrate how much we are prisoners of our own age and its philosophical zeitgeist as those of an older generation. Nevertheless, the overwhelming sense of complexity and diversity attested by both the inner- and extrabiblical evidence compels a recognition of multiple, diverse, and at times contradictory expressions of religious belief and practice within ancient Israel.

Our examination of the pre-Israelite evidence for West Semitic religion in chapters 4 and 5 led to an awareness of the many traditions that anticipate Israel in terms of what it knows of religious expression. Of course, this includes the names and mythic activities of many foreign deities as well as the presence of institutions such as temples, altars, sacrifices, images, prayers, covenants, feasts, and other rituals. However, it also describes the reality of gods at Ugarit, such as El and Baal, who share many of the same characteristics that the Bible associates with Yahweh. Further, even priestly installation rituals and cultic calendars from Emar provide background and surprising parallels to the corresponding biblical texts. Further study of the Late Bronze Age sites in and around the Jordan River suggests the influence of Egypt as well as syncretism with indigenous forms of religious expression. The iconography also shows this as it moves away from the more explicit sexuality of the Middle Bronze Age and toward an emphasis on warfare and its practitioners. The age was one that appreciated the gods of the politically powerful.

The clearly attested polytheism of the Middle and Late Bronze Ages in Palestinian and Syrian archaeology and texts may leave traces in the multiple references to deities in the personal names in the genealogies of Genesis 1–11. The remainder of the Genesis traditions witness to no struggle with other deities. By itself, this may suggest the absence of a conscious issue in Israel's earliest traditions. From Exodus onward, the presence of a single deity for Israel, whose name and people emerge from the southern desert, becomes the unique feature of Israelite religion, however much it may have borrowed from the forms of surrounding cultures. The institutions of priesthood, sanctuary, and covenant all transform existing archaeological and (extrabiblical) textual media to define Israel's relationship with Yahweh as sole (monolatrous, though not necessarily monotheistic), aniconic in representation, and lived out or actualized in a manner that rejected earlier West Semitic deities and yet embraced their cultic objects and actions, whether *maṣṣēbôt* and tent sanctuaries or treaties and blood sacrifices.

In Iron Age I the polytheism of the earlier periods continues with no mention of Yahweh in the extrabiblical texts. The archaeology at first attests to a largely egalitarian culture for twelfth-century BC Israel. It is not governed by a king and the culture and religion are simple insofar as there is little in the way of images and the other materials appear to be cheaper and more basic. The Bible, in Judges and Samuel, attests for an ongoing struggle between Yahweh and the other deities of Bronze Age Canaan. With the appearance of Iron Age II, however, the extrabiblical texts and archaeology and the biblical evidence begin to intersect more frequently than before.

The period from c. 931 BC until 586 BC represents a crucial time for the study and understanding of ancient Israelite religion. Not only is there greater scholarly agreement concerning historical value (greater or lesser, depending on whom one consults) of the biblical literature purporting to describe this time, but there is also available much greater material remains in the archaeological record. Even from the epigraphic finds there is material that is explicitly Israelite and religious. The result is a vast array of data that needs to be surveyed and that is subject to a variety of scholarly interpretations. Nevertheless, a number of common threads emerge.

First, it is clear that ancient Israel was home to a variety of religious beliefs and practices that developed from earlier West Semitic beliefs and practices attested in Bronze Age archives and cult centers. The biblical sources clearly attest to this, using the names of deities known from the earlier periods and many practices that in one way or another connect with earlier archives, with Phoenician and classical sources, and with contemporary epigraphic materials. Among other ways, this inheritance is visible in the traditions of providing food and drink at burials; of the Jerusalem temple architecture; of the use of various figurines, altars and sacrificial system, *maṣṣēbôt*, and incense burners; of the "mating" of the chief male deity with a female consort; of the references to human sacrifice and chthonic rituals; and of the use of priests, prophets, and royalty in religious performances.

Second, there is a sense in which the religion of ancient Israel emerges as a distinctive set of practices and beliefs.[1] Above all there is the exodus tradition of Israel's redemption as slaves from Egypt by its god, and of Yahweh and his unique covenant with them, given in the form of

1. See the definition of religion at the beginning of chapter 1.

a treaty. This is recalled again and again in every major section of the Bible. Yahweh's own revelation of his distinctive name and his origins to the south in the mountains also has no known precedent. The growing emphasis on Yahweh as the sole deity and his intolerance of other gods and goddesses, as well as their cults, is unique. It is not only attested in the Bible but also in the personal names and the overwhelming dominance of Yahweh as a theophoric element. It is found in the texts of the Ketef Hinnom silver strips, the Miqneyahu seal, and the blessings in the attested correspondence found at Lachish and Arad. It is found in the identity of Israel as defined by its enemy in the Moabite stele of King Mesha. Archaeologically, the uniquely aniconic nature of Yahweh cannot be expected to yield much. Yet it may be there in the "gap" on the Taanach cult stand, in the absence of images (first anthropomorphic and later even in the form of designs) on the seals, and in the nature and construction of the sanctuary in the Israelite fortress at Arad. This is true at Arad even if the two *maṣṣēbôt* and incense altars attested to two deities there at one point. They were not apparently in use throughout the monarchy.

A third point is the gradual evolution and change in ancient Israel. Although the texts and archaeology indicate a diversity of religious practice present from the beginning until the end of the period, there are clear signs that as the centuries progressed this people became increasingly devoted to Yahweh alone and to his religion as attested in the biblical texts. However the Judean female figurines are to be understood, these images attest to a different spirit regarding such forms in contrast to earlier and contemporary neighbors. They are modest, without reference to the genitalia. They are available to all, rather than limited to those few who could afford silver, gold, or even bronze forms. They also define Judah, being virtually absent outside the state in the seventh and sixth centuries BC. The near complete absence of male or other human representation and the almost 100 percent usage of Yahweh as the sole theophoric element in the personal names of this period all bear witness to the acceptance of a single deity. This is true however much the kings of Judah and Judeans themselves turned at times to devotion to other deities. The picture is different in the evidence from the northern kingdom of Samaria in the earlier centuries. There the personal names on the Samaria ostraca as well as the diverse architecture of the various cult sites (especially at Dan but also elsewhere) attest to the much greater continuity of religious practice with what preceded it and what could be found at the same time in the neighboring Phoenician states.

Points of similarity, difference, and change are common to all living religions. The significance for ancient Israel remains with those distinctions that grew and developed and that affected not only the subsequent period of this people but also all generations since then. This religion should be seen as more than a singular collection of beliefs and practices arising out of a peculiar concatenation of political and economic factors. It rather held within itself the schema of a faith that could avoid that which was tied only to the temporal, could adopt and transform that which had value from other religions, and could identify and nurture those distinctives that set it apart and enabled it to foster the great monotheistic religions of the Western world and beyond.

Reference List

Aaron, David H. 2006. *Etched in Stone: The Emergence of the Decalogue*. New York: T&T Clark.

Abela, Anthony. 1987. The Genesis Genesis. *Melita Theologica* 39:155–85.

Ackerman, Susan. 1989. "And the Women Knead Dough": The Worship of the Queen of Heaven in Sixth-Century Judah. Pages 109–25 in *Gender and Difference in Ancient Israel*. Edited by P. Day. Minneapolis: Fortress.

———. 1992. *Under Every Green Tree: Popular Religion in Sixth-Century Judah*. Harvard Semitic Monographs 46. Atlanta: Scholars Press.

———. 1993. The Queen Mother and the Cult in Ancient Israel. *Journal of Biblical Literature* 112:385–401.

———. 2002. The Personal Is Political: Covenantal and Affectionate Love (*'āhēb, 'ahăbâ*) in the Hebrew Bible. *Vetus Testamentum* 52:437–58.

Ackroyd, P. R. 1970. *Israel under Babylon and Persia*. London: Oxford University Press.

Aharoni, Yohanan. 1993. Megiddo. *The New Encyclopedia of Archaeological Excavations in the Holy Land*. New York: Simon & Schuster.

Aḥituv, Shmuel. 1984. *Canaanite Toponyms in Ancient Egyptian Documents*. Jerusalem: Magnes.

———. 1996. The Egyptian-Canaanite Border Administration. *Israel Exploration Journal* 46:219–24.

Ahlström, G. W. 1993. *The History of Ancient Palestine from the Palaeolithic Period to Alexander's Conquest*. Journal for the Study of the Old Testament: Supplement Series 146. Sheffield: JSOT Press.

Albani, Matthias. 2004. The Downfall of Helel, the Son of Dawn. Aspects of Royal Ideology in Isa 14:12–13. Pages 62–86 in *The Fall of the Angels*. Edited by C. Auffarth and L. T. Stuckenbruck. Leiden and Boston: Brill.

Albertz, Rainer. 1978. *Persönliche Frömmigkeit und Offizielle Religion: Religionsinterner Pluralismus in Israel und Babylon*. Stuttgart: Calwer Verlag.

———. 1992. *Religionsgeschichte Israels in alttestamentlicher Zeit*. 2 vols. Grundrisse zum Alten Testament 8/1–2. Göttingen: Vandenhoeck & Ruprecht.

————. 1994. *A History of Israelite Religion in the Old Testament Period.* 2 vols. Translated by J. Bowden. Louisville: Westminster/John Knox.

Albertz, Rainer, and Bob Becking, eds. 2003. *Yahwism after the Exile: Perspectives on Israelite Religion in the Persian Era: Papers Read at the First Meeting of the European Association for Biblical Studies, Utrecht, 6–9 August 2000.* Assen: Van Gorcum.

Albright, William F. 1949. *The Archaeology of Palestine.* Harmondsworth: Penguin.

————. 1953. *Archaeology and the Religion of Israel: The Ayer Lectures of the Colgate-Rochester Divinity School.* Baltimore: Johns Hopkins University Press.

————. 1957. *From the Stone Age to Christianity: Monotheism and the Historical Process.* Garden City, NY: Doubleday.

————. 1968. *Yahweh and the Gods of Canaan: A Historical Analysis of Two Contrasting Faiths.* Garden City, NY: Doubleday.

Alexander, T. Desmond. 1995. The Passover Sacrifice. Pages 1–24 in *Sacrifice in the Bible.* Edited by R. T. Beckwith and M. J. Selman. Carlisle: Paternoster.

Alpert-Nakhai, Beth. 1994. What's a Bamah? How Sacred Space Functioned in Ancient Israel. *Biblical Archaeology Review* 20(3):18–29, 77–78.

————. 2001. *Archaeology and the Religions of Canaan and Israel.* Boston: American Schools of Oriental Research.

Alt, Albrecht. 1935. Die Rolle Samarias bei der Entstehung des Judentums. Pages 5–28 in *Festschrift Otto Proksch zum 60. Geburtstag.* Leipzig: A. Deichert and J. C. Hinrichs; repr. pages 316–37 in vol. 2 of A. Alt, *Kleine Schriften zur Geschichte des Volkes Israel.* Munich: C. H. Beck, 1953.

————. 1989. The God of the Fathers. Pages 1–77 in *Essays on Old Testament History and Religion.* Translated by R. A. Wilson. Sheffield: Sheffield Academic Press.

Alter, Robert. 1981. *The Art of Biblical Narrative.* London: Methuen.

————. 1985. *The Idea of Biblical Poetry.* New York: Basic Books.

Anbar, Moshé. 1998. Deux cérémonies d'alliance dans Ex 24 à la lumière des Archives royales de Mari. *Ugarit-Forschungen* 30:1–4.

Anbar, M., and N. Na'aman. 1986–87. An Account Tablet of Sheep from Ancient Hebron. *Tel Aviv* 13–14:3–12.

Andersen, Francis I., and A. Dean Forbes. 1986. *Spelling in the Hebrew Bible.* Rome: Pontifical Biblical Institute.

Anderson, R. T. 1991. The Elusive Samaritan Temple. *Biblical Archaeologist* 54(2):104–107.

Angerstorfer, A. 1982. Ašerah als 'consort of Jahwe' oder Aširtah? *Biblische Notizen* 17:7–16.

Anonymous. 1992. The Pomegranate Scepter Head—From the Temple of the Lord or from a Temple of Asherah? *Biblical Archaeology Review,* May/June, 42–45.

Archer, Gleason L., Jr. 1964. *A Survey of Old Testament Introduction.* Chicago: Moody.

Arnaud, Daniel. 1985a. *Recherches au pays d'Aštata. Emar VI.1. Textes sumériens et accadiens, planches.* Paris: Éditions Recherches sur les Civilisations.

————. 1985b. *Recherches au pays d'Aštata. Emar VI.2. Textes sumériens et accadiens, planches.* Paris: Éditions Recherches sur les Civilisations.

————. 1986. *Recherches au pays d'Aštata. Emar VI.3. Textes sumériens et accadiens, texte.* Paris: Éditions Recherches sur les Civilisations.

—. 1987. *Recherches au pays d'Aštata. Emar VI.4. Textes sumériens et accadiens, textes de la bibliothèque: transcriptions et traductions.* Paris: Éditions Recherches sur les Civilisations.

—. 1991. *Textes syriens de l'âge du Bronze récent.* Aula Orientalis Supplement 1. Barcelona: Editorial AUSA.

—. 2001. Seconde partie: une bibliothèque au sud de la ville. Textes de la «Maison d'Ourtenou» trouvés en 1986, 1988 et 1992. Pages 235–422 in *Études Ougaritiques I. Travaux 1985–1995.* Ras Shamra–Ougarit XIV. Edited by M. Yon and D. Arnaud. Paris: Éditions Recherches sur les Civilisations.

Arnold, Bill T. 1999. Religion in Ancient Israel. Pages 391–420 in *The Face of Old Testament Studies: A Survey of Contemporary Approaches.* Edited by D. W. Baker and B. T. Arnold. Grand Rapids: Baker Academic.

—. 2004. Necromancy and Cleromancy in 1 and 2 Samuel. *Catholic Biblical Quarterly* 66:199–213.

Artzy, Michal. 1991. Nami Land and Sea Project, 1989. *Israel Exploration Journal* 41:194–97.

Asen, Bernhard A. 1996. The Garlands of Ephraim: Isaiah 28: 1–6 and the *marzēaḥ. Journal for the Study of the Old Testament* 71:73–87.

Astour, Michael C. 1979. Yahweh in Egyptian Topographical Lists. Pages 17–34 in *Festschrift für E. Edel.* Ägypten und Altes Testament 1. Edited by M. Görg and E. Push. Bamberg.

Astruc, Jean. 1753. *Conjectures sur les mémoires originaux: dont il paroit Moyse s'est servi pour composer le livre de la Genese: avec remarques qui appuient ou qui éclaircissent ces conjectures.* Brussels: Chez Fricx.

Attridge, H. W., and R. A. Oden Jr. 1981. *Philo of Byblos: The Phoenician History.* CBQ Monograph Series 9. Washington: Catholic Biblical Association.

Aufrecht, Walter. 1989. *A Corpus of Ammonite Inscriptions.* Lewiston, NY: Edwin Mellen.

—. 1999. The Religion of Ammonites. Pages 152–62 in *Ancient Ammon.* Edited by B. MacDonald and R. W. Younkers. Leiden: Brill.

Avigad, Nahman. 1976. *Bullae and Seals from a Post-Exilic Judean Archive.* Qedem 4. Jerusalem: Institute of Archaeology, Hebrew University.

—. 1986. *Hebrew Bullae from the Time of Jeremiah: Remnants of a Burnt Archive.* Jerusalem: Israel Exploration Society.

—. 1990. Two Hebrew "Fiscal Bullae." *Israel Exploration Journal* 40:262–66.

Avigad, Nahman, and Benjamin Sass. 1997. *Corpus of West Semitic Stamp Seals.* Jerusalem: Israel Exploration Society.

Avner, Uzi. 1984. Ancient Cult Sites in the Negev and Sinai Deserts. *Tel Aviv* 11:115–31.

—. 1990. Ancient Agricultural Settlement and Religion in the Uvda Valley in Southern Israel. *Biblical Archaeologist* 53(3):125–41.

—. 1993. *Mazzebot* Sites in the Negev and Sinai and Their Significance. Pages 166–81 in *Biblical Archaeology Today, 1990. Proceedings of the Second International Congress on Biblical Archaeology. Jerusalem, June–July 1990.* Edited by A. Biran and J. Aviram. Jerusalem: Israel Exploration Society.

—. 2001. Sacred Stones in the Desert. *Biblical Archaeology Review*, May/June, 30–41.

Axelsson, L. E. 1987. *The Lord Rose Up from Seir: Studies in the History and Traditions of the Negev and Southern Judah*. Coniectanea Biblica Old Testament Series 25. Lund: Almqvist & Wiksell.

Barkay, Gabriel. 1986. *Ketef Hinnom. A Treasure Facing Jerusalem's Walls*. Jerusalem: Israel Museum.

———. 1990. A Late Bronze Age Egyptian Temple in Jerusalem? *Eretz-Israel* 21:94–106 [Hebrew with English summary, p. 104].

———. 1992. The Priestly Benediction on Silver Plaques from Ketef Hinnom in Jerusalem. *Tel Aviv* 19:139–92.

———. 1993. The Redefining of Archaeological Periods: Does the Date 588/586 B.C.E. Indeed Mark the End of Iron Age Culture? Pages 106–9 in *Biblical Archaeology Today, 1990. Proceedings of the Second International Congress on Biblical Archaeology. Jerusalem, June–July 1990*. Edited by A. Biran and J. Aviram. Jerusalem: Israel Exploration Society.

———. 1994. Tombs and Entombment in Judah during the Biblical Period. Pages 96–164 in *Qbrym wmnhgy qbwrh b'rṣ yśr'l*. Edited by I. Singer. Jerusalem: Yad Yitzhaq Ben Tsvi.

———. 1996. A Late Bronze Age Egyptian Temple in Jerusalem? *Israel Exploration Journal* 46:23–43.

———. 2000. What's an Egyptian Temple Doing in Jerusalem? *Biblical Archaeology Review*, May/June, 48–57, 67.

———. 2003. Mounds of Mystery: Where the Kings of Judah Were Lamented. *Biblical Archaeology Review*, May/June, 32–39, 66, 68.

Barkay, Gabriel, Marilyn J. Lundberg, Andrew G. Vaughn, and Bruce Zuckerman. 2003. The Challenges of Ketef Hinnom: Using Advanced Technologies to Reclaim the Earliest Biblical Texts and Their Context. *Near Eastern Archaeology* 66(4):162–71.

———. 2004. The Amulets from Ketef Hinnom: A New Edition and Evaluation. *Bulletin of the American Schools of Oriental Research* 334:41–71.

Barnett, R. D. 1982. *Ancient Ivories in the Middle East*. Jerusalem: Institute of Archaeology.

Barr, James. 1988. Review of F. I. Andersen and A. D. Forbes, *Spelling in the Hebrew Bible*. *Journal of Semitic Studies* 33:122–31.

———. 2000. *History and Ideology of the Old Testament: Biblical Studies at the End of a Millennium*. Oxford: Oxford University Press.

Barrick, W. Boyd. 1991. The Bamoth of Moab. *Maarav* 7:67–89.

———. 1996. On the Meaning of בֵּית־הַבָּמוֹת and בָּתֵּי־הַ/בָּמוֹת and the Composition of the Kings History. *Journal of Biblical Literature* 115:621–42.

Barstad, Hans M. 1993. No Prophets? Recent Developments in Biblical Prophetic Research and Ancient Near Eastern Prophecy. *Journal for the Study of the Old Testament* 57:39–60.

———. 1994. The Future of the "Servant Songs": Some Reflections on the Relationship of Biblical Scholarship to Its Own Tradition. Pages 261–70 in *Language, Theology and the Bible: Essays in Honour of James Barr*. Edited by S. E. Balentine and J. Barton. Oxford: Clarendon.

———. 1996. *The Myth of the Empty Land: A Study in the History and Archaeology of Judah during the "Exilic" Period*. Symbolae Osloenses Fasciculus Suppletorius 28. Oslo: Scandinavian University Press.

———. 1997. History and the Hebrew Bible. Pages 37–64 in *Can a "History of Israel" Be Written?* Edited by L. L. Grabbe. Journal for the Study of the Old Testament: Supplement Series 245. Sheffield: Sheffield Academic Press.

———. 2003. After the "Myth of the Empty Land": Major Challenges in the Study of Neo-Babylonian Judah. Pages 3–20 in *Judah and the Judeans in the Neo-Babylonian Period*. Edited by O. Lipschits and J. Blenkinsopp. Winona Lake, IN: Eisenbrauns.

Bartlett, J. 1989. *Edom and the Edomites*. Journal for the Study of the Old Testament: Supplement Series 77. Sheffield: Sheffield Academic Press.

Barton, John. 2000. Intertextuality and the "Final Form" of the Text. Pages 33–37 in *International Organization for the Study of the Old Testament. Congress Volume: Oslo, 1998*. Edited by A. Lemaire and M. Saebo. Vetus Testamentum Supplement 80. Leiden: Brill.

———. 2005. The Prophets and the Cult. Pages 111–22 in *Temple and Worship in Biblical Israel*. Edited by J. Day. Library of Hebrew Bible/Old Testament Studies 422. London: T&T Clark.

Baudissin, W. Graf. 1911. *Adonis und Esmun: Eine Untersuchung zur Geschichte des Glaubens an Auferstehungegötter und an Heilgötter*. Leipzig: Hinrichs.

Beck, P. 1982. The Drawings from Ḥorvat Teiman (Kuntillet ʿAjrud). *Tel Aviv* 9:3–68.

Beek, G. van. 1962. Abel. *The Interpreter's Dictionary of the Bible*. New York: Abingdon.

Beit-Arieh, I. 1984. Fifteen Years in Sinai. Israeli Archaeologists Discover a New World. *Biblical Archaeology Review* 10(4):26–54.

Ben-Tor, Amnon. 1992. The Hazor Tablet: Foreword. *Israel Exploration Journal* 42:17–20.

———. 1993a. Hazor. *The New Encyclopedia of Archaeological Excavations in the Holy Land*. New York: Simon & Schuster.

———. 1993b. Tel Qiri. *The New Encyclopedia of Archaeological Excavations in the Holy Land*. New York: Simon & Schuster.

———. 1997. Hazor. *The Oxford Encyclopedia of Archaeology in the Near East*. New York: Oxford University Press.

Benz, Frank L. 1972. *Personal Names in the Phoenician and Punic Inscriptions*. Studia Pohl 8. Rome: Bible Institute Press.

Berge, Kåre. 1990. *Die Zeit des Jahwisten: Ein Beitrag zur Datierung jahwistischer Vätertexte*. Beihefte zur Zeitschrift für die alttestamentliche Wissenschaft 186. Berlin: de Gruyter.

Bergsma, John S., and Scott W. Hahn. 2005. Noah's Nakedness and the Curse on Canaan (Genesis 9:20–27). *Journal of Biblical Literature* 124:25–40.

Berlinerblau, J. 1993. The "Popular Religion" Paradigm in Old Testament Research: A Sociological Critique. *Journal for the Study of the Old Testament* 60:3–26.

Bernhardt, K. 1967. Aschera in Ugarit und im Alten Testament. *Mitteilungen des Instituts Orientforschung* 13:163–74.

Beyer, D. 1980. Notes préliminaires sur les empreintes de sceaux de Meskéné. Pages 265–83 in *Le Moyen Euphrate: Zone de contacts et d'échanges*. Edited by J.-Cl. Margueron. Strasbourg: Université des Sciences Humaines de Strasbourg.

———, ed. 1982. *Meskéné-Emar: Dix ans de travaux, 1972–1982*. Paris: Éditions Recherches sur les Civilisations.

Biddle, M. E. 1990. The "Endangered Ancestress" and Blessing for the Nations. *Journal of Biblical Literature* 109:599–611.

Bietak, Manfred. 1996. *Avaris: Capital of the Hyksos*. London: British Museum.

Bilensi, Jacqueline. 1985. Revising Tell Abu Hawam. *Bulletin of the American Schools of Oriental Research* 257:65–74.

Binger, Tilde. 1995. Asherah in Israel. *Scandinavian Journal of the Old Testament* 9:3–18.

———. 1997. *Asherah: Goddesses in Ugarit, Israel and the Old Testament*. Journal for the Study of the Old Testament: Supplement Series 232. Sheffield: JSOT Press.

Biran, Avraham. 1993. Dan. *The New Encyclopedia of Archaeological Excavations in the Holy Land*. New York: Simon and Schuster.

———. 1994. *Biblical Dan*. Jerusalem: Israel Exploration Society and Hebrew Union College/Jewish Institute of Religion.

Biran, Avraham, and Joseph Naveh. 1993. An Aramaic Stele Fragment from Tel Dan. *Israel Exploration Journal* 43:81–98.

———. 1995. The Tel Dan Inscription: A New Fragment. *Israel Exploration Journal* 45:1–18.

Bird, Phyllis A. 1981. Male and Female He Created Them: Gen. 1:27b in the Context of the Priestly Account of Creation. *Harvard Theological Review* 74:129–59.

———. 1997a. *Missing Persons and Mistaken Identities: Women and Gender in Ancient Israel*. Minneapolis: Fortress.

———. 1997b. The End of the Male Cult Prostitute: A Literary-Historical and Sociological Analysis of Hebrew *Qādēš-Qedēšîm*. Pages 37–80 in *Congress Volume. Cambridge 1995*. Edited by J. A. Emerton. Supplements to Vetus Testamentum Volume 66. Leiden: Brill.

Bledstein, A. J. 1993. Was Eve Cursed? (or Did a Woman Write Genesis?) *Bible Review* 9(1):42–45.

Blenkinsopp, Joseph. 1991. Temple and Society in Achaemenid Judah. Pages 22–53 in *Second Temple Studies: 1. Persian Period*. Edited by P. R. Davies. Journal for the Study of the Old Testament: Supplement Series 117. Sheffield: Sheffield Academic Press.

———. 1992. *The Pentateuch: An Introduction to the First Five Books of the Bible*. The Anchor Bible Reference Library. New York: Doubleday.

———. 1994. The Nehemiah Autobiographical Memoir. Pages 199–212 in *Language, Theology and the Bible. Essays in Honour of James Barr*. Edited by S. E. Balentine and J. Barton. Oxford: Clarendon.

———. 1995a. An Assessment of the Alleged Pre-Exilic Date of the Priestly Material in the Pentateuch. *Zeitschrift für die alttestamentliche Wissenschaft* 108:495–518.

———. 1995b. *Sage, Priest, Prophet: Religious and Intellectual Leadership in Ancient Israel*. Louisville: Westminster John Knox.

———. 2002. The Babylonian Gap Revisited: There Was No Gap. *Biblical Archaeology Review* 28(3):37–38, 59.

———. 2003. Bethel in the Neo-Babylonian Period. Pages 93–107 in *Judah and the Judeans in the Neo-Babylonian Period*. Edited by O. Lipschits and J. Blenkinsopp. Winona Lake, IN: Eisenbrauns.

Bloch-Smith, Elizabeth. 1991. Review of T. J. Lewis, *Cults of the Dead in Ancient Israel and Ugarit*. *Journal of Biblical Literature* 110:327–30.

———. 1992a. The Cult of the Dead in Judah: Interpreting the Material Remains. *Journal of Biblical Literature* 111:213–24.

———. 1992b. *Judahite Burial Practices and Beliefs about the Dead*. Journal for the Study of the Old Testament: Supplement Series 123. JSOT/ASOR Monograph Series 7. Sheffield: JSOT Press.

———. 2002. Life in Judah from the Perspective of the Dead. *Near Eastern Archaeology* 65(2):120–30.

———. 2003. Israelite Ethnicity in Iron I: Archaeology Preserves What Is Remembered and What Is Forgotten in Israel's History. *Journal of Biblical Literature* 122:401–25.

———. 2005. *Maṣṣēbôt* in the Israelite Cult: An Argument for Rendering Implicit Cultic Criteria Explicit. Pages 28–39 in *Temple and Worship in Biblical Israel*. Edited by J. Day. Library of Hebrew Bible/Old Testament Studies 422. London: T&T Clark.

Bloch-Smith, Elizabeth, and Beth Alpert-Nakhai. 1999. A Landscape Comes to Life: The Iron Age I. *Near Eastern Archaeology* 62:62–92, 101–27.

Block, Daniel Isaac. 1979. *The Gods of the Nations: Studies in Ancient Near Eastern National Theology*. Evangelical Theological Society Monograph Series 2. Jackson, MS: Evangelical Theological Society.

———. 1997. *The Book of Ezekiel. Chapters 1–24*. New International Commentary on the Old Testament. Grand Rapids: Eerdmans.

———. 1998. *The Book of Ezekiel. Chapters 25–48*. New International Commentary on the Old Testament. Grand Rapids: Eerdmans.

———. 2004. How Many Is God? An Investigation into the Meaning of Deuteronomy 6:4–5. *Journal of the Evangelical Theological Society* 47:193–212.

Bloom, H. 1990. *The Book of J*. Translated by D. Rosenberg. London: Faber.

Blum, Erhard. 1984. *Die Komposition der Vätergeschichte*. Wissenschaftliche Monographien zum Alten und Neuen Testament 57. Neukirchener: Neukirchen-Vluyn.

———. 1990. *Studien zur Komposition des Pentateuch*. Beihefte zur Zeitschrift für die alttestamentliche Wissenschaft 189. New York: de Gruyter.

Bordreuil, Pierre, and Dennis Pardee. 1990. Le papyrus du marzeaḥ. *Semitica* 38:49–68.

Borger, R. 1959. Gen. iv 1. *Vetus Testamentum* 9:85–86.

Borowski, E. 1995. Cherubim: God's Throne? *Biblical Archaeology Review* 21(4):36–41.

Borowski, O. 1989. The Negev—The Southern Stage for Biblical History. *Bible Review* 5(3):40–44.

Bourke, Stephen J. 1997. Pre-Classical Pella in Jordan: A Conspectus of Ten Years' Work (1985–1995). *Palestine Exploration Quarterly* 129:94–115.

Bretschneider, J. 1991. *Architekturmodelle in Vorderasien und der östlichen Ägäis von Neolithikum bis in das 1. Jahrtausend*. Alter Orient und Altes Testament 229. Kevelaer: Butzon & Bercker.

Brett, Mark G. 1996. *Ethnicity and the Bible*. Biblical Interpretation Series 19. Leiden: Brill.

Briant, Pierre. 2002. *From Cyrus to Alexander: A History of the Persian Empire*. Translated by Peter T. Daniels. Winona Lake, IN: Eisenbrauns.

Bright, John. 1981. *A History of Israel*. 3rd ed. Philadelphia: Westminster.

Brody, Aaron Jed. 1998. *Each Man Cried Out to His God: The Specialized Religion of Canaanite and Phoenician Seafarers*. Harvard Semitic Museum Monographs 58. Atlanta: Scholars Press.

Brooks, Simcha Shalom. 2005. From Gibeon to Gibeah: High Places of the Kingdom. Pages 40–59 in *Temple and Worship in Biblical Israel*. Edited by J. Day. Library of Hebrew Bible/Old Testament Studies 422. London: T&T Clark.

Brown, Shelby. 1991. *Late Carthaginian Child Sacrifice and Sacrificial Monuments in Their Mediterranean Context*. JSOT/ASOR Monograph Series 3. Sheffield: JSOT Press.

Browne, Stanley G. 1986. Leprosy in the Bible. Pages 101–25 in *Medicine and the Bible*. Edited by B. Palmer. Exeter: Paternoster.

Brueggemann, Walter. 1986. *Revelation and Violence: A Study in Contextualization*. The 1986 Père Marquette Theology Lecture. Milwaukee: Marquette University Press.

Budd, Philip J. 1989. Holiness and Cult. Pages 275–98 in *The World of Ancient Israel: Sociological, Anthropological, and Political Perspectives*. Edited by R. E. Clements. Cambridge: Cambridge University Press.

Burnett, Joel S. 2001. *A Reassessment of Biblical Elohim*. SBL Dissertation Series Number 183. Atlanta: Society of Biblical Literature.

Byrne, Ryan. 2004. Lie Back and Think of Judah: The Reproductive Politics of Pillar Figurines. *Near Eastern Archaeology* 67:137–51.

Cahill, Jane M. 2003. Jerusalem at the Time of the United Monarchy: The Archaeological Evidence. Pages 13–80 in *Jerusalem in Bible and Archaeology: The First Temple Period*. SBL Symposium Series. Atlanta: SBL Press.

————. 2004. Jerusalem in David and Solomon's Time. *Biblical Archaeology Review* 30(6):20–31, 62–63.

Cahill, Jane M., and David Tarler. 1993. Tell el-Ḥammah. *The New Encyclopedia of Archaeological Excavations in the Holy Land*. New York: Simon & Schuster.

Callaway, James A. 1993. Khirbet Raddana. *The New Encyclopedia of Archaeological Excavations in the Holy Land*. New York: Simon & Schuster.

Callaway, Joseph A. 1993. Ai. *The New Encyclopedia of Archaeological Excavations in the Holy Land*. New York: Simon & Schuster.

————. 1999. The Name Game: Onomastic Evidence and Archaeological Reflections in Late Judah. *Jian Dao* 2:15–36.

Callaway, Joseph A., and J. Maxwell Miller. 1999. The Settlement in Canaan: The Period of the Judges. Pages 55–89 in *Ancient Israel: From Abraham to the Roman Destruction of the Temple*. Rev. ed. Edited by H. Shanks. Washington, DC: Biblical Archaeology Society.

Campbell, Edward. 1993. Shechem. *The New Encyclopedia of Archaeological Excavations in the Holy Land*. New York: Simon & Schuster.

Carmichael, Calum M. 1995. Forbidden Mixtures in Deuteronomy xxii 9–11 and Leviticus xix 19. *Vetus Testamentum* 45:432–48.

Carr, David M. 1996. *Reading the Fractures of Genesis: Historical and Literary Approaches*. Louisville: Westminster John Knox.

————. 2005. *Writing on the Tablet of the Heart: Origins of Scripture and Literature*. Oxford: Oxford University Press.

Carroll R., M. Daniel. 1992. *Contexts for Amos: Prophetic Poetics in Latin American Perspective*. Journal for the Study of the Old Testament: Supplement Series 132. Sheffield: Sheffield Academic Press.

Carter, Charles E. 1996. A Discipline in Transformation: The Contributions of the Social Sciences to the Study of the Hebrew Bible. Pages 3–36 in *Community, Identity, and Ideology: Social Science Approaches to the Hebrew Bible*. Sources for Biblical and Theological Study 6. Edited by C. E. Carter and C. L. Meyers. Winona Lake, IN: Eisenbrauns.

Cassuto, U. 1961a. *A Commentary on the Book of Genesis. Part I: From Adam to Noah*. Translated by I. Abrahams. Jerusalem: Magnes.

————. 1961b. *The Documentary Hypothesis and the Composition of the Pentateuch: Eight Lectures*. Translated by I. Abrahams. Jerusalem: Magnes.

Castellino, G. R. 1960. Genesis IV 7. *Vetus Testamentum* 10:442–45.

Catastini, A. 1982. Le inscrizioni di Kuntillet ʿAjrud e il profetismo. *Annali dell'Istituto Orientale di Napoli* n.s. 42:127–34.

Causse, Antonin. 1996. From an Ethnic Group to a Religious Community: The Sociological Problem of Judaism. Pages 95–118 in *Community, Identity, and Ideology: Social Science Approaches to the Hebrew Bible*. Sources for Biblical and Theological Study 6. Edited by C. E. Carter and C. L. Meyers. Translated and condensed by D. W. Baker. Winona Lake, IN: Eisenbrauns. Originally published as Du groupe ethnique à la communauté religieuse: Le problème sociologique du judaïsme. *Revue d'histoire et de philosophie religieuses* 14 (1934): 285–335.

Cavanagh, R. R. 1978. The Term "Religion." Pages 1–19 in *Introduction to the Study of Religion*. Edited by T. W. Hall. San Francisco: Harper & Row.

Childs, Brevard S. 1974. *Exodus*. London: SCM.

———. 1986. *Old Testament Theology in a Canonical Context*. Philadelphia: Fortress.

Clifford, R. J. 1990. Phoenician Religion. *Bulletin of the American Schools of Oriental Research* 279:55–64.

Clines, David J. A. 1978. *The Theme of the Pentateuch*. Journal for the Study of the Old Testament: Supplement Series 10. Sheffield: JSOT Press.

Cohen, Chaim. 1993. The Biblical Priestly Blessing (Num. 6:24–26) in the Light of Akkadian Parallels. *Tel Aviv* 20:228–38.

Collins, John J. 1979. Introduction: Towards the Morphology of a Genre. *Semeia* 14:5–9.

———. 1987. The Place of Apocalypticism in the Religion of Israel. Pages 539–58 in *Ancient Israelite Religion: Essays in Honor of Frank Moore Cross*. Edited by P. D. Miller Jr., P. D. Hanson, and S. D. McBride. Philadelphia: Fortress.

———. 1993. *Daniel: A Commentary on the Book of Daniel*. Hermeneia. Minneapolis: Fortress.

———. 1995. Review of G. Hugenberger, *Marriage as a Covenant: A Study of Biblical Law and Ethics Governing Marriage, Developed from the Perspective of Malachi*. *Journal of Biblical Literature* 114:306–8.

———, ed. 1998. *The Encyclopedia of Apocalypticism. Volume 1. The Origins of Apocalypticism in Judaism and Christianity*. New York: Continuum.

———. 2003. Prophecy, Apocalypse, and Eschatology: Reflections on the Proposals of Lester Grabbe. Pages 44–52 in *Knowing the Ending from the Beginning: The Prophetic, the Apocalyptic and Their Relationships*. Edited by L. L. Grabbe. Journal for the Study of the Pseudepigrapha Supplement 46. London: T&T Clark.

Coogan, Michael D. 1987. Canaanite Origins and Lineage: Reflections on the Religion of Ancient Israel. Pages 115–24 in *Ancient Israelite Religion: Essays in Honor of Frank Moore Cross*. Edited by P. D. Miller Jr., P. D. Hanson, and S. D. McBride. Philadelphia: Fortress.

Cook, Stephen L. 1995. Review of R. F. Person, *Second Zechariah and the Deuteronomic School*. *Catholic Biblical Quarterly* 57:780–81.

———. 2004. *The Social Roots of Biblical Yahwism*. Society of Biblical Literature Studies in Biblical Literature 8. Atlanta: SBL Press.

Cooley, Robert E. 1983. Gathered to His People: A Study of a Dothan Family Tomb. Pages 47–58 in *The Living and Active Word of God*. Edited by M. Inch and R. Youngblood. Winona Lake, IN: Eisenbrauns.

Cooper, Alan, and Bernard Goldstein. 1993. The Cult of the Dead and the Theme of Entry into the Land. *Biblical Interpretation. A Journal of Contemporary Approaches* 1:285–303.

Coote, Robert B., and David Robert Ord. 1989. *The Bible's First History*. Philadelphia: Fortress.

Coote, Robert B., and Keith W. Whitelam. 1987. *The Emergence of Early Israel in Historical Perspective*. Sheffield: Almond.

Cross, Frank M. 1970. The Cave Inscription from Khirbet Beit Lei. Pages 299–306 in *Near Eastern Archaeology in the Twentieth Century: Essays in Honor of Nelson Glueck*. Edited by J. A. Sanders. Garden City, NY: Doubleday.

———. 1973. *Canaanite Myth and Hebrew Epic: Essays in the History of the Religion of Israel*. Cambridge, MA: Harvard University Press.

———. 1975. A Reconstruction of the Judean Restoration. *Journal of Biblical Literature* 94:4–18.

———. 2004. Introduction to the Study of the History of the Religion of Israel. Pages 8–11 in *Inspired Speech: Prophecy in the Ancient Near East. Essays in Honour of Herbert B. Huffmon*. Edited by J. Kaltner and L. Stulman. Journal for the Study of the Old Testament: Supplement Series 378. New York: T&T Clark.

———. 2005. The History of Israelite Religion. A Secular or Theological Subject? *Biblical Archaeology Review* 31(3):42–45.

Cross, Frank M., and Hershel Shanks. 1992. Frank Moore Cross: An Interview. Part One. Israelite Origins. *Bible Review* 8(4):22–33, 61–63.

Cryer, Frederick H. 1994. *Divination in Ancient Israel and Its Near Eastern Environment: A Socio-Historical Investigation*. Journal for the Study of the Old Testament: Supplement Series 142. Sheffield: JSOT Press.

Cullican, W. 1968. The Iconography of Some Phoenician Seals and Seal Impressions. *Australian Journal of Biblical Archaeology* 1(1):50–103.

Currid, John D. 1997. *Ancient Egypt and the Old Testament*. Grand Rapids: Baker Academic.

Curtis, Adrian H. W. 1999. Ras Shamra, Minet el-Beida and Ras Ibn Hani: The Material Sources. Pages 5–27 in *Handbook of Ugaritic Studies*. Handbook of Oriental Studies: The Near and Middle East 39. Edited by W. G. E. Watson and N. Wyatt. Leiden: Brill.

Dassow, E. von. 2005. Archives of Alalaḫ IV in Archaeological Context. *Bulletin of the American Schools of Oriental Research* 338:1–69.

Davidson, Robert. 1989. Covenant Ideology in Ancient Israel. Pages 323–47 in *The World of Ancient Israel: Sociological, Anthropological and Political Perspectives*. Edited by R. E. Clements. Cambridge: Cambridge University Press.

Davies, Graham I. 1979. *The Way of the Wilderness*. Cambridge: Cambridge University Press.

———. 1990. The Wilderness Itineraries. Pages 161–75 in *Studies in the Pentateuch*. Edited by J. A. Emerton. Leiden: E. J. Brill.

———. 1991. *Ancient Hebrew Inscriptions. Corpus and Concordance*. Cambridge: Cambridge University Press.

———. 2004. Was There an Exodus? Pages 23–40 in *In Search of Pre-Exilic Israel*. Journal for the Study of the Old Testament: Supplement Series 406. Edited by J. Day. New York: T&T Clark.

Davies, Philip R. 1989. The Social World of Apocalyptic Writings. Pages 251–71 in *The World of Ancient Israel: Sociological, Anthropological and Political Perspectives*. Edited by R. E. Clements. Cambridge: Cambridge University Press.

———. 1992. *In Search of "Ancient Israel."* Journal for the Study of the Old Testament: Supplement Series 148. Sheffield: Sheffield Academic Press.

Davies, W. D., and L. Finkelstein, eds. 1984. *The Cambridge History of Judaism. Volume One: Introduction; The Persian Period*. Cambridge: Cambridge University Press.

Davila, James R. 1995. The Flood Hero as King and Priest. *Journal of Near Eastern Studies* 54:199–214.

Davis, Thomas W. 2004. Theory and Method in Biblical Archaeology. Pages 20–28 in *The Future of Biblical Archaeology: Reassessing Methods and Assumptions*. Edited by J. K. Hoffmeier and A. Millard. Grand Rapids: Eerdmans.

Day, John. 1985. *God's Conflict with the Dragon and the Sea: Echos of a Canaanite Myth in the Old Testament*. University of Cambridge Oriental Publications 35. Cambridge: Cambridge University Press.

———. 1986. Asherah in the Hebrew Bible and Northwest Semitic Literature. *Journal of Biblical Literature* 105:385–408.

———. 1989. *Molech: A God of Human Sacrifice in the Old Testament*. University of Cambridge Oriental Publications 41. Cambridge: Cambridge University Press.

———. 1994. Ugarit and the Bible: Do They Presuppose the Same Canaanite Mythology and Religion? Pages 35–52 in *Ugarit and the Bible. Proceedings of the International Symposium on Ugarit and the Bible, Manchester, September 1992*. Ugaritisch-Biblische Literatur 11. Edited by G. J. Brooke, A. H. W. Curtis, and J. F. Healey. Münster: Ugarit-Verlag.

———. 2000. *Yahweh and the Gods and Goddesses of Canaan*. Journal for the Study of the Old Testament: Supplement Series 265. Sheffield: Sheffield Academic Press.

———. 2004a. Does the Old Testament Refer to Sacred Prostitution and Did It Actually Exist in Ancient Israel? Pages 2–21 in *Biblical and Near Eastern Essays: Studies in Honour of Kevin J. Cathcart*. Journal for the Study of the Old Testament: Supplement Series 375. Edited by C. McCarthy and J. F. Healey. London: T&T Clark.

———, ed. 2004b. *In Search of Pre-Exilic Israel: Proceedings of the Oxford Old Testament Seminar*. Journal for the Study of the Old Testament Supplement Series 406. New York: T&T Clark.

———. 2005a. *Temple and Worship in Biblical Israel*. Library of Hebrew Bible/Old Testament Studies 422. London: T&T Clark.

———. 2005b. Whatever Happened to the Ark of the Covenant? Pages 250–70 in *Temple and Worship in Biblical Israel*. Library of Hebrew Bible/Old Testament Studies 422. Edited by J. Day. London: T&T Clark.

Dearman, J. Andrew. 1993. Baal in Israel: The Contribution of Some Place Names and Personal Names to an Understanding of Early Israelite Religion. Pages 173–91 in *History and Interpretation: Essays in Honour of John H. Hayes*. Journal for the Study of the Old Testament: Supplement Series 173. Edited by M. P. Graham, W. P. Brown, and J. K. Kuan. Sheffield: Sheffield Academic Press.

DeFord, Gabrielle. 1997. Desert Shrines Dedicated to Imageless Gods. *Biblical Archaeology Review* 23(3):49–50.

De Groot, Alon. 1993. Tell Mazar. *The New Encyclopedia of Archaeological Excavations in the Holy Land*. New York: Simon & Schuster.

Demsky, Aaron. 1997. The Name of the Goddess of Ekron: A New Reading. *Journal of the Ancient Near Eastern Society* 25:1–5.

———. 1998. Discovering a Goddess: A New Look at the Ekron Inscription Identifies a Mysterious Deity. *Biblical Archaeology Review* 24(5):53–58.

Demsky, Aaron, and Meir Bar-Ilan. 1988. Writing in Ancient Israel and Early Judaism. Pages 1–38 in *Mikra: Text, Translation, Reading and Interpretation of the Hebrew Bible in Ancient Judaism and Early Christianity*. Edited by M. J. Mulder. Philadelphia: Fortress.

Dever, William G. 1984. Asherah, Consort of Yahweh? New Evidence from Kuntillet 'Ajrud. *Bulletin of the American Schools of Oriental Research* 255:21–37.

———. 1993. Gezer. *The New Encyclopedia of Archaeological Excavations in the Holy Land*. New York: Simon & Schuster.

———. 1995. Will the Real Israel Please Stand Up? Part II: Archaeology and the Religions of Ancient Israel. *Bulletin of the American Schools of Oriental Research* 298:37–58.

———. 1996. Is the Bible Right After All? BAR Interviews William Dever—Part 2. *Biblical Archaeology Review* 22(5):30–37, 74–77.

———. 1999. Archaeology and the Ancient Israelite Cult: How the Kh. El-Qôm and Kuntillet 'Ajrûd "Asherah" Texts Have Changed the Picture. *Eretz-Israel* 26:9*–15*.

———. 2001. *What Did the Biblical Writers Know & When Did They Know It? What Archaeology Can Tell Us about the Reality of Ancient Israel*. Grand Rapids: Eerdmans.

———. 2003. *Who Were the Early Israelites and Where Did They Come From?* Grand Rapids: Eerdmans.

———. 2004. Histories and Non-Histories of Ancient Israel. Pages 65–94 in *In Search of Pre-Exilic Israel*. Edited by J. Day. Journal for the Study of the Old Testament: Supplement Series 406. New York: Continuum.

———. 2005. *Did God Have a Wife? Archaeology and Folk Religion in Ancient Israel*. Grand Rapids: Eerdmans.

Dietrich, M., and O. Loretz. 1992. *"Jahwe und seine Aschera." Anthropomorphes Kultbild in Mesopotamien, Ugarit und Israel*. Ugaritisch-Biblische Literatur 9. Münster: Ugarit.

Dietrich, M., O. Loretz, and J. Sanmartín, eds. 1995. *The Cuneiform Alphabetic Texts from Ugarit, Ras Ibn Hani, and Other Places*. Munster: Ugarit-Verlag.

Dobbs-Allsopp, F. W. et al. 2005. *Hebrew Inscriptions: Texts from the Biblical Period of the Monarchy with Concordance*. New Haven: Yale University Press.

Donner, H., and W. Röllig. 1973–1979. *Kanaanäische und Aramäische Inschriften*. 3 vols. Wiesbaden: Harrassowitz.

Dothan, Moshe. 1993. Nahariya. *The New Encyclopedia of Archaeological Excavations in the Holy Land*. New York: Simon & Schuster.

Douglas, Mary. 1966. *Purity and Danger*. London: Routledge and Keegan Paul.

———. 1993. The Forbidden Animals in Leviticus. *Journal for the Study of the Old Testament* 59:3–23.

———. 1999. *Leviticus as Literature*. Oxford: Oxford University Press.

Dozeman, Thomas B. 1989. *God on the Mountain: A Study of Redaction, Theology and Canon in Exodus 19–24*. Society of Biblical Literature Monograph Series 37. Atlanta: Scholars Press.

———. 2000. Masking Moses and Mosaic Authority in Torah. *Journal of Biblical Literature* 119:21–45.

Drews, Robert. 1993. *The End of the Bronze Age: Changes in Warfare and the Catastrophe ca. 1200 B.C.* Princeton, NJ: Princeton University Press.

Driver, G. R. 1946. Theological and Philological Problems in the Old Testament. *Journal of Theological Studies* 47:156–66.

———. 1973. Affirmation by Exclamatory Negation. *Journal of the Ancient Near Eastern Society of Columbia University* 5:107–14.

Durkheim, Émile. 1915. *The Elementary Forms of Religious Life*. Translated by J. W. Swain. New York: Macmillan.

Dyk, P. J. van. 1990. The Function of the So-Called Etiological Elements in Narratives. *Zeitschrift für die alttestamentliche Wissenschaft* 102:19–33.

Edelman, Diana Vikander. 1986. *The Rise of the Israelite State under Saul.* PhD diss., University of Chicago.

———. 1991. *King Saul in the Historiography of Judah.* Journal for the Study of the Old Testament: Supplement Series 121. Sheffield: JSOT Press.

Eichrodt, Walther. 1961. *Theology of the Old Testament.* 2 vols. Translated by J. A. Baker. London: SCM.

Eisenberg, Emanuel. 1993. Tel Kitan. *The New Encyclopedia of Archaeological Excavations in the Holy Land.* New York: Simon & Schuster.

Eissfeldt, Otto. 1935. *Molk als Opferbegriff in Punischen und Hebräischen um das Ende des Gottes Moloch.* Beiträge zur Religionsgeschichte des Altertums 3. Halle: Max Niemeyer.

Eliade, Mircea. 1949a. *Le mythe de l'éternal retour; archétypes et répétition.* Paris: Gallimard.

———. 1949b. *Traité d'histoire des religions.* Paris: Payot.

———. 1958. *Patterns in Comparative Religion.* Translated by R. Sheed. New York: Sheed & Ward.

———. 1959. *The Sacred and the Profane: The Nature of Religion.* Translated by W. R. Trask. New York: Harcourt, Brace & World.

———. 1974. *The Myth of the Eternal Return: Or, Cosmos and History.* Translated by W. R. Trask. Bollingen Series 46. Princeton, NY: Princeton University Press.

Emerton, John A. 1962. Priests and Levites in Deuteronomy. *Vetus Testamentum* 12:129–38.

———. 1982. New Light on Israelite Religion: The Implications of Inscriptions from Kuntillet ʿAjrud. *Zeitschrift für die alttestamentliche Wissenschaft* 94:2–20.

———. 1988. The Priestly Writer in Genesis. *Journal of Theological Studies* 39:381–400.

———. 1989. Review of Fowler 1988, *Theophoric Personal Names in Ancient Hebrew: A Comparative Study.* *Vetus Testamentum* 29:246–48.

———. 1997. The Biblical High Place in the Light of Recent Study. *Palestine Exploration Quarterly* 129:116–32.

Engle, J. R. 1979. *Pillar Figurines of the Iron Age and Asherah/Asherim.* PhD diss., University of Pittsburgh.

Eph'al, I. 1978. The Western Minorities in Babylonia in the 6th–5th Centuries B.C.: Maintenance and Cohesion. *Orientalia* n.s. 47:74–90.

———. 1982. *The Ancient Arabs. Nomads on the Borders of the Fertile Crescent, 9th–5th Centuries B.C.* Leiden: Brill.

Eshel, E. 1991. 4QDeut—A Text That Has Undergone Harmonistic Editing. *Hebrew Union College Annual* 62:117–54.

Eshel, Itzak, and Kay Prag, eds. 1995. *Excavations by K. M. Kenyon in Jerusalem 1961–1967,* vol. 4. Oxford: Oxford University Press.

Eskenazi, Tamara C. 1988. *In an Age of Prose: A Literary Approach to Ezra-Nehemiah.* Society of Biblical Literature Monograph Series 36. Atlanta: Scholars Press.

———. 1992. Out from the Shadows: Biblical Women in the Postexilic Era. *Journal for the Study of the Old Testament* 54:25–43.

Eslinger, Lyle. 1994. *House of God or House of David: The Rhetoric of 2 Samuel 7.* Journal for the Study of the Old Testament: Supplement Series 164. Sheffield: JSOT Press.

Evans-Pritchard, Edward Evan. 1937. *Witchcraft, Oracles and Magic among the Azande*. Oxford: Clarendon.

———. 1956. *Nuer Religion*. Oxford: Clarendon.

———. 1965. *Theories of Primitive Religion*. Oxford: Clarendon.

Exum, J. Cheryl. 1990. The Centre Cannot Hold: Thematic and Textual Instabilities in Judges. *Catholic Biblical Quarterly* 52:410–31.

———. 1993. *Fragmented Women: Feminist (Sub)versions of Biblical Narratives*. Valley Forge, PA: Trinity Press.

Falconer, Steven E., and Bonnie Magness-Gardiner. 1993. Tell el-Ḥayyat. *The New Encyclopedia of Archaeological Excavations in the Holy Land*. New York: Simon & Schuster.

Farley, Donn Morgan. 1974. *The So-Called Cultic Calendars in the Pentateuch: A Morphological and Typological Study*. PhD diss., Claremont Graduate School. Ann Arbor, MI: University Microfilms.

Faust, Avraham. 2004. "Mortuary Practices, Society and Ideology": The Lack of Iron Age I Burials in the Highlands in Context. *Israel Exploration Quarterly* 54:174–90.

Fenn, Richard K. 2001a. Editorial Commentary: Religion and the Secular; the Sacred and the Profane: The Scope of the Argument. Pages 3–22 in *The Blackwell Companion to Sociology of Religion*. Edited by R. K. Fenn. Oxford: Blackwell.

———. 2001b. The Origins of Religion. Pages 176–93 in *The Blackwell Companion to Sociology of Religion*. Edited by R. K. Fenn. Oxford: Blackwell.

Finkelstein, Israel. 1985. Excavations at Shiloh 1981–1984: Prelimary Report. *Tel Aviv* 12:123–77.

———1988. *The Archaeology of the Israelite Settlement*. Jerusalem: Israel Exploration Society.

———. 1988–1989. The Land of Ephraim Survey 1980–1987: Preliminary Report. *Tel Aviv* 15–16:117–183.

———. 1990. Excavations at Khirbet ed-Dawwara: An Iron Age Site Northeast of Jerusalem. *Tel Aviv* 17:163–208.

———. 1991. The Emergence of Israel in Canaan: Consensus, Mainstream and Dispute. *Scandinavian Journal of the Old Testament* 2:47–59.

———. 1992. Middle Bronze Age "Fortifications": A Reflection of Social Organization and Political Formations. *Tel Aviv* 19:201–20.

———. 1993. Shiloh. *The New Encyclopedia of Archaeological Excavations in the Holy Land*. New York: Simon & Schuster.

———. 1995. The Date of the Settlement of the Philistines in Canaan. *Tel Aviv* 22:213–39.

———. 1996a. The Archaeology of the United Monarchy: An Alternative View. *Levant* 28:177–817.

———. 1996b. Ethnicity and the Origin of the Iron I Settlers in the Highlands of Canaan: Can the Real Israel Stand Up? *Biblical Archaeologist* 59(4):198–212.

———. 1996c. The Philistine Countryside. *Israel Exploration Journal* 46:225–42.

———. 1998. Two Notes on Northern Samaria: The "Einun Pottery" and the Date of the "Bull Site." *Palestine Exploration Quarterly* 130:94–98.

Finkelstein, Israel, and Neil Asher Silberman. 2001. *The Bible Unearthed: Archaeology's New Vision of Ancient Israel and the Origin of Its Sacred Texts*. New York: Free Press.

Fleming, Daniel E. 1992. *The Installation of Baal's High Priestess at Emar. A Window on Ancient Syrian Religion*. Harvard Semitic Studies 42. Atlanta: Scholars Press.

———. 1993. The Etymological Origins of the Hebrew *nābî'*: The One Who Invokes God. *Catholic Biblical Quarterly* 55:217–24.

———. 1995. More Help from Syria: Introducing Emar to Biblical Study. *Biblical Archaeologist* 58(3):139–47.

———. 1997. Six Months of Ritual Supervision by the Diviner (1.124). Pages 436–39 in *The Context of Scripture. Volume 1. Canonical Compositions from the Biblical World.* Edited by W. W. Hallo and K. L. Younger Jr. New York: Brill.

———. 1998. The Biblical Tradition of Anointing Priests. *Journal of Biblical Literature* 117:401–14.

———. 1999a. A Break in the Line: Reconsidering the Bible's Diverse Festival Calendars. *Revue Biblique* 106:161–74.

———. 1999b. If El Is a Bull, Who Is a Calf? Reflections on Religion in Second-Millennium Syria-Palestine. *Eretz-Israel* 26:23*–27*.

———. 1999c. The Israelite Festival Calendar and Emar's Ritual Archive. *Revue Biblique* 106:8–34.

———. 2000a. Mari's Large Public Tent and the Priestly Tent Sanctuary. *Vetus Testamentum* 50:484–98.

———. 2000b. *Time at Emar: The Cultic Calendar and the Rituals from the Diviner's House.* Winona Lake, IN: Eisenbrauns.

———. 2004. Genesis in History and Tradition: The Syrian Background of Israel's Ancestors, Reprise. Pages 193–232 in *The Future of Biblical Archaeology: Reassessing Methodologies and Assumptions.* Edited by J. K. Hoffmeier and Alan Millard. Grand Rapids: Eerdmans.

Flinder, A. 1989. Is This Solomon's Seaport? *Biblical Archaeology Review* 15(4):30–42.

Floyd, Michael H. 1995. The Nature of the Narrative and the Evidence of the Redaction in Haggai. *Vetus Testamentum* 45:470–90.

———. 1996. The Evil in the Ephah: Reading Zechariah 5:5–11 in Its Literary Context. *Catholic Biblical Quarterly* 58:51–68.

Flüglister, N. 1977. Sühne durch Blut—Zur Bedeutung von Leviticus 17, 11. Pages 143–64 in *Studien zum Pentateuch.* Edited by G. Bravlik. Wien: Herder.

Fohrer, Georg. 1972. *History of Israelite Religion.* Translated by D. Green. Nashville: Abingdon.

Fohrer, Georg, and Ernst Sellin. 1968. *Introduction to the Old Testament.* Translated by D. E. Green. Nashville: Abingdon.

Forbes, A. D. 1992. Statistical Research on the Bible. *The Anchor Bible Dictionary.* New York: Doubleday.

Fowler, Jeaneane D. 1988. *Theophoric Personal Names in Ancient Hebrew: A Comparative Study.* Journal for the Study of the Old Testament: Supplement Series 49. Sheffield: JSOT Press.

Foxvog, Daniel A. 1989. A Manual of Sacrificial Procedure. Pages 167–76 in DUMU-E$_2$_DUB-BA-A. *Studies in Honor of Åke W. Sjöberg.* Occasional Publications of the Samuel Noah Kramer Fund 11. Edited by H. Behrens, D. Loding, and M. T. Roth. Philadelphia: University Museum.

Frankel, David. 1994. The Destruction of the Golden Calf: A New Solution. *Vetus Testamentum* 54:330–39.

Frankena, R. 1965. The Vassal Treaties of Esarhaddon and the Dating of Deuteronomy. *Oudtestamentische Studien* 14:122–54.

Frazer, James George. 1911–15. *The Golden Bough: A Study in Magic and Religion*. 3rd ed. 12 vols. London: Macmillan.

Freedman, David Noel. 1987. Yahweh of Samaria and His Asherah. *Biblical Archaeologist* 50(4):241–49.

Freud, Sigmund. 1913. *Totem und Tabu: Einige Übereinstimmungen im Seelenleben der Wilden und der Neurotiker*. Leipzig: H. Heller.

———. 1927. *Die Zukunft einer Illusion*. Leipzig: Internationaler Psychoanalytischer Verlag.

———. 1939. *Moses and Monotheism*. Translated by K. Jones. London: Hogarth Press.

———. 1950. *Totem and Taboo: Some Points of Agreement between the Mental Lives of Savages and Neurotics*. Translated by J. Strachey. London: Routledge & Kegan Paul.

———. 1961. *The Future of an Illusion*. Translated by J. Strachey. New York: W. W. Norton.

Fried, Lisbeth S. 2002. The High Places (*Bâmôt*) and the Reforms of Hezekiah and Josiah: An Archaeological Investigation. *Journal of the American Oriental Society* 122:437–65.

Friedman, Richard Elliott. 1987. *Who Wrote the Bible?* New York: Summit Books.

———. 1991. Is Everybody a Bible Expert? Not the Authors of *The Book of J*. *Bible Review* 7(2):6–18, 50–51.

———. 1996. Some Recent Non-Arguments concerning the Documentary Hypothesis. Pages 87–101 in *Texts, Temples, and Traditions: A Tribute to Menahem Haran*. Edited by M. V. Fox et al. Winona Lake, IN: Eisenbrauns.

———. 1998. *The Hidden Book in the Bible: Restored, Translated, and Introduced*. San Francisco: Harper.

———. 2003. *The Bible with Sources Revealed: A New View into the Five Books of Moses*. San Francisco: Harper.

Fritz, Volkmar. 1977. *Tempel und Zelt. Studien zum Tempelbau in Israel und zum Zeltheiligtum der Priesterschrift*. Neukirchener: Neikirchen-Vluyn.

———. 1993. Open Cult Places in Israel in the Light of Parallels from Prehistoric Europe and Pre-Classical Greece. Pages 182–87 in *Biblical Archaeology Today, 1990. Proceedings of the Second International Congress on Biblical Archaeology. Jerusalem, June–July 1990*. Edited by A. Biran and J. Aviram. Jerusalem: Israel Exploration Society.

Frymer-Kensky, Tikva S. 1992. *In the Wake of the Goddesses: Women, Culture, and the Biblical Transformation of Pagan Myth*. New York: Free Press.

———. 2002. *Reading Women of the Bible*. New York: Schocken Books.

Gabler, Johann P. 2004. An Oration on the Proper Distinction between Biblical and Dogmatic Theology and the Specific Objectives of Each. Pages 497–506 in *Old Testament Theology: Flowering and Future*, Sources for Biblical and Theological Study. Volume 1. Edited by B. C. Ollenburger. Winona Lake, IN: Eisenbrauns.

Gadegaard, N. H. 1978. On the So-Called Burnt Offering Altar in the Old Testament. *Palestine Exploration Quarterly* 110:35–45.

Gal, Z. 1991. The Period of the Israelite Settlement in the Lower Galilee and the Jezreel Valley. *Maarav* 7:101–15.

———. 1992. *Lower Galilee during the Iron Age*. American Schools of Oriental Research Dissertation Series 8. Winona Lake, IN: Eisenbrauns.

Galil, G. 1983. *The Genealogies of the Tribe of Judah*. PhD thesis. Hebrew University, Jerusalem. Hebrew with English summary.

Gane, Roy E. 2004. *Ritual Dynamic Structures*. St. Georgias Dissertation, 14; Religion, 2. Piscataway, NJ: St. Georgias Press.

Garr, W. R. 1992. The Grammar and Interpretation of Exodus 6:3. *Journal of Biblical Literature* 111:385–408.

Garrett, Duane A. 1990. Votive Prostitution Again: A Comparison of Proverbs 7:13–14 and 21:28–29. *Journal of Biblical Literature* 109:681–82.

Geertz, Clifford. 1960. *The Religion of Java*. Glencoe, IL: Free Press.

———. 1968. *Islam Observed: Religious Development in Morocco and Indonesia*. New Haven: Yale University Press.

———. 1971. *Myth, Symbol, and Culture*. Cambridge, MA: American Academy of Arts and Sciences.

———. 1973. *The Interpretation of Cultures*. New York: Basic Books.

Gelb, Ignace J. 1979. Definition and Discussion of Slavery and Serfdom. *Ugarit Forschungen* 11:283–97.

George, Mark. 2002. Yhwh's Own Heart. *Catholic Biblical Quarterly* 64:442–59.

Geraty, Lawrence T. 1997. Tell el-'Umeiri. *The Oxford Encyclopedia of Archaeology in the Near East*. New York: Oxford University Press.

Gerstenberger, Erhard S. 1996. *Leviticus: A Commentary*. Translated by Douglas W. Stott. Louisville: Westminster/John Knox.

Geus, G. H. J. de. 1976. *The Tribes of Israel: An Investigation into Some of the Presuppositions of Martin Noth's Amphictyony Hypothesis*. Assen: Van Gorcum.

Geva, Hillel. 2006. Small City, Few People. *Biblical Archaeology Review* 32(3):66–68.

Gibson, John C. L. 1971–1982. *Textbook of Syrian Semitic Inscriptions*. 3 vols. Oxford: Clarendon.

Gilbert-Peretz, D. 1996. Ceramic Figurines. *Qedem* 35:29–41.

Gilders, William K. 2004. *Blood Ritual in the Hebrew Bible: Meaning and Power*. Baltimore: Johns Hopkins University Press.

Gilula, M. 1978–79. To Yahweh Shomron and His Asherah. *Shnaton* 3–4:129–37 [Hebrew with English summary, 15–16].

Gitin, Seymour. 1992. New Incense Altars form Ekron: Context, Typology, and Function. *Eretz-Israel* 23:43*-49*.

———. 1993. Seventh Century B.C.E. Cultic Elements at Ekron. Pages 248–58 in *Biblical Archaeology Today, 1990. Proceedings of the Second International Congress on Biblical Archaeology. Jerusalem, June–July 1990*. Edited by A. Biran and J. Aviram. Jerusalem: Israel Exploration Society.

———. 2002. The Four-Horned Altar and Sacred Space. Pages 95–123 in *Sacred Time, Sacred Place: Archaeology and the Religion of Israel*. Edited by B. Gittlen. Winona Lake, IN: Eisenbrauns.

———. 2003. Israelite and Philistine Cult and the Archaeological Record in Iron Age II: The "Smoking Gun" Phenomenon. Pages 279–95 in *Symbiosis, Symbolism, and the Power of the Past: Canaan, Ancient Israel, and Their Neighbors through Roman Palestina: Proceedings of the Albright/ASOR Centennial Symposium, Jerusalem, May 29–31, 2000*. Edited by W. G. Dever and S. Gitin. Winona Lake, IN: Eisenbrauns.

Gitin, Seymour, and Mordechai Cogan. 1999. A New Type of Dedicatory Inscription from Ekron. *Israel Exploration Journal* 49:193–202.

Gitin, Seymour, Trude Dothan, and Joseph Naveh. 1997. A Royal Dedicatory Inscription from Ekron. *Israel Exploration Journal* 47:1–16.

Gittlen, Barry M., ed. 2002. *Sacred Time, Sacred Place: Archaeology and the Religion of Israel*. Winona Lake, IN: Eisenbrauns.

Glock, Albert E. 1978. Taanach. *Encyclopedia of Archaeological Excavations in the Holy Land*.

Gnuse, Robert. 1995. Review of M. Douglas, *In the Wilderness: The Doctrine of Defilement in the Book of Numbers*. *Catholic Biblical Quarterly* 57:124–25.

———. 1997. *No Other Gods. Emergent Monotheism in Israel*. Journal for the Study of the Old Testament: Supplement Series 241. Sheffield: JSOT Press.

———. 2000. Redefining the Elohist? *Journal of Biblical Literature* 119:201–20.

Goodfriend, E. A. 1992. Prostitution (OT). *Anchor Bible Dictionary*. New York: Doubleday.

Gordon, Cyrus H. 1988. Notes on Proper Names in the Ebla Tablets. Pages 153–58 in *Eblaite Personal Names and Semitic Name-Giving. Papers of a Symposium Held in Rome July 15–17, 1985*. Edited by A. Archi. Archivi Reali de Ebla Studi 1. Rome: Missione Archeologica Italiana in Siria.

Gordon, Robert P. 1991. Compositeness, Conflation and the Pentateuch. *Journal for the Study of the Old Testament* 51:57–69.

———. 1995. Where Have All the Prophets Gone? The "Disappearing" Israelite Prophet against the Background of Ancient Near Eastern Prophecy. *Bulletin of Biblical Research* 5:67–86.

Goren, Yuval, Shmuel Aḥituv, et al. 2005. A Re-Examination of the Inscribed Pomegranate from the Israel Museum. *Israel Exploration Journal* 55:3–20.

Goren, Yuval, Avner Ayalon, et al. 2005. Authenticity Examination of Two Iron Age Ostraca from the Moussaieff Collection. *Israel Exploration Journal* 55:21–34.

Görg, M. 1976. Jahwe—ein Toponym? *Biblische Notizen* 11:7–14.

Gorman, Frank H., Jr. 1990. *The Ideology of Ritual: Space, Time and Status in the Priestly Theology*. Journal for the Study of the Old Testament Supplement 91. Sheffield: JSOT Press.

Gottwald, Norman K. 1979. *The Tribes of Yahweh. A Sociology of the Religion of Liberated Israel 1250–1050 B.C.E.* Mary Knoll, NY: Orbis Books.

———. 1989. Israel's Emergence in Canaan—BR Interviews Norman Gottwald. *Bible Review* 5(3):26–34.

Grabbe, Lester L. 1994. "Canaanite": Some Methodological Observations. Pages 113–22 in *Ugarit and the Bible. Proceedings of the International Symposium on Ugarit and the Bible Manchester, September 1992*. Ugaritisch-Biblische Literatur 11. Edited by G. J. Brooke, A. H. W. Curtis, and J. F. Healey. Münster: Ugarit-Verlag.

———. 1995. *Priests, Prophets, Diviners, Sages: A Socio-Historical Study of Religious Specialists in Ancient Israel*. Valley Forge, PA: Trinity Press.

———. 2002. "The Comfortable Theory," "Maximal Conservatism" and Neo-Fundamentalism Revisited. Pages 174–93 in *Sense and Sensitivity: Essays on Reading the Bible in Honour of Robert Carroll*. Journal for the Study of the Old Testament: Supplement Series 348. Edited by A. G. Hunter and P. R. Davies. Sheffield: Sheffield Academic Press.

———. 2003. Introduction and Overview. Pages 1–43 in *Knowing the End from the Beginning: The Prophetic, the Apocalyptic and Their Relationships*. Edited by L. L. Grabbe. Journal for the Study of the Pseudepigrapha Supplement 46. London: T&T Clark.

Graf, Karl Heinrich. 1866. *Die Geschichtlichen Bücher des Alten Testaments; Zwei Historisch-Kritische Untersuchungen*. Leipzig: T. O. Weigel.

Grafman, R. 1983. *The Israel Museum Guide*. Jerusalem: Israel Museum.

Greenberg, Moshe. 1983a. *Biblical Prose Prayer: As a Window to the Popular Religion of Ancient Israel*. Berkeley: University of California Press.

———. 1983b. *Ezekiel 1–20: A New Translation with Introduction and Commentary*. The Anchor Bible 22. Garden City, NY: Doubleday.

———. 1997. *Ezekiel 21–37: A New Translation with Introduction and Commentary*. The Anchor Bible 22A. New York: Doubleday.

Greenfield, Jonas C. 1987. The Hebrew Bible and Canaanite Literature. Pages 545–60 in *The Literary Guide to the Bible*. Edited by R. Alter and F. Kermode. Cambridge, MA: Belknap.

Greenspahn, Frederick E. 1994. A Mesopotamian Proverb and Its Biblical Reverberations. *Journal of the American Oriental Society* 114:33–38.

Grosby, Steven. 2002. *Biblical Ideas of Nationality: Ancient and Modern*. Winona Lake, IN: Eisenbrauns.

Gruber, Mayer I. 1986. Hebrew *Qĕdēšāh* and Her Canaanite and Akadian Cognates. *Ugarit-Forschungen* 18:133–48.

Gunkel, H. 1895. *Schöpfung und Chaos in Urzeit und Endzeit: eine religionsgeschichtliche Untersuchung über Gen 1 und Ap Joh 12*. Göttingen: Vandenhoeck & Ruprecht.

———. 1901. *The Legends of Genesis*. Translated by W. H. Carruth. New York: Schocken.

———. 1902. *Genesis übersetzt und erklärt*. Göttingen: Vandenhoeck und Ruprecht.

———. 1903. *Israel und Babylonien: Der Einfluss Babyloniens auf die israelitische Religion*. Göttingen: Vandenhoeck und Ruprecht.

———. 1905. *Ausgewählte Psalmen übersetzt und erklärt*. Göttingen: Vandenhoeck und Ruprecht.

Hackett, J. 1980. *The Balaam Texts from Deir 'Allā*. Harvard Semitic Monographs 31. Chico, CA: Scholars Press.

Hadley, Judith M. 1987. Some Drawings and Inscriptions on Two Pithoi from Kuntillet 'Ajrud. *Vetus Testamentum* 37:180–213.

———. 1989. *Yahweh's Asherah in the Light of Recent Discovery*. PhD thesis, Cambridge University.

———. 1993. Kuntillet 'Ajrud: Religious Centre or Desert Way Station? *Palestine Exploration Quarterly* 125:115–24.

———. 2000. *The Cult of Asherah in Ancient Israel and Judah: Evidence for a Hebrew Goddess*. University of Cambridge Oriental Publications 57. Cambridge: Cambridge University Press.

Hagedorn, Anselm C. 2005. Placing (A) God: Central Place Theory in Deuteronomy 12 and at Delphi. Pages 188–211 in *Temple and Worship in Biblical Israel*. Library of Hebrew Bible/Old Testament Studies 422. Edited by J. Day. London: T&T Clark.

Hägg, Robin. 1993. Open Cult Places in the Bronze Age Aegean. Pages 188–95 in *Biblical Archaeology Today, 1990. Proceedings of the Second International Congress on Biblical Archaeology. Jerusalem, June–July 1990*. Edited by A. Biran and J. Aviram. Jerusalem: Israel Exploration Society.

Hallo, William W. 1990. The Limits of Skepticism. *Journal of the American Oriental Society* 110:187–99.

———. 1991. Information from before the Flood: Antediluvian Notes from Babylonia and Israel. *Maarav* 7:173–81.

———. 1993. For Love Is Stronger than Death. *Journal of the Ancient Near Eastern Society* 22:45–50.

Halpern, Baruch. 1996. The Construction of the Davidic State: An Exercise in Historiography. Pages 44–75 in *The Origins of the Ancient Israelite States*. Journal for the Study of the Old Testament: Supplement Series 228. Edited by V. Fritz and P. R. Davies. Sheffield: Sheffield Academic Press.

Hanson, P. D. 1979. *The Dawn of Apocalyptic*. 2nd ed. Philadelphia: Fortress.

———. 1987. Israelite Religion in the Early Postexilic Period. Pages 485–508 in *Ancient Israelite Religion: Essays in Honor of Frank Moore Cross*. Edited by P. D. Miller Jr., P. D. Hanson, and S. D. McBride. Philadelphia: Fortress.

Haran, Menahem. 1981. Behind the Scenes of History: Determining the Date of the Priestly Source. *Journal of Biblical Literature* 100:321–33.

———. 1993. "Incense Altars"—Are They? Pages 237–47 in *Biblical Archaeology Today, 1990. Proceedings of the Second International Congress on Biblical Archaeology. Jerusalem, June–July 1990*. Edited by A. Biran and J. Aviram. Jerusalem: Israel Exploration Society.

———. 1995. Altar-ed States. Incense Theory Goes up in Smoke. *Bible Review* 11(1):30–37, 48. .

Harris, Marvin. 1996. The Abominable Pig. Pages 135–51 in *Community, Identity, and Ideology: Social Science Approaches to the Hebrew Bible*. Sources for Biblical and Theological Study 6. Edited by C. E. Carter and C. L. Meyers. Winona Lake, IN: Eisenbrauns. Reprinted from M. Harris. *The Sacred Cow and the Abominable Pig: Riddles of Food and Culture*. New York: Simon & Schuster, 1987, 67–87.

Harrison, Roland K. 1969. *Introduction to the Old Testament: With a Comprehensive Review of Old Testament Studies and a Special Supplement of the Apocrypha*. Grand Rapids: Eerdmans.

Hartley, John E. 1992. *Leviticus*. Word Biblical Commentary 4. Waco: Word.

Hartlich, Christian, and Walter Sachs. 1952. *Die Ursprung des Mythosbegriffes in der modernen Bibelwissenschaft*. Tübingen: Mohr Siebeck.

Hauser, A. J. 1980. Linguistic and Thematic Links between Genesis 4:1–16 and Genesis 2–3. *Journal of the Evangelical Theological Society* 23:297–305.

Hayward, C. T. R. 2005. Understandings of the Temple Service in the Septuagint Pentateuch. Pages 385–400 in *Temple and Worship in Biblical Israel*. Library of Hebrew Bible/Old Testament Studies 422. Edited by J. Day. London: T&T Clark.

Heider, G. C. 1985. *The Cult of Molek: A Reassessment*. Journal for the Study of the Old Testament: Supplement Series 43. Sheffield: JSOT Press.

Heimpel, Wolfgang. 2003. *Letters to the King of Mari: A New Translation with Historical Introduction, Notes, and Commentary*. Mesopotamian Civilizations 12. Winona Lake, IN: Eisenbrauns.

Held, Moshe. 1982. Studies in Biblical Lexicography in the Light of Akkadian. *Eretz-Israel* 16:76–85.

Hendel, Ronald S. 1987. *The Epic of the Patriarch: The Jacob Cycle and the Narrative Traditions of Canaan and Israel*. Harvard Semitic Monographs 42. Atlanta: Scholars Press.

———. 1989. Sacrifice as a Cultural System: The Ritual Symbolism of Exodus 24, 3–8. *Zeitschrift für die alttestamentliche Wissenschaft* 101:366–90.

———. 1991. When God Acts Immorally: Is the Bible a Good Book? *Bible Review* 7(3):35–37, 46, 48, 50.

————. 2004. The Nephilim Were on the Earth: Genesis 6:1–4 and Its Ancient Near Eastern Context. Pages 11–34 in *The Fall of the Angels*. Edited by C. Auffarth and L. T. Stuckenbruck. Leiden and Boston: Brill.

Hennessy, J. B. 1985. Thirteenth Century B.C. Temple of Human Sacrifice. Pages 85–104 in *Phoenicia and Its Neighbors: Proceedings of the Colloquium Held 9–10 December 1983 at the Vrije Universiteit Brussels, in cooperation with the Centrum voor Myceense en archaische-Grieke Cultuur*. Edited by E. Gubel and E. Lipiński. Studia Phoenicia 3. Leuven: Uitgeverij Peeters.

Herder, Johann Gottfried. 1782–1783. *Vom Geist der ebräischen Poesie: Eine Anleitung für Liebhaber derselben, und der ältesten Geschichte des menschlichen Geistes*. Dessau.

Herr, Larry G. 1988. Seal. *International Standard Bible Encyclopedia*. Grand Rapids: Eerdmans.

Herzog, Ze'ev. 1997. *Arad Part 2: The Arad Fortress*. Tel Aviv: Hakkibbutz Hammeuchad Publishing House, Israel Exploration Society, Israel Antiquities Authority [Hebrew].

————. 2002. The Fortress Mound at Tel Arad: An Interim Report. *Tel Aviv* 29:3–109.

Hess, Richard S. 1980. *The Structure of the Covenant Code: Exodus 20:22–23:33*. Master's thesis, Trinity Evangelical Divinity School.

————. 1986. Divine Names in the Amarna Correspondence. *Ugarit Forschungen* 18:149–68.

————. 1989a. Cultural Aspects of Onomastic Distribution in the Amarna Texts. *Ugarit Forschungen* 21:209–16.

————. 1989b. The Genealogies of Genesis 1–11 and Comparative Literature. *Biblica* 70:241–54.

————. 1990a. A Comparison of the Onomastica in Genealogical and Narrative Texts of Genesis 1–11. Pages 67–74 in *Proceedings of the Tenth World Congress of Jewish Studies*. Edited by D. Assaf. Jerusalem: World Union of Jewish Studies.

————. 1990b. Genesis 1–2 in Its Literary Context. *Tyndale Bulletin* 41:143–53.

————. 1991a. The Divine Name Yahweh in Late Bronze Age Sources? *Ugarit Forschungen* 23:181–88.

————. 1991b. Lamech in the Genealogies of Genesis. *Bulletin for Biblical Research* 1:21–25.

————. 1992a. Abel; Cain; Enoch; Enosh; Irad; Jabal; Jubal; Lamech; Mehujael; Methushael; Nephilim; Seth; Tubal-Cain; Zillah. *Anchor Bible Dictionary*. New York: Doubleday.

————. 1992b. Review of M. S. Smith, *The Early History of God*. *Themelios* 18(1):27.

————. 1992c. Yahweh and His Asherah? Religious Pluralism in the Old Testament World. Pages 13–42 in *One God, One Lord. Christianity in a World of Religious Pluralism*. Edited by A. D. Clarke and B. W. Winter. 2nd ed. Grand Rapids: Baker Academic.

————. 1993a. *Amarna Personal Names*. American Schools of Oriental Research Dissertation Series 9. Winona Lake, IN: Eisenbrauns.

————. 1993b. Smitten Ant Bites Back: Rhetorical Forms in the Amarna Correspondence from Shechem. Pages 95–111 in *Verse in Ancient Near Eastern Prose*. Alter Orient und Altes Testament 42. Edited by J. C. de Moor and W. G. E. Watson. Neukirchener: Neukirchen-Vluyn.

————. 1993c. *Studies in the Personal Names of Genesis 1–11*. Alter Orient und Altes Testament 234. Neukirchener: Neukirchen-Vluyn.

————. 1994a. Achan and Achor: Names and Wordplay in Joshua 7. *Hebrew Annual Review* 14:89–98.

————. 1994b. Fallacies in the Study of Early Israel: An Onomastic Perspective. *Tyndale Bulletin* 45:339–54.

————. 1994c. One Hundred Fifty Years of Comparative Studies on Genesis 1–11: An Overview. Pages 3–26 in *"I Studied Inscriptions from before the Flood": Ancient Near Eastern, Literary, and Linguistic Approaches to Genesis 1–11*. Sources for Biblical and Theological Study 4. Edited by R. S. Hess and D. T. Tsumura. Winona Lake, IN: Eisenbrauns.

————. 1994d. Recent Studies in Old Testament History: A Review Article. *Themelios* 19(2):9–15.

————. 1994e. The Slaughter of the Animals in Genesis 15:18–21 and Its Ancient Near Eastern Context. Pages 55–65 in *He Swore an Oath: Biblical Themes from Genesis 12–50*. 2nd ed. Edited by R. S. Hess, P. E. Satterthwaite, and G. J. Wenham. Grand Rapids: Baker Academic.

————. 1994f. The Southern Desert. *Archaeology in the Biblical World* 2(2):22–33.

————. 1996a. A Comparison of the Ugarit, Emar and Alalakh Archives. Pages 75–83 in *Ugarit, Religion and Culture: Proceedings of the International Colloquium on Ugarit, Religion and Culture. Edinburgh, July 1994. Essays Presented in Honour of Professor John C. L. Gibson*. Ugaritisch-Biblische Literatur Band 12. Edited by N. Wyatt, W. G. E. Watson, and J. B. Lloyd. Münster: Ugarit-Verlag.

————. 1996b. Asherah or Asheratah? *Orientalia* 65:209–19.

————. 1997. Hurrians and Other Inhabitants of Late Bronze Age Palestine. *Levant* 29:153–56.

————. 1999a. Early Israel in Canaan: A Survey of Recent Evidence and Interpretations. Pages 492–518 in *Israel's Past in Present Research: Essays on Ancient Israelite Historiography*. Sources for Biblical and Theological Study 7. Edited by V. P. Long. Winona Lake, IN: Eisenbrauns. Reprinted from *Palestine Exploration Quarterly* 125 (1993): 125–42.

————. 1999b. The Mayarzana Correspondence: Rhetoric and Conquest Accounts. *Ugarit-Forschungen* 30 (1998): 335–51.

————. 2001. Review Article of Finkelstein and Silberman 2001, *Denver Journal: An Online Review of Current Biblical and Theological Studies* 4:0104. http://www.denverseminary. edu/dj/articles2001/0100/0104.

————. 2002a. Leviticus 10:1: Strange Fire and an Odd Name. *Bulletin for Biblical Research* 12:187–98.

————. 2002b. Literacy in Iron Age Israel. Pages 82–102 in *Windows into Old Testament History: Evidence, Argument, and the Crisis of "Biblical Israel."* Edited by V. P. Long, D. W. Baker, and G. J. Wenham. Grand Rapids: Eerdmans.

————. 2002c. A Reassessment of the Priestly Cultic and Legal Texts. *Journal of Law and Religion* 17:375–91.

————. 2002d. The Book of Joshua as a Land Grant. *Biblica* 83:493–506.

————. 2003a. Israelite Identity and Personal Names in the Book of Judges. *Hebrew Studies* 44:25–39.

————. 2003b. Preliminary Perspectives on Late Bronze Age Culture from the Personal Names in Palestinian Cuneiform Texts. *Dutch Studies in Near Eastern Languages and Literatures* 5(1–2):35–57.

————. 2004a. Genesis 1–3: Egalitarianism with and without Innocence. Pages 79–95 in *Discovering Biblical Equality: Complementarity without Hierarchy*. Edited by R. W. Pirece, R. M. Groothuis, and G. D. Fee. Downers Grove, IL: InterVarsity.

———. 2004b. Multi-Month Ritual Calendars in the West Semitic World. Pages 233–53 in *The Future of Biblical Archaeology: Reassessing Methodologies and Assumptions*. Edited by J. K. Hoffmeier and A. Millard. Grand Rapids: Eerdmans.

———. 2004c. The Name Game: Dating the Book of Judges. *Biblical Archaeology Review* 30(6):38–41.

———. 2005a. Adam, Father, He: Gender Issues in Hebrew Translation. *The Bible Translator* 56(3):144–53.

———. 2005b. Oral Tradition and Written Tradition. Pages 764–67 in *Dictionary of the Old Testament: Historical Books*. Edited by B. T. Arnold and H. G. M. Williamson. Downers Grove, IL: InterVarsity.

———. 2005c. *Song of Songs*, Baker Commentary on the Old Testament Wisdom and Psalms. Grand Rapids: Baker Academic.

———. 2006. Writing about Writing: Abecedaries and Evidence for Literacy in Ancient Israel. *Vetus Testamentum* 56:342–46.

———. Forthcoming a. Aspects of Israelite Personal Names and Pre-Exilic Israelite Religion. To appear in *Papers from the 2004 Groningen Session on Seals and Inscriptions from the Collection of Dr. Shlomo Moussaieff*.

———. Forthcoming b. Leviticus. *The Expositor's Bible Commentary*. Rev. ed. Grand Rapids: Zondervan.

———. Forthcoming c. Going Down to Sheol: A Place Name and Its West Semitic Background. Edited by J. G. McConville. New York: Continuum.

Hess, Richard S., Philip E. Satterthwaite, and Gordon J. Wenham, eds. 1994. *He Swore an Oath: Biblical Themes from Genesis 12–50*. Cambridge: Tyndale House. 2nd ed. Grand Rapids: Baker Academic.

Hess, Richard S., and David T. Tsumura, eds. 1994. *"I Studied Inscriptions from before the Flood": Ancient Near Eastern and Literary Approaches to Genesis 1–11*. Sources for Biblical and Theological Study, 4. Winona Lake, IN: Eisenbrauns.

Hesse, Brian. 1986. Animal Use at Tel Miqne-Ekron in the Bronze Age and Iron Age. *Bulletin of the American Schools of Oriental Research* 264:17–27.

Hestrin, Ruth. 1986. Canaanite Cult Stand. Pages 161–63 in *Treasures of the Holy Land: Ancient Art from the Israel Museum*. Edited by J. P. O-Neill. New York: Metropolitan Museum of Art.

———. 1987a. The Cult Stand from Taʿanach and Its Religious Background. Pages 61–77 in *Phoenicia and the East Mediterranean in the First Millennium B.C.: Proceedings of the Conference Held in Leuven from the 14th to the 16th of November 1985*. Studia Phoenicia V. Orientalia Lovaniensia Analecta 22. Edited by E. Lipiński. Leuven: Peeters.

———. 1987b. The Lachish Ewer and the Asherah. *Israel Exploration Journal* 37:212–23.

———. 1988. A Note on the "Lion Bowls" and the Asherah. *Israel Museum Journal* 7:115–18.

———. 1991. Understanding Asherah: Exploring Semitic Iconography. *Biblical Archaeology Review* 17(5):50–59.

Hestrin, Ruth, and M. Dayagi-Mendels. 1979. *Inscribed Seals: First Temple Period: Hebrew, Ammonite, Moabite, Phoenician and Moabite*. Jerusalem: Israel Museum.

Hill, Andrew E. 1982. Dating Second Zechariah: A Linguistic Examination. *Hebrew Annual Review* 6:105–34.

Himbaza, Innocent. 2004. *Le Décalogue et l'histoire deu texte: Etudes des formes textuelles du Décalogue et leur implications dans l'histoire du texte de l'Ancien Testament*. Orbis Biblicus et Orientalis 207. Göttingen: Vandenhoeck & Ruprecht.

Hoffmeier, James K. 1997. *Israel in Egypt: The Evidence for the Authenticity of the Exodus Tradition*. Oxford: Oxford University Press.

———. 2005. *Ancient Israel in Sinai: The Evidence for the Authenticity of the Wilderness Tradition*. Oxford: Oxford University Press.

Hoffner, Harry A., Jr. 1967. Second Millennium Antecedents to the Hebrew *'ôb*. *Journal of Biblical Literature* 86:385–401.

———. 1997. *The Laws of the Hittites: A Critical Edition*. Leiden: Brill.

Hoglund, Kenneth G. 1991. The Achaemenid Context. Pages 54–72 in *Second Temple Studies: 1. Persian Period*. Journal for the Study of the Old Testament: Supplement Series 117. Edited by P. R. Davies. Sheffield: Sheffield Academic Press.

———. 1992. *Achaemenid Imperial Administration in Syria-Palestine and the Missions of Ezra and Nehemiah*. SBL Dissertation Series 125. Atlanta: Scholars Press.

Holladay, John S., Jr. 1987. Religion in Israel and Judah under the Monarchy: An Explicitly Archaeological Approach. Pages 249–99 in *Ancient Israelite Religion: Essays in Honor of Frank Moore Cross*. Edited by P. D. Miller Jr., P. D. Hanson, and S. D. McBride. Philadelphia: Fortress.

———. 1995. The Kingdoms of Israel and Judah: Political and Economic Centralization in the Iron IIA-B. Pages 368–98 in *The Archaeology of Society in the Holy Land*. Edited by T. E. Levy. New York: Facts On File.

Holland, Thomas A. 1977. A Study of Palestinian Iron Age Baked Clay Figurines with Special Reference to Jerusalem Cave 1. *Levant* 9:121–55.

Holman, Michael W. 2000. The Divine Warrior in His Tent. *Bible Review* 16(6):22–33, 55.

Hopkins, David C. 1993. Pastoralists in Late Bronze Age Palestine: Which Way Did They Go? *Biblical Archaeologist* 56(4):200–11.

Horowitz, Wayne. 1990. The Isles of the Nations: Genesis X and Babylonian Geography. Pages 35–43 in *Studies in the Pentateuch*. Supplements to Vetus Testamentum 41. Edited by J. A. Emerton. Leiden: Brill.

Horowitz, Wayne, and Aaron Shaffer. 1992a. An Administrative Tablet from Hazor: A Preliminary Edition. *Israel Exploration Journal* 42:21–33.

———. 1992b. A Fragment of a Letter from Hazor. *Israel Exploration Journal* 42:165–66.

———. 1992c. Additions and Corrections to "An Administrative Tablet from Hazor: A Preliminary Edition." *Israel Exploration Journal* 42:167.

Hort, Greta. 1957. The Plagues of Egypt. *Zeitschrift für die alttestamentliche Wissenschaft* 69:84–103.

———. 1958. The Plagues of Egypt. *Zeitschrift für die alttestamentliche Wissenschaft* 70:48–59.

Horwitz, L. H. 1986–1987. Faunal Remains from the Early Iron Age Site on Mount Ebal. *Tel Aviv* 13–14:173–89.

Hostetter, Edwin C. 1996. *Nations Mightier and More Numerous: The Biblical View of Palestine's Pre-Israelite Peoples*. BIBAL Dissertation Series 3. Richland Hills, TX: BIBAL Press.

Houk, Cornelius B. 2002. Statistical Analysis of Genesis Sources. *Journal for the Study of the Old Testament* 27(1):75–105.

Houston, Walter. 1993. *Purity and Monotheism: Clean and Unclean Animals in Biblical Law*. Journal for the Study of the Old Testament: Supplement Series 140. Sheffield: JSOT Press.

Houtman, Cornelius. 1993a. *Exodus, Vol. 1*. Historical Commentary on the Old Testament. Kampen: Kok.

———. 1993b. *Der Himmel im Alten Testament: Israels Weltbild und Weltanschauung*. Oudtestamentische Studien 20. Leiden: Brill.

———. 1994. Wie fiktiv ist das Zeltheiligtum von Exodus 25–40? *Zeitschrift für die alttestamentliche Wissenschaft* 106:107–13.

Huehnergard, John. 1999. Etymology and Meaning of Hebrew *nābî'*. *Eretz-Israel* 26:88*–93*.

Huffmon, Herbert B. 1985. Cain, the Arrogant Sufferer. Pages 109–13 in *Biblical and Related Studies Presented to Samuel Iwry*. Edited by A. Kort and S. Morschauser. Winona Lake, IN: Eisenbrauns.

Hugenberger, Gordon Paul. 1993. *Marriage as a Covenant: A Study of Biblical Law and Ethics Governing Marriage, Developed from the Perspective of Malachi*. Vetus Testamentum Supplement 52. Leiden: Brill.

Hughes, Philip E. 1977. *A Commentary on the Epistle to the Hebrews*. Grand Rapids: Eerdmans.

Humphreys, Colin J. 2003. *The Miracles of Exodus*. New York: HarperCollins.

Hurowitz, Victor Avigdor. 1985. The Priestly Account of the Building of the Tabernacle. *Journal of the American Oriental Society* 105:21–30.

———. 1992. *I Have Built You an Exalted House: Temple Building in the Bible in Light of Mesopotamian and Northwest Semitic Writings*. Journal for the Study of the Old Testament: Supplement Series 115. JSOT/ASOR Monograph 5. Sheffield: JSOT Press.

———. 1994. Inside Solomon's Temple. *Bible Review* 10(2):24–37, 50.

———. 1997. Picturing Imageless Deities: Iconography in the Ancient Near East. *Biblical Archaeology Review* 23(3):46–48, 51, 68–69.

———. 2003. The Mesopotamian God Image, From Womb to Tomb. *Journal of the American Oriental Society* 123:147–57.

———. 2005. YHWH's Exalted House—Aspects of the Design and Symbolism of Solomon's Temple. Pages 63–110 in *Temple and Worship in Biblical Israel*. Library of Hebrew Bible/ Old Testament Studies 422. Edited by J. Day. London: T&T Clark.

Hurvitz, A. 1972. *The Transition Period in Biblical Hebrew*. Jerusalem: Bialik Institute (Hebrew).

———. 1988. Dating the Priestly Source in Light of the Historical Study of Biblical Hebrew a Century after Wellhausen. *Zeitschrift für die alttestamentliche Wissenschaft* 100 (Supplement):88–100.

Hutter, M. 1983. Religionsgeschichtliche Erwägungen zur *'elōhîm* in 1 Sam. 28,13. *Biblische Notizen* 21:32–36.

Hutton, Rodney R. 1995. Magic or Street-Theater? The Power of the Prophetic Word. *Zeitschrift für die alttestamentliche Wissenschaft* 107:247–60.

Ilan, T. 1995. On a Newly Published Divorce Bill from the Judean Desert. *Harvard Theological Review* 88:195–202.

Irwin, W. H. 1967. "The Smooth Stones of the Wadi?" Isaiah 57,6. *Catholic Biblical Quarterly* 29:31–40.

Jackson, Kent. 1983. Ammonite Personal Names in the Context of West Semitic Onomasticon. Pages 507–21 in *The Word of the Lord Shall Go Forth: Essays in Honor of David Noel Freedman in Celebration of His Sixtieth Birthday*. Edited by C. L. Meyers and M. O'Connor. Philadelphia: American Schools of Oriental Research.

Jacobsen, Thorkild. 1976. *The Treasures of Darkness: A History of Mesopotamian Religion*. New Haven: Yale University Press.

James, William. 1902. *The Varieties of Religious Experience: A Study in Human Nature, Being the Gifford Lectures on Natural Religion Delivered at Edinburgh in 1901–1902*. New York: Longmans, Green.

Jamieson-Drake, D. W. 1991. *Scribes and Schools in Monarchic Judah. A Socio-Archeological Approach*. Journal for the Study of the Old Testament: Supplement Series 109; Social World of Biblical Antiquity 9. Sheffield: Almond.

Janzen, J. Gerald. 1990. The Character of the Calf and Its Cult in Exodus 32. *Catholic Biblical Quarterly* 52:597–607.

Jarick, John. 2005. The Temple of David in the Book of Chronicles. Pages 365–81. *Temple and Worship in Biblical Israel*. Library of Hebrew Bible/Old Testament Studies 422. Edited by J. Day. London: T&T Clark.

Jaroš, K. 1974. *Die Stellung des Elohisten zur kanaanäischen Religion*. Orbis Biblicus et Orientalis 4. Freiburg: Universitätsverlag; Gottingen: Vandenhoeck & Ruprecht.

Jenson, Philip P. 1992. *Graded Holiness: A Key to the Priestly Conception of the World*. Journal for the Study of the Old Testament: Supplement Series 106. Sheffield: JSOT Press.

———. 1995. The Levitical Sacrificial System. Pages 25–40 in *Sacrifice in the Bible*. Edited by R. T. Beckwith and M. J. Selman. Grand Rapids: Baker Academic.

Ji, C. C. 1995. Iron Age I in Central and Northern Transjordan: An Interim Summary of Archaeology Data. *Palestine Exploration Quarterly* 127:123–40.

Johnston, Philip S. 1994. The Underworld and the Dead in the Old Testament. *Tyndale Bulletin* 45:415–19.

———. 1995. "Left in Hell?" Psalm 16, Sheol, and the Holy One. Pages 213–22 in *The Lord's Anointed. Interpretation of Old Testament Messianic Texts*. Edited by P. E. Satterthwaite, R. S. Hess, and G. J. Wenham. Grand Rapids: Baker Academic.

———. 2002. *Shades of Sheol: Death and Afterlife in the Old Testament*. Downers Grove, IL: InterVarsity.

———. 2003. Figuring Out Figurines. *Tyndale Bulletin* 54(2):81–104.

———. 2005. Death in Egypt and Israel: A Theological Reflection. Pages 94–116 in *The Old Testament in Its World: Papers Read at the Winter Meeting, January 2003, the Society for Old Testament Study and at the Joint Meeting, July 2003, the Society for Old Testament Study and het Oudtestamentische Werkgezelschap in Nederland en België*. Oudtestamentische Studiën 52. Edited by R. P. Gordon and J. C. deMoor. Leiden; Boston; New York: Brill.

———. 2005. Ordeals in the Psalms? Pages 271–91 in *Temple and Worship in Biblical Israel*. Library of Hebrew Bible/Old Testament Studies 422. Edited by J. Day. London: T&T Clark.

Joyce, Paul M. 2005. Temple and Worship in Ezekiel 40–48. Pages 145–63 in *Temple and Worship in Biblical Israel*. Library of Hebrew Bible/Old Testament Studies 422. Edited by J. Day. London: T&T Clark.

Jung, Carl Gustav. 1938. *Psychology and Religion*. New Haven: Yale University Press.

Kaiser, Walter C., Jr. 1978. *Toward an Old Testament Theology*. Grand Rapids: Zondervan.

Kallai, Zecharia. 1993. The King of Israel and the House of David. *Israel Exploration Journal* 43:248.

Kalluveettil, Paul. 1982. *Declaration and Covenant: A Comprehensive Review of Covenant Formulae from the Old Testament and the Ancient Near East.* Analecta Biblica 88. Rome: Biblical Institute Press, 1982.

Kaufman, Stephen A. 1987. The Second Table of the Decalogue and the Implicit Categories of Ancient Near Eastern Law. Pages 111–116 in *Love and Death in the Ancient Near East: Essays in Honor of Marvin H. Pope.* Edited by J. H. Marks and R. M. Good. Guilford, CT: Four Quarters.

———. 1997. A Major New Phoenician Text for the 8th Century BCE—The Incirli Trilingual Inscription. Lecture presented at the Society of Biblical Literature annual meeting, San Francisco, November 23, 1997.

Kaufmann, Yehezkel. 1955. *The History of Israelite Religion from the Beginning until the End of the Second Temple.* 4 vols. Jerusalem: Mosad Bialik (Hebrew).

———. 1960. *The Religion of Israel, from Its Beginnings to the Babylonian Exile.* New York: Schocken.

Keel, Othmar. 1978. *The Symbolism of the Biblical World: Ancient Near Eastern Iconography and the Book of Psalms.* New York: Seabury.

———. 1986. Ancient Seals and the Bible. *Journal of the American Oriental Society* 106:309.

Keel, Othmar, and S. Schroer. 1985. *Studien zu den Stempelsiegeln aus Palästina/Israel.* Orbis Biblicus et Orientalis 67. Göttingen: Vandenhoeck & Ruprecht.

Keel, Othmar, and Christoph Uehlinger. 1992. *Göttinnen, Götter und Gottessymbole: Neue Erkentnisse zur Religionsgeschichte Kanaans und Israels aufgrund bislang unerschlossener ikonographischer Quellen.* Quaestiones Disputatae 134. Freiburg: Herder.

———. 1998. *Gods, Goddesses, and Images of God in Ancient Israel.* Translated by Thomas H. Trapp. Minneapolis: Fortress.

Kempinski, Aharon. 1986. Joshua's Altar—An Iron Age I Watchtower. *Biblical Archaeology Review* 12(1):42, 44–46, 48–49.

———. 1995. From Death to Resurrection: The Early Evidence. *Biblical Archaeology Review* 21(5):56–66, 82.

Kenyon, Kathleen M. 1978. *The Bible and Recent Archaeology.* Atlanta: John Knox.

Kikawada, I. M. 1971. Two Notes on Eve. *Journal of Biblical Literature* 91:33–37.

———. 1983. The Double Creation of Mankind in *Enki and Ninmah*, Atrahasis I 1–351, and Genesis 1–2. *Iraq* 45:43–45.

Kikawada, I. M., and A. Quinn. 1985. *Before Abraham Was. The Unity of Genesis 1–11.* Nashville: Abingdon.

Killebrew, Ann E. 2005. *Biblical Peoples and Ethnicity: An Archaeological Study of Egyptians, Canaanites, Philistines, and Early Israel, 1300–1100 B.C.E.* SBL Archaeology and Biblical Studies Number 9. Leiden: Brill.

King, Philip J. 1988. *Amos, Hosea, Micah—An Archaeological Commentary.* Philadelphia: Westminster.

———. 1993. *Jeremiah. An Archaeological Companion.* Louisville: Westminster/John Knox.

King, Philip J., and Lawrence E. Stager. 2001. *Life in Biblical Israel.* Louisville: Westminster/John Knox.

Kirkpatrick, Patricia G. 1988. *The Old Testament and Folklore Study.* Journal for the Study of the Old Testament: Supplement Series 62. Sheffield: JSOT Press.

Kitchen, Kenneth A. 1979. Egypt, Ugarit, Qatna, and Covenant. *Ugarit Forschungen* 11:453–64.

———. 1989a. The Rise and Fall of Covenant, Law and Treaty. *Tyndale Bulletin* 40:118–35.

———. 1989b. Shishak's Military Campaign in Israel Confirmed. *Biblical Archaeology Review* 15(3):32–33.

———. 1989c. Where Did Solomon's Gold Go? *Biblical Archaeology Review* 15(3):30.

———. 1993. The Tabernacle—A Bronze Age Artifact. *Eretz-Israel* 24:119*–129*.

———. 1994. Genesis 12–50 in the Near Eastern World. Pages 67–92 in *He Swore an Oath: Biblical Themes from Genesis 12–50*. Edited by R. S. Hess, P. E. Satterthwaite, and G. J. Wenham. 2nd ed. Grand Rapids: Baker Academic; Carlisle: Paternoster.

———. 2000a. The Desert Tabernacle. *Bible Review* 16(6):14–21.

———. 2000b. *Documentation for Ancient Arabia. Part II. Bibliographical Catalogue of Texts.* The World of Ancient Arabia Series. Liverpool: Liverpool University Press.

———. 2002. The Controlling Role of External Evidence in Assessing the Historical Status of the Israelite Monarchy. Pages 111–30 in *Windows into Old Testament History: Evidence, Argument, and the Crisis of "Biblical Israel."* Edited by V. P. Long, D. W. Baker, and G. J. Wenham. Grand Rapids: Eerdmans.

———. 2003. *On the Reliability of the Old Testament.* Grand Rapids: Eerdmans.

Kiuchi, N. 1987. *The Purification Offering in the Priestly Literature: Its Meaning and Function.* Journal for the Study of the Old Testament Supplement 56. Sheffield: JSOT Press.

Klein, Joseph P. 1993. How Job Fulfills God's Word to Cain. *Bible Review* 9(3):40–43.

Kletter, Raz. 1996. *The Judean Pillar—Figurines and the Archaeology of Asherah.* BAR International Series 636. Oxford: Tempus Reparatum.

———. 1999. Pots and Polities: Material Remains of Late Iron Age Judah in Relation to Its Political Borders. *Bulletin of the American Schools of Oriental Research* 314:19–54.

———. 2001. Between Archaeology and Theology: The Pillar Figurines from Judah and Asherah. Pages 177–216 in *Studies in the Archaeology of the Iron Age in Israel and Jordan.* Journal for the Study of the Old Testament: Supplement Series 331. Edited by A. Mazar and G. Mathias. Sheffield: Sheffield Academic Press.

Kletter, Raz, and Irit Ziffer. 2003. Yavné. *Hadashot Arkeologiyot* 115:60–62 [Hebrew], 46*–47* [English].

Kleven, Terence. 1994. Up the Waterspout. How David's General Joab Got Inside Jerusalem. *Biblical Archaeology Review* 20(4):34–35.

Klingbeil, Gerald. 2000. The Anointing of Aaron: A Study of Leviticus 8:12 in Its OT and ANE Context. *Andrews University Seminary Studies* 38:231–43.

———. Forthcoming. *Ritual in the Bible.*

Knauf, Ernst Axel. 2000. Jerusalem in the Late Bronze and Early Iron Ages: A Proposal. *Tel Aviv* 27:91–102.

Knight, Douglas A. 1975. *Rediscovering the Traditions of Israel.* 2nd ed. Atlanta: Scholars Press.

Knohl, I. 1995. *The Sanctuary of Silence: The Priestly Torah and the Holiness School.* Minneapolis: Fortress.

Knoppers, Gary N. 1993. *Two Nations under God: The Deuteronomistic History of Solomon and the Dual Monarchies.* 2 vols. Harvard Semitic Monographs 52. Atlanta: Scholars Press.

————. 1995. Prayer and Propaganda: Solomon's Dedication of the Temple and the Deuteronomist's Program. *Catholic Biblical Quarterly* 57:229–54.

————. 1996. Ancient Near Eastern Royal Grants and the Davidic Covenant. *Journal of the American Oriental Society* 116:670–97.

————. 1997. The Vanishing Solomon: The Disappearance of the United Monarchy from Recent Histories of Ancient Israel. *Journal of Biblical Literature* 116:19–44.

Knudtzon, J. A. 1915. *Die El-Amarna-Tafeln mit Einleitung und Erla/uterungen.* 2 Teilen. Leipzig: J. C. Hinrichs. Repr., Aalen: Otto Zeller, 1964.

Koch, K. 1988. Aschera als Himmelskönigin in Jerusalem. *Ugarit Forschungen* 20:385–408.

Kofoed, Jens Bruun. 2002. Epistemology, Historiographic Method, and the "Copenhagen School." Pages 23–43 in *Windows into Old Testament Israel: Evidence, Argument, and the Crisis of "Biblical Israel."* Edited by V. P. Long, D. W. Baker, and G. J. Wenham. Grand Rapids: Eerdmans.

————. 2005. *Text and History: Historiography and the Study of the Biblical Text.* Winona Lake, IN: Eisenbrauns.

Koitabashi, Matahisa. 1998. Music in the Texts from Ugarit. *Ugarit Forschungen* 30:363–96.

Kooij, G. van der. 1993. Tell Deir ʿAlla. *The New Encyclopedia of Archaeological Excavations in the Holy Land.* New York: Simon & Schuster.

Korošec, V. 1931. *Hethitische Staatsverträge. Ein Beitrag zu ihrer juristischen Wertung.* Leipziger rechtswissenschaftliche Studien 60. Leipzig: T. Weicher.

Korpel, M. C. A. 1990. *A Rift in the Clouds.* Ugaritisch-Biblische Literatur 8. Münster: Ugarit Verlag.

Kottsieper, I. 1998. El—Ein aramäischer Gott?—Eine Antwort. *Biblische Notizen* 94:87–98.

Kraemer, David. 1993. On the Relationship of the Books of Ezra and Nehemiah. *Journal for the Study of the Old Testament* 59:73–92.

Kramer, Samuel N. 1968. "The Babel of Tongues": A Sumerian Version. *Journal of the American Oriental Society* 88:108–11.

Kugel, J. L. 1981. *The Idea of Biblical Poetry.* New Haven: Yale University Press.

Kvanvig, Helge S. 1988. *Roots of Apocalyptic: The Mesopotamian Background of the Enoch Figure and of the Son of Man.* Wissenschaftliche Monographien zum Alten und Neuen Testament 61. Neukirchener: Neukirchen-Vluyn.

Laato, Antti. 1994. Zechariah 4,6b–10a and the Akkadian Royal Building Inscriptions. *Zeitschrift für die alttestamentliche Wissenschaft* 106:53–69.

————. 1997. Second Samuel 7 and Ancient Near Eastern Royal Ideology. *Catholic Biblical Quarterly* 59:244–69.

Lafont, Bertrand. 1999. Sacrifices et rituels à Mari et dans la bible. *Revue de Assyriologie* 93:57–77.

Lambert, W. 1975. The Historical Development of the Mesopotamian Pantheon: A Study in Sophisticated Polytheism. Pages 191–200 in *Unity and Diversity: Essays in the History, Literature, and Religion of the Ancient Near East.* Edited by H. Goedicke and J. J. M. Roberts. Baltimore: Johns Hopkins University Press.

————. 1992. Prostitution. Pages 127–57 in *Außenseiter und Randgruppen: Beiträge zu einer Sozialgeschichte des Alten Orients.* Xenia: Konstanzer Althistorische Vorträge und Forschungen, Heft 32. Edited by V. Haas. Konstanz: Universitätsverlag.

————. 2004. Mesopotamian Sources and Pre-Exilic Israel. Pages 352–65 in *In Search of Pre-Exilic Israel*. Journal for the Study of the Old Testament Supplement Series 446. Edited by J. Day. New York: T&T Clark.

————. Forthcoming. A Late Babylonian Tablet. Paper presented at the Society of Biblical Literature International Meeting, July 26, 2004.

Landersdorfer, S. 1916. *Sumerisches Sprachgut im alten Testament*. Leipzig: J. C. Hinrichs.

Lang, Bernhard. 1983. *Monotheism and the Prophetic Minority: An Essay in Biblical History and Sociology*. The Social World of Biblical Antiquity 1. Sheffield: Almond.

Lapp, Paul W. 1969a. The 1968 Excavations at Tell Ta'annek: The New Cultic Stand. *Bulletin of the American Schools of Oriental Research* 195:42–44.

————. 1969b. A Ritual Incense Stand from Taanak. *Qadmoniot* 5:16–17 [Hebrew].

Lapsley, Jacqueline E. 2003. Feeling Our Way: Love for God in Deuteronomy. *Catholic Biblical Quarterly* 65:350–69.

Larkin, Katrina J. A. 1994. *The Eschatology of Second Zechariah: A Study of the Formation of a Mantological Wisdom Anthology*. Contribution to Biblical Exegesis and Theology 6. Kampen: Kok Pharos.

LaRocca-Pitts, E. C. 2001. *"Of Wood and Stone": The Significance of Israelite Cultic Items in the Bible and Its Early Interpreters*. Harvard Semitic Museum Monographs 61. Winona Lake, IN: Eisenbrauns.

Le Déaut, R. 1961. Traditions targumiques dans le corpus Paulinien? (Hebr 11, 4 et 12, 24; Gal 4, 29–30; II Cor 3, 16). *Biblica* 42:28–48.

Lemaire, André. 1976. Priéres en temps de crise: les inscriptions de Khirbet Beit Lei. *Revue Biblique* 83:558–68.

————. 1977. *Inscriptions hébraïques. Tome I. Les ostraca. Littératures anciennes du proche-orient*. Paris: Les éditions du Cerf.

————. 1981. Un inscription paléo-hébraïque sur grenade en ivoire. *Revue Biblique* 88:236–39.

————. 1984. Who or What was Yahweh's Asherah? *Biblical Archaeology Review* 10(6):42–51.

————. 1994a. Déesses et dieux de Syria-Palestine d'après les inscriptions (c. 1000–500 Av. N. E.). Pages 127–58 in *Ein Gott allein? JHWH-verehrung und biblischer Monotheismus im Kontext der Israelitischen und altorientalischen Religionsgeschichte*. Edited by W. Dietrich and M. A. Klopfenstein. Göttingen: Vandenhoeck & Ruprecht.

————. 1994b. La dynastie davidique (*byt dwd*) dans deux inscriptions ouest-sémitiques du IXe 5. av. J.C. *Studi Epigrafici e Linguistici* 11:17–19.

————. 1994c. "House of David" Restored in Moabite Inscription. *Biblical Archaeology Review* 20(3):30–37.

————. 1999. Traditions amorrites et bible: le prophétisme. *Revue Assyriologie* 93:49–56.

————. 2004. Hebrew and West Semitic Inscriptions and Pre-Exilic Israel. Pages 366–85 in *In Search of Pre-Exilic Israel*. Journal for the Study of the Old Testament Supplement Series 446. Edited by J. Day. New York: T&T Clark.

————. 2006. A Re-examination of the Inscribed Pomegranate: A Rejoinder. *Israel Exploration Journal* 56:167–77.

Lemche, Niels Peter. 1993. The Old Testament—A Hellenistic Book? *Scandinavian Journal of the Old Testament* 7:163–93.

———. 1998. *Prelude to Israel's Past: Background and Beginnings of Israelite History and Identity*. Translated by E. F. Maniscalco. Peabody, MA: Hendrickson.

Lenzen, C. J. 1997. Irbid. *The Oxford Encyclopedia of Archaeology in the Near East*. New York: Oxford University Press.

Levenson, Jon D. 1993. *The Death and Resurrection of the Beloved Son: The Transformation of Child Sacrifice in Judaism and Christianity*. New Haven: Yale University Press.

———. 2002. The Resurrection of the Dead and the Construction of Personal Identity in Ancient Israel. Pages 305–22 in *Congress Volume Basel 2001*. Supplements to Vetus Testamentum 92. Edited by A. Lemaire. Leiden: Brill.

Levine, Baruch A. 1963. Ugaritic Descriptive Rituals. *Journal of Cuneiform Studies* 17:105–11.

———. 1965. The Descriptive Tabernacle Texts of the Pentateuch. *Journal of the American Oriental Society* 85:307–18.

———. 1974. *In the Presence of the Lord: A Study of Cult and Some Cultic Terms in Ancient Israel*. Leiden: Brill.

———. 1989. *Leviticus: The Traditional Hebrew Text with the New JPS Translation*. Philadelphia: Jewish Publication Society.

———. 1993a. *Lpny YHWH*—Phenomenology of the Open-Air-Altar in Biblical Israel. Pages 196–205 in *Biblical Archaeology Today, 1990. Proceedings of the Second International Congress on Biblical Archaeology. Jerusalem, June–July 1990*. Edited by A. Biran and J. Aviram. Jerusalem: Israel Exploration Society.

———. 1993b. *Numbers 1–20: A New Translation with Introduction and Commentary*. Anchor Bible 4. New York: Doubleday.

———. 2000. *Numbers 21–36: A New Translation with Introduction and Commentary*. Anchor Bible 4A. New York: Doubleday.

———. 2002. Ritual as Symbol: Modes of Sacrifice in Israelite Religion. Pages 125–35 in *Sacred Time, Sacred Place: Archaeology and the Religion of Israel*. Edited by B. M. Gittlen. Winona Lake, IN: Eisenbrauns.

———. 2003. Leviticus: Its Literary History and Location in Biblical Literature. Pages 11–23 in *The Book of Leviticus. Composition and Reception*. Edited by R. Rendtorff and R. A. Kugler. Vetus Testamentum Supplements 93. Leiden: Brill.

Levinson, Bernard M. 1997. *Deuteronomy and the Hermeneutics of Legal Innovation*. Oxford: Oxford University Press.

———. 2000. The Hermeneutics of Tradition in Deuteronomy: A Reply to J. G. McConville. *Journal of Biblical Literature* 119:269–86.

———. 2006. *Resurrection and the Restoration of Israel: The Ultimate Victory of the God of Life*. New Haven: Yale University Press.

Levy, Thomas E., and Mohammad Najjar. 2006. Edom and Copper—The Emergence of Ancient Israel's Rival. *Biblical Archaeology Review* 32(4):24–35, 70.

Lévy-Bruhl, Lucien. 1922. *La mentalité primitive*. Travaux de l'Année sociologique. Paris: Librairie Félix Alcan.

Lewis, Theodore J. 1987. Death Cult Imagery in Isaiah 57. *Harvard Theological Review* 11:267–84.

———. 1989. *Cults of the Dead in Ancient Israel and Ugarit*. Harvard Semitic Monographs 39. Atlanta: Scholars Press.

———. 1996. The Identity and Function of El/Baal Berith. *Journal of Biblical Literature* 115:401–23.

————. 1998. Divine Images and Aniconism in Ancient Israel. *Journal of the American Oriental Society* 118:36–53.

————. 2002. How Far Can Texts Take Us? Evaluating Textual Sources for Reconstructing Ancient Israelite Beliefs about the Dead. Pages 169–217 in *Sacred Time, Sacred Place: Archaeology and the Religion of Israel*. Edited by B. M. Gittlen. Winona Lake, IN: Eisenbrauns.

Lipiński, Edouard. 1973. Eshmun, "Healer." *Annali dell'Istituto Orientale di Napoli* 23:161–83.

————. 1987. Le dieu Damu dans l'onomastique d'Ébla. Pages 91–99 in *Ebla 1975–1987. Dieci anni di studi linguistici e filologici*. Istituto Universitario Orientale. Dipartimento di Studi Asiatici. Series Minor 27. Edited by L. Cagni. Naples: Istituto Universitario Orientale.

————. 1993a. Les Sémites selon Gen 10,21 et 1 Chr 1,17–23. *Zeitschrift für Althebraistik* 6:193–215.

————. 1993b. The Session Moderator's Introduction. Pages 321–24 in *Biblical Archaeology Today, 1990. Proceedings of the Second International Congress on Biblical Archaeology. Jerusalem, June–July 1990*. Edited by A. Biran and J. Aviram. Jerusalem: Israel Exploration Society.

Lipschitz, Oded. 2005. *The Fall and Rise of Jerusalem: Judah under Babylonian Rule*. Winona Lake, IN: Eisenbrauns.

Lipschitz, Oded, and Manfred Oeming, eds. 2006. *Judah and the Judeans in the Persian Period*. Winona Lake, IN: Eisenbrauns.

Liverani, Mario. 1990. *Prestige and Interest: International Relations in the Near East ca. 1600–1100 B.C.* History of the Ancient Near East Studies 1. Padova: Sargon srl.

Loewenstamm, S. 1967. The Making and Destruction of the Golden Calf. *Biblica* 48:481–90.

————. 1975. The Making and Destroying of the Golden Calf—A Rejoinder. *Biblica* 56:330–48.

————. 1976. Cain and Abel. *Encyclopedia Biblica*.

Lohfink, Norbert. 1995. Bund als Vertrag im Deuteronomium. *Zeitschrift für die alttestamentliche Wissenschaft* 107:215–39.

Long, V. Philips. 1989. *The Reign and Rejection of King Saul: A Case for Literary and Theological Coherence*. Atlanta: Scholars Press.

Loretz, Oswald. 1992a. Die Teraphim als "Ahnen-Götter-Figur(in)en" im Lichte der Texte aus Nuzi, Emar und Ugarit. Anmerkungen zu *ilānū/ilh, ilhm/ʾlhym* und DINGIR.ERÍN.MEŠ/*inš ilm. Ugarit-Forschungen* 24:133–78.

————. 1992b. Ugariter, "Kanaanäer" und "Israeliten." *Ugarit-Forschungen* 24:249–58.

Lucas, Ernest C. 1989. The Origin of Daniel's Four Empires Scheme Re-Examined. *Tyndale Bulletin* 40:185–202.

————. 1990. The Sources of Daniel's Animal Imagery. *Tyndale Bulletin* 41:161–85.

————. 2002. *Daniel*. Leicester: Inter-Varsity Press.

Machinist, Peter. 1976. Literature as Politics: The Tukulti-Ninurta Epic and the Bible. *Catholic Biblical Quarterly* 38:455–82.

————. 1986. On Self-Consciousness in Mesopotamia. Pages 183–202, 511–18 in *The Origins and Diversity of Axial Age Civilizations*. Edited by S. N. Eisenstadt. Albany: State University of New York.

———. 1991. The Question of Distinctiveness in Ancient Israel: An Essay. Pages 196–212 in *Ah Assyria . . . Studies in Assyrian History and Ancient Near Eastern Historiography Presented to Hayim Tadmor*. Edited by M. Cogan and I. Eph'al. Jerusalem: Magnes Press.

Maier, C., and J. Tropper. 1998. El—Ein aramäischer Gott. *Biblische Notizen* 93:77–88.

Maier, W. A., III. 1986. *'Ašerah: Extrabiblical Evidence*. Harvard Semitic Monograph 37. Atlanta: Scholars Press.

Malamat, Abraham. 1989. *Mari and the Early Israelite Experience*. Schweich Lectures. Oxford: Clarendon.

———. 1995. A Note on the Ritual of Treaty Making in Mari and the Bible. *Israel Exploration Journal* 45:226–29.

Margalit, Baruch. 1989. Some Observations on the Inscription and Drawing from Khirbet el-Qôm. *Vetus Testamentum* 39:371–78.

Margueron, Jean-Claude. 1982. Rapport préliminaire sur les 3ᵉ, 4ᵉ, 5ᵉ, et 6ᵉ campagnes de fouille à Meskéné-Emar. *Annales archéologiques arabes syriennes* 32:233–49.

———. 1995. Emar, Capital of Aštata in the Fourteenth Century BCE. *Biblical Archaeologist* 58(3):126–38.

Marks, Herbert. 1995. Biblical Naming and Poetic Etymology. *Journal of Biblical Literature* 114:21–42.

Martin, Bernice. 2001. The Pentecostal Gender Paradox: A Cautionary Tale for the Sociology of Religion. Pages 52–66 in *The Blackwell Companion to Sociology of Religion*. Edited by R. K. Fenn. Oxford: Blackwell.

Martin, W. J. 1955. *Stylistic Criteria and the Analysis of the Pentateuch*. Tyndale Monographs 2. London: Tyndale Press.

Marx, Alfred. 2005. *Les systèmes sacrificiels de l'Ancien Testament: formes et fonctions du culte sacrificiel à Yhwh*. Supplements to Vetus Testamentum 105. Leiden: Brill.

Marx, Karl. 2002. *Marx on Religion*. Edited by J. Raines. Philadelphia: Temple University Press.

Marx, Karl, and Frederick Engels. 2002. *The Communist Manifesto*. Edited by G. Stedman. New York: Penguin.

Maul, Stefan M. 1999. Gottesdienst im Sonnenheiligtum zu Sippar. Pages 285–316 in *Munuscula Mesopotamica. Festschrift für Johannes Renger*. Alter Orient und Altes Testament 267. Edited by B. Böck, E. Cancik-Kirschbaum, and T. Richter. Münster: Ugarit-Verlag.

May, Herbert G., and R. M. Engberg. 1935. *Material Remains of the Megiddo Cult*. Oriental Institute Publication 26. Chicago and London: University of Chicago.

Mayes, A. D. H. 1974. *Israel in the Period of the Judges*. Naperville: A. R. Allenson.

———. 1989. Sociology and the Old Testament. Pages 39–63 in *The World of Ancient Israel: Sociological, Anthropological and Political Perspectives*. Edited by R. E. Clements. Cambridge: Cambridge University Press.

Mazar, Amihai. 1982. The "Bull Site"—An Iron Age I Open Cult Place. *Bulletin of the American Schools of Oriental Research* 247:27–42.

———. 1993. Tell Qasile. *The New Encyclopedia of Archaeological Excavations in the Holy Land*. New York: Simon & Schuster.

———. 1997a. Beth-Shean. *The Oxford Encyclopedia of Archaeology in the Near East*. New York: Oxford University Press.

———. 1997b. Iron Age Chronology: A Reply to I. Finkelstein. *Levant* 29:157–67.

Mazar, Amihai, and John Camp. 2000. Will Tel Rehov Save the United Monarchy? *Biblical Archaeology Review* 26(2):38–51, 75.

Mazar, Eilat. 2006. Did I Find King David's Palace? *Biblical Archaeology Review* 32(1):16–27, 70.

McCarter, P. Kyle, Jr. 1987. Aspects of the Religion of the Israelite Monarchy: Biblical and Epigraphic Data. Pages 137–55 in *Ancient Israelite Religion: Essays in Honor of Frank Moore Cross*. Edited by P. D. Miller Jr., P. D. Hanson, and S. D. McBride. Philadelphia: Fortress.

———. 1996. Pieces of the Puzzle. *Biblical Archaeology Review* 22(2):39–43, 62–63.

———. 1999. The Patriarchal Age: Abraham, Isaac and Jacob. Revised by R. Hendel. Pages 1–31 in *Ancient Israel: From Abraham to the Roman Destruction of the Temple*. Rev. ed. Edited by H. Shanks. Washington, DC: Biblical Archaeology Society.

McCarthy, Dennis J. 1972. *Old Testament Covenant: A Survey of Current Opinions*. Atlanta: John Knox.

———. 1978. *Treaty and Covenant: A Study in Form in the Ancient Oriental Documents and in the Old Testament*. Analecta Biblica 21A. Rome: Biblical Institute Press.

McConville, J. Gordon. 2000. Deuteronomy's Unification of Passover and *Maṣṣôt*: A Response to Bernard M. Levinson. *Journal of Biblical Literature* 119:47–58.

McEvenue, Sean. 1994. A Return to Sources in Genesis 28,10–22? *Zeitschrift für die alttestamentliche Wissenschaft* 106:375–89.

McFall, Leslie. 1991. Was Nehemiah Contemporary with Ezra in 458 BC? *Westminster Theological Journal* 53:263–93.

Mendenhall, George E. 1954. Covenant Forms in Israelite Tradition. *Biblical Archaeologist* 17:20–46, 50–76.

———. 1973. *The Tenth Generation: The Origins of the Biblical Tradition*. Baltimore and London: Johns Hopkins University Press.

———. 2001. *Ancient Israel's Faith and History: An Introduction to the Bible in Context*. Edited by Gary A. Herion. Louisville: Westminster John Knox.

Merling, David, Sr. 1997. *The Book of Joshua: Its Theme and Role in Archaeological Discussions*. Andrews University Seminary Doctoral Dissertation Series 23. Berrien Springs, MI: Andrews University Press.

Merlo, Paolo. 1994. L'Asherah di Yhwh a Kuntillet ʿAjrud. *Studi Epigrafici e Linguistici sul Vicino Oriente antico* 11:21–54.

Merlo, Paolo, and Paolo Xella. 1999. The Ugaritic Cultic Texts: 1 The Rituals. Pages 287–304 in *Handbook of Ugaritic Studies*. Handbook of Oriental Studies: The Near and Middle East 39. Edited by W. G. E. Watson and N. Wyatt. Leiden: Brill.

Meshel, Z. 1978a. Kuntillet ʿAjrûd: An Israelite Religious Center in the Northern Sinai. *Expedition* 20(4):50–54.

———. 1978b. *Kuntillet ʿAjrûd: A Religious Center from the Time of the Judaean Monarchy on the Border of Sinai*. Israel Museum Catalogue 175. Jerusalem: Israel Museum.

———. 1979. Did Yahweh Have a Consort? The New Religious Inscriptions from the Sinai. *Biblical Archaeology Review* 5(2):24–35.

Mettinger, Tryggve N. D. 1976. *King and Messiah: The Civil and Sacral Legitimation of the Israelite Kings*. Coniectanea Biblica Old Testament Series 8. Stockholm: Almqvist & Wiksell.

———. 1988. *In Search of God: The Meaning and Message of the Everlasting Names*. Translated by F. H. Cryer. Philadelphia: Fortress.

————. 1990. The Elusive Essence: YHWH, El and Baal and the Distinctiveness of Israelite Faith. Pages 393–417 in *Die Hebräische Bibel und Ihre zweifache Nachgeschichte: Festschrift für Rolf Rendtorff zum 65. Geburtstag*. Edited by E. Blum et al. Neukirchen-Vluyn: Neukirchener Verlag.

————. 1995. *No Graven Image? Israelite Aniconism in Its Ancient Near Eastern Context*. Coniectanea Biblica Old Testament Series 42. Stockholm: Almqvist & Wiksell.

————. 2001. *The Riddle of the Resurrection: "Dying and Rising Gods" in the Ancient Near East*. Coniectanea Biblica Old Testament Series 50. Stockholm: Almqvist & Wiksell.

Meyers, Carol L. 1987. David as Temple Builder. Pages 357–76 in *Ancient Israelite Religion: Essays in Honor of Frank Moore Cross*. Edited by P. D. Miller Jr., P. D. Hanson, and S. D. McBride. Philadelphia: Fortress.

————. 1988. *Discovering Eve: Ancient Israelite Women in Context*. New York: Oxford University Press.

————. 2002. From Household to House of Yahweh: Women's Religious Culture in Ancient Israel. Pages 277–303 in *Congress Volume Basel 2001*. Supplements to Vetus Testamentum 92. Edited by A. Lemaire. Leiden: Brill.

————. 2005. *Households and Holiness: The Religious Culture of Israelite Women*. Minneapolis: Fortress.

Meyers, Carol L., and Eric M. Meyers. 1987. *Haggai, Zechariah 1–8*. Anchor Bible 25B. Garden City, NY: Doubleday.

————. 1993. *Zechariah 9–14: A New Translation with Introduction and Commentary*. Anchor Bible 25C. New York: Doubleday.

Meyers, Eric M. 1987. The Persian Period and the Judean Restoration: From Zerubbabel to Nehemiah. Pages 510–21 in *Ancient Israelite Religion: Essays in Honor of Frank Moore Cross*. Edited by P. D. Miller Jr., P. D. Hanson, and S. D. McBride. Philadelphia: Fortress.

Middlemas, Jill. 2005. Divine Reversal and the Role of the Temple in Trito-Isaiah. Pages 164–87 in *Temple and Worship in Biblical Israel*. Library of Hebrew Bible/Old Testament Studies 422. Edited by J. Day. London: T&T Clark.

Milgrom, Jacob. 1990. *Numbers*. The New JPS Torah Commentary. Philadelphia: Jewish Publication Society.

————. 1991. *Leviticus 1–16: A New Translation and Commentary*. Vol. 3 of The Anchor Bible. New York: Doubleday.

————. 2000a. *Leviticus 17–22: A New Translation and Commentary*. Vol. 3A of The Anchor Bible. New York: Doubleday.

————. 2000b. *Leviticus 23–27: A New Translation and Commentary*. Vol. 3B of The Anchor Bible. New York: Doubleday.

Millard, Alan R. 1989. Does the Bible Exaggerate King Solomon's Wealth? *Biblical Archaeology Review* 15(3):20–29, 31, 34.

————. 1990. Israelite and Aramean History in the Light of Inscriptions. *Tyndale Bulletin* 41(2):261–75.

————. 1995. The Knowledge of Writing in Iron Age Palestine. *Tyndale Bulletin* 46:207–17.

————. 1997. Observations from the Eponym Lists. Pages 207–15 in *Assyria 1995*. Edited by S. Parpola and R. M. Whiting. Helsinki: Helsinki University Press.

————. 1998a. The History of Israel against the Background of Ancient Near Eastern History. Pages 101–17 in *From the Ancient Sites of Israel: Essays on Archaeology, History and Theology in Memory of Aapeli Saarisalo (1896–1986)*. Iustitia Supplement Series. Edited by T. Eskola and E. Junkkaala. Helsinki: Theological Institute of Finland.

———. 1998b. Review of Niditch 1996, *Oral Word and Written Word: Ancient Israelite Literature*. *Journal of Theological Studies* n.s. 49:699–705.

———. 1999. Owners and Users of Hebrew Seals. *Eretz-Israel* 26:129*–133*.

Miller, J. Maxwell. 1989. The Israelite Journey through (around) Moab and Moabite Toponymy. *Journal of Biblical Literature* 108:577–95.

Miller, Patrick D., Jr. 2000. *The Religion of Ancient Israel*. Louisville: Westminster John Knox.

Miller, Patrick D., Jr., Paul D. Hanson, and S. Dean McBride, eds. 1987. *Ancient Israelite Religion: Essays in Honor of Frank Moore Cross*. Philadelphia: Fortress.

Miroschedji, Pierre de. 1993. Tell el-Farʿah (North): Neolithic Period to Middle Bronze Age. *The New Encyclopedia of Archaeological Excavations in the Holy Land*. New York: Simon & Schuster.

Mizrachi, Y. 1992. Mystery Circles. *Biblical Archaeology Review* 18(4):46–57, 84.

Moberly, R. W. L. 1992a. *Genesis 12–50*. Sheffield: JSOT Press.

———. 1992b. *The Old Testament of the Old Testament: Patriarchal Narratives and Mosaic Yahwism*. Minneapolis: Augsburg Fortress.

———. 1993. Christological Readings of Genesis 22. Pages 143–73 in *He Swore an Oath: Biblical Themes from Genesis 12–50*. Edited by R. S. Hess, P. E. Satterthwaite, and G. J. Wenham. Grand Rapids: Baker Academic.

Modéus, Martin. 2005. *Sacrifice and Symbol: Biblical Šelāmîm in a Ritual Perspective*. Coniectanea Biblica Old Testament 52. Stockholm: Almqvist & Wiksell.

Moffatt, J. 1924. *A Critical and Exegetical Commentary on the Epistle to the Hebrews*. Edinburgh: T&T Clark.

Monson, John. 1999. The Temple of Solomon: Heart of Jerusalem. Pages 1–22 in *Zion, City of Our God*. Edited by R. S. Hess and G. J. Wenham. Grand Rapids: Eerdmans.

———. 2000. The New ʿAin Dara Temple: Closest Solomonic Parallel. *Biblical Archaeology Review* 26(3):20–35, 67.

Moor, Johannes C. de. 1971. *The Seasonal Pattern in the Ugaritic Myth of Baʿlu*. Alter Orient und Altes Testament 16. Neukirchen-Vluyn: Neukirchener Verlag.

———. 1987. *An Anthology of Religious Texts from Ugarit*. Leiden: Brill.

———. 1990a. Lovable Death in the Ancient Near East. *Ugarit Forschungen* 22:233–45.

———. 1990b. *The Rise of Yahwism: The Roots of Israelite Monotheism*. Bibliotheca ephemeridum theologicarum lovaniensium 91. Leuven: Peeters.

———. 1995. A Note on the Ritual of Treaty-Making in Mari and the Bible. *Israel Exploration Journal* 45:226–29.

———. 1997. *The Rise of Yahwism: The Roots of Israelite Monotheism*. Rev. ed. Leuven: Peeters.

Moor, Johannes C. de, and Paul Sanders. 1991. An Ugaritic Expiation Ritual and Its Old Testament Parallels. *Ugarit Forschungen* 23:283–300.

Moore, Michael S. 1994. Review of L. Schmidt, *Studien zur Priesterschrift*. *Catholic Biblical Quarterly* 56:778–80.

Moran, William L. 1963. The Ancient Near Eastern Background of the Love of God in Deuteronomy. *Catholic Biblical Quarterly* 25:77–87.

Morgenstern, Julian. 1956. Jerusalem in 485 B.C. *Hebrew Union College Annual* 27:101–79.

———. 1957. Jerusalem in 485 B.C. *Hebrew Union College Annual* 28:15–47.

———. 1960. Jerusalem in 485 B.C. *Hebrew Union College Annual* 31:1–29.

———. 1967. Jerusalem in 485 B.C. *Hebrew Union College Annual* 37:1–28.

Mosca, Paul. 1975. *Child Sacrifice in Canaanite and Israelite Religion: A Study in Mulk and Molek*. PhD diss., Harvard University.

Moye, R. H. 1990. In the Beginning: Myth and History in Genesis and Exodus. *Journal of Biblical Literature* 109:577–98.

Müller, Friedrich Max. 1975a. *Anthropological Religion*. 1891 Gifford Lectures. New York: AMS Press. (Orig. pub. 1892.)

———. 1975b. *Natural Religion*. 1888–1889 Gifford Lectures. New York: AMS Press. (Orig. pub. 1891.)

———. 1975c. *Physical Religion*. 1890 Gifford Lectures. New York: AMS Press. (Orig. pub. 1892.)

———. 1975d. *Theosophy: or, Psychological Religion*. 1892 Gifford Lectures. New York: AMS Press. (Orig. pub. 1903.)

Müller, H.-P. 1992. Kolloquialsprache und Volksreligion in den Inschriften von *Kuntillet 'Aǧrūd* und *Ḥirbet el-Qōm*. *Zeitschrift für Althebraistik* 5:15–51.

Müller, M. 1993. The Septuagint as the Bible of the New Testament Church. Some Reflections. *Scandinavian Journal of the Old Testament* 7:194–207.

Muth, Richard F. 1997. Economic Influences on Early Israel. *Journal for the Study of the Old Testament* 75:77–92.

Na'aman, Nadav. 1996a. The Contribution of the Amarna Letters to the Debate on Jerusalem's Political Position in the Tenth Century B.C.E. *Bulletin of the American Schools of Oriental Research* 304:17–27.

———. 1996b. Sources and Composition in the History of David. Pages 170–86 in *The Origins of the Ancient Israelite States*. Journal for the Study of the Old Testament: Supplement Series 228. Edited by V. Fritz and P. R. Davies. Sheffield: Sheffield Academic Press.

———. 1997. Cow Town or Royal Capital? Evidence for Iron Age Jerusalem. *Biblical Archaeology Review* 23(4):43–47, 67.

Naveh, J. 1963. Old Hebrew Inscriptions in a Burial Cave. *Israel Exploration Journal* 13:74–92.

———. 1979. Graffiti and Dedications. *Bulletin of the American Schools of Oriental Research* 235:27–30.

Nel, Marius. 2003. Zoroastrianisme en die ontstaan van apokaliptiese denke. *Hervormde Teologiese Studies* 59:1425–42.

Nicholson, E. W. 1973. *Exodus and Sinai in History and Tradition*. Oxford: Blackwell.

———. 1986. *God and His People. Covenant and Theology in the Old Testament*. Oxford: Oxford University Press.

———. 1994. Story and History in the Old Testament. Pages 135–50 in *Language Theology and the Bible. Essays in Honour of James Barr*. Edited by S. E. Balentine and J. Barton. Oxford: Clarendon.

———. 2004. Current "Revisionism" and the Literature of the Old Testament. Pages 1–22 in *In Search of Pre-Exilic Israel*. Journal for the Study of the Old Testament: Supplement Series 406. Edited by J. Day. Oxford: Oxford University Press.

Niditch, Susan. 1996. *Oral Word and Written Word: Ancient Israelite Literature*. Louisville: Westminster John Knox.

————. 1997. *Ancient Israelite Religion*. New York: Oxford University Press.

Niehr, Herbert. 1990. *Der höchste Gott: Alttestamentlicher JWHW-Glaube im Kontext syrisch-kanaanäischer Religion des 1. Jahrtausends v. Chron.* Beihefte zur Zeitschrift für die alttestamentliche Wissenschaft 190. Berlin: de Gruyter.

————. 2003. The Changed Status of the Dead in Yehudi. Pages 136–55 in *Yahwism after the Exile: Perspectives on Israelite Religion in the Persian Era: Papers Read at the First Meeting of the European Association for Biblical Studies, Utrecht, 6–9 August 2000.* Edited by R. Albertz and B. Becking. Assen: Van Gorcum.

Nissinen, Martti. 2003. *Prophets and Prophecy in the Ancient Near East*. SBL Writings from the Ancient World 12. Edited by P. Machinist. Atlanta: Society of Biblical Literature.

Nogalski, James. 1993a. *Literary Precursors to the Book of the Twelve*. Beihefte zur Zeitschrift für die alttestamentliche Wissenschaft 217. Berlin: Walter de Gruyter.

————. 1993b. *Redactional Processes in the Book of the Twelve*. Beihefte zur Zeitschrift für die alttestamentliche Wissenschaft 218. Berlin: Walter de Gruyter.

Noordtzij, A. 1982. *Leviticus*. Translated by R. Togtman. Bible Student's Commentary. Grand Rapids: Zondervan.

Norin, Stig. 1994. Respons zu Lemche, "Ist Es noch möglich die Geschichte des alten Israels zu Schrieben?" *Scandinavian Journal for the Old Testament* 8:191–97.

Noth, Martin. 1928. D*ie israelitischen Personennamen in Rahmen der gemeinsemitischen Namengebung*. Stuttgart: W. Kohlhammer.

————. 1972. *A History of Pentateuchal Traditions*. Englewood Cliffs, NJ: Princeton University Press.

Nougayrol, J. 1968. *Ugaritica V. Textes Sumero-Accadiens des Archives et Bibliotheques Privées de 'Ugarit*. Mission de Ras Shamra 16. Paris: Imprimerie Nationale.

Oded, Bustenay. 1995. Observations on the Israelite/Judaean Exiles in Mesopotamia during the Eighth–Sixth Centuries BCE. Pages 205–12 in *Immigration and Emigration within the Ancient Near East. Festschrift E. Lipiński*. Orientalia Lovaniensia Analecta 65. Edited by K. van Lerberghe and A. Schoors. Leuven: Peeters.

————. 2003. Where Is the "Myth of the Empty Land" to Be Found? History versus Myth. Pages 55–74 in *Judah and the Judeans in the Neo-Babylonian Period*. Edited by O. Lipschits and J. Blenkinsopp. Winona Lake, IN: Eisenbrauns.

Offord, J. 1916. Archaeological Notes on Jewish Antiquities. *Palestine Exploration Fund Quarterly Statement* 138–48.

Oggiano, Ida. 2005. *Dal terreno al divino: Archeologia del culto nella Palestina del I millennio*. Rome: Carrocci Editore.

O'Keefe, Richard A. 2005. Critical Remarks on Houk's "Statistical Analysis of Genesis Sources." *Journal for the Study of the Old Testament* 29:409–37.

Ollenburger, Ben C. 2004. Old Testament Theology before 1933. Pages 3–11 in *Old Testament Theology: Flowering and Future*, Sources for Biblical and Theological Study Vol. 1. Edited by B. C. Ollenburger. Winona Lake, IN: Eisenbrauns.

Olmo Lete, Gregorio del. 1995. The Sacrificial Vocabulary at Ugarit. *Studi Epigrafici e Linguistici* 12:37–49.

————. 1999a. *Canaanite Religion: According to the Liturgical Texts of Ugarit*. Translated by W. G. E. Watson. Bethesda, MD: CDL.

————. 1999b. Chapter Seven: The Ugaritic Cultic Texts 2: The Offering Lists and the God Lists. Pages 305–52 in *Handbook of Ugaritic Studies*. Handbook of Oriental Studies: The Near and Middle East 39. Edited by W. G. E. Watson and N. Wyatt. Leiden: Brill.

———. 2004. The Ugaritic Ritual Texts. A New Edition and Commentary. A Critical As-sessment. *Ugarit-Forschungen* 36:539–648.

Olyan, Saul M. 1988. *Asherah and the Cult of Yahweh in Israel*. SBL Monograph Series 34. Atlanta: Scholars Press.

———. 1993. *A Thousand Thousands Served Him: Exegesis and the Naming of Angels in Ancient Judaism*. Texte und Studien zum Antiken Judentum, 36. Tübingen: Mohr Siebeck.

———. 2000. *Rites and Rank: Hierarchy in Biblical Interpretation*. Princeton, NJ: Princeton University Press.

Oren, Eliezer D. 1993. Tel Haror. *The New Encyclopedia of Archaeological Excavations in the Holy Land*. New York: Simon & Schuster.

Orlinsky, Harry M. 1962. The Tribal System of Israel and Related Groups in the Period of the Judges. Pages 375–87 in *Studies and Essays in Honor of Abraham A. Neuman, President, Dropsie College for Hebrew and Cognate Learning, Philadelphia*. Edited by M. Ben-Horin, B. D. Weinryb, and S. Zeitlin. Leiden: Brill.

Ornan, Tallay. 1995. Symbols of Royalty and Divinity. *Biblical Archaeology Review* 21(4):38–39.

———. 2005. *The Triumph of the Symbol: Pictorial Representations of Deities in Mesopotamia and the Biblical Image Ban*. Orbis biblicus et orientalis 213. Göttingen: Vandenhoeck & Ruprecht.

Otto, Rudolf. 1917. *Das Heilige: Über das Irrationale in der Idee des Göttlichen und Sein Verhältnis Rationalen*. Breslau: Trewendt und Granier.

———. 1923. *The Idea of the Holy: An Inquiry into the Non-Rational Factor in the Idea of the Divine and Its Relation to the Rational*. New York: Oxford University Press.

Pals, Daniel L. 1996. *Seven Theories of Religion*. Oxford: Oxford University Press.

Paran, Meir. 1989. *Forms of the Priestly Style in the Pentateuch: Patterns, Linguistic Usages, Syntactic Structures*. Jerusalem: Magnes, Hebrew University.

Pardee, Dennis. 1988. An Evaluation of the Proper Names from Ebla from a West Semitic Perspective: Pantheon Distribution according to Genre. Pages 119–51 in *Archiv reali di Ebla 1*. Rome: Missione Archaeologica Italiana in Syria.

———. 2000. *Les textes rituels*. Ras Shamra–Ougarit XII. 2 vols. Paris: Éditions Recherches sur les Civilisations.

———. 2002. *Ritual and Cult at Ugarit*. SBL Writings from the Ancient World 10. Atlanta: Society of Biblical Literature.

———. 2005. RIH 98/02: A Preliminary Presentation of a New Song to Athtartu. Lecture at *Ugarit at Seventy-Five, Its Environs and the Bible: Ugaritic and Israelite Religion*. Joint American Oriental Society, Society of Biblical Literature, and American Schools of Oriental Research Midwest Regional Meeting, Trinity International University, Deerfield, IL, February 18, 2005. To be published in the collection of essays from this conference.

Pardee, Dennis, and Pierre Bordreuil. 1992. Ugarit: Texts and Literature. *Anchor Bible Dictionary*. New York: Doubleday.

Pardes, Ilana. 1993. Beyond Genesis 3: The Politics of Maternal Naming. Pages 173–93 in *A Feminist Companion to Genesis*. Edited by A. Brenner. Sheffield: JSOT Press.

Parker, Simon B. 1997. *Stories in Scripture and Inscriptions: Comparative Studies on Narratives in Northwest Semitic Inscriptions and the Hebrew Bible*. Oxford: Oxford University Press.

Patrick, Dale. 1995. The First Commandment in the Structure of the Pentateuch. *Vetus Testamentum* 45:107–18.

Peckham, Brian. 1993. *History and Prophecy: The Development of Late Judean Literary Traditions*. Garden City, NY: Doubleday.

Perlitt, L. 1969. *Bundestheologie im Alten Testament*. Wissenschaftliche Monographien zum Alten und Neuen Testament. Neukirchen: Neukirchener Verlag.

Person, Raymond F. 1993. *Second Zechariah and the Deuteronomic School*. Journal for the Study of the Old Testament: Supplement Series 167. Sheffield: JSOT Press.

Pitard, Wayne T. 1996. The Archaeology of Emar. Pages 13–23 in *Emar: The History, Religion, and Culture of a Syrian Town in the Late Bronze Age*. Edited by M. W. Chavalas. Bethesda, MD: CDL.

———. 1999. The Ugaritic Literary Texts: 4 The Rpum Texts. Pages 259–69 in *Handbook of Ugaritic Studies*. Handbook of Oriental Studies: The Near and Middle East 39. Edited by W. G. E. Watson and N. Wyatt. Leiden: Brill.

———. 2002. Tombs and Offerings: Archaeological Data and Comparative Methodology in the Study of Death in Israel. Pages 145–67 in *Sacred Time, Sacred Place: Archaeology and the Religion of Israel*. Edited by B. M. Gittlen. Winona Lake, IN: Eisenbrauns.

Pomponio, Francesco, and Paolo Xella. 1997. *Les dieux d'Ebla: Etude analytique des divinités éblaïtes à l'epoque des archives royales du IIIe millénaire*. Alter Orient und Altes Testament 245. Münster: Ugarit Verlag.

Pope, Marvin. 1972. A Divine Banquet at Ugarit. Pages 170–203 in *The Use of the Old Testament in the New and Other Essays*. Edited by J. M. Efird. Durham, NC: Duke University.

———. 1973. *Job*. 3rd ed. Anchor Bible 15. Garden City, NY: Doubleday.

———. 1977a. *Song of Songs*. Anchor Bible 7C. Garden City, NY: Doubleday.

———. 1977b. Notes on the Rephaim Texts from Ugarit. Pages 163–82 in *Essays on the Ancient Near East in Memory of J. J. Finkelstein*. Edited by M. J. Ellis. New Haven: Archon.

Porter, Barbara Nevling, ed. 1997. *One God or Many? Concepts of Divinity in the Ancient World*. Transactions of the Casco Bay Assyriological Institute 1. Casco Bay, ME: Casco Bay Archaeological Institute.

Portnoy, S., and D. L. Petersen. 1991. Statistical Differences among Documentary Sources: Comments on "Genesis: An Authorship Study." *Journal for the Study of the Old Testament* 50:3–14.

Potts, T. F. 1984. Bronze and Iron Age Discoveries in Jordan. *Illustrated London News* 272/7037 (December): 82–83.

Potts, T. F., S. M. Colledge, and P. C. Edwards. 1985. Preliminary Report on a Sixth Season of Excavation by the University of Sydney at Pella in Jordan 1983/84. *Annual of the Department of Antiquities of Jordan* 29:181–210.

Pritchard, J. B. 1934. *Palestinian Figurines in Relation to Certain Goddesses Known through Literature*. New Haven: American Oriental Society.

Propp, William H. C. 1999. Monotheism and "Moses": The Problem of Early Israelite Religion. *Ugarit Forschungen* 31:537–75.

Provan, I. 2002. In the Stable with the Dwarves: Testimony, Interpretation, Faith, and the History of Israel. Pages 161–97 in *Windows into Old Testament Israel: Evidence, Argument, and the Crisis of "Biblical Israel."* Edited by V. P. Long, D. W. Baker, and G. J. Wenham. Grand Rapids: Eerdmans.

Puech, Émile. 1986–1987. The Canaanite Inscriptions of Lachish and Their Religious Background. *Tel Aviv* 13–14:17–22.

————. 1992. Palestinian Funerary Inscriptions. *Anchor Bible Dictionary*. New York: Doubleday.

Rad, Gerhard von. 1964. Die Nehemia-Denkschrift. *Zeitschrift für die alttestamentliche Wissenschaft* 76:176–87.

————. 1972. *Genesis. A Commentary*. Translated by J. H. Marks. Rev. ed. London: SCM.

————. 1980. *God at Work in Israel*. Nashville: Abingdon.

Radday, Y., and H. Shore. 1985. *Genesis: An Authorship Study in Computer Assisted Linguistics*. Rome: Biblical Institute Press.

Radday, Y. T., and D. Wickmann. 1975. The Unity of Zechariah Examined in the Light of Statistical Linguistics. *Zeitschrift für die alttestamentliche Wissenschaft* 87:39–55.

Rainey, Anson F. 1970. The Order of Sacrifices in Old Testament Ritual Texts. *Biblica* 51:485–98.

————. *El Amarna Tablets 357–379. Supplement to J. A. Knudtzon Die El-Amarna Tafeln*. 2nd ed. Alter Orient und Altes Testament Band 8. Butzon & Bercker; Neukirchen-Vluyn: Neukirchener Verlag.

————. 1994a. Hezekiah's Reform and the Altars at Beer-sheba and Arad. Pages 333–54 in *Scripture and Other Artifacts. Essays on the Bible and Archaeology in Honor of Philip J. King*. Edited by M. D. Coogan, J. C. Exum, and L. E. Stager. Louisville: Westminster/John Knox.

————. 1994b. Remarks on Donald Redford's "Egypt, Canaan, and Israel in Ancient Times." *Bulletin of the American Schools of Oriental Research* 295:81–85.

————. 1998. Syntax, Hermeneutics and History. *Israel Exploration Journal* 48:239–51.

————. 2002. Down-to-Earth Biblical History. *Journal of the American Oriental Society* 122:542–47.

Rainey, Anson F., and R. Steven Notley. 2006. *The Sacred Bridge: Carta's Atlas of the Biblical World*. Jerusalem: Carta.

Redditt, P. L. 1992. Zerubbabel, Joshua, and the Night Visions of Zechariah. *Catholic Biblical Quarterly* 54:249–59.

————. 1994a. Nehemiah's First Mission and the Date of Zechariah 9–14. *Catholic Biblical Quarterly* 56:664–78.

————. 1994b. The Book of Malachi in Its Social Setting. *Catholic Biblical Quarterly* 56:240–55.

Redford, Donald B. 1992. *Egypt, Canaan and Israel in Ancient Times*. Princeton, NJ: Princeton University Press.

Reed, W. L. 1949. *The Asherah in the Old Testament*. Fort Worth: Texas Christian University.

Reich, Ronny. 1992. The Beth-zur Citadel II—A Persian Residency? *Tel Aviv* 19:113–23.

Reis, Pamela Tamarkin. 2001. Genesis as Rashomon. *Bible Review* 17(3):26–33, 55.

Rendtorff, Rolf. 1986. *The Old Testament: An Introduction*. Philadelphia: Fortress.

————. 1990. *The Problem of the Process of Transmission in the Pentateuch*. Journal for the Study of the Old Testament: Supplement Series 89. Sheffield: JSOT Press.

————. 1993a. The Paradigm Is Changing: Hopes and Fears. *Biblical Interpretation: A Journal of Contemporary Approaches* 1:34–53.

————. 1993b. Two Kinds of P? Some Reflections on the Occasion of the Publishing of Jacob Milgrom's Commentary on Leviticus 1–16. *Journal for the Study of the Old Testament* 60:75–81.

Renfrew, Colin. 1985. Towards a Framework for the Archaeology of Cult Practice. Pages 11–26 in *The Archaeology of Cult: The Sanctuary at Phylakopi*. Edited by C. Renfrew. London: Thames and Hudson.

Renz, Johannes. 1995. *Die Althebräischen Inschriften*. 3 volumes. *Teil 1. Text und kommentar. Teil 2. Zusammenfussende Erörterungen, Paläographie und Glossar. Band 3. Texte und Tafeln*. Darmstadt: Wissenschaftliche Buchgesellschaft.

Rhea, Robert. 1995. Attack on Prophecy: Zechariah 13,1–6. *Zeitschrift für die alttestamentliche Wissenschaft* 107:288–93.

Ricoeur, Paul. 1984. *Time and Narrative*. Chicago: University of Chicago Press.

———. 1999. Humanities between Science and Art. Transcript of Paul Ricoeur's speech at the opening ceremony of the Humanities at the Turn of the Millennium Conference, University of Århaus, June 4, 1999. http://www.hum.au.dk/ckulturf/pages/publications/pr/hbsa.htm.

Ringgren, Helmer. 1966. *Israelite Religion*. Translated by D. Green. Philadelphia: Fortress.

Robben, Antonius C. G. M. 2004. Death and Anthropology: An Introduction. Pages 1–16 in *Death, Mourning, and Burial: A Cross-Cultural Reader*. Edited by A. C. G. M. Robben. Oxford: Blackwell.

Rogerson, John W. 1974. *Myth in Old Testament Interpretation*. Beihefte für die Zeitschrift für die alttestamentliche Wissenschaft 134. Berlin: de Gruyter.

Rooke, Deborah W. 2005. The Day of Atonement as a Ritual of Validation for the High Priest. Pages 342–64 in *Temple and Worship in Biblical Israel*. Library of Hebrew Bible/Old Testament Studies 422. Edited by J. Day. London: T&T Clark.

Rose, Walter H. 2003. Messianic Expectations in the Early Postexilic Period. Pages 165–85 in *Yahwism after the Exile: Perspectives on Israelite Religion in the Persian Era: Papers Read at the First Meeting of the European Association for Biblical Studies, Utrecht, 6–9 August 2000*. Edited by R. Albertz and B. Becking. Assen: Van Gorcum.

Rosenfeld, Amnon, and Shimon Ilani. Appendix: On the Patina and Stable-Isotope Analysis of the Ivory Pomegranate. *Israel Exploration Journal* 56:175–77.

Rothenberg, Benno. 1972a. *Timna. Valley of the Biblical Copper Mines*. New Aspects of Antiquity. London: Thames and Hudson.

———. 1972b. *Were These King Solomon's Mines?* London: Thames and Hudson.

———. 1979. *Sinai. Pharaohs, Miners, Pilgrims and Soldiers*. Berne: Kümmerly & Frey.

Sadeh, M. 1990. Animal Remains from Khirbet ed-Dawwara. *Tel Aviv* 17:209.

Sandys-Wunsch, John, and Laurence Eldredge. 1980. J. P. Gabler and the Distinction between Biblical and Dogmatic Theology: Translation, Commentary and Discussion of His Originality. *Scottish Journal of Theology* 33:133–58.

Sarna, Nahum. 1970. *Understanding Genesis*. The Heritage of Biblical Israel 1. New York: Schocken.

———. 1989. *The JPS Torah Commentary: Genesis*. Philadelphia: Jewish Publication Society.

———. 1999. Israel in Egypt: The Egyptian Sojourn and the Exodus. Pages 33–54 in *Ancient Israel: From Abraham to the Roman Destruction of the Temple*. Rev. ed. Edited by H. Shanks. Washington, DC: Biblical Archaeological Society.

Savran, George W. 2005. *Encountering the Divine: Theophany in Biblical Narratives*. Journal for the Study of the Old Testament Supplement Series 420. New York: T&T Clark.

Sawyer, John F. A. 1986. Cain and Hephaestus. Possible Relics of Metalworking Traditions in Genesis 4. *Abr-Nahrain* 24:155–66.

———, ed. 1996. *Reading Leviticus: A Conversation with Mary Douglas*. Journal for the Study of the Old Testament: Supplement Series, 227. Sheffield: Sheffield Academic Press.

Sawyer, John F. A., and David J. A. Clines, eds. 1983. *Midian, Moab and Edom. The History and Archaeology of Late Bronze and Iron Age Jordan and North-West Arabia*. Journal for the Study of the Old Testament: Supplement Series, 24. Sheffield: JSOT Press.

Schaefer, K. R. 1993. Zechariah 14 and the Composition of the Book of Zechariah. *Revue Biblique* 100:368–98.

———. 1995. Zechariah 14: A Study in Allusion. *Catholic Biblical Quarterly* 57:66–91.

Schäfer-Lichtenberger, Christa. 1993. David und Jerusalem—ein Kapitel biblischer Historiographie. *Eretz-Israel* 25:197*–211*.

———. 1998. PTFJH—Göttin und Herrin von Ekron. *Biblische Notizen* 91:64–76.

Schaper, Joachim. 1995. The Jerusalem Temple as an Instrument of the Achaemenid Fiscal Administration. *Vetus Testamentum* 45:528–39.

Schmidt, Brian B. 1994. *Israel's Beneficent Dead. Ancestor Cult and Necromancy in Ancient Israelite Religion and Tradition*. Forschungen zum Alten Testament 11. Tübingen: Mohr Siebeck. Repr., Winona Lake, IN: Eisenbrauns, 1996.

Schmidt, Ludwig. 1993. *Studien zur Priesterschrift*. Beihefte zur Zeitschrift für die alttestamentliche Wissenschaft 214. Berlin: de Gruyter.

Schmitt, John J. 1995. Yahweh's Divorce in Hosea 2—Who Is That Woman? *Scandinavian Journal of the Old Testament* 9:119–32.

Schmitt, Rüdiger. 2003. Gab es einen Bildersturm nach dem Ezil? Einige Bemerkungen zur Verwendung von Terrakottafigurinen im nachexilischen Israel. Pages 186–98 in *Yahwism after the Exile: Perspectives on Israelite Religion in the Persian Era: Papers Read at the First Meeting of the European Association for Biblical Studies, Utrecht, 6–9 August 2000*. Edited by R. Albertz and B. Becking. Assen: Van Gorcum.

Schniedewind, William M. 1996. Tel Dan Stela: New Light on Aramaic and Jehu's Revolt. *Bulletin of the American Schools of Oriental Research* 302:75–90.

———. 2000. Orality and Literacy in Ancient Israel. *Religious Studies Review* 26(4):327–32.

———. 2004. *How the Bible Became a Book: The Textualization of Ancient Israel*. Cambridge: Cambridge University Press.

Schroer, S. 1987. *In Israel Gab es Bilder: Nachrichten von darstellender Kunst im Alten Testament*. Orbis Biblicus et Orientalis 74. Göttingen: Vandenhoeck & Ruprecht.

Schunck, Klaus D. 1971. Zentralheiligtum, Grenzheiligtum und "Hohenheiligtum" in Israel. *Numen* 18:132–40.

Schwemer, Daniel. 2001. *Die Wettergottgestalten Mesopotamiens und Nordsyriens im Zeitalter der Keilschriftkulturen: Materialen und Studien nach den schriftlichen Quellen*. Wiesbaden: Otto Harrassowitz.

Scurlock, JoAnn. 1997. Ghosts in the Ancient Near East: Weak or Powerful? *Hebrew Union College Annual* 68:77–96.

Seitz, Christopher R. 1998. *Word without End. The Old Testament as Abiding Theological Witness*. Grand Rapids: Eerdmans.

Sellin, E. 1904. *Tell Ta'annek*. Vienna: Denkschriften der Kaiserlichen Akademie der Wissenschaften.

Selman, Martin J. 1995. Sacrifice in the Ancient Near East. Pages 59–74 in *Sacrifice in the Bible*. Edited by R. T. Beckwith and M. J. Selman. Grand Rapids: Baker Academic.

Seow, C. L. 1989. *Myth, Drama, and the Politics of David's Dance*. Harvard Semitic Monographs 46. Atlanta: Scholars Press.

Seybold, K. 1977. Hebel. *Theologisches Wörterbuch zum alten Testament* Stuttgart: Kohlhammer.

Shanks, Hershel. 1994. The Tombs of Silwan. *Biblical Archaeology Review* 20(3):38–51.

———. 1996a. Bed and Breakfast—and Blessings. *Biblical Archaeology Review* 22(4):12.

———. 1996b. Who—Or What—Was Molech? New Phoenician Inscription May Hold Answer. *Biblical Archaeology Review* 22(4):13.

———. 1996c. Review of Eshel and Prag 1995. *Biblical Archaeology Review* 22(4):17–18.

———. 2001. Did the Exodus Really Happen? *Moment* (October): 62–65, 102.

Shanks, Hershel, et al. 1992. *The Rise of Ancient Israel*. Washington, DC: Biblical Archaeology Society.

Shanks, Hershel, and Jack Meinhardt, eds. 1997. *Aspects of Monotheism: How God Is One: Symposium at the Smithsonian Institution October 19, 1996*. Washington, DC: Biblical Archaeology Society.

Shea, William H. 1994. Sargon's Azekah Inscription: The Earliest Extrabiblical Reference to the Sabbath? *Andrews University Seminary Studies* 32:247–51.

Sheler, Jeffrey L. 1999. *Is the Bible True? How Modern Debates and Discoveries Affirm the Essence of the Scriptures*. Grand Rapids: Zondervan.

Shiloh, Yigal. 1993. Megiddo. The Iron Age. *The New Encyclopedia of Archaeological Excavations in the Holy Land*. New York: Simon & Schuster.

Ska, Jean Louis. 1998. *Introduzione alla lettura del Pentateuco: Chiavi per l'interpretazione dei primi cinque libri della Bibbia*. Collana biblica. Rome: Edizioni dehoniane.

Skinner, John. 1930. *A Critical and Exegetical Commentary on Genesis*. 2nd ed. Edinburgh: T&T Clark.

Smart, Ninian. 1960. *World Religions: A Dialogue*. Baltimore: Penguin.

———. 1969. *The Religious Experience of Mankind*. New York: Scribner.

———. 1983. *Worldviews: Cross-Cultural Explorations of Human Beliefs*. New York: Scribner.

———. 1989. *The World's Religions: Old Traditions and Modern Transformations*. Cambridge: Cambridge University Press.

Smelik, K. A. D. 1991. *Writings from Ancient Israel: A Handbook of Historical and Religious Documents*. Edinburgh: T&T Clark.

———. 1995. Moloch, Molekh or Molk-Sacrifice? A Reassessment of the Evidence concerning the Hebrew Term Molekh. *Scandinavian Journal of the Old Testament* 9:133–42.

Smith, Mark S. 1987. God Male and Female in the Old Testament: Yahweh and His "Asherah." *Theological Studies* 48:333–40.

———. 1988. "Seeing God" in the Psalms: The Background to the Beatific Vision in the Hebrew Bible. *Catholic Biblical Quarterly* 50:171–83.

———. 1990a. *The Early History of God: Yahweh and the Other Deities in Ancient Israel*. San Francisco: Harper & Row.

———. 1990b. The Near Eastern Background of Solar Language for Yahweh. *Journal of Biblical Literature* 109:29–39.

———. 1994. Mythology and Myth-Making in Ugaritic and Israelite Literatures. Pages 293–341 in *Ugarit and the Bible. Proceedings of the International Symposium on Ugarit and the Bible. Manchester, September 1992.* Ugaritisch-Biblische Literatur 11. Edited by G. J. Brooke, A. H. W. Curtis, and J. F. Healey. Münster: Ugarit-Verlag.

———. 1996. The Literary Arrangement of the Priestly Redaction of the Exodus: A Preliminary Investigation. *Catholic Biblical Quarterly* 58:25–50.

———. 1998. The Death of "Dying and Rising Gods" in the Biblical World. An Update, with Special Reference to Baal in the Baal Cycle. *Scandinavian Journal of the Old Testament* 12:257–313.

———. 1999. Review of Pomponio and Xella 1997. *Catholic Biblical Quarterly* 61:759–61.

———. 2001a. *The Origins of Biblical Monotheism: Israel's Polytheistic Background and the Ugaritic Texts.* Oxford: Oxford University Press.

———. 2001b. *Untold Stories: The Bible and Ugaritic Studies in the Twentieth Century.* Peabody, MA: Hendrickson.

———. 2003. *The Early History of God: Yahweh and the Other Deities in Ancient Israel.* 2nd ed. Grand Rapids: Eerdmans.

———. 2004. Review Article of Ziony Zevit, *The Religions of Ancient Israel: A Synthesis of Parallactic Approaches. Maarav* 11:145–218.

———. 2005. Like Deities, Like Temples (Like People). Pages 3–27 in *Temple and Worship in Biblical Israel.* Library of Hebrew Bible/Old Testament Studies 422. Edited by J. Day. London: T&T Clark.

Smith, Mark S., and Elizabeth Bloch-Smith. 1988. Death and Afterlife at Ugarit and Ancient Israel. *Journal of the American Oriental Society* 108:277–84.

Smith, William Robertson. 1894. *Lectures on the Religion of the Semites: First Series, the Fundamental Institutions.* New ed. London: Adam and Charles Black.

Snaith, N. 1975. The Meaning of שְׂעִירִים. *Vetus Testamentum* 25:115–18.

Soggin, J. A. 1989. *Introduction to the Old Testament.* 3rd ed. London: SCM.

Sowers, Sidney G. 1996. Did Xerxes Wage War on Jerusalem? *Hebrew Union College Annual* 67:43–53.

Sparks, Kenton L. 1998. *Ethnicity and Identity in Ancient Israel: Prolegomena to the Study of Ethnic Sentiments and Their Expression in the Hebrew Bible.* Grand Rapids: Eisenbrauns.

Speiser, Ephraim A. 1964. *Genesis.* Anchor Bible 1. Garden City, NY: Doubleday.

Spina, F. A. 1992. The "Ground" for Cain's Rejection (Gen 4): ʾᵃdamah in the Context of Gen 1–11. *Zeitschrift für die alttestamentliche Wissenschaft* 104:319–32.

Spronk, Klaas. 1986. *Beatific Afterlife in Ancient Israel and the Ancient Near East.* Alter Orient und Altes Testament 219. Kevelaer: Butzon & Bercker.

———. 1999. The Ugaritic Literary Texts: 5 The Incantations. Pages 270–86 in *Handbook of Ugaritic Studies.* Handbook of Oriental Studies: The Near and Middle East 39. Edited by W. G. E. Watson and N. Wyatt. Leiden: Brill.

Stager, Lawrence E. 1985a. The Archaeology of the Family in Ancient Israel. *Bulletin of the American Schools of Oriental Research* 260:1–35.

———. 1985b. Merenptah, Israel and Sea Peoples: New Light on an Old Relief. *Eretz-Israel* 18:56*–64*.

———. 1991a. When Canaanites and Philistines Ruled Ashkelon. *Biblical Archaeology Review* 17(2):24–37, 40–43.

———. 1991b. Why Were Hundreds of Dogs Buried at Ashkelon? *Biblical Archaeology Review* 17(3):26–42.

———. 1995. The Impact of the Sea Peoples in Canaan (1185–1050 BCE). Pages 332–48 in *The Archaeology of Society in the Holy Land*. Edited by T. E. Levy. New York: Facts on File.

———. 1999. The Fortress-Temple at Shechem and the "House of El, Lord of the Covenant." Pages 228–49 in *Realia Dei: Essays in Archaeology and Biblical Interpretation in Honor of Edward F. Campbell Jr.* Edited by P. H. Williams Jr. and T. Hiebert. Atlanta: Scholars.

———. 2003. The Shechem Temple Where Abimelech Massacred a Thousand. *Biblical Archaeology Review* 29(4):26–35, 66, 68–69.

Stager, Lawrence E., and Samuel Wolff. 1984. Child Sacrifice at Carthage—Religious Rite or Population Control? *Biblical Archaeology Review* 10(1):30–51.

Staubli, Thomas. 1991. *Das Image der Nomaden im Alten Israel und in der Ikonographie seiner sesshaften Nachbarn*. Orbis biblicus et orientalis 107. Göttingen: Vandenhoeck & Ruprecht.

Steen, Eveline J. van der. 1996. The Central East Jordan Valley in the Late Bronze and Early Iron Ages. *Bulletin of the American Schools of Oriental Research* 302:51–74.

Steiner, Margreet. 1993. The Jebusite Ramp of Jerusalem: The Evidence from the Macalister, Kenyon and Shiloh Excavations. Pages 585–88 in *Biblical Archaeology Today, 1990. Proceedings of the Second International Congress on Biblical Archaeology. Jerusalem, June–July 1990*. Edited by A. Biran and J. Aviram. Jerusalem: Israel Exploration Society.

———. 1994. Re-dating the Terraces of Jerusalem. *Israel Exploration Journal* 44:13–20.

Stern, Ephraim. 1977. A Late Bronze Temple at Tell Mevorakh. *Biblical Archaeologist* 40(2):89–91.

———. 1982. *Material Culture of the Land of the Bible in the Persian Period, 538–332 B.C.* Warminster, UK: Aris & Phillips.

———. 1999. Religion in Palestine in the Assyrian and Persian Periods. Pages 245–55 in *The Crisis of Israelite Religion: Transformation of Religious Tradition in Exilic and Post-Exilic Times*. Oudtestamentische Studiën 42. Edited by B. Becking and M. C. A. Korpel. Leiden: Brill.

———. 2001a. *Archaeology in the Land of the Bible, Volume II: The Assyrian, Babylonian, and Persian Periods 732–332 BCE*. Anchor Bible Reference Library. New York: Doubleday.

———. 2001b. Pagan Yahwism: The Folk Religion of Ancient Israel. *Biblical Archaeology Review* 27(3):20–29.

———. 2002. The Babylonian Gap Revisited: Yes There Was. *Biblical Archaeology Review* 28(3):39, 55.

Steymans, H. U. 1995a. *Deuteronomium 28 und die adê zur Thronfolgeregelung Asarhaddons: Segen und Fluch im Alten Orient und in Israel*. Orbis biblicus et orientalis 145. Göttingen: Vandenhoeck & Ruprecht.

———. 1995b. Eine assyrische Vorlage für Deuteronomium 28,20–44. Pages 118–41 in *Bundesdokument und Gesetz: Studien zum Deuteronomium*. Edited by G. Braulik. Herder biblische Studien 4. Freibourg: Herder.

Stiebing, W. H., Jr. 1989. *Out of the Desert? Archaeology and the Exodus/Conquest Narratives*. Buffalo, NY: Prometheus.

———. 1994. Climate and Collapse—Did the Weather Make Israel's Emergence Possible? *Biblical Archaeology Review* 10(4):18–27, 54.

Stockton, E. D. 1974–1975. Phoenician Cult Stones. *Australian Journal of Biblical Archaeology* 2:1–27.

Stolz, F. 1980. Monotheismus in Israel. Pages 143–89 in *Monotheismus im alten Israel und seiner Umwelt*. Biblische Beiträge 14. Edited by O. Keel. Fribourg: Schweizerisches Katholisches Bibelwerk.

Strange, J. 1991. Theology and Politics in Architecture and Iconography. *Scandinavian Journal of the Old Testament* 1:23–44.

Tadmor, Miriam. 1981. Female Relied Figurines of Late Bronze Age Canaan. *Eretz-Israel* 15:79–84 (Hebrew).

———. 1982. Female Cult Figurines in Late Canaan and Early Israel: Archaeological Evidence. Pages 139–73 in *Studies in the Period of David and Solomon and Other Essays*. Edited by T. Ishida. Tokyo: Yamakawa-Shupanshi.

———. 1996. Plaque Figurines of Reclining Women—Use and Meaning. *Eretz-Israel* 24:290–96 (Hebrew).

Talmon, Shemaryahu. 1978. The "Comparative Method" in Biblical Interpretation—Principles and Problems. Pages 320–56 in *Congress Volume: Göttingen 1977*. Vetus Testamentum Supplements 29. Edited by J. A. Emerton. Leiden: Brill.

Tappy, Ron. 1998. Review of R. Kletter, *The Judean Pillar-Figurines and the Archaeology of Asherah*. *Bulletin of the American Schools of Oriental Research* 310:85–89.

———. 2003. Recent Interpretations of Ancient Israelite Religion. *Journal of the American Oriental Society* 123:159–67.

Tappy, Ron E., P. Kyle McCarter, Marilyn J. Lundberg, and Bruce Zuckerman. 2006. An Abecedary of the Mid-tenth Century B.C.E. from the Judaean Shephelah. *Bulletin of the American Schools of Oriental Research* 344:5–46.

Taylor, J. Glen. 1987. Yahweh and Asherah at Tenth Century Taanach. *Newsletter for Ugaritic Studies* 37/38:16–18.

———. 1988. The Two Earliest Known Representations of Yahweh. Pages 557–66 in *Ascribe to the Lord: Biblical & Other Studies in Memory of Peter C. Craigie*. Journal for the Study of the Old Testament: Supplement Series 67. Edited by L. Eslinger and G. Taylor. Sheffield: JSOT Press.

———. 1993. *Yahweh and the Sun. Biblical and Archaeological Evidence for Sun Worship in Ancient Israel*. Journal for the Study of the Old Testament: Supplement Series 111. Sheffield: JSOT Press.

———. 1994. Was Yahweh Worshipped as the Sun? *Biblical Archaeology Review* 20(3):52–61, 90–91.

———. 1996. A Response to Steve A. Wiggins, "Yahweh: The God of the Sun?" *Journal for the Study of the Old Testament* 71:107–19.

Taylor, Joan E. 1995. The Asherah, the Menorah and the Sacred Tree. *Journal for the Study of the Old Testament* 66:29–54.

Tertel, Hans Jürgen. 1994. *Text and Transmission: An Empirical Model for the Literary Development of Old Testament Narratives*. Beihefte zur Zeitschrift für die alttestamentliche Wissenschaft 221. Berlin/New York: de Gruyter.

Theuer, Gabriele. 2000. *Der Mondgott in den Religionen Syrien-Palästinas under besonderer Berücksichtigung von KTU 1.24*. Orbis biblicus et orientalis 173. Göttingen: Vandenhoeck & Ruprecht.

Thompson, Thomas L. 1974. *The Historicity of the Patriarchal Narratives: The Quest for the Historical Abraham*. Beihefte zur Zeitschrift für die alttestamentliche Wissenschaft 133. Berlin: de Gruyter.

————. 1992. *Early History of the Israelite People. From the Written and Archaeological Sources*. Studies in the History of the Ancient Near East 4. Leiden: Brill.

Tigay, Jeffrey H. 1975. An Empirical Basis for the Documentary Hypothesis. *Journal of Biblical Literature* 94:329–42.

————. 1982. *The Evolution of the Gilgamesh Epic*. Philadelphia: University of Pennsylvania.

————, ed. 1985. *Empirical Models for Biblical Criticism*. Philadelphia: University of Pennsylvania.

————. 1986. *You Shall Have No Other Gods: Israelite Religion in the Light of Hebrew Inscriptions*. Harvard Semitic Studies 31. Atlanta: Scholars Press.

————. 1987. Israelite Religion: The Onomastic and Epigraphic Evidence. Pages 157–94 in *Ancient Israelite Religion: Essays in Honor of Frank Moore Cross*. Edited by P. D. Miller Jr., P. D. Hanson, and S. D. McBride. Philadelphia: Fortress.

Tomes, Roger. 1996. "Our Holy and Beautiful House": When and Why Was 1 Kings 6–8 Written? *Journal for the Study of the Old Testament* 70:33–50.

Trible, Phyllis. 1978. *God and the Rhetoric of Sexuality*. Philadelphia: Fortress.

————. 1984. *Texts of Terror: Literary-Feminist Readings of Biblical Narratives*. Philadelphia: Fortress.

Trigger, B. G. 1998. Archaeology and Epistemology: Dialoguing across the Darwinian Chasm. *American Journal of Archaeology* 102:1–34.

Tromp, N. J. 1969. *Primitive Conceptions of Death and the Netherworld in the Old Testament*. Biblica et Orientalia 21. Rome: Pontifical Bible Institute.

Tropper, Josef. 1989. *Nekromantie. Totenbefragung im Alten Orient und im Alten Testament*. Alter Orient und Altes Testament 223. Neukirchener: Neukirchen-Vluyn.

————. 2001. Der Gottesname *Yahwa. Vetus Testamentum* 51:81–106.

Tsukimoto, A. 1985. *Untersuchungen zur Totenpflege (kispum) im alten Mesopotamien*. Alter Orient und Altes Testament 216. Neukirchen-Vluyn: Neukirchener Verlag.

————. 1989. Emar and the Old Testament—Preliminary Remarks. *Annual of the Japanese Biblical Institute* 15:3–4.

Tsumura, D. T. 2005. *The Earth and the Waters in Genesis 1 and 2*. Winona Lake, IN: Eisenbrauns. Repr., Journal for the Study of the Old Testament: Supplement Series 83. Sheffield: Sheffield Academic Press, 1989.

Tubb, Jonathan N. 1993. Tell es-Sa'idiyeh. *The New Encyclopedia of Archaeological Excavations in the Holy Land*. New York: Simon & Schuster.

Tuell, S. S. 1991. The Southern and Eastern Borders of Abar-Nahara. *Bulletin of the American Schools of Oriental Research* 284:51–57.

Turner, L. A. 1990. *Announcements of Plot in Genesis*. Journal for the Study of the Old Testament: Supplement Series 96. Sheffield: Sheffield Academic Press.

Tylor, E. B. 1903. *Primitive Culture: Researches into the Development of Mythology, Philosophy, Religion, Language, Art, and Custom*. 4th ed. London: Murray.

Ulrich, Eugene. 1989. Daniel Manuscripts from Qumran. Part 2: Preliminary Editions of 4QDan[b] and 4QDan[c]. *Bulletin of the American Schools of Oriental Research* 274:3–26.

Ussishkin, David. 1993a. Lachish. *The New Encyclopedia of Archaeological Excavations in the Holy Land*. New York: Simon & Schuster.

————. 1993b. *The Village of Silwan. The Necropolis from the Period of the Judean Kingdom*. Jerusalem: Israel Exploration Society and Yad Izhak Ben-Zvi.

———. 1997. Megiddo. *The Oxford Encyclopedia of Archaeology in the Near East.* New York: Simon & Schuster.

———. 2005. Big City, Few People. *Biblical Archaeology Review* 31(4):26–35.

Van Dam, Cornelis. 1997. *The Urim and Thummim: A Means of Revelation in Ancient Israel.* Winona Lake, IN: Eisenbrauns.

VanderKam, James C. 1991. Joshua the High Priest and the Interpretation of Zechariah 3. *Catholic Biblical Quarterly* 53:553–70.

van der Toorn, Karel. 1989. Female Prostitution in Payment of Vows in Ancient Israel. *Journal of Biblical Literature* 108:193–205.

———. 1990. The Nature of the Biblical Teraphim in Light of the Cuneiform Evidence. *Catholic Biblical Quarterly* 52:203–22.

———. 1992. Prostitution (Cultic). *Anchor Bible Dictionary.* New York: Doubleday.

———. 1993. Saul and the Rise of Israelite State Religion. *Vetus Testamentum* 43:519–42.

———. 1994a. Gods and Ancestors in Emar and Nuzi. *Zeitschrift für Assyriologie und vorderasiatische Archäologie* 84:38–59.

———. 1994b. *From Her Cradle to Her Grave. The Role of Religion in the Life of the Israelite and the Babylonian Woman.* The Biblical Seminar. Sheffield: JSOT Press.

———. 1996a. *Family Religion in Babylonia, Syria, and Israel: Continuity and Changes in the Forms of Religious Life.* Studies in the History and Culture of the Ancient Near East 7. Leiden: Brill.

———. 1996b. Ancestors and Anthroponyms: Kinship Terms as Theophoric Elements in Hebrew Names. *Zeitschift für die alttestamentliche Wissenschaft* 108:1–11.

———. 2002. Israelite Figurines: A View from the Texts. Pages 45–62 in *Sacred Time Sacred Place: Archaeology and the Religion of Israel.* Edited by B. M. Gittlen. Winona Lake, IN: Eisenbrauns.

Vanel, A. 1965. *L'Iconographie du Dieu de l'Orage dans le Proche-Orient Ancien jusqu'au VIIe Siècle avant J.-C.* CRB 7. Paris: Gabalda.

Van Seters, John. 1975. *Abraham in History and Tradition.* London: Yale University Press.

———. 1983a. *In Search of History.* New Haven: Yale University Press.

———. 1983b. The Place of the Yahwist in the History of Passover and Massot. *Zeitschrift für die alttestamentliche Wissenschaft* 95:167–82.

———. 1992. *Prologue to History: The Yahwist as Historian in Genesis.* Louisville: Westminster/John Knox.

———. 1994. *The Life of Moses: The Yahwist as Historian in Exodus-Numbers.* Louisville: Westminster/John Knox.

———. 1997. Solomon's Temple: Fact and Ideology in Biblical and Near Eastern Iconography. *Catholic Biblical Quarterly* 59:45–57.

Van Soldt, W. H. 1991. *Studies in the Akkadian of Ugarit: Dating and Grammar.* Alter Orient und Alter Testament Band 40. Kevelaer: Verlag Butzon & Bercker; Neukirchen-Vluyn: Neukirchener Verlag.

Vatke, Wilhelm. 1835. *Die Religion des Alten Testaments nach den kanonischen Büchern Entwickelt.* Berlin: G. Bethge.

Vaux, Roland de. 1978. *The Early History of Israel.* Translated by David Smith. Philadelphia: Westminster.

Waaler, Erik. 2002. A Revised Date for Pentateuchal Texts? Evidence from Ketef Hinnom. *Tyndale Bulletin* 53(1):29–55.

Wagner, Volker. 1975. Zur Existenz des sogenannten Heiligkeitsgesetzes. *Zeitschrift für die alttestamentliche Wissenschaft* 86:307–10.

Walker, Christopher, and Michael B. Dick. 2001. *The Induction of the Cult Image in Ancient Mesopotamia: The Mesopotamian Mīs pî Ritual*. State Archives of Assyria Literary Texts, Volume 1. Helsinki: Neo-Assyrian Text Corpus Project.

Wallace, H. N. 1990. The Toledot of Adam. Pages 17–33 in *Studies in the Pentateuch*. Supplements to Vetus Testamentum 41. Edited by J. A. Emerton. Leiden: Brill.

Walls, Neal H. 1992. *The Goddess Anat in Ugaritic Myth*. SBL Dissertation Series 135. Atlanta: Scholars Press.

Waltke, B. K. 1986. Cain and His Offering. *Westminster Theological Journal* 48:363–72.

Walton, John H. 1989. *Ancient Israelite Literature in Its Cultural Context: A Survey of Parallels between Biblical and Ancient Near Eastern Texts*. Grand Rapids: Zondervan.

———. 1995. The Mesopotamian Background of the Tower of Babel Account and Its Implications. *Bulletin for Biblical Research* 5:155–75.

———. 2006. *Ancient Near Eastern Thought and the Old Testament: Introducing the Conceptual World of the Hebrew Bible*. Grand Rapids: Baker Academic.

Wapnish, Paula. 1993. Archaeozoology: The Integration of Faunal Data with Biblical Archaeology. Pages 426–42 in *Biblical Archaeology Today, 1990. Proceedings of the Second International Congress on Biblical Archaeology. Jerusalem, June–July 1990*. Edited by A. Biran and J. Aviram. Jerusalem: Israel Exploration Society.

Warning, W. 2001. Terminological Patterns and the Divine Epithet *Shaddai*. *Tyndale Bulletin* 51:149–53.

Watson, W. G. E. 1986. *Classical Hebrew Poetry: A Guide to Its Techniques*. Journal for the Study of the Old Testament: Supplement Series 26. Sheffield: JSOT Press.

Watts, James W. 1995. Rhetorical Strategy in the Composition of the Pentateuch. *Journal for the Study of the Old Testament* 68:3–22.

Webb, Barry G. 1987. *The Book of Judges: An Integrated Reading*. Journal for the Study of the Old Testament: Supplement Series 46. Sheffield: JSOT Press.

Webb, Robert L. 1990. "Apocalyptic": Observations on a Slippery Term. *Journal of Near Eastern Studies* 49:115–26.

Weber, Max. 1946. *From Max Weber: Essays in Sociology*. Translated and edited by H. H. Gerth and C. W. Mills. New York: Oxford University Press.

———. 1952. *Ancient Judaism*. Translated and edited by H. H. Gerth and D. Martindale. Glencoe, IL: Free Press.

Weimar, Peter. 1995. Ex 12,1–14 und die priesterschriftliche Geschichtsdarstellung. *Zeitschrift für die alttestamentliche Wissenschaft* 107:196–214.

Weinfeld, Moshe. 1970. The Covenant of Grant in the Old Testament and in the Ancient Near East. *Journal of the American Oriental Society* 90:184–203.

———. 1972a. Addenda to *JAOS* 90 (1970), p. 184ff. *Journal of the American Oriental Society* 92:468–69.

———. 1972b. *Deuteronomy and the Deuteronomic School*. Oxford: Clarendon.

———. 1984. Kuntillet ʿAjrud Inscriptions and Their Significance. *Studi Epigrafici e Linguistici* 1:121–30.

———. 1991. *Deuteronomy 1–11*. The Anchor Bible 5A. Garden City, NY: Doubleday.

———. 1993. *The Promise of the Land. The Inheritance of the Land of Canaan by the Israelites*. The Taubman Lectures in Jewish Studies. Berkeley: University of California.

———. 1995. *Social Justice in Ancient Israel and in the Ancient Near East*. Minneapolis: Fortress.

———. 1996. Deuteronomy's Theological Revolution. *Bible Review* 12(1):38–41, 44–45.

———. 2004. *The Place of the Law in the Religion of Ancient Israel*. Supplements to Vetus Testamentum 100. Leiden: Brill.

———. 2005. *Normative and Sectarian Judaism in the Second Temple Period*. London: T&T Clark.

Weinstein, J. 1997. Exodus and Archaeological Reality. Pages 87–103 in *Exodus: The Egyptian Evidence*. Edited by E. S. Frerichs and L. H. Lesko. Winona Lake, IN: Eisenbrauns.

Weisman, Z. 1992. The Interrelationship beteween J and E in Jacob's Narrative. *Zeitschrift für die alttestamentliche Wissenschaft* 104:177–97.

Wellhausen, Julius. 1973. *Prolegomena to the History of Ancient Israel*. Gloucester, MA: Peter Smith Reprint.

Wenham, Gordon J. 1978. The Coherence of the Flood Narrative. *Vetus Testamentum* 28:336–48.

———. 1979. *The Book of Leviticus*. New International Commentary on the Old Testament. Grand Rapids: Eerdmans.

———. 1980. The Religion of the Patriarchs. Pages 157–88 in *Essays on the Patriarchal Narratives*. Edited by A. R. Millard and D. J. Wiseman. Leicester, UK: Inter-Varsity.

———. 1981. *Numbers: An Introduction and Commentary*. Tyndale Old Testament Commentaries. Leicester, UK: Inter-Varsity.

———. 1987. *Genesis 1–15*. Word Biblical Commentary 1. Waco, TX: Word.

———. 1991. Method in Pentateuchal Source Criticism. *Vetus Testamentum* 41:84–109.

———. 1994. *Genesis 16–50*. Word Biblical Commentary 2. Waco: Word.

———. 1995. The Theology of Old Testament Sacrifice. Pages 75–87 in *Sacrifice in the Bible*. Edited by R. T. Beckwith and M. J. Selman. Grand Rapids: Baker Academic.

———. 1996. Pentateuchal Studies Today. *Themelios* 22(1):3–13.

———. 1999. Pondering the Pentateuch: The Search for a New Paradigm. Pages 116–44 in *The Face of Old Testament Studies: A Survey of Contemporary Approaches*. Edited by D. W. Baker and B. T. Arnold. Grand Rapids: Baker Academic.

West, G. 1990. Reading "The Text" and Reading "Behind the Text": The "Cain and Abel" Story in a Context of Liberation. Pages 299–320 in *The Bible in Three Dimensions: Essays in Celebration of Forty Years of Biblical Studies in the University of Sheffield*. Journal for the Study of the Old Testament: Supplement Series 87. Edited by D. J. A. Clines, S. E. Fowl, and S. E. Porter. Sheffield: Sheffield Academic Press.

Westermann, C. 1984. *Genesis. 1–11*. Translated by J. J. Scullion. London: SPCK.

Wette, Wilhelm M. L. de. 1815. *Ueber Religion und Theologie: Erläuterungen zu seinem Lehrbuche der Dogmatik*. Berlin: Realschulbuchhandlung.

Whitelam, Keith W. 1991. Between History and Literature: The Social Production of Israel's Traditions of Origin. *Scandinavian Journal of the Old Testament* 2:60–74.

———. 1994. The Identity of Early Israel: The Realignment and Transformation of Late Bronze–Iron Age Palestine. *Journal for the Study of the Old Testament* 63:57–87.

Whitt, William D. 1992. The Divorce of Yahweh and Asherah in Hos 2,4–7,12ff. *Scandinavian Journal of the Old Testament* 6:31–67.

Whybray, R. N. 1987. *The Making of the Pentateuch: A Methodological Study*. Journal for the Study of the Old Testament: Supplement Series 53. Sheffield: Sheffield Academic Press.

Wiggins, Steve A. 1993. *A Reassessment of "Asherah." A Study according to the Textual Sources of the First Two Millennia B.C.E.* Alter Orient und Altes Testament 235. Neukirchener: Neukirchen-Vluyn.

―――. 1996. Yahweh: The God of Sun? *Journal for the Study of the Old Testament* 71:89–106.

Wilhelm, Gernot. 1990. Marginalien zu Herodot, Klio 199. Pages 505–24 in *Lingering over Words. Studies in Ancient Near Eastern Literature in Honor of William L. Moran*. Harvard Semitic Studies 37. Edited by T. Abusch, J. Huehnergard, and P. Steinkeller. Atlanta: Scholars Press.

Willett, E. A. R. 1999. *Women and Household Shrines in Ancient Israel*. PhD diss., University of Arizona.

Williamson, Hugh G. M. 1985. *Ezra, Nehemiah*. Word Biblical Commentary 16. Waco, TX: Word.

―――. 1988. The Governors of Judah under the Persians. *Tyndale Bulletin* 39:59–82.

―――. 1989. The Concept of Israel in Transition. Pages 141–61 in *The World of Ancient Israel: Sociological, Anthropological and Political Perspectives*. Edited by R. E. Clements. Cambridge: Cambridge University Press.

―――. 1991. Ezra and Nehemiah in the Light of the Texts from Persepolis. *Bulletin for Biblical Research* 1:41–61.

―――. 1999. Exile and After: Historical Study. Pages 236–65 in *The Face of Old Testament Studies: A Survey of Contemporary Approaches*. Edited by D. W. Baker and B. T. Arnold. Grand Rapids: Baker Academic.

―――. 2005. Temple and Worship in Isaiah 6. Pages 123–44 in *Temple and Worship in Biblical Israel*. Library of Hebrew Bible/Old Testament Studies 422. Edited by J. Day. London: T&T Clark.

Wilson, Ian. 2005. Merely a Container? The Ark in Deuteronomy. Pages 212–49 in *Temple and Worship in Biblical Israel*. Library of Hebrew Bible/Old Testament Studies 422. Edited by J. Day. London: T&T Clark.

Wimmer, Donald. 1997. Tell Ṣafuṭ. *The Oxford Encyclopedia of Archaeology in the Near East*. New York: Oxford University Press.

Winter, Urs. 1983. *Frau und Göttin: Exegetische und ikonographische Studien zum weiblichen Gottesbild im alten Israel und in dessen Umwelt*. Orbis biblicus et orientalis 53. Göttingen: Vandenhoeck & Ruprecht.

Winward, Stephen. 1976. *A Guide to the Prophets*. Atlanta: John Knox.

Wiseman, Donald J. 1985. *Nebuchadnezzar and Babylon*. 1983 Schweich Lectures. Oxford: Oxford University Press.

―――. 1993. *1 and 2 Kings. An Introduction and Commentary*. Tyndale Old Testament Commentaries. Leicester, UK: Inter-Varsity.

Wolde, Ellen van. 1991. The Story of Cain and Abel: A Narrative Study. *Journal for the Study of the Old Testament* 52:25–41. Repr., pages 48–62 in idem, *Words Become Worlds. Semantic Studies of Genesis 1–11*. Biblical Interpretations Series 6. Leiden: Brill, 1994.

Wolters, Al. 1993. Halley's Comet at a Turning Point in Jewish History. *Catholic Biblical Quarterly* 55:687–97.

———. 1994. *Zōhar hārāqî'a* (Daniel 12.3) and Halley's Comet. *Journal for the Study of the Old Testament* 61:111–20.

———. 1995. Belshazzar's Feast and the Cult of the Moon God Sîn. *Bulletin of Biblical Research* 5:199–206.

Wright, Christopher J. H. 1990. *God's People in God's Land: Family, Land, and Property in the Old Testament*. Exeter, UK: Paternoster.

Wright, David P. 1994. Ritual Analogy in Psalm 109. *Journal of Biblical Literature* 113:385–404.

———. 2001. *Ritual as Narrative: The Dynamics of Feasting, Mourning, and Retaliation Rites in the Ugaritic Tale of Aqhat*. Winona Lake, IN: Eisenbrauns.

———. 2002. Music and Dance in 2 Samuel 6. *Journal of Biblical Literature* 121:201–25.

Wright, J. Edward. 2001. Biblical versus Israelite Images of the Heavenly Realm. *Journal for the Study of the Old Testament* 93:59–75.

Wright, George Ernest. 1950. *The Old Testament against Its Environment*. London: SCM.

———. 1952. *God Who Acts: Biblical Theology as Recital*. London: SCM.

Wyatt, N. 1986. Cain's Wife. *Folklore* 97(1):88–95.

———. 1998. *Religious Texts from Ugarit: The Words of Ilimilku and His Colleagues*. Biblical Seminar 53. Sheffield: Sheffield Academic Press.

———. 1999. The Religion of Ugarit: An Overview. Pages 529–85 in *Handbook of Ugaritic Studies*. Handbook of Oriental Studies: The Near and Middle East 39. Edited by W. G. E. Watson and N. Wyatt. Leiden: Brill.

Xella, Paolo. 1995. Le dieu et "sa" déesse: l'utilisation des suffixes pronominaux avec des théonymes d'Ebla à Ugarit et à Kuntillet 'Ajrud. *Ugarit Forschungen* 27:599–610.

———. 1999. The Ugaritic Cultic Texts: 3. The Omen Texts. Pages 353–58 in *Handbook of Ugaritic Studies*. Handbook of Oriental Studies: The Near and Middle East 39. Edited by W. G. E. Watson and N. Wyatt. Leiden: Brill.

Yadin, Yigael. 1975. *Hazor: The Rediscovery of a Great Citadel of the Bible*. New York: Random House.

———. 1985. Biblical Archaeology Today: The Archaeological Aspect. Pages 21–27 in *Biblical Archaeology Today: Proceedings of the International Congress on Biblical Archaeology, Jerusalem, April 1984*. Edited by J. Amitai. Jerusalem: Israel Exploration Society.

———. 1993. Hazor. *The New Encyclopedia of Archaeological Excavations in the Holy Land*. New York: Simon & Schuster.

Yon, Marguerite. 1997. Ugarit. *The Oxford Encyclopedia of Archaeology in the Near East*. New York: Simon & Schuster.

———. 2003. *The City of Ugarit at Ras Shamra*. Winona Lake, IN: Eisenbrauns.

Young, Edward J. 1956. *An Introduction to the Old Testament*. Grand Rapids: Eerdmans.

Younger, K. Lawson, Jr. 1990. *Ancient Conquest Accounts: A Study in Ancient Near Eastern and Biblical History Writing*. Journal for the Study of the Old Testament: Supplement Series 98. Sheffield: Sheffield Academic Press.

Zadok, R. 1978. *On West Semites in Babylonia during the Chaldean and Achaemenian Periods*. Rev. ed. Jerusalem: H. J. & Z. Wanaarta and Tel-Aviv University.

———. 1979. *The Jews in Babylonia during the Chaldean and Achaemenian Periods according to the Babylonian Sources*. Studies in the History of the Jewish People and the Land of Israel Monograph Series 3. Haifa: University Press.

————. 1980. *Sources for the History of the Jews in Babylonia during the Chaldean and Achaemenian Periods. With an Appendix on West Semitic Names in 1st Millennium Mesopotamia*. Jerusalem: H. J. & Z. Wanaarta and Tel-Aviv University.

————. 1988. *The Pre-Hellenistic Israelite Anthroponymy and Prosopography*. Orientalia Lovaniensia Analecta 28. Leuven: Peeters.

————. 2003. The Representation of Foreigners in Neo- and Late Babylonian Legal Documents (Eighth through Second Centuries B.C.E.). Pages 471–589 in *Judah and the Judeans in the Neo-Babylonian Period*. Edited by O. Lipschits and J. Blenkinsopp. Winona Lake, IN: Eisenbrauns.

Zerafa, Peter Paul. 1993. I Formed a Man with Yahweh. *Melita Theologica. The Review of the Faculty of Theology and the Theology Students' Association Malta* 44:29–31.

Zertal, Adam. 1985. Has Joshua's Altar Been Found on Mt. Ebal? *Biblical Archaeology Review* 11(1):26–43.

————. 1986. How Can Kempinski Be So Wrong! *Biblical Archaeology Review* 12(1):43, 47, 49–53.

————. 1986–1987. An Early Iron Age Cult Site on Mount Ebal: Excavation Seasons 1982–1987. *Tel Aviv* 13–14:105–165.

————. 1991a. Israel Enters Canaan—Following the Pottery Trail. *Biblical Archaeology Review* 17(5):28–47.

————. 1991b. The Trek of the Tribes as They Settled in Canaan. *Biblical Archaeology Review* 17(5):48–49, 75.

————. 1995. Three Iron Age Fortresses in the Jordan Valley and the Origin of the Ammonite Circular Towers. *Israel Exploration Journal* 45:253–73.

————. 1996. *The Manasseh Hill Country Survey: The Eastern Valleys and the Fringes of the Desert*. Tel Aviv: University of Haifa and Ministry of Defense. (Hebrew).

————. 1998. The Iron Age I Culture in the Hill-Country of Canaan—a Manassite Perspective. Pages 238–50 in *Mediterranean Peoples in Transition: Thirteenth to Tenth Centuries B.C.E.* Edited by S. Gitin, A. Mazar, and E. Stern. Jerusalem: Israel Exploration Society.

Zevit, Ziony. 1995. Philology, Archaeology, and a Terminus a Quo for P's *ḥaṭṭāʾt* Legislation. Pages 29–38 in *Pomegranates and Golden Bells: Studies in Biblical, Jewish, and Near Eastern Ritual, Law, and Literature in Honor of Jacob Milgrom*. Edited by D. P. Wright et al. Winona Lake, IN: Eisenbrauns.

————. 2001. *The Religions of Ancient Israel: A Parallactic Approach*. New York: Continuum.

————. 2004. The Biblical Archaeology versus Syro-Palestinian Archaeology Debate in Its American Institutional and Intellectual Contexts. Pages 3–19 in *The Future of Biblical Archaeology: Reassessing Methodologies and Assumptions*. Edited by J. K. Hoffmeier and A. Millard. Grand Rapids: Eerdmans.

Zimhoni, O. 1985. Iron Age Pottery of Tel 'Eton and Its Relation to the Lachish, Tel Beit Mirsim and Arad Assemblages. *Tel Aviv* 12:63–90.

Zoebel, Hans-Jürgen. 1965. *Stammesspruch und Geschichte: Die Angaben der Stammessprüche von Gen 49, Dtn 33 und Jdc 5 über die politischen und kultischen Zustände im damaligen "Israel."* Beihefte zur Zeitschrift für die Alttestamentliche Wissenschaft 95. Berlin: Alfred Töpelmann.

————. 1993. *Altes Testament—Literatursammlung und Heilige Schrift. Gesammelte Aufsätze zur Entstehung, Geschichte und Auslegung des Alten Testaments*. Beihefte zur Zeitschrift für die Alttestamentliche Wissenschaft 212. Edited by J. Männchen and E.-J. Waschke. Berlin and New York: Walter de Gruyter.

Zuckerman, Bruce, and Stephen Kaufman. 1998. Recording the Stela: First Step on the Road to Decipherment. Accessed at http://www.humnet.ucla.edu/humnet/nelc/stelasite/stelainfo.html.

Zwickel, W. 1990. *Räucherkult und Räuchergeräte: Exegetische und archäologische Studien zum Räucheropfer im Alten Testament.* Orbis biblicus et orientalis 97. Göttingen: Vandenhoeck & Ruprecht.

Name Index

Scripture Index

Subject Index

Aaron, 156, 193
Abel's sacrifice, 179–80
Abram
  ancestral religion of,
    149–51
  covenant of, 162, 168–69
  of Harran, 63n59
  meanings of, 178–79
Abydos, 91
Acco, 21
Achan, 206
Ada, 82
Adad, 87
Adah, 144
Adam, 175
Adamma, 82
Adaru, 82
Addu, 86, 89
Admu, 82
Adonis, 258
Ahab, 249
Ahaz, 252
Ahaziah, 249
Ai, 235, 238
ʿAin Dara, 230
Akhenaten, pharoah, 30, 72,
  73, 92, 164
Akkadian, 112
Alalakh, 83, 162
Albertz, Rainer, 66, 72
Albright, William F., 64–65
Alt, Albrecht, 60, 147–48,
  211
altars, 306–7

Amarna tablet, 92, 94–95,
  133, 139
Amaziah, 252
American school, 65
Amman site, 132
Ammon, 21, 74
Ammurapi, 111
Amon-Re, 154
Amos, 70, 256
amulets, 312
Amun, 92
Anat, 100–101, 103n91, 157,
  244, 341–42
ancestral religion in Genesis,
  149–51
Ancient Judaism (Weber), 36
aniconism, 67, 160, 165–66
animal motifs, 137, 315–16
animals, sacrifice of, 184–89
Annunitum, 87
anthropology, 25–26
Apis cult, 153–54
apocalypticism, 343–46
Aqhat, 96, 198
Arad, 283, 299, 303–4
Aramea, 20n14
archaeology and religious
  analysis, 38–39
Asa, 251
ʾăšērîm, 269
Ashdod, 238
Asherah
  and Astarte, 322
  condemned in Bible, 75, 76
  epithets in Genesis, 151–52

female figurines depicting,
  308–11
importance neglected,
  73–74
in Kuntillet ʿAjrud texts,
  12–13, 14, 67, 283–89
in personal names of Pal-
  estine, 140
prophets, 254–55
on seals, 317
seventy sons of, 147
at Ugarit, 98–99
Ashkelon site, 18, 136, 139,
  155–57
Ashtar, 82
Ashtaroth, 103, 243
Ashteroth-Karnaim, 243
Ashurbanipal, 268
Asiatic variant, theory of, 27
Aspects of Monotheism
  (Shanks and Meinhardt),
  73–74
Assyria, 20n14
Assyrian royal annals, 50n15
Astarte, 75, 99, 103, 135,
  243, 250, 317, 322
Astruc, Jean, 45
Aten, cult of, 72, 92, 164
Athaliah, 251
Athirat, 98–99, 147
Athtar, 102
atonement, 106–7, 186–87
Axial Age theory, 72
Azande peoples, 34
Azariah, 252